T0214481

Lecture Notes in Computer Science   11010

Commenced Publication in 1973
Founding and Former Series Editors:
Gerhard Goos, Juris Hartmanis, and Jan van Leeuwen

More information about this series at http://www.springer.com/series/7409

Anup Basu · Stefano Berretti (Eds.)

Smart Multimedia

First International Conference, ICSM 2018
Toulon, France, August 24–26, 2018
Revised Selected Papers

 Springer

Editors
Anup Basu
University of Alberta
Edmonton, AB, Canada

Stefano Berretti
Dipartimento di Ingegneria
Università degli Studi di Firenze
Florence, Italy

ISSN 0302-9743   ISSN 1611-3349 (electronic)
Lecture Notes in Computer Science
ISBN 978-3-030-04374-2   ISBN 978-3-030-04375-9 (eBook)
https://doi.org/10.1007/978-3-030-04375-9

Library of Congress Control Number: 2018962151

LNCS Sublibrary: SL3 – Information Systems and Applications, incl. Internet/Web, and HCI

This Springer imprint is published by the registered company Springer Nature Switzerland AG
The registered company address is: Gewerbestrasse 11, 6330 Cham, Switzerland

Preface

Welcome to the proceedings of the First International Conference on Smart Multimedia. The idea behind this conference originated from the need to bring together smart algorithm design and various multimedia technologies ranging from smart sensing to haptics. We organized this conference with only one track to facilitate exchanges between researchers from various communities (e.g., deep learning, signal processing, computer vision, robotics, and medical multimedia processing) who focus on different topics. We hope this will help initiate new interdisciplinary collaborations and accelerate projects that need expertise in multiple disciplines.

In the long term, we would like to go beyond collecting big data and using such data for learning, to understanding what smartness really means and how many animals in nature can learn and generalize from a limited number of examples.

In our first year of the conference, we received around 100 submissions; around 30% could be accepted in the regular tracks owing to limited space. In addition, two excellent tutorials covering the topics of "Haptics for Smart Multimedia" and "Domain Adaptation for Computer Vision" were included. Papers in the conference were organized into 11 sessions, and the Springer LNCS proceedings containing the papers are arranged following these sessions into 10 topics. The topics in the proceedings include: Social, Affective and Cognition Analysis; Person-centered Smart Multimedia; Haptic and Robots for Smart Multimedia; MR, 3D, Underwater Image Processing; When Smart Signal Processing Meets Smart Sensing; Visual Behavior Analysis; Video Analysis; Learning; and Low-level Vision. These areas cover a broad range of disciplines on the wider field of smart multimedia.

We thank several donors for our premier conference on Smart Multimedia whose gifts not only assisted in covering the cost of organizing the conference, but also made the variety of social events possible.

October 2018

Stefano Berretti
Anup Basu

Organization

General Chairs

N. Thirion-Moreau   SeaTech
A. Leleve   INSA, Lyon, France
A. Basu   University of Alberta, Canada

Program Chairs

S. Berretti   UFlorence, Italy
M. Daoudi   IMT Lille Douai

Area Chairs

S. Panchanathan   Arizona University, USA
A. El-Saddik   University of Ottawa, Canada
W. Pedrycz   University of Alberta, Canada
M. Kankanhalli   NUS, Singapore
J. Wu   University of Windsor, Canada

Industrial Program Chairs

Li Cheng   A-Star, Singapore
Tao Wang   SAS, USA
H. Azari   Microsoft, USA
G.-M. Su   Dolby, USA
F. Zhai   Huawei, Hong Kong, SAR China

Finance Chair

Lihang Ying   Together Inc.

Special Sessions Chair

S. Nahavandi   Deakin University, Australia

Special Sessions Assistant

S. Soltaninejad   University of Alberta, Canada

Registration Chair

Yo-Ping Huang   Taipei University, Taiwan

Publicity Co-chairs

P. Atrey   University of Albany, USA
Jun Zhou   Griffith University, Australia

Submissions Chair

S. Mukherjee   University of Alberta, Canada

Web Chair

X. Sun   University of Alberta, Canada

Advisor

P. Bonfils   University of Toulon, France

Program Committee

ICSM 2018 Program Committee

Ajmal Mian   University of Western Australia
Alan Wee-Chung Liew   Griffith University, Australia
Alexander Schwing   University of Illinois at Urbana-Champaign, USA
Allan Jepson   University of Toronto, Canada
Andrea Prati   University of Parma, Italy
Ashirbani Saha   Duke University, USA
Audrey Minghelli   University of Toulon, France
Bin Wang   Griffith University, Australia
Chengcai Leng   University of Alberta, Canada
Cheston Tan Yin Chet   Institute for Infocomm Research, Singapore
Chidansh Bhatt   FxPal, USA
Chunhua Shen   University of Adelaide, Australia
Claudio Ferrari   University of Florence, Italy
Claudio Tortorici   Khalifa University of Science, Technology and
                             Research, UAE
Costantino Grana   University of Modena and Reggio Emilia, Italy
Cyril Prissette   University of Toulon, France
David Fofi   University of Bourgogne Franche-Comté (UBFC),
                             France
Dibyendu Mukherjee   Epson Canada Ltd.
Djamila Aouada   University of Luxembourg, Luxembourg
Eric Moreau   University of Toulon, France

Contents

MR, 3D, Underwater Image Processing

When Smart Signal Processing Meets Smart Sensing

Visual Behavior Analysis: Methods and Applications

Low-Level Vision

Miscellaneous

Social, Affective and Cognition Analysis

Tactile Facial Action Units Toward Enriching Social Interactions for Individuals Who Are Blind

Troy McDaniel[✉], Samjhana Devkota, Ramin Tadayon,
Bryan Duarte, Bijan Fakhri, and Sethuraman Panchanathan

Center for Cognitive Ubiquitous Computing, School of Computing, Informatics,
and Decision Systems Engineering, Arizona State University,
Tempe, AZ 85281, USA
{troy.mcdaniel, rtadayon, bjduarte, panch}@asu.edu

Abstract. Social interactions mediate our communication with others, enable development and maintenance of personal and professional relationships, and contribute greatly to our health. While both verbal cues (i.e., speech) and non-verbal cues (e.g., facial expressions, hand gestures, and body language) are exchanged during social interactions, the latter encompasses more information ($\sim 65\%$). Given their inherent visual nature, non-verbal cues are largely inaccessible to individuals who are blind, putting this population at a social disadvantage compared to their sighted peers. For individuals who are blind, embarrassing social situations are not uncommon due to miscommunication, which can lead to social avoidance and isolation. In this paper, we propose a mapping between visual facial expressions, represented as facial action units, which may be extracted using computer vision algorithms, to haptic (vibrotactile) representations, toward discreet and real-time perception of facial expressions during social interactions by individuals who are blind.

Keywords: Social assistive aids · Assistive technology
Visual-to-tactile mapping · Sensory substitution · Facial action units

1 Introduction

Social interactions are a fundamental part of the human experience, paramount to our ability to communicate effectively, establish and maintain personal and professional relationships, and live healthy lives. During a social interaction, both verbal and non-verbal cues are exchanged to communicate information. Non-verbal social cues account for approximately 65% of the information exchanged [1], and include facial expressions, hand gestures, body language, eye gaze, interpersonal distance, and appearance. It is the inherent visual nature of non-verbal cues that poses significant social barriers for individuals who are blind.

We take for granted the contribution of non-verbal cues in social interactions; for example, eye gaze enables communication partners to effectively and efficiently direct questions or attentional focus; facial expressions help communicate more complex emotional states such as sarcasm; and copying the body language of communication

A. Basu and S. Berretti (Eds.): ICSM 2018, LNCS 11010, pp. 3–14, 2018.
https://doi.org/10.1007/978-3-030-04375-9_1

partners conveys agreement and interest. These subtleties of non-verbal communication are not available to individuals who are blind, creating a social disadvantage when interactions involve sighted peers. Limited access to social non-verbal cues increases miscommunication, leading to embarrassing social situations, which may increase the likelihood of social avoidance and the development of poor social skills, which is a leading cause of psychological problems such as depression and social anxiety [2]. This work aims to break down social barriers for individuals who are blind by improving access to non-verbal cues, beginning with facial expressions.

To accomplishment this aim, we propose a mapping between visual facial expressions, and their haptic (vibrotactile) counterparts. Facial expressions may be represented at different levels of abstraction: from more literal representations, such as facial action units, to more symbolic representations that convey emotional content. Our approach focuses on facial action units for the following reasons: (i) Using the Facial Action Unit Coding System (FACS) [3], any facial expression can be broken down into its fundamental building blocks called facial action units, which provides a reliable and descriptive language for communication; (ii) It is known which facial action units occur most frequently among the six basic emotions (happy, sad, surprise, anger, fear, and disgust) [4], which can help narrow the number of facial action units for consideration in an effort to reduce user training without sacrificing efficacy; and (iii) Software [5–7] are now freely or commercially available for real-time, accurate extraction of facial action units, which now warrants attention on how these action units can be delivered to users once extracted. In this paper, we propose a novel set of tactile facial action units that builds upon our previous work. We also present a user study involving individuals who are blind, to evaluate the learnability, distinctness and naturalness of the proposed mapping.

2 Related Work

Social assistive aids for improving access to non-verbal communicative cues for individuals who are blind have received very little attention. Researchers have proposed algorithms for extracting and/or delivering non-verbal cues of gaze, interpersonal distance/direction, facial expressions and emotions. Qiu et al. [8] proposed the Tactile Band, a vibrotactile band worn around the head for conveying the gaze signals of a sighted interaction partner to an individual who is blind. The mapping of gaze to the Tactile Band encompasses both glances and fixations: When an interaction partner glances at the face of an individual who is blind, a short, subtle vibration is felt; when an interaction partner fixates longer on the face of the blind interaction partner, a repeating vibration pattern is felt.

Previously, we proposed the use of a haptic belt for conveying the direction [9] of an interaction partner from the point of view of a user who is blind, and their interpersonal distance [10], i.e., the distance between the user and the partner. Direction was mapped to body site around the waist, stimulated through the use of vibrotactile actuators spaced equidistantly along the length of the belt. Distance was mapped to different vibrotactile rhythms representing categories of intimate, personal, social and public space. Both direction and distance estimates were driven by a real-time face detection algorithm applied to video from a discreetly embedded camera in a pair of sunglasses.

Compared to other non-verbal cues, facial expressions have received more attention in the context of social assistive aids for individuals who are blind. Krishna et al. [11] mapped the six basic emotions to spatiotemporal vibrotactile stimulation patterns displayed on the back of the hand using a custom-built device called the VibroGlove. Pattern designs were inspired by mouth shapes: For example, expressions of happiness and surprise were represented by vibrations following the shape of a smile and circle, respectively. Buimer et al. [12] mapped the six basic emotions to body site through the use of a waist worn belt embedded with vibrotactile actuator spaced around the left and right sides of the body. Réhman et al. [13] mapped expressions of happy, sad, and surprise to three axes on the back of a chair, with a direct correlation between where the vibrotactile stimulation occurred along each axis and the intensity of the corresponding expression. Rahman et al. [14] focused on a small set of behavioral expressions (e.g., yawn, closed lips, smile, open lips, sleepy, looking away) and dimensions of affect (valence, arousal, and dominance), conveyed to users through speech output.

The first attempt to explore tactile representations of facial action units is our own past work [15], in which a visual-to-tactile mapping was proposed for facial action units for use in social assistive aids for individuals who are blind. There are several limitations of this work that our proposed approach aims to overcome: (i) The chosen set of facial action units did not include all of the most commonly occurring action units among the six basic emotions, and some chosen action units do not occur at all among the six basic emotions; (ii) Some patterns were redundant, and therefore, not needed in the final set; and (iii) The pattern set was not evaluated with individuals who are blind.

3   Proposed Mapping

Our proposed set of tactile action units is shown in Fig. 1, designed for use with a two-dimensional vibrotactile display to create richer patterns that vary both spatially and temporally. Compared to [15], the proposed set provides better coverage of action units (AUs) occurring across the six basic emotions [4], particularly for emotions of surprise, fear, anger and disgust. Using [15] as a starting point, we removed four redundant patterns (variations on AU2 and AU4) as well as three more patterns (AU13, AU22, AU23) since they do not occur frequently across the six basic emotions. We then kept the remaining patterns from [15] and added new patterns for AU7, AU10, AU20, AU25 and AU27 to achieve better coverage of the six basic emotions.

We then conducted extensive pilot testing with an individual who is blind to assess the distinctness and intuitiveness of the proposed mapping before conducting a full evaluation. Based on pilot test results, patterns for AU1, AU5, AU9, and AU12 from [15] were redesigned for ease of recognition and naturalness, and only patterns for AU4, AU6, AU15, and AU26 from [15] remained unchanged.

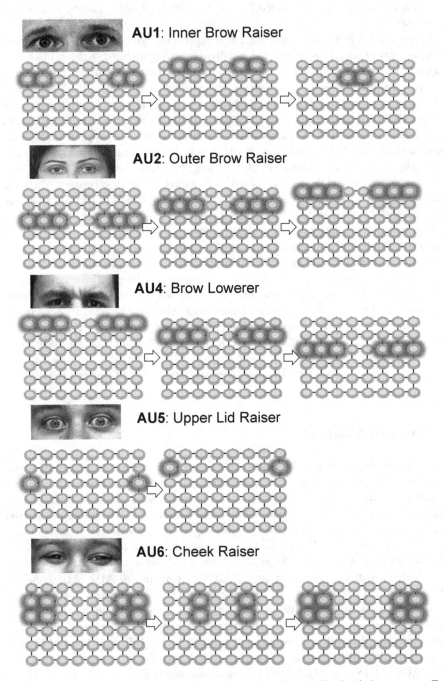

Fig. 1. Proposed mapping between facial action units and vibrotactile stimulation patterns. For each action unit, the drawing depicts the sequence (indicated by arrows) of actuated vibration motors (indicated by highlights) on the 6 × 8 vibrotactile display.

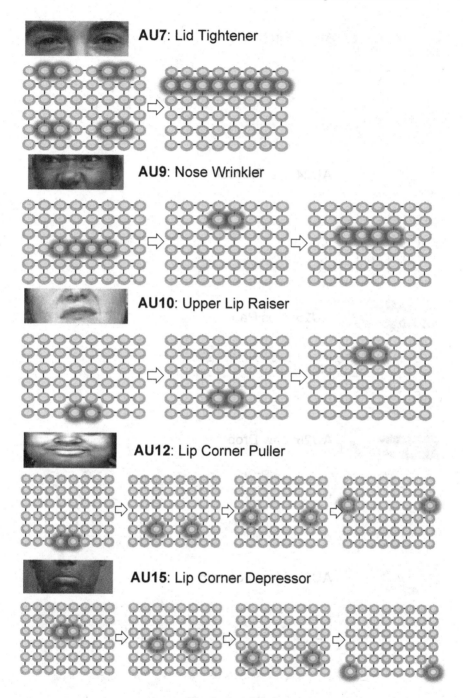

Fig. 1. (*continued*)

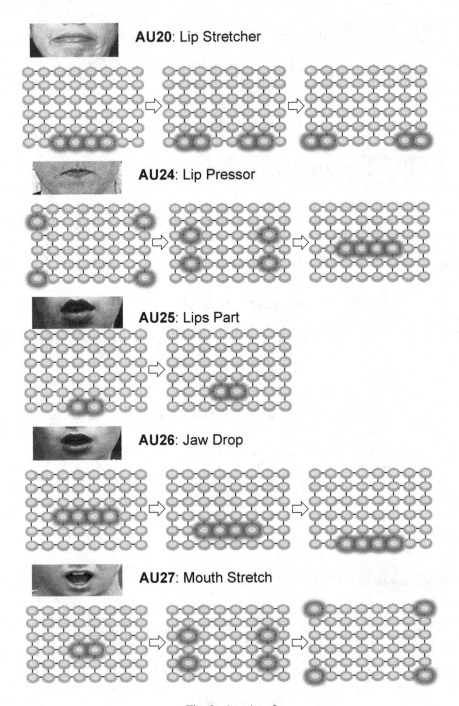

Fig. 1. (*continued*)

4 User Study

4.1 Aim

Our aim is to evaluate our proposed tactile facial action units with individuals who are blind for distinctness and naturalness. Whereas in [15] we used a fixed-choice paradigm that relied upon relative identification between two face images, we employ an absolute identification (AI) design to gauge performance within a setting similar to what would be encountered during social interactions. In AI tasks, patterns are recognized individually, allowing a much more accurate assessment of learnability and ease of recognition.

4.2 Participants

We recruited 14 individuals who self-identify as blind or visually impaired for our IRB-approved study. Of the 14, 5 were male, 9 were female; 9 were born blind, 5 became blind later in life; and ages ranged 21 to 62 (M: 40, SD: 10).

4.3 Apparatus

Our two-dimensional vibrotactile display used in this study was built using the design specifications from [15]. Our display is a matrix of 6 rows and 8 columns of vibration motors (3.3 V eccentric rotating mass pancake motors). Motors are spaced 2 cm apart horizontally, and 4 cm apart vertically. Vibration motors are attached to the back of mesh chair to enable closer contact with participants' skin. All hardware components were built in-house using printed circuit boards and Arduino products. All software for controlling the display was written in Python.

4.4 Procedure

Each participant was first given an overview of the purpose of the study, and then asked to complete an informed consent form followed by a subject information form to collect demographic information. All participants received $25 to compensate them for their time. During the entire study, action units were identified and described using layman terminology as follows: AU1 "Raise only inner parts of eyebrows"; AU2 "Raise eyebrows"; AU4 "Lower eyebrows"; AU5 "Raise eyelids"; AU6 "Raise cheeks"; AU7 "Squint eyes"; AU9 "Wrinkle up nose"; AU10 "Raise upper lip"; AU12 "Pull lip corners up into smile"; AU15 "Pull lip corners down into frown"; AU20 "Pull lips tight toward corners of mouth"; AU24 "Press lips tightly together"; AU25 "Slightly part lips"; AU26 "Drop jaw"; and AU27 "Open mouth wide".

Next, each participant underwent a familiarization phase during which each pattern was described in layman terms and presented using the vibrotactile display. Three vibration durations (pulse widths) were evaluated: 250, 500, and 750 ms. In [15], pulse widths of 250, 500, 750, 1000 ms were evaluated with sighted individuals; no statistically significant difference was found. Here, we aim to explore a subset of the shortest durations with individuals who are blind. The gap between vibrotactile pulses was

50 ms. All 15 patterns were presented while keeping the pulse width constant at 750 ms. This process was repeated for 500 ms, and then finally, 250 ms. Participants were allowed to ask for patterns to be repeated during the familiarization phase.

During the training phase, each participant was tasked with recognizing randomly presented tactile facial action units. The training phase consisted of 45 trials (15 patterns × 3 durations). Correct guesses were confirmed; incorrect guesses were corrected. To proceed to the testing phase, each participant had to score 80% or better (i.e., correctly guess at least 36 out of the 45 trials) during training. At most, the training phase could be repeated three times. If a participant underwent all four training phases, and still could not score 80% or better, they were allowed to proceed to testing, but their testing data was not included in analysis.

The testing phase was similar to training, except that during the 45 trials, no feedback was given to participants regarding whether their guess was right or wrong. During testing, no repeat presentations were allowed. Immediately following the testing phase, participants were asked to complete a post-experiment questionnaire with two Likert-scale questions: The first question asked participants to rate the ease of recognizing each pattern (15 ratings total); and the second question asked participants to rate the naturalness of the mapping for each pattern (again, 15 ratings total).

4.5   Results

Of the 14 participants, 10 passed the training phase by at maximum the fourth try. The following analysis includes only the aforementioned 10 participants. The mean number of training phase attempts was M: 2.1 (SD: 0.56). A total of 945 training trials

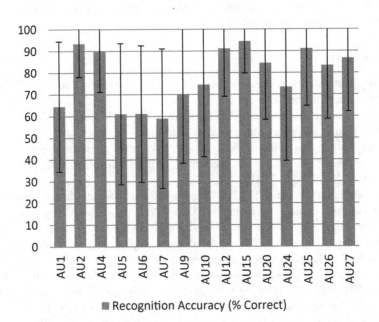

Fig. 2. Mean recognition accuracy per action unit (AU). Error bars are standard deviations.

(participant responses) were recorded; five of these trials were omitted from analysis due to equipment malfunctions: three trials from participant #6 and two trials from participant #11. A total of 1,350 testing trials were recorded; four trials were omitted

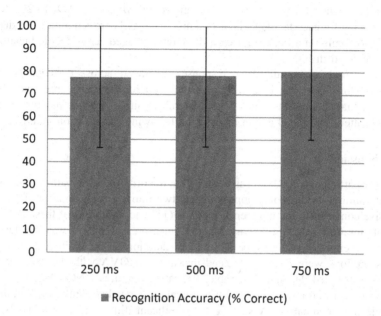

Fig. 3. Mean recognition accuracy per pattern duration. Error bars are standard deviations.

Table 1. Part (A). Ease of recognizing tactile facial action units. Part (B). Naturalness of mapping. Ratings based on Likert scale: 1 (very hard) to 5 (very easy).

Questions	Mean (A)	SD (A)	Mean (B)	SD (B)
AU1: Inner Brow Raiser	2.3	1.15	2.8	1.31
AU2: Outer Brow Raiser	4.2	1.13	4.4	0.69
AU4: Brow Lowerer	4.3	1.05	4.5	0.70
AU5: Upper Lid Raiser	3.8	0.78	3.5	0.84
AU6: Cheek Raiser	3.3	1.41	3.3	0.94
AU7: Lid Tightener	2.8	0.91	3.2	1.03
AU9: Nose Wrinkler	3.3	1.25	3.4	1.17
AU10: Upper Lip Raiser	3.4	1.26	3.8	1.03
AU12: Lip Corner Puller	4.7	0.67	4.9	0.31
AU15: Lip Corner Depressor	4.6	0.96	4.9	0.31
AU20: Lip Stretcher	4.4	1.26	4.8	0.42
AU24: Lip Pressor	4	1.15	4.4	0.69
AU25: Lips Part	4	1.24	3.9	0.87
AU26: Jaw Drop	4.7	0.94	4.8	0.42
AU27: Mouth Stretch	4.5	0.97	4.8	0.42

from analysis due to equipment malfunctions: one trial from participant #6, one trial from participant #9, and two trials from participant #7.

We define *recognition accuracy* as the number of correctly guessed testing trials out of the total number of testing trials. Recognition accuracy averaged across participants, tactile facial action units, and durations was M: 78.5%, SD: 13.2%. Recognition accuracy for each tactile facial action unit, averaged across durations, is depicted in Fig. 2. Recognition accuracy for each duration, averaged across tactile facial action units, is depicted in Fig. 3.

Table 1 summarizes subjective responses, averaged across participants, to the questions "How easy was it to recognize the vibration patterns represented by the following facial action units?" and "How natural (intuitive) was the mapping between vibration pattern and facial action unit for the following facial action units?".

4.6 Discussion

While four participants did not pass training, the majority of participants (10 out of 14) did pass training, needing only approximately two training trials on average, which is impressive considering the number of patterns (15) and variations of these patterns in terms of duration (3). A two-way repeated measures ANOVA was conducted to compare the effect of pattern type and pattern duration on recognition accuracy. All data assumptions were met for repeated measures ANOVA with the exception of a normally distributed dependent variable. Repeated measures ANOVAs are robust to non-normal distributions, especially for extremely low p values, and therefore, this test is reliable in our situation. A statistically significant difference was found between recognition accuracies for pattern type (i.e., type of tactile facial action unit), F $(4,126) = 3.34$, $p < 0.001$, indicating some patterns were more difficult to recognize than others. Indeed, from Fig. 2, we can see that a few action units, namely AU1, AU5, AU6, AU7 and AU9, had lower mean recognition accuracies, 70% or less, compared to other action units. This result is further corroborated by subjective feedback. Lower mean Likert scale ratings were found for these action units, both in terms of ease of recognition (Table 1A) and naturalness (Table 1B).

Of the 32 times AU1 "Inner Brow Raiser" was misclassified, AU9 "Nose Wrinkler" was incorrectly guessed 15 times. Indeed, the designs for AU1 and AU9 shown in Fig. 1 do indicate similar vertical movements, which could have been the source of confusion. To differentiate from AU1, AU9 will be redesigned to convey a more centrally located stimulation with only upward movement. Of the 34 times AU5 "Upper Lid Raiser" was misclassified, AU7 "Lid Tightener" was incorrectly guessed 15 times. Figure 1 does show some similarities: Both patterns consist of two pulse sequences and largely vary vertically. AU7 will be redesigned to convey a more downward stimulation, representing squinting, rather than upward motion. Of the 35 times AU6 "Cheek Raiser" was misclassified, AU1 "Inner Brow Raiser" and AU9 "Nose Wrinkler" were incorrectly guessed 7 and 11 times, respectively. It is interesting to note pattern AU9 "Nose Wrinkler" was frequently misclassified as AU6 "Cheek Raiser" (15 out of 27 times) as well. The aforementioned misclassifications may be due to similar stimulation locations between AU1, AU6, and AU9, as shown in Fig. 1. AU6 will be lowered for better alignment with the cheeks to reduce similarities. Finally,

AU7 "Lid Tightener" had much variation in its 37 misclassifications with AU6 "Cheek Raiser" being misclassified most often at 9 times. Again, this may be due to similarity between locations, which may be reduced once AU6 is lowered.

No statistically significant difference was found between recognition accuracies for duration, $F(2,18) = 0.918$, $p = 0.417$, indicating that participants could just as easily recognize the patterns of short durations compared to long durations. This result confirms a similar finding in [15], and is important considering how fast paced and dynamic social interactions are, necessitating quick delivery of tactile facial action units to achieve real-time perception. Moreover, no statistically significant interaction effect between pattern type and duration was found, $F(28,252) = 0.539$, $p = 0.974$.

5 Conclusion and Future Work

This paper presented a novel set of tactile facial action units that improves upon previous work to enhance social interactions for individuals who are blind. Moreover, this work represents the first effort to evaluate tactile facial action units with individuals who are blind. Our presented research study revealed both useful feedback and promising results: (i) Individuals who are blind were able to quickly learn the proposed patterns in just two short training phases on average; (ii) Participants found most of the proposed tactile facial action units easy to recognize and natural; and (iii) A few patterns were found to need minor redesigns, which will be done and tested in future work, described below.

As part of future work, we aim to explore: (i) How feedback gathered during this research study can be used to further enhance the distinctness and naturalness of the proposed tactile facial action units. In particular, we aim to focus on improving the design of those patterns participants found most difficult to recognize in the current study. In this paper, we've already outlined specific design changes we plan to carry out and retest; (ii) Performance differences between individuals who were born blind (i.e., congenitally blind) and individuals who became blind later in life (i.e., acquired blindness). Our study included both populations (specifically, 9 individuals who were born blind, and 5 individuals who became blind later in life), and their performance will be compared as part of future work. Our intent is to understand whether preexisting visual experiences of facial expressions play a role in an individual's ability to learn, recognize and understand tactile facial action units; (iii) Conduct a follow-up research study to investigate how well tactile facial action units (e.g., "Brow Lowerer", "Nose Wrinkler", "Cheek Raiser", etc.) contribute toward real-time recognition and under-standing of the basic emotions (e.g., happy, sad, surprise, fear, anger, and disgust) and even higher level cognitive states such as sarcasm; and (iv) Explore how the proposed tactile facial action units may be combined with verbal cues (speech) for multimodal perception of facial expressions and emotions. The current findings represent an important first step toward ultimately designing tactile facial action units for use in more realistic conversational situations involving speech.

References

1. Knapp, M.L.: Nonverbal Communication in Human Interaction. Harcourt College, San Diego (1996)
2. Segrin, C., Flora, J.: Poor social skills are a vulnerability factor in the development of psychosocial problems. Hum. Commun. Res. **26**(3), 489–514 (2000)
3. Ekman, P., Friesen, W.V., Hager, J.C.: The Facial Action Coding System: A Technique for the Measurement of Facial Movements. Consulting Psychologists, Palo Alto (2002)
4. Valstar, M.F., Pantic, M.: Biologically vs. logic inspired encoding of facial actions and emotions in video. In: IEEE International Conference on Multimedia & Expo, pp. 325–328 (2006)
5. Seeing Machines. https://www.seeingmachines.com. Accessed 24 Nov 2017
6. IMOTIONS. https://imotions.com. Accessed 24 Nov 2017
7. De la Torre, F., et al.: IntraFace. In: 11th IEEE International Conference and Workshops on Automatic Face and Gesture Recognition, pp. 1–8 (2015)
8. Qiu, S., Rauterberg, M., Hu, J.: Designing and evaluating a wearable device for accessing gaze signals from the sighted. In: Antona, M., Stephanidis, C. (eds.) UAHCI 2016, Part I. LNCS, vol. 9737, pp. 454–464. Springer, Cham (2016). https://doi.org/10.1007/978-3-319-40250-5_43
9. McDaniel, T., Krishna, S., Balasubramanian, V., Colbry, D., Panchanathan, S.: Using a haptic belt to convey non-verbal communication cues during social interactions to individuals who are blind. In: IEEE Haptics Audio-Visual Environments and Games Conference, pp. 13–18 (2008)
10. McDaniel, T., Villanueva, D., Krishna, S., Colbry, D., Panchanathan, S.: Heartbeats: a methodology to convey interpersonal distance through touch. In: ACM Conference on Human Factors in Computing Systems, pp. 3985–3990 (2010)
11. Krishna, S., Bala, S., McDaniel, T., McGuire, S., Panchanathan, S.: VibroGlove: an assistive technology aid for conveying facial expressions. In: ACM Conference on Human Factors in Computing Systems, pp. 3637–3642 (2010)
12. Buimer, H.P., Bittner, M., Kostelijk, T., van der Geest, T.M., van Wezel, R.J.A., Zhao, Y.: Enhancing emotion recognition in vips with haptic feedback. In: Stephanidis, C. (ed.) HCI 2016, Part II. CCIS, vol. 618, pp. 157–163. Springer, Cham (2016). https://doi.org/10.1007/978-3-319-40542-1_25
13. Réhman, S.U., Liu, L.: Vibrotactile rendering of human emotions on the manifold of facial expressions. J. Multimedia **3**(3), 18–25 (2008)
14. Rahman, A., Anam, A.I., Yeasin, M.: EmoAssist: emotion enabled assistive tool to enhance dyadic conversation for the blind. Multimedia Tools Appl. **76**(6), 7699–7730 (2017)
15. Bala, S., McDaniel, T., Panchanathan, S.: Visual-to-tactile mapping of facial movements for enriched social interactions. In: IEEE International Symposium on Haptic, Audio and Visual Environments and Games, pp. 82–87 (2014)

Affectional Ontology and Multimedia Dataset for Sentiment Analysis

Rana Abaalkhail, Fatimah Alzamzami[✉], Samah Aloufi[✉],
Rajwa Alharthi[✉], and Abdulmotaleb El Saddik[✉]

Multimedia Communications Research Laboratory, University of Ottawa,
Ottawa, ON, Canada
{rabaa006,falza094,salou102,ralha081,elsaddik}@uottawa.ca

Abstract. Ontology is able to understand the association between concepts and the relationships within contents. We argue that, ontology could compete with machine learning in detecting sentiments contained in textual messages. Current ontology-based sentiment models are domain specific, which limits their ability to adapt to different domains. In this work, we propose a general sentiment ontology (Affectional Ontology) using various sentiment lexicons and psychological-based resources. To provide an efficient evaluation on the Affectional Ontology, we propose a domain-free sentiment multimedia dataset (DFSMD). Our DFSMD was constructed with high standard annotation criteria. The results of our work show the effectiveness of the proposed ontology in capturing the sentiment, when compared to the machine learning approach. The proposed DFSMD is publicly available and can be used in various sentiment analysis problems without the restrictions of particular domains or aspects.

Keywords: Ontology · Machine learning · Sentiment analysis
Multimedia · Dataset

1 Introduction

Although lexicon-based and machine learning approaches have developed a strong reputation in the area of sentiment analysis, there still exists a gap in the semantic understanding of textual content. Ontology has the ability to capture the semantic association between concepts and the relationships within contents. With such an ability, the requirements of manual annotation in machine learning approaches can be resolved. As a result, the sentiment analysis community is moving towards an ontological approach to represent a common-sense knowledge base [20]. Fortunately, ontology-based sentiment analysis has proven to have a richer semantic representation than lexicons [20]. Also, it addresses the fact that a single message might contain different notions of the same aspect. Therefore, a more elaborate understanding of the sentimental content can be obtained. Contrary to ontology, machine learning approaches understand the sentiment of

© Springer Nature Switzerland AG 2018
A. Basu and S. Berretti (Eds.): ICSM 2018, LNCS 11010, pp. 15–28, 2018.
https://doi.org/10.1007/978-3-030-04375-9_2

messages as a whole, without semantically dividing and analyzing the messages. In this paper, we investigate the capability of the ontological approach against machine learning algorithms for sentiment analysis on social media. We argue that the ontological approach could compete with machine learning algorithms to capture a more comprehensive sentiment behaviour from sparse and informal textual contents in social media.

Existing studies on ontology-based sentiment analysis focus on domain onto-logical approaches [16,22]. Sentimental and emotional keywords used in the construction of the ontology were collected from domain-specific datasets. In other words, existing domain sentiment ontologies were created based on the emotional words related to domain-specific datasets. This results in a limitation when trying to adapt a domain ontology to various different domains. In this paper, we overcome this drawback and propose the Affectional Ontology (AFO) that represent wide range of emotions vocabularies. Our proposed ontology is able to capture a sentiment from unstructured-informal messages on social media, regardless of what the subject of the message is. Since we propose a general sentiment ontology for sentiment analysis, it is valid to evaluate its performance on a domain-free dataset. Actually, it is an efficient approach to show the capability of our proposed ontology in detecting sentimental opinions from social contents. To the best of our knowledge, all the publicly available datasets used for sentiment analysis are domain-specific, where the dataset collection is based on specific subjects, emotions, or events. Therefore, we propose to create a domain-free sentiment multimedia dataset (DFSMD) with high quality messages and annotation labels. Our DFSMD follows high standard criteria for the data collection and annotation procedures. This will ensure a consistency in the evaluation of our ontology against the machine learning algorithms. The results of this paper support our argument that the ontological approach can compete with machine learning algorithms in detecting sentiments contained in social media messages, with a performance accuracy of 66% for the ontological approach and 64% for machine learning.

The rest of the paper is organized as follows. Section 2 discusses the related works on ontology-based sentiment analysis and some existing sentiment datasets. Section 3 provides a detailed description of the construction of our domain-free sentiment multimedia dataset DFSMD. Section 4 describes the development of the proposed general sentiment ontology AFO. Experiments and evaluation of the proposed methods are discussed in Sect. 5. Finally, Sect. 6 concludes the paper with possible future directions.

2   Related Work

Previous studies have shown the ability of the ontological approach in capturing the sentiments in social media textual contents [1]. However, most of the studies are considered domain ontologies for sentiment analysis. A mobile-product sentiment ontology was created to understand customer opinions on mobile products using related reviews shared on social media, as well as a mobile website. The opinions (i.e. sentiments) are stored with the descriptions of the product's features in the defined ontology [16]. Similarly, Sam and Chatwin [22] have proposed an ontology based sentiment analysis approach to understand the behaviour of electronic-product consumers. The ontology was created using the vocabulary, data features, and emotions from customers reviews related to electronic products and shared on online social networks. In their domain ontology, they focused on the common emotional keywords associated with reviews of electronic products. Authors in [14] suggested to take advantage of domain ontology to provide a deeper understanding of a sentiment within a single message. Their proposed ontology-based sentiment model is able to provide a more elaborate sentiment regarding different notions contained in a single post for a specific subject. The limitation of domain sentiment ontologies has been tackled in the work [26] by proposing to build a general fine-grained emotion ontology (Emotive ontology), without considering emotional keywords associated with any particular aspect. The Emotive ontology has the ability to understand the emotional behaviour of various events, services, and products using textual content shared on social media. We decided to follow a similar approach in order to build a general sentiment ontology that provides a sentiment label for messages, regardless of subject domains. Even though the Emotive ontology [26] was created to capture emotions from textual content, its performance evaluation is limited for three reasons: (1) the dataset was small containing only 150 tweets, (2) it was annotated by only two users, (3) the tweet collection was event related. We have observed these limitations with the current publicly available datasets used in the sentiment analysis research domain.

A closer look at the existing publicly available datasets reveals a number of limitations that restrict our purpose for this study. One of the major limitations in some of the existing datasets is the focus on the polarity or the valence of the tweets, thus ignoring the neutral sentiment class. For example, Go et al. in [8] constructed a large Twitter training dataset with 1.6 million tweets using positive and negative emoticons as noisy labels. Authors in [18] used similar labeling approach for positive and negative sentiment however they added a neutral class using 44 newspaper and magazine accounts. In another work, Davidov et al. [5] utilized 50 hashtags and 15 smileys as labels for sentiment and no-sentiment categories. For the sentiment category, two human-judges manually labeled the 50 hashtags and used them to collect tweets and construct a hashtag-based sentiment dataset. Ten Amazon Mechanical Turk workers labeled 15 smileys with mood states that were used to collect tweets and construct a smiley-based sentiment dataset. For the no-sentiment category, they randomly selected tweets with no hashtags or smileys. Besides the limitation of being restricted to sentiment and no-sentiment labels, relying on hashtags and mood smileys might not truly reflect the sentiment of the tweet. Moreover, tweets in some of the existing datasets were retrieved and labeled with respect to trending topics, specific events or products. For instance, in [8] test data, they manually labeled a set of 177 negative tweets and 182 positive tweets that were collected using queries related to specific companies, events, locations, music, movies, people and products. Sanders dataset[1], the Dialogue Earth Twitter Corpus[2] and the Health Care Reform datase [24] are other domain specific datasets that are publicly available. Tweets included in these datasets are manually labeled for sentiment with respect to specific topics. For example, Apple, Google, Microsoft and Twitter in the Sanders dataset, weather and gas prices in the Dialogue Earth Twitter Corpus, and 8 targets including: Health care, Reform, Obama, Democrats, Republicans, Tea party, Conservatives, Liberals, and Stupak in the Health Care Reform dataset. Even SemEval [21], a well-known dataset that is widely used to evaluate sentiment analysis methods, is constructed based on 200 English trending topics and popular events. In addition to the above limitations, the annotation methodology for most of the manually annotated datasets have some ambiguities. Authors in [8,24] did not report a detailed description of the data collection and annotation procedures such as the annotators' selection criteria, the number of annotators, their demographic information, and the agreement among them. Aiming to overcome the above limitations and to complement the existing sentiment datasets, we are proposing a domain free sentiment multimedia dataset (DFSMD).

3   Domain-Free Sentiment Multimedia Dataset (DFSMD)

In this section, we describe the procedure for the construction of the DFSMD, including data collection, preparation and annotation.

3.1   Dataset Collection

Twitter APIs were used to collect our set of tweets. The fetching process was free of keywords, in order to respect our purpose of creating a generalized dataset independent of topics and emotions. The tweets were collected worldwide from five different dates, chosen randomly to ensure that many of the topics and events discussed daily were covered. To ensure that the content of all tweets was appropriate and distinct, we created a filter to exclude tweets with inappropriate, non useful content (i.e. tweets with only hashtags or links), and retweets. The collection process included only English tweets, since English was the common language among participating annotators. Each tweet entity is described with a set of attributes including creation time, message, tweet user, location and an image. Note that not all the tweets necessarily come with images or a location. A total of 70,228 tweets were collected during the data collection.

3.2   Dataset Preparation

The collected data from the previous section was noisy and contained tweets with non-useful content. As a result, we performed two runs of cleaning. First,

---

[1] http://www.sananalytics.com/lab.
[2] www.dialogueearth.org.

we created three cleaners: (1) to remove mentions to ensure text granularity, (2) to remove links since annotators won't open them, (3) to remove duplications. We used regular expressions to ensure the quality of the cleaning process. Second, we manually read and evaluated the tweets and excluded all the tweets with meaningless contents (i.e tweets auto-generated by applications). The same is applied to tweeted images; we excluded the tweets that came with inappropriate or unrelated images. A sample of 39,000 tweets (i.e. out of 70,228 raw collected tweets) was randomly selected for the manual evaluation. Three English speakers participated in evaluating and choosing the useful tweets. Each evaluated 13,000 tweets that had been cleaned using the first cleaning step. A total of 12,800 tweets were selected for the annotation process.

3.3   Dataset Annotation

Our dataset annotation was designed based on a set of criteria for both anno-tators and questions. Quality control was considered as a tool to monitor the behaviour of annotators and to ensure the quality of the data being annotated. To access an acceptable number of sentimental opinions on our tweet set, we used a survey method as a way to acquire as many annotators as possible. To ensure the quality of the resulting annotations, we carefully decided on three main aspects: annotators, questions, and tweet subsets.

Annotators. In order to create a dataset with high quality annotation, we required that all annotators speak fluent English and possess a high level of edu-cation. Many studies reflect the fact that the way people express their opinions and perceive other people's opinions are subject to cultural and gender differ-ences [7,27]. Accordingly, annotators of both genders and of different cultural backgrounds should be considered in order to limit the bias in the annotation.

An email invitation was sent to email list provided by university of Ottawa. The invitation included a questionnaire asking for personal and demographic information. According to our criteria, 58 out of 65 participants were qualified to participate. 24% of the participants are native and 76% fluent English speakers. The participants are of both genders (57% male, 43% female) and of different cultural backgrounds (East Asian 33%, South Asian 38%, Middle Eastern 21%, African 7%, and North American 1%).

Questions. Each tweet message was associated with a sentiment question on a 3-level scale (positive, neutral, negative). On each tweet message evaluation, there was a confidence question on a 5-level scale, ranging from 1 (i.e. not con-fident) to 5 (i.e. very confident). If a tweet came with an image or images, the same questions are asked to evaluate the sentiment of the image(s). In addition, a third question is asked to evaluate if the image(s) is related to the tweet, fol-lowed by a confidence question for evaluating the answer. The reason for adding the confidence question in our survey is to show the strength of the sentiment evaluation provided by the annotators. This will be used for two purposes: (1) as a factor to resolve disagreements between annotators, if they exist, (2) as an indicator to exclude tweets with unclear sentiment.

Tweets Subsets. The tweet dataset was divided into 20 subsets. Every annotator was assigned to only one group. Therefore, each tweet group had at least four annotators. Previous studies suggested that average of 4 non-expert annotators are required for annotation tasks [23]. Our strategy of dividing the tweets into groups was to ensure that the annotation process was not tedious for our participants. Therefore, they were able to provide a high level of concentration in order to carefully evaluate tweets and provide consistent sentiment understanding.

In an effort to increase the speed of the annotation process while also ensuring consistency, annotators were provided with a web-based annotation tool. Guidelines were provided to the annotators explaining the annotation task as well as some examples of annotated tweets for reference. The most important guideline focused on asking the annotators to evaluate the feeling/opinion of the authors when they posted these tweets. Annotators needed to register an account on the survey website. We proposed this service so that the annotators could stop the annotation at any time and resume safely where they had stopped, at a later time. Only one tweet was displayed at a time. The message and image(s), if any, were shown to the annotators along with the questions and the answer fields. A hidden timer started once a tweet was displayed and stopped when the next tweet was shown. We provided a counter for each annotator to give them a sense of their progression. Once annotators were done with their tweets, the results were saved under their identity.

The annotation process was split into three phases where the first and second phases are combined and then followed by the third one. The first phase acts as a qualification phase, intended to test the annotators' efficiency and exclude the annotators whose work did not meet the required standards. An annotator is qualified if she labels in agreement with a domain-expert. All annotators were provided with tt test tweets (i.e. 200 in our case), obtained from a dataset annotated by three expert psychologists [2]. They were asked to annotate the test tweets with one of the three sentiment states: positive, neutral, negative. Their results were then compared with the sentiment labels of the psychologists to measure the qualification agreement $agr(a)$ as shown in Eq. 1

$$agr(a) = \frac{n}{tt} * 100 \tag{1}$$

where a is an annotator, n is the number of matched sentiment labels between annotator a and psychologists, and tt is the size of the test tweets.

Table 1. DFSMD statistics

Labels	Tweets number	Images number
Positive	6,683	4,851
Negative	2,275	966
Neutral	2,983	4,427

In the second phase, the actual annotation was performed in two rounds, giving the annotators enough time to rest between the rounds. In each round, annotators were divided into ten groups, each with at least four individuals. For each group, the assigned annotators were given 640 tweets and asked to answer the sentiment questions (3.3). Note that each group had a distinct set of tweets. To preserve the quality of our dataset, we combined the test tweets with the to-be-annotated tweets, as a quality control technique. This way we ensured the annotator's mental state was constant when evaluating both types of tweets, and hence eliminating possible biases. As a result, a sentiment evaluation with the same standard for both types of tweets could be obtained. The duration timer is another quality control metric we considered in the annotation process. A hidden timer started when a tweet was displayed and ended when the next tweet was shown. Its role was to measure the time annotators took to evaluate tweets, ensuring that they took enough time to carefully review each tweet before assigning an appropriate label.

Based on the qualification agreement measurement and the duration timer results, three annotators were excluded. They showed a lower agreement rate (less than 50%) with the psychologists, and in comparison to the majority of the other annotators, who agreed on more than 50% of the tweets. The low agreement rate could have been a result of these annotators selecting the labels randomly, which could be evidenced by examining the timers, or caused by language barriers, which could lead to difficulties in understanding the tweet's slang, idiom or context. The other 55 annotators were considered as qualified and could move to the third annotation phase.

The third phase involved the construction of our final dataset, DFSMD. We constructed the DFSMD based on the following rules: the label was assigned to each tweet within the dataset based on a majority vote among annotators in each of the 20 groups. In 1,848 cases, tweets equally achieved sentiment disagreements. For instance, two annotators thought that a tweet was positive and another two thought that it was neutral. In such cases, we resolved this conflict by considering the confidence answers that the annotators provided. If the confidence score of all the annotators of one opinion x_1 was greater than the other opinions x_2 or x_3, then opinion x_1 was the sentiment of the corresponding tweet. A total of 859 (i.e. out of 1,848 tweets with disagreement) were excluded from the dataset due to the inability to resolve the disagreement between the annotators. Table 1 shows the sentiment distribution of DFSMD. The DFSMD[3] is released for public use.

4   Affectional Ontology Development

We proposed AFO for sentiment analysis as a general domain ontology. Since human sentiments are related to feelings, we considered using psychological based resources to create the ontology. In addition, we used non-ontological resources such as lexicons and thesaurus. The ontology development has four main steps:

---

[3] http://www.mcrlab.net/datasets/dfsmd/.

- Incorporate language dictionaries and psychological theories vocabularies.
- Add the Sentiment Strength from SentiStrength and AFINN.
- Start the ontology conceptualization.
- Model the data by using RDF/OWL.

The ontology development starts with the knowledge acquisition phase, which involves knowing the information and resources for ontology development. Sentiments reflect human affective states, which means the emotional state of the person towards a topic. Affective states include emotions, mood, and sentiments. As a result, words that describe emotions can be used to express human sentiments [3].

We used many language dictionaries and lexicons such as WordNet[4], WordNet-Affect[5], NRC Word-Emotion Association Lexicon[6], SenticNet 4.0[7], EmoSenticNet[8], Harvard General Inquirer lexicon[9], and MPQA Subjectivity lexicon[10]. Besides, we used vocabulary from AFINN[11], and SentiStrength[12] AFINN, and SentiStrength are dictionaries that has a list of English words rated for valence with an integer between that range from +1 to +5 for positive words, −1 to −5 for negative words, and 0 for neutral. In addition, we used the Oxford English Dictionary[13] to extend the list of synonyms. An important point is that these dictionaries contain slang words that can be used in micro-blogging sites like Twitter.

Moreover, we utilized emotion words from psychological theories such as Parrott [19], Frijda [6], and Cowie [4] To be able to cover a comprehensive emotion vocabularies that can appear in different events and domains.

After that, we extracted the emotion word sentiment strength from SentiStrength and AFINN.

After we considered the ontology sentiment vocabulary resources, we started with the ontology conceptualization phase in order to model the ontology. We grouped the terms into classes and subclasses (concepts), and verbs and properties. The class "Affective State" represents the human sentiment state. The class "Affective State Model" represents the classes about the sentiment analysis classification. Also, "Affective State Annotation" represents the sentiment annotation type. The Affective State class connects with the Affective State Model through "isModelFor", and "hasModel" relationships. As well, the Affective State class connects with Affective State Annotation through "isAnnotatedBy", and "isAnnotatedFor" relationships.

---

[4] https://wordnet.princeton.edu/.
[5] http://wndomains.fbk.eu/wnaffect.html.
[6] http://saifmohammad.com/WebPages/NRC-Emotion-Lexicon.htm.
[7] http://sentic.net/.
[8] https://www.gelbukh.com/emosenticnet/.
[9] http://www.wjh.harvard.edu/~inquirer/.
[10] http://mpqa.cs.pitt.edu/lexicons/subj_lexicon/.
[11] http://www2.imm.dtu.dk/pubdb/views/publication_details.php?id=6010.
[12] http://sentistrength.wlv.ac.uk/.
[13] https://en.oxforddictionaries.com/.

After the conceptualization phase, we used Protégé[14] for the ontology development. Figure 1 shows AFO visualization. It shows the class - subclass hierarchy, object properties, and data properties. The Positive Negative Neutral Category is considered as a subclass of Discrete Model, because it classifies the sentiments as words that are grouped into families that share similar characteristics. The "Affective State Annotations" class was created with three individuals: negative affective state, positive affective state, and neutral affective state. Moreover, we added individuals for each subclass of "Positive Negative Neutral Category", which are the words that were extracted from the dictionaries, the lexicons, and the psychological theories. In addition, we create a data property "Strength score" with a range of xsd:integer$[\geq -5, \leq 5]$. The AFO was evaluated through the Pellet[15] reasoner to check the ontology's inconsistencies that may lead to incorrect semantic understanding.

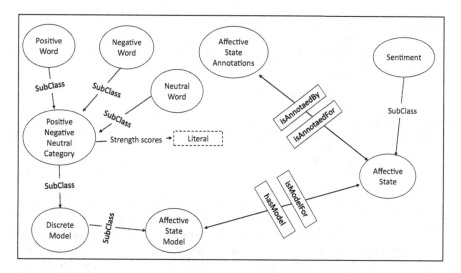

Fig. 1. AFO visualization. Oval shape represents class and subclass. Rectangle shape represents object property. Round-dotted rectangle represents data property.

5   Evaluation

The aim of our experiment is to evaluate the performance of our proposed ontology AFO compared to machine learning approach. Our evaluation is divided into two parts: AFO sentiment analysis and a comparison against machine learning algorithms. Both experiments are evaluated on our proposed DFSMD dataset. Accuracy and F-score are the metrics used for the performance evaluation.

---

[14] http://protege.stanford.edu/.
[15] https://www.w3.org/2001/sw/wiki/Pellet.

5.1   AFO Sentiment Analysis

Ontology sentiment analysis has two main steps: (1) Query the ontology (AFO) with SPARQL Query[16], (2) Calculate the sentence sentiment

Table 2. Example of tweets sentiment analysis result of AFO

Sentence (Tweet)	Word strength value by SPARQL query	Tweet sentiment result
A very pleasant weekend it is pleasant real	AFO :very 0 AFO :pleasant 3 AFO :weekend 0 AFO :is 0 AFO :pleasant 3 AFO :real 0 Final result 3	Positive
Exam answer fails these are so funny	AFO :exam 0 AFO :answer 0 AFO :fails −3 AFO :are 0 AFO :so 0 AFO :funny 2 Final result −1	Negative
Low quality selfie low quality person	AFO :low −2 AFO :quality 0 AFO :selfie 0 AFO :low −2 AFO :quality 0 AFO :person 0 Final result −2	Negative

We took extra step regarding the data Preparation by converted any presence of emojis into text. Since nowadays people often express their feelings by using emojis, consequently, emojis had an effect on the result of the sentence sentiment [10]. We converted the emojis in the data to an equivalent word by using the Emoji Sentiment Ranking[17] and Home of Emoji Meaning[18]. In addition, spelling correction was applied to the text.

Then, we applied sentiment analysis on a sentence level. As result, for each tweet we ran SPARQL query to get the sentiment strength for the words that affect the overall sentence sentiment. For example, we ignored the pronouns and the articles in the sentence. We used parameterized SPARQL query to apply a query against the ontology. We also used Jena JAVA API, which is a java framework that provides support for manipulating and query RDF models. We then

---

[16] http://www.w3.org/TR/rdf-sparql-query/.

[17] http://kt.ijs.si/data/Emoji_sentiment_ranking/.

[18] https://emojipedia.org/.

calculated the sentiment score by adding the biggest value from the positive words and the smallest value from the negative words in the sentence. The biggest value in the positive range is 5, and the smallest value in the negative range is -5. Table 2 shows some examples of tweet sentiment analysis results using AFO which has achieved a performance accuracy of 66%.

5.2 Ontology vs Machine Learning

We have used our proposed (DFSMD) dataset to train machine learning classifiers. We randomly divided DFSMD into two groups: 60% for training and 40% for testing. Sentiment analysis is a standard classification problem that consists of two main steps: feature extraction and classifier learning. For the feature extraction step, we utilized the following features:

1. Bag-of-Word (BOW) feature: a tweet is represented as a feature vector, where each element corresponds to a term in a pre-defined set of vocabulary. We used the Term Frequency-Inverse Document Frequency (TF-IDF) schema. We used three different models of the BOW feature: Uni-gram, Bi-gram and Uni-Bi gram. For all sets of vocabulary, we included words that occur in at least five tweets in our training dataset.
2. Lexicon-based feature: we utilized different existing word sentiment lexicons: Bing Liu's Opinion Lexicon (OL) [13], NRC Hashtag Sentiment lexicon (NRC) [12], emoticons [9], and emojis [17] sentiment lexicons.

For the classifier learning step, we used three popular algorithms in text analysis in default settings: Linear Support Vector Machine (SVM), Multinomial Naïve Bayes (MNB), and Random Forest (RF) to compare their performance.

The results are illustrated in Table 3. When comparing the performance of BOW features, we have observed that Uni-Bi gram achieves the best performance. The performance of different classifiers decreased when using lexicon features compared to BOW features. Combining BOW features with all four lexicons' features used in our experiment has boosted the performance from 63% to ≈65%, as seen in Table 3. Comparing the performance results of the classifiers, we can see that SVM and MNB have achieved a comparable performance. The experimental results of the best machine learning model compared to the ontological method is shown in Table 4. As the results show, the ontological method surpasses the performance of the machine learning approach. This is due to the fact that AFO is designed to cover a wide range of sentiment words from language dictionaries and psychological-based resources.

Table 3. Performance of SVM, MNB, and RF classifiers using different features

Feature		SVM		MNB		RF	
		Avg. accuracy	Avg. F-score	Avg. accuracy	Avg. F-score	Avg. accuracy	Avg. F-score
BOW	Uni-gram	0.629	0.62	0.626	0.57	0.607	0.60
	Bi-gram	0.564	0.44	0.564	0.44	0.561	0.44
	Uni-Bi gram	0.6305	0.62	0.628	0.57	0.611	0.60
Lexicon	OL	0.584	0.49	0.583	0.49	0.584	0.49
	NRC	0.571	0.46	0.567	0.47	0.563	0.49
Emoticons+Emojis		0.564	0.42	0.565	0.44	0.568	0.43
Lexicons+Emoticons+Emojis		0.608	0.55	0.599	0.58	0.566	0.55
BOW+Lexicons+Emoticons+Emojis		0.647	0.64	0.649	0.64	0.617	0.61

Table 4. Comparison of ontology and machine learning methods

Method	Avg. accuracy	Avg. F-score
Ontology	0.660	0.66
Machine learning	0.647	0.64

6 Conclusion

In this work, we proposed to create AFO, a general ontology for sentiment analysis. The development of the AFO ontology incorporates various sentiment lexicons and psychological-based resources in order to capture the semantic representation of the sentiment expressed in social media content. Moreover, we introduced a domain-free sentiment multimedia dataset (DFDMS), which consists of 11,941 tweets and their 10,244 associated images annotated as positive, negative or neutral. The annotation procedure was performed manually and followed high standard annotation criteria and measurement to ensure the dataset quality. The DFSMD dataset is publicly available to be used in the development and evaluation of various textual and visual sentiment analysis methods. The experimental evaluation on the DFSMD dataset demonstrates the effectiveness of the AFO in detecting sentiment compared to machine learning method. In this work, we only considered sentiment affective states when building our ontology. Thus, for future work we will extend the AFO to cover other affective states such as emotion and mood.

References

1. Abaalkhail, R., Guthier, B., Alharthi, R., El Saddik, A.: Survey on ontologies for affective states and their influences. Semant. Web, 1–18 (2016). https://doi.org/10.3233/SW-170270
2. Alharthi, R., Guthier, B., Guertin, C., El Saddik, A.: A dataset for psychological human needs detection from social networks. IEEE Access **5**, 9109–9117 (2017). https://doi.org/10.1109/ACCESS.2017.2706084

3. Jurafsky, D., Martin, J.H., Lexicons for sentiment and affect extraction. In: Speech and Language Processing, pp. 326–344. Pearson London (2014). https://doi.org/10.1162/089120100750105975

4. Cowie, R., Douglas-Cowie, E., Apolloni, B., Taylor, J., Romano, A., Fellenz, W., et al.: What a neural net needs to know about emotion words. Comput. Intell. Appl. **404**, 5311–5316 (1999)

5. Davidov, D., Tsur, O., Rappoport, A.: Enhanced sentiment learning using Twitter hashtags and smileys. In: Proceedings of the 23rd International Conference on Computational Linguistics: Posters, pp. 241–249. Association for Computational Linguistics (2010)

6. Frijda, N.H.: The Emotions. Cambridge University Press (1986). https://doi.org/10.1017/9781316275221

7. Fujita, F., Diener, E., Sandvik, E.: Gender differences in negative affect and well-being: the case for emotional intensity. J. Pers. Soc. Psychol. **61**(3), 427 (1991)

8. Go, A., Bhayani, R., Huang, : L.: Twitter sentiment classification using distant supervision. CS224N Project Report, Stanford, vol. 1, no. 2009, p. 12 (2009)

9. Hogenboom, A., Bal, D., Frasincar, F., Bal, M., De Jong, F., Kaymak, U.: Exploiting emoticons in polarity classification of text. J. Web Eng. **14**(1–2), 22–40 (2015)

10. Hogenboom, A., Bal, D., Frasincar, F., Bal, M., de Jong, F., Kaymak, U.: Exploiting emoticons in sentiment analysis. In: Proceedings of the 28th Annual ACM Symposium on Applied Computing, pp. 703–710. ACM (2013). https://doi.org/10.1145/2480362.2480498

11. Hovy, E.H.: What are sentiment, affect, and emotion? Applying the methodology of michael Zock to sentiment analysis. In: Gala, N., Rapp, R., Bel-Enguix, G. (eds.) Language Production, Cognition, and the Lexicon. TSLT, vol. 48, pp. 13–24. Springer, Cham (2015). https://doi.org/10.1007/978-3-319-08043-7_2

12. Kiritchenko, S., Zhu, X., Mohammad, S.M.: Sentiment analysis of short informal texts. J. Artif. Intell. Res. **50**, 723–762 (2014). https://doi.org/10.1613/jair.4272

13. Hu, M., Liu, B.: Mining and summarizing customer reviews. In: Proceedings of the Tenth ACM SIGKDD International Conference on Knowledge Discovery and Data Mining, KDD 2004, pp. 168–177. ACM, New York (2004).https://doi.org/10.1145/1014052.1014073

14. Kontopoulos, E., Berberidis, C., Dergiades, T., Bassiliades, N.: Ontology-based sentiment analysis of Twitter posts. Expert Syst. Appl. **40**(10), 4065–4074 (2013). https://doi.org/10.1016/j.eswa.2013.01.001

15. Mohammad, S.M., Turney, P.D.: Crowdsourcing a word-emotion association lexicon. Comput. Intell. **29**(3), 436–465 (2013). https://doi.org/10.1111/j.1467-8640.2012.00460.x

16. Nithish, R., Sabarish, S., Kishen, M.N., Abirami, A., Askarunisa, A.: An ontology based sentiment analysis for mobile products using tweets. In: 2013 Fifth International Conference on Advanced Computing (ICoAC), pp. 342–347. IEEE (2013). https://doi.org/10.1109/ICoAC.2013.6921974

17. Novak, P.K., Smailović, J., Sluban, B., Mozetič, I.: Sentiment of emojis. PloS One **10**(12), e0144296 (2015)

18. Pak, A., Paroubek, P.: Twitter as a corpus for sentiment analysis and opinion mining. In: LREc, vol. 10 (2010). https://doi.org/10.17148/ijarcce.2016.51274

19. Parrott, W.G.: Emotions in Social Psychology: Essential Readings. Psychology Press, Hove (2001)

20. Ravi, K., Ravi, V.: A survey on opinion mining and sentiment analysis: tasks, approaches and applications. Knowl.-Based Syst. **89**, 14–46 (2015). https://doi.org/10.1016/j.knosys.2015.06.015

21. Rosenthal, S., Farra, N., Nakov, P.: Semeval-2017 task 4: sentiment analysis in Twitter. In: Proceedings of the 11th International Workshop on Semantic Evaluation (SemEval-2017), pp. 502–518 (2017)
22. Sam, K.M., Chatwin, C.: Ontology-based sentiment analysis model of customer reviews for electronic products. In: Encyclopedia of Information Science and Technology, 3rd edn, pp. 892–904. IGI Global (2015). https://doi.org/10.4018/978-1-4666-5888-2.ch085
23. Snow, R., O'Connor, B., Jurafsky, D., Ng, A.Y.: Cheap and fast—but is itgood?: evaluating non-expert annotations for natural language tasks. In: Proceedings of the Conference on Empirical Methods in Natural Language Processing, pp. 254–263. Association for Computational Linguistics (2008)
24. Speriosu, M., Sudan, N., Upadhyay, S., Baldridge, J.: Twitter polarity classification with label propagation over lexical links and the follower graph. In: Proceedings of the First Workshop on Unsupervised Learning in NLP, pp. 53–63. Association for Computational Linguistics (2011)
25. Strapparava, C., Valitutti, A., et al.: Wordnet affect: an affective extension of wordnet. In: LREC, vol. 4, pp. 1083–1086 (2004)
26. Sykora, M.D., Jackson, T., O'Brien, A., Elayan, S.: Emotive ontology: extracting fine-grained emotions from terse, informal messages (2013)
27. Wierzbicka, A.: Emotions Across Languages and Cultures: Diversity and Universals. Cambridge University Press, Cambridge (1999). https://doi.org/10.1017/CBO9780511521256

Predicting Student Seating Distribution Based on Social Affinity

Zhao Pei[1,2](✉), Miaomiao Pan[2], Kang Liao[2], Miao Ma[2], and Chengcai Leng[3]

[1] Key Laboratory of Modern Teaching Technology, Ministry of Education,
Xi'an, China
zpei@snnu.edu.cn
[2] School of Computer Science, Shaanxi Normal University, Xi'an, China
[3] School of Mathematics, Northwest University, Xi'an, China

Abstract. Learning students social affinity and modeling their social networks are beneficial for instructors to design proper pedagogical strategies. Students seating distribution contains social data and can be used for analysing their social relationships. In this paper, we propose a method to automatically construct the class social network and predict the position of a student's seat in class. First, we determine the positions of each student in a classroom by utilizing the center projection principle and linear fitting algorithms. The intimate relationship between students is captured to model their social network based on Euclidean distance. Then, we learn the social affinities from the Social Affinity Map (SAM) which clusters the relative positions of surrounding students. Based on this, students' seating distribution can be predicted successfully with accuracy reaching 82.1%.

Keywords: Social network · Center projection · Seating prediction

1 Introduction

In educational environments social interaction between students plays an important role in promoting efficient learning. It means that students can effectively share information and learn from each other. Understanding how social interaction works is beneficial for instructors to design better pedagogical strategies. Therefore, a large amount of effort has been spent on collecting immense social data for students.

We believe that the distribution of seats in a class contains important social relations between students [1]. In universities, students can select their seats

This work is supported by the National Natural Science Foundation of China (No. 61501286, No. 61402274, No. 61672333, No. 61702251), The Key Research and Development Program in Shaanxi Province of China (No. 2018GY-008), the Natural Science Basic Research Plan in Shaanxi Province of China (No. 2015JQ6208, No. 2018JM6068, No. 2018JM6030), the Fundamental Research Funds for the Central Universities (No. GK201702015) and the China Scholarship Council.

A. Basu and S. Berretti (Eds.): ICSM 2018, LNCS 11010, pp. 29–38, 2018.
https://doi.org/10.1007/978-3-030-04375-9_3

freely when in class, which is the reflection of the evolution of social relations between students. As a result, a new method to collect social data is to record students' seating distribution for each class.

In this paper, we utilize class social network to model intimate relationships between students and predict their seating positions. The framework of our study consists of two parts: constructing class social networks and predicting the average distribution of students' seats. First, we need to acquire enough social data. In data collection, the instructor takes a photo of the students at the beginning of the class, and in each class, a single image including all the students faces is captured. This image not only can extract students' social data, but also can be used for class attendance via face recognition. Then, the AdaBoost algorithm with skin-color model [2] is used to detect and recognize the students' faces in the photo taken in class. Following this, the center projection principle and linear fitting algorithms are used for locate students' position. Relationship between students can be determined by the Euclidean distance of their locations. Later, we modify the SAM [3] to build the eight neighbors around each student. In this way, the habit of how students choose companions are recorded. Finally, the prediction of the seating distribution can be obtained after a long-term accumulation of the statistics of seating distribution. The seating distribution prediction is based on the assumption that if two students are friends, their seats are close.

It is proved that both the arrangement of seats in class and the distribution of students affect the learning performance of students [4–6]. Usually the students who sit together are more aware of each others behavior. Once a student is absent for no reason, it is more efficient for the instructor to ask the student who has a good relationship with him or her, rather than the whole class.

There are two major contribution of this paper:

1. We automatically determine the positions of students based on the center projection principle and linear fitting algorithms.
2. We modify the feature descriptor to capture the adjacent seat of each student to learn the social affinities, and propose a prediction method of the seating distribution.

2   Related Work

Human social behavior has attracted significant research attentions, with many positive results being proposed [7–9]. Alahi et al. [3] proposed a descriptor named as SAM which bind people in a crowded space to learn the various social affinities. They find that pedestrians mobility is effected by their neighbors and utilize SAM to predict their destinations. Their experiments showed great improvement in performance through the use of SAM features. Hong et al. [10] proposed a group recommendation method based on social affinity and trustworthiness, with outstanding performance compared to other methods.

Social Network Analysis (SNA) can be used for investigating people's collaboration patterns [11,19]. With rapid advancement of technology, there are also many applications of social networks in education management [12,13]. For example, one can take advantage of SNA to promote student interactions that accelerate the learning process [14]. Becheru et al. [15] proposed a conceptual knowledge extraction framework to extract information from student social networks that satisfy an instructor's pedagogical needs. Halawa et al. [16] created a data model to predict student personality type and learning performance based on the Myers-Briggs Type Indicator (MBTI) theory. This model makes the learning process more personalized for students and avoids the one-size-fits-all learning model problem in the field of education.

However, these research findings are based on the virtual network environment rather than real life at school. Thus, it may lead to a contradictory conclusion. This necessitates a good method which can be easily applied to real-life classroom. The classroom's seating distribution influences the climate and students relationships with each other [17,18]. A well-considered seating distribution can improve students' behavior and learning performance. Wei [20] proposed multimedia technology which can recognize the positions and identities of the students in a classroom to solve the problem of large-scale social data collection. They also designed the in-class social networks which consists of student-to-student and student-to-teacher interactions to analyze the co-learning patterns among students. However, this method is not fully automatic in identification. The number of row and column seats in the classroom need to be manually marked. In addition, since this method is based on image stitching and alignment algorithms, some requirements must be satisfied when acquiring the data. For example, all images must be taken in the same classroom, and two images should have enough overlapping regions for stitching.

3   Social Network Construction

In this section, we aim to model students' class social networks. We achieve this by analyzing the distribution of the seats and finding intimate relationship between students. We develop a social affinity feature which captures eight neighbors around each student.

Taking into account the fact that students are greatly affected by friends when they choose their seats in class, those who sit close to a target student tend to have a close relationship with the target student. For example, we observe that there are two students sitting together twelve times among the total 26 records of attendances in a semester. Figure 1 shows the four scenes where they sit together. Upon inquiry, we learn that they are really close partners in their daily lives.

3.1   Student Localization

In order to acquire social data, the instructor needs to take photos before class, including all the students in the classroom during the whole semester. After each class, the instructor submits the photo to the attendance taking website which is developed by us. The faces in the image are automatically detected

Fig. 1. Two students with close relationship often sit together, there are four scenes shown in the image (a) (b) (c) (d).

by the website. To improve the accuracy of student identification, students are asked to login on the website with their ID to confirm their face and complete attendance as well. Then, center projection principle algorithms are utilized for student localization. First, we pick out the student who seat in the leftmost column and the rightmost column in the classroom. Second, we regard them as discrete points, and use a linear fitting algorithm for these discrete points. We obtain two linear equations with least squares method. The least square formula is as follow:

$$k = \frac{\sum xy - \frac{1}{N}\sum x \sum y}{\sum x^2 - \frac{1}{N}\left(\sum x\right)^2}, \tag{1}$$

where k denotes the slope of the linear equation, N denotes the total number of fitting points, x and y denote for the horizontal and vertical coordinates of students respectively.

Fig. 2. In this figure, the leftmost and the rightmost seats lines are marked with yellow lines. The intersection point P is the center projection point of the classroom. (Color figure online)

According to the principle of central projection, each line (we abstract each column of seats into a straight line) is extended infinitely at the same point, which is called the center projection point. The intersection point of the two straight lines is the center projection point of the classroom. The coordinates of the center projection point can be obtained from the linear equation of two arbitrary column seat lines in the two-dimensional coordinate system. In this paper, we utilize linear equations of the leftmost and the rightmost seat lines to calculate the center projection point (see Fig. 2).

We regard each column of seat in a classroom as a straight line through the center projection point, then locate the student to determine which students belong to the same column. However, since the physical stature and seating position of every student is different, the position of the students in a specific column is not precisely distributed on the same line. To address this problem, we use the angle measure evaluation method (AMEM) to judge whether students belong to the same column. Specifically, for each student, we calculate the slope of the line which goes through the central projection point and the coordinates of this student's seat. Then, we pick out the adjacent students obtained in the previous step. The angle between two lines is measured by:

$$\tan\theta = \left| \frac{(k_2 - k_1)}{(1 + k_1 \times k_2)} \right|,\tag{2}$$

where θ denotes the angle of two lines, and k_1 and k_2 are the slopes of two lines respectively. Finally, we select the students who have the minimum tangent as in the same column with a specific student.

Fig. 3. The illustration of eight neighbors around a student.

Based on the Euclidean distance between two points, we can determine students who are adjacent to each student. In general, we choose four adjacent students for each student. That is, we pick out four student whose seats are one of the four seats with the least Euclidean distance from the center students seat. The number of adjacent seats can be changed according to the number of students in the classroom.

3.2 Deskmate Matching

We classify the adjacent seats into three relations: deskmate, front-rear desk, and diagonal desk. In most situations, seats are often arranged as long rows which are close to others. In this kind of situation, the deskmate of this type of seat

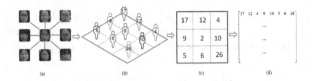

Fig. 4. Illustration of how to build a Social Affinity Map. The student in the center of the left picture is labeled as 2, around her there are eight adjacent students in sequence, namely, 17, 12, 4, 9, 10, 5, 6, 26. These eight IDs exist in this students model as one attendance.

includes the left and right sides. In the three adjacent seat relations above, the most intimate relationship between students is the deskmate relationship. So, we need to identify all pairs of deskmates from an image.

To identify all the pairs of deskmates from a class, we need linear fitting of each column of seats. Matching deskmates can be formulated as a judgment process as:

$$f(a, b) = w \times h(a, b) + (1 - w) \times g(a, b), \tag{3}$$

where a and b denote the coordinates of the students in two adjacent columns, respectively. $h(a, b)$ denotes the Euclidean distance between points a and b. $g(a, b)$ denotes the absolute value of slope of the line through the points a and b. w denotes the coefficient of proportionality, and the value in the range (0,1). $f(a, b)$ denotes the weight used to measure whether two students are deskmates, and the larger the value is, the lower the probability of the two students to be deskmates. For each student, calculate the weight of each adjacent column, the students with the least weight are selected as their deskmates.

In this section, we use the central projection principle and linear fitting algorithms to construct students class social network. Compared to other existing methods, this method is fully automated. In addition, the method can address the issue of images taken in different classrooms; such as, the desk movement and different columns and rows in classrooms. After "student localization" and "deskmate matching" for plenty of images, the final social network of the students can be constructed to predict the seat distribution.

4   Average Seat Distribution Prediction

Students' social affinities are mostly determined by the proximity of students to each other in a class. That is why good friends usually sit together. We modify a feature descriptor SAM [7] to learn the in-class social affinities. Our model records the positions of eight neighbouring students around each one, as shown in the Fig. 3. In the direction, they are front, back, left, right, and four diagonal relations. In the example shown in Fig. 4, around the student whose ID is 2, this student's eight adjacent students in sequence are 17, 12, 4, 9, 10, 5, 6, 26. This means we build a model for each student to record the eight people sitting around for each attendance. Therefore, the model denotes as M can be calculated by:

$$M = \begin{bmatrix} C_{0,0} & C_{0,1} & \cdots & C_{0,7} \\ C_{1,0} & C_{1,1} & \cdots & C_{1,7} \\ \vdots & \vdots & \ddots & \vdots \\ C_{n,0} & C_{n,1} & \cdots & C_{n,7} \end{bmatrix}, \tag{4}$$

where $C_{i,j}$ denotes a student who is sitting at the student's next j desk in $i\text{-}th$ attendance.

In Sect. 3 we obtain all the students' position data and social affinities in the classroom. Based on this foundation, students' seat distribution can be predicted. For predicting the distribution of seats, we should determine some of the students' seats first. We choose the students who have the lowest frequency of changing their seats and place them to the seat where he or she is most likely to sit. The set of placed students is denoted as A, and the proportion of students in set A is about 1/3 of the total number of students in the class. The scale of proportion needs to be adjusted appropriately when the number of students is different or the classroom is changed. Following this we extract a student whose seat is the most frequently adjacent to anyone in A according to SAM, and place him or her on their adjacent seats and add to set A. This step is repeated to get the final seat distribution result. In the process of predicting the seat distribution we utilize a greedy algorithm, i.e., each placement of students is the most appropriate choice in the current situation.

Figure 5 shows the predictive process intuitively, (a) shows the seat distribution after one third of students have been fixed. Then we place the remaining students one by one with a greedy algorithm. For example, consider the student who with the red border has the most times seating together with the student on her left. Thus, the student with the red border can be fixed as shown in Fig. 5(b). The remaining steps are similar in principle.

In order to verify the accuracy of seat distribution prediction, we need to collect a large amount of attendance data over a long period of time. We take photos in different classrooms and periods to avoid the impact of accidental data on the prediction accuracy. When evaluating the performance of the prediction of seat distribution, we leave one part of the photos as a test dataset. To simplify the distribution of students' seats in a classroom, we divide the classroom into eight areas according to the spatial locations. Figure 6 shows schematics for partitioned areas for rectangular classrooms. Through similarity comparison between the predicted results and the actual positions, we can evaluate the accuracy of the prediction. If a student's two results belong to the same area, it means that this student's seat is correctly predicted. The accuracy of the prediction is calculated as follows:

$$s = \frac{l}{D}, \tag{5}$$

where D denotes the total number of students, and l denotes the number of students whose predicted position and actual position belong to the same area.

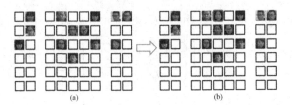

Fig. 5. Illustration of how to predict a student's seat. The squares represent seats in the classroom. (a) shows the seating distribution after a third of the students are fixed. (b) predicts the seat position of the student with red border. (Color figure online)

5   Experimental Results

We took photos of attendance for each class over a semester, and finally got 26 attendance images. These photos are split into two parts, 25 photos are used as the experimental dataset to construct the social network, while the other one photo is used as the test image to validate the prediction of seat distribution. In the classroom, students are encouraged to choose seats freely so as to observe seat distribution among students.

To evaluate the accuracy of "deskmate matching," we use the method in Sect. 3 to analyze each photo and get all pairs of deskmates. Through artificial comparisons, in this experiment there are 33 students for whom matching deskmates are correct (39 students in total), i.e., the accuracy of deskmate matching method is 84.3%.

The SAM model is filled with the student coordinate data obtained in Sect. 3, then the seat distribution of test dataset can be predicted by the method in Sect. 4. The correct number of students in this experiment of seat distribution prediction is 32 (39 students for all), so the accuracy of prediction is 82.1%.

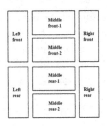

Fig. 6. Illustration of how to divide the rectangular classroom into eight areas.

In this section, we quantify the social relationship as a model and apply it for prediction of students' seat distribution. It can help instructors quickly find the proper student to inquire why his deskmate is absent, keep abreast of the absence of students and avoid accidents. In addition, the prediction results of seat distribution represent the trend of students' future choice of seats. Then, students' future learning trends can be understood, and timely guidance and help for students can be provided.

6 Conclusion

We acquired social data from attendance images with high efficiency to construct class social networks and explore the social affinities between students. A pilot study for the prediction of students' seat distribution was conducted, and the experimental results show the accuracy to be 82.1%. The representative seat distribution data will provide the data sources for studies relating to pedagogical research. We believe that with more social data, more valuable information can be extracted. In future work, we plan to extend our research on social networking. For example, the potential relevance of a student's performance considering his or her neighbouring groups is worth future investigation.

References

1. Mohamed, A., Kamal, M.: Association of student's position in a classroom and student's academic performance using ANOVA. In: Proceedings of the 2015 15th International Conference on e-Learning, pp. 392–395 (2015)
2. Ji, S., Lu, X., Xu, Q.: Fast face detection method combining skin color feature and adaboost. In: Proceedings of the 2014 International Conference on Multisensor Fusion and Information Integration for Intelligent Systems (MFI), pp. 1–5 (2014)
3. Alahi, A., Ramanathan, V., Li, F.F.: Socially-aware large-scale crowd forecasting. In: Proceedings of the 2014 IEEE Conference on Computer Vision and Pattern Recognition (CVPR), pp. 2211–2218 (2014)
4. Shin-ike, K., Lima, H.: A method for determining classroom seating arrangements by using a genetic algorithm. In: Proceedings of the 2012 12th International Conference on Control, Automation and Systems (ICCAS), pp. 29–33 (2012)
5. Mc Gowan, A., Hanna, P., Greer, D.: Learning to program-does it matter where you sit in the lecture theatre? In: Proceedings of the 2017 40th International Convention on Information and Communication Technology, Electronics and Microelectronics (MIPRO), pp. 624–629 (2017)
6. Zeng, S., Zhang, J.,: Analyse social influence on student motivation based on social activity network. In: Proceedings of the 2016 IEEE International Conference on Service Operations and Logistics, and Informatics (SOLI), pp. 133–138 (2012)
7. Ji, Q.G., Chi, R., Lu, Z.M.: Anomaly detection and localisation in the crowd scenes using a block-based social force model. IET Image Process. **12**, 133–137 (2012)
8. Qian, Y., Yuan, H., Gong, M.: Budget-driven big data classification. In: Barbosa, D., Milios, E. (eds.) CANADIAN AI 2015. LNCS (LNAI), vol. 9091, pp. 71–83. Springer, Cham (2015). https://doi.org/10.1007/978-3-319-18356-5_7
9. Cao, N.B., et al.: Destination and route choice models for bidirectional pedestrian flow based on the social force model. IET Intell. Transp. Syst. **11**, 537–545 (2017)
10. Hong, M., Jung, J.J., Camacho, D.: GRSAT: a novel method on group recommendation by social affinity and trustworthiness. Cybern. Syst. **48**(3), 140–161 (2017)
11. Isba, R., Woolf, K., Hanneman, R.: Social network analysis in medical education. Med. Educ. **51**, 81–88 (2017)

12. Chvanova, M.S., Hramov, A.E., Khramova, M.V.: Is it possible to improve the university education with social networks: the opinion of students and teachers. In: Proceedings of the 2016 IEEE Conference on Quality Management, Transport and Information Security, Information Technologies (IT&MQ&IS), pp. 33–38 (2016)

13. Krouska, A., Troussas, C., Virvou, M.: Social networks as a learning environment: developed applications and comparative analysis. In: Proceedings of the 2017 8th International Conference on Information, Intelligence, Systems& Applications (IISA), pp. 1–6 (2017)

14. Al-Oqily, I., Abdallah, E., Abdallah, A.: Mobile intra-campus student social network. In: Proceedings of the 2017 IEEE Jordan Conference on Applied Electrical Engineering and Computing Technologies (AEECT), pp. 1–4 (2017)

15. Becheru, A., Popescu, E.: Using social network analysis to investigate students' collaboration patterns in eMUSE platform. In: Proceedings of the 2017 21st International Conference on System Theory, Control and Computing (ICSTCC), pp. 266–271 (2017)

16. Halawa, M.S., Shehab, M.E., Hamed, E.M.R.: Predicting student personality based on a data-driven model from student behavior on LMS and social networks. In: Proceedings of the 2015 15th International Conference on Digital Information Processing and Communications (ICDIPC), pp. 294–299 (2015)

17. Gremmen, M.C., van den Berg, Y., Segers, E., Cillessen, A.H.: Considerations for classroom seating arrangements and the role of teacher characteristics and beliefs. Soc. Psychol. Educ. **19**, 1–26 (2016)

18. Li, X., Zhang, Y., Bai, Y.Q., Chiang, F.K.: An investigation of university students classroom seating choices. J. Learn. Spaces (2017)

19. Upreti, M., Kumar, V.: Learning the student's sufferings using social networks. In: Proceedings of the 2017 International Conference on Computing, Communication and Automation (ICCCA), pp. 319–322 (2017)

20. Wei, X.Y., Yang, Z.Q.: Mining in-class social networks for large-scale pedagogical analysis. In: Proceedings of the 20th ACM International Conference on Multimedia, pp. 639–648 (2012)

Spatio-Temporal Eye Gaze Data Analysis to Better Understand Team Cognition

Nasim Hajari[1]([✉]), Wenjing He[2], Irene Cheng[1], Anup Basu[1], and Bin Zheng[2]

[1] MRC Center, Department of Computing Science, University of Alberta,
Edmonton, Canada
hajari@ualberta.ca
[2] SSRL Lab, Department of Surgery, University of Alberta,
Edmonton, Canada

Abstract. Studying and understanding team performance is very important for sports, games, health and any applications that involve a team of users. It is affected by team behaviour or cognition. Usually a team with a good shared cognition can perform better and achieve the set goal faster. Having a good team with a good shared behaviour is even more crucial in health care environments, especially for laprascopic surgery applications. Analyzing team cognition is a new area of research. In this paper, we study the team cognition between two surgeons, who performed a laparascopic simulation operation, by analyzing their eye tracking data spatially and temporally. We used Cross Recurrence Analysis (CRA) and overlap analysis to find spatio-temporal features that can be used to distinguish between a good performer team and a bad performer team. Dual eye tracking data for twenty two dyad teams were recorded during the simulation and then the teams were divided into good performer and poor performer teams based on the time to finish the task. We then analyze the signals to find common features for good performer teams. The results of this research indicates that the good performer teams show a smaller delay as well as have a higher overlap in the eyegaze signals compared to poor performer teams.

Keywords: Spatio-temporal data analysis · Team cognition

1 Introduction

Teamwork is critical in many working environments such as sports, games and healthcare. However, current assessment tools for teamwork are based on subjective assessments. Minimally invasive surgery is one application of teamwork, which is getting more popular. It has extensive benefits over conventional surgery such as shorter hospital stay and faster recovery time. Laparoscopic surgeries are mostly performed by teams of two or more surgeons [3]. In a laparoscopic surgery team, an assistant usually controls the primary surgeon's vision by manipulating a laparoscope through the surgery site. As several studies suggest, having

© Springer Nature Switzerland AG 2018
A. Basu and S. Berretti (Eds.): ICSM 2018, LNCS 11010, pp. 39–48, 2018.
https://doi.org/10.1007/978-3-030-04375-9_4

a relatively untrained assistant in the team may affect the primary surgeon's course of action and decision making due to non-optimal display of the surgical site [7,9,19]. These factors, further imposed upon the surgeon, who is already carrying considerable ergonomic difficulties related to laparoscopy, may eventually lead to overt surgical errors that compromise patient safety [2,7]. Therefore, teamwork in laparoscopic surgery is crucial and needs to be explored. It has been shown that a trained laparoscopic team can achieve better results in terms of operation time, patient care and overall cost [11]. However, the available training programs are mainly focused on individuals, and surgeons are evaluated on an individual basis [4,5,18]. Although team cognition is believed to be the foundation for team performance, there is no direct and objective way to measure it, especially in the healthcare setting. In fact, the lack of objective assessment tools has been a major barrier in promoting surgical team training [10,14,17].

One method to assess team collaboration is video analysis. [20] analyzed a simulation of an endoscopic cutting task performed by two operators. This study showed that team performance is highly correlated with team collaboration. In the recent years people used eye tracking systems to study different features of health care providers. A procedural and objective method to assess surgeon's skill is through eye gaze analysis. This method has been studied and well reported in the literature [1]. Studies such as [6,12,15] showed the difference between gaze pattern's of good and bad surgeon. Eye gaze data analysis is also useful in understanding surgeon's workload [16,21] as well as surgeon's interaction and team behaviour [8]. Khan and Zheng [12] used dual eye-tracking system to examine the spatial similarity in eye gaze data between two surgeons, through gaze overlap. One problem is phase difference and delay between team members. In other words, people may look at the same location on different time. To understand team cognition better, one needs to consider both spatial and temporal feature of eye gaze data.

In this paper, we study the spatial features of surgeons' gaze from elite and poor performance teams through overlap analysis. We also adopt CRP algorithms to analyze the temporal features of dual eye tracking signals recorded simultaneously from two human operators. Using both features, one can reveal more reliable evidence for shared cognition of surgeons in laparoscopic surgery. We hypothesize that there is a relationship between task completion time, recurrence rate, time delay and overlap between eye gaze signals for good performance team and bad performance team during the simulated surgery task. This is helpful in developing a novel method for assessment of the level of team cognition.

2   Background and Related Work

Cross Recurrence Plot (CRP) is a useful statistical tool to study and analyze two signals with different phase spaces. More importantly it can find the matched sequences between signals and so is a reliable tool for dynamic, short and complex data series. It is due to recurrence, which is an important property of non-stationary systems. Using CRP one can visualize the dynamic behaviour of the

systems as well as analyze the recurrence rate (RR), which can be explained by
Eq. 1 as it is explained in [13].

$$RR = \frac{1}{N^2} \sum_{i,j=1}^{N} R_{i,j} \tag{1}$$

where N is the number of points on the phase space trajectory, i and j belong
to the two different data series that we are studying and eventually $R_{i,j}$ is the
RP as defined by Eq. 2.

$$R_{i,j} = \Theta(\epsilon_i - \|\overrightarrow{x_i} - \overrightarrow{x_j}\|) \tag{2}$$

where $\overrightarrow{x_i}$ and $\overrightarrow{x_j}$ are the phase space trajectories of time series i and time series
j respectively. The states of a natural or engineering dynamic system usually
change over time. A state of a system x can be described by its d state variables,
$x_1(t), x_2(t), \ldots, x_d(t)$. The vector $(x(t))$ in a d-dimensional space is called phase
space. The system's evolving state over time traces a path, which is called the
phase space trajectory of the system.

RR can be used to find delay between two time serie as explained in [8].
Another method to find time delays is using cross-correlation between the two
signals. In this paper we use cross-correlation to find delays between the two eye
gaze signals. More technical details will be presented in the Measurement and
Data Analysis section.

3   Experimental Setup

This section explains the experimental setup and data collection procedure. The
study was performed in the Surgical Simulation Research Lab at the University
of Alberta. Methods used in this exper-iment were reviewed and approved by
the Health Research Ethics Board of the University of Alberta. Consent was
ob-tained from each participant before entering the study.

3.1   Participants

Participants included 17 university students, office staff, and visiting scholars of
which none have received special train-ing on laparoscopic surgery. They were
asked to form 22 dy-ad teams to perform a simple object transportation task
under the simulated surgical environment using the laparoscopic technique.

3.2   Apparatus

The experimental set up includes three main components. The first one is a
laparoscopic training box measuring $30 \times 30 \times 20$ cm (Fig. 1a). Inside this box the
distances of the home plate to different pins are labeled (Fig. 1a). The second
component is two 17" video monitors, which display the image captured by

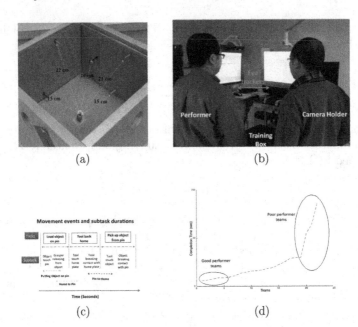

(a)   (b)

(c)   (d)

Fig. 1. (a) The black box setup; (b) The experimental setup; (c) Procedure and task description; (d) Completion time of the orange pin task for 22 teams. (Color figure online)

a laparoscope and a webcam. Finally, two high-resolution remote eye-trackers were set up in an orthogonal arrangement (Fig. 1b). More technical details of the experimental setup is shown in [8]

The task was to pick up an object (plastic cylinder, 2.0×1.5 cm) using a pair of laparoscopic graspers from the bottom floor of a laparoscopic training box (Fig. 1a), then transport to a pin located on one side-wall of the training box. After loading the cylinder onto the pin, participants need to bring the grasper back to the home base at the bottom floor of the training box. There were a total of five different colored pins located at the different side-walls. Figure 1c explains the steps required during each task. For this study, data analysis was performed on the task of reaching and loading the orange pin where eye-tracking yielded consistent data. In addition, the travel distance between the home base and the orange pin was about 20 cm, which provided a sufficient space to observe collaborative behaviors.

4   Measurement and Data Analysis

We analyzed the good and poor performer teams based on the spatial feature, which is gaze overlap percentage, as well as temporal features, which reports when the highest cross recurrence rate occurs between two team members' gaze signals. We also calculated the delay between two team members using cross-correlation.

To get a distinctive category of good performer and poor performer teams, we chose the top and bottom 25% of the teams based on the completion time of the orange pin task, which is shown as two closed regions in Fig. 1(d). We mainly focused on the tool transportation period for analysis purposes. We specifically considered the periods for tool transports from the orange pin to home and from home to the orange pin. Note that both orange and pink pins have the greatest distance from the home plate. However, we chose the orange pin in this paper because the separation between good performer and poor performer teams is more visible for this pin. The following subsections describe the spatial, temporal and delay analysis in more detail.

4.1 Spatial Data Analysis (Gaze Overlap)

We calculated the pixel overlap of the camera driver and the performer to study the spatial features. The gaze overlap analysis is explained in [8]. As studies [12] shown the level of gaze overlap is highly correlated with the level of expertise. Previous studies [12,15] suggested that a visual angle of at least 3° is required to mark eye gaze data as mismatch, therefore we set the threshold to 50 pixels, which indicates a gaze separation of almost 5° visual angle for our setup and resolution. In other words if the Euclidean distance between the location of two gaze signals is smaller than 50 pixels then both members are almost looking at the same location. The white circle in Fig. 2(a) demonstrates the overlapping area in the simulation environment and the red horizontal line in Fig. 2(b) shows a 50 pixel separation threshold on the difference between two gaze signals (blue curve).

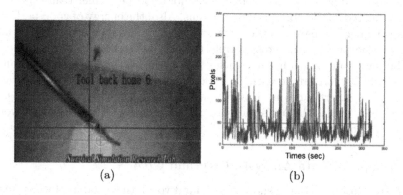

(a)   (b)

Fig. 2. (a) The overlay on dual eye tracking data on one frame of the video; (b) The eye-gaze overlap analysis as shown in [8]. (Color figure online)

4.2 Cross-Correlation and Delay Analysis

We used cross correlation to calculate the delay between team members. Cross-correlation of two signals $X = (X_t)$ and $Y = (Y_t)$ is the function that gives the correlation of the two signals at different time points. It displaced one signal relative to another. Please note that cross-correlation of two signals is similar to convolution of two functions. It is used as a measure of similarity between two signals. Also, it can detect if two signals have a lag relative to each other for the time delay analysis. Equation 3 shows how to calculate cross-correlation.

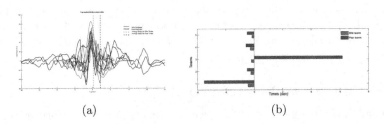

(a)   (b)

Fig. 3. (a) Distribution of phase delay between good performers and poor performers; (b) The delay distribution for good performers and poor performers.

$$(X \star Y)(\tau) = \int_{-\infty}^{\infty} X^*(t)\, Y(t + \tau)\, dt, \tag{3}$$

Please note that X^* is the conjugate of signal X. The maximum cross-correlation between the two signals is the point in time where two signals are best aligned. This represents the delay between the two signals. Figure 3(a) shows the distribution of the phase delay for good performer and poor performer teams. As the dotted lines show the average delay for good performer teams are much lower compared to the poor performer teams. Also, the energy of good performer teams is higher compared to the poor performer teams. The energy is the magnitude of the peak of the cross-correlation curve. Figure 3(b) shows the delay distribution. Note that a negative delay means that the camera holder is ahead of time, which is a characteristic of a good performer team and is an indication that they are expert surgeons. However, in the poor performer teams the positive average delay means the performer gaze signal is ahead of time. In other words, the camera holder is a novice.

4.3   Temporal Data Analysis, CRP and CRA

The first column of Fig. 4 shows CRP for two of the good performer teams and the second column belongs to poor performer teams. The diagonal area corresponds to the recurrence rate. As these figures demonstrate, the plots for elite teams reveal more recurrence area and also appear to be denser and more clustered, while the plots for the poor performer teams are more random and do not show the overlap patches very well. We also used CRA to get the numerical value for recurrence rates for both elite and poor performer teams. The results were presented in Fig. 5. The overall recurrence rate for good performer teams is higher compared to the poor performer teams.

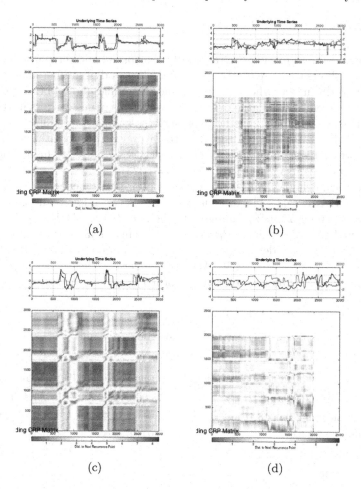

Fig. 4. (a, c) Cross Recurrence Plot for good performer teams; (b, d) Cross Recurrence Plot for poor performer teams.

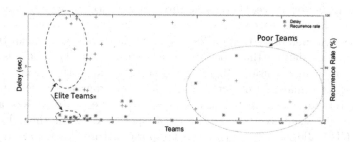

Fig. 5. The recurrence rate and delay distribution for poor performer and good performer teams.

5   Results

In this subsection we present the results of both spatial and temporal data analysis. Table 1 shows the gaze overlap percentage for good performer and poor performer teams during the whole procedure and the orange-pin tool transportation periods. The average total gaze overlap between two team members in the good performer team is higher than the poor performer team (Elite: 35.87 ± 4.84%; Poor: 28.74 ± 6.34%; P = 0.018), while the average transportation overlap for good performer teams is 50.97 ± 9.22%, which is significantly higher than the poor performer teams (29.56 ± 18.15%; P = 0.023).

The average delay for good performer and poor performer teams is presented in Table 1. CRA reveals a higher recurrence rate between two team members for elite teams (78.06 ± 25.93%) compared to the poor teams (34.41% ± 34.42; P = 0.0412). Further analysis shows that two team members in poor teams displayed a 2.75 ± 2.94 sec gaze delay; whereas the delay dropped to 0.3 ± 0.12 sec for good performer teams; P = 0.032. Also, the camera holder leads the performer in the elite teams while in the poor performer teams the performer leads the camera holder.

Table 1. Comparison of different features for good performer and poor performer teams.

	Transportation overlap (%)	Recurrence rate (%)	Delay (sec)
Elite teams	50.97 ± 9.22	78.06 ± 25.93	0.3 ± 0.12
Poor teams	29.56 ± 18.15	4.41 ± 34.42	2.27 ± 2.94
P value	0.023	0.0412	0.032

6   Discussion and Future Work

Using CRP and CRA to describe team cognition in healthcare environment is a new area of research. Although team cognition is believed to be the foundation for team performance, there is no direct and objective way to measure it, especially in the healthcare setting. In fact, the deficiency in tools for objective team assessment has been a major barrier in promoting surgical team training. Previous studies showed that spatial features such as overlap analysis can be a measure of team cognition [10,14,17]. However, due to the dynamic nature of the eye-gaze signals, gaze overlapping calculated from spatial feature is not sufficient. Temporal features of gaze signals should be analyzed too, as team members might scan over the same surgical spot at different time slops. The CRP and CRA allows us to capture this temporal feature. Therefore, we believe they provide a more powerful tool for spatio-temporal analysis and refer better to shared cognition than the gaze overlapping. The results presented in this paper support our hypothesis that the top performance team displayed higher recurrence rate (Figs. 4, 5). Specifically, two members in good performer teams scanned over the same surgical spot almost simultaneously, whereas members in the poor performance teams failed to scan over the same surgical spot at the same time. One of them, often the camera holder is behind the operator. Generally the delay would be higher and recurrence rate and overlap would be lower for teams with longer completion time. This study analyzed the teams based on completion time. However, the design of study should include expert surgeons in the elite teams, and compare their performance to team comprised by novice surgeons. We plan to perform a new study by including surgeons with different level of surgical expertise. Based on the results of our study, dual eye-tracking and CRP/CRA is demonstrated to be a powerful tool for revealing team cognition, and can help to improve the training quality of a surgical team.

References

1. Atkins, M.S., Tien, G., Khan, R.S., Meneghetti, A., Zheng, B.: What do surgeons see capturing and synchronizing eye gaze for surgery applications. Surg. Innov. **20**(3), 241–248 (2013)
2. Berguer, R., Forkey, D., Smith, W.: Ergonomic problems associated with laparoscopic surgery. Surg. Endosc. **13**(5), 466–468 (1999)
3. Cassera, M.A., Zheng, B., Martinec, D.V., Dunst, C.M., Swanström, L.L.: Surgical time independently affected by surgical team size. Am. J. Surg. **198**(2), 216–222 (2009)
4. Dunkin, B., Adrales, G., Apelgren, K., Mellinger, J.: Surgical simulation: a current review. Surg. Endosc. **21**(3), 357–366 (2007)
5. Feldman, L.S., Sherman, V., Fried, G.M.: Using simulators to assess laparoscopic competence: ready for widespread use? Surgery **135**(1), 28–42 (2004)
6. Flin, R., Maran, N.: Identifying and training non-technical skills for teams in acute medicine. Qual. Saf. Health Care **13**(suppl 1), i80–i84 (2004)
7. Gallagher, A.G., Al-Akash, M., Seymour, N.E., Satava, R.M.: An ergonomic analysis of the effects of camera rotation on laparoscopic performance. Surg. Endosc. **23**(12), 2684–2691 (2009)
8. Hajari, N., Cheng, I., Zheng, B., Basu, A.: Determining team cognition from delay analysis using cross recurrence plot. In: EMBC 2016, pp. 3482–3485 (2016)
9. Haveran, L.A., et al.: Optimizing laparoscopic task efficiency: the role of camera and monitor positions. Surg. Endosc. **21**(6), 980–984 (2007)
10. Healey, A., Undre, S., Vincent, C.: Developing observational measures of performance in surgical teams. Qual. Saf. Health Care **13**(suppl 1), i33–i40 (2004)
11. Kenyon, T.A., Lenker, M.P., Bax, T., Swanstrom, L.: Cost and benefit of the trained laparoscopic team. Surg. Endosc. **11**(8), 812–814 (1997)
12. Khan, R.S., Tien, G., Atkins, M.S., Zheng, B., Panton, O.N., Meneghetti, A.T.: Analysis of eye gaze: do novice surgeons look at the same location as expert surgeons during a laparoscopic operation? Surg. Endosc. **26**(12), 3536–3540 (2012)
13. Marwan, N., Romano, M.C., Thiel, M., Kurths, J.: Recurrence plots for the analysis of complex systems. Phys. Rep. **438**(5), 237–329 (2007)
14. Salas, E., Wilson, K.A., Burke, C.S., Priest, H.A.: Using simulation-based training to improve patient safety: what does it take? Jt. Comm. J. Qual. Patient Saf. **31**(7), 363–371 (2005)

15. Tien, G., Atkins, M.S., Jiang, X., Khan, R., Zheng, B.: Identifying eye gaze mismatch during laparoscopic surgery. Stud. Health Technol. Inform. **184**, 453–457 (2012)
16. Tien, G., Zheng, B., Atkins, M.S.: Quantifying surgeons' vigilance during laparoscopic operations using eyegaze tracking. In: MMVR, pp. 658–662 (2011)
17. Undre, S., Sevdalis, N., Healey, A.N., Darzi, S.A., Vincent, C.A.: Teamwork in the operating theatre: cohesion or confusion? J. Eval. Clin. Pract. **12**(2), 182–189 (2006)
18. Zheng, B., Denk, P., Martinec, D., Gatta, P., Whiteford, M., Swanström, L.: Building an efficient surgical team using a bench model simulation: construct validity of the legacy inanimate system for endoscopic team training (lisett). Surg. Endosc. **22**(4), 930–937 (2008)
19. Zheng, B., Janmohamed, Z., MacKenzie, C.: Reaction times and the decision-making process in endoscopic surgery. Surg. Endosc. Other Interv. Tech. **17**(9), 1475–1480 (2003)
20. Zheng, B., Verjee, F., Lomax, A., MacKenzie, C.: Video analysis of endoscopic cutting task performed by one versus two operators. Surg. Endosc. Other Interv. Tech. **19**(10), 1388–1395 (2005)
21. Zheng, B., Jiang, X., Tien, G., Meneghetti, A., Panton, O.N.M., Atkins, M.S.: Workload assessment of surgeons: correlation between NASA TLX and blinks. Surg. Endosc. **26**(10), 2746–2750 (2012)

Person-Centered Smart Multimedia: Serving People with Disabilities to the General Population

Person-Centric Multimedia: How Research Inspirations from Designing Solutions for Individual Users Benefits the Broader Population

Sethuraman Panchanathan, Ramin Tadayon, Hemanth Venkateswara$^{(\boxtimes)}$,
and Troy McDaniel

Center for Cognitive Ubiquitous Computing (CUbiC), Arizona State University,
Tempe, USA
{panch,rtadayon,hemanthv,troy.mcdaniel}@asu.edu
https://cubic.asu.edu/

Abstract. While Human-Centered Multimedia Computing (HCMC) improves upon traditional multimedia computing paradigms by accounting for the differences among populations of humans, inter-personal differences between, and intra-personal differences within, populations have created the need for a new paradigm which is sensitive to the needs of a specific user, task and environment. The paradigm of Person-Centered Multimedia Computing (PCMC) addresses this challenge by focusing the design of a system on a single user and challenge, shifting the focus to the individual. It is proposed that this paradigm can then extend the applicability of multimedia technology from the individual user to the broader population through the application of adaptation and integration. These concepts are discussed within the context of disability, where variations among individuals are particularly prevalent. Examples in domain adaptation and autonomous rehabilitative training are presented as proofs-of-concept to illustrate this process within PCMC.

Keywords: Person-centric computing · Coadaptive design
Human-computer interaction · Domain adaptation

1 Introduction

For decades of its existence, multimedia design research has emphasized the development of technology to serve the broader population. In doing so, solutions to challenges at the highest level of user homogeneity had prevailed in favor of encompassing as large a user base as possible. Far from being all-encompassing, however, these solutions have often left many users unable to fully benefit from their use, and still more unable to use them entirely. In perhaps no greater a scenario is this more prevalent than that of users with disabilities; since the focus of design had been on the technology itself rather than the one using it,

© Springer Nature Switzerland AG 2018
A. Basu and S. Berretti (Eds.): ICSM 2018, LNCS 11010, pp. 51–65, 2018.
https://doi.org/10.1007/978-3-030-04375-9_5

those who did not match the ambiguous template of "user", whether due to the inability to interface with the technology or to do so as effectively as other users who did not share their disability, found themselves at a disadvantage.

To address this fragmentation in the population benefiting from multimedia technology, new computing paradigms have emerged to restore the equilibrium between user and technology in design. The first of these paradigms is that of Human-Centered Multimedia Computing (HCMC) [16]. Human-Centered Multimedia Computing emphasizes the human as the central focus of the process of designing a computing interface. In doing so, this philosophy forces the researcher and designer to be sensitive to the characteristics that define populations of human beings. For example, we differ in our cultures, societal attributes, economies, behaviors, needs, goals and environments. The key advancement of HCMC is the ability for technology to be able to detect, adapt to and accommodate these variations between humans [6]. It is critical to note that this paradigm shift did not occur spontaneously; it is the result of years of advancement in technology and multimedia research, yielding new technologies that have the capability of capturing and utilizing a great deal of information about their users.

Despite the dramatic improvement yielded by HCMC in the applicability of multimedia solutions to a larger variety of individuals, there is still a gap in usability and accessibility that emerges from the fact that in many cases, users of technology vary greatly even at the individual level, and beyond this, even a single individual can change significantly over time. The paradigm of Person-Centered Multimedia Computing (PCMC) addresses this challenge by fully transitioning the focus of design from the technology to the individual [24]. Where HCMC seeks to incorporate inter-societal and inter-population variations in design, PCMC seeks instead to account for inter-personal and even intra-personal variations. The goal of this paradigm is to begin the design process with a challenge posed by a specific individual, yielding a design process wherein the two are integrated at every step. Hence, the technology developed using PCMC guarantees accessibility, usability, and often optimality for an individual. Typically, this fine-tuned design comes at the price of rendering the technology inflexible toward a broader audience. However, it is proposed that individually-inspired design which meets the explicit needs of individuals, using the methods of adaptation and integration, can also meet the implicit needs of a much broader audience. To demonstrate how these two methods expand the impact of the PCMC paradigm beyond what is possible even in HCMC, two example solutions from the Center for Cognitive Ubiquitous Computing are presented, along with the findings in each.

2 Person-Centric Multimedia in Disability Research

The field of disability research is a perfect platform for the application of person-centric design because it is one of the richest sources of intrapersonal variation. Disability is not necessarily a status that divides populations binarily; any individual may be abled in a given context or environment and disabled in another.

For example, in a dark environment, an individual who is blind may actually have a significant advantage in ability over his or her sighted peers due to the heightened sensitivity of the other senses developed as a result of the condition [26]. Hence, disability is largely a matter of the individual, the task and the context, and with this understanding, not only are there variations between individuals but also within a single individual over time. Nevertheless, even by the standard policies used to define disability in today's society, it affects a significant portion of the world's population. In the United States alone, an estimated 12.8 percent of the population are classified as individuals with disabilities (www.disabilitystatistics.org). To these individuals, it is of critical importance that an interface is accessible, yet in interfaces designed without the individual nature of disability in mind, accessibility is often nothing more than an afterthought, if it is considered at all [30].

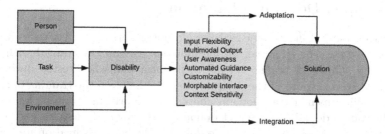

Fig. 1. The process by which person-centric design accounts for disability to provide an accessible, usable interface.

An overview of how person-centric computing weaves accessibility into the design process is given in Fig. 1. Two critical components of the process, adaptation and integration, allow for the applicability of the solution to transition smoothly from context to context. These components are defined and explained below within the example scenarios of domain adaptation and autonomous at-home rehabilitative training.

3   Adaptation: Transition to the Broader Public

Within person-centric computing, it is assumed that with any given technology or interface, it is inevitable that an individual will adapt, or attempt to adapt, to a particular technology over the duration of its use. For example, a new update to an individual's smart phone interface may change the layout of the menu, requiring that the user learn the latest way to navigate the software on the device. Person centric computing puts into practice the notion that a machine should also be able to detect and respond to variations in a user or context, and to constantly and frequently learn about and adapt to the user in a similar manner to which the user adapts to the machine. As the human and computer coadapt in this manner, a more reliable and robust interaction between the two is formed [12]. Therefore, when the task, the context, or even the user change, the system designed under PCC principles should evolve in turn to handle this change.

Adaptation in a system can manifest itself in a variety of ways, depending on the intended goal. For example, in the case of accessibility, adaptation might be applied at the input/output level, where the system may, for example, include redundancy of information in feedback across multiple modalities [17] or allow the user to control the way information is exchanged in the interaction [18]. Within a single user, the interface may change in complexity over time as it detects that the user's skill level or comfort level increases [1]. In addition to users, a system may, for example, adapt to a variety of domains, as presented in the following example of domain adaptation.

4   Example: Domain Adaptation

Data driven models in machine learning do not generalize well across different domains of data. For example, an autonomous driving car trained with data having only sunny-day traffic will fail to perform well when tested during the night. This is on account of the domain difference between the training data and the test environment data. Domain adaptation algorithms transfer knowledge from the source domain to a target domain in the form of models, feature representations and classifiers in order to develop efficient classification models for the target domain. These algorithms play a crucial role in being able to adapt systems across different data distributions. Person-centered algorithms trained using annotated data from a single individual can similarly be adapted to data from a wider population even in the absence of annotations. In this section, we discuss a model for unsupervised domain adaptation that adapts a classifier trained on a source dataset to data from a target domain with a different distribution. We evaluate this adaptation algorithm with face-expression and head-pose estimation datasets.

4.1   Nonlinear Domain Alignment

We first outline the problem of domain adaptation by considering two domains; source domain $\mathcal{D}_s$ and target domain $\mathcal{D}_t$. The source domain consists of data points $\mathbf{X}_S = [\mathbf{x}_1^s, \ldots, \mathbf{x}_{n_s}^s] \in \mathbb{R}^{d \times n_s}$ with associated labels $Y_S = [y_1^s, \ldots, y_{n_s}^s]$. The target domain has data points $\mathbf{X}_T = [\mathbf{x}_1^t, \ldots, \mathbf{x}_{n_t}^t] \in \mathbb{R}^{d \times n_t}$ and associated labels which are unknown; $Y_T = [y_1^t, \ldots, y_{n_t}^t]$. The data points $\mathbf{x}_i^s$ and $\mathbf{x}_i^t \in \mathbb{R}^d$ and the labels y_i^s and $y_i^t \in \{1, \ldots, C\}$. We define $\mathbf{X} := [\mathbf{x}_1, \ldots, \mathbf{x}_n] = [\mathbf{X}_S, \mathbf{X}_T]$ with $n = n_s + n_t$. The goal is to estimate the labels Y_T under the constraint that the source and target data come from different joint distributions; $P_S(X, Y) \neq P_T(X, Y)$.

A common procedure to align the features of the source and the target is by projecting them to a subspace. The Kernel-PCA (KPCA) estimates a nonlinear basis to account for nonlinear variations in the data. Data is mapped to an infinite-dimensional subspace defined by $\Phi(\mathbf{X}) = [\phi(\mathbf{x}_1), \ldots, \phi(\mathbf{x}_n)]$ before estimating the projection. $\phi : \mathbb{R}^d \rightarrow \mathcal{H}$ is the mapping function and $\mathcal{H}$ is the reproducing kernel hilbert space (RKHS). The similarity between data points $\mathbf{x}$ and $\mathbf{y}$ is represented by the dot product between the mapped representations $k(\mathbf{x}, \mathbf{y}) = \phi(\mathbf{x})^\top \phi(\mathbf{y})$. The similarities between all pairs of points is denoted by the kernel matrix $\mathbf{K} = \Phi(\mathbf{X})^\top \Phi(\mathbf{X}) \in \mathbb{R}^{n \times n}$. The kernel matrix is used to estimate the projection matrix $\mathbf{A}$ which is then used to project the data points to a common subspace. The projection matrix $\mathbf{A}$ is estimated by solving,

$$\max_{\mathbf{A}^\top \mathbf{A} = \mathbf{I}} \operatorname{tr}(\mathbf{A}^\top \mathbf{K} \mathbf{H} \mathbf{K}^\top \mathbf{A}), \tag{1}$$

where, $\mathbf{H}$ is the $n \times n$ dimension centering matrix given by $\mathbf{H} = \mathbf{I} - \frac{1}{n}\mathbf{1}$, and $\mathbf{I}$ is an identity matrix and $\mathbf{1}$ is an $n \times n$ dimension matrix of 1s. The projection matrix $\mathbf{A} \in \mathbb{R}^{n \times k}$, is the matrix of coefficients and the nonlinear projected data is given by $\mathbf{Z} = [\mathbf{z}_1, \ldots, \mathbf{z}_n] = \mathbf{A}^\top \mathbf{K} \in \mathbb{R}^{k \times n}$.

In order to reduce the source and target domain disparity, we apply Maximum Mean Discrepancy (MMD) [14], to align the projected features of the source and target. Incorporating the MMD, the projection matrix can now be estimated using the formulation,

$$\min_{\mathbf{A}} \left\| \frac{1}{n_s} \sum_{i=1}^{n_s} \mathbf{A}^\top \mathbf{k}_i - \frac{1}{n_t} \sum_{j=n_s+1}^{n} \mathbf{A}^\top \mathbf{k}_j \right\|_{\mathcal{H}}^2 = \operatorname{tr}(\mathbf{A}^\top \mathbf{K} \mathbf{M} \mathbf{K}^\top \mathbf{A}), \tag{2}$$

where $\mathbf{M}$, is the MMD matrix which is given by,

$$(\mathbf{M})_{ij} = \begin{cases} \frac{1}{n_s n_s}, & \mathbf{x}_i, \mathbf{x}_j \in \mathcal{D}_s \\ \frac{1}{n_t n_t}, & \mathbf{x}_i, \mathbf{x}_j \in \mathcal{D}_t \\ \frac{-1}{n_s n_t}, & \text{otherwise,} \end{cases} \tag{3}$$

Since the goal is to estimate the target data labels, Y_T, we need to estimate a projection where the data points are easily classified. We introduce laplacian eigenmaps to perform similarity based embedding. We cluster data points based on label similarity where data points having the same class label are clustered together ensuring easy classification. Data point similarity is captured using the $(n \times n)$ adjacency matrix $\mathbf{W}$, where,

$$\mathbf{W}_{ij} := \begin{cases} 1 & y_i^s = y_j^s \text{ or } i = j \\ 0 & y_i^s \neq y_j^s \text{ or labels unknown.} \end{cases} \tag{4}$$

When the sum of squared distances between projected data points (weighted by the adjacency matrix) is minimized, the projected data is clustered by class labels. This is expressed as a minimization problem,

$$\min_{\mathbf{Z}} \frac{1}{2} \sum_{ij} \left\| \frac{\mathbf{z}_i}{\sqrt{d_i}} - \frac{\mathbf{z}_j}{\sqrt{d_j}} \right\|^2 \mathbf{W}_{ij} = \min_{\mathbf{A}} \operatorname{tr}(\mathbf{A}^\top \mathbf{K} \mathbf{L} \mathbf{K}^\top \mathbf{A}). \tag{5}$$

where, $\mathbf{L}$, denotes the symmetric positive semi-definite graph laplacian matrix with $\mathbf{L} := \mathbf{I} - \mathbf{D}^{-1/2}\mathbf{W}\mathbf{D}^{-1/2}$, $\mathbf{I}$ is an identity matrix and $\mathbf{D}$, the $(n \times n)$ dimension diagonal matrix with the diagonal entries given by $d_i = \sum_k \mathbf{W}_{ik}$ and $d_j = \sum_k \mathbf{W}_{jk}$. Here, $||\mathbf{z}_i/\sqrt{d_i} - \mathbf{z}_j/\sqrt{d_j}||^2$, is the normalized squared Euclidean distance between the projected data points $\mathbf{z}_i$ and $\mathbf{z}_j$, which are clustered together when $\mathbf{W}_{ij} = 1$, (as they belong to the same category). The projected data is given by $\mathbf{Z} = \mathbf{A}^{\top}\mathbf{K}$.

4.2   Optimization Problem

We bring together the concepts of projection, domain alignment and similarity embedding to determine the projection matrix in the following optimization problem. Maximizing Eq. (1) while simultaneously minimizing Eqs. (2) and (5) is achieved by maintaining Eq. (1) constant and minimizing Eqs. (2) and (5). The optimization problem is defined as,

$$\min_{\mathbf{A}^{\top}\mathbf{KDK}^{\top}\mathbf{A}=\mathbf{I}} \operatorname{tr}(\mathbf{A}^{\top}\mathbf{KMK}^{\top}\mathbf{A}) + \operatorname{tr}(\mathbf{A}^{\top}\mathbf{KLK}^{\top}\mathbf{A}) + ||\mathbf{A}||_F^2. \tag{6}$$

where, the last term is the regularizer (Frobenius norm) ensuring a smooth projection matrix. The constraint on $\mathbf{A}$ (in place of equation $\mathbf{A}^{\top}\mathbf{KHK}^{\top}\mathbf{A} = \mathbf{I}$), is introduced to avoid the projection mapping onto a trivial subspace whose dimensions are less than k, [3]. Equation (6) is solved by introducing the Lagrangian given by,

$$\begin{aligned} L(\mathbf{A}, \mathbf{\Lambda}) = &\operatorname{tr}(\mathbf{A}^{\top}\mathbf{KMK}^{\top}\mathbf{A}) + \operatorname{tr}(\mathbf{A}^{\top}\mathbf{KLK}^{\top}\mathbf{A}) \\ &+ ||\mathbf{A}||_F^2 + \operatorname{tr}((\mathbf{I} - \mathbf{A}^{\top}\mathbf{KDK}^{\top}\mathbf{A})\mathbf{\Lambda}), \end{aligned} \tag{7}$$

with Lagrangian constants denoted by the diagonal matrix, $\mathbf{\Lambda} = diag(\lambda_1, \ldots, \lambda_k)$. Setting the derivative $\frac{\partial L}{\partial \mathbf{A}}$ to 0, we arrive at the generalized eigen-value problem,

$$\left(\mathbf{KMK}^{\top} + \mathbf{KLK}^{\top} + \mathbf{I}\right)\mathbf{A} = \mathbf{KDK}^{\top}\mathbf{A}\mathbf{\Lambda}. \tag{8}$$

The k-smallest eigen-vectors of Eq. (8) yield the projection matrix $\mathbf{A}$. The domain aligned projected features are then obtained by $\mathbf{Z} = \mathbf{A}^{\top}\mathbf{K}$. We note that a classifier can be trained with only the source data points in the projected data because we only have labels for the source data. However, since the source and target data points are aligned using MMD, we can assume that the source classifier can be used to determine the labels for the projected target data.

4.3   Experiments

In our original work [34], we test our model across different applications like digit recognition, object recognition, facial expression recognition and head-pose recognition. We present only a subset of the results that are relevant for social interaction. At CUbiC, we have spent over a decade designing social assistive aids for individuals who are blind in order to make social situations more accessible for these users. Our work focuses on vision-based analysis of facial expressions and other visual non-verbal social cues such as gestures and gaze. These cues are extracted from video, captured using a discreet wearable camera, and conveyed to the user through haptics and/or audio. The optimization problem in [34] is also a more generalized version of Eq. (6) and the results are based on the generalized model. For our experiments, we evaluated our model using facial expression recognition and head-pose applications that are relevant for social interaction.

MMI-CKPlus Datasets: The MMI [25], and CKPlus [21] are Facial Expression recognition datasets from which we choose 6 categories of facial expression, viz., *anger, disgust, fear, happy, sad* and *surprise*. We generate two domains, CKPlus and MMI, by selecting video frames with the most intense expressions from the two datasets. A pre-trained deep neural network (VGG-F [4]), was used to extract features (4096-dimensional) from the $fc7$ layer. PCA was applied to reduce the feature dimensions to 500.

PIE Dataset: The "Pose, Illumination and Expression" (PIE) dataset consists of face images (32×32 pixels) of 68 individuals with varying head-pose, illumination and expression. Along the lines of [20], we create 3 domains based on head-pose, viz. P05 (C05, left pose), P07 (C07, upward pose), P09 (C09, downward pose).

Table 1. Classification accuracies (%) for domain adaptation experiments on facial expression and head pose datasets. {CK+ → MMI implies CK+ is source domain and MMI is the target domain. The best results in every experiment (col) are highlighted in **bold**.

Expt	CK+ → MMI	MMI → CK+	P05 → P07	P05 → P09	P07 → P05	P07 → P09	P09 → P05	P09 → P07	Avg
SA	31.12	39.75	26.64	27.39	25.42	47.24	23.26	41.87	32.84
CA	31.89	37.74	40.33	41.97	41.51	53.43	35.47	47.08	41.18
GFK	28.75	37.94	26.21	27.27	25.27	47.37	21.88	43.09	32.22
TCA	**32.72**	31.33	40.76	41.79	41.78	51.47	34.69	47.70	40.28
TJM	30.35	40.62	10.80	7.29	16.63	21.69	14.98	27.26	21.20
JDA	29.78	28.39	58.81	54.23	57.62	62.93	50.96	57.95	50.08
NET	29.97	**45.83**	**77.84**	**70.96**	**74.55**	**77.08**	**73.98**	**79.01**	**66.15**

In our experiments, we compare the target data recognition accuracies with popular domain adaptation methods such as, Subspace Alignment (SA) [10] Correlation Alignment (CA) [31], Geodesic Flow Kernel (GFK) [13], Transfer Component Analysis (TCA) [23], Transfer Joint Matching (TJM) [19] and Joint Distribution Adaptation (JDA) [20]. Our model is denoted as Nonlinear Embedding Transform (NET). The results we present are based on the generalized model discussed in [34]. The recognition accuracies are depicted in Table 1. The table contains entries for the target data recognition accuracies. The source and target data are projected to a common domain based on solving Eq. (8). A classifier is trained using the projected source data and the labels for the target data are estimated with this classifier. The NET algorithm provides the best target data classification accuracies compared to the other methods.

The NET algorithm has a straightforward procedure to transfer facial expression recognition and head-pose estimation algorithms across different users. We can apply the NET algorithm to adapt a classification model trained for one user to other users (broader population). This is especially relevant when there is a lack of annotated data in the target dataset. Domain adaptation algorithms help to transfer knowledge from models trained on a population subset to broader populations in the absence of annotated data.

5   Integration: Stealth in Coadaptive Design

While it is of critical importance to design a system which can adapt to a user, it is just as critical to ensure that this adaptation is performed in a way which seamlessly integrates with the task and context under which the user interacts with this system. This integration should account for the complexity of the task and the interests of the user, and attempt to unify these components in a way that minimizes the burden of adaptation of the user to the technology. For example, the user's task of adapting to haptic feedback from a system designed to convey facial expressions is far less daunting when the haptic patterns are representative of natural facial expressions and directly map to those expressions [2]. When this integration is correctly performed, the adaptation mechanisms of a system are abstracted from the user in such a way that he or she may be completely unaware that they are being used, leading to a state called "stealth adaptation", named after the concept of "stealth assessment" [28].

In general, the most effective way to integrate stealth adaptation into a system is to find the most natural abstraction of the intended task of an individual given the interaction medium and its constraints and limitations, and to leverage these in design. How complex is the user's input? What metaphors can be drawn to ease the task of learning on the user? These challenges are presented here in the context of at-home upper extremity motor rehabilitation in the development of a system known as the Autonomous Training Assistant.

5.1   Example: The Autonomous Training Assistant

Overview. The Autonomous Training Assistant (ATA) is a system designed for the automation of guided at-home motor exercise during rehabilitation. The need for this system arose from the explicit need of a single individual, who was hemiparetic as a result of cerebral palsy resulting in one impaired arm and one fully-functioning arm, to complete a series of stick training exercises at home assigned by his martial arts trainer who uses self-defense training as a context for rehabilitative therapy. For this individual, conventional at-home repetitive practice did not provide the in-depth feedback on performance that was provided

Fig. 2. Overview illustration of the Autonomous Training Assistant system (right) and example game (left).

by the trainer in live exercise sessions between the two individuals, resulting in a less effective learning environment at-home.

Consequently, the two individuals expressed the need for a system that could utilize serious games [9] to deliver, a guided, automated exercise experience at home. While this was an explicit need exhibited by this individual, it touches upon a greater challenge in the world of rehabilitation: while frequent exercise in the home is necessary for steady recovery [29], lack of guidance in this environment can lead to reduced compliance to at-home exercise in the long term and, by extension, can slow the progress of the rehabilitation program [27] by dropping the individual outside of the zone of proximal development [35].

A system was developed consisting of a game interface using the Unity platform, a Microsoft Kinect V2 sensor to allow the system to track an individual's joint movements and facial expressions in real-time, and custom exercise equipment, entitled "The Intelligent Stick", equipped with an accelerometer and gyroscope for real-time motion trajectory tracking and haptic motors for vibrotactile feedback on performance as a user attempts an exercise task.

An overview of the ATA system, as originally shown in [32], is illustrated in Fig. 2. To use the system, the user simply picks up the Intelligent Stick and activates the game on Unity. The system then integrates the user's assigned at-home exercises into a game environment where the exercises are used as input to complete the game, and performance in the game is directly reflective of performance at the motion task. Three categories of feedback, as previously derived in [33], are provided to the user. Feedback on posture indicates how correctly the user's body is aligned during exercise, while feedback on progression indicates how accurately the motion itself is performed and pacing indicates how close to the ideal speed the user is moving.

Person-Centric Design. Person-centric design and adaptation principles were employed extensively throughout the creation of the ATA system. The Intelligent Stick device was designed to be modular, allowing for parts to be swapped in and out as necessary. This allows, for example, the use of customized grips for users with a variety of grip strengths, or various shapes and sizes to match the task and context for each user's training. The inspiration for this design was that the main user in this project required a custom grip with a strap so that his impaired hand could be secured on the stick during use. It was evident from this stage of the design process that the input mechanism to the system should be flexible enough to account for high individual variability both between individuals who have various tasks and upper extremity strength levels, and within a single individual's grip strength and exercise types over time.

Furthermore, the mechanism for feedback was designed with the individual in mind. The categories of posture, progression and pacing were derived by directly observing live sessions between the individual and trainer and recording the type of feedback provided by the trainer to the individual during these sessions. The goal of this process was to construct a framework for the evaluation of upper-extremity motor performance that was detailed enough to accurately capture the training program of this particular individual while being broad and flexible enough to encompass some of the most popular standard assessment methods in the field [11, 36]. The process of extracting these metrics is detailed in [33].

Finally, the game design process reflected person-centric philosophy by tailoring gameplay specifically to the individual and the task, as described below.

Stealth Adaptation. The approach taken toward stealth integration of adaptation elements in this work draws upon work by Shute et al. entitled "stealth assessment" in academic serious games, where assessment of the subject was performed behind the scenes and integrated directly into the gameplay [28]. To do this, the Evidence Centered Design (ECD) framework is applied [22]. This consists of three models: a task model specifying the type of real task that needs to be performed, a competency model specifying the metrics that indicate competency at that task (in this case, posture, progression and pacing) and an evidence model linking in-game metrics to task performance metrics in the competency model.

In this work, we extend this model to include adaptation. Three popular forms of Dynamic Difficulty Adaptation (DDA) [15] are explored: Bayes net refers to the usage of a Bayesian network to independently track each category of performance and to adapt independently to that category, while hit-rate stabilization refers to the attempt to stabilize the subject at a particular hit-rate, or success rate with respect to the task being performed, and clustering refers to the assignment of a skill level of "high", "normal" or "low" to a user's performance based on his or her history of performance at the same motor task. In all three cases, high performance results in an increase in difficulty to maintain challenge while low performance results in a reduction of difficulty.

Evaluation. To evaluate the system for the subject, the ECD framework was employed as the main method of integration. The subject was asked by the trainer to complete a swinging arc motion from the lower right to the upper left of the body. Due to the complexity of this motion, the fruit slicing game pictured

Fig. 3. Screenshot of the Island Fruit game in the case study of the ATA.

in Fig. 3 was developed wherein the sword would be abstracted virtually as a sword intended to slice fruit. Three fruit objects were deployed in the air in each round of a session, and these fruit adapted to the subject's pacing requirement by changing their falling speed, the progression requirement by changing their size, and the postural requirement by being unslicable when the user's impaired arm was off of the intelligent stick. The task of completing the arc motion was thus abstracted to the task of slicing three fruit objects as they fall through the air in virtual space. Three forms of adaptation (Bayes-net, hit-rate stabilization with target hit-rate = 2 fruit sliced, and clustering) and one control condition with no adaptation were experienced by the subject. The subject began with a 1-min tutorial, then played in four 5-min sessions with 10-min breaks inbetween sessions to account for possible learning or fatigue effects.

To determine how well each of the adaptation styles described above fit the needs of the user in this case study, an evaluation was performed using "flow-state", or the ratio in which the subject is considered fully engaged in gameplay to total game time. "Flow" in this context is simply the state in which an individual is given the appropriate level of difficulty in gameplay to match his or her skill level, facing challenges that are neither too difficult (resulting in frustration) or too easy (resulting in boredom) for the player [5]. Flow-state was extracted in this study by leveraging the real-time facial tracking of the Kinect camera. Facial data was fed into a process which would determine the individual's facial expression as a vector of 7 values representing its belief that the user is expressing each of the seven basic emotions contained within the Facial Action Coding System (FACS) [8]. This data was then mapped into a single flow-state output using a method similar to [7]. For each 5-min session, one flow-state value (either "boredom", "anxiety", "flow" or "unknown") was extracted every ten seconds of gameplay for a total of 30 samples in each session.

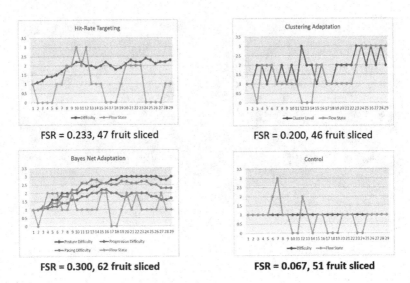

Fig. 4. Flow-state ratio for three adaptation methods (Bayes-net, Hit-rate stabilization, and Clustering) and control condition for Island Fruit game.

Results. Results of the study are shown in Fig. 4. The highest flow-state ratio of 0.300 was yielded in the condition wherein the user was evaluated independently on posture, progression, and pacing using a Bayes net, and each component of performance was then adapted to separately. This finding was also validated by the fact that the subject also demonstrated the highest performance in this condition, and provided the most positive subjective feedback and self-reporting of engagement during gameplay in this particular session. While these results are not reflective of the general effectiveness of these adaptation approaches over larger populations, they have indicated that there is a potential relationship worthy of exploring between the implementation of stealth adaptation in rehabilitative games to the level of engagement and long-term compliance, by extension, of an individual using such a system.

6   Conclusions

The works presented here serve as proofs-of-concept for the highly successful application of person-centric computing within the disability space. With careful design, it is demonstrated that solutions inspired by unique individuals in multimedia need not restrict themselves to those individuals, and can instead benefit the broader population in the same manner that many interfaces which were originally designed to target particular individuals with disabilities have done historically. Under this novel paradigm, individual empowerment fostered by a smart, learning, coadapting interface can redefine the way we view disability in human-computer interaction. Specifically, it can be interpreted in this domain as a spectrum of ability which can be modulated both by the individual and by the technology to create a space in which any individual is "able" to benefit from interacting with this technology.

Acknowledgements. The authors thank Arizona State University and National Science Foundation for their funding support. This material is partially based upon work supported by the National Science Foundation under Grant Nos. 1069125 and 1116360.

References

1. Afergan, D., et al.: Dynamic difficulty using brain metrics of workload. In: Proceedings of the 32nd Annual ACM Conference on Human Factors in Computing Systems, pp. 3797–3806. ACM (2014)
2. Bala, S., McDaniel, T., Panchanathan, S.: Visual-to-tactile mapping of facial movements for enriched social interactions. In: 2014 IEEE International Symposium on Haptic, Audio and Visual Environments and Games (HAVE), pp. 82–87. IEEE (2014)
3. Belkin, M., Niyogi, P.: Laplacian eigenmaps for dimensionality reduction and data representation. Neural Comput. **15**(6), 1373–1396 (2003)
4. Chatfield, K., Simonyan, K., Vedaldi, A., Zisserman, A.: Return of the devil in the details: delving deep into convolutional nets. In: BMVC (2014)
5. Chen, J.: Flow in games (and everything else). Commun. ACM **50**(4), 31–34 (2007)
6. Cooley, M.: Human-centered design. In: Information Design, pp. 59–81 (2000)
7. Craig, S.D., D'Mello, S., Witherspoon, A., Graesser, A.: Emote aloud during learning with autotutor: applying the facial action coding system to cognitive-affective states during learning. Cogn. Emot. **22**(5), 777–788 (2008)
8. Ekman, P., Rosenberg, E.L.: What the Face Reveals: Basic and Applied Studies of Spontaneous Expression Using the Facial Action Coding System (FACS). Oxford University Press, Oxford (1997)
9. Fernandez-Cervantes, V., Stroulia, E., Oliva, L.E., Gonzalez, F., Castillo, C.: Serious games: rehabilitation fuzzy grammar for exercise and therapy compliance. In: 2015 IEEE Games Entertainment Media Conference (GEM), pp. 1–8. IEEE (2015)
10. Fernando, B., Habrard, A., Sebban, M., Tuytelaars, T.: Unsupervised visual domain adaptation using subspace alignment. In: CVPR, pp. 2960–2967 (2013)
11. Fugl-Meyer, A.R., Jääskö, L., Leyman, I., Olsson, S., Steglind, S.: The post-stroke hemiplegic patient. 1. A method for evaluation of physical performance. Scand. J. Rehabil. Med. **7**(1), 13–31 (1975)
12. Gallina, P., Bellotto, N., Di Luca, M.: Progressive co-adaptation in human-machine interaction. In: 2015 12th International Conference on Informatics in Control, Automation and Robotics (ICINCO), vol. 2, pp. 362–368. IEEE (2015)
13. Gong, B., Shi, Y., Sha, F., Grauman, K.: Geodesic flow kernel for unsupervised domain adaptation. In: IEEE CVPR (2012)
14. Gretton, A., Smola, A., Huang, J., Schmittfull, M., Borgwardt, K., Schölkopf, B.: Covariate shift by kernel mean matching. In: Dataset Shift in Machine Learning, vol. 3, no. 4, p. 5 (2009)
15. Hunicke, R.: The case for dynamic difficulty adjustment in games. In: Proceedings of the 2005 ACM SIGCHI International Conference on Advances in Computer Entertainment Technology, pp. 429–433. ACM (2005)

16. Jaimes, A., Sebe, N., Gatica-Perez, D.: Human-centered computing: a multimedia perspective. In: Proceedings of the 14th ACM International Conference on Multimedia, pp. 855–864. ACM (2006)

17. Jewitt, C., Bezemer, J., O'Halloran, K.: Introducing Multimodality. Routledge, Abingdon (2016)

18. Jorritsma, W., Cnossen, F., van Ooijen, P.M.: Adaptive support for user interface customization: a study in radiology. Int. J. Hum.-Comput. Stud. **77**, 1–9 (2015)

19. Long, M., Wang, J., Ding, G., Sun, J., Yu, P.: Transfer joint matching for unsupervised domain adaptation. In: CVPR, pp. 1410–1417 (2014)

20. Long, M., Wang, J., Ding, G., Sun, J., Yu, P.S.: Transfer feature learning with joint distribution adaptation. In: Proceedings of the IEEE International Conference on Computer Vision, pp. 2200–2207 (2013)

21. Lucey, P., Cohn, J.F., Kanade, T., Saragih, J., Ambadar, Z., Matthews, I.: The extended Cohn-Kanade dataset (CK+): a complete dataset for action unit and emotion-specified expression. In: CVPR, pp. 94–101. IEEE (2010)

22. Mislevy, R.J., Haertel, G., Riconscente, M., Rutstein, D.W., Ziker, C.: Evidence-centered assessment design. In: Mislevy, R.J., Haertel, G., Riconscente, M., Rutstein, D.W. (eds.) Assessing Model-Based Reasoning using Evidence- Centered Design. SS, pp. 19–24. Springer, Cham (2017). https://doi.org/10.1007/978-3-319-52246-3_3

23. Pan, S.J., Tsang, I.W., Kwok, J.T., Yang, Q.: Domain adaptation via transfer component analysis. IEEE Trans. Neural Netw. **22**(2), 199–210 (2011)

24. Panchanathan, S., Chakraborty, S., McDaniel, T., Tadayon, R.: Person-centered multimedia computing: a new paradigm inspired by assistive and rehabilitative applications. IEEE MultiMedia **23**(3), 12–19 (2016)

25. Pantic, M., Valstar, M., Rademaker, R., Maat, L.: Web-based database for facial expression analysis. In: ICME. IEEE (2005)

26. Rauschecker, J.P.: Compensatory plasticity and sensory substitution in the cerebral cortex. Trends Neurosci. **18**(1), 36–43 (1995)

27. Shaughnessy, M., Resnick, B.M., Macko, R.F.: Testing a model of post-stroke exercise behavior. Rehabil. Nurs. **31**(1), 15–21 (2006)

28. Shute, V.J., Kim, Y.J.: Formative and stealth assessment. In: Spector, J.M., Merrill, M.D., Elen, J., Bishop, M.J. (eds.) Handbook of Research on Educational Communications and Technology, pp. 311–321. Springer, New York (2014). https://doi.org/10.1007/978-1-4614-3185-5_25

29. Smith, D., et al.: Remedial therapy after stroke: a randomised controlled trial. Br. Med. J. (Clin. Res. Ed.) **282**(6263), 517–520 (1981)

30. Stephanidis, C.: User interfaces for all: new perspectives into human-computer interaction. In: User Interfaces for All-Concepts, Methods, and Tools, vol. 1, pp. 3–17 (2001)

31. Sun, B., Feng, J., Saenko, K.: Return of frustratingly easy domain adaptation. In: ICCV, TASK-CV (2015)

32. Tadayon, R.: A person-centric design framework for at-home motor learning in serious games. Ph.D. thesis, Arizona State University (2017)

33. Tadayon, R., et al.: Interactive motor learning with the autonomous training assistant: a case study. In: Kurosu, M. (ed.) HCI 2015. LNCS, vol. 9170, pp. 495–506. Springer, Cham (2015). https://doi.org/10.1007/978-3-319-20916-6_46

34. Venkateswara, H., Chakraborty, S., McDaniel, T., Panchanathan, S.: Model selection with nonlinear embedding for unsupervised domain adaptation. In: KnowPros Workshop - Proceedings of the AAAI Conference on Artificial Intelligence (2017)

35. Vygotsky, L.: Zone of proximal development. In: Mind in Society: The Development of Higher Psychological Processes, vol. 5291, p. 157 (1987)
36. Wolf, S.L., Catlin, P.A., Ellis, M., Archer, A.L., Morgan, B., Piacentino, A.: Assessing wolf motor function test as outcome measure for research in patients after stroke. Stroke **32**(7), 1635–1639 (2001)

Deep Reinforcement Learning Methods for Navigational Aids

Bijan Fakhri[1], Aaron Keech[3], Joel Schlosser[3], Ethan Brooks[3],
Hemanth Venkateswara[1(✉)], Sethuraman Panchanathan[1], and Zsolt Kira[2,3]

[1] School of Computing, Informatics, and Decision Systems Engineering,
Arizona State University, Tempe, AZ 85281, USA
hkdv1@asu.edu

[2] School of Interactive Computing, Georgia Tech, 85 5th St. NW, Atlanta, GA, USA

[3] Georgia Tech Research Institute, 250 15th St. NW, Atlanta, GA, USA

Abstract. Navigation is one of the most complex daily activities we engage in. Partly due to its complexity, navigational abilities are vulnerable to many conditions including Topographical Agnosia, Alzheimer's Disease, and vision impairments. While navigation using solely vision remains a difficult problem in the field of assistive technology, emerging methods in Deep Reinforcement Learning and Computer Vision show promise in producing vision-based navigational aids for those with navigation impairments. To this effect, we introduce GraphMem, a Neural Computing approach to navigation tasks and compare it to several state of the art Neural Computing methods in a one-shot, 3D, first-person maze solving task. Comparing GraphMem to current methods in navigation tasks unveils insights into navigation and represents a first step towards employing these emerging techniques in navigational assistive technology.

Keywords: Navigation · Assistive technology
Reinforcement learning · Topographical agnosia

1 Introduction

From navigating the rooms and hallways of one's own home to navigating a large city, the cognitive functions involved in negotiating an environment to arrive at a predetermined destination are delicate, complex, and in many ways innate. Specialized components of the brain (head direction cells, place cells, grid cells, and border cells) have been shown to be integral to navigation [25]. Although the ability to navigate endows people with independence and self determination, many circumstances can lead to complications in navigation, and a surprising number of people experience such complications. The World Health Organization estimates that 253 million people worldwide have a vision impairment [4] and 21 to 25 million people have Alzheimer's Disease worldwide [7], both of which are known to cause navigation issues [24] among many other conditions.

A. Basu and S. Berretti (Eds.): ICSM 2018, LNCS 11010, pp. 66–75, 2018.
https://doi.org/10.1007/978-3-030-04375-9_6

Navigation itself is a complicated processes, requiring multisensory integration over time and space and a strong dependence on memory. Researchers have determined that efficiently storing and recalling the relationship of landmarks in space is essential to spacial cognition, and thus navigation [24]. There also exists large individual differences in navigation performance: an individual's acuity towards environmental cues, computational mechanisms, and spatial representations that are involved in navigation all are responsible for their navigational aptitude [30]. With so many factors affecting navigational ability, there exists real demand for assistive technology in the space of navigational aids. While the advent of ubiquitous GPS has already benefited many with navigational impairments, small scale and indoor navigation remains a challenge. There does though exist promise in the application of emerging computer vision based technologies for navigational aids.

Deep Learning (DL) and Convolutional Neural Networks (CNNs) have recently emerged to solve complex vision-based tasks [16, 18]. Coupled with reinforcement learning, these methods have been shown to learn increasingly complex behavior solely from images [3, 22, 23, 29], from playing Atari games to continuous control. This begs the question: can deep reinforcement learning techniques be employed in assistive technology to aid in navigation? In this paper, we survey the state of the art in Deep Reinforcement Learning methods suited for the high complexity of visual navigation, and present our own technique, GraphMem, designed for such tasks. We also compare the performance of these methods with our own first-person, vision based navigation task built on the ViZDoom 3D research platform [17], shown in Fig. 1. Our results provide insight into how assistive devices can benefit from emerging methods in Artificial Intelligence and provide a platform for future integration into assistive technology.

Fig. 1. Agent's point of view in ViZDoom.

2 Related Works

While Deep Q-Networks, Policy Gradients, and related deep reinforcement learning (DRL) methods [3, 21] have achieved super-human performance in many previously difficult domains, some seemingly simple tasks have remained out of reach. Specifically, problems with long-term temporal dependencies have proven difficult [28]. Navigation is one such problem; for example, in a first-person maze solving task, it is essential to recognize where you have already been in order to effectively trim the search space.

Several recent papers have validated the ability of deep networks to make sense of 3D environments using visual information, specifically with a focus on navigation tasks. Supervised methods have been developed such as [11], where authors trained a network to infer space through which a robot may travel unobstructed, in order to generate a trajectory for navigating the environment. While there has been success with supervized methods, reinforcement learning paradigms are of predominant interest to our goal, because agent-environment interaction is integral to navigation. Such approaches can be found in the work of [31], where the authors used a double-Q network (D3QN) to achieve obstacle avoidance and path planning in a reinforcement learning setting. DeepMind also showed in "Learning to Navigate in Cities Without a Map" [19] how natural images can be tamed with CNNs paired with LSTMs in vision-based navigation problems. Researchers in [32] also explored transfer between navigation tasks, training the model to navigate one environment and subsequently transferring its learning to a new environment in which the walls and objective have been modified. This work is similar to RL^2 [6], a model which achieves a sizable performance increase of 25.5% between the first and second attempts at the same maze. Our task is similar, but with the added complexity of random start positions between the first and second attempt at a maze. While RL^2 was able to store information in its hidden state, it did not make use of addressable external memory. Due to the complexity of spacial navigation tasks in terms of relational connectivity, we chose to explore methods with the capacity for more complex computation: Memory Augmented Neural Networks (MANNs). DeepMind's work in "Learning to Navigate in Complex Environments" [20] used a stacked LSTM model to solve randomized mazes. While the authors do not employ MANNs in their tests, they stress their applicability to problems of this complexity.

MANNs, sometimes termed "Neural Computers", are characterized by models utilizing an external and addressable memory space [8,9]. This allows them to store and recall information relevant to solving problems that require integrating and processing information over time and space more effectively than standard recurrent networks. For this reason MANNs trained in a Reinforcement Learning setting will be the focus of this work. Specifically, we selected the Differential Neural Computer (DNC) [9] and TARDIS [10] as MANNs to compare to our model, GraphMem. As a baseline, we also compare to a standard feed-forward multilayered perceptron (MLP) and an LSTM [13] based model. There has been work on MANNs used in navigation problems: in [26], authors used a MANN, similar to a Neural Turing Machine [8]. The model was tested in a Minecraft-style maze with discrete movement [15]. Authors also emphasized the use of memory in reinforcement learning tasks in [12], demonstrating the ability of Neural Computers to learn memory-based control tasks. Of these, the most pertinent to the task discussed in this paper is the "water maze" task, in which the agent must first find a hidden objective through random exploration and then subsequently find it again, taking advantage of memories from the initial exploration. Taking inspiration from graph-based representations [2, 27], we propose a MANN with graph-like external memory, with the intuition that the spacial connectedness of 3D environments lends itself to a graph-like representation, hence GraphMem.

3   Proposed Method

3.1   GraphMem

In this section we introduce GraphMem, a Memory Augmented Neural Network (MANN) with a novel graph-like external memory (Fig. 2). The choice of a graph structure for the external memory was inspired by the notion that the strong spacial connectivity of 3D environments would be best represented in memory with strong connectivity. Like most MANNs, GraphMem takes in an observation $\mathbf{x}_t$ at time t from the environment and outputs a distribution on actions $\mathbf{a}_t$ to take at time step $t + 1$. The magnitude of the ith element $\mathbf{a}_t[i]$ corresponds to the model's confidence in that action relative to all other actions. Observations are transformed into action probabilities by feeding the observation into a CNN, producing state representation vector $\phi_t \leftarrow \text{CNN}(\mathbf{x}_t)$. The representation is fed through the Memory Module generating a context vector $\mathbf{c}_t \leftarrow \text{MM}(\phi_t)$. The context vector represents information read from the memory that is relevant to the current observation. The context vector and state representation are then both fed to the policy (a fully connect neural network), which outputs action probabilities $\mathbf{a}_t \leftarrow \pi(\mathbf{c}_t, \phi_t)$. When the state representation ϕ_t passes through the Memory Module, the module reads from and writes to the memory, determining what to store from ϕ_t and where to store it. Information can thus be stored to be recalled when necessary. This process is outlined below.

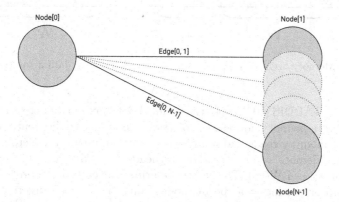

Fig. 2. GraphMem's memory consists of nodes and edges. Information can both be stored in nodes and edges, encouraging relational reasoning.

GraphMem extends the memory structure of the Neural Turing Machine and its successors [8–10] by modelling external memory as a fully connected graph, illustrated in Fig. 2, instead of a sequential array. In practice, the memory graph consists of two arrays, one containing the node data and the other containing the edge data. Figure 3 illustrates the substructures of the memory graph. The node array $\mathbf{N}_{\text{ode}} \in \mathbb{R}^{N \times (A+W)}$ is of size $N \times (A + W)$ where N is the number of nodes, A is the address field size, and W is the word size. The edge array $\mathbf{E}_{\text{dge}} \in \mathbb{R}^{N^2 \times W}$ is of size $N^2 \times W$, each edge connects a distinct pairs of nodes. The node array's address field is initialized with unique, sparse random vectors. The content field is initialized with zeros, as well as the edge array. At each time step, GraphMem writes to a single graph node and a single graph edge. The node it writes to is based on a content addressing scheme based on content, while the edge it writes to must be the edge connecting the node written to during the previous time step and the node being written to at the current time step. For example, if GraphMem writes to $\mathbf{N}_{\text{ode}}[i]$ at time t and $\mathbf{N}_{\text{ode}}[j]$ at time $t+1$, the edge it writes to at time $t+1$ is $\mathbf{E}_{\text{dge}}[i,j]$. The discrete and graph-like addressing forces GraphMem to discritize its observations and encourages the network to store information relating observations made in close proximity in both time and space in the edges, an ability indispensable to modeling 3D environments.

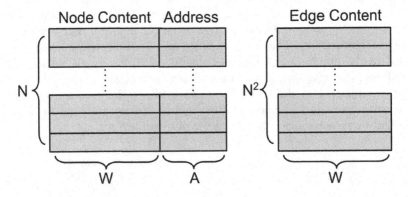

Fig. 3. Memory architecture: node data array (left), edge data array (right).

Similar to TARDIS [10], we use the Gumbel Softmax reparameterization trick [14] for discrete memory addressing to retain the ability to differentiate end-to-end. During memory reads and writes, the state representation vector ϕ_t passes through the Memory Module read/write heads (LSTMs) resulting in address logits vector $\mathbf{w}_t \leftarrow \text{RW}(\phi_t)$. This vector describes the categorical probabilities of reading from or writing to a specific node. Equations 1 and 2 describe how the address logits vector $\mathbf{w}_t$ is transformed into a one-hot vector $\mathbf{m}_t \in \mathbb{R}^N$ describing the memory address of the node to read or write from.

$$\mathbf{g}_t \leftarrow gumbel(\mathbf{w}_t) \tag{1}$$

$$\mathbf{m}_t = (one\_hot(argmax(\mathbf{g}_t)) - \mathbf{g}_t) + \mathbf{g}_t \tag{2}$$

Equation 2 features an *argmax* and *one_hot* operation, which are not differentiable. To circumvent this, the gradient only flows through $\mathbf{g}_t$, the last term, bypassing $(one\_hot(argmax(\mathbf{g}_t)) - \mathbf{g}_t)$. This estimates the derivative while allowing backpropagation through a discrete addressing mechanism. Details of the Gumbel Softmax function are described in [14].

3.2   Maze Task

The ViZDoom maze task was designed to reveal how effectively an agent can re-navigate to a location it has been to before, having started at a new location. Figure 4 shows a bird's eye view of the map and screenshots of the agent's point of view. Notice, the maze is not "simply connected" as it features detached walls that can fool more simple maze solving algorithms. The goal of this task is to find the "health pack" hidden in the maze. Each episode consists of two phases. For each phase the agent spawns in a random room and must search the maze for a "health pack". The agent is rewarded, on a per-episode basis, proportionally to the number of steps it takes to reach the goal ("health pack"). The fewer total steps taken (phase1 + phase2), the higher the agent's reward. In both phases of an episode the agent is given the same maze, so that the agent can make use of what was learned about the maze in Phase 1 when looking for the "health pack" in Phase 2. It is important to note that the agent is rewarded in proportion to the summation of steps taken in each phase. The agent will thus learn to minimize the total number of steps and in no way is directed to use its memory to optimize the second encounter. At the conclusion of an episode, both the locations of the "health pack" and furniture in the rooms is randomized, so that the agent must learn a policy that memorizes the maze's composition using its external memory only. This is to prevent the agent from memorizing the maze using the parameters of the model, which is slow and poorly replicates a real navigation scenario.

Fig. 4. Blueprint of the maze (left) Screenshots of the rooms (middle, right).

The maze environment consists of 9 rooms connected by hallways (shown in Fig. 4). All of the walls are identical. The only unique features in the rooms are pieces of "furniture" placed in the rooms, one piece of furniture per room. The goal is also placed in a random room at a random offset from the center of the room. This makes seeing the goal from across the maze non-trivial. Because the hallways are narrower than the rooms, furniture and the goal are not necessarily visible from another room. The agent may also get "caught" on the walls of the room, so the agent must learn efficient movement as well as an efficient exploration policy to maximize its reward. The maze was designed to be non-simply connected, meaning agents that cannot identify and address loop closures may loop indefinitely.

3.3   Training

We trained all of the models using the Asynchronous Advantage Actor-Critic (A3C) algorithm [22], which allows for training a model using many distinct instances of the environment in parallel. Parameter updates from the distinct instances are applied asynchronously to a master copy of the policy, which is periodically copied down to the worker copies of the policy that are interacting with the environment. The gradient is describe in Eq. 3, with policy π, return R_t, value function V, and model parameters θ. The model entropy $H(\pi(\mathbf{x}_t; \theta'))$ is also considered in the gradient to discourage premature convergence to sub-optimal policies (scaled by hyperparameter $\beta = 10^{-4}$).

$$\nabla_{\theta'} \log \pi(\mathbf{a}_t | \mathbf{x}_t; \theta')(R_t - V(\mathbf{x}_t; \theta_v)) + \beta \nabla_{\theta'} H(\pi(\mathbf{x}_t; \theta')) \tag{3}$$

The models were trained on a 12-core Xeon machine with an Nvidia GTX 1080ti using TensorFlow 1.3.0 [1]. Each model was trained for 30 million time steps ($\sim$12 h). Figure 5 shows the training graphs for all models. It is interesting to note that all models show meager performance until 10–15M time steps of training. For our tests, we used the DeepMind implementation of the Differential Neural Computer [9]. The LSTM and MLP models used were public A3C [22] implementations proven to work on OpenAI Gym benchmark suite [5] environments. We used our own implementation of TARDIS as a public version was not available at the time of writing.

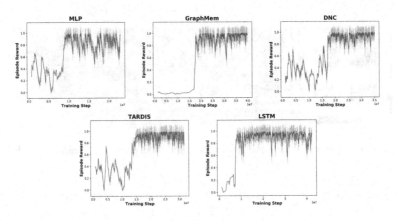

Fig. 5. Training graphs for all models.

4   Results

After training, all models were subjected to 123456 episodes of testing. During testing, the parameters of the network were frozen by disabling backpropagation and the models were subjected to the maze environment for evaluation. Figure 6 illustrates the average number of steps taken by the models in solving the maze tasks as well as the percentage improvement of steps between Phase 1 and Phase 2 of an episode. TARDIS and DNC proved to be the fastest models, while GraphMem was the slowest and the MLP and LSTM remain in middle of the pack. With regards to leveraging memory, GraphMem saw the greatest percentage improvement (percentage difference in number of steps between Phase 1 and Phase 2) of all the models, followed by LSTM. It is surprising to note that the two other MANNs were unable to capitalize on having already seen the maze, both models performed about as well as the memoryless MLP model (Table 1).

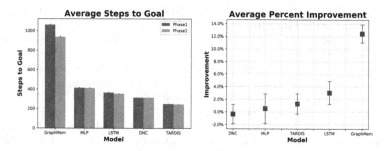

Fig. 6. Average steps to goal (left) percent improvement from Phase 1 to Phase 2 (right) both with 95% confidence intervals.

Table 1. Results with 95% confidence intervals.

	Phase1 $\bar{\mu}_{steps}$	Phase2 $\bar{\mu}_{steps}$	Steps sum	Improvement
TARDIS	248.92 ± 2.82	245.67 ± 2.88	494.59 ± 4.03	$1.29 \pm 1.61\%$
DNC	312.97 ± 3.39	314.06 ± 3.34	627.03 ± 4.75	$-0.36 \pm 1.52\%$
MLP	414.54 ± 6.57	412.27 ± 6.68	826.81 ± 9.37	$0.52 \pm 2.33\%$
LSTM	364.74 ± 4.85	353.56 ± 4.74	718.31 ± 6.78	$3.05 \pm 1.83\%$
Ours	1060.24 ± 8.43	938.76 ± 7.95	1999.00 ± 11.59	$11.45 \pm 1.41\%$

5   Conclusion and Future Work

Vision-based navigation remains a difficult problem in assistive technology. While Deep Reinforcement Learning methods for navigation are still in their infancy, this work highlights some promising approaches towards that goal. Improved methods will be beneficial in compensating for navigational difficulties faced by people with disabilities. Future work will emphasize memory access and content analysis - with the goal of human interpretable memory contents. We also intend to explore integrating this work or similar models with wearable computers, in order to provide real-time navigational assistance to users that are blind or have other vision impairments.

References

1. Abadi, et al.: TensorFlow: Large-Scale Machine Learning on Heterogeneous Distributed Systems (2016)
2. Allamanis, M., Brockschmidt, M., Khademi, M.: Learning to Represent Programs with Graphs. In: ICLR (2018)
3. Bengio, Y.: Continuous control with deep reinforcement learning. Foundations and Trends®. Mach. Learn. **2**(1), 1–127 (2009)
4. Bourne, R.R.A., et al.: Magnitude, temporal trends, and projections of the global prevalence of blindness and distance and near vision impairment: a systematic review and meta-analysis. Lancet Global Health **5**(9), e888–e897 (2017)
5. Brockman, G., et al.: OpenAI Gym (2016)
6. Duan, Y., Schulman, J., Chen, X., Bartlett, P., Sutskever, I., Abbeel, P.: RL2: fast reinforcement learning via slow reinforcement learning. arXiv, pp. 1–14 (2016)
7. Duthey, B.: Background Paper 6.11 Alzheimer Disease and other Dementias, Update on 2004. World Health Organization, pp. 1–77, February 2013
8. Graves, A., Wayne, G., Danihelka, I.: Neural Turing Machines. arXiv, pp. 1–26, October 2014
9. Graves, A., et al.: Hybrid computing using a neural network with dynamic external memory. Nat. Res. (2016)
10. Gulcehre, C., Chandar, S., Bengio, Y.: Memory Augmented Neural Networks with Wormhole Connections. arXiv, pp. 1–27 (2017)
11. Gupta, S., Davidson, J., Levine, S., Sukthankar, R., Malik, J.: Cognitive mapping and planning for visual navigation. In: CVPR (2017)
12. Heess, N., Hunt, J.J., Lillicrap, T.P., Silver, D.: Memory-based control with recurrent neural networks (2015)
13. Hochreiter, S., Urgen Schmidhuber, J.: Long short-term memory. Neural Comput. **9**(8), 1735–1780 (1997)
14. Jang, E., Gu, S., Poole, B.: Categorical Reparameterization with Gumbel-Softmax. In: International Conference on Learning Representations, pp. 1–13 (2017)
15. Johnson, M., Hofmann, K., Hutton, T., Bignell, D.: The Malmo platform for artificial intelligence experimentation. In: IJCAI International Joint Conference on Artificial Intelligence, January 2016, pp. 4246–4247 (2016)
16. Karpathy, A., Li, F.F.: Deep visual-semantic alignments for generating image descriptions. In: Proceedings of the IEEE Computer Society Conference on Computer Vision and Pattern Recognition, vol. 39, no. 4, pp. 3128–3137 (2015)

17. Kempka, M., Wydmuch, M., Runc, G., Toczek, J., Jaskowski, W.: ViZDoom: a doom-based AI research platform for visual reinforcement learning. In: IEEE Conference on Computational Intelligence and Games, CIG (2017)
18. Krizhevsky, A., Sutskever, I., Hinton, G.E.: ImageNet classification with deep convolutional neural networks. In: Advances In Neural Information Processing Systems, pp. 1–9 (2012)
19. Mirowski, et al.: Learning to Navigate in Cities Without a Map (2018)
20. Mirowski, P., et al.: Learning to navigate in complex environments. ICLR (2017)
21. Mnih, V., et al.: Human-level control through deep reinforcement learning. Nature **518**(7540), 529–533 (2015)
22. Mnih, et al.: Asynchronous methods for deep reinforcement learning. arXiv preprint, vol. 48, pp. 1–28. arXiv:1602.01783v1 [cs.LG] (2016)
23. Mnih, V., et al.: Playing Atari with deep reinforcement learning. arXiv (2013). https://www.cs.toronto.edu/~vmnih/docs/dqn.pdf
24. Monacelli, A.M., Cushman, L.A., Kavcic, V., Duffy, C.J.: Spatial disorientation in Alzheimer's disease: the remembrance of things passed. Neurology **61**(11), 1491–1497 (2003)
25. Moser, M.B., Rowland, D.C., Moser, E.I.: Place cells, grid cells, and memory. Cold Spring Harb. Perspect. Biol. **7**(2), a021808 (2015)
26. Oh, J., Chockalingam, V., Singh, S., Lee, H.: Control of Memory, Active Perception, and Action in Minecraft. arXiv:1605.09128 [cs] (2016)
27. Sanchez-Gonzalez, A., et al.: Graph networks as learnable physics engines for inference and control (2018)
28. Santoro, A., Bartunov, S., Botvinick, M., Wierstra, D., Lillicrap, T.: One-shot Learning with Memory-Augmented Neural Networks. arXiv:1605.06065 [cs], May 2016
29. Schulman, J., Levine, S., Jordan, M., Abbeel, P.: Trust region policy optimization. In: ICML 2015, p. 16, February 2015
30. Wolbers, T., Hegarty, M.: What determines our navigational abilities? Trends Cogn. Sci. **14**(3), 138–146 (2010)
31. Xie, L., Wang, S., Markham, A., Trigoni, N.: Towards Monocular Vision based Obstacle Avoidance Through Deep Reinforcement Learning. Robotics: Science and Systems Workshop 2017: New Frontiers for Deep Learning in Robotics (2017)
32. Zhang, J., Springenberg, J.T., Boedecker, J., Burgard, W.: Deep reinforcement learning with successor features for navigation across similar environments. In: IEEE International Conference on Intelligent Robots and Systems, September 2017, pp. 2371–2378 (2017)

Haptic and Robots for Smart Multimedia Applications

A Pneumatic Haptic Probe Replica for Tele-Robotized Ultrasonography

Ibrahim Abdallah[1], Fabrice Gatwaza[1], Nicolas Morette[2], Arnaud Lelevé[1(✉)],
Cyril Novales[2], Laurence Nouaille[2], Xavier Brun[1], and Pierre Vieyres[2]

[1] Univ Lyon, INSA Lyon, Laboratoire Ampère (UMR 5005), 69621 Lyon, France
arnaud.leleve@insa-lyon.fr
[2] Univ. Orléans, INSA-CVL, PRISME, EA 4229 Bourges, France
pierre.vieyres@univ-orleans.fr
http://www.ampere-lab.fr, https://www.univ-orleans.fr/prisme

Abstract. This paper introduces a pneumatic haptic device to remotely control a slave ultrasound probe-holder robot. This device should orientate this probe according to the sonographer's examination needs, while rendering the force applied by it on the patient's body, in order to provide a realistic examination environment as *in situ*. Previous designs with electric actuators were limited in terms of torque, dimensions and ergonomics, which actually did not match end-users' remote ultrasonography requirements. This paper describes the mechatronic design of an haptic pneumatic probe replica and preliminary control laws for it to perform as a Variable Stiffness Actuator (VSA). This approach is original and experimental results are provided to validate its feasibility.

Keywords: Medical robotics · Haptics · Variable Stiffness Actuator
Pneumatics

1 Introduction

Nowadays, more than one out of four emergency admissions requires an ultrasound examination. This non-radiative and relatively low-cost imaging technique is routinely used to help physicians to deliver a preliminary diagnosis. Depending on state health policies, an ultrasound imaging diagnosis is performed either by trained physicians or by specialized sonographers. In both cases, the physician/sonographer must be close to the patient to maintain and hold the ultrasound probe on the designated anatomic area to perform the examination. The sonographer integrates the position of the probe and the motion of his hand to analyze the resulting 2D ultrasound images. Since the late 1990s, in order to deliver equitable healthcare in medically isolated settings, several concepts of remote robotized ultrasonography have been developed, giving the sonographer the ability to move an ultrasound probe on a distant patient [5,7,10,20]. TER [22] or Masuda [11] used fixed robots attached to a table. Current trends are light body-mounted robots [13,14]: a paramedic holds the robot on the patient body

© Springer Nature Switzerland AG 2018
A. Basu and S. Berretti (Eds.): ICSM 2018, LNCS 11010, pp. 79–89, 2018.
https://doi.org/10.1007/978-3-030-04375-9_7

while the distant sonographer controls the probe orientation using a dedicated input device, as in Fig. 1.

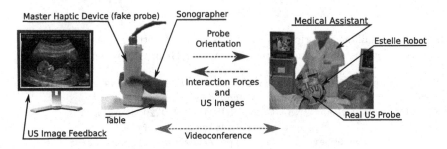

Fig. 1. Remote echography.

Ergonomics is a critical requirement as the sonographers should not be disturbed by the distance with their patient in order to only focus on the medical procedure. Hence, master devices have to provide sonographers with full transparency to perform a robotized remote ultrasound scanning as if they were next to the patient. The master device must be adapted to the sonographer's hand and to his/her expertise. Devices such as SensAble Phantom perform 3D/6D motions and can render force feedback [5]. However, their kinematic chain is totally different from the one offered by the standalone ultrasound probes sonographers are used to. This means that the practitioner has to adapt his/her hand motions to the proposed input devices, which therefore disturbs the medical act. We proposed in [6] to provide the sonographer with a master ultrasound probe with no mechanical link with the environment, similar to a standard ultrasound probe. The practitioner was able to hold it and move it (on a table) as he/she would manipulate a real ultrasound probe on a patient body. With this master probe concept, trained doctors or specialized sonographers should need less training to control the distant robot [19].

Also, when performing a robotized ultrasound examination, sonographers need to feel the interaction between the ultrasound probe and the patient's body. Indeed, they need to feel when they touch hard body parts and when the body-probe interaction stiffness changes. This is even more true at distance as the practitioner does not have a direct view of the patient (only through a web camera). The master probe should thus be actuated to render the interaction forces (and stiffness) between the real remote ultrasound probe and the patient's body. This is a real ergonomic and technological challenge: it is important to preserve weight and dimensions comparable to standard ultrasound probes. We identified the following requirements:

- a reversible mechanism with small dimensions (12 cm long, 6.5 cm wide and 3.5 cm thick at most),
- in the z direction (orthogonal to the patient's skin), a continuous force feedback level around 15 N,

– a maximum force of 25 N, a stroke of 50 mm, with a maximum velocity of 200 mm/s.

The devices we could find in the literature use various small electric actuators with the lowest possible inertia, but are unsuccessful in meeting all the aforementioned requirements. Neither a DC-motor [12], nor a custom brushless motor [4], nor a linear motor [21] were able to provide the combined characteristics. For instance, when using standard electric actuators, planetary or harmonic gears have a reduction factor of n for the rotation velocity which magnifies the inertia of the rotor by a factor n^2; this leads to the equivalent inertia of a 20 kg mass which makes the probe too sluggish.

In this paper, we propose to use a pneumatic cylinder as actuator to satisfy the end-users' requirements for the haptic input device to perform remote robotized ultrasonography. This approach is novel for this kind of application. This device is designed to be introduced in a bilateral control scheme (proposed earlier in [20]), controlling a remote robot which holds a real ultrasound probe. Performances of some basic control laws are evaluated in order to render, at the sonographer (master) site, the force applied on the remote patient's body by the real ultrasound probe, and the stiffness rendering.

The paper is organized as follows: Section 2 introduces the tele-echography system used in this project. Section 3 introduces the new mechanical design and Sect. 4 provides experimental results.

2 The Melody Teleoperation System

The tele-echography device developed by PRISME laboratory (see Fig. 2) was industrialized under patent in a French company called AdEchoTech. The Melody robot dedicated to tele-echography is now commercialized for hospitals. The system is divided into two parts: a slave robot on the patient side and a hand-free probe replica on the sonographer side without any mechanical connection between the two. A TCP/IP connection links the two parts.

Fig. 2. Adechotech melody system.

In order to perform a haptic control, we enhanced the aforementioned Melody robot by replacing the electric motor which performs the longitudinal (z) real probe motion by a linear motor. This ensures the reversibility of this motion and provides enough power (velocity and contact force) without any gear reducer. Moreover we added a force sensor which measures the reactive force of the patient's body on the ultrasound probe.

On the sonographer's side, we first designed electrically actuated probe replicas. Unfortunately, the various designs (with DC [12], brushless [21], custom direct drive or linear [21] motors) were mechanically irreversible, provided too slow dynamics, or were too heavy. Indeed, electrical motors struggle to provide linear fast motions on the one hand, and high forces at low speed on the other hand, all in a light and compact design without heating issues. This is why we propose a pneumatic actuation.

3   Design of a Pneumatic Haptic Probe Replica

3.1   Variable Stiffness Actuation

In order to reproduce a variable stiffness with an actuator, many Variable Stiffness Actuator (VSA) solutions have been proposed in the literature [3,8,9]. However, these solutions do not fit the sonographers' and remote ultrasound scanning requirements. Unlike electric actuators, pneumatic cylinders are low-cost off-the-shelf components and are easy to embed. They provide a natural passive compliance due to the pressurized air contained inside their two chambers. Moreover, by modifying these pressure levels, one can vary the pneumatic stiffness in real-time over a large range of values starting from 0.1 N/mm according to [18].

For instance, Semini et al. [16] introduced a VSA based on position-controlled hydraulic cylinders. Abry et al. [1] proposed a finer control law to handle the global closed loop compliance of a pneumatic cylinder using a backstepping approach. In this case, high frequency disturbances are absorbed by the natural compliance of the pressurized chambers while the control loop adjusts its stiffness. Senac et al. [17] reused these works to design a syringe simulator in the context of epidural needle insertion simulation. This approach will be adapted later to the needs of our project to enhance its performance.

3.2   Pneumatic Design

Pneumatic cylinders offer non-linear dynamics, which require more complex control laws, but on the other hand, provide a natural compliance due to the compressibility of the air in the chambers. This compliance is an important property that we expect from this haptic interface in order to satisfy the force rendering requirements. Position or force control of pneumatic cylinders is well mastered nowadays in the fluid power community, as detailed in [2,15].

In order to provide a guided active translation in the longitudinal direction between the socket and the body of the master probe, one asymmetric pneumatic cylinder (Pneumatic Union® CS 10 E) was integrated beside a low friction slider. The cylinder rod is linked with the socket (see Fig. 3). Two miniature piezoelectric 100 PSI pressure sensors (40PC series from Honeywell®, Canada) are located near the cylinder supplies through a T air connection to measure the cylinder chamber pressures. This is the closest location we could find with off-the-shelf pneumatic components. The rod position is provided by a lightweight (20 g) position sensor (LP804-2 by Omega Engineering) located beside the cylinder. Its range is 51 mm. The cylinder is supplied with a 5:2 Festo® MPYE-5-M5-010-B servovalve. A dSPACE® DS1104 board is used to control the servovalve and to sample the sensor values.

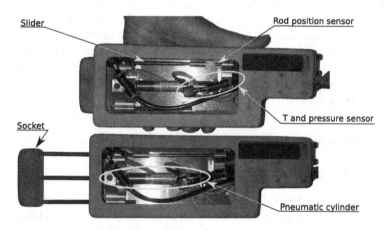

Fig. 3. Haptic pneumatic probe (with the rod completely in (top picture) and out (bottom picture).

The whole probe measures 120 mm high, 65 mm wide and 35 mm deep, and weighs 240 g. It is bulky compared to modern ultrasonography probes. Nevertheless, this prototype was designed for the purposes of a feasibility study. Hence off-the-shelf low-priced components have been preferred over ergonomic constraints. Future designs will take ergonomics into account more comprehensively.

3.3 Haptic Interface Force Control

In order to feed back interaction forces from the slave robot, the pneumatic actuator has to be controlled accordingly. A low level force tracking control has been set up. It controls the force exerted by the pneumatic actuator on the probe socket. As the socket of the probe is held in contact with a stable horizontal surface, the reaction force makes the upper part of the probe shift it up, in order to reproduce the variable interaction force between the real patient and the real ultrasound probe measured on the remote robot.

The global vertical (positive upward) force exerted on the hand of the practitioner is given by:

$$f_g(t) = f_p(t) - b\,\dot{z}_m(t) - f_{dry}(t) - M_u g \tag{1}$$

where f_p is the force exerted by the pneumatic cylinder on the rod (in the extension direction of the rod), b the viscous friction coefficient, z_m the position of the upper part ($z_m = 0$ when the rod is completely retracted, m subscript means "master"), f_{dry} the dry friction force, M_u the mass of the upper part of the probe and g the acceleration of gravity. Note that the $M_u g$ component is null when the rod is completely retracted as the upper part rests on the bottom part and the upper and lower parts rest on the force sensor.

The controller must track a desired force $f_d(t)$. To feed back this force (and reciprocally, the force exerted by the probe replica on the hand of the holder), the probe must push on a force sensor, attached to the horizontal surface, which measures the force applied by the probe on the table. The measured force also includes the weight of the replica but the main internal disturbances including frictions are thus naturally rejected in the control loop.

4   Experimental Validation

4.1   Force Tracking

Experiments were performed with a PI controller ($K_p = 0.1$ and $K_i = 4.10^{-3}$, see Fig. 4). The probe replica was held by an operator, standing on a force sensor (a ±100 N ELPF Load Cell model, manufactured by Measurement Specialties, Inc.) as visible in Fig. 5. So the force measured by the sensor f_m is directly fed back to the controller. Note that in the following measures, the mass of the replica was not accounted for but it will be so in the future.

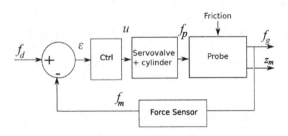

Fig. 4. Force controller for the master probe.

To evaluate the force tracking in realistic conditions (see next section), the desired force f_d was expressed as a function of the vertical position of the probe as:

$$f_d(t) = K_d(z_{m_{out}} - z_m(t)) \tag{2}$$

where $K_d = 400$ N/m was the desired stiffness, $z_{m_{out}} = 50$ mm is the position of the probe when the rod is completely out and z_m is its instantaneous position measured by the probe internal position sensor. The supply pressure was 4 bar.

Force sensor

Fig. 5. Experimental setup: the probe held by an operator and standing on a force sensor.

Figure 6 displays the desired and measured interaction forces, the tracking error and the position of the probe. One can observe a globally correct force tracking obtained with a simple PI controller. The worst performances are obtained for small force values below 10 N where the relative error rises up to 50%. Over 10 N, the mean relative error is around 10%.

The probe can render larger forces: during the experiments, a force of 27 N could be obtained. The maximal speed was not evaluated during these experiments. The performances in terms of force tracking are mitigated. Higher gains generate oscillations. A better tracking control should be tested with nonlinear controllers such as in [17]. Also, the noise visible in the force error signal of Figure 6 results from a small sampling resolution of the force sensor signal (ADC range is ± 10 V while the sensor signal uses a range of $[0\,\text{V}, 1.6\,\text{V}]$ for this application). An analogic preamplification of this signal should diminish it.

4.2 Stiffness Reproduction

In addition to feedback interaction forces, the master probe, handled by the sonographer, must reproduce a desired stiffness estimated by the slave robot, equipped with a force sensor measuring the interaction forces between the skin

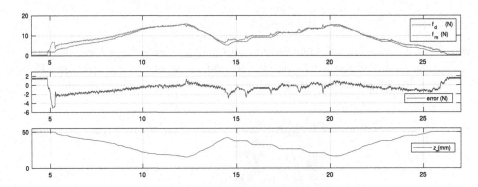

Fig. 6. Force tracking experimental results.

and the real ultrasound probe. The desired stiffness estimated by the slave robot site is as follows:

$$K_d = \frac{\Delta f_e}{\Delta z_s} \qquad (3)$$

where Δf_e is the variation of the measured force applied by the slave robot on the patient skin, and Δz_s is the variation of the position of the real probe in the axis orthogonal to the patient skin (z grows when the probe pushes harder against the skin), between each sample. This raw estimation should be further filtered and frozen when there is no motion. The estimated stiffness is transmitted through a TCP/IP network (satellite private link, Internet, etc). The controller of the master probe then computes a desired force to be applied by the actuator f_d following Eq. (2).

To evaluate the performance of the probe, we successively applied a range of desired stiffness (50, 100, 200, 400, 800, 1500 N/m) and asked the operator to "palpate" the table through the force sensor (see Fig. 7). We reconstructed the apparent stiffness by rearranging Eq. (2):

$$K_{eval} = -\frac{\Delta f_m}{\Delta z_m} \qquad (4)$$

where Δf_m is the variation of the force measured by the force sensor on the master side, and Δz_m is the variation of the position of the probe replica in the axis orthogonal to the patient skin, between each sample. After having removed some outliers due to short times where the probe did not move, the relative mean error RME is less than 4% (see Eq. (5) and Table 1). Taking into account that this stiffness reproduction is performed by force tracking, not by stiffness tracking, the resulting performance is satisfactory.

$$RME = \frac{|K_{eval} - K_{des}|}{K_{des}} \qquad (5)$$

Table 1. Relative mean error for various values of desired stiffness.

K_{des} [N/m]	RME (%)
50	1.3
100	1.7
200	1.8
400	1.8
800	2.0
1500	3.3

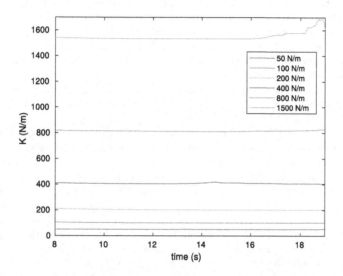

Fig. 7. Resulting stiffness for $K_{des} \in 50, 100, 200, 400, 800, 1500$ N/m.

Conclusion

This paper introduced a prototype of a pneumatic haptic probe to be used as a master input device in a teleoperated robotized ultrasonography system. Previous attempts to build hands-free haptic probes with electric actuators did not meet the end-users' specifications, which led us to study a pneumatic actuation. As the experimental results show, the use of a pneumatic actuator controlled as a Variable Stiffness Actuator makes it possible to reproduce a desired stiffness. Still, the force tracking is not yet sufficiently precise. This performance may still be enhanced by choosing a robust nonlinear controller such as in [17]. The reversibility of the probe replica, its strength >25 N, its stroke of 50 mm and its maximum velocity >200 mm/s already comply with our mechanical requirements. It is still a little over-sized, as off-the-shelf devices were used. However, this should be solved by selecting some smaller parts and/or custom-building other ones. Also, the use of this solution will require use of a compressed air supply. When not available, a compressed air cylinder can be used for this purpose. A study of the air consumption during typical ultrasonography sessions performed by radiologists will help us to determine its required capacity. Future experimentations featuring the whole teleoperation loop will be held to evaluate the overall quality of the whole system. Also, these results will be accompanied by a psychometric study determining whether users are able to recognize common medical cases.

References

1. Abry, F., Brun, X., Sesmat, S., Bideaux, E.: Non-linear position control of a pneumatic actuator with closed-loopstiffness and damping tuning. In: Proceedings of the European Control Conference 2013 (2013)
2. Falcao Carneiro, J., Gomes de Almeida, F.: Using two servovalves to improve pneumatic force control in industrial cylinders. Int. J. Adv. Manuf. Technol. **66**(1–4), 283–301 (2013)
3. Cestari, M., Sanz-Merodio, D., Arevalo, J.C., Garcia, E.: Ares, a variable stiffness actuator with embedded force sensor for the atlas exoskeleton. Ind. Robot.: Int. J. **41**(6), 518–526 (2014)
4. Charron, G., et al.: Robotic platform for an interactive tele-echographic system: the prosit anr-2008 project. In: Proceedings of Hamlyn Symposium on Medical Robotics, London, UK, May 2010
5. Conti, F., Park, J., Khatib, O.: Interface design and control strategies for a robot assisted ultrasonic examination system. In: Khatib, O., Kumar, V., Sukhatme, G. (eds.) Experimental Robotics. Springer Tracts in Advanced Robotics, vol. 79, pp. 97–113. Springer, Heidelberg (2014). https://doi.org/10.1007/978-3-642-28572-1_7
6. Courreges, F., Novales, C., Poisson, G., Vieyres, P.: Modelisation, commande geometrique et utilisation d'un robot portable de tele-echographie: teresa. J. Eur. Syst. Autom. (JESA) **43**(1), 165–196 (2009). ISSN 12696935
7. Gourdon, A., Poignet, P., Poisson, G., Vieyres, P., Marche, P.: A new robotic mechanism for medical application. In: Proceedings of the IEEE/ASME International Conference on Advanced Intelligent Mechatronics (AIM 1999), pp. 33–38 (1999)
8. Groothuis, S.S., Rusticelli, G., Zucchelli, A., Stramigioli, S., Carloni, R.: The variable stiffness actuator vsaUT-II: mechanical design, modeling, and identification. IEEE/ASME Trans. Mechatron. **19**(2), 589–597 (2014)
9. Jafari, A., Tsagarakis, N.G., Sardellitti, I., Caldwell, D.G.: A new actuator with adjustable stiffness based on a variable ratio lever mechanism. IEEE/ASME Trans. Mechatron. **19**(1), 55–63 (2014)
10. Krupa, A., Folio, D., Novales, C., Vieyres, P., Li, T.: Robotized tele-echography: an assisting visibility tool to support expert diagnostic. IEEE Syst. J. **PP**(99), 1–10 (2014)
11. Masuda, K., Kimura, E., Tateishi, N., Ishihara, K.: Three dimensional motion mechanism of ultrasound probe and its application for tele-echography system. In: Proceedings of the IEEE/RSJ International Conference on Intelligent Robots and Systems, vol. 2, pp. 1112–1116 (2001)
12. Mourioux, G., Novales, C., Smith-Guerin, N., Vieyres, P., Poisson, G.: A free haptic device for tele-echography. In: Proceedings of International Workshop on Research and Education in Mechatronics (REM 2005), Annecy, June 2005
13. Najafi, F., Sepehri, N.: A novel hand-controller for remote ultrasound imaging. Mechatronics **18**(10), 578–590 (2008)

14. Nouaille, L., Vieyres, P., Poisson, G.: Process of optimisation for a 4 DOF tele-echography robot. Robotica **30**, 1131–1145 (2012)
15. Abd, R., Rahman, L.H., Sepehri, N.: Design and experimental study of a dynamical adaptive backstepping–sliding mode control scheme for position tracking and regulating of a low-cost pneumatic cylinder. Int. J. Robust Nonlinear Control. **26**(4), 853–875 (2016)
16. Semini, C., Tsagarakis, N.G., Guglielmino, E., Focchi, M., Cannella, F., Caldwell, D.G.: Design of HyQ-a hydraulically and electrically actuated quadruped robot. Proc. Inst. Mech. Eng. Part J. Syst. Control Eng. **225**, 831–849 (2011)
17. Senac, T., Lelevé, A., Moreau, R.: Control laws for pneumatic cylinder in order to emulate the loss of resistance principle. In: IFAC 2017 World Congress, Proceedings of the 20th World Congress of the International Federation of Automatic Control, Toulouse, France, July 2017. IFAC (2017)
18. Takaiwa, M., Noritsugu, T.: Development of pneumatic human interface and its application for compliance display. In: Proceedings of 26th Annual Conference of the IEEE Industrial Electronics Society (IECON 2000), pp. 806–811, vol. 2 (2000)
19. Vieyres, P., et al.: The next challenge for world wide robotized tele-echographyexperiment (wortex 2012): from engineering success to healthcare delivery. In: Proceedings of TUMI II, Congreso Peruano de Ingeniera Biomedical Bioingeniera, Biotecnologica y Fisica Medica, Lima, Peru, May 2013
20. Vieyres, P., Poisson, G., Courreges, F., Smith-Guerin, N., Novales, C., Arbeille, P.: A tele-operated robotic system for mobile tele-echography: the Otelo project. In: Istepanian, R.S.H., Laxminarayan, S., Pattichis, C.S. (eds.) M-Health. Topics in Biomedical Engineering, pp. 461–473. Springer, Boston (2006). https://doi.org/10.1007/0-387-26559-7_35
21. Vieyres, P., et al.: An anticipative control approach and interactive gui to enhance the rendering of the distal robot interaction with its environment during robotized tele-echography: interactive platform for robotized tele-echography. Int. J. Monit. Surveill. Technol. Res. **1**(3), 1–19 (2013)
22. Vilchis Gonzales, A., et al.: TER: a system for robotic tele-echography. In: Niessen, W.J., Viergever, M.A. (eds.) MICCAI 2001. LNCS, vol. 2208, pp. 326–334. Springer, Heidelberg (2001). https://doi.org/10.1007/3-540-45468-3_39

Haptic Vision: Augmenting Non-visual Travel and Accessing Environmental Information at a Distance

Bryan Duarte, Troy McDaniel[(⊠)], Ramin Tadayon,
Samjhana Devkota, Gracie Strasser, CeCe Ramey,
and Sethuraman Panchanathan

Center for Cognitive Ubiquitous Computing (CUbiC), School of Computing,
Informatics, and Decision Systems Engineering, Arizona State University,
Tempe, AZ 85281, USA
{bjduarte, troy.mcdaniel, rtadayon, panch}@asu.edu

Abstract. Independent travel is essential to an individual's ability to lead a healthy and successful life. For individuals who are blind and low vision, however, access to critical safety and way-finding information is limited to the objects within their immediate vicinity. Due to the versatility and information obtained through its use, the long white cane remains the most widely used method of non-visual travel. Non-visual travelers are able to use a cane to interrogate objects to obtain perceptual information allowing them to identify physical characteristics such as position, distance, texture, and slope, but only in close proximity. This work aims to augment current methods of non-visual travel to extend the distance at which a non-visual traveler can obtain information about their surroundings. We propose a relative mapping between the angular direction and distance of an object with respect to the orientation of the user, displayed using a two-dimensional matrix of haptic (vibrotactile) motors. A preliminary experiment revealed that blind and low vision subjects could identify objects and their angular direction and distance through the sense of touch.

Keywords: Haptics · Sensory substitution · Non-visual travel

1 Introduction

An individual who is blind or low vision obtains critical safety and navigational information about their surroundings through the use of a long white cane, guide dog, and/or human guide. Although the number of individuals who travel with the long white cane as their primary method of travel is unknown, it is estimated that only 2% of non-visual travelers use a guide dog as their primary means of travel [1]. Of the estimated 2% who primarily use a guide dog for travel, they must also be capable of utilizing another form of independent travel such as the white cane. In addition to the three non-technical modalities for non-visual travel, there are three sub-categories of assistive technology available to augment or substitute vision during travel. An electronic travel aid (ETA) is a device developed to provide sensory substitution by gathering real-time data about objects in the environment and conveying that information to the user through an available modality. An electronic orientation aid (EOA) is a device designed to provide orientation information prior to or during travel as a sensory augmentation tool. A position locator device (PLD) is used to provide way-finding information during travel as in the use of Global Positioning System (GPS), which typically delivers guidance information through speech output.

While specialized training is available to equip someone who is blind with the skills and confidence necessary to live an independent life, there are still limitations present by the nature of a visual disability where assistive technology is critical. For example, when traveling by cane, obstacles above the reach of the cane go undetected by the traveler until they collide with the object. Consequently, a collision of this type often results in injury to areas of the body such as the head [2]. In addition to the potential for injury, a non-visual traveler is largely unable to obtain information about their surroundings such as: objects of interest (e.g., landmarks) out of reach of the cane; the position or movements of other travelers; and obstacles at a distance for timely decision-making to ensure safety.

While the topic of electronic travel aids has seen much focus over the last couple of decades, there has been little effort to understand the needs of individuals who are blind for assistive travel aids. To gain a deeper understanding of the techniques, methods, and cues non-visual travelers utilize when traveling independently, we surveyed 90 individuals who identify as blind or low vision. In conjunction to the survey, we interviewed 15 orientation and mobility professionals who all hold a certification from an accredited university or agency to help identify the techniques, methods, and cues used in traveling safely and independently with a cane. These need-finding efforts have helped us identify the information most useful for non-visual travel as well as the optimal modality to present the information.

2   Related Work

Besides the sense of touch demonstrating promise as an alternative modality for communication, particularly in the field of sensory substitution, the skin also has the advantage of offering a discreet and personal information delivery channel that is potentially less obtrusive compared to modalities of vision and hearing. Moreover, information may be displayed to any part of the body, or the entire body itself, thereby allowing opportunities for a rich dimension upon which to design stimuli.

In contrast to the use of haptics to convey visual information to non-visual travelers, other modalities have been explored including speech synthesizers and audio tones [3, 4]. In addition to these outdoor travel aids, systems, such as Toward [5], have been designed to provide access to visual information through speech and audio while indoors. Speech and audio output have been vastly explored in the context of non-visual travel aids mainly due to the detail in which information may be conveyed through this modality. Moreover, individuals who are blind or low vision are familiar with accessing information on a computer or smart phone through the use of a screen reader or Text To Speech Engine (TTS). Unfortunately, speech and audio output obstructs hearing, and consequently, this may interfere with a non-visual traveler's ability to interact with his or her surroundings, as well as other patrons, and to remain safe when positioning to cross a street.

Within the last decade, more focus has been placed on the use of haptics as a viable modality for providing access to visual information for non-visual travelers. Palleja et al. [6] developed a tactile belt to present information extracted from a bioinspired electronic white cane using LIDAR and a tri-axial accelerometer. Mann et al. [7] proposed a system for blind navigation using a wearable range camera and a helmet embedded with vibrotactile actuators that vibrate in the direction of an approaching object to assist with obstacle avoidance. Head level collisions have been addressed by other ETAs such as the Wearable Collision Warning System for the Blind [8].

These projects demonstrate the potential for haptics in ETAs, but more work is required. Efforts thus far have been limited to communicating one or two dimensions of situational awareness information to users; in particular, obstacle angle and/or distance. In this work, we explore the mapping of three spatial dimensions (elevation, angle, and distance) to a user relative of his or her orientation and position using visual-to-tactile sensory substitution. Through pilot testing, we first identified a promising mapping for these three dimensions, described next in Sect. 3. We then conducted a user study with individuals who are blind to assess the intuitiveness and ease-of-recognition of the proposed mappings, described in Sect. 4.

3 Proposed Approach

3.1 Hardware Design

The final hardware design will be a wearable two-dimensional vibrotactile display that wraps around the torso with actuators at the back, centered at the spine. The back was chosen to maximize the surface area of the skin for which information may be presented two dimensionally. As a preliminary first step to evaluate the proposed mapping, described in Sect. 3.2, we choose to conduct an experimental study using a vibrotactile device, the Haptic Chair, depicted in Fig. 1, that we previously built [9]. Using an existing device allowed us to focus on the design and testing of the conceptual mappings, the findings of which will ultimately inform the design of the final wearable hardware implementation. The Haptic Chair consists of an ergonomic mesh chair embedded with a 6×8 two-dimensional array of 3 V DC pancake (ERM) motors. Motors are spaced 2 cm horizontally and 4 cm vertically (measured center-to-center). This spacing was chosen based on results of van Erp's [10] study exploring vibrotactile spatial acuity on the abdomen and back. The wearable version of the display will be similar in design. Actuators are attached to custom printed circuit boards, which are connected over I^2C, and controlled using an Arduino FIO.

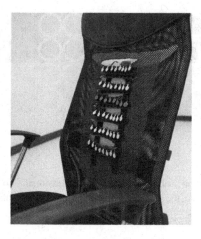

Fig. 1. Haptic Chair with close-up of two-dimensional vibrotactile display consisting of six rows and eight columns of vibrating pancake motors.

3.2 Software Design and Conceptual Mapping

Software for controlling the Haptic Chair was written in Python, and actuation scripts were composed as JSON files, which can be quickly created for rapid prototyping and evaluation. Actuation scripts for the following mappings were created and used with a custom-built GUI, also developed in Python, for the research study in Sect. 4. To map three-dimensional positions to a two-dimensional haptic display, mappings must be intuitive and intelligible. Furthermore, mappings should use the egocentricity of the human body as a focal point allowing for angular position to be perceived relative to the orientation and position of the user. To convey three-dimensional data through a two-dimensional interface, we designed the mappings based on situational metaphors. Below, we first describe the mapping for each dimension—elevation, angle, and distance—and then we describe how these dimensions are combined into three-dimensional patterns.

Three levels of elevation are used, and each level is mapped to a different object: (i) Low elevation describes a chair; (ii) Mid elevation describes a vehicle; and (iii) High elevation describes a person. Each mapping of elevation is relative to the user allowing for the system to be intuitive universally across genders, ages, and body types. These objects correspond to actuating the bottom two rows (chair); middle two rows (vehicle); or top two rows (person) of the display, depicted in Fig. 2. These objects (or obstacles depending on the context) were chosen as they are commonly encountered by individuals who are blind during transit; but their representations are intended to be situational metaphors, and therefore, elevation cues may be mapped to other objects based on context; for example, an object at low elevation could refer to bench when the user is in a park setting, or a low hanging branch during a hike.

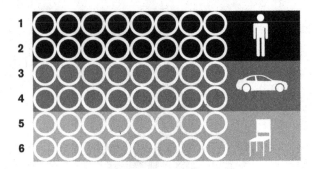

Fig. 2. Mapping of elevation (object) to a two-dimensional vibrotactile array: 'Person', 'Vehicle', and 'Chair' actuate the top (1 & 2), middle (3 & 4), and bottom (5 & 6) rows, respectively.

To map angular position, we utilized the egocentricity of the human body to describe angles of an object relative to the user's orientation, depicted in Fig. 3: 0° is described by activating motors directly in line with the spine; 45° angles are described by activating motors just to the immediate left or right of the egocentric center-point of the spine; and 90° angles are described by activating motors at the edges, furthest away from the center-point of the spine.

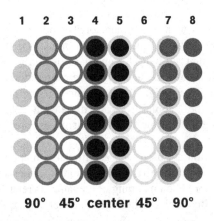

Fig. 3. Mapping of angles to a two-dimensional vibrotactile display. Assuming number begins at the user's right side when seated in the Haptic Chair, '90° right' actuates the blue columns (1 & 2); '45° right' actuates the pink circled columns (2, 3, & 4), '0°' (center) actuates the black columns (4 and 5); '45° left' actuates the orange circled columns (5, 6, & 7), and '90° left' actuates the purple columns (7 & 8). (Color figure online)

In previous work [11], we designed a vibrotactile rhythm based on the analogy of a heartbeat to convey interpersonal distance within a vision-based social assistive aid for individuals who are blind. The mapping of interpersonal distances to heartbeat rhythms is based on the following metaphor: as your social partner approaches you, the interaction between you and your partner becomes more intimate and engaging, and therefore, the tempo of your heartbeat increases. The rhythms were found to be easy to learn and intuitive, so we adopted a similar approach here. In this work, the tempo of the heartbeat is used to indicate the closeness of an object: when objects are far away, the tempo is slow; when objects are close, the tempo is fast. The study of interpersonal distance across cultures and social groups is known as proxemics [12]. In American culture, there are four zones: (i) Intimate space (0–18 inches); (ii) Personal space (1.5–4 feet); (iii) Social space (4–12 feet); and (iv) Public space (12 or more feet). In this work, the above mapping is adjusted to take into account that we are augmenting current non-visual travel aids, not replacing them. The average distance someone can interrogate with the use of a white cane is roughly five feet in front of them. Furthermore, if an object is within reach of the traveler, we presume they are already engaged with the object and are no longer in need of the information. Therefore, distance information begins at 10 feet (roughly the end of social space), followed by 15 feet (roughly, the beginning of public space), then 20 feet (well into public space), and finally, 25 feet, which is no longer conveyed as a heartbeat, but rather, a sonar pulse to convey that the object is far from interaction. When an object's distance enters the range of personal space, a constant vibration replaces the rhythm to alert the user. Figure 4 depicts these heartbeat rhythms.

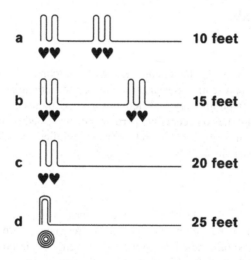

Fig. 4. Vibrotactile rhythms for communicating object distance. Heartbeat rhythms (a–c) consist of a heartbeat separated by varying gaps. A single heartbeat consists of two quick pulses: each pulse is 50 ms separated by a 50 ms gap to simulate a single heartbeat. (a) Heartbeats are separated by a 300 ms gap. (b) Heartbeats are separated by a 650 ms gap. (c) Heartbeats are separated by a 1500 ms gap. (d) Instead of a heartbeat, a single pulse of 50 ms is used to simulate a sonar pulse, with sonar pulses separated by 1500 ms.

The aforementioned individual dimensions of elevation, angle, and distance are combined to build a three-dimensional vibrotactile stimulation pattern. Three examples of how these individual dimensions are combined into a multidimensional representation are shown in Fig. 5.

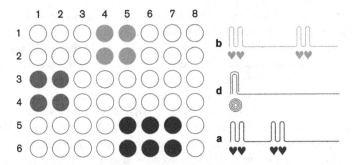

Fig. 5. Three examples to demonstrate how the proposed multidimensional patterns are displayed. The leftmost motors would be at the left side of your back, and vice versa. The depicted groups of actuated motors (red, green, and blue) each represent a different object at a specific angle and distance. To convey a 'Person' at '0° (center)' and '15 ft', motors (red group) at the intersection of rows 1 & 2 and columns 4 & 5 are actuated using rhythm (b). To convey a 'Vehicle' at '90° left' and '25 ft', motors (green group) at the intersection of rows 3 & 4 and columns 1 & 2 are actuated using rhythm (d). To convey a 'Chair' at '45° right' and '10 ft', motors (blue group) at the intersection of rows 5 & 6 and columns 5, 6, & 7 are actuated using rhythm (a). (Color figure online)

4   Research Study

4.1   Aim

This study aims to explore the distinctness and naturalness of three-dimensional vibrotactile patterns representing objects at a distance for individuals who are blind or visually impaired. As a preliminary first step, this study explores absolute identification (AI) of static (non-moving) objects while participants are seated in a chair. Subsequent studies will explore moving objects and relative identification in a wearable form factor, described further in Sect. 5.

4.2   Participants

Twelve individuals who self-identified as blind or visually impaired were recruited for this IRB-approved research study. Of the 12, 4 are male, 5 are female, and 1 is transgender; 3 acquired blindness later in life, and 7 were born blind; ages ranged from 29 to 63 (*M*: 43.6, *SD*: 11.8); and 7 of the 12 participants have used the Haptic Chair previously as part of their participation in an unrelated study at CUbiC.

4.3   Apparatus

The Haptic Chair hardware, software, and conceptual mappings described in Sect. 3 were used in this study with some adjustment to the patterns to accommodate experimental procedures, described in Sect. 4.4. A GUI was built to easily send individual dimensions as well as three-dimensional patterns to the Haptic Chair and record participant responses.

4.4   Procedure

Participants were first introduced to the purpose of the study, given $25 compensation for their willingness to participate, and requested to provide informed consent. Participants then completed three stages: familiarization, training, and testing, each described below. Following these three stages, participants completed a questionnaire to rate the ease of recognition and naturalness of the vibrotactile patterns.

The familiarization phase began with introducing participants to the dimension of distance and its four values: '10 ft', '15 ft', '20 ft', and '25 ft'. The analogy of a heartbeat was described, and the following example was given: "The heartbeat pattern plays at a faster rate (tempo) the closer an object is to you. For example, at 10 ft, the heartbeat will feel faster than it will at 20 ft. At 25 ft, the object is so far away, you no longer feel the rhythm as a heartbeat, but instead, a simple sonar pulse". All four rhythms were presented to the user in order from '10 ft' to '25 ft' with elevation and angle kept constant at 'Vehicle' and '0°', respectively. Participants were allowed to request rhythms be repeated. All four rhythms were then repeated two more times. Each rhythm is designed to have exactly three heartbeats (or in the case of '25 ft', three sonar pulses) to ensure participants do not count beats to recognize distance.

Next, participants were introduced to the dimension of elevation and the associated three objects: 'Person', 'Vehicle", and 'Chair'. All three elevations were presented to the user in order from 'Chair' to 'Person' with distance and angle kept constant at '10 ft' and '0°', respectively. Participants were allowed to request elevations be repeated. All three elevations were then repeated two more times. Finally, participants were introduced to the dimension of angle and its five values: '90° left', '45° left', '0° (center)', '45° right', and '90° right'. All five angles were presented to the user in order from '90° left' to '90° right' with distance and elevation kept constant at '10 ft' and 'Vehicle', respectively. Participants were allowed to request angles be repeated. All five angles were then repeated two more times.

Next, during training, each unique combination of the three dimensions were randomly presented to participants for 60 presentations (or trials) total (4 distances × 3 elevations × 5 angles = 60 trials). Patterns were presented as multidimensional stimuli (Fig. 5) rather than individual dimensions to assess absolute identification under more realistic conditions such as those that would be encountered in the wild. For each trial, participants had to guess the elevation, angle, and distance encoded in the presented pattern. The experimenter confirmed correct guesses, and corrected incorrect guesses. For incorrect guesses, the experiment allowed participants to feel the pattern again. To pass training and move to testing, participants had to score 80% or better (at least 48 out of 60 trials correctly guessed). If a participant did not pass training, he or she had to complete another 60 trials of training before moving to testing. The testing phase is similar to training except that all participants complete a single pass of all 60 randomly presented trials, during which the experimenter provides no feedback concerning correct or incorrect guesses, with no repeats allowed.

4.5   Results

Of the 12 participants, the data of two participants were omitted due to experimenter error resulting in data loss during Participant 4's study, and equipment malfunction during Participant 9's study. Of the remaining 10 participants, 600 trials were captured, but due to experimenter error, two of these data points were lost, resulting in the successful recording of 598 trials (participant responses). The vibration motor at column 1, second row from the bottom stopped working beginning with Participant 7 due to a hardware failure. Therefore, experiments involving Participant 7 through 12 did not use this motor, but due to the nature of the mapping, redundant information still allowed participants to recognize patterns involving this motor (the vibration motor could not be repaired as it was not a mechanical failure, but rather, an issue with the actuator's microprocessor, and given that the Haptic Chair uses custom PCBs with surface mounted devices, the hardware could not be easily repaired). Of the 10 participants, 6 passed the training phase on the first try; the remaining 4 participants needed the second training phase before moving to testing.

In this paper, we define *recognition accuracy* as the percentage of correctly guessed trials out of total trials. Recognition accuracy of the complete, multidimensional vibrotactile pattern, averaged across participants, was M: 57%, SD: 49.5%. Recognition accuracy of the individual dimension of elevation, averaged across participants, was M: 91.8%, SD: 27.4%. Recognition accuracy of the individual dimension of angle, averaged across participants, was M: 74%, SD: 43.8%. Recognition accuracy of the individual dimension of distance, averaged across participants, was M: 78.2%, SD: 41.2%. Individual recognition accuracies of the three elevations are depicted in Fig. 6. Individual recognition accuracies of the five angles are depicted in Fig. 7. Individual recognition accuracies of the four distances are depicted in Fig. 8.

Table 1 presents subjective responses from the post-experiment questionnaire. Likert-scale responses to questions assessing the ease of recognition and intuitiveness of the proposed patterns were averaged across participants.

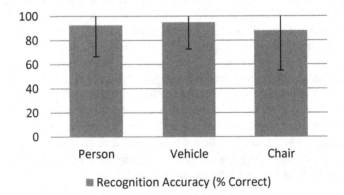

Fig. 6. Mean recognition accuracy per elevation (object). Error bars are standard deviations.

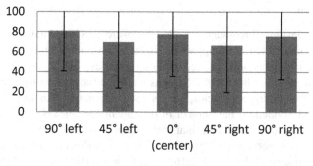

Fig. 7. Mean recognition accuracy per angle. Error bars are standard deviations.

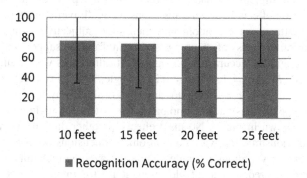

Fig. 8. Mean recognition accuracy per distance. Error bars are standard deviations.

Table 1. Responses to questionnaire. (A) Ease of recognizing individual dimensions. (B) Naturalness of mapping for individual dimensions. Likert scale: 1 (very hard) to 5 (very easy).

Questions	M (A)	SD (A)	M (B)	SD (B)
Chair	4.0	1.0	4.2	1.0'
Vehicle	4.4	0.7	4.3	0.6
Person	4.7	0.6	4.3	0.8
90° left	2.9	1.3	3.3	1.2
45° left	2.5	1.1	2.9	1.1
0° (center)	3.9	1.3	4.3	0.9
45° right	2.5	0.9	3.0	1.0
90° right	3.0	1.4	3.5	1.4
10 feet	4.0	1.3	4.3	0.8
15 feet	3.6	0.7	4.0	0.8
20 feet	3.5	0.8	3.7	0.8
25 feet	4.1	0.7	4.2	0.8

4.6   Discussion

A $3 \times 5 \times 4$ design, three-way repeated measures (RM) Analysis of Variance (ANOVA) was conducted to compare the effects of individual dimensions, and inter-actions between dimensions, on recognition accuracy. All data assumptions for RM ANOVA were met. Three RM ANOVAs were conducted, one for each dependent variable (three recognition accuracies, one for each dimension). An alpha value of 0.01 was selected and divided by the number of dependent variables ($k = 3$) to account for the multiple significance tests. The final alpha value used was 0.003.

For elevation (object) recognition accuracies, no significant differences were found for type of elevation (object), $F(2,16) = 4.18$, $p = 0.035$; angle, $F(4,32) = 0.65$, $p = 0.631$; or distance, $F(3,24) = 0.19$, $p = 0.902$; nor any two- or three-way inter-actions. These results show that no particular pattern for elevation was more difficult to recognize. Indeed, the recognition accuracies of Fig. 6 corroborate this finding. Moreover, the other dimensions had no effect on the perception of elevation, nor were there any interaction effects between dimensions. Overall, participants performed well at recognizing patterns for elevation, and their high subjective ratings for ease of recognition and intuitiveness of mapping, shown in Table 1, support this.

For angle recognition accuracies, no significant differences were found for type of elevation (object), $F(2,16) = 1.481$, $p = 0.257$; angle, $F(4,32) = 1.615$, $p = 0.194$; or distance, $F(3,24) = 1.546$, $p = 0.228$; nor any two- or three-way interactions. No main effect for angle type demonstrates that no particular pattern for angle was more difficult to recognize, as shown in Fig. 7. No main effects for other dimensions, and no inter-action effects, demonstrate that variations in other dimensions do not change the dif-ficultly of perceiving variations in angle. While the average recognition accuracy for angle is lower compared to that of elevation, it is still impressive considering the limited training participants were exposed to, the difficulty of the task of absolute identification (compared to relative identification in general), and the number of pat-terns to recognize (5 angles compared to only 3 elevations). In this regard, participants rated the ease of recognizing and the naturalness of the mapping lower compared to elevation (Table 1). While recognition accuracy could potentially improve with fewer angles, this simplification would decrease the resolution of the system.

Lastly, for distance recognition accuracies, no significant differences were found for type of elevation (object), $F(2,16) = 0.687$, $p = 0.517$; angle, $F(4,32) = 2.594$, $p = 0.055$; or distance, $F(3,24) = 1.244$, $p = 0.316$; nor any two- or three-way inter-actions. Similar to the other dimensions, no particular rhythm was more difficult to recognize, which is corroborated by Fig. 8. Moreover, no main effects for other dimensions, nor interaction effects, were found, showing that other dimensions did not influence participants' perception of rhythm. Similar to the average recognition accu-racy for angle, accuracy is lower compared to that of elevation. Even so, participants' performance is still impressive given the number of rhythms, limited training, and absolute identification task. The average recognition accuracy for distance was higher compared to angle (with lower standard deviation), and this objective outcome is corroborated by the subjective results of Table 1, showing that participants rated the ease of recognizing distance and the naturalness of its mapping higher compared to angle on average (*M*: 3.8 compared to 2.9 for distance and angle, respectively—Part A; and *M*: 4 compared to 3.4. for distance and angle, respectively—Part B).

5 Conclusion and Future Work

We proposed a conceptual mapping of three-dimensional environmental information to a two-dimensional vibrotactile display toward augmenting current methods for non-visual travel. A preliminary experiment showed that individuals who are blind are able to learn and recognize static (non-moving) representations of the proposed multidimensional patterns. These results form the basis for future work in two ways: (i) to recognize dynamic (moving) objects, which will be more commonly encountered in the wild, users will first need to learn static representations. The static representations of the current work have shown promise for relative identification of moving objects. (ii) The back as a body site for communication showed potential for accurate and intuitive perception of three-dimensional information.

Acknowledgements. This material is partially based upon work supported by the National Science Foundation under Grant No. 1069125.

References

1. National Federation of the Blind. https://nfb.org/blindness-statistics. Accessed 30 Mar 2018
2. Manduchi, R., Kurniawan, S.: Mobility-related accidents experienced by people with visual impairment. Insight Res. Pract. VI Blind. 4(2), 44–54 (2011)
3. Shoval, S., et al.: Auditory guidance with the navbelt—a computerized travel aid for the blind. IEEE Trans. Syst. Man Cybern. Part C 28(3), 459–467 (1998)
4. Ivanchenko, V., et al.: Staying in the crosswalk: a system for guiding visually impaired pedestrians at traffic intersections. Assist. Tech. Res. Ser. 25, 69–73 (2009)
5. Tian, Y., et al.: Toward a computer vision-based way finding aid for blind persons to access unfamiliar indoor environments. Mach. Vis. Appl. 24(3), 521–535 (2013)
6. Pallejà, T., et al.: Bioinspired electronic white cane implementation based on a LIDAR, a tri-axial accelerometer and a tactile belt. Sensors 10(12), 11322–11339 (2010)
7. Mann, S., et al.: Blind navigation with a wearable range camera and vibrotactile helmet. In: 19th ACM International Conference on Multimedia, pp. 1325–1328 (2011)
8. Jameson, B., Manduchi, R.: Watch your head: a wearable collision warning system for the blind. Sensors, 1922–1927 (2010)
9. McDaniel, T., Bala, S., Rosenthal, J., Tadayon, R., Tadayon, A., Panchanathan, S.: Affective haptics for enhancing access to social interactions for individuals who are blind. In: Stephanidis, C., Antona, M. (eds.) UAHCI 2014. LNCS, vol. 8513, pp. 419–429. Springer, Cham (2014). https://doi.org/10.1007/978-3-319-07437-5_40
10. van Erp, J.B.: Vibrotactile spatial acuity on the torso: effects of location and timing parameters. In: Joint Eurohaptics Conference and Haptics Symposium, pp. 80–85 (2005)
11. McDaniel, T., et al.: Heartbeats: a methodology to convey interpersonal distance through touch. In: ACM Conference on Human Factors in Computing Systems, pp. 3985–3990 (2010)
12. Hall, E.T.: The Hidden Dimension. Double Day & Company Inc., New York (1966)

Robotic Catheter for Endovascular Surgery Using 3D Magnetic Guidance

Amir Pournajib[(✉)] and Anup Basu

Department of Computing Science, University of Alberta, Edmonton, Canada
{pournaji, basu}@ualberta.ca

Abstract. Endovascular surgery is an alternative for invasive medical procedures that is becoming widely deployed for many procedures. One of the main challenges of this method is using X-ray before and during the surgery. X-ray side effects are significant for surgeons who are regularly exposed while performing surgeries. Improving the accuracy, efficiency and safety of intraoperative X-rays is very challenging. Furthermore, manual navigation of surgical tools, lack of 3D visualization, and lack of intelligent planning and automatic tracking of the end-effector are critical challenges that have not allowed automatic endovascular surgery to be feasible. In this project, our goal is to develop hardware and software platforms to make a computer assisted robotic surgery system that reduces the need for X-rays during surgery. Also the system can work remotely which means surgeons do not need to be physically next to the patient during an endovascular surgery. The goal is to also overcome the difficulties encountered during manual navigation; and, to improve the speed and experience of performing endovascular surgeries. Experimental results demonstrate the promise and preliminary outcomes of our research.

Keywords: Endovascular surgery · Magnetic sensor · Arduino board
Catheter

1 Introduction

Cardiovascular diseases (CVDs) are the first cause of death around the globe. It is estimated that 17.5 million people died from these kind of diseases in 2012, accounting for 31% of all global deaths; the main causes being coronary heart disease (about 7.4 million) and stroke (about 6.7 million) [1]. Although improvements in computer based technologies have significantly reduced the need for user intervention, image segmentation in medical applications is still a balance between automation and user interaction. This is why modern segmentation methodologies aim at automation, accuracy, reproducibility, and efficiency, while allowing for necessary intervention by the user, who tunes the results of the segmentation process [2]. The current surgical procedure relies on capturing 2D X-ray images at regular time intervals from a fixed view-point during the surgery, and mapping the 2D images onto a pre-scanned static 3D model. Without seeing the navigation space in 3D, the surgeon often has difficulty in following the center line without putting unnecessary pressure on the artery walls. Therefore, in order to support accurate and safe navigation of the surgical tools inside a

© Springer Nature Switzerland AG 2018
A. Basu and S. Berretti (Eds.): ICSM 2018, LNCS 11010, pp. 102–109, 2018.
https://doi.org/10.1007/978-3-030-04375-9_9

patient, the capability of visualizing the navigation path in a 3D space is crucial. There are three main approaches for segmentation of 3D objects. The first one is manual tracing in which a human operator delineates each 2D slice in a volume; an approach that is time consuming and not feasible for a large volume of data. The second approach is fully-automatic segmentation in which no human intervention is required; however, it suffers from sensitivity to parameterization and variation of biological structures among different subjects [3]. Researchers have recently become interested in semi-automated methods in which computer-based segmentation is facilitated by minimal human interaction [4].

In this work, we develop an electro-mechanical system to accurately guide mechanically controlled surgical tools from a close distance, and a visualization interface to assist in monitoring and controlling of the process. The simulated surgical process includes the bending and navigation of a surgical catheter using the feedback from the sensor and interface. For tracking the position and speed of a catheter, magnetic motion capture sensor and servomotor feedback have been used to provide feedback to a catheter-driving mechanism. The device can also help in autonomous catheter insertion for major vasculature surgeries. Catheter insertion speed control and path reconstruction experiments were performed with the hardware system and a user interface was built to simulate surgery. One of the major problems that could occur during a surgery is buckling of the catheter tip. In our system the 3D magnetic feedback was attached to the tip of catheter to detect buckling and send the catheter tip backward to correct the problem.

The remainder of this paper is organized as follows: The Sect. 2 explains the method. The Sects. 3 and 4 describe the experimental results and conclusion.

2   Method

The proposed automated catheter tracking system has two main components which are the hardware and the software interface. These components are outlined below. The framework of the proposed system is shown in Fig. 1.

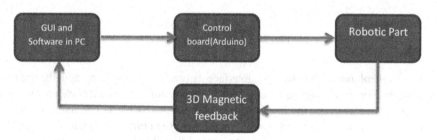

Fig. 1. Framework of the proposed system.

2.1   Hardware

The hardware component consists of three parts:

- Robotic elements
- Control board
- 3D Magnetic feedback

The *Robotic part* is responsible for catheter movement. As can be seen in Fig. 2 there are two servo motors of which one is for back and forth movement of the catheter and the other one is for rotation of the tip. The back and forth movements consisting of two gears which have been tightening together and there is a groove in the middle of them. The groove has been filled by rubber and catheter pass throw two gears. There is a servo motor which is connected to one of the gears and is responsible for making movement back and forth. By using this part we can move the catheter super accurate and also we can control the speed. Since the servo has its own feedback by itself all feedback is not just by magnetic sensor. It will help the system to have less lag and be more accurate.

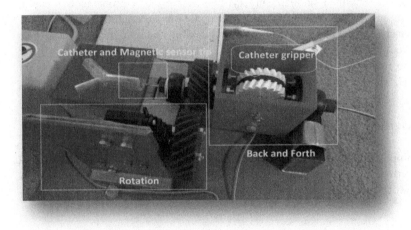

Fig. 2. Robotic components.

The *Control board* handles the interface between our software and the robotic components. For the control part the Arduino board is utilized since it is cheap and easy to use (Fig. 3). For programming the control board C++ is used. The main benefit of using Arduino is that it gives us a serial interface to the computer. It has seven analog to digital converters, with which one can control the PWM motor and also the servo motor. After this we can turn on the power so that the system is ready to use. Since this platform is going to be used in the surgery room, it needs to be capable of recovering very fast even if the system crashes.

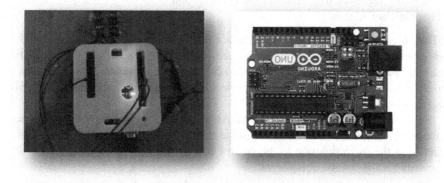

Fig. 3. The Arduino board used in our system.

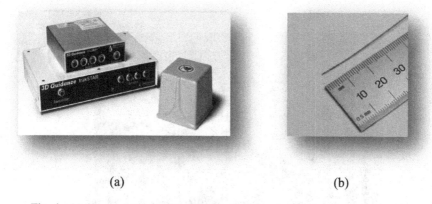

(a)   (b)

Fig. 4. (a) 3D magnetic feedback system (b) 3D magnetic feedback sensor wire.

3D Magnetic Feedback is an essential part of this project. It is a device to get feedback of the exact position of the catheter tip, and it is attached to the catheter so that the catheter tip and sensor tip have the same position. Some components of the magnetic feedback system are shown in Fig. 4. The driveBAY™ and trakSTAR™ electromagnetic (EM) 6DoF tracking solutions from Ascension Technology Corporation provides a cost-effective, high accuracy position and orientation tracking technology for integration into the most innovative and realistic medical training and surgical rehearsal simulators, with no line of sight requirements [5].

2.2 Software Component

The software system consists of four parts:

- Communication with the magnetic sensor;
- Communication with the control board;

- Analyzing feedback data and lead the catheter; and,
- Graphic User Interface.

The *Magnetic sensor* has its own interface protocol in C++. We implemented the main program in visual C++, because it is easier to communicate with the magnetic sensor this way. The magnetic sensor needs 12v DC power supply for which we used a personal computer power supply in this project. For connecting to the computer, USB connection was used.

The *Control board* in this system is the Arduino board which was programed once for the system. After this, for any action in the robotic component we need to send data to and from the main program to the control board. The control board interprets the commands for the robotic component.

The *Leading Catheter* in this project could be either manual or automatic. Since we have feedback on the movement and orientation of the catheter tip we can simply instruct the system to go to a destination. If necessary, the system can automatically correct itself using the 3D magnetic feedback. Even if buckling happens, it is easy to detect.

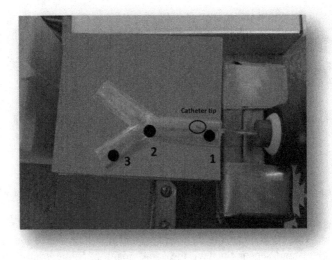

Fig. 5. Movement of catheter in the transparent vessel

According to Fig. 5 and our physical and image processing measurement we know the distance between Point 1 and Point 2 in Fig. 5. As we have mentioned before, we have two kinds of feedback: Magnetic feedback and also Servo motor feedback. These two types of feedback help the system to be more accurate. For example, if the servo sensor shows that the catheter is going forward and magnetic sensor shows no movement, it means that the tip is buckling. In this situation the robotic part will pull the catheter back to the last joint, which in this example is Point 1.

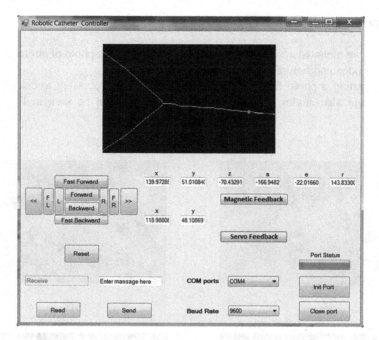

Fig. 6. Graphical user interface.

The *Graphic user interface* or GUI is a type of interface that allows users to interact with the robotic component and get feedback from the magnetic sensor and also the servo motor.

As can be seen in Fig. 6 in the GUI one can choose the desired serial port and send a command to the control board. At the same time one can see the feedback of the catheter from both sensors.

Fig. 7. Camera on the top of object.

3 Experimental Results

In this part we mounted a camera on top of the system to take a photo of our transparent vessel just once and before any movement (Fig. 7).

After getting a photo from the vessel we used image processing to calculate the distances and also angles between vectors (Fig. 8). As can be seen in Fig. 6, we

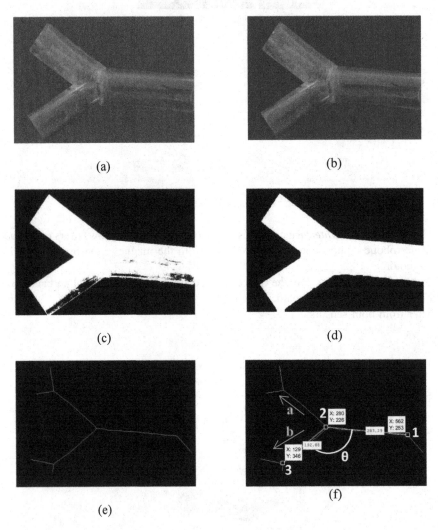

Fig. 8. (a) Original image. (b) Binary image. (c) Thresholded binary image. (d) Removing black spots with morphological functions. (e) Thinning the white part with morphological functions. (f) Calculating the length of each part.

processed the image to get the line of path for sending the command to robotic module. For getting the angle between two vectors the following formula was used.

$$\cos \theta = \frac{U.V}{||U||||V||} \tag{1}$$

Which according to Fig. 6 U and V are:

$$U = (X_1 - X_2)i - (Y_1 - Y_2)j \tag{2}$$

$$V = (X_3 - X_2)i - (Y_3 - Y_2)j \tag{3}$$

Now we have all distances and also angles. For going from Point (1) to Point (3) according to Fig. 8 we send the command to the robotic part to move from Point (1) to Point (2). After reaching to point (2) it will rotate to make up angle (θ) and after rotation the catheter will go to direction (b).

4 Conclusion

There are wide ranges of cardio disease which need to be cured by using endovascular surgery. In this procedure the catheter needs to be guided through the patient's vessel, manually by the doctors. Since, manual navigation of a catheter is prone to error which is too risky for the patients; thus, an automatic endovascular surgery system is needed to replace invasive medical procedures. In this work, a prototype system consisting of hardware and software parts has designed. Two type of feedback was used for this system; one of them is servo sensor and the other one is magnetic sensor feedback. Furthermore, the proposed system automatically guides the catheter through the simulated transparent vessels with different speeds and positions using the feedback from the Magnetic and servo sensors. Experimental results illustrate the accuracy and efficiency of the proposed surgical system.

References

1. Radaelli, A.G., Peiro, J.: On the segmentation of vascular geometries from medical images. Int. J. Numer. Methods Biomed. Eng. 26(1), 3–34 (2010)
2. Bekkers, E., Duits, R., Berendschot, T., ter Haar Romeny, B.: A multi-orientation analysis approach to retinal vessel tracking. J. Math. Imaging Vis. 49(3), 583–610 (2014)
3. Kumar, R.P., Albregtsen, F., Reimers, M., Edwin, B., Langø, T., Elle, O.J.: Three-dimensional blood vessel segmentation and centerline extraction based on two-dimensional cross-section analysis. Ann. Biomed. Eng. 43(5), 1223–1234 (2015)
4. Mura, M., et al.: A computer-assisted robotic platform for vascular procedures exploiting 3D US-based tracking. Comput. Assist. Surg. 21(1), 63–79 (2016)
5. https://www.ascension-tech.com/products

Haptic Training in a Virtual Environment to Train Cognitive Functions of Medical Students: Work in Progress

Nemanja Babic[1], Charles Barnouin[2], Benjamin De Witte[3], Arnaud Lelevé[1(✉)], Richard Moreau[1], Minh Tu Pham[1], and Xavier Martin[4]

[1] Univ Lyon, INSA Lyon, Ampère (UMR 5005), 69621 Lyon, France
arnaud.leleve@insa-lyon.fr
[2] Univ Lyon, Univ Lyon 1, LIRIS, 69622 Lyon, France
benji.dewitte@gmail.com
[3] Univ Lyon, Univ Lyon 1, LIBM, 69622 Lyon, France
[4] Univ Lyon, Faculte de Medecine, 69373 Lyon, France
xavier.martin@chu-lyon.fr
http://www.ampere-lab.fr, http://www.libm.fr,
https://www.univ-lyon1.fr/ecole-de-chirurgie-616440.kjsp

Abstract. This paper introduces the development of exercises to be embedded in a lightweight laparoscopic haptic simulator to help surgeons starting their training to Minimal Invasive Surgery (MIS) gestures. These exercises were created by observing professionals in operation rooms and by isolating key gestures, which have been combined to create desired trajectories with a slow learning curve. These exercises combine memory, new gestures, new environments and new visual feedback so that the trainees' cognitive load remains low. This favors an effective training. Hence, the simulator displays a simple 3D virtual environment in order to focus on the gestures and trajectories, performed on an haptic device by means of real MIS tool handles. Its ludic dimension, which make it a Serious Game, should help users to make progress in their first gesture training in order to continue on more evolved medical simulators. This paper introduces the software architecture analysis and the methods used for creating the exercises.

Keywords: Medical robotics · Haptics · Virtual reality · Training

1 Introduction

The need for simulation in medical training is particularly relevant in Mini Invasive Surgery (MIS) where the operation field is not directly visible by the surgeon as his two tools operate inside the patient's body: the surgeon uses an endoscope to watch them operating. This medical approach allows the patient to recover faster than with open surgery but it makes the operation more difficult for the surgeon who has an indirect effect on tools (fulcrum effect) and an indirect view

© Springer Nature Switzerland AG 2018
A. Basu and S. Berretti (Eds.): ICSM 2018, LNCS 11010, pp. 110–120, 2018.
https://doi.org/10.1007/978-3-030-04375-9_10

of his gestures. Indeed, the surgeon lacks depth perception of the operation field (through the endoscope), and is provided with a reduced visual field. Also, this technique implies to learn how to manipulate new surgical tools. Training and evaluating MIS medical gesture is therefore a difficult task.

As a result of various technological advances, the medical students are offered a more valuable and superior education than the previous generation. One of these advancements are the medical simulation platforms which train the medical staff, to decrease mistakes or accidents during medical practices (e.g. surgery). Medical simulators offer a convenient way to learn by trial and error, and are a growing solution for overcrowded medical student populations having too few opportunities to perform hands-on training during their curriculum.

Computer based simulators use haptic interfaces and calculators to provide a realistic feeling to the user and a greater number of cases without having to change worn out parts. Thanks to their software part, they offer various parameters, which enable them to reproduce an infinite number of study cases and more particularly the difficult ones. It has been validated that the skills acquired on simulators can be transferred to real operations [4] and more particularly for advanced tasks [7].

However, as these simulators tend to be very complex to use and expensive (so not sufficiently widespread), the medical training teams we work with in *Universite de Lyon*, identified that their students were not sufficiently efficiently trained. This is why, alongside the use of these "high resolution" simulators, their medical students undergo a training in laparoscopy using the traditional surgical "black box". The surgical "black box" is simply a portable system which reproduces the patient body by confining the operating scene into a box equipped with trocars and an endoscope, as in real MIS operations. In general, additional sensors allow the training staff to get instant visual feedback, which makes it easier to identify any mistake.

The first simulators visible in the literature provided a visual feedback of the gestures through a monitor while the users manipulated their tools in a virtual environment [1,9]. Later on, researches have focused on improving the quality of textures to make them more life-like [5]. As haptic feedback was missing for a full immersion in the virtual world, simulators having both visual and haptic feedback was created [10]. They are currently used in the training of medical students, for example LapSim® in Lyon's medical school. Students can then experience even rare surgical cases without jeopardizing patients' safety. These simulators are usually expensive and, as a result, cannot be freely used by every student. It hinders the continual practice necessary to learn a new medical gesture. Also, our colleagues identified an issue in the medical education field: the transition between the surgical "black box" and the medical simulators. Once completing the "black box" training, the medical students are still having trouble using the simulators. This is due to a cognitive overload.

To fix this issue, we developed a less complex virtual environment with haptic feedback. This environment fills the cognitive gap that exists between the "black box" and the medical simulators. The virtual environment consists of simple but significant exercises to train the cognitive functions of medical students. It is expected that after this training, the students will perform with greater skills on more evolved medical simulators, such as those reviewed in [6].

This paper is organized as follows: Sect. 2 introduces the requirements this simulator should fulfill to be efficient in the training. Section 3 describes its software and hardware structure, and Sect. 4 briefly depicts the exercises.

2   Requirements

The main objective of the work presented in this paper is to create "low cognitive" exercises taking place in Virtual Reality and to be performed by means of two haptic devices (one per hand). Force feedback must be implemented in each exercise in order to reproduce tool-environment interactions typical in MIS operations. Three exercises should be realized:

1. An exercise involving cubes of various sizes and colors, to be simultaneously manipulated by two haptic devices, in order to construct a specific model (e.g. pyramid).
2. An exercise proposing a circuit composed of various static objects. This exercise should consist of two levels and three different views (front, side and top) each, giving a total of six different circuits that must be implemented. An evaluation of the progress is to be carried out at the end of each circuit, providing several motion quality metrics (e.g. time required, number of undesired collisions).
3. An exercise where the virtual environment features a muscular tissue and an elastic string in order to create various kinds of surgical knots. The string should be manipulated with two haptic devices if needed. The user should feel the forces when pulling the string and pushing it inside the tissue.

These specifications were provided by a group of medical doctors of *Universite de Lyon*, in order to train their medical students and enhance there cognitive capacity. They were reworked by the LIBM team who has strong skills in gesture training. They were then submitted and validated by the Head of Lyon Surgery Department.

3   Simulator Structure Study

In this paper, the investigation was mostly focused on the implementation of different exercises in a virtual world with haptic devices. Two software frameworks were selected and compared: Gazebo over ROS on the one side, and Chai3d library on the other side. Assessment functions were integrated in order to evaluate the progress of users, at the end of the second exercise.

3.1   Software

Two frameworks were selected to develop such exercises necessitating a Virtual World in 3 dimensions linked to two haptic devices: Gazebo over ROS and Chai3d library.

ROS and Gazebo: The Robot Operating System (ROS)[1] is an open-source collection of software frameworks for robot software development. Indeed, it is a meta-operating system for the robot, between an operating system and a middleware. ROS can simply be illustrated as the combination of 4 parts: plumbing, tools, capabilities and ecosystem. The plumbing which is at the lowest level allows the programs to communicate between each other by providing the publish–subscribe messaging infrastructure. This set of tools offers many important features such as robot 3D visualization through RVIZ application, introspection, debugging, testing and more. ROS provides a collection of libraries that incorporates robot functionalities such as the advanced manipulation and path-grasp planning which enables the robot to recognize objects and react accordingly.

Gazebo[2] is a software for robot simulation. It offers a dynamic simulation environment with high-performance physics engines such as Open Dynamic Engine (ODE). Moreover, it contains an advanced 3D graphics rendering engine: OGRE. In that manner, realistic rendering of the environment is made possible such as in Fig. 1. Various sensors and plug-ins are available from laser range-finders, cameras, contact sensors, force-torque and many more can be found in the Gazebo API. Gazebo communicates through ROS and allows the user to change or acquire various information from the simulated world. The SDF[3] data provides the robots visual and physical elements to Gazebo, which then creates services for the described robot. These services can be accessed by ROS nodes using service calls.

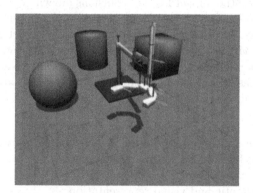

Fig. 1. Simple shapes and gripper in Gazebo

The following list is a summary of the pros and cons of using ROS and Gazebo.

– Pros

---

[1] See http://www.ros.org/.

[2] See http://gazebosim.org/.

[3] SDF: Simulator Description Format.

- Possibility to build robots with multiple links and joints.
- Several degrees of freedom (DOF) for the robot.
- Force feedback (collision detection) not limited to a single point.
- Rich libraries, features, API, etc.
- Scalable: works in big projects.
- Powerful software.
  – Cons
- Implementation of dual user haptic device on ROS (Linux OS).
- Modeling limitations: no pulleys, ropes, nor flexible materials.
- Focused on robot simulation; in our case, there is no robot.

Chai3d: Chai3d[4] is an open source set of C++ libraries for computer haptics, visualization and interactive real-time simulation. It has been designed in C++ to make it easier and more natural for computer programmers to create applications that integrate the force feedback ability with 3D modeling.

Chai3d provides a large number of force rendering algorithms, supports several commercial devices, contains two dynamic engine for simulation and uses Open GL for graphic rendering. It is also possible to import 3D mesh files in the virtual environment. The two dynamic engine present are the ODE (Open Dynamic Engine) for rigid bodies and the GEL dynamics engine for deformable body simulation.

The Force Rendering Algorithms Module in Chai3d enables the communication between an haptic device and the virtual environment. Chai3D embeds functions to compute the impact force of collisions anywhere in space depending on the position and velocity of the device, but also to compute it when it is in contact with meshes. In other words, it computes the interaction force between the device and any virtual object. Another interesting feature that Chai3d offers is the Haptic Effects Module which enables to add viscosity to a surface to model a tissue or to increase the frequency (vibration) in order to alert the user that he is in contact with a certain object for example.

- Pros
  - Simple communication with haptic devices (supports multiple devices).
  - Useful set of libraries for haptic development.
  - Supports flexible/deformable objects.
  - Focused on haptic and visual representation.
- Cons (at the time of the realization of this project)
  - Force feedback limited to the interactions between the tool tip (a simple volume) and any shape in the scene. Self-collision is not detected, which may complicate the design of exercise #3 with suture threads to tie.

---

[4] See http://www.chai3d.org/.

Comparison: Chai3d was chosen taking into account the requirements for the exercises to be implemented in this project, even if ROS+Gazebo offers much more programing resources and a more evolved collision detection function than Chai3d. First, Gazebo does not support deformable objects, which is an limitation in the modeling of surgical suture, such as in the third exercise. Secondly, the intercommunication between ROS and the haptic devices is not developed as in Chai3d. The incapability of simultaneous manipulation of two haptic devices on a single machine (at the time of the start of this work, in 2015) was an issue. In turns, this limits the efficiency of some exercises to train cognitive functions. Also, Gazebo is more complex to use as it is intended for robot simulation. Indeed, developing simple exercises for cognitive training with Chai3d is much more straightforward. Moreover, Chai3d integrates at once both the haptic technology and the visual representation of objects. It supports multiple devices by detecting them automatically. The GEL Dynamics Engine is useful to model deformable objects. Also, the 2D and 3D graphical rendering and the system-level I/O is achieved with the OpenGL[5] and GLUT[6] libraries which are effective. Finally, our colleagues of the medical staff found it much more user friendly when interacting with the virtual environment.

Hence, Chai3d was considered a better choice to progressively prepare students for the medical simulators.

3.2   Hardware

The simulator reproduces a black box with real MIS tools. Yet, the tips of the tools are connected, inside the box, each one to a Geomagic Touch Haptic Device (formerly Sensable Phantom Omni) such as illustrated on the left of Fig. 2. A screen displays the virtual operating scene rendered by Chai3d, imitating the endoscope visual feedback.

4   Exercises

This section sums up the exercises developed during this project. Each exercise involves a different degree of cognitive difficulty.

This simulator was designed by observing surgeons in operation rooms and by isolating key gestures with the help of the Fundamentals of Laparoscopic Surgery [3]. Prono-supination, elbow flexion and extension, wrist rotations and index finger rotations were the basic anatomical movements analyzed. The exercises require the user to regularly perform these anatomical gestures. This way, they should improve their dexterity, precision, speed and other mental abilities, in the field of laparoscopic surgery. Provided MIS exercises combine memory work, gestures, and guarantee that the trainees' cognitive load remains low.

---

[5] OpenGL (Open Graphics Library) is cross-platform API for rendering 2D and 3D graphics.

[6] GLUT (OpenGL Utility Toolkit) is a library of utilities for OpenGL used for system-level I/O.

Fig. 2. On the left: a geomagic touch haptic device, on the right: the complete simulator with two devices hidden in the box, handled by a trainee.

Otherwise, it may negatively impact their ability to learn medical gestures [8]. Hence, it was decided to keep the exercises and the virtual environment simple, to focus on the gestures and trajectories.

4.1   Exercise 1

The exercise #1 is the easiest in terms of cognitive difficulty and the objective is to build different 3D structures with cubes. It demonstrates the 3D interaction between the haptic arms - user - and the virtual environment. Figure 3 shows how cubes of different sizes and colors can be manipulated to recreate a certain structure (e.g. pyramid). In that way, medical students can train their cognitive abilities by building different structure with both hands. This exercise is the first level for the cognitive training. Many functions are integrated in this exercise:

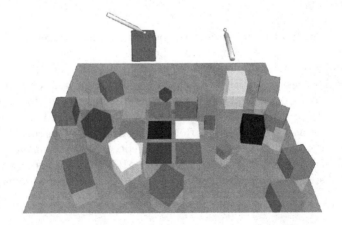

Fig. 3. Exercise 1: dual-user haptic interaction of cubes

- Sensation of weight for each cube.
- 3 dimensional perception (e.g. depth perception).
- Contact force at the tip of the tool.
- Collision detection and dynamics when colliding.
- The gravity can be enabled or disabled.
- Using two haptic devices simultaneously.

However, the exercise #1 is limited with manipulations of cubes by only one tool simultaneously. Once a cube is grasped by a first tool, the second tool cannot grasp it as well.

4.2   Exercise 2

The Exercise #2 is divided in two different levels and three different views (camera position). This gives a total of 6 different models to work with. The goal of the second exercise is to complete a circuit as fast as possible and without touching other objects. This exercise consists of a virtual world containing various static objects. It embeds two levels and three different views for each level. Its purpose is to train the dexterity and precision of the users when manipulating a tool. As shown in Figs. 4 for level A and 5 for level B, the user must complete a circuit where the objects act like obstacles. For example, passing through each ring (level B) or doing a circular movement around the cylinder without touching it.

When starting the exercises a video clip of the circuit is shown and the students must remember the various paths (involving short term memory). In addition, the collision with each object and the time required to complete the circuit is calculated and reported once the circuit is finished.

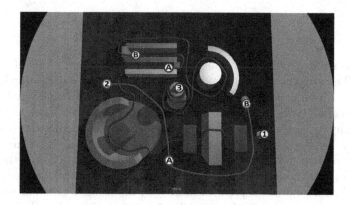

Fig. 4. Circuit to complete in Exercise # 2 Level A, endoscopic view.

Following criteria were chosen to provide an accurate assessment: time of completion and number of collisions. However, a few points should be improved:

- To find a solution on how to evaluate the collision with vibrating objects (which overestimates the number of collisions).
- To find a solution on how to count simultaneous collisions, e.g. when tool collides with an object while already being in contact with the ground.
- To find an additional criterion to assess the smoothness of the trajectories. An adaptation of the works introduced in [2], in the context of obstetrical gesture assessment, is in progress.

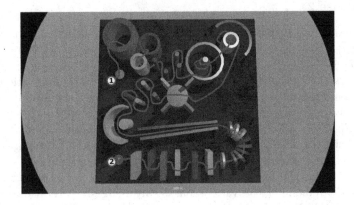

Fig. 5. Circuit to complete in Exercise # 2 Level B, endoscopic view.

4.3   Exercise 3

Finally, the third exercise is considered the most difficult in terms of cognitive intensity. The purpose of Exercise #3 is to manipulate a string in order to tie knots such as in surgical suture. The exercise #3 incorporates a deformable string and a muscular tissue in a virtual environment. A force feedback is rendered when pulling and pushing the string. The sensation of inserting the string into the tissue is rendered as well. Figure 6 shows the skeleton of the string and the integration of dual haptic devices. Since it is not possible to "grab" the string, the program was structured such that the end of the string follows the tool – sphere – when the button is pressed. Moreover, the Hooke's Law was integrated in the program to model the force feedback between the end of the string and the cursor. However, some critical points must be improved: detecting a collision between the string and a solid object, and detecting its self collision, which is mandatory to reproduce knots.

Fig. 6. Exercise # 3: surgical knot.

Conclusion

This paper introduces the development of exercises to be displayed to the trainees in a laparoscopic haptic simulator to help surgeons starting their training to Minimal Invasive Surgery (MIS) gestures. These exercises were created by observing professionals in operation rooms and isolating key gestures which have been combined to create trajectories with a slow learning curve. This training simulator aims at helping trainees who want to acquire by themselves the necessary MIS practical skills. Its low-cost design should facilitate its spreading and availability at large scale so that students can use it freely. It will also be useful to assess their progress by means of an integrated autonomous and automatic objective assessment tool. Once sufficient skills have been acquired, trainees should be more efficient on higher fidelity simulators such as LapSim. This paper presented a description and comparison of the available softwares, besides the hardware structure of this simulator. The implementation of two exercises for cognitive training was detailed. The third one still requires work to be effective. Experimental results are being performed to determine whether a progression between novices, unexperimented interns and expert users could be detected. Also, complementary experiments are necessary to determine whether this simulator is more efficient than other existing solutions (from basic box trainer to more evolved active simulators) to train medical students on first MIS training levels.

Acknowledgements. Authors would like to thank the University of Ottawa SIRI program which helped Nemanja Babic realize this work during his internship in Ampere lab in Lyon.

References

1. Chaudhry, A., Sutton, C., Wood, J., Stone, R., McCloy, R.: Learning rate for laparoscopic surgical skills on MIST VR, a virtual reality simulator: quality of human-computer interface. Ann. R. Coll. Surg. Engl. **81**(4), 281 (1999)
2. Cifuentes, J., Boulanger, P., Pham, M.T., Moreau, R., Prieto, F.: Automatic gesture analysis using constant affine velocity. In: Engineering in Medicine and Biology Society (EMBC), 2014 36th Annual International Conference of the IEEE, pp. 1826–1829. IEEE (2014)

3. Fried, G.M.: FLS assessment of competency using simulated laparoscopic tasks. J. Gastrointest. Surg. **12**(2), 210–212 (2008)
4. Hyltander, A., Liljegren, E., Rhodin, P.H., Lönroth, H.: The transfer of basic skills learned in a laparoscopic simulator to the operating room. Surg. Endosc. **16**(9), 1324–1328 (2002)
5. James, D.L., Pai, D.K.: DyRT: dynamic response textures for real time deformation simulation with graphics hardware. In: ACM Transactions on Graphics (TOG), vol. 21, no. 3, pp. 582–585. ACM (2002)
6. Julian, D., Tanaka, A., Mattingly, P., Truong, M., Perez, M., Smith, R.: A comparative analysis and guide to virtual reality robotic surgical simulators. Int. J. Med. Robot. Comput. Assist. Surg. 14(1), e1874-n/a, e1874 RCS-17-0115.R2 (2018)
7. Panait, L., Akkary, E., Bell, R.L., Roberts, K.E., Dudrick, S.J., Duffy, A.J.: The role of haptic feedback in laparoscopic simulation training. J. Surg. Res. **156**(2), 312–316 (2009)
8. Van Merriënboer, J.J.G., Sweller, J.: Cognitive load theory in health professional education: design principles and strategies. Med. Educ. **44**(1), 85–93 (2010)
9. Westwood, J.D., Hoffman, H.M., Stredney, D., Weghorst, S.J.: Validation of virtual reality to teach and assess psychomotor skills in laparoscopic surgery: results from randomised controlled studies using the MIST VR laparoscopic simulator. In: Medicine Meets Virtual Reality: Art, Science, Technology: Healthcare and Evolution, p. 124 (1998)
10. Woodrum, D.T., Andreatta, P.B., Yellamanchilli, R.K., Feryus, L., Gauger, P.G., Minter, R.M.: Construct validity of the LapSim laparoscopic surgical simulator. Am. J. Surg. **191**(1), 28–32 (2006)

MR, 3D, Underwater Image Processing

Towards Maritime Videosurveillance Using 4K Videos

V. Marié[1,2(⊠)], I. Bechar[1], and F. Bouchara[1]

[1] Aix Marseille Univ, Université de Toulon, CNRS, LIS, UMR 7020, Marseille, France
{vincent.marie,ikhlef.bechar,frederic.bouchara}@univ-tln.fr
[2] CS Systemes D'information, Paris, France
vicent.marie@c-s.fr

Abstract. This paper develops a novel approach to automatic maritime target recognition in the framework of near real-time maritime videosurveillance using super-resolved (i.e.; 4K) videos captured either with a static or with a moving video camera. The challenge of achieving a robust 4K video-based surveillance system is twofold. Firstly, the 4K video resolution (3840×2160 px.) constrains considerably the amount of videoprocessing for meeting the near real-time requirement. Secondly, maritime environment is very dynamic and highly unpredictable, thereby, rendering target extraction a difficult task. Therefore, the proposed approach attempts to leverage both temporal and spatial video information for achieving fast and accurate target extraction. In fact, since, the object rigidity assumption is implemented parsimoniously, i.e.; at key video locations, its real-time implementation, first, enables to quickly extract potential (sparse) target locations. Furthermore, we have shown, experimentally using many maritime videos, that maritime targets generally exhibit richer textural variations than dynamic background at different scales. Thus, secondly, a still image based multi-scale texture discrimination algorithm carried out around previously extracted key video locations allows to achieve final target extraction. An experimental study we have conducted both using our own maritime video datasets and publicly available video datasets have demonstrated the feasibility of the proposed approach.

Keywords: Maritime videosurveillance · 4K video
Spatiotemporal approach

1 Introduction

With the important recent advances in camera technologies and in computing resources, maritime videosurveillance has become an important research topic. The latter finds several real-world applications among which we can mention optimal monitoring of maritime traffic [3,9,21], seacoast security [18], prevention

Supported by the French Defense Agency (DGA), CIFRE no. 0004/2015/DGA.

© Springer Nature Switzerland AG 2018
A. Basu and S. Berretti (Eds.): ICSM 2018, LNCS 11010, pp. 123–133, 2018.
https://doi.org/10.1007/978-3-030-04375-9_11

of fraudulent maritime activities [7,16], situation awareness and prevention of asymetric threats (i.e.; a commercial or military ship being threatened by small maritime vehicles such as jetskis and inflatable boats). For instance, in the latter context, it is highly desired to be able to detect as early as possible small targets, hence, the need for highly performing computer vision hardware (e.g.; 4K video cameras) and software.

Although videosurveillance in controlled environments using conventional (e.g.; CIF) video formats is, now, a quite well understood computer vision topic, maritime videosurveillance still poses many challenges to the computer vision community. Indeed, traditionally, background subtraction algorithms [13,20,24,25] have achieved best state of the art performances in terms of detection accuracy and computational efficiency. Furthermore, in the goal of accounting for low video SNR, thereby, achieving more accurate object recognition, robust background subtraction algorithms–attempting to exploit small image neighborhoods, instead of single pixels–have been developed [6]. When the camera is moving and if the background is static, then a coupling of a background subtraction technique with a fast motion compensation algorithm, generally, yields very good results [23]. Nevertheless, the latter category of approaches is hardly applicable in maritime video-surveillance because of the dynamic background (e.g.; sea). Alternative approaches attempting to take advantage of spatiotemporal coherence of objects have been proposed [14,15]. More recently, deep learning based approaches have achieved astounding results in various application contexts, and in maritime vision in particular [4,8]. Nevertheless, our experiments have shown that the latter only achieve mitigated performances on maritime videos, above all, for detection of small and lowly contrasted targets. This can be partly explained by the fact that the latter category of techniques do not attempt to take advantage of the temporal video dimension in the goal of accounting for low maritime object contrast, and hence, for achieving better maritime object recognition performances.

In the contexts of maritime situation awareness and airborne maritime videosurveillance, every bit of a maritime scene is moving, including the camera, the background (i.e.; sea) and, obviously, maritime objects. Clearly, in such a context, none of the aforementioned techniques is suited. Consequently, novel computer vision algorithms using as little assumptions as possible are needed. Indeed, this work is part of a bigger research project aiming at developing state of the art maritime videosurveillance algorithms to automated situation awareness, and especially, for the fight against asymetric threats. Obviously, early detection of small ships requires near real-time processing of high definition video, typically 4K videos in our case. Therefore, in the remainder of this paper, we describe the approach that we have developed for maritime object extraction using 4K videos. The main contribution of this paper resides in the fact that video processing is carried out around key video locations while taking advantage both of the spatial and temporal video dimensions for achieving accurate and fast maritime target extraction.

2 General Method Overview

The main idea behind the proposed spatiotemporal approach to object recognition using 4K videos is motivated as follows. On the one hand, what mostly distinguishes a real-world object from a dynamic background is rigidity. On the other hand, we first hypothesize, then, we show experimentally using several maritime video datasets that maritime objects, generally, present richer textural features than maritime background. Furthermore, in the goal of achieving a near real-time 4K maritime videosurveillance system, we have efficiently implemented the latter idea with respect to the temporal and spatial dimensions of a video, respectively. Basically, a temporal algorithm allows to extract potential target keypoint locations as rigid ones using long-term keypoint tracking. Then, a spatial algorithm performs texture discrimination in the vicinity of the latter in the goal of achieving final target extraction. The workflow of the proposed approach is outlined in Fig. 1.

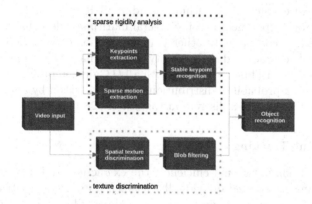

Fig. 1. Workflow of the proposed spatiotemporal approach.

3 Rigidity Analysis via Long-Term Keypoint Tracking

The key idea of exploiting the object rigidity hypothesis to achieve object extraction in video is not new. For instance, the authors in [22] have proposed a fundamental matrix based approach for performing multiple objects extraction in video. However, a major drawback of the fundamental matrix based type of approaches lays in their combinatorial nature, plus, in the difficulty of establishing enough "good" keypoint inter-frame correspondences. The latter issue is aggravated when the background is dynamic and/or the camera is moving which turns out to be, generally, the case in maritime videos. An alternative approach proposed in [2] attempts to estimate a dense rigidity criterion based on a timely $3D$ analysis of dense optical flow. But, the latter is hardly applicable in our case

due to unreliability of optical flow. Thus, we have proposed an alternative approach to rigidity analysis restricted to key video locations via keypoint tracking.
Indeed, extraction of keypoints in individual frames, and establishment of their
inter-frame correspondences is an easy, fast, and reliable process. Moreover, it
makes sense to hypothesize that rigid object pixels tend to undergo less textural
change in the course of time than dynamic background. Therefore, our approach
to rigidity analysis using video consists in assessing the temporal textural variation at video keypoint locations via their long-term tracking as it will be in
described in detail, hereafter.

3.1 Keypoint Extraction

The proposed approach to rigidity analysis in video begins with the extraction
of key video locations. The latter are further tracked over time before they
are declared as potential object keypoints, otherwise, permanently abandoned
because they are, eventually, ranked as background. We have tested different
existing keypoint extraction algorithms including SURF [1], ORB [19], and SIFT
[11]. However, our experiments– using several maritime videos–have shown that
SIFT outperforms considerably other existing keypoint extraction techniques
both in terms of accuracy and repeatability, thus, we have finally opted for SIFT.
The SIFT descriptor is, first, convolved with a $1D$ Gaussian profile ($\sigma = 2$), then,
transformed into a probability distribution via mere division by a normalization
constant, finally, stored in a discrete histogram of 128 bins.

3.2 Keypoint Tracking

For the sake of computational efficiency, the extracted SIFT keypoints in the
first video frame are tracked individually between frames using optical flow and
the Kalman filter. The state vector of the Kalman filter consists here of the
concatenation of the subpixel position (x_t, y_t) of a SIFT keypoint and its $2D$
velocity vector (u_t, v_t), in such a way that, the sate vector of the Kalman filter
writes as $Y_t = (x_t, y_t, u_t, v_t)^T$, but, of which one may only observe a noisy version
denoted by Z_t. Thus, the SIFT keypoint dynamic model writes as

$$\begin{cases} x_{t+1} = x_t + u_t + \epsilon_{t+1}^{(1)} \\ y_{t+1} = y_t + v_t + \epsilon_{t+1}^{(2)} \\ u_{t+1} = u_t + w_{t+1}^{(1)} \\ v_{t+1} = v_t + w_{t+1}^{(2)} \\ Z_{t+1} = Y_{t+1} + W_{t+1} \end{cases}$$

where it has been assumed that $\epsilon_{t+1}^{(1)}$, $\epsilon_{t+1}^{(2)}$, $w_{t+1}^{(1)}$, and $w_{t+1}^{(2)}$ stand for four independent Gaussian random variables, W_T stands a 4-dimensional random Gaussian
vector, last, subscript t denotes the time. Furthermore, we have used the method

developed in [5] for achieving robust optical flow estimation, and hence, accurate SIFT keypoint tracking. In short, such an optical flow estimation technique is based on the inversion of the Hessian matrix and which just happens to be well conditioned at SIFT keypoints. We refer the reader to [5,11] for more details.

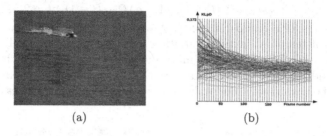

(a)   (b)

Fig. 2. Sparse rigidity estimation based on keypoint tracking. (a) Tracking of SIFT keypoints across 250 4K frames; (b) Temporal evolution of the proposed rigidity measure for different classes of SIFT keypoints. In blue: wave; in green: wake; in red: object. (Color figure online)

3.3 Keypoint Rigidity Analysis and Classification

As aforementioned, SIFT keypoint classification as object *versus* background is based on the estimation of the long-term variation of the dynamic of the SIFT descriptor. Furthermore, since, we have modeled the latter in our approach as a probability distribution, it makes sense to use the Kullback-Leibler pseudo-Distance (KLpD) for deriving a measure of normalized SIFT keypoint textural variation. For obvious reasons, the latter is fairly correlated with any measure of rigidity, for rigid object regions are bound to undergo little textural change over time. Moreover, by basing a rigidity measure on a distance between probability distributions, one guarantees invariability against common geometric deformations of objects.

In fact, we have proposed a slight modification to the original KLpD for obtaining a symmetric and robust measure of textural variation over time, and which, overall, can account for the possible presence of near-zero values in a normalized SIFT descriptor, and slight shifts in the latter(mainly due to discretization). Thus, suppose two probability distributions P and Q, and define the divergence measure between P and Q as $D_{KL}(P||Q) = \sum_i D_i(P,Q)$ where one has $\forall i$:

$$D_i(P,Q) = \inf\left\{ \left|P(i)\log\frac{P(i)}{Q(i)}\right|, \left|Q(i)\log\frac{Q(i)}{P(i)}\right|\right\}$$

Robustness of $D_{KL}(P||Q)$ resides in that, given any couple of real positive numbers x and y, if $\inf\{x,y\} \to 0$, then $\inf\{|x\log\frac{x}{y}|, |y\log\frac{y}{x}|\} \to 0$, thereby, mitigating the contributions from too distinct couples of bins of P and Q, respectively. Next, assume an arbitrary SIFT keypoint at time t, and denote by P_t the corresponding normalized SIFT descriptor. Then, a real-time implementation of above formula is achieved keypoint-wise by simply propagating it across frames via the moving average trick according to the following update scheme: $\hat{D}_{KL}(t) = \begin{cases} D_{KL}(P_1||P_0), \text{if } t = 1 \\ \alpha D_{KL}(P_t||P_{t-1}) + (1-\alpha)\hat{D}_{KL}(t-1), \forall t = 2, \ldots \end{cases}$, where $\alpha \in (0, 1)$ stands for a real parameter that we have experimentally tuned to 0.1. An example of temporal textural variation for three classes of SIFT keypoints (wave, wake, and object) in a 4K maritime video is presented in Fig. 2. One can notice, indeed, that the temporal KLpD profile of object keypoints quickly decreases, whereas, its wave and wake counterparts keep higher values over time.

(a)   (b)

Fig. 3. Results of texture discrimination in a maritime video. In green: image blocks ranked as background; in blue: image blocks ranked as object. (Color figure online)

The final stage, then, consists, in merely classifying every tracked SIFT keypoint either as object or background based on its estimated value of $\hat{D}_{KL}(t)$. Such a classification algorithm, thus, attempts to divide the set of real (1D) points consisting of all the values of $\hat{D}_{KL}(t)$ for each SIFT keypoint into two separate clusters (i.e.; as background vs object). This is efficiently achieved by means of the expectation maximization (EM) algorithm by computing the mixture of two Gaussians which best fits the set of keypoint-wise values of $\hat{D}_{KL}(t)$.

4   Spatial Texture Discrimination

Since, the above rigidity based approach only yields sparse object regions, one, moreover, needs perform some image processing in order to identity full object zones. As mentioned earlier, this is achieved in the present approach based on the analysis of texture. The intuition behind the latter consists in that objects exhibit much richer textural features (e.g.; discontinuities, etc) independently of the scale, whereas, dynamic background is generally characterized with monotonous texture, and hence, poorer textural variation. In this paper, we have used the RFA descriptor [10] which has the advantage to be invariant against rotation and translation. The latter is computed in small overlapping image regions for capturing textural features across an image. Next, in order to capture textural variation, we perform a PCA on the matrix consisting of a column-wise alignment of the RFA vectors in a given image region in the goal of extracting the main directions of textural variation. Our experiments have demonstrated that, generally, only two or three principal components are enough for summing up most (i.e.; $\geq 90\%$) of the textural information. Thus, we have opted for the latter value (3), in such a way that, the output of this step consists of a $3D$ vector containing the three most significant eigen values of the PCA matrix. The latter is further used to feed a K-means classifier for computing two clusters, likely, corresponding to object and background, respectively.

Final maritime object extraction is merely achieved by merging image blocks– ranked as object by the texture discrimination algorithm and containing at least one stable SIFT keypoint– using the connected components algorithm. Furthermore, for the sake of accuracy and efficiency, we have implemented the latter algorithm using a multi-resolution scheme. In a nutshell, this consists in running the algorithm on a pyramid of downscaled images (by a factor of 2 with respect to each image dimension), before finally merging the results found at different scales of a 4K image for extracting full object zones. An example of the obtained results of the latter approach on a 4K maritime video is presented in Fig. 3.

5 Experimental Work

The proposed method is implemented in C++ using the OpenCV library[1], and runs in near real-time for 4K videos at an average rate of 6 images per min on an Intel CPU architecture (i5 2.2Gh).

We have chosen to show in Fig. 4 results of the proposed method using a maritime videos we have captured using a 4K fix security camera, and that we have named Video 4, throughout this experimental section. One can observe that, despite the fact that the camera is not moving, in contrast to our method, the KNN method produces awful oversegmentations resulting in many false detections. This can be explained by the fact that the mixture of Gaussians model is not well suited to maritime background.

We have also conducted a comparative study of the proposed approach against some existing well known videosurveillance approaches [25] [24], *Lin et al.* [10], and *Moo Yi et al.* [23]. However, since, we have not found any publicly available 4K video datasets with ground truth, we have only been able to test the proposed method using the following publicly available lower resolution videos:

---

[1] http://opencv.org/downloads.html.

- *Singapore Maritime Dataset (SMD)* [17]: this dataset provides several onshore RGB video sequences captured with a $70D$ Canon camera (1080×1920 px.) and showing vessels evolving in a maritime scene,
- *UCSD Background Subtraction* dataset [12]: this dataset provides several videosurveillance sequences (344×224 px.) presenting dynamic backgrounds.

We have chosen to use the F-measure of which formula is given by

$$F\text{-}measure = \frac{1}{n} \sum_{i=1}^{n} 2 * \frac{\text{Prec}_i * \text{Rec}_i}{\text{Prec}_i + \text{Rec}_i}$$

where i stands for the frame index, $Prec_i = TP_i/TP_i + FP_i$ and $Rec_i = TP_i/TP_i + FN_i$ where TP, FP and FN stand for the number of true positives, the number of true negatives and the number of false negatives, respectively.

The comparison results are summed up in Table 1 (using our 4K video datasets), Tables 2 and 3 (using publicly available video datasets).

One can observe that our method achieves best performances in terms of the F-measure which, in some sense, means that it achieves the best false positive *vs.* false negative trade-off. This can be explained by the fact that, in contrast to other existing approaches, the proposed approach in this paper is based on the useful rigid nature of maritime objects as opposed to non-rigidity of maritime background, moreover, such a rigidity hypothesis turns out to be particularly useful for eliminating wake regions.

Table 1. F-measure results using 4K videos.

Seq	Frame number	Our method	KNN
Video1	94	**0.81**	6.27e−7
Video2	95	**0.93**	1.55e−7
Video3	64	**0.6**	1.5e−6
Video4	95	**1**	5.7e−6

Table 2. F-measure results using the Singapore maritime dataset

Seq	Num. frame	Our method
MVI_1610_VIS	537	0.727642
MVI_1646_VIS	514	0.656212

Table 3. F-measure results using the UCSD dataset.

Seq.	bottle	jump	skiing	birds
Num. frame	25	75	105	65
Our method	**0.76**	**0.64**	**0.33**	**0.36**
RFA	0.58	0.63	0.18	0.1
KNN [25]	0.54	0.39	0.08	0.048
MOG2 [24]	0.259	0.27	0.02	0.015
Dual-mode SGM	0.004	0.0032	0.027	0.09

(a) T = 0   (b) T = 100

(c) T = 200

Fig. 4. Results of the proposed approach using Video 4.

6   Conclusion

We have described a novel spatiotemporal approach to maritime target recognition approach using 4K maritime videos. The approach is mainly based on the notion of object rigidity and the property that, generally, maritime objects are texturally richer than maritime background. Moreover, for the sake of computational efficiency, first, we have proposed a parsimonious implementation of the rigidity measure by assessing the temporal deformation of the SIFT descriptor at key video locations. Second, we have developed a multi-resolution scheme for extracting full object zones based both on rigidity analysis and spatial discrimination. The present method has been implemented on a CPU architecture and achieves near real-time performances, however, the former is highly parallelizable. Thus, as future work, we will develop a GPU implementation of the present approach for achieving real-time maritime video-surveillance using 4K videos.

References

1. Bay, H., Ess, A., Tuytelaars, T., Van Gool, L.: Speeded-up robust features (SURF). Comput. Vis. Image Underst. **110**(3), 346–359 (2008)
2. Bechar, I., Lelore, T., Bouchara, F., Guis, V., Grimaldi, M.: Object segmentation from a dynamic background using a pixelwise rigidity criterion and application to maritime target recognition. In: ICIP, pp. 363–367 (2014)
3. Bechar, I., Lelore, T., Bouchara, F., Guis, V., Grimaldi, M.: Toward an airborne system for near real-time maritime video-surveillance based on synchronous visible light and thermal infrared video information fusion. In: OCOSS (2013)
4. Cruz, G., Bernardino, A.: Aerial detection in maritime scenarios using convolutional neural networks. In: Blanc-Talon, J., Distante, C., Philips, W., Popescu, D., Scheunders, P. (eds.) ACIVS 2016. LNCS, vol. 10016, pp. 373–384. Springer, Cham (2016). https://doi.org/10.1007/978-3-319-48680-2_33
5. Farnebäck, G.: Two-frame motion estimation based on polynomial expansion. In: Bigun, J., Gustavsson, T. (eds.) SCIA 2003. LNCS, vol. 2749, pp. 363–370. Springer, Heidelberg (2003). https://doi.org/10.1007/3-540-45103-X_50
6. Gallego, J., Pardas, M., Haro, G.: Bayesian foreground segmentation and tracking using pixel-wise background model and region based foreground model. In: ICIP 2009, vol. 50, pp. 566–571 (2015)
7. Grimaldi, M., Bechar, I., Lelore, T., Guis, V., Bouchara, F.: An unsupervised approach to automatic object extraction from a maritime video scene. In: IPTA, pp. 378–383 (2014)
8. Liu, Y., Cui, H.Y., Kuang, Z., Li, G.Q.: Ship detection and classification on optical remote sensing images using deep learning. In: ITM Web Conference, vol. 12, p. 05012 (2017)
9. Leggat, J., Litvak, T., Parker, I., Sinha, A., Vidalis, S., Wong, A.: Study on persistent monitoring of maritime, great lakes and St. lawrence seaway border regions. Contract report DRDC CSS CR, 2011–2028 (2011)
10. Lin, S.C.F., Wong, C.Y., Jiang, G., Rahman, M.A., Kwok, N.M.: Radial fourier analysis (RFA) image descriptor. In: 2014 11th International Conference on Fuzzy Systems and Knowledge Discovery (FSKD), pp. 814–819, August 2014. https://doi.org/10.1109/FSKD.2014.6980942
11. Lowe, D.G.: Distinctive image features from scale-invariant keypoints. Int. J. Comput. Vision **60**(2), 91–110 (2004)
12. Mahadevan, V., Vasconcelos, N.: Spatiotemporal saliency in dynamic scenes. IEEE Trans. Pattern Anal. Mach. Intell. **32**(1), 171–177 (2010)
13. Mittal, A., Paragios, N.: Motion-based background subtraction using adaptive kernel density estimation. In: CVPR, pp. 302–309 (2004)
14. Narayana, M., Hanson, A., Learned-Miller, E.: Coherent motion segmentation in moving camera videos using optical flow orientations. In: ICCV, pp. 1577–1584 (2013)
15. Oneata, D., Revaud, J., Verbeek, J., Schmid, C.: Spatio-temporal object detection proposals. In: Fleet, D., Pajdla, T., Schiele, B., Tuytelaars, T. (eds.) ECCV 2014. LNCS, vol. 8691, pp. 737–752. Springer, Cham (2014). https://doi.org/10.1007/978-3-319-10578-9_48
16. Pires, N., Guinet, J., Dusch, E.: ASV: an innovative automatic system for maritime surveillance. Navigation **58**(232), 1–20 (2010)
17. Prasad, D.K., Rajan, D., Rachmawati, L., Rajabally, E., Quek, C.: Video processing from electro-optical sensors for object detection and tracking in a maritime environment: a survey. IEEE Trans. Intell. Transp. Syst. **18**, 1993–2016 (2017)

18. Rhodes, B.J., et al.: SeeCoast: persistent surveillance and automated scene understanding for ports and coastal areas. In: SPIE, vol. 6578, no. 1, p. 65781 (2007)
19. Rublee, E., Rabaud, V., Konolige, K., Bradski, G.: ORB: an efficient alternative to SIFT or SURF. In: Proceedings of the 2011 International Conference on Computer Vision, ICCV 2011, pp. 2564–2571. IEEE Computer Society (2011)
20. Sheikh, Y., Javed, O., Kanade, T.: Background subtraction for freely moving cameras. In: ICCV, pp. 1219–1225 (2009)
21. Smith, A., Teal, M.: Identification and tracking of marine objects in nearinfrared image sequences for collision avoidance. In: 7th International Conference on Image Processing and Its Applications, pp. 250–254 (1999)
22. Vidal, R., Soatto, S., Sastry, S.: Segmentation of dynamic scenes from the multibody fundamental matrix. In: Proceedings of the Workshop on Analysis of Dynamic Scenes (2002)
23. Moo Yi, K., Yun, K., Wan Kim, S., Jin Chang, H., Young Choi, J.: Detection of moving objects with non-stationary cameras in 5.8ms: bringing motion detection to your mobile device. In: CVPR Workshops, pp. 27–34. IEEE Computer Society (2013)
24. Zivkovic, Z.: Improved adaptive Gaussian mixture model for background subtraction. In: Proceedings of the 17th International Conference on Pattern Recognition, ICPR 2004. vol. 2, pp. 28–31, August 2004
25. Zivkovic, Z., van der Heijden, F.: Efficient adaptive density estimation per image pixel for the task of background subtraction. Pattern Recogn. Lett. **27**, 773–780 (2006)

A Heterogeneous Image Fusion Algorithm Based on LLC Coding

Bing Zhu[1(✉)], Weixin Gao[1], Xiaomeng Wu[1], and Ruixing Yu[2]

[1] Xi'an Shiyou University,
Xi'an 710065, Shaanxi Province, People's Republic of China
Bzhu@xsyu.edu.cn
[2] Northwestern Polytechnical University,
Xi'an 710072, Shaanxi Province, People's Republic of China

Abstract. Most image fusion algorithms are not good at batch processing. To address this, we propose a LLC coding based image fusion algorithm, by which multiple infrared and visible light images can be fused and identified. The images were encoded and several image features were extracted by those codes. It was judged whether the images could be merged by the coincidence of the non-zero coding counterpart obtained from comparing the LLC coding of two heterogeneous images. The max-pooling criterion was employed to fuse the features extracted from images by maximizing the complementary information and minimizing the redundant information. Consequently the SVM classifier was used to classify and identify the target. The simulated results show the accuracy of our proposed method.

1 Introduction

Image fusion has gained increasing importance over the past decades. During the process, much more information contained in the heterologous images are combined, and a certain algorithm which can maximize the complementary information and minimize the redundant information is required to keep complementary information of the images. Such an algorithm can help to get more information through the fusion process.

Image fusion algorithms can be divided into three different levels: pixel-level fusion, feature-level fusion and decision-level fusion. Pixel-level fusion is the most widely used.

Image sparse coding is usually employed to extract image features. Sparse coding method applied to the study of mechanism of biological vision system, Field and Olshausen [1] proposed the well-known sparse coding model which expresses input stimulus images by linear superposition of base functions. This method emphasizes the similarity of processed image and original. The similarity can be judged by minimizing mean square error, and this emphasizes response of the algorithm to be sparse. Many researchers have used sparse coding models to achieve comparative results in many applications such like denoising of digital images, image compression, image reconstruction, super resolution analysis, and face recognition. Many scholars have further optimized the sparse coding model: Li Zhiqing proposed sparse coding based method to structural similarity so that the reconstructed image block maintains structural

A. Basu and S. Berretti (Eds.): ICSM 2018, LNCS 11010, pp. 134–144, 2018.
https://doi.org/10.1007/978-3-030-04375-9_12

information of the original image block as much as possible [2]. After training using sufficient number of input images, a set of basis functions can be used to optimize and obtain the corresponding response from a piece of image. Thus, such a response is called sparsely encoded features for a single image block. Yang [3] used the sparse coding theory for image representation based on local features, based on using bag-of-word and spatial pyramid models for replacing sparse coding (SC) in Vector Quantization(VQ) to extract image features. Consequently such a process had been used for image retrieval successfully. Yu [4] et al. proposed the method of Local Coordinate Coding (LCC Coding), and improved the SC method proposed by Yang. This made the correspondence of coding basis more accurate. Wang [5] et al. improved the LLC method, and proposed locality-constrained Linear Coding (LLC Coding), which makes the constraints of the Coding base of sparse Coding and the image retrieval results more accurate. Previous researches on sparse coding totally focused on image retrieval and classification. However, very few researchers focused on image fusion with sparse Coding method, which is explored in this paper. Most image fusion algorithms can only deal with two images at one step, this paper proposed a Locality-constrained Linear Coding(LLC) based images fusion algorithm, which can fusion much more than two infrared and visible images at one step.

The LLC encoding method was employed to extract the image feature at beginning. Then according to the non-zero coding of the LLC to determine we decide if it is necessary for the processed images to be fused. If yes, a specific fusion method is used. The accuracy of the algorithm was validated by simulation results, and the target recognition rate of the algorithm was used as the evaluation criterion. The conclusion of simulation is that the recognition rate of the processed images were better than that of unprocessed images.

2 Sparse Coding Theory

Local coordinate coding requires the use of the smoothing function $f(x)$ in high dimensional space $\mathbb{R}^d$.

Definition 1 (Lipschitz smoothing function): in $\mathbb{R}^d$, if $\alpha, \beta > 0$ and $p \in (0, 1]$ are assumed to satisfy equations $|f(x') - f(x)| \leq \alpha|x - x'|$ and $|f(x') - f(x) - \nabla f(x)^T(x' - x)| \leq \beta\|x - x'\|^{1+p}$ for any $x, x', f(x)$ is called Lipschitz smoothing function.

Definition 2.2 (coordinate coding): (γ, B) represents coordinate coding, where $B \subset \mathbb{R}^d$ is the set of anchor points, and γ is the mapping betweet $x \in \mathbb{R}^d$ and $|\gamma_v(x)|_{v\in B} \in R^{|B|}$, and satisfies $\sum_v r_v(x) = 1$. This represents the following approximation to $x \in \mathbb{R}^d$:$\gamma(x) = \sum_{v\in B} \gamma_v(x)v$. In addition, for all $x \in \mathbb{R}^d$, the norm for defining the coordinate encoding is: $\|x\|_\gamma = (\sum_{v\in B} \gamma_v(x)^2)^{1/2}$.

The key point of the concept of coordinate coding is that if the coordinate coding has sufficient locality, a nonlinear function can be approximated by a linear function. So, we can get the following "linearized" lemma:

Lemma 2.1 (linearization): Suppose (γ, B) is an arbitrary coordinate encoding in $\mathbb{R}^d$, and f is a Lipschitz smoothing function about (α, β, p). For all $x \in \mathbb{R}^d$, there exists:

$$\left| f(x) - \sum_{v \in B} \gamma_v(x) f(v) \right| \leq \alpha \|x - \gamma(x)\| + \beta \sum_{v \in B} |\gamma_v(x)| \|v - \gamma(x)\|^{1+p} \tag{1}$$

It can be seen from the above formula that the nonlinear function $f(x)$ in $\mathbb{R}^d$ is represented by a coded linear function $\sum_{v \in B} \gamma_v(x) f(v)$, and $|f(v)|_{v \in B}$ denotes the set of coefficients obtained through data estimation. The upper limit of the approximation error is determined by the right side of the inequality. There are two terms: the first term $\|x - \gamma(x)\|$ indicates that x must be close to its physical approximation $\gamma(x)$, and the second term indicates that the coding must be local. The code γ quality of B can be measured by the right side of the inequality.

For convenience, the following definitions about coding locality are given.

Definition 2.3 (locally): given α, β, p and encoded (γ, B), define

$$Q_{\alpha,\beta,p}(\gamma, B) = \mathrm{E}_x \left[\alpha \|x - \gamma(x)\| + \beta \sum_{v \in B} |\gamma_v(x)| \|v - \gamma(x)\|^{1+p} \right] \tag{2}$$

In $Q_{\alpha,\beta,p}$, α, β, p is an adjustment parameter, and we set $\alpha = \beta = p = 1$. Because the quality function $Q_{\alpha,\beta,p}(\gamma, B)$ depends only on unlabeled data, it can actually be optimized using unlabeled data, and thus we can easily determine (γ, B).

From the LCC approach, locality is more essential than sparsity, and locality necessarily leads to sparseness, but sparsity does not necessarily lead to locality. LLC uses local constraints instead of LCC's sparse constraints to improve the efficiency of the optimization problem. The LLC encoding method is defined as follows:

Definition 2.4: Let X be a set of D-dimensional local descriptors, $X = [x_1, x_2 \cdots x_N] \in \mathbb{R}^{D \times N}$, given a codebook $B = [b_1, b_2 \cdots b_M] \in \mathbb{R}^{D \times M}$ with M table items, all data x_i can be converted to an M-dimensional encoding. The coding guidelines for LLC are as follows:

$$\min \sum_{i=1}^{N} \|x_i - Bc_i\|^2 + \lambda \|d_i \odot c_i\|^2 \tag{3}$$

Where, for any i, we have $1^T c_i = 1$. $\odot$ represents the product of the corresponding elements of the vector, and $d_i \in \mathbb{R}^M$ is the local adaptor. Its purpose is to use b_i close to x_i to represent x_i as far as possible, so as to reflect the locality. d_i is defined as follows:

$$d_i = \exp\left(\frac{dist(x_i, B)}{\sigma}\right) \tag{4}$$

In the above formula, $dist(x_i, B) = [dist(x_i, b_1), dist(x_i, b_2), \cdots, dist(x_i, b_M)]^T$, $dist(x_i, b_j)$ is the Euclidean distance between x_i and b_j. σ is the weight attenuation factor of the local adaptor.

In order to better identify the image, when coding the same area, the descriptors used should be consistent as far as possible. The LLC method uses regular item $\|d_i \odot c_i\|^2$ with the following features:

1. Better refactoring. As shown in the figure below, one descriptor for a Vector Quantization (VQ) method corresponds to one encoding base. Each descriptor of the LLC method is represented by a plurality of code bases adjacent to it, which improves reconfiguration (Fig. 1).

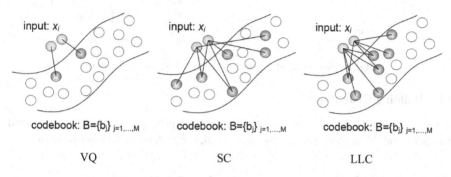

VQ   SC   LLC

Fig. 1. Comparison of VQ, SC, and LLC methods

2. Local smooth sparsity. Compared with LLC, Sparse Coding (SC) method also has good reconfiguration due to the use of multiple Coding bases. However, the regular terms in SC are not smooth, which is due to the sparsity. Thus, it is necessary to learn complete coding bases in the coding. For similar input, it is possible to choose the coding base representation with a large gap. The LLC method assures similar input with similar coding bases due to the limitations of longer distance bases.
3. Resolvability. The optimization function of LLC method has analytic solution, so it doesn't need to carry out complex iteration like SC method, so the computational efficiency is greatly improved.

3   Image Coding Algorithm Based on LLC Coding

The general image fusion algorithm only performs fusion processing on two images. For a large number of hetero-images to be fused, the processing efficiency is poor. Therefore, this paper chooses the method of extracting hetero-images features based on LLC coding and fuses the extracted hetero-images features. This can handle a large number of registered infrared and visible light images.

LLC coding is based on a codebook to encode the entire image and extract image features. Before fusion, it is necessary to build a codebook, then process the image, extract the LLC coding features, and quickly compare the features of the hetero-images by using the non-zero coding counterpart of the hetero-images LLC features to judge whether fusion is needed.

The fusion flow diagram is shown in Fig. 2:

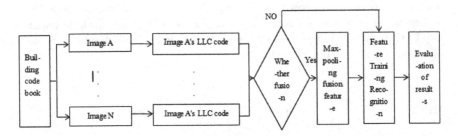

Fig. 2. Feature-level fusion flow chart based on LLC coding

3.1 Building Code Book

When constructing a codebook, the most important principle is that the constructed codebook should be more encompassing and can make sparse coding better. In order to

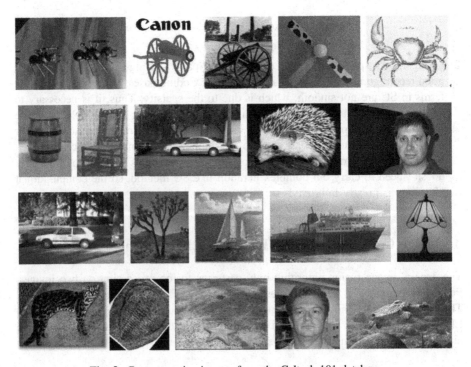

Fig. 3. Representative images from the Caltech-101 database

make the code book more comprehensive, the Caltech-101 image classification database was selected as the training set. Figure 3 shows some of the images in the database.

First the SIFT algorithm is used to extract image features. The image source is a Caltech-101 database. A number of images are randomly selected, and the image sub-blocks (size $N \times N$) are cut out. The 128-dimensional SIFT features of these image sub-blocks are extracted. Next, the extracted SIFT features are K-means clustered. Finally, the cluster centers of each type of K-means clustering are selected as the words in the dictionary, that is, the entries in the codebook.

3.2 Spatial Pyramid Matching

In the process of SIFT feature extraction, the spatial relationship between image features is not considered, and only features in each image sub-block are concatenated to form new features. The dimension of the SIFT feature is proportional to the image size, and the LLC code is based on the SIFT feature, so the LLC code length is also proportional to the image size. This is very unfavorable for image fusion. Therefore, in order to normalize the image coding length of the LLC, a spatial pyramid matching (SPM) method is used to process the image features.

In this article, L = 2, the basic flow of SPM is as follows:

(1) At different scales of $l = 0, 1, 2$, images are divided into $2^l * 2^l$ separate regions Seg_{l-i};

(2) In the 21 well-divided image sub-blocks, a 128-dimensional SIFT feature is extracted from each image sub-block, and LLC feature coding is performed;

(3) Perform the max-pooling operation on the LLC feature code c_{l-i-j} in each Seg_{l-i}, and obtain the final output feature $\tilde{c}_{l-i}$ of Seg_{l-i}, that is, $\tilde{c}_{l-i} = \max(c_{l-i-1}, \cdots, c_{l-i-1}, \cdots, c_{l-i-N})$. Among them, $\max(\cdot)$ denotes taking the maximum of the corresponding bit of $c_{l-i-1}, \cdots, c_{l-i-1}, \cdots, c_{l-i-N}$ by column, and the dimension of $\tilde{c}_{l-i}$ is the same as c_{l-i-j};

(4) Concatenate all 21 $\tilde{c}_{l-i}$ to get the final classification feature c_{out}, that is, $c_{out} = [\tilde{c}_{0-1}, \cdots, \tilde{c}_{l-1}, \cdots, \tilde{c}_{2-21}]$. The characteristic dimension of c_{out} must be $21 \times k$, where k is the number of bases in the codebook for LLC coding. In this paper, the characteristic dimension of c_{out} is $21 \times 1024 = 21504$-dimensional.

3.3 Determine Whether the Image Needs Fusion

The image features are obtained using LLC coding. According to the principle of LLC coding, this vector contains non-zero coding and zero coding. Non-zero coding represents image features, and the non-zero coding corresponding coding base can also represent image features. Therefore, by comparing the coding base corresponding to the non-zero code in the heterologous image, it can be judged whether the image contains complementary information or redundant information. If the comparison result is that the bases corresponding to the non-zero codes are approximately the same, indicating that there is little complementary information among the image features, the judgment features do not need to be fused, and the fusion image can provide all the required information. If the comparison result is that the bases corresponding to the non-zero code are only partially the same, it means that the complementary information between the features is more and the redundant information is less, then the images need to be merged and feature level fusion is performed.

Table 1 lists the partial LLC feature codes of the two to-be-fused images. It can be seen that there are three feature coding cases corresponding to the same coding base, one is all 0, indicating that the image does not contain such feature information; One is not 0, which means that the image contains redundant information; Another kind is not all 0, indicating that the image contains complementary information. After many experiments, the thresholds for the fusion of the images can be determined. If the coincidence rate of the non-zero coded corresponding bases reaches 85% or more, no fusion is needed; if less than 85%, the next fusion operation is performed.

Table 1. LLC features of different spectrum images

Image A	0.009	0.014	0.021	0.000	0.000	0.000	0.007	0.000	0.000
Image B	0.018	0.012	0.019	0.000	0.000	0.005	0.010	0.003	0.003

3.4 Fusion Rules

After the completion of image LLC coding, the final classification features of the heterogenous images can be fused through SPM operation. Suppose the output feature of image LLC after SPM processing is $c_{spm}^i, i = 1, 2, \cdots T$, Where T is the number of image sub-blocks in SPM. The fusion feature obtained by fusing is T. The fusion feature of each c_{spm}^i is $\tilde{c}f$. The fusion rule is based on the max-pooling method to fuse c_{spm}^i, obtain the initial fusion feature cf, that is, $cf = \max(c_{spm}^1, c_{spm}^2, \cdots, c_{spm}^T)$, and then normalize cf to obtain the final fusion feature $\tilde{c}f = cf/\|cf\|_2$, where $\|\|_2$ denotes obtaining the l_2-norm.

In order to verify that the feature of the max-pooling fusion image is optimal, two different method fusion features are adopted, namely the min-pooling and sum-pooling methods. The comparison between these two methods and max-pooling is that the fusion feature f is obtained in a different way. In the min-pooling method, fusion is performed on c_{spm}^i to obtain fusion feature $cf = \min(c_{spm}^1, c_{spm}^2, \cdots, c_{spm}^T)$; In the sum-pooling method, c_{spm}^i is merged to obtain a fusion feature $cf = \text{sum}(c_{spm}^1, c_{spm}^2, \cdots, c_{spm}^T)$.

4   Experimental Results and Analysis

In the experimental process, because of the large number of images required by this method, the existing database with a large number of images is basically an image retrieval aspect. There was no complete open source heterogeneous image fusion database, which was a challenge for the performing the work described in this paper. Therefore, Photoshop was used to transform the visible image into the infrared image, and build a fusion database. The advantage of self-built image fusion database is that we can freely choose the target to be recognized, and create a complete heterogeneous image fusion database. Moreover, since infrared image is completed by PS operation of visible image, it ensures that the image to be fused is completely accurate.

Some samples in the image fusion database are shown in Fig. 4. The first column and the third column are visible images; the second column and the fourth column are

(a) Representative background sample

(b) Representative automobile samples

(c) Representative aircraft samples

(d) Representative sample ships

(e) Representative tank samples

Fig. 4. Self-built database of some five types of samples

the corresponding infrared images. All images are divided into five categories: back-grounds, automobiles, airplanes, ships, and tanks. They contain 140, 370, 394, 360, and 330 images, respectively, of which half are infrared and visible light images. The number of samples used for training in each type of sample is 30, and the rest are used as test samples.

The research content of this paper is heterogeneous image fusion based on LLC encoding, which belongs to the feature-level fusion method. The fusion result is image feature and cannot be reconstructed into a complete visual image. Therefore, the method of calculating the mean square error, mutual information and other evaluation indicators based on the pixels of the entire image is not applicable. In this paper, according to the support vector machine (SVM) method, the fused image features are trained and identified, and compared with the pre-fusion results. We use recognition accuracy rate as a measure of the improvement brought about by our fusion method.

In order to verify the target recognition effect of this method, the background is also used as a kind of sample, which is input into the SVM as the automobile, aircraft, ship, and tank target to perform training identification. Before the images are fused, SVM is used to classify unfused images. Table 2 lists the results of image recognition accuracy.

Table 2. Image recognition accuracy before fusion

Category	Background	Car	Aircraft	Ship	Tank	Mean
Recognition accuracy	0.8375	0.7603	0.7386	0.8453	0.7663	0.7896

As can be seen from Table 2, the accuracy of the identification of ship targets is the highest, followed by the background, tank, and car targets. The aircraft target is the lowest in recognition rate. The average recognition accuracy of the image before fusion is 0.79. In practice, we prefer the target recognition rate to be as high as possible to strike the target more accurately. Therefore, image feature fusion is needed to improve the recognition accuracy. Table 3 shows the result of recognition accuracy after image fusion.

Table 3. Recognition accuracy after image fusion

Fusion method	Background	Car	Aircraft	Ship	Tank	Mean
Max-pooling	0.9171	0.8514	0.7868	0.9072	0.8436	0.8612
Min-pooling	0.9171	0.7816	0.8701	0.8744	0.8345	0.8556
Sum-pooling	0.9186	0.8465	0.7706	0.9117	0.8406	0.8576

As can be seen from Table 3, the average accuracy of recognition after image fusion has increased by 9.07% compared with that before fusion. Among the three different fusion method results, from the mean analysis, the max-pooling recognition rate is the highest, followed by the sum-pooling, and the min-pooling method has the lowest recognition rate. From a single target identification analysis, car and tank targets are the best for max-pooling, background and ship targets are the best for sum-pooling, and aircraft targets are best for min-pooling. The objective of min-pooling is the worst for cars, ships, and tanks. The accuracy of background-target max-pooling and min-pooling is the same, and the sum-pooling effect of aircraft targets is the worst. This is also about the same as the result obtained from the point of view of the mean analysis.

The results obtained in Tables 2 and 3 are from the mean and from the individual target identification analysis, and the results obtained are basically the same. The characteristics of each type of target are different, and the characteristics of the coding features are also different. Therefore, there are differences in the accuracy of recognition for different target types and fusion methods. However, as can be seen from the data in the table, using the feature training before fusion, the differences among the three fusion methods of various targets are the smallest, and the max-pooling method works best, mainly because it is similar to the human visual perception system.

In summary, the max-pooling method fusion feature has the highest recognition accuracy. This also proves that image fusion is necessary. The image fusion method based on LLC coding proposed in this paper can effectively improve the recognition accuracy.

5   Conclusion

A LLC coding based image fusion method was introduces in this paper. The method can fuse a large number of infrared and visible light images at same time. The method comprises the step of: construction of codebooks and LLC coding principles, spatial pyramid matching to normalize image features, heterologous image LLC coding and fusion methods. Finally, the simulation and analysis are performance to illustrate the advantages of this method in image fusion. The target recognition rate of images processed by the algorithm were greater than that of unprocessed images. Because it is difficult to find a database that meets the criteria, Photoshop is used to build the database required for integration.

Acknowledgements. Sponsored by Shaanxi Provincial Department of Education Scientific Research Plan Special Project (17JK0599), National Natural Science Foundation of China (41604122), Xi'an shiyou University Youth Science and Technology Innovation Fund project (2015BS18), Aviation Science Fund Project (20160153001), SAST Foundation (Grant No. SAST2015040), Xi'an Government Science and Technology Plan Project (2017081CGRC044 (XASY007))

References

1. Olshausen, B.A., Field, D.J.: Emergence of simple-cell receptive field properties by learning a sparse code for natural images. Nature **381**(6583), 607–609 (1996)
2. Li, Z.-Q., Shi, Z.-P., Li, Z.-X., Shi, Z.-Z.: Structural similarity sparse coding and image feature extraction. Pattern Recognit. Artif. Intell. **23**(1), 17–22 (2010)

3. Yang, J., Yu, K., Gong, Y., Huang, T.: Linear spatial pyramid matching using sparse coding for image classification. In: Proceedings of CVPR 2009 (2009)
4. Yu, K., Zhang, T., Gong, Y.: Nonlinear learning using local coordinate coding. In: Proceedings of NIPS09 (2009)
5. Wang, J., Yang, J., Yu, K., Lv, F., Huang, T., Gong, Y.: Locality-constrained linear coding for image classification. In: CVPR10 (2010)

Towards the Identification of Parkinson's Disease Using only T1 MR Images

Sara Soltaninejad[✉], Irene Cheng, and Anup Basu

Department of Computing Science, University of Alberta, Edmonton, Canada
soltanin@ualberta.ca

Abstract. Parkinson's Disease (PD) is one of the most common types of neurological diseases caused by progressive degeneration of dopaminergic neurons in the brain. Even though there is no fixed cure for this neurodegenerative disease, earlier diagnosis followed by earlier treatment can help patients have a better quality of life. Magnetic Resonance Imaging (MRI) has been one of the most popular diagnostic tool in recent years because it avoids harmful radiations. In this paper, we investigate the plausibility of using MRIs for automatically diagnosing PD. Our proposed method has three main steps: (1) Preprocessing, (2) Feature Extraction, and (3) Classification. The FreeSurfer library is used for the first and the second steps. For classification, three main types of classifiers, including Logistic Regression (LR), Random Forest (RF) and Support Vector Machine (SVM), are applied and their classification ability is compared. The Parkinson's Progression Markers Initiative (PPMI) data set is used to evaluate the proposed method. The proposed system prove to be promising in assisting the diagnosis of PD.

1 Introduction

Parkinson's Disease (PD) is the second most important neurodegenerative disease after Alzheimer's Disease (AD) that affects middle aged and elderly people. The statistical information presented by Parkinson's News Today [1] shows that an estimated seven to ten million people worldwide have Parkinson's disease. PD causes a progressive loss of dopamine generating neurons in the brain resulting in two types of symptoms, including motor and non-motor. The motor symptoms are bradykinesia, muscles rigidity, tremor and abnormal gait [2], whereas non-motor symptoms include mental disorders, sleep problems, and sensory disturbance [3]. Even though there are some medical methods of diagnosing and determining the progress of PD, the results of these experiments are subjective and depend on the clinicians' expertise. On the other hand, clinicians are expensive and the process is time consuming for patients [4]. Neuroimaging techniques have significantly improved the diagnosis of neurodegenerative diseases. There are different types of neuro imaging techniques of which Magnetic Resonance Imaging (MRI) is one of the most popular because it is a cheap and non-invasive method. People with PD exhibit their symptoms when they lose almost 80%

© Springer Nature Switzerland AG 2018
A. Basu and S. Berretti (Eds.): ICSM 2018, LNCS 11010, pp. 145–156, 2018.
https://doi.org/10.1007/978-3-030-04375-9_13

of their brain dopamine [5]. All of these facts prove the urgent need to have a Computer Aided Diagnosis (CAD) system for an automatic detection of this type of disease. In recent years machine learning has shown remarkable results in the medical image analysis field. The proposed CAD system in neuro disease diagnosis uses different types of imaging data, including Single-Photon Emission Computed Tomography (SPECT) (Prashanth et al. [6]), diffusion tension imaging (DTI), Positron Emission Tomography (PET) (Loane and Politis [7]) and MRI. In this study, the goal is to utilize a structural MRI (sMRI) for developing an automated CAD to early diagnose of PD. Focke et al. [8] proposed a method for PD classification using MR Images. The proposed method in [8] used Gray Matter (GM) and White Matter (WM) individually with an SVM classifier. Voxel-based morphometry (VBM) has been used for preprocessing and feature extraction. The reported results show poor performance (39.53%) for GM and 41.86% for WM. Babu et al. [9] proposed a CAD system for diagnosing PD. Their method include three general steps: feature extraction, feature selection, and classification. In the first part, the VBM is used over GM to construct feature data. For the feature selection, recursive feature elimination (RFE) was used to select the most discriminative features. In the last step, projection based learning and meta-cognitive radial basis function was used for classification, which resulted in 87.21% accuracy. The potential biomarker for PD is identified as the superior temporal gyrus. The limitation in this work is that VBM is univariate and RFE is computationally expensive. Salvatore et al. [9], proposed a method that used PCA for feature extraction. The PCA was applied to normalized skull stripped MRI data. Then, SVM was used as the classifier, resulting in 85.8% accuracy. Rana et al. [10] extracted features over the three main tissues of the brain consisting of WM, GM and CSF. Then, they used t-test for feature selection and in the next step, SVM for classification. This resulted in 86.67% accuracy for GM and WM and 83.33% accuracy for CSF. In their other work [11], graph-theory based spectral feature selection method was applied to select a set of discriminating features from the whole brain volume. A decision model was built using SVM as a classifier with a leave-one-out cross-validation scheme, giving 86.67% accuracy. The proposed method in [4] was not focused on just individual tissues (GM, WM and CSF); rather, it considered the relationship between these areas because the morphometric change in one tissue might affect other tissues. $3D$ LBP was used as a feature extraction tool that could produce structural and statistical information. After that, minimum redundancy and maximum relevance with t-test are used as a feature selection methods to get the most discriminative and non-redundant features. In the end, SVM is used for classification giving 89.67% accuracy. In [13], the low level features (GM, cortical volume, etc.) and the high level features (region of interest (ROI) connectivity) are combined to perform a multilevel ROI feature extraction. Then, filter and wrapper feature selection method is followed up with multi kernel SVM to achieve 85.78% accuracy for differentiation of PD and healthy control (HC) data. Adeli et al. [14] propose a method for early diagnosis of PD based on the joint feature-sample selection (JFSS) procedure, which not only selects the best subset of most discriminative features, but also it is choosing the best sample to build a classification model. They have utilized the robust regression method and further develop a robust classification model for designing the CAD for PD diagnosis. They have used MRI and SPECT images for evaluation on both synthetic and publicly available PD datasets which is shown high accuracy classification.

In this paper, a CAD is presented for diagnosing of PD by using MR T1 Images. The general steps of the proposed method is shown in Fig. 1 including preprocessing, feature extraction and classification.

The remaining sections of this paper are structured as follows: Sects. 2 and 3 presents materials and methods, which provides details of the dataset, preprocessing and the proposed method for PD classification. The experimental results and discussion are provided in Sect. 4. Section 5 shows the conclusion.

2   Dataset

The data used in the preparation of this article is the T1-weighted brain MR images obtained from the PPMI database (www.ppmi-info.org/data). PPMI is a large-scale, international public study to identify PD progression biomarkers [15]. The data that is used in our study contains the original T1 MR image of 598 samples with 411 Parkinson disease (PD) and 187 healthy control (HC). Furthermore, the data also includes demographic or clinical information on the age and sex of the subjects. The summary of the data base is presented in Table 1. Based on the demographic information in this table, the balance of dataset is presented for the two type of classes which are PD and HC.

Table 1. Demographics of the PPMI

Data type	Class		Sex		Age		
	PD	HC	F	M	(25–50)	(50–76)	(75–100)
Number of subjects	411	187	217	381	81	472	45

3   Proposed Method

The framework of our proposed method presented in Fig. 1 that includes 3 general steps: 1 - Preprocessing; 2 - Feature Extraction; and 3 - Classification. The goals of CAD system are:

1. Extract the volume based features from the MR T1 images using FreeSurfer.
2. Comparing the capability of different type of classifier for diagnosis PD.

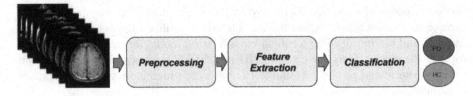

Fig. 1. The general framework of the proposed methods.

3.1 Preprocessing

Preprocessing is an essential step in designing the CAD system providing an informative data for the next steps. In this paper, we used several preprocessing steps to compute the volumetric information of the MRI subject's. The FreeSurfer image analysis suite is used to perform preprocessing of the 3D MRI data. FreeSurfer is a software packageto analyze and visualize structural and functional neuroimaging data from cross-sectional or longitudinal studies [16]. He FreeSurfer library is proposed to do cortical reconstruction and subcortical volumetric segmentation and preprocessing including the removal of non-brain tissue (skull, eyeballs and skin), using an automated algorithm with the ability to successfully segment the whole brain without any user intervention [17]. FreeSurfer is the software for structural MRI analysis for the Human Connectome Project which the documentation can be downloaded on-line (http://surfer. nmr.mgh.harvard.edu/). In total 31 preprocessing steps has been done by using FreeSurfer which some of them are shown in Fig. 2.

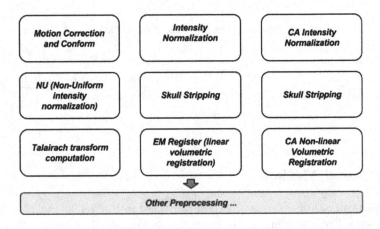

Fig. 2. Preprocessing steps.

There are two types of failures occurring in the preprocessing step: hard failures and soft failures. Hard failures apply to the subjects for whom preprocessing has not been successful; soft failures apply to the subjects who have been pre-processed but there are some problems in the preprocessing results which affect the results of the next analysis. Out of 568 subjects MRIs, 507 images were successfully preprocessed. Other images were excluded from the dataset due to poor quality of the original images or unknown CDR labels.

3.2 Feature Extraction

After preprocessing using FreeSurfer, a list of volume based features is extracted from different regions of the brain. These features were captured from the regions segmented through brain parcellation using FreeSurfer. Some of the features collected in the left and right hemispheres of the brain are listed below:

1. Left and right lateral ventricle
2. Left and right cerebellum white matter
3. Cerebrospinal fluid (CSF)
4. Left and right hippocampus
5. Left and right hemisphere cortex
6. Estimated total intra cranial (eTIV)
7. Left and right hemisphere surface holes.

The extracted feature data is based on Eq. 1.

$$FeatureData = \begin{bmatrix} f_{11} & f_{12} \ f_{13} \cdots f_{1n} \\ f_{21} & x_{22} \ x_{23} \cdots f_{2n} \\ \cdots \\ f_{s1} & f_{s2} \ f_{s3} \cdots f_{sn} \end{bmatrix} \quad (1)$$

where s is the number of subjects and n is the number of extracted features for that subject. In this study, n is 507 and m is 139.

Furthermore, there are two other types of features provided by the PPMI dataset : each subject's age and sex. Thus, these two pieces of biographical information could be added to the extracted feature from FreeSurfer.

3.3 Classification

In this part, our goal is to use the extracted volume based features to classify the MRI data into two classes of PD and HC. In our study, three types of supervised classification algorithms are used. Next, each classification method is described:

– **Logistic Regression (LR):**
  Logistic regression (LR) is a statistical technique which is used in machine learning for binary classification. LR belongs to the group of MaxEnt classifiers known as the exponential or log-linear classifiers [18]. LR belongs to the family of classifiers known as the exponential or log-linear classifiers [18]. It is following three general steps including: Extraction of weights features from the input, Taking log, and linearly combination of them [19].

- **Random Forest (RF):**
  Random forests (RF) is an ensemble learning method for classification, regression and other tasks. This method is presented by Breiman [18], which creates a set of decision trees (weak classifier) from randomly selected subset of training data. It then aggregates the votes from different decision trees to decide the final class of the test object. In the current stage of this research, we tested how accurate decisions can be made by RF with the data coming from a the PD's MRI volumes.
- **Support Vector machine (SVM):**
  Support vector machine (SVM) [20] is a well-known supervised machine learning algorithm for classification and regression. It performs classification tasks by making optimal hyperplanes in a multidimensional space that distinguish different class of data. This classification method is more popular because its easier to use, has higher generalization performance and little tunning comparing to other classifier. In our case, the kernel SVM is used.

There is a set of parameters for each classifier that needs to be tuned in order to have a fair comparison.

4   Results and Discussion

In this section, we present the experimental results of the different steps of the proposed CAD system to diagnose PD is presented. First, using FreeSurfer, the preprocessing step prepares the MRI data for the next steps. Figure 3 shows the MRI for subject 3102 and the resulting image after preprocessing.

After preprocessing with FreeSurfer, a list of volume-based features is extracted for each subject. Also, age and sex are provided for the PPMI data on their website as of the patients' demographic information. Some evaluation has been done over the set of extracted features in terms of their discrimination ability. Since PD is an age related disease, the distribution of data in terms of age is plotted. Figure 4 shows the distribution of age in the dataset for the subjects with PD and HC labels. The distribution of all the extracted features is plotted in terms of their ability to divide the data into two classes, PD and HC. Some of these distributions are shown in Fig. 5. As can be seen in Fig. 5(a), the subjects with PD have higher cerebellum cortex volume compared to the healthy ones. Furthermore, the distribution in Fig. 5(b) and (c) illustrate that when people are in the PD category, their putamen and CSF volume size is intended to be enlarged. Figure 5(d) shows that the right lateral ventricle volume in PD is noticeably higher than in the normal subjects. Another set of evaluations was performed over the extracted features. Data distribution for each pairs of features are plotted based on the corresponding class. Figure 6 shows the distribution of data based on the two pairs of features including Left pallidum vs right cerebellum cortex and right cerebellum cortex vs left cerebellum cortex. In both of them, two features tend to have bigger value when the subject is PD.

As explained in the previous section, three types of classifiers are used in this study. These algorithm are run over 507 samples with 141 features. The number

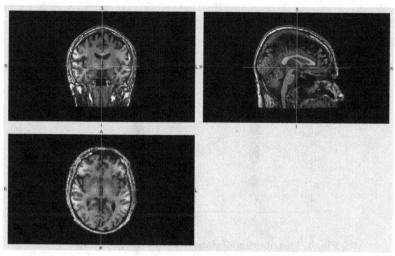

(a) Original MR image.

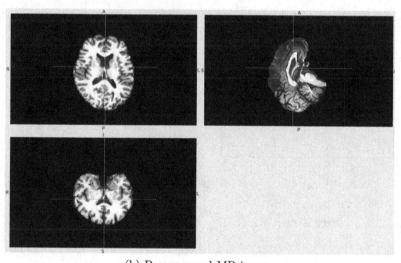

(b) Preprocessed MR image.

Fig. 3. Preprocessing results for one of the subjects.

of PD and control samples in this set of subjects are 340 for PD and 167 for HC. Since there is not enough balance for the data, we did data augmentation to b balance it. Since, the number of HC (negative) samples is not enough, we increase these samples just by creating a new set of negative samples calculated by subtracting the mean value from the current negative feature values. After doing data augmentation, the total number of samples is 673 with 341 PD (positive samples) and 332 HC (negative samples). Internal and external cross validation is applied with $K = 10$ for external and $k = 5$ for internal (parameter

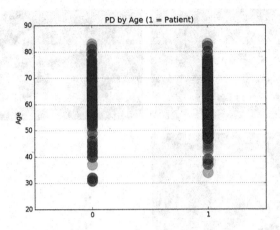

Fig. 4. Distribution of data in terms of age feature.

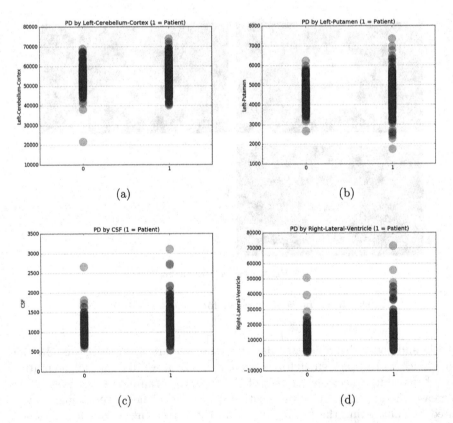

Fig. 5. Data distributions in terms of the class labels and corresponding features, which are: (a) Left cerebellum volume. (b) Left putamen. (c) CSF. (d) Right lateral ventricle.

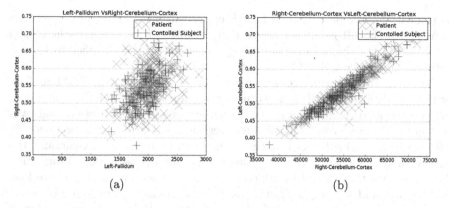

Fig. 6. Data distribution based on the pair of features: (a) Left pallidum vs right cerebellum cortex. (b) Right cerebellum cortex vs left cerebellum cortex.

tunning cross validation). The number of selected samples for the training part is 536 and for the test part, 67. The number of PD and HC in each group is presented in Table 2.

Table 2. Data balance in training and testing parts.

	PD	Hc	Total
Training	307	229	536
Test	34	33	67

As mentioned before, the classification algorithm needs a set of parameters for tunning which is selected as follows:

- logistic Regression (LR):
  Regularization $= [1e-1, 1e-2, 1e-3, 1e-4, 1e-5]$, Tolerance $= [1e-1, 1e-2, 1e-3, 1e-4, 1e-5]$
- Random Forest (RF):
  Number of estimator $=[5, 10, 15, 20, 25]$, Max depth $= [2-10]$
- Support Vector Machine (SVM):
  $C = [0.1, 1, 10, 100, 1000]$, Gamma $= [10, 1, 1e-1, 1e-2, 1e-3, 1e-4]$, kernels $= [linear, rbf, poly]$.

The evaluation metrics used in this paper for comparing the results of the classification algorithms include accuracy for training and testing data and AUC (area under ROC curve). Table 3 shows the general comparison between these methods which is achieved by averaging the accuracy over 10-fold cross validation. In the table there are two sets of results related to using age/sex feature or the classification built only on the extracted volume based features from FreeSurfer.

As you can see, the best result is for RF either with age/sex feature or without it. Although the LR result is close to that. However, if we compare the results based on the training accuracy showing the ability of the classifier to learn a feature from the data, SVM-linear is the best one.

Based on the literature review, most studies use SPM with VBM toolbox for data analysis and MRI data feature extraction not only for PD evaluation, but also for other neuro diseases. In this paper, one of the important goals was to evaluate FreeSurfer in terms of preprocessing and feature extraction over T1 MR Images for PD subjects using machine learning techniques. Generally, the experimental results show that the classification models need more information about the data that should be added to the current features as, these are low-level features and we need a set of high-level features as well. In future research, we are going to determine the useful general features that can be combined with the volume based features extracted from the PPMI data.

Table 3. Comparing performance of different classifiers

Methods/criteria	Age/sex feature	Train accuracy	Test accuracy	AUC
RF	No	0.7667	0.7419	0.7398
RF	Yes	0.7944	0.7576	0.7545
LR	No	0.7673	0.7373	0.7319
LR	Yes	0.7705	0.7502	0.7479
NN	No	0.6757	0.6665	0.6642
NN	Yes	0.7006	0.6825	0.6791
SVM with rbf kernel	No	0.5044	0.5044	0.5
SVM with rbf kernel	Yes	0.5044	0.5044	0.5
SVM with linear kernel	No	0.7698	0.7091	0.7086
SVM with linear kernel	Yes	0.8015	0.7146	0.7138

5   Conclusion

We presented an automatic MRI based CAD system for diagnosing Parkinson's Disease (PD), the second common neuro degenerative disease affecting elderly people. This disease is exposed by the loss of neuro-transmitters that control body movements. Currently, there is no cure other than earlier diagnosis with better and more efficient treatment for patients. We used MR T1 images from the public PPMI PD dataset and FreeSurfer for feature extraction and preprocessing. The decision model for classification of the extracted feature data is based on LR, RF, and SVM methods. In the experimental results, we compare the ability of these three types of classifiers to diagnose PD. The results show that using MRI only has a potential for diagnosing PD. This approach will avoid exposing the brain to harmful radiation based scans. In future work, the efficiency of the proposed method could be improved by adding high level features to the current ones. In addition, the classification rate with MRI needs to be improved to get close to rate achieved by those using raditation based scanning.

References

1. https://parkinsonsnewstoday.com/parkinsons-disease-statistics/
2. Fox, S.H., et al.: The movement disorder society evidence-based medicine review update: treatments for the motor symptoms of Parkinson's disease. Mov. Disord. **26**(S3), S2–S41 (2011)
3. Chaudhuri, K.R., Schapira, A.H.: Non-motor symptoms of Parkinson's disease: dopaminergic pathophysiology and treatment. Lancet Neurol. **8**(5), 464–474 (2009)
4. Rana, B., et al.: Relevant 3D local binary pattern based features from fused feature descriptor for differential diagnosis of Parkinson's disease using structural MRI. Biomed. Signal Process. Control **34**, 134–143 (2017)
5. Adeli, E., et al.: Joint feature-sample selection and robust diagnosis of Parkinson's disease from MRI data. NeuroImage **141**, 206–219 (2016)
6. Prashanth, R., Roy, S.D., Mandal, P.K., Ghosh, S.: Automatic classification and prediction models for early Parkinson's disease diagnosis from SPECT imaging. Expert Syst. Appl. **41**, 3333–3342 (2014)
7. Politis, M., Loane, C.: Serotonergic dysfunction in parkinson's disease and its relevance to disability. Sci. World J. **11**, 9 (2011). Article ID 172893
8. Focke, N.K., et al.: Individual voxel-base subtype prediction can differentiate progressive supranuclear palsy from idiopathic Parkinson syndrome and healthy controls. Hum. Brain Mapp. **32**(11), 1905–1915 (2011)
9. Babu, G.S., Suresh, S., Mahanand, B.S.: A novel PBL-McRBFN-RFE approach for identification of critical brain regions responsible for Parkinson's disease. Expert Syst. Appl. **41**(2), 478–488 (2014)
10. Salvatore, C., et al.: Machine learning on brain MRI data for differential diagnosis of Parkinson's disease and progressive supranuclear palsy. J. Neurosci. Methods **222**, 230–237 (2014)
11. Rana, B., et al.: Regions-of-interest based automated diagnosis of Parkinson's disease using T1-weighted MRI. Expert Syst. Appl. **42**(9), 4506–4516 (2015)
12. Rana, B., et al.: Graph-theory-based spectral feature selection for computer aided diagnosis of Parkinson's disease using T1-weighted MRI. Int. J. Imaging Syst. Technol. **25**(3), 245–255 (2015)
13. Peng, B., et al.: A multilevel-ROI-features-based machine learning method for detection of morphometric biomarkers in Parkinson's disease. Neurosci. Lett. **651**, 88–94 (2017). ISSN 0304–3940
14. Adeli, E., et al.: Joint feature-sample selection and robust diagnosis of Parkinson's disease from MRI data. NeuroImage **141**, 206–219 (2016)
15. https://ida.loni.usc.edu/home
16. https://surfer.nmr.mgh.harvard.edu/fswiki

17. Worker, A., et al.: Cortical thickness, surface area and volume measures in Parkinson's disease, multiple system atrophy and progressive supranuclear palsy. PLoS One **9**(12), e114167 (2014)
18. Breiman, L.: Random forests. Mach. Learn. **45**(1), 5–32 (2001)
19. Martin, J., Jurafsky, D.: Speech and Language Processing. Prentice Hall, Upper Saddle River (2000)
20. Vapnik, V.: The Nature of Statistical Learning Theory. Springer, New York (1995). https://doi.org/10.1007/978-1-4757-2440-0

Atlas-Free Method of Periventricular Hemorrhage Detection from Preterm Infants' T1 MR Images

Subhayan Mukherjee$^{(\boxtimes)}$, Irene Cheng, and Anup Basu

University of Alberta, Edmonton, AB T6G 2R3, Canada
{mukherje,locheng,basu}@ualberta.ca

Abstract. Detection of hemorrhages in the periventricular white matter region of infant brains is crucial since if left untreated it causes neuro-developmental deficits in later life. However, noise and motion artefacts are introduced while scanning infant brains due to small brain size and movement during scanning. Furthermore, a vast majority of traditional brain lesion detection algorithms which require accurate segmentation of the white matter region often rely on brain atlases to guide the segmentation. However, reliable brain atlases are hard to obtain for preterm infant brains which undergo rapid structural changes. To address this gap in published literature, we propose a novel method for hemorrhage detection which does not require a brain atlas. Instead of attempting accurate segmentation, the proposed method detects the ventricles and then samples a region of white matter around the ventricles. Based on the normal distribution of intensities in this tissue sample, the outliers are designated as hemorrhages. Heuristics based on size and location of the detected outliers are used to eliminate false positives. Results on an expert-annotated dataset demonstrate the effectiveness of the proposed method.

Keywords: Periventricular hemorrhage · Segmentation
Magnetic resonance imaging · Preterm infant · Atlas-free

1 Introduction

1.1 Motivation and Clinical Significance

The premature infant brain's immaturity makes it inherently more susceptible to injury [16] often leading to developmental deficits or even fatalities in subsequent stages of life [8]. Degree of prematurity of the infant is positively correlated with likelihood of brain damage. Near the center of brain, in each half, there exists

---

Supported by CIHR, NeuroDevNet, Alberta Innovates (iCORE) Research Chair program, and NSERC. DICOM slices with marked ground truth for preterm neonates' periventricular hemorrhage detection provided by Dr. Steven Miller and his team at SickKids Hospital, Toronto, Canada.

A. Basu and S. Berretti (Eds.): ICSM 2018, LNCS 11010, pp. 157–168, 2018.
https://doi.org/10.1007/978-3-030-04375-9_14

a C-shaped cavity having cerebrospinal fluid, called the lateral ventricles. The area of the premature infant brain most vulnerable to injury is the "periventricular" area, which is a brain tissue rim lining the outside of each lateral ventricle. A dense network of thin, fragile (prone to rupture) blood vessels called capillaries are present in each periventricular area. Unfortunately, more premature infants have more of these capillaries [2]. During premature birth, the fetus is abruptly expelled from the controlled environment of the uterus to the hostile, highly stimulating environment outside. The resulting shock and physiological stress causes the capillaries to rupture. Initially, "periventricular" hemorrhage or "PVH" occurs as the immediate periventricular areas start bleeding. Continued bleeding creates an expanding volume of blood which severs the adjacent lateral ventricles, thus causing an "intraventricular" hemorrhage or "IVH."

The periventricular areas serve two important purposes:

1. The brain's outer layers (cerebral cortex) is formed by new brain cells which form and develop in the periventricular areas, and gradually move to form the outer layers. The cerebral cortex handles several vital functions of the brain, including learning and intelligence, behavior and personality, and speech. It also has considerable influence on control and strength of muscles.
2. Periventricular areas serve as passages for motor nerve signals to the muscles originating from the cerebral cortex.

PVH/IVH may cause brain injury via several mechanisms. If damaged new brain cells developing in the periventricular area ultimately move outward and get embedded inside the cerebral cortex, they impair the functions and distort the structure of the cerebral cortex. Unfortunately, the infant does not even start using various parts of the cerebral cortex for months or even years after birth. Thus, the developmental issues arising out of the aforementioned damages to the cerebral cortex are not even apparent until later stages of life. Nonetheless, the implications of cerebral cortex damage are debilitating: learning and language difficulties, arrested mental development, behavioral and personality disorders, convulsions, etc.

This emphasizes the need for both early detection and long-term developmental follow-up for high-risk infants [5,13].

Early detection is possible by examining images of high-risk infants' brains acquired using scanning devices like Magnetic Resonance Imaging (MRI). To make this possible, the different types of brain tissues in an image need to be identified in order to look for abnormalities.

1.2   Computational and Signal Processing Challenges

Brain tissue segmentation usually refers to the separation of brain MR images into three prominent parts, viz. Grey Matter (GM), White Matter (WM) and Cerebro-Spinal Fluid (CSF) to identify physiological abnormalities. It also facilitates volumetric studies and quantitative analyses [3]. Seizures, strokes, brain infections and injuries are often hard to determine by manual expert examination due to its volume. Also, it is subjective; interpretation may change from one expert to another, or be different even for the same expert at different times.

Automated brain extraction and segmentation of MR images of the adult brain has received considerable attention in previous decades. But, the same is not true for neonates or preterm infants, because of several practical challenges in obtaining MR images of their brains and analysing them:

1. Lack of any anatomical map or "atlas" for the brain, which can guide the segmentation process. This is because the brain is undergoing rapid structural and physiological changes during maturation.
2. Most infants move constantly during the MRI scan process, which is inherently (highly) sensitive to patient movement. It induces motion artefacts, blurring, etc. in the MR images.
3. Infant brains are smaller in size and the duration of MRI scanning is also shorter. This results in a low Contrast-to-Noise ratio (CNR), low Signal-to-Noise ratio (SNR) and low spatial resolution.
4. Dynamic changes in the contrast between grey matter (GM) and white matter (WM) in both T1- and T2-weighted images (T1w and T2w) during brain maturation. Most parts of the infant brain are non-myelinated at birth, where WM appears less intense in T1 images and more intense in T2 images, whereas this trend is reversed for a fully myelinated adult brain (contrast inversion).

MR studies of neonatal periventricular-intraventricular hemorrhage (PIVH) are scarce. Acute MR findings of adult and neonatal hemorrhage are considered similar. However, the medical community believes that, due to rapid myelination and maturation of the premature infant brain, subacute and chronic MR appearance of hemorrhagic evolution in premature infants are possibly quite distinct from those in adults [1].

Brain MRI segmentation research is highly varied in terms of their intent, design, implementation and outcome. Any such algorithm can be classified mainly based on these criteria:

1. Extent of brain tissue segmentation; and,
2. Level of prior knowledge incorporated.

Based on these criteria, segmentation approaches can be classified as Low-level algorithms which only separate the skull from the rest of the brain in the MR image, and High-level algorithms which further segment and classify the tissues inside the brain. Based on their usage of prior information (atlases), they can be further classified as follows:

1. Atlas-based: Uses pre-segmented brain atlases which guide the algorithm in areas of low contrast and help distinguish tissues of similar intensities. However, the atlases need to be registered onto the test MR image, which is difficult, given the structural variations of the infant brain.
2. Augmented atlas-based: As predefined atlases may not account for variability between subjects, these methods use longitudinal data in segmentation or patch-based sparse representation to obtain subject-specific atlases.

3. Atlas-free: Uses local contrast and geometric traits, brain morphology and tissue connectivity to aid segmentation. The strength of atlas-free methods is that they can accommodate changes in anatomy of the developing brain (such as for infants), as they are not bound by constraints imposed by the atlas.

Generally, algorithms which aim to extract a large number of classes of brain tissues rely on brain atlases and probabilistic methods. However, for neonatal and preterm infant brains, atlases are often unavailable, and hence in such scenarios, atlas-free methods are the most suitable ones to consider.

1.3   Our Contributions

Although PIVH in preterm infants has recently started gaining increased attention, attempts at detecting such abnormalities have been (fully or partly) through manual examination by radiologists or subject matter experts [1,2,5, 8,13]. However, such manual examination has its own limitations, as outlined earlier.

We are the first to propose a fully automated method to detect periventricular hemorrhage from preterm infants' brain MR images. Our method also addresses the challenges arising from unavailability of reliable preterm infant brain atlases by removing the requirement of accurate segmentation of brain tissues. This also makes our method computationally very efficient. In contrast, conventional brain lesion detection methods are often segmentation-based (thus, time-consuming) and/or require a reliable brain atlas, as described next, under "Related Works".

2   Related Works

The first method we surveyed [11] is an atlas-free fully automated method to segment brain MR images using self-organizing maps (SOMs) and Genetic Algorithms (GAs). A novel SOM clustering mechanism is also presented which defines cluster borders by considering the relationship between the input and output spaces. During preprocessing, they remove the background noise in the MR image, which may have been introduced due to variations in the amplitude or phase of the radio frequency used to obtain the MR image. Background noise removal was done using a Binary Mask, and the binary threshold was determined using Ostu's method, by minimizing the intra-class variance of the signal and noise voxels. Then, 24 important 1st order statistical features (intensity, mean and variance) and 2nd order statistical features (energy, entropy, contrast etc.) were extracted. Most discriminatory features were selected using a GA. Next, the SOM was trained using the selected features in an unsupervised way. Then a label (e.g. type of brain tissue) was assigned to each SOM unit. The proposed method was tested on the Internet Brain Image Repository (IBSR). It performed better than CGMM in classifying WM and CSF, and gave promising results on high-resolution MR images.

The next method we surveyed [4] first segments the brain tissues into GM, WM and CSF using Bayesian segmentation and then improves the results using domain knowledge obtained from experts in the form of heuristics. For applying the heuristics, the eight adjacent pixels of each pixel (its neighbours) are considered. A sample heuristic is: If "neighbours are WM", then "new centre is WM". The method assumes Normal Distribution of grey values in all tissues and uses Expectation Maximization (EM) to maximize the likelihood probability of tissues. The authors tested their proposed method on 30 simulated MR images of Brainweb and 30 real MR images of ADNI. They compared their output against the expert-segmented versions of these images in terms of sensitivity and specificity of each tissue type.

$$sensitivity = \frac{True\ Positives}{True\ Positives + False\ Negatives} \tag{1}$$

$$specificity = \frac{True\ Negatives}{True\ Negatives + False\ Positives} \tag{2}$$

In the next surveyed method [7] the authors propose an effective way of implementing the initial step in the brain MR image segmentation process, viz. skull-stripping. The proposed hybrid skull-stripping algorithm, based on the adaptive balloon snake (ABS) model has two steps:

1. Pixel clustering using probabilistic fuzzy C-means (FPCM). The output of this step is a labelled image which clearly demarks the brain boundary.
2. Based on the FPCM result, a contour is initialized outside the surface of the brain. This contour is evolved as guided by an ABS model.

However, the ABS method employed here has one limitation: it ends up splitting the contours in multi-object segmentation.

In yet another work [6] the authors propose "MSmetrix", an automatic method of MRI-based lesion segmentation. This method is independent of the protocol used for image acquisition and does not require any training data. Their approach involves segmenting 3D T1-weighted and FLAIR MR Images into WM, GM and CS in a probabilistic model, and treating WM lesions as outliers. The method assumes Gaussian distribution for the image intensities for each tissue class. However, this method uses an MNI-atlas for skull stripping and GM, WM, CSF classification. Accuracy of the proposed MSmetrix method output is ascertained by comparing it with segmentations (by experts) for 20 MRI datasets of MS (multiple sclerosis) patients. The experimental results indicate a significant spatial overlap (Dice score) between the MSmetrix output and expert segmentation.

Based on the literature survey we can infer that in general, an ideal candidate algorithm for preterm hemorrhage detection should have the following characteristics:

1. Not be overly dependent on the atlas: This is because the preterm brain is constantly undergoing major changes in physiology and anatomy, and hence a

"reliable" atlas for preterm brains is impractical to construct/obtain. Unreliable atlases guiding the segmentation process will result in poor segmentation results.

2. Be able to handle low-resolution images: This is because infant brains are smaller in size, and the MR scan duration is short, so the resulting MR images suffer from low spatial resolution and partial volume effect on voxels.

3. Be robust to noise and motion artefacts: This is because most infants move constantly during the MR scan, which results in motion artefacts and low SNR.

4. Be automated as far as possible (without human intervention), as MR data is voluminous and hence it is not feasible to provide too much intervention by human experts.

3   Proposed Method

For periventricular hemorrhage detection, we have to search for abrupt intensity variations (hyper-intensities) in the white matter region of the brain near the periphery of the ventricles (hence the term *peri*ventricular). Since the intensities in the white matter should be normally distributed, we assume that the hemorrhage will be an "outlier" with respect to the range of white matter intensities. We mark an area around the ventricles to estimate the range of white matter intensities.

3.1   Separating Brain from Background

We use Ostu's method [12] for separating the brain from the (noisy) background of the DICOM slice. Ostu's method separates an input grey-scale image into foreground and background by determining a global threshold. It tries to minimize the intra-class variance of foreground and background pixels by iterating trough all the possible thresholds in the image to find the threshold that gives the smallest within class variance. To find the within class variance Otsu's method uses the formula:

$$\sigma_W^2 = W_b \sigma_b^2 + W_f \sigma_f^2 \tag{3}$$

where σ is the variance and W is the weight for the foreground and background of the image. The weight for the foreground is found by adding all the pixels in the foreground and dividing the sum with the total number of pixels. The same is done for the background (sum of background pixels).

Thus, employing Ostu's method, we obtained a binary image where the foreground in white and the background in black. The *holes* in the foreground were filled using the appropriate morphological operator, giving a foreground mask.

$$M_f = I > Th_O \tag{4}$$

Here, I is the input image and Th_O is the binary threshold obtained by running Ostu's method on I.

Similarly, the background mask M_b is obtained by taking the complement of M_f. Using the background mask, we "clean" the background by setting it to 255 (white). Thus, we remove the unwanted intensity variations (noise) in the background, which may interfere with the subsequent processing of the image. The rationale behind setting the background to white (and not black) will be explained later.

$$M_b = \overline{M_f} \tag{5}$$

3.2 Ventricle Detection

We detect the ventricle as blobs inside the brain using the MSER algorithm [9]. But the MSER algorithm also detects other parts of the brain (as regions) which do not form part of the ventricles. We filter out these regions by making the assumption that detected regions which are farthest from the boundary of the brain and have lower intensity (T1 images) are more likely to constitute the ventricles.

Detailed steps of ventricle detection are explained below. First, we calculate the following matrices:

D_p

The distance transform [15] of M_b (using the city-block distance measure) normalized to the $[0, 1]$ range. Distance transform of each point inside the brain gives its distance to the nearest point lying on the brain boundary (background mask). Thus, the points lying more towards the centre of the brain (where we expect to find the ventricles) tend to get higher values.

I_c

The normalized complement of I. Since I is a grey-scale image, this means $I_c = 255 - I$, and then I_c is normalized to the $[0, 1]$ range. Since the points inside the ventricles will have a low intensity (T1 images), the inverted image will have those points having a high intensity. Also, referring back to an earlier step in which the background was marked white, it can be easily inferred that in the inverted image, the background will be inverted to black, and thus have a "zero" value.

L_p

The $[0, 1]$ normalized *Hadamard* product of the matrices D_p and I_c, that is $L_p = D_p \bullet I_c$. This essentially means that we are multiplying the distance transform of each point with its (inverted) intensity. Thus, going by the above descriptions of D_p and I_c, we can infer that the points lying inside the ventricle will have very high values for L_p. Thus L_p can be regarded as the "confidence" measure for any given point inside the brain to be part of the ventricles.

Next, we run the MSER algorithm on I. The linear implementation [10] makes it one of the fastest region detectors. It is also affine invariant, has good repeatability and performs well on images containing homogeneous regions with distinctive boundaries. Let us assume that the MSER extracts R regions from

I, denoted as r_1, r_2, r_3, ..., r_R. For each region r_i, we calculate the "average confidence" C_i, which is the average of L_p values for the pixels belonging to r_i. Thus, our problem reduces to finding the "maximal set of optimal regions" $S_v = \{r_1, r_2, ..., r_v\}$ forming the ventricles.

We model the above as an optimization problem to be solved using Genetic Algorithm. For each region r_i, we have to make a *binary* choice of either to include it in a *candidate solution*, or leave it out. So, we represent a candidate solution as a *bit string*. We define a *fitness function* on a candidate solution:

$$F_s = N_s * C_1 * C_2 * ... * C_{N_s} \tag{6}$$

where N_s is the number of regions selected and C_j refers to the confidence of the selected region j. Thus, a GA returns the *optimal* choice of regions S_v which are *most likely* to constitute the ventricles.

We also define a mask M_v for all pixels p_i belonging to the ventricles (as determined by a GA).

$$M_v = \{p_i \in r_j \,\forall\, r_j \in S_v\} \tag{7}$$

3.3   Normal Distribution of WM Intensities

Next, we consider the white matter region around the ventricles. Let D_v be the distance transform of M_v. Since we are not "segmenting" the WM region, we simply chose a contour that follows the relation:

$$|D_p - D_v| \leqslant 1 \tag{8}$$

This generates a contour, whose points are halfway between the ventricles and the brain boundary. Thus, the region mask M_w *enclosed* by the contour is mostly WM with the ventricles as "holes". Sometimes, parts of ventricles undetected by MSER (or GA) are also included in M_w, but as we will see later, they also end up in the range of *outlier* intensities, as we assume a normal distribution for WM.

Next, considering the pixels described by M_w we calculate their Median, M_d and Median Absolute Deviation, M_a. Then, any grey level g in the image I is a potential hemorrhage candidate if:

$$g > M_d + 2 * \frac{M_a}{0.6745} \tag{9}$$

We use the *median* instead of the *mean*, as the former is more robust to outliers. Also, as mentioned earlier, the parts of the ventricles undetected by MSER (or GA) lie in the range of values of g satisfying:

$$g < M_d - 2 * \frac{M_a}{0.6745} \tag{10}$$

Future research may be directed towards *improving* ventricle detection results following this heuristic.

Continuing with hemorrhage detection, next, we define a mask M_c for the potential hemorrhage candidates, such that pixels of image I whose grey level g satisfies Eq. 9 belong to M_c. We enumerate the 8-connected *objects* found in M_c by following the steps below:

1. Run-length encode the input image.
2. Scan the runs, assigning preliminary labels, storing label equivalences in a local equivalence table.
3. Resolve the equivalence classes.
4. Relabel the runs based on the resolved equivalence classes.

Let us assume that the above procedure returns a set of objects $S_w = \{O_1, O_2, ..., O_w\}$. Next, we compute the sizes of the corresponding objects as $\{N_{O_1}, N_{O_2}, ..., N_{O_w}\}$. We disregard the *largest* 5% objects, as they are most likely to be outliers, like (parts of) the skull boundary. Next, we perform a *binary* classification ("big" and "small") of the remaining objects based on their sizes, using the K-means clustering algorithm. We initialize the starting means (or "centroids") of the K-means algorithm with the sizes of the smallest and the largest object (among the remaining 95%). The assumption here is that the hemorrhage always fall in the "small" category, while the "big" category contains brain tissue boundaries. Using the process shown above, we further enforce the constraint that a hemorrhage cannot lie close to the skull.

4   Results and Discussion

Following majority of recent brain tissue segmentation methods, we use Anisotropic Diffusion as a preprocessing step to de-noise brain MR images. The parameters used were $\frac{1}{7}$ for the integration constant, 3 for the gradient modulus threshold and the 2nd conduction coefficient function proposed by Perona & Malik [14], because this set of parameter values gave best results. The number of iterations was set to 15.

Figure 1 shows hemorrhage detection results on three representative DICOM slices of a preterm infant brain provided by SickKids Hospital in Toronto. There are false positives mostly due to noise, but only one false negative (Slice 3, left hemorrhage) which also reflects in the quantitative results in Table 1.

A closer examination of the false positive detections reveals that they often have similar visual characteristics as the true positive detections. The best example of this is the false positive detection adjacent to the lower-right corner of the right ventricle in Slice 3 (Fig. 1). Thus, circumventing these false detections necessitates additional clinical criteria beyond the already applied heuristics and image processing techniques, and can thus be explored as future work.

While interpreting the quantitative results it should be noted that even a small increase in the number of true positive hemorrhage detections results in a large increase in the sensitivity score, and the opposite is true for false positives and specificity. The reason is that, in our preterm brain hemorrhage detection based on the given ground truth, the total number of positives is very small

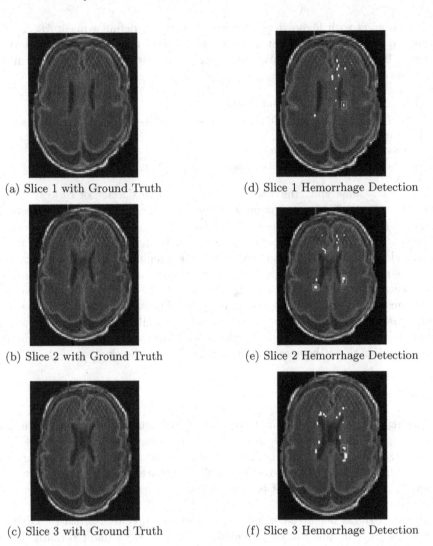

(a) Slice 1 with Ground Truth   (d) Slice 1 Hemorrhage Detection

(b) Slice 2 with Ground Truth   (e) Slice 2 Hemorrhage Detection

(c) Slice 3 with Ground Truth   (f) Slice 3 Hemorrhage Detection

Fig. 1. Periventricular hemorrhage detection using proposed method on DICOM slices obtained from SickKids Hospital, Toronto. Red squares mark true positives. (Color figure online)

Table 1. Periventricular hemorrhage detection quantitative results

Slice#	Sensitivity	Specificity
1	1.0000	0.9972
2	1.0000	0.9970
3	0.5056	0.9904

compared to the total number of negatives (healthy brain tissue). Thus, the numerical values of sensitivity and specificity should be interpreted in light of the actual number of true positives and false positives while assessing the relative performance of the proposed method.

4.1 Time Performance

Our per-slice average serial execution time was around 1 second for a Dell Inspiron 15R N5010 notebook running Matlab R2015b on Windows 7 on a Intel core $i3$ 2.26 GHz processor with 4 GB RAM.

5 Conclusion

We proposed a fast, unsupervised, atlas-free method to detect periventricular hemorrhages. The results show satisfactory performance of the proposed method. Our future research will focus on reduction in number of false detections and combining hemorrhage detection from adjacent DICOM slices to improve accuracy.

6 Compliance with Ethical Standards

The "Standard Protocol Approvals, Registration, and Patient Consents" at the BC Children's Hospital in Vancouver was followed for obtaining all clinical data related to this work. A written informed consent from the legal guardian of each participating neonate was obtained. This study was reviewed and approved by the Clinical Research Ethics Board at the University of British Columbia and BC Children's and Women's Hospitals.

All procedures performed in studies involving human participants were in accordance with the ethical standards of the institutional and/or national research committee and with the 1964 Helsinki declaration and its later amendments or comparable ethical standards.

References

1. Asao, C., Korogi, Y., Kondo, Y., Yasunaga, T., Takahashi, M.: Neonatal periventricular-intraventricular hemorrhage: subacute and chronic MR findings. Acta Radiol. **42**(4), 370–375 (2001)
2. Ballabh, P.: Intraventricular hemorrhage in premature infants: mechanism of disease. Pediatr. Res. **67**(1), 1–8 (2010)
3. Devi, C.N., Chandrasekharan, A., Sundararaman, V., Alex, Z.C.: Neonatal brain-MRI segmentation: a review. Comput. Biol. Med. **64**, 163–178 (2015)
4. Farzan, A.: Heuristically improved bayesian segmentation of brain MR images. Sci. World J. **9**(3), 5–8 (2014)
5. Iyer, K.K., et al.: Early detection of preterm intraventricular hemorrhage from clinical electroencephalography. Crit. Care Med. **43**(10), 2219–2227 (2015)

6. Jain, S., et al.: Automatic segmentation and volumetry of multiple sclerosis brain lesions from MR images. NeuroImage: Clin. **8**, 367–375 (2015)

7. Liu, H.T., Sheu, T.W.H., Chang, H.H.: Automatic segmentation of brain mr images using an adaptive balloon snake model with fuzzy classification. Med. Biol. Eng. Comput. **51**(10), 1091–1104 (2013)

8. Marba, S.T.M., Caldas, J.P.S., Vinagre, L.E.F., Pessoto, M.A.: Incidence of periventricular/intraventricular hemorrhage in very low birth weight infants: a 15-year cohort study. J. Pediatr. **87**, 505–511 (2011)

9. Matas, J., Chum, O., Urban, M., Pajdla, T.: Robust wide-baseline stereo from maximally stable extremal regions. Image Vis. Comput. **22**(10), 761–767 (2004)

10. Nistér, D., Stewénius, H.: Linear time maximally stable extremal regions. In: Forsyth, D., Torr, P., Zisserman, A. (eds.) ECCV 2008. LNCS, vol. 5303, pp. 183–196. Springer, Heidelberg (2008). https://doi.org/10.1007/978-3-540-88688-4_14

11. Ortiz, A., Gorriz, J., Ramirez, J., Salas-Gonzalez, D.: Improving MR brain image segmentation using self-organising maps and entropy-gradient clustering. Inf. Sci. **262**, 117–136 (2014)

12. Otsu, N.: A threshold selection method from gray-level histograms. IEEE Trans. Syst. Man Cybern. **9**(1), 62–66 (1979)

13. Ou, X., et al.: Impaired white matter development in extremely low-birth-weight infants with previous brain hemorrhage. Am. J. Neuroradiol. **35**(10), 1983–1989 (2014)

14. Perona, P., Malik, J.: Scale-space and edge detection using anisotropic diffusion. IEEE Trans. Pattern Anal. Mach. Intell. **12**(7), 629–639 (1990)

15. Rosenfeld, A., Pfaltz, J.L.: Sequential operations in digital picture processing. J. ACM **13**(4), 471–494 (1966)

16. Simon, N.P.: Periventricular/intraventricular hemorrhage (PVH/IVH) in the premature infant. http://www.pediatrics.emory.edu/divisions/neonatology/dpc/pvhivh.html. Accessed 02 Apr 2018

When Smart Signal Processing Meets Smart Sensing

When Smart Signal Processing Meets Smart Imaging

Bihan Wen[(✉)] and Guan-Ming Su

Dolby Laboratories, Sunnyvale, USA
{bihanwen,guanmingsu}@ieee.org

Abstract. With the advancement of modern sensing and imaging technologies, people can acquire measurements more effectively and efficiently for data of various modalities. Meanwhile, the new imaging technologies also bring challenges for the corresponding signal processing systems, in order to achieve high-quality image reconstruction and rendering. To fully utilize the advanced imaging schemes, we need smart signal processing methodologies. In this paper, we will cover some recent trends on techniques for high dynamic range (HDR) imaging, compressed sensing, computational imaging, as well as the image recovery methods with data-driven regularizers. Related works and examples are presented, to illustrate new problems and challenges of signal processing in the context of modern sensing systems.

Keywords: High dynamic range · Compressed sensing
Image processing · Computational imaging · Machine learning

1 Introduction

Imaging refers to the procedure of image measurement acquisition and image formation. In contrast to traditional imaging, a signal processing scheme, with advanced algorithms and computational resources, is usually integrated with the modern imaging pipeline. Conventional signal and image processing tools focus on solving general image problems, without considering the specific imaging modalities, leading to suboptimal solutions in sophisticated imaging pipelines. To enhance the capability, or to overcome hardware limitations of modern imaging systems, smart signal processing technologies are required, which (1) solve the image problems associated with the specific imaging schemes, and (2) are jointly designed or optimized in the complete imaging pipeline.

Modern imaging systems typically aim to acquire measurements for the target images more effectively, or efficiently. On one hand, for the consumer market and products, e.g., television (TV), smart phone, cinema, computer gaming, etc, generating high-quality images to provide better visual experience is always the first priority. Ultra-high-definition (UHD) TV enables displays with higher resolution, and more recently, the advent of High dynamic range (HDR) technologies

© Springer Nature Switzerland AG 2018
A. Basu and S. Berretti (Eds.): ICSM 2018, LNCS 11010, pp. 171–182, 2018.
https://doi.org/10.1007/978-3-030-04375-9_15

provides potential for expanded contrast and wide color gamut. Conventional signal processing tools, especially with legacy devices, usually fail to handle new color space, or electro-optical transfer functions (EOTFs), e.g., the Perceptual Quantizer (PQ). The challenge is to design smart signal processing methods which overcome the limitation of legacy devices, while utilizing the potential of new sensing technology effectively. On the other hand, modern imaging schemes improve sensing efficiency, by reducing the system complexity, data-acquisition time, or radiation does. Thus, new challenges arise at the problems of image reconstruction from incomplete or corrupted measurements, e.g., compressed sensing, magnetic resonance imaging (MRI), fluorescence spectroscopy, multi-spectral imaging, computational topology (CT), Positron emission tomography (PET), inverse scattering, etc.

Numerous new data modeling approaches and signal processing algorithms have recently been proposed for advanced imaging systems, which demonstrate superior performance in a wide range of applications. It is important to summarize and survey the related methods, as well as study their relationships in the context of emerging imaging schemes. This article provides an overview of recent works on smart signal processing methodologies for highly effective or efficient imaging systems, and highlights the new challenges for signal processing in these emerging sensing schemes. In particular, we cover recent trends on techniques for HDR imaging, compressed sensing, image recovery with various image priors, and image modeling with machine learning approaches. We present examples to demonstrate advantages of smart signal processing algorithms for new imaging system in related works, with illustrations and experimental results.

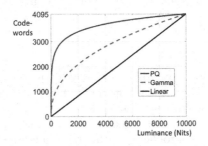

Fig. 1. The plot of PQ, gamma, and linear EOTFs curves.

2 Emerging Imaging Technologies

2.1 High Dynamic Range Imaging

From the cathode ray tube (CRT) to 4K UHD TV, huge efforts have been made by developers to increase the resolution of displays. Recently, more attention has been drawn to the advent of high dynamic range (HDR) imaging technologies. Instead of providing "more pixels" like UHD, HDR imaging offers "better pixels" with expanded contrast and wide color gamut, comparing to the traditional standard dynamic range (SDR) imaging. New technologies and specifications have been applied in HDR imaging systems, which are different from those used in conventional SDR:

- New EOTFs have been proposed and used in international standards for HDR, in order to provide optimized visual quality. For example, the PQ curve [20, 23] is now widely used for HDR videos, while the traditional Gamma curve is typically applied for SDR videos. Figure 1 shows a comparison of PQ, Gamma, and Linear EOTFs.

- Raw (or uncompressed) encoding system for HDR imagery requires at least 12 bits of tonal resolution [12, 21]. However, conventional codecs, data formats, as well as transmission interfaces are still limited up to 10 bits.

- New color spaces, e.g., ITP color space [17], are used in HDR for more effective content representation with wider color gamut. Whereas SDR signals are typically delivered in Y'CbCr space, which works differently in signal quantization and compression.

- In consumer market, diverse HDR displays usually have different specifications, e.g., brightness levels, EOTFs (e.g., PQ [20], HLG [3], etc), color spaces, etc. The challenge is how to efficiently and effectively transmit and process video content, while preserving colorists' intent across all specifications [15].

Directly applying conventional signal processing tools for HDR usually results in problems such as coding deficiency, serious image artifacts, etc. [32]. Smarter approaches have been proposed in recent works to jointly optimize signal processing algorithms with the HDR imaging systems, sometimes subject to various constraints due to legacy devices [12, 15, 17, 32].

2.2 Compressed Sensing

Nyquist-Shannon sampling theory provides the number of samples needed to reconstruct the signal, based on the signal frequency constraints. However, given additional image priors, e.g., sparsity, much fewer samples than the sampling theorem are required for (perfect) signal reconstruction [6]. The powerful signal processing technique for recovering the signal or image with lower sampling rates than with Nyquist's Law, is widely known as compressed sensing (CS) [9]. In general, CS seeks for the solutions to ill-posed inverse problems, by solving underdetermined linear systems [6, 9]. For imaging problems, the aim is to estimate the underlying image data $x \in \mathbb{C}^n$ from its degraded measurements $y \in \mathbb{C}^l$ ($l < n$). The general form of the measurement is $y = Ax + e$, where $A \in \mathbb{C}^{l \times n}$ denotes the sensing operator associated with the advanced imaging system, and $e \in \mathbb{C}^l$ denotes the additive noise.

Given the measurement and the sensing operator, CS solves the following optimization problem

$$(\text{P1}) \quad \hat{x} = \operatorname*{argmin}_{x} \|Ax - y\|_2^2 + \Re(x),$$

where $\mathfrak{R}(\cdot)$ is the regularizer based on image priors, e.g., sparsity. With different forms of the operator A, (P1) generalizes various modern imaging problems, ranging from image restoration (e.g., image denoising [28], inpainting [31], and super-resolution [16]) to computational imaging for medical applications (e.g., MRI, CT, and PET). To achieve image recovery, CS algorithms apply effective $\mathfrak{R}(\cdot)$'s, which need to (1) exploit image priors of the underlying x, and (2) satisfy the incoherence condition of the specific A, based on the isometric property [10]. As an ill-posed problem, $\mathfrak{R}(\cdot)$ is usually the key factor to successful signal processing algorithms, which needs to be jointly optimized with the emerging imaging system.

2.3   Image Priors

Image priors play important roles in many of the emerging imaging applications. Popular methods make use of image models, such as sparsity [11,28], joint sparsity [19], low-rankness [14,29], intensity histogram [27], image statistics [32], etc. Choice of a particular image prior in signal processing algorithms depends on both the imaging modality, and the distribution of image data. Sparsity, for example, is one of the popular image priors used in CS. Early works [7] exploited image properties using fixed models, e.g., analytical transforms or dictionaries. As advanced imaging schemes demand high-quality image restoration, data-driven approaches have been proposed in recent works, to adapt the image models to images or image patches [11]. For imaging systems of high-dimensional multimedia data, such as videos, volumetric data, or spectral images, smart signal processing schemes exploit the data correlation in multi-dimensional space, to achieve accurate image modeling. Recent works [30] applied more advanced tools, including tensor decomposition, or high-dimensional transform learning, as effective regularizers in the corresponding image restoration scheme. While algorithms based on many popular image priors require fixed-size image I/O, other priors, such as intensity histogram, enables size invariant image restoration tools [27].

3   Smart Image Processing

We introduce recent works on smart image processing for emerging imaging systems. In practice, there are usually system constraints, such as legacy devices, so that only part of the modules in the pipeline can be modified. Figure 2(a) illustrates the imaging pipelines with, and without the legacy system constraint. The signal processing modules to be designed are highlighted in blue. Thus, we categorize the smart image processing algorithms based on whether legacy system constraints are imposed. The various smart algorithms are all designed to (1) reduce system complexity, or (2) improve image recovery quality. Figure 2(b) summarizes the algorithms discussed in this paper according to their objectives.

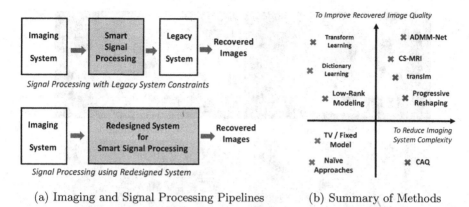

(a) Imaging and Signal Processing Pipelines   (b) Summary of Methods

Fig. 2. An overview: (a) the flowcharts of imaging pipelines with legacy system constraint (top), and using resigned system (bottom); (b) a summary of surveyed signal processing methods based on their objectives. The conventional methods, smart methods with legacy system constraint, and those without constraint are highlighted in green, blue, and red, respectively. (Color figure online)

3.1 Signal Processing with Legacy System Constraints

Ideally, the whole signal processing module needs to be designed and optimized jointly for the emerging sensing system, in order to achieve superior performance in applications. Such approach, however, can be very expensive, time consuming, and not scalable in practice. We take applications in HDR imaging as examples for this scenario, jointly optimizing signal processing module typically leads to redesigning the whole codec. Several smart signal processing techniques have been proposed to avoid major cost, by performing affordable operations to effectively handle new imaging systems. We discuss several recent works in the following:

Statistics Transfer. New EOTFs have been widely used for HDR imaging, which are typically different from those used in SDR, in order to provide good visual quality. However, applying new EOTFs alters image local statistics (e.g., standard deviation of image patches) of HDR videos from those of SDR data [32]. Figure 3 illustrates the difference of local statistics of the SDR and HDR images, by applying Gamma and PQ EOTFs, respectively. There are important applications, such as content-aware retargeting [1] and compression [25], which are highly sensitive to the change of image local statistics (see examples in Sect. 4.1). The algorithms of such applications are typically optimized for SDR data. They may have been embedded in the existing signal processing modules, and distributed to the user side. Therefore, smarter signal processing techniques aim to preserve the quality of various image and video applications results (e.g., images without noticable visual artifacts), while avoiding heavy post-processing or major system modification. For example, the recently proposed transIm

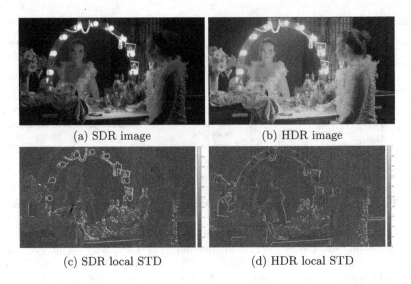

(a) SDR image   (b) HDR image

(c) SDR local STD   (d) HDR local STD

Fig. 3. Visual comparison of one frame of video *showgirl02*: the image displayed in (a) HDR and (b) SDR, as well as their local standard deviation (STD) maps in (c) and (d), respectively.

scheme [32] tackled such challenge by altering the local statistics of HDR images, to match the corresponding ones of the SDR images. This is achieved by injecting or suppressing less perceivable noise which is orthogonal to image content via sparse modeling [32]. Thus, the "manipulated" HDR images are still visually close to the original ones, while their local statistics are close to their SDR pairs (see examples in Sect. 4.1). As all operations of transIm are at the encoder side, and they are affordable for typical HDR systems.

Content-Aware Quantization. Fixed encoding for HDR imagery requires 12-bit-depth format for transmission and codec, whereas the mainstream systems in consumer market usually support up to only 10 bits. Due to the well-established networks and infrastructures, upgrading the entire existing systems to 12 bits is expensive. Thus, smart signal processing is required, to enable HDR using the current-generation imaging and transmission pipeline. Recent work [12] proposed Content-Aware Quantization (CAQ) technique for HDR data, which apply adaptive re-quantization scheme for each individual image. Different from the conventional quantization scheme, CAQ adaptively estimates the image local statistics, and predicts the required bits for quantization of each image, at each intensity segment [12]. The usage of bit depth is thus optimized for each individual HDR image, and thus the whole quantization scheme becomes more efficient. Furthermore, Wong et al. [33] provided analysis and demonstrated the importance of the re-quantization step for information reduction in the video codec, in order to achieve end-to-end high coding efficiency. Therefore, by applying smart signal processing tools, such as CAQ, the HDR data with a tone resolution of 12 bits, can be reduced to the constrained bit depth, e.g. 10 bits, such that the HDR images and videos can be stored and transmitted in the current SDR pipeline.

Image Reshaping. As an emerging technology, great amount of HDR videos have been produced, and there are various types of HDR standards and displays in the market, which typically apply different specifications, e.g., EOTFs, brightness levels, color spaces. To achieve the best visual quality for each type of displays, broadcasting companies grade the HDR videos for different HDR specifications. However, as the same contents have been broadcasted, it is inefficient to transmit multiple bitstreams for various HDR displays simultaneously, due to the utility and bandwidth limitation. A smarter approach to improve the transmission efficiency, is to apply image reshaping, which is an re-quantization method which generates images which are optimized for certain type of displays in terms of visual quality. Kadu et al. [15] proposed a progressive coding scheme for HDR videos across displays. Meta data that are used to generate different reshaping functions are embedded into a base-layer bitstream, such that its different overlapping portions are used to generate different reshaping functions across displays [15]. By progressively reusing prediction coefficients, the proposed scheme is capable of decoding meta data from bitstream, thus rendering videos on devices with varied dynamic ranges [15].

3.2   Redesigned System for Smart Signal Processing

Without legacy system constraint or hardware limitation, various new algorithms have been proposed to achieve superior results in image processing applications. Smart signal processing system aims to optimize the algorithms for the specific imaging modality, as well as adapting to the image data to be recovered (i.e., data-driven algorithms). Such systems have demonstrated advantages for applications such as image restoration and compressed imaging.

Data-Driven Image Restoration. Image restoration, e.g., denoising, inpainting, deblurring, super-resolution, etc, is essential in image processing, which also improves robustness in various high-level computer vision applications [16]. Conventional algorithms exploit image properties using total variation (TV) [2,24], or fixed transforms [7,8]. These recovery methods apply regularizers which adapt to neither the specific sensing system nor the images of interest, which usually result in degraded performance in emerging imaging systems. Recent data-driven methods demonstrated improved results of image restoration applications using sparse modeling, including dictionary learning (DL) [11,19] and transform learning (TL) [28,29]. Besides, natural images are known to have self-similarity, i.e., image local textures are typically similar to other structures within the same image [14,29]. The non-local methods are capable of exploiting such properties using popular image models such as low-rankness [14], joint sparsity [19], or collaborative filtering [8]. In addition to exploiting only image internal structures, recent advance of deep neural networks, including fully connected networks [5], convolutional neural networks (CNN) [36], U-Net [16], recurrent neural network (RNN) [26], etc, have demonstrated great potential to learn image models from training dataset with an end-to-end approach.

Compressed Sensing Magnetic Resonance Imaging. Modern imaging systems aim to recover image from under-sampled measurements, which lead to ill-posed inverse problems. In MRI applications, CS-based MRI scheme results in faster scanning rate and low-complexity system [22]. However, directly applying conventional magnetic resonance (MR) image recovery algorithms, e.g., zero-filling, results in low-quality images which potentially affect the clinical applications. Therefore, designing good regularzers based on effective image models becomes critical in CS-based MRI. Previous works on Sparse MRI algorithms [18] applied Wavelets and TV as the regularizer for MR images. However, since the MRI scheme is significantly different from those for natural images, it is natural to apply regularizers which are adaptive to both the MR images, and the specific CS sampling patterns. Recent works on CS-based MRI proposed to incorporate DL [22] and TL [31] schemes, which are more effective than conventional methods using fixed models. On the other hand, Gleichman and Eldar [13] proposed useful analysis on how the learned model should be constrained by the sensing scheme. More recently, Yang et al. [34] proposed ADMM-Net, which is an unrolled deep neural network [4] for CS MRI. It further improves the quality of the reconstructed MR images using the CS scheme.

4   Applications and Experiments

In this section, we demonstrate two applications, namely statistics transfer scheme for HDR images, and compressed sensing based MRI, as examples using the smart signal processing techniques discussed in the previous section. We show that (1) the conventional methods generate degraded results in the HDR and MRI applications, and (2) smart algorithms are effective and outperform the heuristic approaches, providing superior results in these applications.

4.1   Content-Aware Image Retargeting

As discussed in Sect. 3.1, the local statistics are altered in HDR images due to different EOTFs used, comparing to those used in SDR images [32]. There are many important applications, such as content-aware image retargeting, which are sensitive to image local statistics. One popular example is seam carving [32], which is capable of resizing images while maintaining its major contents and information, without introducing major artifacts or distortions. The seam carving algorithm achieves visually appealing results, by gradually adding or removing "seams" of less important contents, which are determined by image local standard deviation. However, as the seam carving algorithms are optimized for SDR images, they usually generated degraded results when directly applying them to

(a) resized HDR image w/o transIm   (b) resized HDR image with transIm

Fig. 4. Resized images (with 300 columns removed) of one frame of HDR video *show-girl02* by applying the seam carving [1] algorithm: (a) without applying transIm [32] as preprocessing, and (b) with transIm applied as preprocessing.

HDR images. Figure 4(a) shows one example of seam carving result after reducing the size of an HDR image. The resized image has image distortion of the important content as shown in the zoom-in region. Without changing the image visual look, we apply transIm [32] to pre-process the HDR image, so that the local statistics of the HDR image becomes similar to SDR. Figure 4(b) shows the corrected seam carving result with transIm, in which the major distortion and artifacts are removed effectively.

4.2   Compressed Sensing MRI

We present MR image reconstruction results in CS-based MRI systems, as an example of efficient imaging applications, using various smart image processing algorithms. We simulated the complex MR measurements, by taking the discrete Fourier transform (DFT) of the magnitude of the testing image (shown in Fig. 5(f)), using an 5× undersampled pseudo radial sampling mask in k-space(shown in Fig. 5(a))[1]. We apply MR image reconstruction algorithms, including methods using naive zero-filling, dictionary learning (DLMRI) [22], transform learning (FRIST) [31], as well as ADMM-Net [34] which is a deep learning method. Figure 5 compares the reconstructed MR images using the aforementioned algorithms. To quantitatively evaluate the reconstruction results, we calculate the Peak Noise-to-Signal Ratio (PSNR) of the reconstructed images shown in Fig. 5(b)–(e). The naive zero-filling method recovered the MR image by directly taking inverse DFT of the undersampled K-space measurements, which leads to results with noticeable artifacts. The data-driven methods, namely DL-MRI [22] and FRIST [31], generated significantly better MR images, by using learned sparsity-based regularizers. The ADMM-Net algorithm [34] further improved the results by training a deep neural network for image reconstruction, achieving the highest PSNR of the reconstructed image among selected methods.

---

[1] We apply the example sampling mask associated with ADMM-Net [35], such that the trained ADMM-Net model can be directly applied.

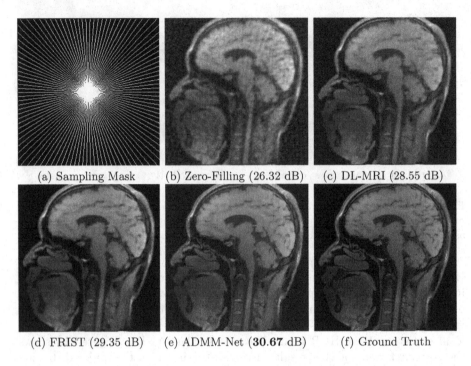

(a) Sampling Mask   (b) Zero-Filling (26.32 dB)   (c) DL-MRI (28.55 dB)

(d) FRIST (29.35 dB)   (e) ADMM-Net (**30.67** dB)   (f) Ground Truth

Fig. 5. CS MRI from the simulated MR data with (a) the 5× undersampling pseudo radial mask in K-space: the results using (b) Zero-filling, (c) DLMRI [22], (d) FRIST [31], (e) ADMM-Net [34], and (f) the ground true image.

5   Conclusion

In this paper, we presented an overview of recent works on smart signal processing techniques for smart imaging systems. We demonstrated that conventional signal processing methods are usually limited, and perform poorly in advanced imaging applications. Thus, it is important to design smart signal processing algorithms which are jointly optimized for imaging systems, as well as the image data. We introduced emerging imaging technologies, such as high dynamic range imaging, and compressed sensing. Recently proposed smart signal processing algorithms are surveyed and categorized based on whether there are legacy system constraints in existing imaging pipelines. We presented experimental results for seam carving and compressed sensing MRI, to evaluate various popular smart signal processing algorithms. We visually and quantitatively demonstrate the significant improvement of imaging results using smart algorithms, over those by conventional approaches.

References

1. Avidan, S., Shamir, A.: Seam carving for content-aware image resizing. ACM Trans. Graph. (TOG) **26**(3), 10 (2007)
2. Beck, A., Teboulle, M.: Fast gradient-based algorithms for constrained total variation image denoising and deblurring problems. IEEE Trans. Image Process. **18**(11), 2419–2434 (2009)
3. Borer, T., Cotton, A.: A "display independent" high dynamic range television system. In: International Broadcasting Convention. IET (2015)
4. Boyd, S., Parikh, N., Chu, E., Peleato, B., Eckstein, J., et al.: Distributed optimization and statistical learning via the alternating direction method of multipliers. Found. Trends Mach. Learn. **3**(1), 1–122 (2011)
5. Burger, H.C., Schuler, C.J., Harmeling, S.: Image denoising: can plain neural networks compete with BM3D? In: IEEE Conference on Computer Vision and Pattern Recognition (CVPR), pp. 2392–2399. IEEE (2012)
6. Candes, E.J., Romberg, J.K., Tao, T.: Stable signal recovery from incomplete and inaccurate measurements. Commun. Pure Appl. Math. **59**(8), 1207–1223 (2006)
7. Chang, S.G., Yu, B., Vetterli, M.: Adaptive wavelet thresholding for image denoising and compression. IEEE Trans. Image Process. (TIP) **9**(9), 1532–1546 (2000)
8. Dabov, K., Foi, A., Katkovnik, V., Egiazarian, K.: Image denoising by sparse 3-D transform-domain collaborative filtering. IEEE Trans. Image Process. (TIP) **16**(8), 2080–2095 (2007)
9. Donoho, D.L.: Compressed sensing. IEEE Trans. Inf. Theory **52**(4), 1289–1306 (2006)
10. Donoho, D.L.: For most large underdetermined systems of linear equations the minimal ℓ_1-norm solution is also the sparsest solution. Commun. Pure Appl. Math. **59**(6), 797–829 (2006)
11. Elad, M., Aharon, M.: Image denoising via sparse and redundant representations over learned dictionaries. IEEE Trans. Image Process. **15**(12), 3736–3745 (2006)
12. Froehlich, J., Su, G.M., Daly, S., Schilling, A., Eberhardt, B.: Content aware quantization: requantization of high dynamic range baseband signals based on visual masking by noise and texture. In: IEEE International Conference onImage Processing (ICIP), pp. 884–888. IEEE (2016)
13. Gleichman, S., Eldar, Y.C.: Blind compressed sensing. IEEE Trans. Inf. Theory **57**(10), 6958–6975 (2011)
14. Gu, S., Xie, Q., Meng, D., Zuo, W., Feng, X., Zhang, L.: Weighted nuclear norm minimization and its applications to low level vision. Int. J. Comput. Vis. **121**(2), 183–208 (2017)
15. Kadu, H., Song, Q., Su, G.M.: Single layer progressive coding for high dynamic range video. In: Picture Coding Symposium (2018)
16. Liu, D., Wen, B., Liu, X., Huang, T.S.: When image denoising meets high-level vision tasks: a deep learning approach (2017)
17. Lu, T., et al.: ITP colour space and its compression performance for high dynamic range and wide colour gamut video distribution. ZTE Commun. **14**(1), 32–38 (2016)
18. Lustig, M., Donoho, D., Pauly, J.M.: Sparse MRI: The application of compressed sensing for rapid MR imaging. Magnetic resonance in medicine **58**(6), 1182–1195 (2007)
19. Mairal, J., Bach, F., Ponce, J., Sapiro, G., Zisserman, A.: Non-local sparse models for image restoration. In: IEEE 12th International Conference on Computer Vision, ICCV, pp. 2272–2279 (2009)

20. Miller, S., Nezamabadi, M., Daly, S.: Perceptual signal coding for more efficient usage of bit codes. SMPTE Motion Imaging J. **122**(4), 52–59 (2013)
21. Nezamabadi, M., Miller, S., Daly, S., Atkins, R.: Color signal encoding for high dynamic range and wide color gamut based on human perception. In: Color Imaging XIX: Displaying, Processing, Hardcopy, and Applications, vol. 9015, p. 90150C. International Society for Optics and Photonics (2014)
22. Ravishankar, S., Bresler, Y.: MR image reconstruction from highly undersampled k-space data by dictionary learning. IEEE Trans. Med. Imaging **30**(5), 1028–1041 (2011)
23. Recommendation ITU-R BT2100-0: image parameter values for high dynamic range television for use in production and international programme exchange, July 2016
24. Rudin, L.I., Osher, S., Fatemi, E.: Nonlinear total variation based noise removal algorithms. Phys. D: Nonlinear Phenom. **60**(1–4), 259–268 (1992)
25. Ström, J., et al.: High quality HDR video compression using HEVC main 10 profile. In: Picture Coding Symposium (PCS), pp. 1–5. IEEE (2016)
26. Tai, Y., Yang, J., Liu, X., Xu, C.: MemNet: a persistent memory network for image restoration. In: Proceedings of International Conference on Computer Vision (ICCV) (2017)
27. Wen, B., Harshad, K., Su, G.: Inverse Luma/Chroma mappings with histogram transfer and approximation, April 5 2018, US Patent App. 15/725, 101
28. Wen, B., Ravishankar, S., Bresler, Y.: Structured overcomplete sparsifying transform learning with convergence guarantees and applications. Int. J. Comput. Vis. **114**(2), 137–167 (2015)
29. Wen, B., Li, Y., Bresler, Y.: When sparsity meets low-rankness: transformlearning with non-local low-rank constraint for image restoration. In: IEEE International Conference on Acoustics, Speech and Signal Processing (ICASSP), pp. 2297–2301. IEEE (2017)
30. Wen, B., Li, Y., Pfister, L., Bresler, Y.: Joint adaptive sparsity and low-rankness on the fly: an online tensor reconstruction scheme for video denoising. In: IEEE International Conference on Computer Vision (ICCV), vol. 1 (2017)
31. Wen, B., Ravishankar, S., Bresler, Y.: FRIST- flipping and rotation invariant sparsifying transform learning and applications. Inverse Probl. **33**(7), 074007 (2017)
32. Wen, B., Su, G.M.: Transim: transfer image local statistics across EOTFS for HDR image applications. In: International Conference on Multimedia and Expo (ICME). IEEE (2018)
33. Wong, C.W., Su, G.M., Wu, M.: Impact analysis of baseband quantizer on coding efficiency for HDR video. IEEE Signal Process. Lett. **23**(10), 1354–1358 (2016)
34. Yang, Y., Sun, J., Li, H., Xu, Z.: Deep ADMM-Net for compressive sensing MRI. In: Advances in Neural Information Processing Systems, pp. 10–18 (2016)
35. Yang, Y., Sun, J., Li, H., Xu, Z.: Deep-ADMM-Net. https://github.com/yangyan92/Deep-ADMM-Net (2017). gitHub repository
36. Zhang, K., Zuo, W., Chen, Y., Meng, D., Zhang, L.: Beyond a gaussian denoiser: residual learning of deep CNN for image denoising. IEEE Trans. Image Process. **26**(7), 3142–3155 (2017)

A Regularized Nonnegative Third Order Tensor decomposition Using a Primal-Dual Projected Gradient Algorithm: Application to 3D Fluorescence Spectroscopy

Karima El Qate[1]([⊠]), Mohammed El Rhabi[2], Abdelilah Hakim[1], Eric Moreau[3], and Nadàge Thirion-Moreau[3]

[1] LAMAI, FSTG Marrakech, University of Cady Ayyad, Marrakesh, Morocco
karima.elqate@gmail.com, abdelilah.hakim@gmail.com
[2] Applied Mathematics and Computer Science Department, Ecole des Ponts ParisTech (ENPC), Paris, France
mohammed.el-rhabi@enpc.fr
[3] Aix Marseille Université, Université de Toulon, CNRS UMR 7020, LIS, Marseille, France
{thirion,moreau}@univ-tln.fr

Abstract. This paper investigates the use of Primal-Dual optimization algorithms on multidimensional signal processing problems. The data blocks interpreted in a tensor way can be modeled by means of multi-linear decomposition. Here we will focus on the Canonical Polyadic Decomposition (CPD), and we will present an application to fluorescence spectroscopy using this decomposition. In order to estimate the factors or latent variables involved in these decompositions, it is usual to use criteria optimization algorithms. A classical cost function consists of a measure of the modeling error (fidelity term) to which a regularization term can be added if necessary. Here, we consider one of the most efficient optimization methods, Primal-Dual Projected Gradient.

The effectiveness and the robustness of the proposed approach are shown through numerical examples.

Keywords: Constrained optimization
Nonnegative tensor decomposition · Primal-Dual · Regularization
Projected gradient

1 Introduction

This work deals with the Canonical Polyadic Decomposition (CPD) problem which has received much attention in the last ten years in various fields, ranging from telecommunications to chemometrics, spectral unmixing, neuroimaging, machine learning and Signal Processing for Biomedical Engineering. The CPD

© Springer Nature Switzerland AG 2018
A. Basu and S. Berretti (Eds.): ICSM 2018, LNCS 11010, pp. 183–192, 2018.
https://doi.org/10.1007/978-3-030-04375-9_16

is a compact and flexible model which consists of decomposing a tensor into a minimal sum of rank-1 tensors. Initially developed by Harshman in psychometry [1], it was later referred to as Canonical Decomposition (Candecomp) [2], Parallel Factor Model (Parafac) [3,4], and Topographic Components Model [5].

Many researchers have addressed the problem of computing the CPD of multi-way arrays, rewriting it as an optimization problem and more precisely as a minimization problem involving a sum of a (not necessarily convex) differentiable function and a (not necessarily differentiable) convex function:

$$\underset{z \in \mathbb{R}^N}{minimize} \quad \underbrace{F(z)}_{Fidelity} + \quad \underbrace{R(z)}_{Regularization} \tag{1}$$

The most popular approach is resorted to an iterative Alternating Least Squares (ALS) procedure [2]. Other iterative algorithms based on first and second order optimization methods such as gradient or conjugate gradient have also been proposed ([6,7] for a full comparison of computation cost). Recently, a set of iterative algorithms based on a reduced functional has been introduced in [8]. In this article, we consider the minimization of a function which is the sum of a convex differentiable function F and a convex function R, which is not differentiable. A standard approach in this context consists of using the Primal-Dual Projected Gradient algorithm, which alternates a subgradient step. This proposed scheme differs from the other classical methods because it allows to obtain efficient combinatorial algorithms, in terms of approximation factor and calculation time. The main idea is to work simultaneously on the primal and the dual by finding an adequate solution for the dual, then to improve it at each step by optimizing an associated restricted primal problem.

The rest of the paper is organized as follows: Sect. 2 introduces a reminder of the principles of 3D fluorescence spectroscopy, and its links with the CPD problems. Section 3 describes the general principles of Primal-Dual Projected Gradient Algorithm. In Sect. 4, we will explain how it can be used to solve the CPD problem and we will provide the resulting algorithm. Finally, Sect. 5 provides some numerical results and a discussion on the algorithm performance.

2   Problem Statement: CPD of Fluorescent Data

2.1   3D Fluorescence Spectroscopy

Whether it appears disturbing or playful, the phenomenon of fluorescence stirs our curiosity as much as it captures our gaze. This transitory manifestation results from the interactions between light and matter. When these are illuminated by incident light, some elements emit some of the energy at different wavelengths. The intensity of this fluorescence light varies as a function of the wavelengths of the incident light and the light emitted. The shape of these variations forms the fluorescence spectrum of the illuminated element and can be measured using a spectrofluorometer. We can distinguish two types of fluorescence spectrum: excitation and emission spectra. Therefore, spectroscopic fluorescence analysis is based on the processing of these signals. By successively, using the two monochromator of the Spectrofluorometer (in excitation and in emission), it is possible to measure the emission spectra for different excitation wavelengths. The Fluorescence Excitation-Emission Matrices (FEEM) are thus obtained [9]. When a first order approximation of the Beer-Lambert law [10] is considered (for weak or low absorbance of the fluorophores), the intensity measured at (λ_e, λ_f) can be written as:

$$I(\lambda_e, \lambda_f, k) = C\phi I_0(\lambda_e)\gamma(\lambda_f)\varepsilon(\lambda_e)c_k \tag{2}$$

where C is a constant depending on the device, $I_0(\lambda_e)$ is the intensity of the light source, ϕ is the fluorescence quantum yield, ε denotes the relative absorbance spectrum (sometimes called the excitation spectrum), λ_f is the fluorescence emission wavelength, λ_e stands for the excitation wavelength, γ is the fluorescence relative emission spectrum and c_k is the concentration of the fluorophore in the sample number k. In the case of a mixture of N fluorophores, we obtain a generalized version of Eq. 2

$$I(\lambda_e, \lambda_f, k) = CI_0(\lambda_e) \sum_{n=1}^{N} \phi_n \gamma_n(\lambda_f)\varepsilon(\lambda_e)c_{k,n} \tag{3}$$

where $c_{k,n}$ stands for the concentration of n-th fluorescent solute in the k-th sample. The goal is to estimate the individual spectra of each fluorophore using the Canonical Polyadic Decomposition.

2.2 CP Decomposition of 3-Way Arrays

We thus have a data set, denoted by X, containing the measurements of a physical quantity x_{ijk} function of three parameters, i, j, k. A trilinear model [11, 12] of X consists of a linear combination of three variables a, b and c depending respectively on i, j, k and a common parameter n such that:

$$x_{ijk} = \sum_{n=1}^{N} a_{in}b_{jn}c_{kn}, \quad \forall(i, j, k) \tag{4}$$

where the three involved matrices $A = (a_{in}) \in \mathbb{R}^{I \times N}$, $B = (b_{jn}) \in \mathbb{R}^{J \times N}$ and $C = (c_{kn}) \in \mathbb{R}^{K \times N}$ are the so-called loading matrices, whose N columns are the loading factors.

Matrix Writing. The data can be grouped in a single matrix by unfolding the tensor X in a preferred direction [13]. We denote by $X_{(1)}^{I,KJ}$ the matrix (I, KJ) representing the tensor unfolded in the direction i. We then look for the matrix relation existing between $X_{(1)}^{I,KJ}$ and the three matrices to be determined. For this, we introduce a special tensor product called Khatri-Rao product denoted by $(\odot)$, such that for two matrices A and C having the same number of columns N, we have:

$$A \odot C = [a_{:1} \otimes c_{:1} \ a_{:2} \otimes c_{:2} \ldots a_{:N} \otimes c_{:N}]$$

where $\otimes$ refers to the Kronecker product. $X_{(1)}^{I,KJ}$ can then be written as:

$$X_{(1)}^{I,KJ} = A(C \odot B)^T \tag{5}$$

It is possible to unfold X according to j into a matrix $X_{(2)}^{J,KI}$, or again according to k into a matrix $X_{(3)}^{K,IJ}$. Thanks to the same reasoning, we obtain the two following formulas:

$$X_{(2)}^{J,KI} = B(C \odot A)^T, \ \ X_{(3)}^{K,JI} = C(B \odot A)^T \tag{6}$$

These three relations will allow us to estimate A, B and C.

In the particular case of Fluorescence Spectroscopy analysis, X contains different FEEMs corresponding to mixtures of N fluorophores in various proportions, then a_{in} represents the fluorescence factor (the product of the concentration and the quantum yield) of the fluorophore n, b_{jn} represents the value of the emission spectrum of the fluorophore n at the wavelength j and c_{kn} represents the value of the excitation spectrum of the fluorophore n at the wavelength k.

3   Primal-Dual Projected Gradient Algorithm

An efficient approach for solving the aforementioned general minimization problem (1) consists of using the Primal-Dual Projected Gradient Algorithm. We refer the interested reader to [14–16] for further details.

Using the Fenchel-Legendre transform, the previous minimization problem can be formulated as the search for a saddle point, more precisely, we have the following proposition:

Proposition 1. *Each of the following two problems admit a solution*

1. $\widehat{z_1} \in \underset{z_1 \in Z_1}{\arg\min} f_0(z_1) + f_1(Kz_1)$
2. $\widehat{z_2} \in \underset{z_2 \in Z_2}{\arg\max} - (f_0^*(-K^*z_2) - f_1^*(z_2))$

The first is called "primal problem" and the second is called "dual problem". In addition, we have:

$$\min_{z_1 \in Z_1} f_0(z_1) + f_1(Kz_1) = \max_{z_2 \in Z_2} - (f_0^*(-K^*z_2) - f_1^*(z_2)) \tag{7}$$

Let us now give one of the essential theorems in this context

Theorem 1. *Let $f_0 : U \to \mathbb{R}$ be a closed and convex functional on the set U, f_1 a closed and convex functional on the set V and let $K : U \to V$ be a continuous linear operator. Then we have the following equivalence:*

$$\underbrace{\min_{z \in U}\{f_0(z) + f_1(Kz)\}}_{Primal} = \underbrace{\min_{z \in U}\max_{\varphi \in V^*}\{< Kz, \varphi > -f_1^*(\varphi) + f_0(z)\}}_{Primal-Dual} \qquad (8)$$

where z and φ are the primal and dual variables, respectively, f_1^* is the convex conjugate of f_1, V^* is the dual space of V, and $< \cdot, \cdot >$ is the inner product.

Variational Problem. We will now see how the primal-dual problem of Theorem (1) can be written as a variational problem.

Before considering the specific problems, we first introduce a general saddle point problem notation

$$\min_{u \in U}\max_{v \in V}\{\mathbf{L}(u, v)\} \qquad (9)$$

where U and V are closed convex, and $\mathbf{L}$ is a convex-concave function defined over $U \times V$. In particular, $\mathbf{L}(\cdot, v)$ is convex for every $v \in V$, and $\mathbf{L}(u, \cdot)$ is concave for every $u \in U$.

Now we reduce the problem of approximating a saddle point (9) of $\mathbf{L}$ on $U \times V$, the resolution of the associated variational inequality find $z^* \in X := U \times V$ s.t

$$< z - z^*, H(z^*) > \geq 0 \quad \forall z \in Z \qquad (10)$$

where

$$z = \begin{pmatrix} u \\ v \end{pmatrix} \quad \text{and} \quad H(z) = \begin{pmatrix} \partial_u \mathbf{L}(u, v) \\ -\partial_v \mathbf{L}(u, v) \end{pmatrix}$$

Projected Gradient Method. Now, we will see how the preceding variational inequality (10) can be solved using the gradient projection method, for this we give the following proposition.

Proposition 2. *Let r be a positive parameter and Z a convex set. An element z^* is solution of (10) if and only if*

$$z^* = P_Z(z^* - rH(z^*)) \qquad (11)$$

where $P_Z(z)$ denote the orthogonal projection of the point z onto the nonempty, close, convex set Z.

Now we will use the fixed-point method to solve the last equation defined in the previous proposition:

Given $z \in Z$ compute the solution at step $n + 1$ by iterating the scheme

$$z_{n+1}^* = P_Z(z_n^* - rH(z_n^*)) \qquad (12)$$

4   Application to the Penalized Nonnegative Third Order Tensor Factorization Problem

4.1   Proposed Algorithm

Estimate $\widehat{A}, \widehat{B}$ and $\widehat{C}$ of A, B and C results from

$$\underset{A \in \mathbb{R}^{I \times N}}{minimize} \ \mathbf{F}(A,B,C) + \mathbf{R}_1(A) \quad s.t. \quad A \geq 0. \tag{13}$$

$$\underset{B \in \mathbb{R}^{J \times N}}{minimize} \ \mathbf{F}(A,B,C) + \mathbf{R}_2(B) \quad s.t. \quad B \geq 0. \tag{14}$$

$$\underset{C \in \mathbb{R}^{K \times N}}{minimize} \ \mathbf{F}(A,B,C) + \mathbf{R}_3(C) \quad s.t. \quad C \geq 0. \tag{15}$$

where

$$
\begin{aligned}
\mathbf{F}(A,B,C) &= \frac{1}{2} \parallel X_{(1)}^{I,KJ} - A(C \odot B)^T \parallel_F^2 \\
&= \frac{1}{2} \parallel X_{(2)}^{J,KI} - B(C \odot A)^T \parallel_F^2 \\
&= \frac{1}{2} \parallel X_{(3)}^{K,JI} - C(B \odot A)^T \parallel_F^2
\end{aligned}
\tag{16}
$$

and $\parallel \cdot \parallel_F$ denotes the Frobenius norm. We opt for the following regularization terms

$$\mathbf{R}_1(A) = \alpha_A \parallel A \parallel_1, \ \ \mathbf{R}_2(B) = \alpha_B \parallel B \parallel_1 \ \ and \ \ \mathbf{R}_3(C) = \alpha_C \parallel C \parallel_1 \tag{17}$$

where α_A, α_B and α_C are non negative regularization parameters, and $\parallel \cdot \parallel_1$ is the l_1-norm.

Now we will follow the steps of the previous paragraph to solve our optimization problem. It becomes obvious, by comparing our following optimization problem with the primal-dual model in Theorem (1), we get the following notation:

$$f_0(A) = \frac{1}{2} \parallel X_{(1)}^{I,KJ} - A(C \odot B)^T \parallel_F^2 \tag{18}$$

$$f_1(KA) = \alpha_A \sum_{i,n} |A(i,n)| \tag{19}$$

Now, we define the functionals:

$$
\begin{array}{ccc}
K : U \to V & & f_1 : V \to \qquad \mathbb{R} \\
A \mapsto A & and & Y \mapsto \sum_i \sum_n f(Y(i,n))
\end{array}
\tag{20}
$$

with $U = \mathbb{R}_+^{I \times N}$ and $V = \mathbb{R}_+^{I \times N}$ two reflexive spaces and $f : \mathbb{R} \to \mathbb{R}, f(x) = |x|$. The conjugate f^* of the function f is found as:

$$
\begin{array}{cc}
f^* : \mathbb{R} \to & \mathbb{R} \\
s \mapsto & \begin{cases} 0 & \text{if } |s| \leq 1 \\ +\propto & \text{if } |s| > 1 \end{cases}
\end{array}
\tag{21}
$$

and therefore the convex conjugate f_1^* of f is

$$f_1^* : V \to \quad\quad \mathbb{R}$$
$$Y \mapsto \sum_i \sum_n f^*(Y(i,n)) \tag{22}$$

Thus, using Theorem (1), we now get the equivalent primal-dual problem:

$$\min_{A \in U} \max_{Y \in V^*} \{\alpha_A < A, Y > + \frac{1}{2} \parallel X_{(1)}^{I,KJ} - A(C \odot B)^T \parallel_F^2\} \tag{23}$$

where $V^* = \{Y \in \mathbb{R}_+^{I \times N}; \sum_{i,n} |Y(i,n)| \leq 1\}$

Using the notation in (10) we get for each (i,n)

$$H(A,Y) = \begin{pmatrix} \alpha_A Y - \left(X_{(1)}^{I,KJ} - A(C \odot B)^T\right)(C \odot B) \\ -\alpha_A A \end{pmatrix} \tag{24}$$

Now by proceeding the last step which is used to apply the projection algorithm, and to provide a current estimate $(A^{(k+1)}, Y^{(k+1)})$ at iteration step $k+1$, we obtain the following algorithm:

Algorithm

Initialize $A^{(0)}$, $Y^{(0)}$.
Repeat

1. $Y^{(k+1)} = P_{V^*}\{Y^{(k)} + r_1 \alpha_A A^{(k)}\}$
2. $A^{(k+1)} = P_U\{A^{(k)} - r_2[\alpha_A Y^{(k+1)}(X_{(1)}^{I,KJ} - A(C \odot B)^T)(C \odot B)]\}$

until convergence

Where r_1, r_2 small positive constants. We do exactly the same for the estimation of matrices B and C.

   Note, that the nonnegativity of the factors is ensured by the projection onto the subspaces U and V^*, introduced in the algorithm above.

5   Numerical Simulations

The purpose of this subsection is to evaluate the performance of the Primal Dual Gradient Projected algorithm on synthetic data tensor built as follows: emission and excitation spectra and the three resulting Fluorescence Excitation Emission Matrices of three fluorophores, in our case tyrosine, phenylalanine and tryptophan have been downloaded at the following address: http://omlc.ogi.edu/spectra/PhotochemCAD/index.html. In the case of a perfect trilinear model and a known rank, our algorithm is able to recover the true solution. Moreover, by comparing our algorithm with Conjugate Gradient algorithm (with regularization terms l_1) and Gradient algorithm (with regularization terms l_1), we observe that our algorithm is the less computer time consuming ($\alpha_A = \alpha_B = \alpha_C = 0.01$ and $r1 = 0.01, r2 = 1/700$)(Table 1).

Table 1. Computer elapsed time (in second) for the different methods after 10000 iterations

Primal Dual	Conjugate gradient	Gradient
9.1984	28.6114	28.1782

In Fig. 1, we have given the 3 FEEM of reference, and the 3 FEEM obtained by application of primal-dual algorithm with regularization terms.

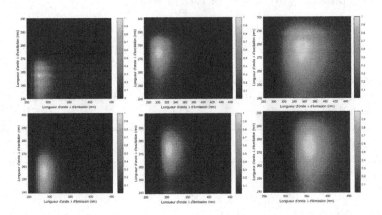

Fig. 1. Reference FEEM (top), the estimated FEEM (bottom) using Primal-Dual Projected Gradient

In Fig. 2, we have given the reference emission spectrum, and the estimated emission spectra using our algorithm starting from a random initialization ($\alpha_A = \alpha_B = \alpha_C = 0.01$)) and ($r_1 = 0.01, r_2 = 1/700$).

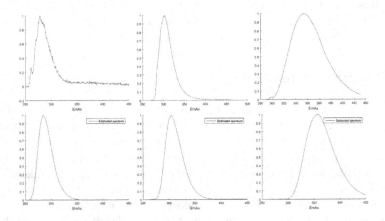

Fig. 2. Reference spectrum (top), the estimated emission spectra (bottom): phenylalanine, tyrosine and tryptophan

In Fig. 3, we have given the reference excitation spectrum, and the estimated excitation spectra using our algorithm starting from a random initialization $(\alpha_A = \alpha_B = \alpha_C = 0.01))$ and $(r_1 = 0.01, r_2 = 1/700)$.

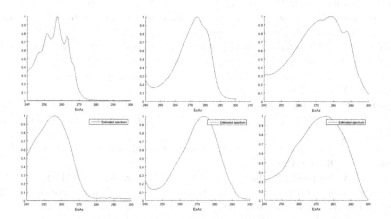

Fig. 3. Reference spectrum (top), the estimated excitation spectra (bottom): phenylalanine, tyrosine and tryptophan

6   Conclusion

Our work has investigated the problem of the nonnegative CPD of three-way array (third order tensors) arising in a variety of disciplines in the sciences and engineering. In particular, we have shown its interest in the field of 3D fluorescence spectroscopy. Efficiently, to solve that problem we have suggested Primal-Dual Projected Gradient Algorithm. Numerical results have proven the interest of the proposed approach.

References

1. Harshman, R.A.: Foundations of the PARAFAC procedure: models and conditions for an "explanatory" multi-modal factor analysis. UCLA Working Papers in Phonetics, vol. 16, pp. 1–84 (1970)
2. Carroll, J.D., Chang, J.J.: Analysis of individual differences in multidimensional scaling via an N-way generalization of "Eckart-Young" decomposition. Psychometrika **35**(3), 283–319 (1970)
3. Harshman, R.A., Lundy, M.E.: PARAFAC: parallel factor analysis. Comput. Stat. Data Anal. **18**(1), 39–72 (1994)
4. Harshman, R.A., Lundy, M.E.: The PARAFAC model for three-way factor analysis and multidimensional scaling. Res. Methods Multimode Data Anal. **46**, 122–215 (1984)
5. Mocks, J.: Topographic components model for event-related potentials and some biophysical considerations. IEEE Trans. Biomed. Eng. **35**(6), 482–484 (1988)

6. Tendeiro, J., Dosse, M.B., Berge, T., Jos, M.F.: First and second-order derivatives for CP and INDSCAL. Chemom. Intell. Lab. Syst. **106**(1), 27–36 (2011)
7. Acar, E., Dunlavy, D.M., Kolda, T.G., et al.: Scalable tensor factorizations with missing data. In: Proceedings of the 2010 SIAM International Conference on Data Mining. Society for Industrial and Applied Mathematics, pp. 701–712 (2010)
8. Kindermann, S., Navasca, C.: News algorithms for tensor decomposition based on a reduced functional. Numer. Linear Algebr. Appl. **21**(3), 340–374 (2014)
9. Coble, P.G.: Characterization of marine and terrestrial dom in seawater using excitation-emission matrix spectroscopy. Mar. Chem. **52**, 325–346 (1996)
10. Smilde, A., Bro, R., Geladi, P.: Multi-way Analysis: Applications in the Chemical Sciences. Wiley, Hoboken (2005)
11. Royer, J.-P., Thirion-Moreau, N., Comon, P.: Computing the polyadic decomposition of nonnegative third order tensors. EURASIP Signal Process. **91**(9), 2159–2171 (2011)
12. Hitchcock, F.L.: The expression of a tensor or a polyadic as a sum of products. J. Math. Phys. **6**, 165–189 (1927)
13. Cichocki, A., Zdunek, R., Phan, A.H., Amari, S.I.: Non Negative Matrix and Tensor Factorizations: Application to Exploratory Multi-way Data Analysis and Blind Separation. Wiley, Hoboken (2009)
14. Chambolle, A., Pock, T.: A first-order primal-dual algorithm for convex problems with applications to imaging (2010)
15. Zhu, M., Chan, T.: An efficient primal-dual hybrid gradient algorithm for total variation image restoration, Technical report, UCLA CAM Report 08–34 (2008)
16. Ekeland, I., Roger, T.: Convex analysis and variational problems, vol. 28. SIAM (1999)

Adaptive Dithering Using Curved Markov-Gaussian Noise in the Quantized Domain for Mapping SDR to HDR Image

Subhayan Mukherjee[1]([✉]), Guan-Ming Su[2], and Irene Cheng[1]

[1] University of Alberta, Edmonton, AB T6G 2R3, Canada
{mukherje, locheng}@ualberta.ca
[2] Dolby Laboratories Inc., Sunnyvale, CA 94085, USA
guanmingsu@ieee.org

Abstract. High Dynamic Range (HDR) imaging is gaining increased attention due to its realistic content, for not only regular displays but also smartphones. Before sufficient HDR content is distributed, HDR visualization still relies mostly on converting Standard Dynamic Range (SDR) content. SDR images are often quantized, or bit depth reduced, before SDR-to-HDR conversion, e.g. for video transmission. Quantization can easily lead to banding artefacts. In some computing and/or memory I/O limited environment, the traditional solution using spatial neighborhood information is not feasible. Our method includes noise generation (offline) and noise injection (online), and operates on pixels of the quantized image. We vary the magnitude and structure of the noise pattern adaptively based on the luma of the quantized pixel and the slope of the inverse-tone mapping function. Subjective user evaluations confirm the superior performance of our technique.

Keywords: High dynamic range · Image coding · Image quality
Dithering · Gaussian noise

1 Introduction

High Dynamic Range (HDR) imaging technology with 12+ bits per color channel is becoming commonplace [1]. Traditional 8-bit Standard Dynamic Range (SDR) imaging only has a peak brightness of 100 nits and narrower color gamut compared to HDR (peak brightness of 1000+ nits and a wider color gamut). However, consumers can only make the most of this technology when more HDR content is widely available to the public. Current videos are mostly distributed at 8-bit depth. Although modern cameras can capture 12-/16-bit, videos are quantized to 8 bits SDR for compression and transmission. In order to watch SDR videos on HDR displays, the challenge is to up-convert the 8 bits content effectively for visualization, e.g. apply inverse tone-mapping operator [2–7]. HDR videos generated by these methods often suffer from false contours called banding/ringing artifacts, arising due to the Mach band effect [8, 9]. 8-bit SDR video has a maximum of 256 code-words. Consequently, the output HDR video also has a maximum of 256 code-words when we deploy single-channel mapping. But in order to show a banding-free image on a 1000+ nits display, 12-bit (i.e., 4,096)

© Springer Nature Switzerland AG 2018
A. Basu and S. Berretti (Eds.): ICSM 2018, LNCS 11010, pp. 193–203, 2018.
https://doi.org/10.1007/978-3-030-04375-9_17

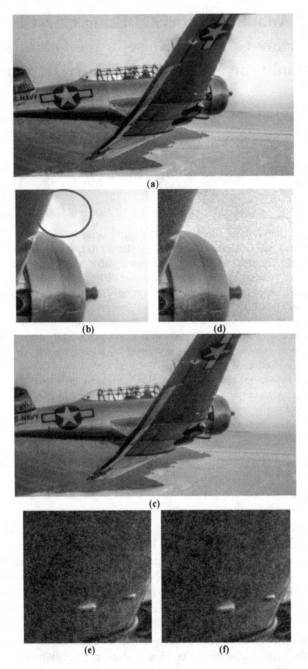

Fig. 1. (a): A quantized Image and (b) a cropped region with banding. (c): Output of (a) from our method and (d) the corresponding cropped area. (e): Circular Noise, compared with (f): Curved Noise. This example shows that our curved noise method gives a better blending result and de-bands quantized images effectively. Note that (a–f) are tone-mapped [28] for illustration in printed form or on a SDR display (realistic visualization is only possible on a HDR display).

code-words, is necessary [1]. Dithering techniques aim to mask banding by placing a combination of pixels with different colors in the neighborhood to perceptually mask banding artefacts [10].

Traditional dithering methods can be adaptive or non-adaptive. The former uses both the pixel and its neighborhood information, whereas the latter uses only the pixel. Both approaches need to access the original high bit-depth and un-quantized pixel values [10–21]. However, many applications, e.g., video-on-demand, require content compression or data quantization before transmission. We proved mathematically that adding zero-mean noise can only remove banding from un-quantized data, but not from quantized signal. Furthermore, in some computing and/or memory I/O limited environment, the traditional solution using spatial neighborhood information is not feasible. Thus, our contribution lies in proposing a two-stage dithering method in the quantized domain, which is composed of two components: (1) the offline Curved Markov Gaussian noise pattern generation stage, and (2) the online luma/tone curve modulated noise injection stage.

1.1 Background

Since video transmission on mobiles is commonplace and HDR capable mobiles are increasingly popular in the consumer market, we consider the mobile GPU computing environment, where computation capacity is limited and accessing neighbor information is expensive in terms of memory I/O and processing time. Such environment limits the usage of filtering and prediction of false contour based on neighborhood information [22–27, 30]. Our method performs pixel-wise dithering on quantized images (display end), without the need to detect texture structure in the neighborhood. One application scenario, where only quantized images are available, is a video decoder which decodes 10-bit streams and outputs 8 bits signal (bit depth interface between two connected hardware chips are different) and another case is when 8-bit streams are received (e.g. 8-bit AVC/HEVC bit stream). In this context, the input quantized images undergo inverse tone-mapping to output HDR content of significantly higher bit-depth for display on the mobile device.

2 Proposed Computational Model

The proposed method is designed to process the computational expensive noise pattern generation offline, and to inject minimal noise to mask banding adaptively online. Figure 1(a-d) illustrate our de-banding result, which keeps the image visually pleasant. Figure 1(a, b) highlight how banding is visible especially in texture-less regions, e.g., sky, but is less visible in textured regions, e.g., airplane. Figure 1d shows the result of our noise injection, which is adaptively adjusted based on the degree of banding of the input. We simulate quantization by right shifting the original SDR input by 2 bits and then left-shifting it by 2 bits. Thus, the input is still 10 bits, but has very sparsely distributed code-words (banding). The output HDR image uses 16 bits per channel, but its code-words are normalized to the [0, 1) range. We consider a generic SDR-to-HDR conversion scheme where the luma channel is inverse tone-mapped using a look-up table. We label this look-up table BLUT (Backward Look-Up Table) as it is used to get back the HDR from the SDR image. But the chroma channels are processed using non-BLUT methods (i.e., we dither chroma channels without assuming any look-up tables). The range of luma intensities near the top and bottom of the code-word range are clipped, as shown in Fig. 2a. This process of restricting the intensity range is commonly used in the Society of Motion Picture and Television Engineers (SMPTE) [29]. In the rest of this paper, we label the highest SDR intensity in the lower flat region as Y_0 and the lowest SDR intensity in the upper flat region as Y_1 respectively.

In our experiments, images are in the Y-C_b-C_r color space, where Y is luma. C_b and C_r are the two chroma channels. We consider the inverse tone-mapping function as a one-to-one mapping between the SDR and HDR intensities in the Y channel. The advantage is to compute only once for each frame and store the result in BLUT, indexed by the SDR code-words. We consider that the original SDR uses 10 bits in each channel, and thus has 1024 code-words with integer values in the range [0, 1023]. Due to 8-bit quantization per channel, our method's input has only 256 code-words.

An example of BLUT is shown in Fig. 2a, where the horizontal axis has SDR code-words and the vertical axis has normalized HDR code-words. We found via testing that the smallest SDR intensity, with corresponding normalized HDR intensity greater than

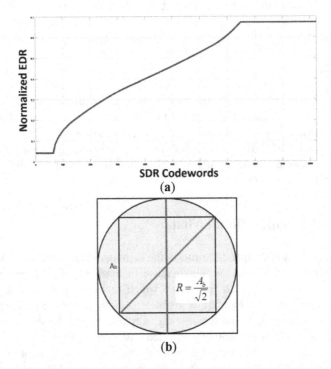

Fig. 2. (a) BLUT for the Y channel from a sunset scene, and (b) Extraction of the square block in a circular noise pattern.

0.625, can be taken as the starting intensity for highlight region. On a 4,000 nits display, this HDR intensity would be 3,000 nits. We denote the corresponding SDR intensity 'Y_h', all individual SDR intensities t and the set of all SDR intensities $T = \{t_0,$ $t_1, t_2, ..., t_{1023}\}$. Now, let the lower flat region be $BLUT_{Down} = \{t < Y_0\}$, the low-lights & mid-tones region be $BLUT_{Mid} = \{Y_0 \leq t < Y_h\}$, the highlight region before reaching the upper flat region be $BLUT_{High} = \{Y_h \leq t < Y_1\}$, and the upper flat region be $BLUT_{Up} = \{t \geq Y_1\}$. In this way, we partition BLUT into four mutually exclusive regions:

$$T = \{BLUT_{Down} \cup BLUT_{Mid} \cup BLUT_{High} \cup BLUT_{Up}\}.$$

2.1   Simple Two-State Markov Gaussian Noise Generation

Experimental analysis showed that when simple Gaussian noise is used for dithering, it masks the banding artefacts more effectively if the mean and standard deviation of the Gaussian distribution is increased, but at the same time it makes the image progressively noisier. Better results can be obtained by creating noise patterns, which has a global zero mean property, though locally the noise patterns have non-zero means to break banding. Using Markov chain to build state transition, where each state has non-zero mean noise can achieve this local non-zero mean.

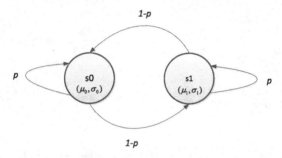

Fig. 3. Two-state Markov-Gaussian noise generator

As shown in Fig. 3, apply Markov Gaussian signal to generate noise for each pixel, we need to know the previous pixel's state. Based on the previous state and an intra-state probability p, we can stay in the same state or move to another state with an inter-state probability $1 - p$. In each state, s, we can generate a Gaussian noise with mean μ_s, variance σ_s, i.e. (μ_0, σ_0) for state 0 and (μ_1, σ_1) for state 1. We use the value $\mu_0 = 2, \sigma_0 = 1, \mu_1 = -2, \sigma_1 = 1$ in our implementation, as these values gave the best results. By comparing (a) and (b) in Fig. 4, we can see that a higher intra-state transition probability can generate longer texture, and have better ability to destroy the banding artefact, but make the image noisier.

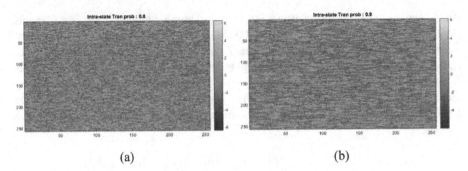

Fig. 4. Two-state Markov Gaussian Noise with intra-state transition probabilities (a) 0.8 and (b) 0.9. Note that higher transition probability has higher masking effect.

2.2 Limitation of Simple Markov Gaussian Noise

A limitation of the two-state Markov Gaussian noise is that it generates noise patterns ("stripes") in only two fixed directions: horizontal and vertical. But, such patterns look unnatural, and the effectiveness of de-banding depends on the angle at which the stripes meet the false contours.

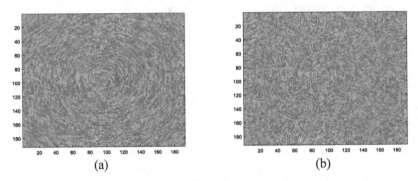

Fig. 5. Convert (a) Circular to (b) Curved Markov-Gaussian Noise; Block size = 200 × 200; Trans. Prob. = 0.815.

This motivated us to adopt the curved noise pattern instead of straight, in order to blend the patterns into the image content naturally. We first obtain concentric circles from the noise generator's output. In each circle, starting from the point on its circumference subtending the least angle θ (counter-clockwise) w.r.t the horizontal axis, we copy the output of the noise generator to that pixel. The length, 'L' of the sequence, which the noise generator should generate to construct a square block of circular noise of size $A_b \times A_b$ is:

$$L = 2\pi \sum_{v=0}^{N_m} \left(\left(\frac{A_b}{\sqrt{2}} \right) - v \right) \tag{1}$$

where $N_m = (R - 1)$, and R $= 200/\sqrt{2} \sim 142$ (we use square blocks of each side length $A_b = 200$). This metric is illustrated in Fig. 2b. Radius of the biggest circle is R. Figure 5a shows an example of circular noise pattern. Although Fig. 5 shows only one value of transition probability (0.815), our method in fact adaptively determines this value based on the slope of the BLUT in the current image.

2.3   Curved Markov Gaussian Noise from Circular Pattern

To generate a curved pattern from a circular pattern, we partition the square block of circular noise into four equal-sized *quadrants* or sub-blocks. We process each quadrant as an independent image and choose the same set of points at each quadrant as sites for Voronoi tessellation to generate irregular sized patches, called Voronoi cells (Fig. 6).

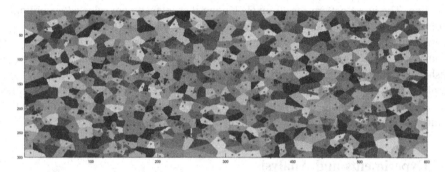

Fig. 6. Voronoi Tessellation of arbitrary matrix with adjacent cells shown in different colors; sites (*): red dots. (Color figure online)

Since Voronoi tessellation is deterministic, we have one-to-one correspondence between the cells in all quadrants with respect to their shapes and sizes. Now, for each cell in each quadrant, we replace its content with that of any randomly selected cell from its corresponding set of four co-located cells across all quadrants. We integrate the quadrants to get the curved pattern block shown in Fig. 5b. The blocks are concatenated to get the noise matrix. Experiments showed that block size of 200 × 200 gave high-quality result, with a typical number of sites $(N_s) = 300$. Note that swapping square or rectangular blocks (instead of Voronoi cells) with each other generates blocky artefacts in curved noise, but randomizing site locations across frames ensures that noise patterns vary smoothly and the video looks more natural.

2.4   Noise Injection and Transition Probability

Noise patterns are generated offline only once and stored. When system boots up, they are loaded to memory. For noise injection, a higher transition probability gives better de-banding effect, but makes the image noisier. We can also increase the variance of noise to get rid of more banding, but making the image noisier at the same time. We define:

$$D = Q + s \cdot N_p \qquad (2)$$

where 's' is the noise variance and N_p is the matrix containing the generated noise pattern. Q is the quantized image with banding artefacts. We inject noise to produce the dithered image D. Noise patterns, fetched from memory, have transition probabilities given by:

$$P_T = \{0.545 + k * 0.045\} \text{ where } k = [0, 1, 2 \ldots 9].$$

An effective way to compute the transitional probability for any given intensity is to use the slope of BLUT, where the intensity is an indication of the potential degree of banding. The noise pattern for all pixels having that intensity are selected accordingly from memory, and blended into the image. Note that wherever the BLUT has a steep slope, adjacent SDR intensities are mapped to HDR intensities, which are far apart from each other. This increases the possibility of banding artefacts in the backward reshaped (HDR) image. Thus, in regions where the banding is more noticeable, we apply higher intra-state transition probability to inject more structured noise. The fine granularity of probabilities in P_T ensures that the aggregated noise pattern applied to the entire quantized image does not have abrupt variations in adjacent regions.

3   Experiments and Analysis

In order to understand the visual impact of banding caused by the SDR-to-HDR conversion, we observed the Y, C_b, and C_r channels in the output images on a 4,000 nits PULSAR HDR display. We created five video sequences[1] and selected 20 scenes from these sequences, with varying degrees of banding and luma intensities, and generated our test dataset of 120 frames (6 frames per scene). User evaluations were conducted by twelve subjects[2], who have computing science or engineering background. Images were randomly selected and shown in pairs on the PULSAR display with the light turned off in the room. Subjects were asked to decide the preferred image, or no preference, and enter the answer using a Google Form. If there was a preference, the subject was asked whether the preferred image was slightly better or much better than the other, and (optionally) whether the preferred image had lesser banding and/or lesser noise than the other. Based on the questionnaire, we could account for human errors when rating the subjective opinions. Five image pairs were shown in different order in each test as per Table 1. To avoid bias, the noise types were not revealed to the subjects. Note that, our proposed method is *adaptive* because it performs BLUT-slope modulated dithering. It does not need to use neighborhood information, which is needed in the traditional adaptive methods. The non-adaptive version of our curved

---

[1] There are no public HDR datasets containing banding.

[2] At least four subjects should be included, per T-REC P.910 (https://www.itu.int/rec/T-REC-P.910/en).

noise technique uses fixed variance and fixed transition probability, but the adaptive version gives a better result.

Table 1. Image pairs displayed randomly to subjects

Test-ID	ImageA	ImageB
Test-1	Simple Gaussian noise	Proposed adaptive method noise
Test-2	Proposed adaptive method noise	Non-adaptive curved noise method
Test-3	Low-Pass filtered Gaussian noise	Proposed adaptive method noise

The subjective opinion scores were assigned these values:

1. If a method is preferred by the subject as "much better than the other method" then it gets a score of +2
2. If a method is preferred by the subject as "slightly better than the other method" then it gets a score of +1
3. In case of "NO preference", both methods get a score of 0.

Test results (Difference of Mean Opinion Scores, or DMOS) are shown in Table 2. Raw subjective scores collected for calculating these DMOS scores are available at: http://webdocs.cs.ualberta.ca/~mukherje/DMOS_RAW.xlsx.

Table 2. DMOS scores from subjective test results

Test-ID	Test-1	Test-2	Test-3
DMOS	1.067	0.717	1.033

The positive DMOS values of the adaptive method are promising. Subjective opinions showed that our method does not cause detrimental side-effect on image quality and the noise patterns generated by our dithering method are perceptually smooth across successive frames, which is important for video delivery.

3.1 Time Performance

We tested the serial implementation of our method in MATLAB running on Windows 10 64-bit, x64-based AMD FX-4350 4.2 GHz CPU, 16 GB RAM PC. We generated a set of Markov-Gaussian noise patterns with different intra-state probability. This offline step is computational intensive (11.79 s), but is done only once, stored and loaded to memory for the online noise injection stage. Adaptively selecting noise pattern, adjusting the noise magnitude and injecting to a 1920×1080 pixels frame takes 4.36 s. Faster performance can be achieved by converting the MATLAB code to a more efficient platform, e.g. C/C++.

4 Conclusion

We propose a pixel-based curved pattern dithering method for SDR-to-HDR conversion. In contrast to traditional methods, our adaptive approach works directly on quantized images without using spatial neighborhood information. Our method is more effective in some computing and/or memory I/O limited environment. Computational expensive noise generation step is performed offline. Subjective tests conducted on HDR display showed that our method de-bands significantly better compared to using other types of Gaussian noise with or without low-pass filter.

References

1. Miller, S., Nezamabadi, M., Daly, S.: Perceptual signal coding for more efficient usage of bit codes. In: Annual Technical Conference Exhibition, pp. 1–9. SMPTE (2012)
2. Reinhard, E., Heidrich, W., Debevec, P., Pattanaik, S., Ward, G., Myszkowski, K.: High Dynamic Range Imaging: Acquisition, Display, and Image-Based Lighting, 2nd edn. Morgan Kaufmann, Burlington (2010)
3. Dufaux, F., Callet, P.L., Mantiuk, R., Mrak, M.: High Dynamic Range Video: From Acquisition, to Display and Applications. Academic Press, New York (2016)
4. Rempel, A.G., et al.: Ldr2Hdr: on-the-fly reverse tone mapping of legacy video and photographs. In: SIGGRAPH. ACM (2007)
5. Banterle, F., Ledda, P., Debattista, K., Chalmers, A.: Inverse tone mapping. In: 4th International Conference on Computer Graphics and Interactive Techniques in Australasia and Southeast Asia, New York, NY, USA, pp. 349–356 (2006)
6. Kuo, P.-H., Tang, C.-S., Chien, S.-Y.: Content-adaptive inverse tone mapping. In: International Conference on Visual Communications and Image Processing (VCIP), pp. 1–6. IEEE (2012)
7. Chen, Q., Su, G.-M., Yin, P.: Near constant-time optimal piecewise LDR to HDR inverse tone mapping. In: SPIE 9404, 94 040O–11 (2015)
8. Gonzalez, R.C., Woods, R.E.: Digital Image Processing, 3rd edn. Pearson, London (2007)
9. Foley, H., Matlin, M.: Sensation and Perception, 5th edn. Psychology Press, London (2009)
10. Nguyen, T.Q., Kay, J., Pasquale, J.: Fast source-based dithering for networked digital video. In: High-Speed Networking and Multimedia Computing. SPIE (1994)
11. Bayer, B.E.: An optimum method for two-level rendition of continuous tone picture. In: International Conference on Communications, pp. (26–11)–(26–15). IEEE (1973)
12. Floyd, R., Steinberg, L.: An adaptive algorithm for spatial gray scale. In: Society for Information Display Symposium Digest of Technical Papers, pp. 36–37 (1975)
13. Foley, J., van Dam, A., Feiner, S., Hughes, J.: Computer Graphics: Principles and Practice, 2nd edn. Addison-Wesley, Boston (1990)
14. Jarvis, J.F., Judice, C.N., Ninke, W.H.: A survey of techniques for the display of continuous tone pictures on bilevel displays. Comput. Graph. Image Process. 5, 13–40 (1976)
15. Judith, J.N., Jarvis, J.F., Ninke, W.: Using ordered dither to display continuous tone pictures on an AC plasma panel. In: Proceedings of the Society for Information Display, Q4, pp. 161–169 (1976)
16. Heckbert, P.: Color image quantization for frame buffer display. Comput. Graph. 16(3), 297–307 (1982)

17. Netravali, A., Haskell, B.G.: Digital Pictures: Representation and Compression. Plenum Press, New York (1988)
18. Roberts, L.G.: Picture coding using pseudo-random noise. IRE Trans. Inf. Theory **8**, 145–154 (1962)
19. Stoffel, J.C., Moreland, J.F.: Survey of electronic techniques for pictorial image reproduction. IEEE Trans. on Commun. **29**(12), 1898–1925 (1981)
20. Ulichney, R.: Digital Halftoning. MIT Press, Cambridge (1987)
21. Ulichney, R.: Video rendering. Digit. Tech. J. **5**(2), 9–18 (1993)
22. Su, G.-M., Chen, T., Yin, P., Qu, S.: Guided post-prediction filtering in layered VDR coding. U.S. Patent 8,897,581 B2 (2014)
23. Su, G.-M., Qu, S., Daly, S.: Adaptive false contouring prevention in layered coding of images with extended dynamic range. U.S. Patent 8,873,877 B2 (2014)
24. Daly, S.J., Feng, X.: Decontouring: prevention and removal of false contour artifacts. In: Proceedings of SPIE, vol. 5292, pp. 130–149. SPIE (2004)
25. Lee, J.W., Lim, B.R., Park, R.-H., Kim, J.-S., Ahn, W.: Two-stage false contour detection using directional contrast and its application to adaptive false contour reduction. IEEE Trans. Consum. Electron. **52**(1), 179–188 (2006)
26. Bhagavathy, S., Llach, J., Zhai, J.: Multi-scale probabilistic dithering for suppressing banding artifacts in digital images. In: International Conference on Image Processing, pp. IV-397–IV-400. IEEE (2007)
27. Huang, Q., Kim, H.Y., Tsai, W.J., Jeong, S.Y., Choi, J.S., Kuo, C.C.J.: Understanding and removal of false contour in HEVC compressed images. IEEE Trans. Circuits Syst. Video Technol. **99**, 1 (2016)
28. Mantiuk, R., Myszkowski, K., Seidel, H.-P.: A perceptual framework for contrast processing of high dynamic range images. ACM Trans. Appl. Percept. **3**(3), 286–308 (2006)
29. Miller, S.: 2017 Update on High Dynamic Range Television. SMPTE Motion Imaging J. **126** (7), 94–96 (2017)
30. Song, Q., Su, G.M., Cosman, P.: Hardware-efficient debanding and visual enhancement filter for inverse tone mapped high dynamic range images and videos. In: International Conference on Image Processing. IEEE (2016)

Visual Behavior Analysis: Methods and Applications

A Flexible Method for Time-of-Flight Camera Calibration Using Random Forest

Chi Xu[1,2] and Cheng Li[3,4(✉)]

[1] School of Automation, China University of Geosciences, Wuhan 430074, China
[2] Hubei Key Laboratory of Advanced Control and Intelligent Automation
for Complex Systems, Wuhan 430074, China
xuchi@cug.edu.cn
[3] Bioinformatics Institute, A*STAR, Singapore 138671, Singapore
chengli@bii.a-star.edu.sg
[4] Department of Electrical and Computer Engineering, University of Alberta,
Edmonton, Canada

Abstract. A learning based approach is proposed to calibrate the geometric distortion of a Time-of-Flight (ToF) camera. Our method is flexible as it requires only a ToF camera and a standard camera calibration chessboard. We treat the noise model of a ToF camera as a black box, and employ random forest to automatically learn the underlying unique noise model. The geometric property of the point-cloud can be effectively restored by the learned distortion model. The method can be used in a range of computer vision applications including e.g. hand pose estimation.

Keywords: ToF camera · Calibration · Random forest

1 Introduction

Commodity-level Time-of-Flight (ToF) cameras become increasingly important in a wide range of computer vision applications including hand pose estimation [25], video matting [26], and 3D scene analysis, among others. ToF camera produces a depth image at a time, where each pixel value encodes the distance to the corresponding 3D point in the scene. Usually, a ToF camera has been pre-calibrated by the manufacturer [1], where the calibration process will consider len distortion, distance deviation, as well as temperature drift. Ideally this calibration will enable the apparatus readily to be used as a precise 3D sensor. Unfortunately, the processed images are still not accurate enough for many computer vision applications. As illustrated in Figs. 1 and 5, noticeable geometric

This work was supported by the Fundamental Research Funds for Central Universities, China University of Geosciences (Wuhan) (No. CUG170692), by the National Natural Science Foundation of China under Grants 61876170, and by the R&D project 2018GY121 of CRRC Zhuzhou Locomotive Co., Ltd.

© Springer Nature Switzerland AG 2018
A. Basu and S. Berretti (Eds.): ICSM 2018, LNCS 11010, pp. 207–218, 2018.
https://doi.org/10.1007/978-3-030-04375-9_18

distortion of up to around 30 mm is often observed, which becomes more severe when working with relative small objects such as human hands. The situation is further compromised by the fact that an end user can only access to the processed depth images while the raw data is usually unavailable, as is typical with other consumer electronics.

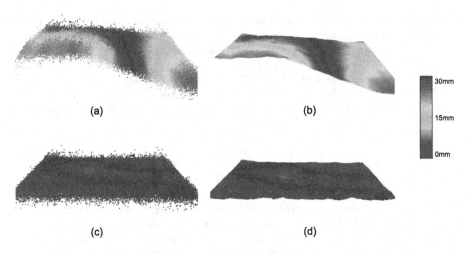

Fig. 1. (a) The point-cloud of a flat plane captured by a ToF camera. Significant geometric distortion and white noise can be observed. (b) The white noise is removed by a Gaussian filter. (c) The geometry of the point-cloud is restored after calibration, and (d) the smoothed result. The color denotes the measure of geometric distortion. (Color figure online)

In this work, we directly address this problem with a particular emphasis on enabling the follow-up computer vision applications. In other words, we aim at directly calibrating the processed ToF depth images as provided by the manufacturer. Another implication is that the calibrated depth image is expected to preserve local geometric and topological properties of the scene objects, e.g. to retain the 3D shape of a hand or the flatness of a chessboard, which are crucial for computer vision tasks. The calibration procedure needs to be fast and simple, so the camera can be mobile and easily used in different settings. As a trade-off, it is acceptable for a calibrated depth image to be less precise in term of its global 3D locations.

With the above context in mind, we propose a learning-based approach using random forest to calibrate the ToF depth images. The main contributions of our approach are two-folds: (1) Our approach is flexible and requires as input only a short video of placing the classic calibration chessboard as multiple 3D spaces. It is also efficient, and easy to use. (2) Random forest is used in camera calibration. It enables us to learn from empirical observations the complex geometric distortion model of the ToF camera without prior assumptions on the model.

Specifically, we note that this model is naturally treated as a black box in our context for the following reasons: The raw data is unavailable to the end user, while we only have access to a depth image processed through a proprietary pre-calibration; The structure of the underlying distortion model is complex and nonhomogeneous; For a non-expert user, it is difficult to construct a proper model from the working principle of a particular ToF camera.

It is worth-mentioning that learning-based methods have been used to process ToF images. For example, a boosting-based learning method has been used in [22] to super-resolve ToF images, and a random forest based method is used in [19] to obtain a better confidence map.

1.1   Related Work

ToF cameras are known to contain multiple sources of noises [8] which collectively distort the 3D distance measurements as presented in its depth image. Some of the noise sources systematically distort the optical ray directions and/or the measured depths, including noises that introduced by IR demodulation, integration time, amplitude ambiguity, or temperature drift. They are the main focus of ToF calibration. To model these distortions, Lindner and Kolb [16] used uniform B-splines, while a polynomial model is used by Schiller et al. in [20]. Similarly, Kahlmann et al. [12] measured the distortions which are subsequently stored as look-up tables (LUTs). Kim et al. [13] also present an approach to correct these distortions. Importantly, it has been shown in Cui et al. [4] that the depth distortion of ToF cameras is in fact *scene dependant*. As a result, it is necessary to calibrate a ToF camera for every new scene. Furthermore, it is also crucial to obtain ground-truth 3D locations to facilitate the camera calibration process. To address this issue, a multi-spline model was proposed by Fuchs and Hirzinger in [7] where a robotic arm is utilized to provide precise 3D measurements. In [28] the depth from stereo and ToF cameras was fused using the triangulation from the stereo cameras as ground truth. In [18], a convolutional neural network to correct multipath interference error. In [11] a 2.5D pattern board with irregularly placed holes is used for calibration, and the range error profiles along the calibrated distance are classified according to their wiggling shapes. In [24] a fast solution is proposed to calibrate the geometric relationships across an arbitrary number of RGB-D cameras on a network.

We note in the passing that there are however a few noise sources [8] that will not be addressed by the calibration process discussed in our context, and the affected measurements are thus regarded as outliers. These sources include the so called flying pixels that mostly presented around the object boundaries, as well as noises due to motion blur or intensity values.

2   Our Approach

To form a depth pixel value in a ToF depth image, its corresponding IR (Infrared) ray is projected onto the surface of the 3D object, with its reflected light being

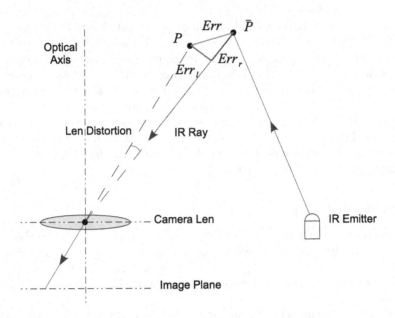

Fig. 2. The measurement error of a ToF camera Err (shown in green) between the real position $\bar{P}$ and the measured position P can be decomposed into two components: The len distortion error Err$_l$ (denoted in red) caused by the camera len that distorts the IR ray direction; meanwhile, the depth distortion error along this IR ray Err$_r$ is illustrated in blue. (Color figure online)

detected by the sensor. By measuring the phase difference between the radiated and reflected IR waves, the distance from the point on object to the camera is thus calculated.

As illustrated in Fig. 2, the measurement error of a 3D point is the distance between its real position and the estimated position. This error can be decomposed into two components: (1) the len distortion error Err$_l$ (denoted as red) caused by camera len which distorts the direction of the IR ray. (2) the depth distortion error along the IR ray Err$_r$ (denoted as blue). This facilitates us to devise separate calibration processes to address each of the error components, as follows.

2.1   Len Distortion

The len distortion can be readily calibrated by a standard toolbox in OpenCV library [2] based on the work of Zhang [27]. We just briefly describe the len distortion model here. The len distortion includes radial and tangential factors. Commonly, it is modelled as a 4th order polynomial, i.e.

$$\begin{cases} x_d = x(1 + k_1 r^2 + k_2 r^4) + 2p_1 xy + p_2(r^2 + 2x^2) \\ y_d = y(1 + k_1 r^2 + k_2 r^4) + 2p_2 xy + p_1(r^2 + 2y^2) \end{cases}, \tag{1}$$

where (x, y) are normalized image coordinate, (x_d, y_d) are distorted image coordinate, $r^2 = x^2 + y^2$, (k_1, k_2) are radial distortion parameters, and (p_1, p_2) are tangential distortion parameters. Normally, the tangential factor is negligible.

2.2 Depth Distortion

The geometric distortion of a ToF camera is primarily caused by the distortion on depth direction, the main focus of our approach. The calibration of depth distortion is addressed by utilizing a regression random forest model.

Training Data Collection. Our learning based approach demands the collection of training data. It can be conveniently collected by placing a standard calibration chessboard in front of a ToF camera from different positions and orientations, which results in a video that contains about 150 depth images and the corresponding confidence maps. $1.6M$ pixels are then randomly selected from these captured training images, where each pixel is considered as a training example. We wold like to emphasize that our data collection phase is simple and easy to be carried out by a non-expert, as it involves only a ToF camera and a printed chessboard.

The displacement from the measured depth to the real depth is used as the annotation or label of its training instance. In other words, the annotation of a pixel is defined as $y := \bar{d} - d$, where $\bar{d}$ is the real depth at the pixel, and d is the measured depth. The ground-truth of $\bar{d}$ is obtained by solving a Perspective-n-point problem (PnP) [15] using the key-points of a chessboard: Key-points are extracted from the confidence map. The 3D position and orientation of the chessboard plane can be solved by a PnP solver. Then the depth value $\bar{d}$ is obtained by the intersection of the projection ray of the pixel and the 3D calibration plane. In our experiment, the resolution of the ToF camera is 320×240, and experimental results show that the ground-truth is accurate enough for an effective calibration.

Random Forest. A random forest, in particular a regression forest, is an ensemble of regression decision trees, which maps high dimensional input space into a simpler continuous output space [3]. Each decision tree is built from a set of annotated training examples. Starting from the root, the tree is recursively constructed by selecting a binary test at each non-leaf node, called the split node. According to the result of the test, the training patches are distributed to either the left or the right child.

Binary Test. The feature of a pixel is defined as $x := (u, v, d, c)$, where (u, v) are the 2D image coordinates, d is the measured depth value, and c is the confidence value in the confidence map. The binary test is simply defined as

$$test(f, t) = \begin{cases} 1 & x(f) > t \\ 0 & \text{otherwise} \end{cases},$$

where f is the index of the feature, and t is a randomly selected threshold.

Split Criteria. The accuracy of a random forest is closely related to the split criteria in use. Similar to those in [5,6], at every split node, we select a random subset of features $\mathcal{F} := \{f_i\}_{i=1}^s$, and for each feature selected, a set of candidate thresholds $\mathcal{T} := \{t_j\}_{j=1}^T$ are further generated. Let $\mathcal{I}(f,t)$ denote the information gain, as:

$$\mathcal{I}(f,t) = |S|\,H(S) - \sum_{k \in \{l,r\}} |S_k|\,H(S_k), \qquad (2)$$

where $|\cdot|$ counts the set size, S is the set of training examples arriving at the current node, which is split into two subsets S_l and S_r according to the $test(f,t)$ and $H(\cdot)$ denotes the standard Shannon entropy [3]. The best test (f^*,t^*) is chosen from these s features and accompanying t thresholds by maximizing the information gain:

$$(f^*,t^*) = \arg \max_{f \in \mathcal{F}, t \in \mathcal{T}} \mathcal{I}(f,t). \qquad (3)$$

The first term of Eq. (2) is fixed, so maximizing the information gain leads to minimizing the sum of the entropies from its child trees, which can be interpreted as the pursuit of more compact clusters in the course of tree constructions.

3   Experiments

Experimental Setup: Without loss of generality, a near range ToF camera Softkinetic DS325 is used in our experiments. The resolution of the camera is 320×240, and the diagonal field-of-view is $87°$. The working distance of the camera is from $150\,mm$ to $1000\,mm$ [1], which provides the working range of our calibration. Consider a pixel of the depth image, and let P denote the estimated 3D position, and $\bar{P}$ its real position. The depth error metric is defined as $\mathrm{Err} = ||P - \bar{P}||_2$, i.e. the Euclidean distance between the two points. Test dataset contains 120 unseen test images, where the ground-truths are obtained in the same manner as described in Sect. 2.2.

Table 1. The depth error of the compared methods (unit is mm).

	Mean	Median	Std.
Raw data	20.1813	18.2874	13.1291
Lindner et al. [17]	14.3707	12.1679	11.2198
Ours	8.94757	6.39804	9.17156

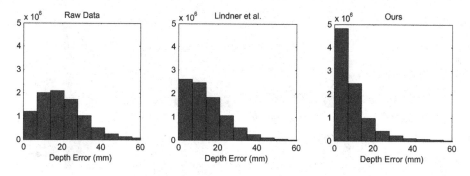

Fig. 3. The distribution of the depth error.

Accuracy: The depth errors of the competing methods are shown in Table 1. We compare our method to the wigging compensation method of Lindner et al. [17], a well known method for ToF camera calibration. The depth error of the raw data is also included here to establish a baseline. The method of [17] reduces the mean error from 20.2 mm to 14.4 mm, while our method considerably reduces the mean error down to 9.9 mm. The distributions of the depth error are also plotted in Fig. 3. Clearly, the depth error of the raw data primarily distributed in range [10 30] mm, which is primarily in range [0 20] mm for [17], and further down to [0 10] mm in our approach. This convincingly demonstrates the effectiveness of our learning based approach in depth error reduction. Meanwhile, as displayed in Fig. 1, the geometric distortion of the point-cloud can be effectively removed by our approach. Note that the error of the calibrated depth map is primary due to the white noise of the CMOS sensor whose standard deviation is 9.17 mm. In Fig. 1, the flat plane looks like a thick blanket in the point-cloud because of the white noise of ToF sensor.

Table 2. The depth error of our approach at different camera-object distances (unit is mm).

Distance	250	400	550	700	850	1000
Mean	6.2380	7.1962	8.6373	9.4522	9.5263	9.5306
Median	4.6765	5.3411	6.1458	6.5416	6.5706	6.5716
Std.	6.5852	7.1768	8.9960	10.0418	10.1488	10.1580

Distance: The estimation error of our method at different distances are shown in Table 2. When the distance form the target to the camera is 250 mm, the mean depth error is 6.2 mm. When the distance increases, the estimation error increases as well. The nearer the target to the camera is, the more accurate the estimation result is.

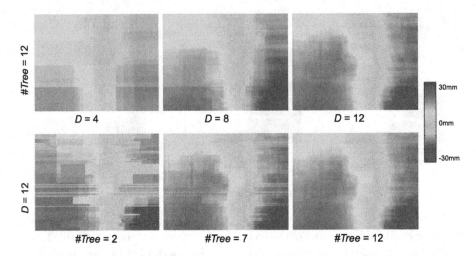

Fig. 4. The estimated distortion pattern varies with respect to the parameters of the random forest. In which "#$Tree$" denotes the number of trees in forest, and "D" denotes the depth of the tree. The slice of the distortion pattern is taken at distance 200 mm.

Table 3. The mean depth error varies with respect to two parameters of the random forest, i.e. the depth of tree (D) and the number of trees in the forest (#$Tree$). The unit of the depth error is mm.

#Tree	Depth of tree (D)					
	3	6	9	12	15	18
2	11.7176	10.4085	9.5966	9.1324	9.2395	9.1452
4	11.5214	9.9856	9.5349	8.9851	9.0726	9.0387
6	11.0451	9.7783	9.3518	8.9656	8.9995	9.0204
8	10.9337	9.7072	9.2873	8.9712	8.9929	9.0310
10	10.6910	9.6385	9.2427	8.9640	8.9628	9.0015
12	10.7243	9.6219	9.2032	**8.9476**	8.9436	8.9818
14	10.6035	9.6095	9.1921	8.9484	8.9359	8.9634
16	10.8630	9.6834	9.2375	8.9820	8.9559	8.9626
18	10.8635	9.7706	9.2246	8.9829	8.9529	8.9527
20	10.7632	9.7601	9.2310	8.9787	8.9449	8.9464

Parameters of the Forest: The random forest has two important parameters, i.e. the depth of tree (D), and the number of trees in the forest (#$Tree$). The mean depth error of our method are shown in Table 3 by varying these two parameters. When the depth of tree increases, the accuracy of random forest increases accordingly. When the depth of tree reaches 12, the performance stops increasing. Therefore, we set $D = 12$ in our experiments. The more trees in the forest, the better the performance is. $\#Tree = 12$ is a good trade-off between performance and complexity,

The estimated geometric distortion pattern also varies with respect to these two parameters (see Fig. 4). Depth of tree (D) is closely related to the resolution of the estimation. The deeper the tree is, the more details can be discovered by the forest. $\#Tree$ is closely related to the stability of the estimation. When $\#Tree = 2$, the estimated pattern is very noisy. But the stability of the estimation result can be effectively improved when $\#Tree = 12$.

Execution Time: The experiments are performed on a normal desktop computer with Intel i7 CPU. As the random forest contains 12 trees, our method is not real-time, and it takes 395 ms to calibrate one image. This can nevertheless be solved by saving the estimated geometric distortion patterns into a LUT, where the efficiency can be improved to 5 ms per frame. Moreover, our method is memory efficient. The size of each tree is less then 50 KB, and the size of the LUT is 16 MB.

Application: One useful application of our method is hand pose estimation. As in Fig. 5, the geometric distortion of ToF camera will affect the estimation accuracy of hand pose. As the distortion is non-linear, the displacement of different fingers may be different, and the angle between the two fingers is also affected as can be seen in Fig. 5(c).

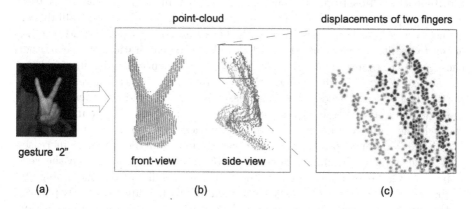

Fig. 5. (a) The hand gesture "2" in confidence map, (b) the point-clouds in the front-view and the side-view, (c) a zoomed in window of the two fingers. The blue points denote the point-cloud of the raw data, and the brown points denote the calibrated result. In (c) the displacement of the left finger is much bigger than that of the right finger because the geometric distortion of ToF camera is non-linear. Note that the angle between the two fingers is also changed by the distortion. (Color figure online)

4 Discussion

Distortion Pattern: The geometric distortion pattern of the softkinetic ToF camera is irregular in 3D space. A series of estimated distortion patterns are shown in Fig. 6 as we take slices at several different distances along the optical axis of the camera. It is reported in [10] that, the geometric distortion pattern of kinect is approximately radical. This model works very well for kinect like depth cameras, and their toolbox is widely used by the community. But we found that the radical distortion assumption does not hold in ToF cameras such as softkinetic.

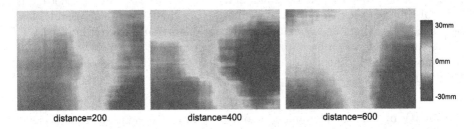

Fig. 6. The geometric distortion patterns at different distances along the optical axis of the camera.

Calibration Chessboard: Standard camera calibration chessboard is used in both steps of our method. In the step of camera len distortion calibration, we use a chessboard contains 7×5 grids, because more key-points lead to more accurate result. In the second step of depth distortion calibration, we use another chessboard contains only 4×3 grids. Since the confidence map is dim when the chessboard is far from the camera, the less grids are used, the more stably the pattern can be recognized. That is the reason we use less grids. Readers may find more details about chessboard detection of ToF camera in [9]. One may wonder that whether the accuracy will be reduced with less key-points. Actually, 12 key-points are enough to produce accurate estimation, and the accuracy increases very little with more than 12 key-points [15]. It is noted that, when the key-points are planar or quasi singular, the PnP solver suffers from the ambiguity problem [15,23]. This problem is serious when the plane is approximately parallel to the camera image plane. It is suggested that this orientation in data collection should be avoided. When the angle between the chessboard and the camera image plane exceeds $10°$, the PnP solver could stably find out a global minimum by verifying local minima.

Other Noise Source: This work primarily focuses on the geometric distortion of the ToF camera. The ToF camera also contains many other noise sources, such as: (1) flying pixel [14], (2) temperature drift [21], and (3) intensity related error [17]. These noises can be dealt with independently. A large amount of dedicated researches focus on these error sources, and these issues are not included in the scope of this paper.

5 Conclusion

A new method is proposed to calibrate the geometric distortion of ToF camera using random forest. As the distortion pattern of ToF camera is complex and irregular, random forest is a powerful tool to discover the geometric distortion model. The proposed method is flexible, and the calibration process needs only a ToF camera and a standard chessboard. The training data is collected by observing the chessboard from different viewpoints and distances, and it can be easily performed by a non-expert user. The proposed method can be helpful to improve the accuracy of computer vision applications using ToF camera.

References

1. Softkinetic (2012). http://www.softkinetic.com
2. Bradski, G.: The OpenCV library. Doct. Dobbs J. **25**(11), 120–126 (2000)
3. Breiman, L.: Random forests. Mach. Learn. **45**(1), 5–32 (2001)
4. Cui, Y., Schuon, S., Chan, D., Thrun, S., Theobalt, C.: 3D shape scanning with a time-of-flight camera. In: CVPR (2010)
5. Denil, M., Matheson, D., de Freitas, N.: Narrowing the gap: random forests in theory and practice. In: ICML (2014)
6. Fanelli, G., Gall, J., Van Gool, L.: Real time head pose estimation with random regression forests. In: CVPR (2011)
7. Fuchs, S., Hirzinger, G.: Extrinsic and depth calibration of ToF-cameras. In: CVPR (2008)
8. Hansard, M., Lee, S., Choi, O., Horaud, R.: Time-of-Flight Cameras: Principles, Methods and Applications. Springer, London (2013). https://doi.org/10.1007/978-1-4471-4658-2
9. Hansard, M., Horaud, R., Amat, M., Evangelidis, G.: Automatic detection of calibration grids in time-of-flight images. Comput. Vis. Image Underst. **121**, 108–118 (2014)
10. Herrera, C., Kannala, J., Heikkilä, J., et al.: Joint depth and color camera calibration with distortion correction. IEEE TPAMI **34**(10), 2058–2064 (2012)
11. Jung, J., Lee, J.Y., Jeong, Y., Kweon, I.S.: Time-of-flight sensor calibration for a color and depth camera pair. IEEE Trans. Pattern Anal. Mach. Intell. **37**(7), 1501–1513 (2015)
12. Kahlmann, T., Remondino, F., Ingensand, H.: Calibration for increased accuracy of the range imaging camera SwissRangerTM. Image Eng. Vis. Metrol. (IEVM) **36**(3), 136–141 (2006)
13. Kim, Y.M., Chan, D., Theobalt, C., Thrun, S.: Design and calibration of a multi-view TOF sensor fusion system. In: CVPR Workshops (2008)
14. Lenzen, F., et al.: Denoising strategies for time-of-flight data. In: Grzegorzek, M., Theobalt, C., Koch, R., Kolb, A. (eds.) Time-of-Flight and Depth Imaging. Sensors, Algorithms, and Applications. LNCS, vol. 8200, pp. 25–45. Springer, Heidelberg (2013). https://doi.org/10.1007/978-3-642-44964-2_2

15. Li, S., Xu, C., Xie, M.: A robust O(n) solution to the perspective-n-point problem. IEEE Trans. Pattern Anal. Mach. Intell. **34**(7), 1444–1450 (2012)

16. Lindner, M., Kolb, A.: Calibration of the intensity-related distance error of the PMD ToF-camera. In: Optics East, p. 67640W. International Society for Optics and Photonics (2007)

17. Lindner, M., Schiller, I., Kolb, A., Koch, R.: Time-of-flight sensor calibration for accurate range sensing. Comput. Vis. Image Underst. **114**(12), 1318–1328 (2010)

18. Marco, J., et al.: DeepToF: off-the-shelf real-time correction of multipath interference in time-of-flight imaging. ACM Trans. Graph. **36**(6), 1–12 (2017)

19. Reynolds, M., Dobos, J., Peel, L., Weyrich, T., Brostow, G.: Capturing time-of-flight data with confidence. In: CVPR (2011)

20. Schiller, I., Beder, C., Koch, R.: Calibration of a PMD-camera using a planar calibration pattern together with a multi-camera setup. Int. Arch. Photogramm. Remote Sens. Spat. Inf. Sci. **37**, 297–302 (2008)

21. Schmidt, M.: Analysis, modeling and dynamic optimization of 3D time-of-flight imaging systems. Ph.D. thesis, Univ. Heidelberg (2011)

22. Schuon, S., Theobalt, C., Davis, J., Thrun, S.: LidarBoost: depth superresolution for ToF 3D shape scanning. In: CVPR (2009)

23. Schweighofer, G., Pinz, A.: Robust pose estimation from a planar target. IEEE Trans. Pattern Anal. Mach. Intell. **28**(12), 2024–2030 (2006)

24. Su, P.C., Shen, J., Xu, W., Cheung, S.S., Luo, Y.: A fast and robust extrinsic calibration for RGB-D camera networks? Sensors **18**(1), 235 (2018)

25. Tang, D., Chang, H., Tejani, A., Kim, T.K.: Latent regression forest: structured estimation of 3D articulated hand posture. In: CVPR (2014)

26. Wang, L., Gong, M., Zhang, C., Yang, R., Zhang, C., Yang, Y.H.: Automatic real-time video matting using time-of-flight camera and multichannel poisson equations. IJCV **97**(1), 104–21 (2012)

27. Zhang, Z.: A flexible new technique for camera calibration. IEEE TPAMI **22**(11), 1330–1334 (2000)

28. Zhu, J., Wang, L., Yang, R., Davis, J.: Fusion of time-of-flight depth and stereo for high accuracy depth maps. In: CVPR (2008)

A Survey on Vision-Based Hand Gesture Recognition

Taiqian Wang[1], Yande Li[1], Junfeng Hu[2], Aamir Khan[2], Li Liu[2(✉)], Caihong Li[1], Ammarah Hashmi[3], and Mengyuan Ran[2]

[1] School of Information Science and Engineering, Lanzhou University, Lanzhou 730000, China
{wangtq16,liyd2016,licaihong}@lzu.edu.cn
[2] School of Software Engineering, Chongqing University, Chongqing 401331, China
{junfenghu,dcsliuli}@cqu.edu.cn, amir@gmail.com, 1174099667@qq.com
[3] School of Software Engineering, Beijing Institute of Technology, Beijing 100080, China
1995ammarahhashmi@gmail.com

Abstract. Hand gesture recognition is regarded as an important part of artificial intelligence. A great effort was put into human-computer interaction so that hand gesture recognition is gradually becoming a developed technology. In light of the utilization of mouse and keyboard, the increasing needs of human-computer interaction cannot be met; hindrance turns out to be increasingly genuine. In this paper, we reviewed previous investigations of vision-based gesture recognition and summarized their findings. This paper compares the most common human-computer interaction products in recent years, which can be used to capture gesture data. Then we started with the classification of gestures and summarized the research of visual gesture recognition based on static and dynamic gestures. The gesture representations we summarized includes appearance-based and 3D model-based methods. We also introduced the applications of the two kinds of hand gestures recognition in the papers of recent years. A possible classification methods was put forward to improve the performance of gesture recognition. The goal of this paper is to summarize the current technology and research results and compare the differences and the advantage of different hand gesture recognition methods, which will contribute to the following research.

Keywords: Interaction products · Hand gesture recognition
Gesture representation · Application · Classification

1 Introduction

The information society is evolving rapidly. Although the common human-computer interaction devices we use at present (such as mouse and keyboard) offer us an approach to interact with electronic products, we are trying to find

© Springer Nature Switzerland AG 2018
A. Basu and S. Berretti (Eds.): ICSM 2018, LNCS 11010, pp. 219–231, 2018.
https://doi.org/10.1007/978-3-030-04375-9_19

a better way to use these devices, which brings us less hinder and fewer restrictions. Then, an efficient way named hand gesture recognition [10] appears. Hand gesture recognition has two main research directions [2]. Human-computer interaction devices such as smart home devices and somatosensory devices came into our lives and bring us different experiences. The use of hands can let us communicate with a computer more intuitively.

Contrasted with whatever is left of the body, hands assume an essential part to communicate. Both vision-based and contact-based types of researches about hand gesture recognition [33] have been achieved in a specific environment. This paper presents and contrasts previous articles on the survey of gesture recognition. Many articles have been published for a few years and lack the summary of the latest research. Whether it is a new survey article or an old survey article the common feature is that the introduction of visual gesture recognition is very comprehensive, and each technical point has a detailed summary.

Likewise, there are a few issues with these past surveys. For example, the study of gestures does not have statistics based on categories, the correspondence between gesture categories, classification techniques and technical application is not clear, the common gestures recognized in references are not summarized. These problems are the main goals of this paper, which will make researchers choosing more appropriate techniques in a specific scene and offer some advice to improve the performance of the technology.

In this paper, we cut our topic in the classification of gesture and investigated the common methods and applications. Section 2 provides related work, which includes previous surveys of hand gesture recognition, the implementation of gesture recognition, the products of human-computer interaction. Section 3 presents the details about gesture recognition. In Sect. 4, the recognition of static hand gesture is discussed. Section 5 presents dynamic hand gesture recognition. Section 6 provides the applications of hand gesture recognition. Section 7 discusses future perspectives for hand gesture recognition. Section 8 summarizes the survey.

2 Related Work

Before doing our survey, we did a related work about hand gesture recognition, which made us to determine the direction of our work. The main content of this section is to summarize the previous survey, the implementation and the productions of hand gesture recognition.

In order to solve limitation, real-time, robustness of a hand gesture recognition application, researchers face a lot of difficulties [23]. In terms of vision-based hand gesture recognition, the operation is more likely to be affected by the surrounding environment in comparison with contact based human-hand gesture recognition. Because of its limitation of equipment design, contact based hand gesture recognition needs to think much more of the wearer's sense of experience. To some extent, the two research directions of human-hand gesture recognition both have their merits and demerits, which are summarized in Table 1.

As far as feasibility is concerned, vision-based hand gesture recognition is a hotter and more difficult research direction compared with contact-based hand gesture recognition. Some different approaches were tested by researchers for vision based recognition. Enumerate previous related statistics as Table 2.

Table 1. A contrast between vision-devices and contact-devices.

Criterion	Comfortable	Healthy	Accurate	Robust	Flexible (use)	Flexible (configure)
Vision-devices	✓	✓	✓		✓	
Vision-devices			✓	✓		✓

Table 2. Some analysis from the surveys of the previous people.

Ref.	Published year	Scope of analysis	Key findings
Chaudhary et al. [3]	2011	Comprehensive review of nearly 50 papers which focuses on the soft computing such. Focusing on human computer interaction. Dividing approaches of image treating	Soft computing such as fuzzy logic, artificial neural network offers a way to define new a uncertain thing. Fingertip detection and joints of hand detection have been used by researchers
Suarez and Murphy [28]	2012	A survey of 37 papers which discusses depth-based gesture recognition systems. Hand localization, gesture classification	Find two methods for segmentation, three methods for tracking, and five method for classification. The release of the Kinect turns the focus of depth-based gesture recognition to application
Rautaray and Agrawal [23]	2012	A survey focusing on the detection, tracking, recognition, the three main steps of hand gesture recognition [23]. Analysis of the existing gesture recognition system	The techniques of hand gesture recognition are sensitive to environmental factors. Some efficient systems to overcome current technical defects
Hasan and Abdul-Kareem [8]	2013	Discussion on different application areas. Reviews of human computer interaction (HCI). Presentation about static and dynamic hand gesture recognition	Representations of appearance -based gesture are better recognized than 3D-based gesture

(continued)

Table 2. (*continued*)

Ref.	Published year	Scope of analysis	Key findings
Lad [16]	2013	Paper reviews application fields of real time hand gesture recognition. Feature extraction, classification. Static background	Neural network can be well used to control some devices in compound background. The presented system in their paper can categorize different simple hand gestures
Ruffieux et al. [25]	2014	A comprehensive survey on datasets creation of gesture recognition field. Proposing selection and creation of datasets when recognize a gesture	The available datasets in hand gesture recognition. Presenting the potential usage of the datasets. The lack of information in most reviewed datasets
Itkarkar and Nandi [11]	2016	Comprehensive review 2D and 3D imaging techniques in hand gesture recognition. Real-time application [11]. Rate of recognition. Limitations in gesture recognition	Vision-based gesture recognition is better than contact based gesture recognition when make a gesture. Precision and performance of the system may be different when the device becomes a product for different customers

Many people may think of the advanced somatosensory devices such as Kinect [15,18] and RealSense, which are based on image sensors [17,35]. Although combined with advanced technology, the two devices have a very strict requirement for the environment when we use them, which will affects the user's experience to some extent. Utilizing pressure is the hardest to acknowledge as a result of that the diverse pressure between individuals' qualities is too huge. The image sensing based somatosensory devices such as Leap Motion and Kinect and EMG sensor [36] devices based gesture recognition system [4] gradually entered the public view, which promoted the development of these techniques. We did a survey about the hand gesture recognition products that appeared in recent years. The comparison about these products appears as Table 3.

In specific implementation of gesture recognition, there are generally three ways: EMG, light sensation and pressure. Comparison of three ways of hand gesture recognitions realization from three dimensions: power consumption, environmental sensitivity and recognition difficulty are shown as follows in Table 4.

From the point of view of existing products, the experience of them isn't sufficient. Hand gesture recognition technology also has a long way to go. Following paper discusses vision-based hand gesture recognition based on gesture classification and presents the application of gesture recognition.

Table 3. Comparison of human-computer interaction products

Product	Kinect	RealSense	Leap motion	MYO
Wear way	Put it on the plane. A limited distance	Put it on the plane. A limited distance	Put it on the plane. A limited distance	Wear it on the wrist
Tracking detection	Multiplayer or object	Hands, fingers, face and object	Hands or fingers	Wrist muscle movement
Implementation method	Light sensation	Light sensation	Light sensation	EMG
SDK support	Yes	Yes	Yes	Yes
Developing documents	Adequate	Medium/adequate	Adequate	Adequate
Advantages and disadvantages	The precision of gesture recognition is not high	Multi function	High finger recognition. Only can recognize the movement of hands	It's not affected by the environment, but it needs to be worn

Table 4. Comparison between the three recognition methods.

Criterion	Power consumption	Environmental sensitivity	Recognition difficulty
EMG	Medium	Medium	Low
Light sensation	High	High	Medium
Pressure	Low	Low	High

3 Review of Gesture Recognition

Detection, tracking and recognition consist of the three parts of hand gesture recognition techniques. The techniques of vision based hand gesture recognition are shown in Fig. 1. In terms of vision-based recognition, we have static and dynamic gesture [32,34] recognition to discuss in this paper. The recognition process [27] can be generally divided into two steps, one is the feature extraction stage, the other is the classification stage. Figure 2. shows the progress of the phases of hand gesture recognition.

3.1 Gesture Representations

The gestures that we collected by somatosensory devices and so on have two kinds of representations: appearance-based and 3D model-based methods [1]. Motion-based methods and 2D static model-based methods are the two subcategories of appearance-based gesture representation methods. The common applications of two dimensional model are deformable gabarit-based models, color based model and silhouette geometry-based models, which are the variants of two dimensional model.

Vision-based 2D recognition system has three steps such as segmentation [11], feature extraction and recognition. 2D based static model uses appearance-based hand gesture representation strategies. 2D based static methods use tags to track motion and contour geometry.

3D geometric model, 3D skeleton model and 3D textured volumetric model are the three different techniques of three-dimensional model [1, 19]. Gesture representation based on 3D model defines three dimensional spatial descriptions of human hands through automated time representation. The timing characteristics of gestures are divided into pre stroke stage, stroke stage and post stroke stage by the automatization.

3.2   Hand Gesture Recognition Techniques

Static gesture recognition always use linear classifier and non-linear classifier, and the techniques of dynamic gesture recognition consists of Time Delay Neural Network, Dynamic Time Warping, Finite State Machine, Hidden Markov Model (HMM) and the common methods Convolutional Neural Network (CNN). We found that the most commonly used gesture recognition methods in the papers are HMM, SVM, CNN, etc.

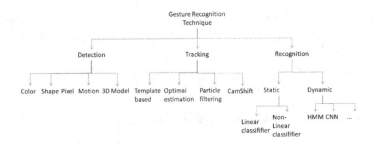

Fig. 1. Vision-based gesture recognition techniques

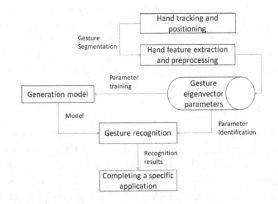

Fig. 2. Flow chart based on static visual gesture recognition system

4   A Survey on the Research of Static Hand Gesture

The hand gesture that researchers always use in their experiment consists of the two kinds of the gestures. Based on 2D color image recognition technology, the focus of early gesture recognition is static gesture. Static gesture recognition [11] identifies the shape features by a gesture at a time point, which doesnt observe the movement of hands.

Vision-based hand gesture recognition should meet three prerequisites, which includes robustness, accuracy and real-time. Previous static gesture recognition using two-dimensional gesture recognition technology is equivalent to put gestures on a plane, which can express very limited meaning, such as OK and numbers.

Researchers pay more attention to the application and improvement of classification algorithm to improve hand gesture recognition in accuracy and robustness. In Table 5, there is a survey we did about the researches on static hand gesture recognition, which is based on vision.

Table 5. Researches on static hand gesture

Ref.	Technique	Gesture number	Dataset (recognition of gesture)	Limitation	Average accuracy
Trigueiros et al. [31]	SVM	25 hand gestures	Portuguese sign language (A, B, C, D, etc.)	Camera is the limitation	99.4%
Tang [29]	DBN, CNN, HOG + SVM	36 hand gestures	Hand posture for American sign language (1, 2, 3, 4, A, B, etc.)	Without specific requirements on uniform-colored or stable background	DBN (98.12%), CNN (94.17%), HOG + SVM (87.58%), device (Kinect)
Naguri and Bunescu [22]	CNN	Six types of hand gestures	Custom gesture dataset recorded by a Leap Motion (circle, swipe, correct, etc.)	Limits of scope	F-measure (97.0%) device (Leap Motion)
Tewari et al. [30]	CNN + RNN	5 hand gestures	60000 sample of labelled images of five pose classes (up, down, etc.)	Limits of images. The self-occlusion of the hand.	88.80% device (Kinect)

(continued)

Table 5. (*continued*)

Ref.	Technique	Gesture number	Dataset (recognition of gesture)	Limitation	Average accuracy
Devineau [5]	CNN	14 hand gestures/28 hand gestures	DHG dataset from the SHREC 2017 3D shape retrieval contest (grab, tab, swipe, left, etc.)	Limits of scope	91.28%/84.35%
Gao et al. [7]	CNN	24 hand gestures	The ASL database (A, B, C, etc.)	Changing illumination and complicated background	93.3%

5   A Survey on the Research of Dynamic Hand Gesture

With the development of camera and sensor technology, the depth information of gesture can be captured. Researchers pay more attention to dynamic gesture recognition. A series of actions make up dynamic gestures focus on in a period of time, which increase time information and dynamic characteristics.

Dynamic gesture recognition is the combination of these simple static gestures to express the meaning of their combination. With the improvement of the equipment, three dimensional gesture recognition technology is more accurate and deeper than two-dimensional. Using the method of Structure Light, Time of Flight and Multi-camera to restore the entire three-dimensional space, and get the depth information of the object. To solve the problem of shadowing and so on, some experiments of researchers also use two or more cameras to capture images at the same time. We investigated articles on dynamic gesture recognition in resent years, and summarized the research with reference value in Table 6.

Table 6. Researches on dynamic hand gesture

Ref.	Techniques	Gesture number	Dataset (recognition of gesture)	Limitation	Average accuracy
Trigueiros et al. [31]	HMM	25 hand gestures	Gestures defined and used in the Referee CommLang (GOAL, CANCEL, etc.)	Camera is the limitation	93.7%

(*continued*)

Table 6. (*continued*)

Ref.	Techniques	Gesture number	Dataset (recognition of gesture)	Limitation	Average accuracy
Tewari et al. [30]	CNN + RNN	4 hand gestures	60000 sample of labelled images of five pose classes (accept, decline, etc.)	Limits of images. The self-occlusion of the hand	89.50%, device (Kinect)
Liu et al. [20]	DBN	8 hand gestures	The dataset includes the palm posture from 500 video sequences (a, c, an upright triangle, etc.)	Noisy environment	98.0%
Rokade-Shinde and Sonawane [24]	A proposed method combined with PCA	10 hand gestures	300 videos of two persons (11 to 20 digits)	Limits of images	94%
Zhang et al. [37]	A method that includes fuzzy pattern recognition method and the number of track points	9 hand gestures	100 data samples for each kind of gestures (chose, erase, page add, etc.)		95.9%

6   Applications of Vision-Based Hand Gesture Recognition

The primary motivation behind the specialized research is to give this innovation a chance to assume a part throughout everyday life. Therefore, how to apply gesture recognition technology to applications is also a problem that researchers need to consider after researching this technology. Although key issues in gesture recognition were not well solved at present, such as: there are a large number of hand-crossing and overlapping movements in sign language used by deaf and dumb people.

Researchers did a lot of gesture recognition applications so far. Although many of these applications are only at the laboratory stage. It will also provide many ideas for future research. Our application survey on gesture recognition is shown in Table 7.

Table 7. Application of vision-based gesture recognition

Application	Challenge	Example
Sign recognition [9, 14]	Design visual descriptors that can capture human gesture	Kishore et al. [14] presents 3D motionlets method. Huang et al. [9] proposes a continuous symbol recognition framework named LS-HAN
Robot control [6]	Predictive gesture recognition rate	Fujii et al. [6] proposes a gesture recognition system, which is used to develop a service robot
Game control [13]	Real-time and the capture of human gesture.	Kalpakas et al. [13] presents a interactive computer-based board games
Virtual reality environment [21]	Insufficient natural interaction	Liu et al. [21] proposes Hu Moment-based Gesture Recognition Method, which applies to virtual reality interaction
Electronic control [12]	Limit of recognition range	Jing et al. [12] uses six gestures to implement the control application in the presentation

7   Future Perspectives for Hand Gesture Recognition

At present, the most commonly used gesture recognition method is a feedforward neural network named Convolutional Neural Network. The artificial neurons of CNN can respond to a portion of the peripheral units and perform well for large image processing. However, CNN needs a lot of pictures to train or reuse part of the neural network trained by massive data. But CapsNet uses much less training data to generalize. CNN cannot deal with fuzziness very well.

A capsule network is made up of capsules, which is a small group of neurons. A capsules can learn to examine a specific object within a certain area of a picture. In the CapNet, the details of the attitude information, such as the exact location of the object, the rotation, the thickness, the inclination, the size and so on, are saved in the network without the first loss and recovery. Slight changes in the input bring small changes in output and information is saved, which allows CapsNet to use a simple and unified architecture to deal with different visual tasks.

A paper about the introduction of the CapsNet architecture named Dynamic Routing between Capsules [26] was published by Sabour et al. The architecture achieves the most advanced performance on MNIST, and achieves much better results than CNN on the MultiMNIST dataset. Through investigation, we found that capsule network can solve many problems of CNN, which makes that it has the possibility to replace CNN in the future. CapsNet also has a great potential in the direction of gesture recognition research.

8   Conclusion

Most of the mature human-machine interaction applications are visually based. Wearable interaction is still in the exploration stage. Because of the reason that wearable technology is not mature enough, only a few entrepreneurs are making wearable gesture recognition products. If there are great breakthroughs in chip technology, material technology and battery technology in the future, the material will be good enough to make people to wear these devices without feeling, which dont have an influence on making a gesture. Thus, contact based human-hand gesture recognition will have more support to be researched. As far as the present situation is concerned, The recognition of hand sign based on vision has more value to research and it also has more products and applications to support research.

Acknowledgement. This work was supported by grants from the Fundamental Research Funds for the Key Research Programm of Chongqing Science & Technology Commission (grant no. cstc2017rgzn-zdyf0064), the Chongqing Provincial Human Resource and Social Security Department (grant no. cx2017092), the Central Universities in China (grant nos. 2018CDXYRJ0030, CQU0225001104447), Science and Technology Innovation Project of Foshan City, China (grant no. 2015IT100095), the Fundamental Research Funds for the Central Universities (grant no. lzujbkey-2016-br03), CERNET Innovation Project (grant no. NGII20150603) and Science and Technology Planning Project of Guangdong Province, China (grant no. 2016B010108002).

References

1. Al-Shamayleh, A.S., Ahmad, R., Abushariah, M.A.M., Alam, K.A., Jomhari, N.: A systematic literature review on vision based gesture recognition techniques. Multimed. Tools Appl. **77**(21), 28121–28184 (2018)
2. Badi, H., Fadhel, M., Sabry, S., Jasem, M.: A survey on humanncomputer interaction technologies and techniques. Int. J. Data Sci. Anal. **3**(2), 1–11 (2017)
3. Chaudhary, A., Raheja, J.L., Das, K., Raheja, S.: A survey on hand gesture recognition in context of soft computing. In: Meghanathan, N., Kaushik, B.K., Nagamalai, D. (eds.) CCSIT 2011. CCIS, vol. 133, pp. 46–55. Springer, Heidelberg (2011). https://doi.org/10.1007/978-3-642-17881-8_5
4. Chen, Y., Huang, H., Xu, W., Center, T.I.: Gesture recognition system based on wearable accelerometer. Autom. Inf. Eng. (2015)
5. Devineau, G., Xi, W., Moutarde, F., Yang, J.: Deep learning for hand gesture recognition on skeletal data (2018)
6. Fujii, T., Lee, J.H., Okamoto, S.: Gesture recognition system for human-robot interaction and its application to robotic service task. Lect. Notes Eng. Comput. Sci. **2209**(1), 63–68 (2014)

7. Gao, Q., Liu, J., Ju, Z., Li, Y., Zhang, T., Zhang, L.: Static hand gesture recognition with parallel CNNs for space human-robot interaction. In: Huang, Y.A., Wu, H., Liu, H., Yin, Z. (eds.) ICIRA 2017. LNCS (LNAI), vol. 10462, pp. 462–473. Springer, Cham (2017). https://doi.org/10.1007/978-3-319-65289-4_44

8. Hasan, H., Abdul-Kareem, S.: Retracted article: humanccomputer interaction using vision-based hand gesture recognition systems: a survey. Neural Comput. Appl. **25**(2), 251–261 (2014)

9. Huang, J., Zhou, W., Zhang, Q., Li, H., Li, W.: Video-based sign language recognition without temporal segmentation (2018)

10. Huang, Y.A., Wu, H., Liu, H., Yin, Z.: Erratum to: intelligent robotics and applications. In: Huang, Y.A., Wu, H., Liu, H., Yin, Z. (eds.) ICIRA 2017. LNCS (LNAI), vol. 10463, p. E1. Springer, Cham (2017). https://doi.org/10.1007/978-3-319-65292-4_78

11. Itkarkar, R.R., Nandi, A.V.: A survey of 2D and 3D imaging used in hand gesture recognition for human-computer interaction (HCI). In: IEEE International WIE Conference on Electrical and Computer Engineering, pp. 188–193 (2017)

12. Jing, S., Jiao-Yan, A.I.: The real-time dynamic gesture recognition based on computer vision technology and its application for powerpoint control. Comput. Technol. Autom. (2013)

13. Kalpakas, A.C., Stampoulis, K.N., Zikos, N.A., Zaharos, S.K.: 2D hand gesture recognition methods for interactive board game applications. In: Proceedings of the International Conference on Signal Processing and Multimedia Applications, SIGMAP 2008, Porto, Portugal, 26–29 July 2008, pp. 325–331 (2015)

14. Kishore, P.V.V., Kumar, D.A., Sastry, A.S.C.S., Kumar, E.K.: Motionlets matching with adaptive kernels for 3D Indian sign language recognition. IEEE Sens. J. **PP**(99), 1–1 (2018)

15. Kumar, P., Gauba, H., Roy, P.P., Dogra, D.P.: Coupled HMM-based multi-sensor data fusion for sign language recognition. Pattern Recogn. Lett. **86**(C), 1–8 (2017)

16. Lad, M.: Soft computing approaches for hand gesture recognition. Int. J. Comput. Sci. Eng. Inf. Technol. Res. **3**(4), 55–58 (2013)

17. Lee, K., et al.: Four DoF gesture recognition with an event-based image sensor. In: Consumer Electronics, pp. 293–294 (2012)

18. Li, S., Xu, K., Zhang, H.: Research on virtual Guzheng based on Kinect. In: International Conference on Computer-Aided Design, Manufacturing, Modeling and Simulation, p. 040010 (2018)

19. Liang, B., Zheng, L.: Three dimensional motion trail model for gesture recognition. In: IEEE International Conference on Computer Vision Workshops, pp. 684–691 (2013)

20. Liu, N., Aziz, M.A.A.: A robust deep belief network-based approach for recognizing dynamic hand gestures. In: International Bhurban Conference on Applied Sciences and Technology, pp. 199–205 (2016)

21. Liu, Y., Yin, Y., Zhang, S.: Hand gesture recognition based on HU moments in interaction of virtual reality. In: International Conference on Intelligent Human-Machine Systems and Cybernetics, pp. 145–148 (2012)

22. Naguri, C.R., Bunescu, R.C.: Recognition of dynamic hand gestures from 3D motion data using LSTM and CNN architectures. In: IEEE International Conference on Machine Learning and Applications, pp. 1130–1133 (2017)

23. Rautaray, S.S., Agrawal, A.: Vision based hand gesture recognition for human computer interaction: a survey. Artif. Intell. Rev. **43**(1), 1–54 (2015)

24. Rokade-Shinde, R., Sonawane, J.: Dynamic hand gesture recognition. In: International Conference on Signal and Information Processing (2017)

25. Ruffieux, S., Lalanne, D., Mugellini, E., Abou Khaled, O.: A survey of datasets for human gesture recognition. In: Kurosu, M. (ed.) HCI 2014. LNCS, vol. 8511, pp. 337–348. Springer, Cham (2014). https://doi.org/10.1007/978-3-319-07230-2_33

26. Sabour, S., Frosst, N., Hinton, G.E.: Dynamic routing between capsules (2017)

27. Su, B., Wu, H., Sheng, M.: Human action recognition method based on hierarchical framework via Kinect skeleton data. In: International Conference on Machine Learning and Cybernetics, pp. 83–90 (2017)

28. Suarez, J., Murphy, R.R.: Hand gesture recognition with depth images: a review, pp. 411–417 (2012)

29. Tang, A., Lu, K., Wang, Y., Huang, J., Li, H.: A real-time hand posture recognition system using deep neural networks. ACM Trans. Intell. Syst. Technol. 6(2), 1–23 (2015)

30. Tewari, A., Taetz, B., Grandidier, F., Stricker, D.: A probabilistic combination of CNN and RNN estimates for hand gesture based interaction in car. In: IEEE International Symposium on Mixed and Augmented Reality (2017)

31. Trigueiros, P., Ribeiro, F., Reis, L.P.: Vision-based Portuguese sign language recognition system. In: Rocha, Á., Correia, A.M., Tan, F.B., Stroetmann, K.A. (eds.) New Perspectives in Information Systems and Technologies, Volume 1. AISC, vol. 275, pp. 605–617. Springer, Cham (2014). https://doi.org/10.1007/978-3-319-05951-8_57

32. Wu, X., Yang, C., Wang, Y., Li, H., Xu, S.: An intelligent interactive system based on hand gesture recognition algorithm and kinect, vol. 2, no. 4, pp. 294–298 (2012)

33. Wu, X., Yang, C., Wang, Y., Li, H., Xu, S.: An intelligent interactive system based on hand gesture recognition algorithm and kinect. In: Fifth International Symposium on Computational Intelligence and Design, pp. 294–298 (2013)

34. Yang, X.W., Feng, Z.Q., Huang, Z.Z., He, N.N.: A gesture recognition algorithm using hausdorff-like distance template matching based on the main direction of gesture. Appl. Mech. Mater. **713–715**(3), 2156–2159 (2015)

35. Zhang, B., Yun, R., Qiu, H.: Hand gesture recognition in natural state based on rotation invariance and OpenCV realization. In: Zhang, X., Zhong, S., Pan, Z., Wong, K., Yun, R. (eds.) Edutainment 2010. LNCS, vol. 6249, pp. 486–496. Springer, Heidelberg (2010). https://doi.org/10.1007/978-3-642-14533-9_50

36. Zhang, X., Chen, X., Li, Y., Lantz, V., Wang, K., Yang, J.: A framework for hand gesture recognition based on accelerometer and EMG sensors. IEEE Trans. Syst. Man Cybern. Part A Syst. Hum. 41(6), 1064–1076 (2011)

37. Zhang, Z., He, X., Chen, Z., Wu, K.: Research on dynamic gesture recognition algorithm based on multi-touch human-computer interaction devices in classroom teaching. In: International Conference on Machinery, Materials and Information Technology Applications (2017)

Video Analysis

Research on Path Planning Method of an Unmanned Vehicle in Urban Road Environments

Yu Ruixing[1(✉)], Zhu Bing[2], Cao Meng[1], Zhao Xiao[3], and Wang Jiawen[3]

[1] Northwestern Polytechnical University, Xian 710072, Shaanxi Province, People's Republic of China
yrxgigi@nwpu.edu.cn
[2] Xi'an Shiyou University, Xian 710065, Shaanxi Province, People's Republic of China
[3] Shanghai Institute of Satellite Engineering, Shanghai 201109, People's Republic of China

Abstract. Path planning is one of the crucial technologies for autonomous driving of unmanned vehicle. It is considerably difficult for unmanned vehicles to perform a path planning assignment in an urban environment due to the complexity of the environmental constraints. In order to solve this problem, a new path planning method is introduced in this paper. We did not regard the unmanned vehicle as a particle, but selected the front-wheel-drive model combined with the mechanical constrains to calculate the path of the vehicle. The constraints of the external environment and mechanical limitations are introduced into different objective functions. This paper also proposes an algorithm based integration of the A* and Stochastic Fractal Search (SFS) algorithms. The integrated algorithm searches for the optimal path, which is the shortest path to the target location of the vehicle's rear axle mid-point in the raster map, with the help of the A* algorithm. Then, based on the shortest path the SFS algorithm generates the vehicle path, which contains the vehicle status information. Finally, the A* and SFS algorithms are compared under the same simulation environment when searching for a path of the vehicle's rear suspension. The results simulated on MATLAB R2012a show that the composite method we propose is effective in solving the path planning problem in an urban environment.

Keywords: Path planning · Stochastic Fractal Search · A* algorithm
Grid map · Dynamic programming

1 Introduction

Most widely used algorithms in path planning are based on grid maps, such as the A* algorithm and the D* algorithm. The features of these grid based methods are that they can get the trajectory of the vehicle with high accuracy but sacrifice real-time performance. Artificial potential fields can solve this shortcoming, and is simple in structure

© Springer Nature Switzerland AG 2018
A. Basu and S. Berretti (Eds.): ICSM 2018, LNCS 11010, pp. 235–247, 2018.
https://doi.org/10.1007/978-3-030-04375-9_20

and fast in computation. Many scholars have tried to improve the traditional algorithms in recent years [1–5]. In 2009, Yang K used the rapidly exploring random trees (RRT) algorithm to deal with the path planning problem in a chaotic environment [6]. In 2013, Subramanian [7] used the potential energy gradient theory to simulate path planning of an autonomous robot using the multipoint potential field method (MPPF). According to their simulation results, this method achieved good results. Two scholars in South Korea divided the working space of unmanned vehicles into triangular areas to solve the problem of vehicle obstacle avoidance on a two-dimensional plane [5]. The above three teams simplified the vehicle into a single particle to simplify the path planning problem. However, the vehicle may be in a complex environment, especially the urban road driving environment in China. The urban driving environment in China is more complicated than in other developed countries, and the environment features include: complex types of vehicles on roads, mixture of motor vehicles and non-motor vehicles, large number of road intersections and mix of people and traffic at intersections. Therefore, it is often not feasible to treat the vehicle as a particle. For these reasons, the vehicle model selection in this paper is based on the front-wheel-drive model without side-slip.

In order to solve the problem of unmanned vehicle path planning in complex urban environments David [8] in 2017 generated a vehicle trajectory through a simulated online testing and verification platform. But this was just the generation of the trajectory and did not further study the real-time status information of the vehicle. J [9] proposed a new artificial potential field method, which took into account both the boundary conditions of the road and the vehicle as well as the vehicle kinematics model. However, the vehicle had a constant motion model, which limits the application of this method. Rahman [10] considered the vehicle's own state information and obstacle information separately, and achieved good results when dealing with obstacles in complex scenes. But their method is only valid for static obstacles. In 2016, Shao Zhijiang [11] proposed a trajectory planning algorithm based on Stochastic Fractal Search (SFS). From the simulation results, this method can deal with the trajectory planning of unmanned vehicles in complex environment very well. However, it usually takes several hours to obtain a collision-free trajectory including the vehicle state information. This is too long for use in a real car.

From the above research results, we saw that unmanned vehicles under the complicated urban road conditions still face a lot of difficulties that a single path planning algorithm cannot deal with. We combine the A* algorithm with the SFS to take the advantages of the speed of A* and the advantages of SFS algorithm in dealing with many constrained optimization problems. First, the candidate driving path is searched by the A* algorithm, finding the shortest path from the midpoint of the vehicle rear wheel axis to the target position. However, A* can only get vehicle location coordinates, but lacks of other state information like steering angle, direction angle and speed. Fortunately, the SFS algorithm helps to get these state information. Most trajectory planning algorithms put vehicle environmental constraints and mechanical constraints into one objective function, this increases the complexity of the objective function and takes more time. Therefore, in this paper we separate vehicle environmental constraints and mechanical constraints into two different objective functions.

The rest of this paper is organized as follows: Sect. 2 introduces the theory behind the algorithm theory in detail. Section 3 introduces the selection of simulation conditions, including the simulation of the car model, the vehicle termination conditions, the dynamic optimization of vehicle parameters and discretization. Section 4 explains why we chose the A* algorithm for mid-path generation of a vehicle's rear wheel axis, and compares the advantages of A* with the SFS algorithm. Finally, we show the effectiveness of the algorithm through simulations.

2   A* and SFS Combined Path Planning Algorithm

The flowchart of the integrated A* and SFS path planning algorithm is shown in Fig. 1. First, we establish the road environment map models of the vehicle and select the appropriate rasterization factor to rasterize them. The road environment map model includes the edge of the road and the obstacles that affect the normal driving of the vehicle. Then, we generate the vehicle travel environment map model. We set the start point and the end point of the vehicle in the environment map model and calculate the locus of the vehicle's rear wheel axis center point P using the A* algorithm considering the vehicle external environment constraints. After obtaining the trajectory of point P, the vehicle model without side-slip front-wheel drive is selected, and finally a collision-free feasible path with the vehicle's state information is obtained by the SFS algorithm.

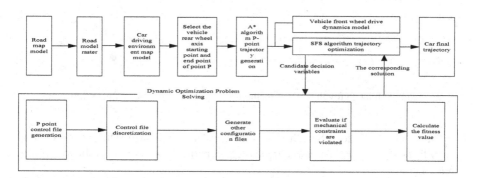

Fig. 1. Overall algorithm flow chart.

2.1   Using A* Algorithm to Generate P-Point Trajectory

The A* algorithm is an efficient way to get the shortest path in a static environment. The method is based on a raster map. We set the start and end points in the raster map and find a minimum of the cost function expressed as follows:

$$f(n) = g(n) + h(n) \tag{1}$$

Where f(n) is the estimated cost from the start to the end point via the state n. g(n) is the actual cost from the start point to the state n in the grid map, and h(n) is the estimated cost of the best path from state n to the end point. The A* algorithm's process can be described as follows: it always choose the cell with the lowest total cost of f(n), when moving to the next cell. Then, it repeat above process until the end point is reached and gets the final path with the lowest cost.

In this paper, we use the four-neighborhood cost algorithm. The A* algorithm can quickly search the shortest path in a raster map. However, due to the limitation of A* we only get the position information of a feasible path. If we want to get the state information at every moment of the vehicle in the path tracking stage, we need to use other algorithms. In this paper we use SFS to get the state of the vehicle.

2.2 Stochastic Fractal Search Algorithm

Random fractals are an objects' attribute of self-similar growth at all scales. The random fractal pattern is formed in combination with the Diffusion Limited Aggregation (DLA) method. An example of a simple DLA random fractal application is considering a cluster on a plane, with the initial (seed) particle located at the origin. Other particles are then generated randomly around the origin and cause diffusion. To simulate the diffusion process, a mathematical algorithm like random walk has been employed. The diffusing particle sticks to the seed particle which is made from it. This process is repeated until a cluster is formed. While forming the cluster, the probability of a particle being stuck to the end is increased compared to the ones that penetrate the interior. Therefore, this property leads a cluster to the branch-like structure (Fig. 2).

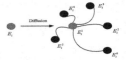

Fig. 2. A simple fractal growth by DLA method.   **Fig. 3.** Particle diffusion.

The Stochastic Fractal Search theory includes fractal growth (DLA) and potential energy theory. In short, the random fractal search in order to solve the problem includes three criteria:

- Each particle has an electrical potential energy.
- Each particle diffuses to create some other random particles, and the energy of the seed particle is divided among generated particles.
- Only few of the best particles remain in each generation, and the rest of the particles are disregarded.

As shown in Fig. 3, the diffusion of primary particles will randomly generate several new particles at different positions around the primary particles. And the Gaussian distribution is a random walk used in the growth of the Diffusion-limited

Aggregation (DLA) by the Stochastic Fractal Search algorithm. In general, a series of Gaussian walks that participate in the diffusion process is given by:

$$GW_1 = Gaussian(\mu_{BP}, \sigma) + (\varepsilon \times BP - \varepsilon' \times P_i) \tag{2}$$

$$GW_2 = Gaussian(\mu_p, \sigma) \tag{3}$$

Where ε and ε' are random numbers uniformly distributed between [0, 1]. BP and p_i are denoted as the position of the best point and the i-th point in the group respectively. In Eq. (2) two Gaussian parameters are μ_{BP} and σ. μ_{BP} is equal to BP. In Eq. (3) the Gaussian parameters are μ_p and σ. And the standard deviation of Gaussian parameters is computed by Eq. (4):

$$\sigma = |(\log(g)/g) \times (P_i - BP)| \tag{4}$$

In Eq. (4) the term $\log(g)/g$ is used to decrease the size of Gaussian jumps, as the number of generations increase.

We are looking for the optimal path from the start to the end point, which can be seen as a d-dimensional global optimization problem. During the initialization process, each point is initialized randomly generated according to the minimum and maximum limits of the constraint vector. The initialization equation of the point j is:

$$P_j = LB + \varepsilon \times (UB - LB) \tag{5}$$

where LB and UB are the lowest and highest bounds of the constraint vector, respectively. As stated in previous equations, ε is a uniformly distributed random number which is restricted to the contiguous area between [0, 1]. After initializing all points, the fitness of each point is computed to attain the best point (BP) among all points. The fitness can be calculated by Eq. (13). According to the property in the diffusion procedure, all points are randomly wandering to explore the search space in their current location. On the other hand, two statistical procedures aimed to increase the better space exploration are considered. The first statistical procedure considers each individual vector index, and the second statistical method is then applied to all points.

For the first statistical procedure, all the points are ranked based on the value of the fitness function. Each point in the group is then given a probability value which obeys a simple uniform distribution following the equation below:

$$P_{ai} = \frac{rank(p_i)}{N} \tag{6}$$

Where rank(Pi) is the rank of point Pi, and N is the total number of all points in the group. In fact, Eq. (6) shows that the bigger the fitness value is, the higher the probability. This equation helps intermediate fitness points increase the chance of entering the next iteration and also helps to have good fitness value in the next iteration. For each point Pi in a group, if $Pa_i \leq \varepsilon$ is satisfied, the j-th component of Pi is updated according to Eq. (7), otherwise it remains unchanged.

$$p_i'(j) = P_r(j) - \varepsilon \times (P_t(j) - P_i(j)) \tag{7}$$

Where Pi is the new modified position of Pi. Pr and Pt are randomly selected points in the group, ε is the random number selected from the uniform distribution in the continuous space [0, 1].

With regard to the first statistical procedure which is carried out on the components of the points, the second statistical change is aimed to change the position of a point considering the position of other points in the group. This property improves the quality of exploration, and it satisfies the diversification property. Before starting the second procedure, once again, all points obtained from the first statistical procedure are ranked based on Eq. (6). Similar to the first statistical process, if the condition $Pa_i < \varepsilon$ is held for a new point P_i', the current position of P_i' is modified according to Eqs. (8) and (9), otherwise no update occurs. Equations (8) and (9) are presented as follows:

$$P_i'' = P_i' - \hat{\varepsilon} \times (P_t' - BP), \quad \varepsilon' \leq 0.5 \tag{8}$$

$$P_i'' = P_i' + \hat{\varepsilon} \times (P_t' - P_r'), \quad \varepsilon' > 0.5 \tag{9}$$

where P_t' and P_r' are randomly selected points obtained from the first procedure, and $\hat{\varepsilon}$ are random numbers generated by the Gaussian Normal distribution. The new point P_i'' is replaced by P_i' if its fitness function value is better than P_i'.

3 Simulation Settings

3.1 Simulation Car Model

The front wheel drive of the car model is based on the basic assumption of no sideslip. The kinematic model of the car is shown in Fig. 4, and the kinematic description equation of the car is as follows:

$$\begin{cases} \frac{dx(t)}{dt} = v(t) \cdot \cos \theta(t) \\ \frac{dy(t)}{dt} = v(t) \cdot \sin(t), t \in [0, t_f] \\ \frac{d\theta(t)}{dt} = \frac{v(t) \cdot \tan \phi(t)}{L} \end{cases} \tag{10}$$

where t refers to time, t_f indicates the unknown terminal moment of the entire movement. (x, y) denotes the mid-point of rear wheel axis (point P in Fig. 4), θ is the orientation angle, V refers to the linear velocity of point P and ϕ refers to the steering angle of front wheels. Moreover, as illustrated in Fig. 4, L denotes the wheelbase length, N denotes the front overhang length, M is the rear overhang length and 2B is the tractor width.

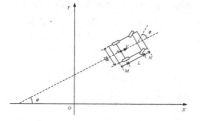

Fig. 4. Car kinematics model.

Fig. 5. Obstacles in a cluttered environment.

3.2 Car Termination Conditions

The edge of the city road and obstacles are represented by gray rectangles. The target location is represented by non-filled rectangular gridlines, as shown in Fig. 5. In order to better simulate the complex environment of the vehicle, the obstacles in the simulation are generated randomly.

As shown in Fig. 6, the rectangle Q and the rectangular area ABCD have the following relation:

$$(0 < \overrightarrow{AQ} \cdot \overrightarrow{AB} < \overrightarrow{AB} \cdot \overrightarrow{AB}) \bigcap (0 < \overrightarrow{AQ} \cdot \overrightarrow{AD} < \overrightarrow{AD} \cdot \overrightarrow{AD}) = 1 \qquad (11)$$

If Eq. (11) is established, then the point Q is within the rectangle ABCD; if Eq. (11) is not true, the point Q is outside the rectangle ABCD. Therefore, in the process of simulation, the condition that the car reaches the target location can be considered as the car's four vertices are all within the target location rectangle.

Fig. 6. Points and rectangular area collision schematic.

3.3 Dynamic Optimization and Discretization

A numerical approach is proposed to solve the formulated dynamic optimization problem. The numerical approach includes two stages: discretization and optimization. In the former, all the continuous-time state and control profiles in time are discretized into finite periods. Through this, the original infinite-dimensional problem is transformed into a finite-dimensional nonlinear programming (NLP) problem, which is solved in the latter stage.

To discretize the unknown control variable (such as $v(t), \phi(t), x(t), y(t), \theta(t)$) and t_f, First, the time domain $[0, t_f]$ is divided equally into N_{fp} intervals $\{[t_{i-1}, t_i] | i = 1, 2, \cdots, N_{fp}\}$, where $t_{N_{fp}} = t_f, t_0 = 0$ and the length of each interval is t_f / N_{fp}. Thereafter, (k+1) interpolation points are chosen in each interval to form a Lagrange polynomial. The piecewise polynomials on all the intervals form an estimation of the ground truth of a control profile. Specifically, one can set (k+1) interpolation points $\{Z_{i0}, Z_{i1}, \cdots, Z_{ik}\}$ to describe $v(t)$ in the i th interval $[t_{i-1}, t_i]$ via the following Lagrange polynomial:

$$v(t_{i-1} + (t_i - t_{i-1}) \cdot \tau) = \sum_{j=0}^{k} (z_{ij} \cdot \prod_{k=0, \neq j}^{k} \frac{(\tau - \tau_k)}{(\tau_j - \tau_k)}) \tag{12}$$

where $\tau \in [0, 1]$, $\tau_0 = 0$ and $0 < \tau_i \leq 1$ $(j = 1, 2, \cdots, k)$. Each τ_i refers to a Gauss point, which can be calculated offline when K is given. In this way, $v(t)$ is discretized. And in a similar way, the steering angle of the front wheel of the car $\phi(t)$ can also be discretized. According to Eq. (10), the orientation angle of the car $\theta(t)$ can be similarly transformed. In this way, the state quantities constrained by continuous time at any time can be discretized, and the original dynamic optimization problem can be transformed into a large scale NLP problem.

3.4   Optimization Stage

Due to the mechanical constraints, some of the car's state quantities cannot be unbounded. For example, the line speed of the car $v(t)$, is actually $|v(t)| \leq v_{\max}$, so for a certain time t_i, if $v^i > v_{\max}$, then do the following corresponding processing $v^i = v_{\max}$. This adjustment fundamentally guarantees the feasibility of the whole maneuver.

In addition to the bounded constraints imposed on the control profiles, complicated constraints of the state profiles that cannot be simply addressed by this adjustment still exist. Satisfactions of these complicated constraints are ensured through inaccuracy penalty. Violations of two types of constraints are penalized: (i) collision avoidance and (ii) terminal condition achievement. In handling the collision-avoidance constraints, we check every discretized moment and accumulate the violation amount in collision $\psi_{collision}$. The violation amount is taken as an important index that guides the optimizer to seek for improvements. The penalty amount is determined as:

$$\psi = \begin{cases} 0, & \text{if } \psi_{collision} + \psi_{destination} = 0 \\ Value_{l \arg e} + \psi_{collision} + \psi_{destination}, & \text{if } \psi_{collision} + \psi_{destination} > 0 \end{cases} \tag{13}$$

Where $Value_{l \arg e}$ is a relatively large number. If no violation of these two fundamental restrictions occurs, ψ should be equal to 0; otherwise, ψ is larger than the positive constant $Value_{l \arg e}$, which is set sufficiently large to guarantee that the fitness of any feasible solution is smaller than any infeasible solution.

The rough interpolation points as well as t_f are chosen as decision variables, because they determine the control profiles directly. Later, when the state variables are obtained through integral, constraint violations are examined, evaluated and then incorporated in the concerned optimization criterion through inaccuracy penalty.

4 Simulations

4.1 Determining the Trajectory Generation Algorithm P

We considered the mid-point P of the vehicle rear axle alone. The real-time route search algorithm is used to generate the trajectory of the point P. The specific operation is to generate the trajectory of P with the real-time algorithm first, and then the car model is generated by the relationship between P and the car model, and the trajectory of the car is generated according to the trajectory and constraints on P (the maximum steering angle, the maximum speed and obstacles).

We use the more representative of the real-time path search algorithm A*, artificial potential field algorithm (APF) and rapidly exploring random trees (RRT). In this section, we set up the road model, set the same start and end points, and use the three algorithms to simulate the same scene as in Fig. 7. It can be seen from Fig. 7 that for the same starting point, RRT generates longer paths and takes more time than the former two algorithms. Combining with the mechanical constraints of the car, we know that RRT is not suitable for the trajectory planning of the car. There is a certain difference between A * and APF, and the time difference between them is not big, but it is more advantageous to deal with multi-obstacle scene A *. For example, as shown in Fig. 8, when the car turns around, the A * algorithm can figure out the car's turn-around path while APF cannot. In summary, we use A* to generate P point trajectory.

As shown in Fig. 9, for the same start and end point we set, the red line is the path of the point P calculated by A*. The green line is iterated 3000 times using the SFS algorithm and takes 4 h to calculate the point P. From Fig. 10, we see that the path searched by the SFS algorithm collides with the rightmost obstacle. Obviously, the A* algorithm is more efficient in path computation (Table 1).

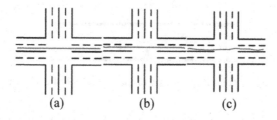

Fig. 7 (a) A* algorithm path (b) APF algorithm path (c) RRT algorithm path.

Table 1. Time comparison.

Algorithm	Time (s)
A*	0.2381
APF	0.4684
RRT	1.659003

(a) A * finds the path.   (b) APF cannot find the path.

Fig. 8. Trajectory planning of vehicle turning problem.

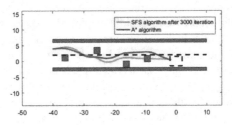

Fig. 9. A* finds the path of P (red trajectory) and SFS algorithm iterates 3000 times to find the path of P (green track) (Color figure online).

4.2 Complex Algorithm Simulation

The integrated algorithm includes two parts: the first part is the vehicle's rear wheel axis point P trajectory generation. We come up with a separate point P trajectory generation. The objective function only includes the environment constraint information of the vehicle. In this step, we use A *, and the shortest path of the trolley is the optimization target. The simulation results are shown in Fig. 10.

Fig. 10. The trajectory of point P in the axis of the rear wheel of a vehicle by A* algorithm.

The second part of the composite algorithm is based on the first part of the P-point trajectory, combined with the car's dynamic model and the car's own mechanical constraints, using the SFS algorithm to generate the vehicle state information. The state information including the car's orientation angle, P point's line speed and steering angle of the front wheel of the car. The car's parameters and SFS algorithm's specific parameters are shown in Table 2, the vehicle's final trajectory is shown in Fig. 11, and Fig. 12 is the car's the steering angle, the line speed of P and the front wheel steering angle.

Table 2. The simulation parameters.

Parameter	Description	Setting
N	The car's front suspension	0.25 m
M	Rear suspension of the car	0.25 m
2B	The width of the car	2.00 m
L	Wheelbase of the car	1.50 m
Vmax	The maximum car line speed	3.0 m/s
Φmax	Car maximum steering angle	0.714 rad
Nfp	Number of finite intervals	5
K+1	Interpolation point number	4
$[\tau_0, \tau_1, \cdots, \tau_k]$	Vector contains Gaussian interpolation points	[0, 0.16, 0.65, 1]

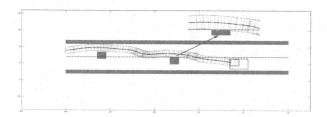

Fig. 11. The car trajectory P trolley track using SFS algorithm.

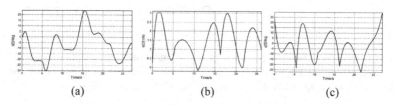

(a)   (b)   (c)

Fig. 12. The amount of car state changes from start to end over time ((a) the change of direction angle, (b) the change of velocity, (c) the change of front wheel steering angle).

4.3   Composite Algorithm and SFS Algorithm Comparison

For the same start and end point the composite algorithm and SFS algorithm generated point P's path as shown in Fig. 13, with the path length shown in Table 3.

It can be seen from Table 3 that the path generated by the composite algorithm is shorter, and the two algorithms of the car orientation angle, P line speed and front wheel steering angle of the three state information is shown in Fig. 14.

From Fig. 14, the change range of the orientation angle and the steering angle of the front wheel in the composite algorithm is smaller than that of the simple SFS algorithm. Moreover, the path generated by composite algorithm is shorter in Table 3. The shortest path is generated by the optimized target, so the compound algorithm proposed in this paper is better than the simple SFS algorithm.

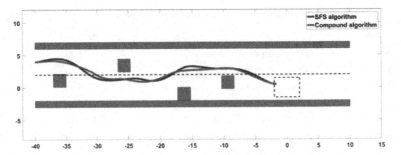

Fig. 13. Compound algorithm path and SFS algorithm path.

Table 3. Compound algorithm and SFS algorithm path length.

Algorithm	Path length (m)
Compound algorithm	40.14
SFS algorithm	39.71

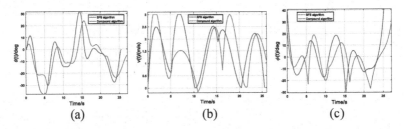

(a)   (b)   (c)

Fig. 14. Comparison of two algorithm vehicle status information ((a) the direction angle of car, (b) the speed of car, (c) the front wheel steering angle of car. The red line is for compound algorithm, while the blue line is for SFS algorithm) (Color figure online).

5 Conclusion

This paper considered path planning of unmanned vehicles in an urban road environment. We proposed a composite (integrated) algorithm that combines the A* algorithm with the SFS algorithm. Combined with the constraints on the vehicle's environment, the shortest collision-free path of the mid-point of the rear axle of the vehicle was planned by A *. On the basis of the shortest path, the SFS algorithm was used to generate the car's motion state information. From the simulation results the composite algorithm proposed in this paper can successfully plan paths for unmanned vehicles in urban road environments.

Acknowledgements. This work was sponsored by Aviation Science Fund Project (20160153001), SAST Foundation (Grant No.SAST2015040), Shaanxi Provincial Department of Education Scientific Research Plan Special Project (17JK0599), Xi'an Shiyou University Youth Science and Technology Innovation Fund project (2015BS18).

References

1. Wei, S., Zhengda, M.: Smooth path design based on improved A* algorithm. J. Southeast Univ. (Nat. Sci.) **s1**, 155–161 (2010)
2. Koenig, S., Likhachev, M.: Improved fast replanning for robot navigation in unknown terrain. In: IEEE International Conference on Robotics and Automation, vol. 1, pp. 968–975 (2002)
3. Nyerges, Á., Tihanyi, V.: Trajectory Planning for Automated Vehicles – A Basic Approach. In: Jármai, K., Bolló, B. (eds.) VAE 2018. LNME, pp. 403–412. Springer, Cham (2018). https://doi.org/10.1007/978-3-319-75677-6_35
4. Lau, G.T.L.: Path planning algorithms for autonomous border patrol vehicles. School of Graduate Studies, Theses (2012)
5. Pamosoaji, A.K., Hong, K.S.: A path-planning algorithm using vector potential functions in triangular regions. IEEE Trans. Syst. Man Cybern. Part B **43**(4), 832–842 (2013)
6. Yang, K., Gan, S.K., Sukkarieh, S.: An Efficient Path Planning and Control Algorithm for RUAV's in Unknown and Cluttered Environments. In: Valavanis, K.P., Beard, R., Oh, P., Ollero, A., Piegl, L.A., Shim, H. (eds.) Selected papers from the 2nd International Symposium on UAVs, vol. 57, pp. 1–4. Springer, Dordrecht (2009). https://doi.org/10.1007/978-90-481-8764-5_6
7. Saravanakumar, S., Asokan, T.: Multipoint potential field method for path planning of autonomous underwater vehicles in 3D space. Intell. Serv. Robot. **6**(4), 211–224 (2013)
8. González, D., Pérez, J., Milanés, V.: Parametric-Based Path Generation for Automated Vehicles at Roundabouts. Pergamon Press, Inc., Oxford (2017)
9. Ji, J., Khajepour, A., Melek, W.W., et al.: Path planning and tracking for vehicle collision avoidance based on model predictive control with multiconstraints. IEEE Trans. Veh. Technol. **66**(2), 952–964 (2017)
10. Rahman, M.A.: Multi agent coordinated path planning using imporved artificial potential field-based regression search method. Dissertations and Theses, Gradworks (2014)
11. Li, B., Shao, Z.: Precise trajectory optimization for articulated wheeled vehicles in cluttered environments. Adv. Eng. Softw. **92**, 40–47 (2016)

Detecting Attention in Pivotal Response Treatment Video Probes

Corey D. C. Heath[✉], Hemanth Venkateswara, Troy McDaniel,
and Sethuraman Panchanathan

Center for Cognitive Ubiquitous Computing, Arizona State University,
Tempe, AZ 85287, USA
{corey.heath,hemanthv,troy.mcdaniel,panch}@asu.edu

Abstract. The benefits of caregivers implementing Pivotal Response Treatment (PRT) with children on the Autism spectrum is empirically supported in current Applied Behavior Analysis (ABA) research. Training caregivers in PRT practices involves providing instruction and feedback from trained professional clinicians. As part of the training and evaluation process, clinicians systematically score video probes of the caregivers implementing PRT in several categories, including if an instruction was given when the child was paying adequate attention to the caregiver. This paper examines how machine learning algorithms can be used to aid in classifying video probes. The primary focus of this research explored how attention can be automatically inferred through video processing. To accomplish this, a dataset was created using video probes from PRT sessions and used to train machine learning models. The ambiguity inherent in these videos provides a substantial set of challenges for training an intelligence feedback system.

Keywords: Pivotal Response Treatment · Dyadic behavior
Attention detection · Untrimmed video · Autism Spectrum Disorder

1 Introduction

Individuals with Autism Spectrum Disorder (ASD) often have challenges in developing communication and social skills. Pivotal Response Treatment (PRT) is an Applied Behavior Analysis (ABA) technique that has empirical research backing its effectiveness. PRT is a dyadic interaction where an interventionist engages with a recipient to aid the recipient in acquiring new target skills. PRT is exemplified by providing learning opportunities in a natural context using objects or activities selected by the recipient as motivational reinforcement [1]. Training primary caregivers to implement PRT has been proven to help caregiver and child stress levels and help the child gain communication skills [2]; however, training and supporting caregivers requires the time of experienced clinicians. The research presented in this paper examines initial steps in aiding the evaluation and feedback of caregivers' implementation of PRT.

PRT research and training relies on video probes to provide analysis of the interventionist's fidelity to implementation. The videos require a significant time commitment by a behavioral analyst to provide effective evaluation of the interventionist's

© Springer Nature Switzerland AG 2018
A. Basu and S. Berretti (Eds.): ICSM 2018, LNCS 11010, pp. 248–259, 2018.
https://doi.org/10.1007/978-3-030-04375-9_21

performance. Providing automated analysis of the video data would reduce the cost of evaluation, and provide the opportunity to collect data on long term progression.

Video probes present a challenge for automated analysis. Ideally, the videos should depict the interventionist (the caregiver), and the recipient (the child), both of whom should be completely in frame, unobscured, and facing the camera. This is not always the case. These videos are often filmed using handheld digital cameras or cell phone cameras. The resulting videos are often low resolution, unstable, and occasionally have the interventionist or the recipient out of the frame. The video probes are often recorded at home in an unstructured environment and with inconsistent backgrounds, which could provide a challenge for computer vision based algorithms [3]. Additionally, because PRT is based on integrating learning opportunities within activities selected by the treatment recipient, there are no standardized actions or activities reflected in the videos.

This paper explores how PRT performance data can be extracted from the video probes automatically to reduce the processing time for clinicians and provide feedback to PRT interventionists. The research presented focuses on one evaluation metric utilized for feedback - gaining the recipient's attention. This is an important step in training the interventionist to provide proper instruction.

The contribution of this work includes a new labeled dataset consisting of body pose data from PRT video probes. As part of this we examine strategies for preparing data and approximating data gaps in natural, untrimmed videos, along with methods for building spatio-temporal (ST) graphs for dyadic interactions. Additionally, the implementation of a machine learning model for detecting attention is explored, through the comparison of Support Vector Machine (SVM) implementations using Euclidean based data and a pretrained convolutional neural network (CNN) model with AlexNet weights fine-tuned with pixel data from video probe still frames. These implementations are intended to serve as a baseline for future innovation. Ultimately, we present how automated detection of attention can be used to aid clinicians and caregivers reviewing PRT video probes.

2 Related Work

Technology for supporting and training individuals to implement PRT have focused on remote instruction and online training [4, 5], without automated components. This work is the first known attempt to provide automated analysis of PRT.

ST graphs have been used for structuring input features in several recent works. Jain et al. [6] explored creating an RNN that utilizes ST graph representations of human activities. Their goal was to create a general model for human activity detection, motion forecasting, and maneuver anticipation for driving data. A similar approach using human skeletal model data and an RNN for motion forecasting was published by Fragkiadaki et al. [7]. Chen and Grauman [8] examined different ways of linking ST graphs while using a SVM implementation for classifying human activities.

Deep learning approaches have been explored in numerous recent publications. Ma et al. [9] explored combining a CNN with a long short-term memory architecture for human activity detection in untrimmed video. Zhao et al. [10] used CNN and RNN architectures to create a comparative model, where the classification with the highest competency was used to predict a class label. Working with children with ASD, Jazouli et al. [11] implemented a neural network for classifying self-stimulating behaviors. The approach presented in this paper differs from the these works in that it examines dyadic behaviors.

ST graphs based on human body pose data were used for detecting actions of multiple individuals by Zhang et al. [12], Sener and Ikizler-Cinbis [13], and Van Gemeren et al. [14]. Zhang et al., and Sener and Ikizler-Cinbis both used multiple instance learning techniques for classifying interaction between people. Van Gemeren et al. examined connecting subgraphs of two individuals and detecting interactions in untrimmed videos using an SVM based classifier.

Detection of joint attention and levels of engagement are a subset of dyadic behavior recognition that is related to the work presented in this paper. Gaze estimation and proximity were primary features used to detect if people were engaged as a group by Bazzani et al. [15], and to determine joint attention between two individuals by Duffner and Garcia [16]. Pusiol et al. [17] used egocentric cameras to evaluate joint attention between children and caregivers. Rajagopalan, Murthy, et al. [18], and Rajagopalan, Morency, et al. [19] examined video sessions between a child and a clinician to classify the child's level of engagement. Presti et al. [20] employed a Hidden Markov Model (HMM) on recognized gestures in order to classify reciprocal behaviors in dyadic interactions.

The problem discussed in this paper differs from the research examining dyadic behavior mentioned above. PRT is based on following the recipient's lead on activities, making activity recognition difficult, and it requires an approach for detecting attention generalized outside of specific actions. Another key difference is the dataset. The publications mentioned above used datasets that either resemble security footage, were created under laboratory conditions, came from scripted television, or utilized egocentric or multiple camera perspectives. Video probes from PRT sessions are filmed using a single, handheld camera with subjects filmed at a closer distance than typical security footage. These constraints add additional complexity to the problem and require greater flexibility in proposed solutions.

3   Proposed Method

A dataset consisting of labeled video segments of PRT sessions was created and a feature set of body and facial landmark points was extracted for each individual in the videos. This feature set was then examined for completeness and a procedure was run to approximate missing information. The augmented feature set was then used to train a nu-SVM model to classify video sequences based on the attention of the recipient. The SVM model was evaluated using a leave-one-out strategy where two videos were reserved as a validation set for each training iteration. The remaining sections describe the dataset and evaluation methodologies that were employed.

3.1 Data and Feature Sets

Fourteen videos were selected at random from a PRT study [21] to create a dataset for detecting a child's attention to his or her caregiver. Each of seven caregiver-child dyads were in two videos, a baseline video recorded before the caregiver received instruction in PRT and a post-study video recorded at the end of the training. To represent the types of videos that could be expected, no regard was paid to quality or levels of occlusion. The videos depict the child and caregiver engaged in various activities including playing with assorted toys and games, spinning in a chair, moving about the room, and watching videos on a cell phone. Each video was recorded by a clinician in a room at an ASD resource center.

The videos were divided into 30 frame increments for labeling. Labels were assigned according to the attentive state of the child in accordance with PRT literature [1, 22]. Attention can be labeled regarding who is in control of the motivator - the toy or activity the child wishes to engage with. The segments were labeled as 'attentive' if the caregiver controlled the motivator, and the child was not engaged in an activity, was looking at the parent or was reaching toward the caregiver at any time during the video clip. The segment was labeled 'inattentive' if the child controlled the motivator, was moving about the room, or was engaged in a solitary activity. Segments were labeled as 'shared attention' if the caregiver and child were engaged in a joint activity, or if the caregiver had control of a motivator in a way that seizing control is not disruptive to the activity. Segments were ignored if either the child or caregiver were not visible.

OpenPose [23] was used to extract spatial information. OpenPose provides Cartesian data points for body and facial landmarks for individuals identified in the videos. Eighteen body points are detected including the eyes, nose, neck, and major limb joints. Seventy points from facial landmarks are also recorded. Figure 1 depicts a frame from an instructional video [24] with an overlay of the OpenPose features. In addition to the OpenPose data, relationships between data points were calculated to create an expanded feature set.

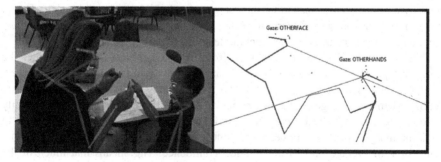

Fig. 1. The frame on the left is a screenshot from [24] with an overlay of the face and body points detected by OpenPose. The OpenPose points along with the gaze estimation and hand coordination vectors are shown on the left.

To overtly capture the interaction between the two individuals in each frame, the Euclidean distance between the individuals' hands was calculated and provided as an additional feature for classification. The goal was to capture common motions that could be indicative of attention, such as the child reaching toward an object in the caregiver's hand or the child playing with an object on his or her own.

Visual attention is an important feature for determining an individual's focus. An individual's gaze was estimated by calculating the Euler angles of the face using 15 of the facial features and an approximated camera perspective based on frame dimensions. The pitch and yaw angles were used to create a point projected away from the individual's face, creating a vector approximating gaze. Euclidean distance is used to determine if the vector intersects with the other person's hands or face. If a specific target was not identified, the gaze would be approximated as looking toward or away from the opposing individual.

The right side from Fig. 1 illustrates features calculated from the spatial data. The two individuals are connected by their left and right hand. An additional vector is depicted extending from the individuals' faces to estimate their gaze. The expected gaze target is displayed above each individual. This figure also shows that body points can overlooked by OpenPose due to occlusion. The individual on the left is missing the points on their left arm and lower body. Her face was also not recognized in enough detail to adequately plot, resulting in a relative scatter of individual points, include two points between the two figures. The right arm of the individual on the right was not detected, however, OpenPose was able to correctly discern the individual's face, as shown by more accurate plotting of points around the head.

Missing body point locations were estimated by looking forward a set number of frames for a value, then averaging the difference over the frames to fill missing values. If a value was not found in the set number of frames, the last known value is used for each remaining frame in the segment. If facial features were not detected, a gaze approximation was calculated using the eye, nose, and neck values from the body point set. If those points were also not detected, the gaze target value was set to 'unknown'.

The basic video attributes are presented in Table 1, showing the number of 30 frame segments given each label. The majority of the segments were able to be classified by a human. This means that the caregiver and child were visible in the frame, and their interaction was discernible. The ignored segments were not used in the remaining analysis or to train the machine learning models.

Presented in Table 1 are the statistics from using OpenPose. The data shows the ability of OpenPose to extract body and facial features from the videos. As expected, OpenPose data displays marginal results. On average only 66% of the body points are identified with an average confidence of 56%. Much of this could be attributed to only the top portion of individuals being in the shot, along with the tendency of caretakers to be on the margins of video frame. More concerning is the lack of confidence in facial features, at an average of 23% recognition confidence. This means that much of the gaze estimation will be undertaken using the less precise locations of the eyes and ears presented in the body point results from OpenPose.

Figure 2(a) shows the percentage of frames in each probe by the number of individual people OpenPose identified. This data illustrates that OpenPose overwhelmingly recognized only one individual in the frame despite human vetting removing segments where only the child or the caregiver were present. This is likely due to partial occlusion of one of the individuals. In addition to failing to find two people in the frames, there are a significant number of frames where three or more individuals were recognized. This could be due to additional individuals in the background, or to objects being incorrectly recognized as human features.

Table 1. Label counts for 30 frame increments for each video probe are presented along with proportions and confidence levels for body and facial point detection from OpenPose.

Video probe	Attentive	Shared	Inattentive	Ignored	Body det.	Body conf.	Face det.	Face conf.
Dyad1 Base	182	43	371	5	0.72	0.58	0.76	0.13
Dyad1 Post	170	23	266	156	0.62	0.55	0.60	0.08
Dyad2 Base	178	4	254	170	0.62	0.56	0.87	0.36
Dyad2 Post	11	585	14	0	0.69	0.59	0.80	0.35
Dyad3 Base	146	258	190	10	0.63	0.50	0.85	0.26
Dyad3 Post	203	101	133	167	0.53	0.56	0.79	0.33
Dyad4 Base	80	0	278	260	0.74	0.57	0.79	0.23
Dyad4 Post	261	22	285	33	0.74	0.56	0.83	0.23
Dyad5 Base	35	144	415	17	0.72	0.57	0.95	0.34
Dyad5 Post	144	66	372	29	0.72	0.53	0.78	0.17
Dyad6 Base	95	180	215	125	0.55	0.54	0.63	0.10
Dyad6 Post	135	26	317	127	0.59	0.52	0.63	0.13
Dyad7 Base	94	110	167	236	0.62	0.55	0.82	0.24
Dyad7 Post	119	246	221	24	0.68	0.59	0.91	0.32

These statistics were improved by implementing the procedure for estimating missing data detailed in the methodology section of this paper. Figure 2(b) shows that this process could reconstruct the data to favor having two individuals in the frame. This means that periods of occlusions resulting in the failure to detect an individual were relatively sparse and the data could be approximated within set parameters. This process also caused the completeness of the body points to rise on average across the videos to 74%.

Due to the variety of activities the caregiver and child could participate in, identifying action poses was not feasible, and the feature set needed to be generalized. Based on observation and current literature [1, 22] it was determined that the coordination of the individuals' hands and gaze would be the most diagnostic features for detecting attention. Rate of movement was also a consideration, as the child would need to be relatively still to be attentive. To emphasize this, magnitude between body landmarks in adjoining frames was included in samples instead of the spatial value. Prior to calculating features, each of the spatial points was rescaled by the frame dimensions of the video and normalized to the neck point of the individual. The position of the child in the frame relative to the caregiver was known prior to processing. This information was used to organize the data so that the caregiver always represents the first person in the feature set.

The feature set used for training the SVM models consisted of a movement score for each individual, the Euclidean distance between the hands of the individuals, a gaze target and a flag indicating reaching behavior. The 30 frame video segments that were labeled were subdivided into six samples. The five frames in each sample where condensed to provide a summary of the activity depicted over the frames. Each of the six samples were given the same label as the 30 frame segment they were extracted from.

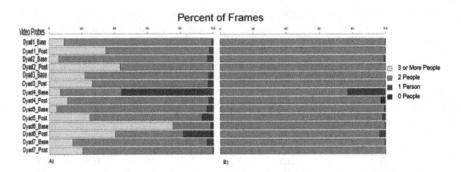

Fig. 2. (A) The bar graph shows the number of people detected by OpenPose in each video. The bars illustrate the percent of frames by the number of people detected. (B) Shows the percentages after processing.

The movement scores were calculated by taking the average magnitude between points in adjoining frames. Unrecognized points were not included in the average. The averages from the frame differences were summed to provide a score for the sample. It is expected that movement scores will be higher when the child is inattentive.

Distances were calculated between the individual's own hands and the hands of the other individual in the frame, resulting in six features. It is hypothesized that when the child's hands are close to one another and far from the caregiver's hands, the child is engaged in an individual activity and is inattentive. If the caregiver's hands and the child's hands are in close proximate, they are likely engaged in a shared activity.

Gaze target estimates are presented as a set of binary features for each frame. This accounts for 10 of the features in the feature set, with five possible targets for each individual. These include looking at the other person's hands or face, looking at the other person's body, looking toward the person or looking away. The gaze was set 'unknown' if insufficient data was present for an estimation. For the amalgamated feature, the gaze binary values were averaged over the frames in the sample.

The final feature is a flag indicating if the child is reaching. This was determined using the angles between the child's shoulder, elbow, and wrist. For the flag to be true in the sample, each of the frames must indicate the child was reaching.

3.2   Attention Classification

A nu-SVM [25] with a radial basis function kernel was used to evaluate classification tasks using the expanded feature set. The base and post videos for each dyad were used as a validation set, while the remaining data was used for training resulting in seven individual model tests.

Two additional feature sets were used as a baseline to compare the results. The Red Green Blue (RGB) pixel values from individual video frames were used to finetune an AlexNet CNN [26, 27] with pretrained weights. The pretrained weights were used to initialize the CNN before training it to classify the PRT images. The finetuning was evaluated using 'leave-one-out' validation for two videos for each dyad. A second baseline feature set consisted of the raw spatial values extracted from OpenPose and used to train an SVM [25]. These baselines differ in that the AlexNet implementation must contend with the background variation and extract the meaningful pose information, whereas the spatial data represents the cartesian location of major body points. The data was processed to approximate missing body points and remove additional individuals as mentioned above. Both data sets were created using every fifth frame from each of the labeled 30 frame segments and organized, resulting in six subsamples for each labeled segment in congruency with the expanded feature set.

4   Results and Discussion

The results of the model evaluations reveal the complexity of the problem space. Overall accuracy for each approach is low, and varies substantially between validation sets as depicted in Table 2. In the table, the accuracy metric shows the proportion of correct to incorrect predictions on the validation dataset. Segment accuracy is the classification of the 30 frame segments that were originally labeled, as determined by the majority classification of the six subsamples. It combines shared and attentive classifications to reflect the system's ability to discern when an instruction could be given.

Table 2. Proportion of correct label predictions for RGB, spatial, and expanded data for each validation set.

Evaluation	Dyad1	Dyad2	Dyad3	Dyad4	Dyad5	Dyad6	Dyad7
AlexNet RGB accuracy	0.46	0.39	0.37	0.55	0.55	0.40	0.33
AlexNet RGB segment acc.	0.49	0.37	0.37	0.59	0.59	0.52	0.57
SVM Spatial accuracy	0.32	0.31	0.32	0.43	0.40	0.34	0.34
SVM spatial segment acc.	0.41	0.53	0.60	0.51	0.47	0.50	0.62
SVM expanded accuracy	0.43	0.37	0.42	0.51	0.50	0.49	0.41
SVM expanded segment acc.	0.52	0.51	0.54	0.60	0.63	0.57	0.56

The low average accuracies show that there is a significant variation in the data, making generalization of patterns for classification needed for successful predictions difficult. The dataset is imbalanced, favoring inattentive behavior. This was addressed by undersampling the larger classes to be equal size with the smallest, resulting in a reduction of the samples that could be used to train the models. Additionally, samples only needed to display attention for part of the segment to be classified as attentive. This could lead to subsamples of the attentive segments being similar in composition to inattentive or shared attention samples.

Class distributions were not evenly spread across the videos, making training a model that performs adequately on each set difficult. This is particularly apparent in Dyad2 and Dyad7, which have large quantities of shared attention samples. The shared activity largely depicted in the Dyad2 Post video is the child sitting in the caretaker's lap, watching a movie on a cellphone. This is different from other shared activities that often had the child and caregiver facing each other, with the motivator, a toy or game, in between them. Similarly, in the Dyad7 Post video the child and caregiver are sitting across the table from one another playing a game. The distance in between them is much greater and there are longer periods of inaction than in other examples of shared activities.

The worst performance was exhibited by the spatial feature set at 35% average accuracy, which is not significantly different from what would be expected with random label assignments. As this data only contained the coordinate location of the individuals, there was little for the algorithm to generalize to form an effective classifier. The inclusion of this feature set was to provide a baseline to compare the results from the CNN model and expanded feature set.

The AlexNet CNN performed better than the spatial feature set at an average of 43% accuracy across the validation sets. This illustrates that the pretrained network could extract features from the still frames to improve classification above random, however, the data still exhibited significant variation to prevent strong predictions. The image background alone does not likely account for the variation. Each video was filmed in rooms, often the same room, at the same ASD resource facility, and the same toys were used in different videos. Since the toys would be associated with different states of attention, this could have aided the classification.

The intention of the expanded feature set was to generalize the features of each state of attention to provide a classification regardless of the activity. At an average of 46% accuracy, this was not sufficiently achieved. The variability among activities caused some scenarios to be in the validation set that did not have an adequate equivalent in the training set. More data may be needed to ensure that a wider range of activities is encompassed in both sets.

The precision of OpenPose could potentially be problematic. Table 2 illustrates that prediction confidence levels are low, particularly regarding facial features. Since the expanded feature set is reliant on extracting information from these points, it is important that recognition be uniform for each sample. The detected position of body parts could vary between videos base on the quality of the video, the proximity of the individual to the camera, whether the person has his or her back to the camera, or other extenuating factors such as clothing. These issues will be compounded by the wobble inherent in videos from handheld cameras. Each of the 30 frame increments in the video were processed through OpenPose independently. It is likely that processing the entire video would improve the precision of detection through OpenPose's tracking algorithms.

The two-dimensionality of the data was problematic for detecting the target of the individual's gaze. One problematic scenario occurred when the child was playing with a toy while the parent stood behind the child and watched. The child gaze is on the toy, however because of the parent in the background, the child's gaze would be incorrectly attributed to looking at the parent. Similar issues can also be attributed to a lack of the ability to infer eye direction. For instance, a child facing the camera, but looking down at the cellphone in his caregiver's hand is in a shared state of attention, whereas a child looking directly at the camera is not attending the parent. The difference in head position is not discernible from the OpenPose data causing misidentification of gaze. This may be addressed by incorporating RBG data of the individuals' heads as a substitute for attempting to determine a gaze target.

Table 3. Illustration of how attention classification aligns with behavior in the video probes. The first two minutes of Dyad5 Post video probe has been broken into 30 s increments.

Time (s)	Description	Attentive	Inattentive	Acc. (%)
1–30	The child looks about the room while the caregiver offers a choice of toys. The caregiver offers a different choice of toys and the child responds	13	17	63
31–60	The child plays with the toy. The caregiver offers a choice of accessories. The child chooses and continues solo play	8	22	70
61–90	The caregiver offers a new choice of accessories. The child chooses, but then asks for a different piece. After receiving the piece, he continues playing	8	22	83
91–120	The child continues solo play. Then watches the caregiver rummage through accessories. The child is offered a choice but does not respond correctly and the caregiver holds the toy until a new response is given	12	18	93

The goal of this research is to maximize the feedback that can be provided to the PRT interventionist while reducing the amount of time necessary for expert review of the video probes. Even with the low classification accuracies, this system could provide benefit to a clinician reviewing the videos. Table 3 contains a description of 2 min from the Dyad5 Post video probe along with the attention classifications. Each second of the video is classified. The predictions are correlated with the activities in the video, and show that the child was largely engaged in solo play with intermittent periods of attention toward the caregiver. By providing this information to the clinician they could gauge the relative attention of the child throughout the video along with finding moments were the caregiver should be providing instruction. This also provides a metric that can be viewed across multiple videos to gain an understanding of whether the caregiver is improving at seizing the child's attention. This example illustrates that in the scheme of attention, accuracy to a one second precision is unnecessary. A more robust approach will likely need to account for greater lengths of time, and encompass a broader understanding of the temporal features for detecting attention. This is particularly important for shared attention states as they are generally sustained for a long period of time compared to attentive states.

5 Conclusion

Video probes are an integral part of evaluating people learning PRT. The current manual process is limited by the costs of having behavioral analysts extract relevant data. These videos provide an opportunity for improving the training process for learning PRT, as well as expanding the field of dyadic human activity detection and classification. PRT video probes provide a complex problem for computer vision due to the unpredictability of the camera stability, the mobility and occlusion of the individuals in the video, and the range of activities that could be performed. The research examined three data representations using two different machine learning algorithms to detect dyadic attention in untrimmed videos to serve as a baseline for future research. Greater exploration into extracting important diagnostic and temporal features is needed to improve classification predictions.

Acknowledgement. The authors thank Arizona State University and National Science Foundation for their funding support. This material is partially based upon work supported by the National Science Foundation under Grant No. 1069125.

References

1. Koegel, R.L.: How to teach pivotal behaviors to children with autism: a training manual (1988)
2. Lecavalier, L., Smith, T., Johnson, C., et al.: Moderators of parent training for disruptive behaviors in young children with autism spectrum disorder. J. Abnorm. Child Psychol. **45** (6), 1235–1245 (2017)
3. Brutzer, S., Høferlin, B., Heidemann, G.: Evaluation of background subtraction techniques for video surveillance. In: IEEE CVPR, pp. 1937–1944 (2011)
4. Machalicek, W., O'Reilly, M.F,, Rispoli, M., et al.: Training teachers to assess the challenging behaviors of students with autism using video tele-conferencing. Educ. Train. Autism Dev. Disabil. **45**(2), 203–215 (2010)
5. Vismara, L.A., McCormick, C., Young, G.S., et al.: Preliminary findings of a telehealth approach to parent training in autism. J. Autism Dev. Disord. **43**(12), 2953–2969 (2013)
6. Jain, A., Zamir, A.R., Savarese, S., Saxena, A.: Structural-RNN: deep learning on spatio-temporal graphs. In: IEEE CVPR, pp. 5308–5317 (2016)
7. Fragkiadaki, K., Levine, S., Felsen, P., Malik, J.: Recurrent network models for human dynamics. In: IEEE ICCV, pp. 4346–4354 (2015)
8. Chen, C.Y., Grauman, K.: Efficient activity detection in untrimmed video with max-subgraph search. IEEE Trans. Pattern Anal. Mach. Intell. **39**(5), 908–921 (2017)
9. Ma, S., Sigal, L., Sclaroff, S.: Learning activity progression in LSTMs for activity detection and early detection. In: IEEE CVPR, pp. 1942–1950 (2016)

10. Zhao, R., Ali, H., van der Smagt, P.: Two-stream RNN/CNN for action recognition in 3D videos. arXiv preprint arXiv:1703.09783 (2017)

11. Jazouli, M., Elhoufi, S., Majda, A., Zarghili, A., Aalouane, R.: Stereotypical motor movement recognition using microsoft kinect with artificial neural network. World Acad. Sci. Eng. Technol. Int. J. Comput. Electr. Autom. Control Inf. Eng. 10(7), 1270–1274 (2016)

12. Zhang, Y., Liu, X., Chang, M.-C., Ge, W., Chen, T.: Spatio-temporal phrases for activity recognition. In: Fitzgibbon, A., Lazebnik, S., Perona, P., Sato, Y., Schmid, C. (eds.) ECCV 2012. LNCS, vol. 7574, pp. 707–721. Springer, Heidelberg (2012). https://doi.org/10.1007/978-3-642-33712-3_51

13. Sener, F., Ikizler-Cinbis, N.: Two-person interaction recognition via spatial multiple instance embedding. J. Vis. Commun. Image Represent. 32, 63–73 (2015)

14. Van Gemeren, C., Poppe, R., Veltkamp, R.C.: Spatio-temporal detection of fine-grained dyadic human interactions. International Workshop on Human Behavior Understanding, pp. 116–133. Springer, Cham (2016). https://doi.org/10.1007/978-3-319-46843-3_8

15. Bazzani, L., Cristani, M., Tosato, D., Farenzena, M., et al.: Social interactions by visual focus of attention in a three-dimensional environment. Expert Syst. 30(2), 115–127 (2013)

16. Duffner, S., Garcia, C.: Visual focus of attention estimation with unsupervised incremental learning. IEEE Trans. Circ. Syst. Video Technol. 26(12), 2264–2272 (2016)

17. Pusiol, G., Soriano, L., Frank, M.C., Fei-Fei, L.: Discovering the signatures of joint attention in child-caregiver interaction. In: Proceedings of the Cognitive Science Society, vol. 36 (2014)

18. Rajagopalan, S.S., Murthy, O.R., Goecke, R., Rozga, A.: Play with me measuring a child's engagement in a social interaction. In: IEEE FG, pp. 1–8, IEEE (2015)

19. Rajagopalan, S.S., Morency, L.-P., Baltrusaitis, T., Goecke, R.: Extending long short-term memory for multi-view structured learning. In: Leibe, B., Matas, J., Sebe, N., Welling, M. (eds.) ECCV 2016. LNCS, vol. 9911, pp. 338–353. Springer, Cham (2016). https://doi.org/10.1007/978-3-319-46478-7_21

20. Presti, L., Sclaroff, S., Rozga, A.: Joint alignment and modeling of correlated behavior streams. In: IEEE ICCV, pp. 730–737, IEEE (2016)

21. Signh, N.: The effects of parent training in pivotal response treatment (PRT) and continued support through telemedicine on gains in communication in children with autism spectrum disorder. Degree of Doctor of Medicine, University of Arizona, April 2014. http://arizona.openrepository.com/arizona/handle/10150/315907

22. Suhrheinrich, S., Reed, S., Schreibman, L., Bolduc, C.: Classroom Pivotal Response Teaching for Children with Autism. Guilford Press, New York (2011)

23. Cao, Z., Simon, T., Wei, S.E., Sheikh, Y.: Realtime multi-person 2D pose estimation using part affinity fields. In: IEEE CVPR, IEEE (2017)

24. Considine, B.: https://www.youtube.com/watch?v=VwoAYir7Vsk. Accessed 30 Apr 2018

25. Pedregosa, F., Varoquaux, G., Gramfort, A., et al.: Scikit-learn: machine learning in Python. J. Mach. Learn. Res. 12, 2825–2830 (2011)

26. Kratzert, F.: https://kratzert.github.io/2017/02/24/finetuning-alexnet-with-tensorflow.html. Accessed 30 Apr 2018

27. Krizhevsky, A., Sutskever, I., Hinton, E.: ImageNet classification with deep convolutional neural networks. In: Advances in Neural Information Processing Systems, pp. 1097–1105 (2012). https://doi.org/10.1145/3065386

Person Authentication by Air-Writing Using 3D Sensor and Time Order Stroke Context

Lee-Wen Chiu[1], Jun-Wei Hsieh[2(✉)], Chin-Rong Lai[1],
Hui-Fen Chiang[2], Shyi-Chy Cheng[2], and Kuo-Chin Fan[1]

[1] National Central University, Taoyuan City 32001, Taiwan
[2] National Taiwan Ocean University, Keelung City 202, Taiwan
shieh@email.ntou.edu.tw

Abstract. This paper proposes touch-less system to use air-written signatures for person authentication. This smart system can verify a person's ID without using any mouse, touch panels, or keyboards. It benefits from a 3D sensor to capture a user's signature in air and then verifies his ID via a novel reverse time-ordered shape context. This backward representation can effectively filter out redundant lifting-up strokes and thus simplify the matching process as a path finding problem. As features to analyze a user's signature more accurately, the rates of turning point and curvature are also embedded into this representation. Then, with a weighting scheme, the path finding problem can be solved in real time via a dynamic time warping technique. Another challenging problem is the multiplicity problem which means a signature is not always written the same due to users' practices and moods. Thus, an agglomerative hierarchical clustering scheme is adopted to cluster users' signatures into different subclasses. Each subclass represents different within-class variations. Another key issues is the criterion to determine the threshold for verifying and then passing a user's signature. Experimental results proves the average within-class distance can gain the best accuracy. The proposed solution achieves quite satisfactory authentication accuracy (more than 93.5%) even though no starting gesture is required.

Keywords: Air-writing ideographic signature · Identity authentication
Shape context · Dynamic time warping

1 Introduction

Person authentication is the process of determining whether a person is who he claims to be by validating his identity documents. The identity documents can be roughly divided into two types, i.e., non-biometric elements and biometric ones. The former ones include passwords, PIN (personal identification number), ID card, security token, cell phone with hardware token, software token, or cell phone holding a software token. The major advantages of this authentication method are: (i) simpleness; (ii) low cost; (iii) easy use for mobile devices. However, the identity documents are not based on users' unique individual characteristics and thus easily faces the risk of being stolen, lost, or hacked. To avoid the problem of sharing, guessing, duplication, or fraud, biometric authentication will be another good choice. Two kinds of biometric attributes

A. Basu and S. Berretti (Eds.): ICSM 2018, LNCS 11010, pp. 260–273, 2018.
https://doi.org/10.1007/978-3-030-04375-9_22

can be used for authentication, i.e., physical biometrics and behavioral ones. The former ones include DNA, fingerprints, face recognition, and eye scans (iris, retina). The later ones include voice recognition and handwritten signatures. Unlike physical biometrics, a behavioral biometric feature is much less invasive and cannot be easily stolen or duplicated. Thus, this paper investigates the possibility and robustness of air-writing in person authentication.

The authentication based on writing signature can be finished off-line or on-line. For the off-line system, the time-order or writing speed information of each signature is usually missed and thus two signatures are compared majorly based on their shape similarity. For the on-line system, a signature is compared based on not only its shape but also its time order of writing. Because the correct time order or writing speed is not easily imitated, it is more difficult for hackers to hack an on-line system than the off-line one. The input devices of most on-line systems to capture users' signatures focus on touch panels. For example, in [1], Forhad et al. converted signature trajectories into strings and then matched them by calculating their edit distances for person authentication. In [2], Zhang et al. proposed a finger-writing-in-the-air system by combining skin, depth, and background information to segment and track fingertips and their positions via Kinect. In [3], Tsuchida et al., used motion vectors and self-defined dynamic programming matching to calculate the highest similarity between two data samples. In [4], Chiang et al. considered each writing trajectory as a one-stroke finger gesture and modified the DTW algorithm as a path finding algorithm to recognize all possible individual numerals. In [5], Qu, Zhang, and Tian used a tracking technique to extract six features including fingertip position, displacement, velocity, acceleration, tilt angle, and path angle of fingertip to represent and recognize characters written in air. Furthermore, Su et al. [6] proposed a SVM-based hand-gesture recognition system to recognize numbers written in air via Kinect for home appliance control. In [7], Beg, Khan, and Baig proposed a real time pointing system which allows sketching and writing of English texts over air in front of mobile camera. In [8], Aggarwa et al. used the K-means clustering method to partition and quantize zones of fingers into vectors which were then classified into different characters via SVMs. As to authentication using air-writing, there are fewer frameworks proposed in the literature. Schick, Morlock, and Amma [9] combined HMM and a 3D tracking technique to recognize characters handwritten in air. In [10], Tian et al. proposed an authentication system to allow users to write their passwords in 3D space via Kinect devices. However, this approach performed the authentication task majorly based on passwords rather than biometric features. In [11], Milanova and Xie used Fourier descriptors and moments with invariance properties to match writing signatures for authentication. However, the used Fourier descriptor and moment feature are not robust to noise and redundant strokes.

Aiming at addressing the above challenges, this paper proposes a novel air-writing authentication system to recognize users' signatures without using any pen-starting-lift

Fig. 1. Flowchart of the proposed air-writing recognition system.

signal. Figure 1 shows the flowchart of our proposed air-writing authentication system. When a user writes his signature in air, some redundant trajectories will usually appear at the beginning of this signature. To release this problem, this paper proposes a novel reverse time-ordered shape context to represent an air-writing trajectory in a backward way. This backward representation can effectively filter out them and thus simplify the matching process as a path finding problem. Then, with a weighting scheme, the path finding problem can be solved in real time via a dynamic time warping technique. In addition to shape context, the rates of turning point and curvature are also embedded into this representation as features to analyze a user's signature more accurately. Then, the path finding problem can be solved in real time via a dynamic time warping technique. Another challenging problem is the multiplicity problem which means a signature is not always written the same due to users' practices and moods. To enhance the robustness of our system, an agglomerative hierarchical clustering scheme is then adopted to cluster users' signatures into different subclasses. Each subclass can capture different within-class variations to represent the same user's signatures more accurately. Another key issues is the threshold to determine whether a user's signature is passed or not. Experimental results proves the average within-class distance can gain the best accuracy. The evaluated performance shows that the proposed solution achieves quite satisfactory authentication accuracy (more than 93.5%) even though no starting gesture is required.

2 Motion Trajectory Extraction

The proposed system uses a 3D sensor to capture human hand motions. Figure 2 shows a sequence of writing trajectory for a Chinese family name "Wong". To represent an air-writing trajectory T, different turning points should be extracted along T and then used for authentication.

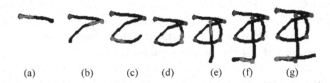

(a)   (b)   (c)   (d)   (e)   (f)   (g)

Fig. 2. An air-writing trajectory captured for authentication. (a)–(g): sequential writing trajectories for a Chinese family name "Wong" or "王".

Let $\alpha(p)$ be an angle of a point p on T. As shown in Fig. 3, the angle α can be determined by two specified points q and r which are selected from both sides of p along T and satisfy that

$$d_{\min} \leq |p - q| \leq d_{\max} \text{ and } d_{\min} \leq |p - r| \leq d_{\max}, \tag{1}$$

where d_{min} and d_{max} are two thresholds and set to $|T|/30$ and $|T|/20$, respectively, and $|T|$ the length of T. The term d_{min} is a smoothing factor used to reduce the effect of noise from T. With q and r, the angle $\alpha(p)$ can be decided by

$$\alpha(p) = \cos^{-1} \frac{(p-q) \bullet (p-r)}{\|p-q\|\|p-r\|}, \tag{2}$$

where $\bullet$ denotes an inner product operation. If α is less than a threshold τ_α, i.e., $150°$, the point p is selected as a turning point. It is also expected that two turning points should be far from each other. This enforces that the distance between any two control points should be larger than the threshold d_{min} (defined in Eq. (1)). If two candidates p_1 and p_2 are close to each other, i.e., $\|p_1 - p_2\| \le d_{min}$, the one (denoted by a green color) with a smaller angle α is chosen as the best turning point. All the remained turning points are pushed into a stack for recording.

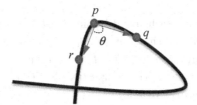

Fig. 3. Angle calculation of a turning point p on a trajectory T.

3   Air-Writing Representation

Given a writing trajectory T, we can adopt the shape context (SC) [12] to characterize its shape. However, the SC technique cannot well record the time order information of T. To capture this information, in what follows, a novel representation technique is proposed for trajectory comparison and air-wring authentication.

3.1   Shape Context

The SC technique [12] projects T onto a log-polar coordinate and then labels each point on T. We use m to represent the number of shells used to quantize the radial axis and n to represent the number of sectors that we want to quantize in each shell. Given a reference point r selected from T, we construct a vector histogram $H_r^T = (h_r(1), \ldots, h_r(k), \ldots, h_r(mn))$, in which $h_r(k)$ is the number of trajectory points in the kth bin when r is considered as the origin, i.e.,

$$h_r(k) = \#\{q|\, q \ne r,\, (q-r) \in bin^k\}, \tag{3}$$

where bin^k is the kth bin of the log-polar coordinate. Then, given two histograms, H_p^T and H_q^T, their distance can be measured by a Chi-square distance as the form:

$$\xi(H_p^T, H_q^T) = \sum_{i=1}^{mn} \frac{(H_p^T(k) - H_q^T(k))^2}{H_p^T(k) + H_q^T(k) + 1}. \tag{4}$$

3.2   Time-Order Shape Context

Assume there are M points collected from a trajectory T, i.e., $T = \{p_0, p_1, \ldots, p_t, \ldots, p_{M-1}\}$, where p_t is written later than p_{t-1}. From p_t, we can construct its corresponding shape context $H_{p_t}^T$. Then, a Full Time-order Context (FTC) can be constructed to describe T as follows:

$$FTC(T) = \left\{ H_{p_0}^T, \ldots, H_{p_t}^T, \ldots, H_{P_{M-1}}^T \right\}. \tag{5}$$

As shown in Fig. 4, for each tracked point p_t of '王', its corresponding shape context $H_{p_t}^T$ is constructed and shown in (b). All $H_{p_t}^T$ form the descriptor $FTC(T)$ to describe '王'. The disadvantage of $FTC(T)$ is very time-consuming in matching because all points on T are used. The complexity of $FTC(T)$ can be reduced if $H_{p_t}^T$ is extracted only from the strokes of T.

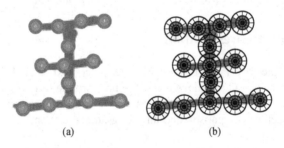

(a)   (b)

Fig. 4. Full time-order shape contexts of '王'. (a) Time-order air-written points of '王'. (b) Full time-order shape contexts of '王'.

Assume there are $(N_T + 1)$ turning points extracted from T, i.e., $C^T = \{c_0, c_1, \ldots, c_t, \ldots, c_{N_T}\}$. It is noticed that $N_T << M$. Two adjacent turning points c_t and c_{t+1} in C^T can form the tth stroke S_t^T in T. Let S^T denote the set of stokes collected from T, i.e., $S^T = \{S_0^T, \ldots, S_t^T, \ldots, S_{N_T-1}^T\}$. As shown in Fig. 5, four strokes can be extracted along '王'. Each stroke S_t^T can generate two shape contexts from its starting point c_t and ending one c_{t+1}. Let U_t^T be the union of $\{S_0^T, \ldots, S_t^T\}$, i.e., $U_t^T = \bigcup_{i=0}^{t} S_i^T$. Examples of U_t^T are shown in Fig. 5, where different stokes are denoted by different colors. Based on U_t^T, we can create a Stroke-based Time-order Context (STC) to describe T:

$$STC(T) = \left\{ \mathbb{H}^{U_0^T}, \mathbb{H}^{U_1^T}, \ldots, \mathbb{H}^{U_t^T}, \ldots, \mathbb{H}^T \right\}, \tag{6}$$

where $\mathbb{H}^{U_t^T} = \left\{ \boldsymbol{H}_{c_0}^{U_t^T}, \ldots, \boldsymbol{H}_{c_{t+1}}^{U_t^T} \right\}$. Noticed that $\boldsymbol{H}_{c_0}^{U_1^T}$ and $\boldsymbol{H}_{c_0}^{U_2^T}$ are different even though their origins are the same because U_1^T and U_2^T are with different shapes. Different versions of $\mathbb{H}^{U_t^T}$ for '圭' are shown in Fig. 6. After integration, the whole STC descriptor to describe '圭' is (a) + (b) + (c) + (d).

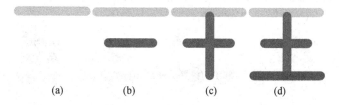

(a)   (b)   (c)   (d)

Fig. 5. Four strokes for '圭'. (a) U_0^T. (b) U_1^T. (c) U_2^T. (d) U_3^T.

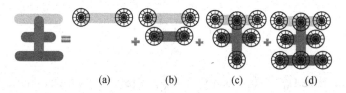

(a)   (b)   (c)   (d)

Fig. 6. Different versions of '圭' in the STC representation. (a) $\mathbb{H}^{U_0^T}$. (b) $\mathbb{H}^{U_1^T}$. (c) $\mathbb{H}^{U_2^T}$. (d) $\mathbb{H}^{U_3^T}$.

3.3 Reverse Time-Order Stroke Representation

In real conditions, a user often inputs his air-writings from an unknown lifting position which will result in some redundant strokes. For example, in Fig. 7(a), there are four strokes extracted from 'y'. The first stroke in Fig. 7(a) (formed by p_0 and p_1) is redundant for air-writing authentication. To tackle the above problem, a novel reverse time order stroke representation is proposed in this paper to represent an air-written signature more accurately.

This representation stacks all turning points and then pops them to get different strokes in a reverse time order. Let Ω^T denote the set of reverse time-order strokes of T, *i.e.*,

$$\Omega^T = \bigcup_{t=0}^{N_T-1} S_t^T. \tag{7}$$

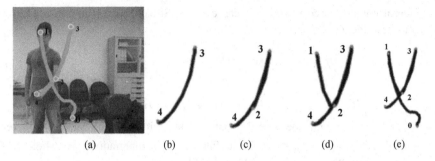

Fig. 7. Reverse time order stroke representation of a trajectory 'y'. (a) Original Image. (b) Ω_0^T. (c): Ω_1^T. (d): Ω_2^T. (e): Ω_3^T.

Fig. 8. Reverse Stroke-based time-order context (STC) for describing '王'.

In addition, let Ω_t^T denote the tth version of Ω^T, *i.e.*,

$$\Omega_t^T = \bigcup_{i=N_T-t-1}^{N_T-1} S_i^T.$$

Then, we have $\Omega_0^T = S_{N_T-1}^T$ and $\Omega_1^T = S_{N_T-1}^T \bigcup S_{N_T-2}^T$. With Ω_t^T, different evolved versions of T can be generated until a complete one. Figure 7(b)–(e) shows an example of the reverse time order stroke representation of a 'y' signature. It is noticed that Ω_2^T corresponds to the correct 'y' character without including any redundant lifting strokes. Clearly, the correct version of the analyzed signature will be evolutionally generated without including any redundant strokes. Figure 8 shows an example of this method to describe '王'. With the sets $\{\Omega_2^T\}_{t=0,\ldots,N_T-1}$, a reverse Stroke-based Time-order Context (*rSTC*) can be constructed for recognizing a signature T more correctly. The reverse representation is similar to $STC(T)$ (see Eq. (5)) but with a reverse time order. This *rSTC* descriptr for air-writing recognition is defined as follows:

$$rSTC(T) = \left\{ \mathbb{H}^{\Omega_0^T}, \mathbb{H}^{\Omega_1^T}, \ldots, \mathbb{H}^{\Omega_2^T}, \ldots, \mathbb{H}^T \right\}, \tag{8}$$

where $\mathbb{H}^{\Omega_t^T} = \left\{ H_{c_{N_T}}^{\Omega_t^T}, \ldots, H_{c_{N_T-t-1}}^{\Omega_t^T} \right\}$. An example of this *rSTC* descriptor to describe '王' is shown in Fig. 8.

3.4   Representation by Velocity and Curvature

For a signature written in air, a hacker might easily copy its shape but should feel very difficultly to imitate its writing velocities and angles turning between stokes. Thus, they can form important biometric features for authentication. From T, its writing velocity at time t can be defined as follows:

$$V(T(t)) = \frac{T(t+\Delta t) - T(t)}{\Delta t} = (x'(t), y'(t))^t$$

For the turning angle, we can use "curvature" (denoted by κ) to measure how fast a curve is changing its direction at a given point. Given a point $T(t)$, its κ is the inverse of the radius of a circle fitted at it and defined as

$$\kappa(T(t)) = \frac{|x''(t)y'(t) - x'(t)y''(t)|}{[(x'(t))^2 + (y'(t))^2]^{3/2}}. \tag{9}$$

Then, for each point $T(t)$ in T, it includes three kinds of features for authentication,

$$(X_{T(t)}^T, V(T(t)), \kappa(T(t)))^t, \tag{10}$$

where $X_{T(t)}^T$ is one of time-order contexts described in Sects. 3.2 or 3.3.

4   Air-Writing Authentication

Let T_D and T_Q denote two air-written trajectories; one from the database and another from the writer. Then, different features can be extracted from T_D and T_Q for authentication. In what follows, the task to measure their distance will be discussed.

4.1   Distance Measure

Let N_D and N_Q be the numbers of control points extracted from T_D and T_Q, respectively. Then, from T_D, a set of control points can be extracted, i.e.,

$$C^{T_D} = \{p_0, p_1, \ldots, p_i, \ldots, p_{N_D}\}. \tag{11}$$

Similarly, from T_Q, another set of control points can be extracted, i.e.,

$$C^{T_Q} = \{q_0, q_1, \ldots, q_j, \ldots, q_{N_Q}\}. \tag{12}$$

Given two control points p_i and q_j, their distance can be measured as follows:

$$\mathbf{d}_X(p_i, q_j) = w_X \varepsilon_X(X_{p_i}^{T_D}, X_{q_j}^{T_Q}) + w_{vel}d_{vel}(V(p_i), V(q_j)) + w_{cur}d_{cur}(\kappa(p_i), \kappa(q_j)), \tag{13}$$

where X is the used shape descriptor, $d_{vel}()$ the velocity distance between $V(p_i)$ and $V(q_j)$, and $d_{cur}()$ the distance between $\kappa(p_i)$ and $\kappa(q_j)$. If the STC descriptor is adopted, $\varepsilon_X(X_{P_i}^{T_D}, X_{q_j}^{T_Q})$ will become

$$\varepsilon_X(X_{p_i}^{T_D}, X_{q_j}^{T_Q}) = \frac{1}{|C_j^{T_Q}|} \sum_{q \in C_j^{T_Q}} \min_{p \in C_i^{T_D}} \xi(H_p^{U_i^{T_D}}, H_q^{U_j^{T_Q}}), \tag{14}$$

where $C_t^T = \{c_k|c_k : \text{the } k\text{th control point of } T, k = 0, \dots, t\}$ and $|C_t^T| = t+1$. If the rSTC descriptor is adopted, $\varepsilon_X(X_{P_i}^{T_D}, X_{q_j}^{T_Q})$ will have the form

$$\varepsilon_X(X_{p_i}^{T_D}, X_{q_j}^{T_Q}) = \frac{1}{|\tilde{C}_j^{T_Q}|} \sum_{q \in \tilde{C}_j^{T_Q}} \min_{p \in \tilde{C}_i^{T_D}} \xi(H_p^{\Omega_i^{T_D}}, H_q^{\Omega_j^{T_Q}}), \tag{15}$$

where $\tilde{C}_t^T = \{c_k|c_k : \text{the } k\text{th control point of } T \text{ from } k = N_T \text{ to } N_T - t - 1\}$ and $|\tilde{C}_t^T| = t+1$. $d_{vel}()$ and $d_{cur}()$ in Eq. (13) are defined, respectively, as follows:

$$d_{vel}(V(p_i), V(q_j)) = (V(p_i) - V(q_j))^2, \tag{16}$$

and

$$d_{cur}(\kappa(p_i), \kappa(q_j)) = (\kappa(p_i) - \kappa(q_j))^2. \tag{17}$$

In Eq. (13), the weights w_X, w_{vel}, and w_{cur} balance the contributions among the context X, the velocity, and the curvature features, respectively.

4.2 Dynamic Time Warping

In real cases, a signature will often be written at different speeds even by the same user. To deal with this time-scaling change problem, the DTW technique is adopted in our system to measure the distance between T_D and T_Q. Assume the DTW distance between $T_D[p_0, \dots, p_i]$ and $T_Q[q_0, \dots, q_j]$ is denoted by $DTW_X[p_i, q_j]$ where X is the used descriptor. Its value can be easily calculated with the recursive form

$$DTW_X[p_i, q_j] = \mathbf{d}_X[p_i, q_j] + \min(DTW_X[p_{i-1}, q_j], DTW_X[p_i, q_{j-1}], DTW_X[p_{i-1}, q_{j-1}]), \tag{18}$$

where $\mathbf{d}_X[p_i, q_j]$ is defined in Eq. (13) and will be different according to the descriptor X. By recursively performing Eq. (18), we can get the distance between T_D and T_Q, i.e., $DTW_X[|T_D|, |T_Q|]$ with a dynamic programming technique.

4.3 Reverse Representation with Weighting

In real implementations, if each stroke is with different importance, the distance in Eq. (18) can be measured more accurately. As discussed previously, the lifting strokes written early tend to be redundant in matching. It means the stroke written later is considered more important than the early one. For the ith stroke S_i, this paper enforces its importance W_i being proportional to i as follows:

$$W_i \propto i, \ i \in [1, N]. \tag{19}$$

Because $\sum_{i=1}^{N} W_i = 1$, we have $W_i = \frac{2i}{N(N+1)}$. With W_i, Eq. (18) can be modified as

$$DTW_X[p_i, q_j] = W_i \mathbf{d}_X[p_i, q_j] + \min(DTW_X[p_{i-1}, q_j],$$
$$DTW_X[p_i, q_{j-1}], DTW_X[p_{i-1}, q_{j-1}]). \tag{20}$$

Because the importance of each stroke is considered d, each air-written signature can be more accurately compared.

4.4 Agglomerative Hierarchical Clustering

In real cases, a user's signatures written at different times are not totally the same. To capture this within-class variations, this paper uses more than one models to represent a user's signatures via an agglomerative hierarchical clustering scheme.

Assume there are N signatures collected from the same user. Considering each signature as a cluster first, the closest cluster pairs are then successively merged into another new cluster so that fewer than N sets are obtained. This merging process is repeated until the minimum distance between all pairs of clusters is greater than a predefined threshold. Then, no more clusters can be further merged or the number of clusters reduced to the number desired. There are three ways of calculating the distance between any two clusters $\mathbb{C}_i$ and $\mathbb{C}_j$. They can be defined as follows:

1. The distance of the closest two points in two clusters each; that is,

$$\mathbf{d}_{\min}(\mathbb{C}_i, \mathbb{C}_j) = \min_{p \in \mathbb{C}_i, q \in \mathbb{C}_j} DTW_X(p, q). \tag{21}$$

2. The distance of the farthest two points in two clusters each; that is,

$$\mathbf{d}_{\max}(\mathbb{C}_i, \mathbb{C}_j) = \max_{p \in \mathbb{C}_i, q \in \mathbb{C}_j} DTW_X(p, q). \tag{22}$$

3. The average distance of all pairs of points in two clusters each; that is,

$$\mathbf{d}_{avg}(\mathbb{C}_i, \mathbb{C}_j) = \frac{1}{|\mathbb{C}_i||\mathbb{C}_j|} \sum_{p \in \mathbb{C}_i, q \in \mathbb{C}_j} DTW_X(p, q), \tag{23}$$

where $|C|$ denotes the number of elements in C.

After clustering, the centers of all obtained clusters are used to represent the signature variations from the same user. Assume C is a subclass in $\mathbb{C}_i$. There are three ways to define the distance between P and $\mathbb{C}_i$; that is, the minimum, maximum, and average measurements. The "minimum" distance between P and $\mathbb{C}_i$ is defined as

$$d_{\min}^{class}(p, \mathbb{C}_i) = \min_{C \in \mathbb{C}_i} \min_{q \in C} DTW_X(p, q). \tag{24}$$

The maximum distance between P and $\mathbb{C}_i$ is

$$d_{\max}^{class}(p, \mathbb{C}_i) = \min_{C \in \mathbb{C}_i} \max_{q \in C} DTW_X(p, q). \tag{25}$$

The average one is defined as:

$$d_{avg}^{class}(p, \mathbb{C}_i) = \min_{C \in \mathbb{C}_i} \frac{1}{|C|} \sum_{q \in C} DTW_X(p, q). \tag{26}$$

5   Experimental Results

To evaluate the performance of our method, a dataset including 1326 signatures is adopted in this paper. Figure 9 shows some examples of signatures written in air for authentication from nine users. All the signatures were randomly collected during three months for capturing the signature variations from the same user.

Fig. 9. Samples of signatures written in air for authentication.

Table 1. Accuracy comparisons among different parameters without clustering and weightings.

Distance	Min	Min	Min	Max	Max	Max	Avg	Avg	Avg
Threshold	Max	Min	Avg	Max	Min	Avg	Max	Min	Avg
Accuracy	34.5	61.3	65.5	58.9	59.1	60.2	41.7	59.6	79.2

To determine whether a signature is passed through the ith class $\mathbb{C}_i$, this paper uses three methods to define the passing threshold. The first one is to choose the minimum distance between all pairs in $\mathbb{C}_i$ as the threshold $T_{\mathbb{C}_i}^{\min}$, *i.e.,*

$$T_{\mathbb{C}_i}^{\min} = \min_{p,q\in\mathbb{C}_i,p\neq q} DTW_X(p,q). \tag{27}$$

The second one $T_{\mathbb{C}_i}^{\max}$ is to choose the maximum distance between all pairs in $\mathbb{C}_i$, i.e.,

$$T_{\mathbb{C}_i}^{\max} = \max_{p,q\in\mathbb{C}_i} DTW_X(p,q). \tag{28}$$

The third threshold $T_{\mathbb{C}_i}^{avg}$ is to choose the average distance between all pairs in $\mathbb{C}_i$. The first set of experimental results evaluates the accuracy comparisons of our method among different thresholds without clustering. There are three methods to calculate the distance between a query P and a class $\mathbb{C}_i$, i.e., $d_{\min}$, $d_{\max}$, and d_{avg}, and three thresholds for passing check. Thus, there are nine combinations for accuracy comparisons. Table 1 shows the accuracy comparisons among the nine combinations without clustering and weighting. Clearly, when the threshold is fixed, the worst performance is got from $d_{\min}$. When the distance measure is fixed, $T_{\mathbb{C}_i}^{\max}$ got the worst performance because $T_{\mathbb{C}_i}^{\min}$ can reject more fake signatures than $T_{\mathbb{C}_i}^{\max}$. The best performance is got from the combinations of d_{avg} and $T_{\mathbb{C}_i}^{avg}$. As described before, the accuracy of authentication can be further improved if each stoke is compared with weights. Table 2 shows the same comparisons but measuring strokes weights. Compared with Table 2, the accuracy improvement is more than 4%. The best accuracy is 84.6% from the last column.

Table 2. Accuracy comparisons without clustering but with weightings.

Distance	Min	Min	Min	Max	Max	Max	Avg	Avg	Avg
Threshold	Max	Min	Avg	Max	Min	Avg	Max	Min	Avg
Accuracy	38.6	66.1	72.0	65.6	65.4	65.4	46.1	65.4	84.6

In Tables 1 and 2, the adopted descriptor is $STC(T)$ (see Eq. (6)). Actually, if a reverse forward time-order representation $rSTC(T)$ (see Eq. (8)) is adopted, the accuracy can be further improved. Table 3 shows the similar comparisons but with the descriptor $rSTC(T)$ in a reverse time-order way. Clearly, $rSTC(T)$ performs much better than $STC(T)$ because the former can filter out most redundant starting strokes.

Table 3. Accuracy comparisons without clustering in a reverse representation.

Distance	Min	Min	Min	Max	Max	Max	Avg	Avg	Avg
Threshold	Max	Min	Avg	Max	Min	Avg	Max	Min	Avg
Accuracy	45.3	73.2	75.8	70.3	70.8	71.3	50.3	70.7	87.5

Actually, there are various within-class changes in signatures even from the same user. To tackle this problem, this paper adopts an agglomerative hierarchical clustering scheme to cluster a user's signatures into different subclasses. Table 4 shows the accuracy comparisons among different distance measures and thresholds if the clustering scheme is adopted with $\mathbf{d}_{\min}(\mathbb{C}_i, \mathbb{C}_j)$ (see Eq. (21)). When the distance measure is fixed, the threshold $T_{\mathbb{C}_i}^{avg}$ performs better than other thresholds $T_{\mathbb{C}_i}^{\max}$ and $T_{\mathbb{C}_i}^{\min}$. In addition, the distance measure $d_{\min}^{class}$ performs the best because it can let a query be closer to its corresponding class than $d_{\max}^{class}$ and d_{avg}^{class}. Table 5 shows the same comparisons but $\mathbf{d}_{\max}(\mathbb{C}_i, \mathbb{C}_j)$ (see Eq. (22)) is adopted to merge classes. Table 6 shows the same accuracy comparison but $\mathbf{d}_{avg}(\mathbb{C}_i, \mathbb{C}_j)$ (see Eq. (23)) is adopted. In Tables 5 and 6, $T_{\mathbb{C}_i}^{avg}$ still performs better than $T_{\mathbb{C}_i}^{\max}$ and $T_{\mathbb{C}_i}^{\min}$. For all clustering strategies, the best performance is got from the measure $\mathbf{d}_{\min}(\mathbb{C}_i, \mathbb{C}_j)$ because signatures in a category can be more accurately clustered into their corresponding subclasses. Similar to Table 4, in Tables 5 and 6, $d_{\min}^{class}$ performs better than $d_{\max}^{class}$ and d_{avg}^{class}. The best accuracy is 89.4%, got from Table 4.

Table 4. Accuracy comparisons if Eq. (21) is adopted for clustering.

Distance	Min	Min	Min	Max	Max	Max	Avg	Avg	Avg
Threshold	Max	Min	Avg	Max	Min	Avg	Max	Min	Avg
Accuracy	52.5	67.7	89.4	78..8	65.3	65.4	63.7	65.6	79.6

Table 5. Accuracy comparisons if Eq. (22) is adopted for clustering and weightings.

Distance	Min	Min	Min	Max	Max	Max	Avg	Avg	Avg
Threshold	Max	Min	Avg	Max	Min	Avg	Max	Min	Avg
Accuracy	67.0	68.7	86.2	78.2	65.2	65.9	74.0	65.6	77.7

Table 6. Accuracy comparisons with clustering via Eq. (23) and weightings.

Distance	Min	Min	Min	Max	Max	Max	Avg	Avg	Avg
Threshold	Max	Min	Avg	Max	Min	Avg	Max	Min	Avg
Accuracy	78.0	65.3	88.6	78..0	65.3	65.7	68.4	65.7	80.3

The adopted descriptors in Table 4 are $STC(T)$ (see Eq. (6)). As described before, if a reverse forward time-order representation $rSTC(T)$, the accuracy can be further improved. In Tables 4, 5, and 6, the best performances were got from the distance measure $d_{\max}^{class}$ and the threshold $T_{\mathbb{C}_i}^{avg}$. Thus, the same parameter setting was adopted in this evaluation. Table 7 shows the comparisons between the descriptors $STC(T)$ and $rSTC(T)$. Clearly, the worse accuracy in $rSTC(T)$ is still better than the best accuracy in $STC(T)$. The best accuracy of our system is more than 93.5%.

Table 7. Accuracy comparisons among the forward way and the reverse time-order one.

Descriptor	STC			rSTC		
Clustering	Min	Max	AVG	Min	Max	AVG
Dist/Thres	Min/AVG	Min/AVG	Min/AVG	Min/AVG	Min/AVG	Min/AVG
Accuracy	89.4	86.2	88.6	93.6	89.5	90.6

References

1. Chen, M.Y., Alregib, G., Juang, B.-H.: Air-writing recognition—part I: modeling and recognition of characters, words, and connecting motions. IEEE Trans. Hum. Mach. Syst. **46** (3), 403–413 (2016)
2. Zhang, X., et al.: A new writing experience: finger writing in the air using a kinect sensor. IEEE Multimed. **20**, 85–93 (2013)
3. Tsuchida, K., Miyao, H., Maruyama, M.: Handwritten character recognition in the air by using leap motion controller. In: Stephanidis, C. (ed.) HCI 2015. CCIS, vol. 528, pp. 534–538. Springer, Cham (2015). https://doi.org/10.1007/978-3-319-21380-4_91
4. Chiang, C.-C., Wang, R.-H., Chen, B.-R.: Recognizing arbitrarily connected and superimposed handwritten numerals in intangible writing interfaces. Pattern Recognit. **61**, 15–28 (2016)
5. Qu, C.Z., Zhang, D.Y., Tian, J.: Online kinect handwritten digit recognition based on dynamic time warping and support vector machine. J. Inf. Comput. Sci. **12**(1), 413–422 (2015)
6. Su, C.-Y., et al.: Kinect-based midair handwritten number recognition system for dialing numbers and setting a timer. In: IEEE International Conference on Systems, Man and Cybernetics, pp. 2127–2130 (2014)
7. Be, S., Khan, M.F., Baig, F.: Text writing in Air. J. Inf. Disp. **14**(4), 137–148 (2013)
8. Aggarwa, R., et al.: Online handwriting recognition using depth sensors. In: IEEE International Conference on Document Analysis and Recognition (ICDAR) (2015)
9. Schick, A., Morlock, D., Amma, C.: Vision-based handwriting recognition for unrestricted text input in mid-air. In: Proceedings of the 14th ACM international conference on Multimodal Interaction, pp. 217–220 (2012)
10. Tian, J., Qu, C., Xu, W., Wang, S.: KinWrite: handwriting-based authentication using kinect. In: Proceedings of the 20th Annual Network and Distributed System Security Symposium (2013)
11. Ciao, G., Milanova, M., Xie, M.: Secure behavioral biometric authentication with leap motion. In 4th International Symposium on Digital Forensics and Security, pp. 25–27 (2016)
12. Belongie, S., Malik, J., Puzicha, J.: Shape context: a new descriptor for shape matching and object recognition. In: Advances in Neural Information Processing Systems, pp. 831–837 (2001)

Synthetic Vision Assisted Real-Time Runway Detection for Infrared Aerial Images

Changjiang Liu[1,2(✉)], Irene Cheng[2], and Anup Basu[2]

[1] Key Lab of Enterprise Informationization and Internet of Things of Sichuan Province, Sichuan University of Science and Engineering, Zigong 643000, Sichuan, China
liuchangjiang@189.cn
[2] Department of Computing Science, University of Alberta, Edmonton, AB T6G 2H1, Canada
{locheng,basu}@ualberta.ca

Abstract. This paper presents a new real-time runway detection based on synthetic vision and level set method. It mainly focuses on the initial level set function and time performance. As for the initial level set function, three-thresholding segmentation is derived to obtain the subset of the runway, which serves as an initial curve to induce the initial level set function. As for time performance, a ROI (Region of Interest) based evolution method is proposed. Analysis of experimental results and comparisons with existing algorithms demonstrate the efficiency and accuracy of the proposed method.

Keywords: ROI propagation · Three-thresholding · Segmentation Synthetic vision · Level set method

1 Introduction

Approaching and landing under the conditions of low visibility and night vision are important issues in aviation safety. The instrument landing system (ILS) [5] is currently the predominant navigation technology used to assist in low visibility approach and take-off operations. However, it is not economically feasible to equip all airports. Therefore, enhanced vision system (EVS) and synthetic vision system (SVS) are the key technologies being considered. SVS generates a rendered image of the 3D scene topography, which simulates what pilots actually see in that position and pose derived from airborne high precision navigation data.

Runways, as a type of important landmark, are a focus of analysis. In common mechanisms of runway detection used by existing methods, image edges are detected, followed by extracting line segments via the hough transform. This approach works in remote sensing images. However, for onboard aerial images

A. Basu and S. Berretti (Eds.): ICSM 2018, LNCS 11010, pp. 274–281, 2018.
https://doi.org/10.1007/978-3-030-04375-9_23

during approach and landing, coupled with line segments, like roads, vehicles and fields, these techniques have trouble distinguishing candidate airport patches [12]. Among contour extraction techniques, the level set method [8] is quite novel. Li *et al.* [7] presented a new variational formulation of geometric active contours that forces the level set function to be close to a signed distance function, and therefore completely eliminated the costly re-initialization of traditional level set methods. In practical applications, level set methods are computationally expensive. Some researchers focused on the fast marching level set method [10, 11], which uses narrow bands to make only points close to the curve evolved.

In experiments on infrared runways, the touch zone is very close to runways which makes it hard to differentiate between the two regions without edge information. The structure of runways is illustrated in Fig. 1. How to detect only one object of interest in real time is an important issue; i.e., we want to detect only the runway, not including touch zones and other regions. In this paper, we generalize Otsu's thresholding method to trichotomize the region overlapping a virtual runway (see Fig. 2); thus, we obtain the initial curve to be evolved by level set methods. Furthermore, a ROI based scheme is proposed to speed up level set methods.

Fig. 1. Typical runway structure in infrared images.

The remainder of the paper is organized as follows. Generation of synthetic vision is presented in Sect. 2. Section 3 gives a brief overview of level set evolution without re-initialization proposed by Li *et al.* [7]. Our proposed ROI-based level set method for runway detection is presented in Sect. 4, which focuses on evolving the initial curve and fast implementation of the proposed method. Experimental results and comparison with existing methods are outlined in Sect. 5. Finally, concluding remarks are given in Sect. 6.

2   Generation of Synthetic Vision

An overview of generation of synthetic vision is shown in Fig. 2, where the region bounded by the quadrilateral in green is the virtual runway. First, a digital elevation model (DEM) and a high resolution map texture are prepared to construct the three-dimensional terrain model. Simultaneously, the high precision airport runway model is constructed by 3D modeling tools. Following this, the GPS provides the onboard camera with position information and AHRS provides the pose information. Finally, three-dimensional engineering tools render a 3D model to generate a virtual image. The setup simulates a virtual camera traversing the world in response to incoming navigation sensor data.

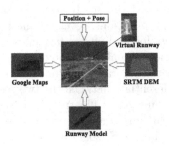

Fig. 2. Generation of synthetic vision (Color figure online)

3   Level Set Evolution Without Re-initialization

The authors in [1] showed that any function ϕ satisfying $|\nabla\phi| = 1$ is the signed distance function plus a constant. Thus, Li *et al.* [7] defined the following integral:

$$\mathcal{P}(\phi) \triangleq \int_{\Omega} \frac{1}{2}(|\nabla\phi| - 1)^2 dxdy \tag{1}$$

as a metric to depict how close a function $\phi \in \mathcal{R}^2$ is to a signed distance function, where ∇ is the gradient operator. Furthermore, they proposed a level set evolution without re-initialization. We briefly review these models next. Ref. [7] gives a new variational formulation:

$$\mathcal{E}(\phi) \triangleq \mu\mathcal{P}(\phi) + \lambda\mathcal{L}_g(\phi) + \nu\mathcal{A}_g(\phi) \tag{2}$$

where $\mu > 0$ is a parameter controlling the effect of penalizing the deviation of ϕ from a signed distance function, $\lambda > 0$ and ν are constants.

The energy functional $\mathcal{L}_g(\phi)$ in (2) computes the length of the zero level set of ϕ in the conformal metric and the term $\mathcal{L}_g(\phi)$ is defined by:

$$\mathcal{L}_g(\phi) \triangleq \int_{\Omega} g\delta(\phi)|\nabla\phi|dxdy \tag{3}$$

where g is the edge indicator function. Let I be an image, the term g is defined by:

$$g \triangleq \frac{1}{1 + |\nabla G_\sigma * I|^2} \tag{4}$$

where G_σ is the Gaussian Kernel with standard deviation σ.

The energy functional $\mathcal{A}_g(\phi)$ in (2) can be viewed as the weighted area of $\Omega_\phi^- \triangleq \{(x,y)|\phi(x,y) < 0\}$, and the term $\mathcal{A}_g(\phi)$ is defined by:

$$\mathcal{A}_g(\phi) \triangleq \int_\Omega gH(-\phi)dxdy \tag{5}$$

where H is the Heaviside function.

In order to solve the functional $\mathcal{E}$ which minimizes (2), the following evolution equation was proposed:

$$\frac{\partial \phi}{\partial t} = -\frac{\partial \mathcal{E}}{\partial \phi} \tag{6}$$

where the Gateaux derivative of the functional $\mathcal{E}$ in (2) can be written as:

$$\frac{\partial \mathcal{E}}{\partial \phi} = -\mu \left[\triangle\phi - \text{div}\left(\frac{\nabla\phi}{|\nabla\phi|}\right) \right] - \lambda\delta(\phi) \,\text{div}\left(g\frac{\nabla\phi}{|\nabla\phi|}\right) - \nu g\delta(\phi) \tag{7}$$

where $\triangle$ is the Laplacian operator. Combining (7) with (6), evolution equation of the level set function ϕ proposed in [7] can be given by:

$$\begin{cases} \frac{\partial \phi}{\partial t} = \mu \left[\triangle\phi - \text{div}\left(\frac{\nabla\phi}{|\nabla\phi|}\right) \right] + \lambda\delta(\phi) \,\text{div}\left(g\frac{\nabla\phi}{|\nabla\phi|}\right) + \nu g\delta(\phi) \\ \phi(0,x,y) = \phi_0(x,y) \end{cases} \tag{8}$$

where ϕ_0 is the initial level set function. The sign of coefficient ν is dependent on the relative position of the initial contour to the object of interest. If the initial contours are placed outside the object, ν takes positive values, otherwise it takes negative values to speed up the evolution.

4   Proposed ROI-based Level Set Method for Runway Detection

4.1   Initial Contour Based on Three-Thresholding Segmentation

Considering the characteristic of runway detection for aerial images, the initial level set function ϕ_0 in (8) is crucial in terms of accuracy and efficiency. In this paper, the IR runway region bounded by the virtual runway (see Fig. 2), generated by synthetic vision, provides a coarse localization of the IR runway, which is regarded as the ROI. Gray value difference of separated parts in the runway structure motivates us to trichotomize the pixels of the ROI into three classes: background, touch zone and runway subset. Three-thresholding segmentation method is proposed in the following context. Subsequently, the ϕ_0 is induced by the subregion. By iterations following the evolution equation, the initial contour is expanded to the final runway.

Denoting the vertices of the virtual runway by $P_i(x, y), i = 1, 2, 3, 4$, the ROI can be represented as the convex hull of the vertex point set $V \triangleq \{P_1, P_2, P_3, P_4\}$:

$$\text{ROI} \triangleq \left\{ \sum_{i=1}^{4} \alpha_i P_i | \alpha_i \geq 0 \ (i = 1, \ldots, 4) \text{ and } \sum_{i=1}^{4} \alpha_i = 1 \right\} \quad (9)$$

Assume that we trichotomized the pixels of the ROI into three classes C_0 (background), C_1 (touch zone) and C_2 (runway subset) by two thresholds at levels k_1 and k_2, where $g_{\min} \leq k_1 < k_2 \leq g_{\max}$. Analogous to the term "binary thresholding method" [9], we call the aforementioned process three-thresholding method. Henceforth, the pixels of the ROI are trichomized into three classes:

$$g(x, y) \triangleq \begin{cases} 255 \ f(x, y) \geq k_2 & (C_2) \\ 128 \ k_1 \leq f(x, y) < k_2 & (C_1) \ (x, y) \in \text{ROI} \\ 0 \ f(x, y) < k_1 & (C_0) \end{cases} \quad (10)$$

where $f(x, y)$ is the gray value of the infrared input image at location (x, y) and $g(x, y)$ is the corresponding output.

The class C_2 is considered as the probable subset of the runway in the infrared image. Furthermore, we find the contours in the subregion mentioned above and the contour whose area is the largest is selected as the final initial contour. We denote the region supported by the contour with Ω_0 and the image domain as $\Omega \triangleq \{(x, y) | 1 \leq x \leq W, 1 \leq y \leq H\}$. Therefore, the initial level set function ϕ_0 is induced by:

$$\phi_0(x, y) \triangleq \begin{cases} -\rho, (x, y) \in \Omega_0 - \partial\Omega_0 \\ 0, (x, y) \in \partial\Omega_0 \\ \rho, (x, y) \in \Omega - \Omega_0 \end{cases} \quad (11)$$

where $\rho > 0$ is a constant, $\partial\Omega_0$ represents the initial contour, $\Omega_0 - \partial\Omega_0$ represents the area inside the initial contour and $\Omega - \Omega_0$ represents the area outside the initial contour in the image domain.

4.2   ROI Based Level Set Method Without Re-Initialization

How to create a fast level set method for runway detection to meet real time performance is a challenging problem.

There is a product rule of divergence operator [6]: if φ is a scalar valued functional, and $\mathbf{F}$ is a vector field, then

$$\text{div}(\varphi\mathbf{F}) = \nabla\varphi \cdot \mathbf{F} + \varphi \ \text{div}(\mathbf{F})$$

Recall the evolution equation in (8), based on the above rule it will be given by:

$$\begin{cases} \frac{\partial\phi}{\partial t} = \mu\left[\Delta\phi - \text{div}\left(\frac{\nabla\phi}{|\nabla\phi|}\right)\right] + \nu \ g\delta(\phi) \\ \quad + \lambda \ \delta(\phi)\left(\nabla g \cdot \frac{\nabla\phi}{|\nabla\phi|} + g \ \text{div}\left(\frac{\nabla\phi}{|\nabla\phi|}\right)\right) \\ \phi(0, x, y) = \phi_0(x, y), (x, y) \in \Omega \end{cases} \quad (12)$$

For the purpose of analysis, denote $\triangle \phi \triangleq L$, $\frac{\nabla \phi}{|\nabla \phi|} \triangleq \mathbf{N}$, div$\left(\frac{\nabla \phi}{|\nabla \phi|}\right) =$ div$(\mathbf{N}) \triangleq K$. Note that in Eq. (12), the terms g and ∇g do not vary during the iterative procedure. However, the terms L, $\mathbf{N}$ and K are updated in every iteration. Considering this issue, we propose a rectangular ROI to implement level set methods without re-initialization. Assuming that the ROI in the n-th iteration is $\Omega_n \subset \Omega$ and $\phi_{i,j}^n \triangleq \phi(ih, jh, n\tau)$, where a discrete grid in the domain Ω with spacing h and τ is the time step, we can write:

$$
\begin{cases}
\phi_{i,j}^{n+1} = \phi_{i,j}^n + \tau \left[\mu(L_{i,j}^n - K_{i,j}^n) + \nu \, g_{i,j} \delta_\varepsilon(\phi_{i,j}^n) \right. \\
\qquad \left. + \lambda \, \delta_\varepsilon\left(\phi_{i,j}^n\right) \left((\nabla g)_{i,j} \cdot \mathbf{N}_{i,j}^n + g_{i,j} K_{i,j}^n \right) \right], \\
\qquad (ih, jh) \in \Omega_n \\
\phi_{i,j}^0 = \phi_0(ih, jh), (ih, jh) \in \Omega_0
\end{cases}
\tag{13}
$$

After n iterative evolutions based on (13), the level set function is $\phi_{i,j}^n$. Hence, the region in which an object of interest lies is given by $A^n \triangleq \{(ih, jh)|\phi_{i,j}^n \leq 0\}$, whose minimal upright bounding rectangle is given by:

$$
B^n \triangleq \{(x, y) | x_{\min}^n \leq x \leq x_{\max}^n, y_{\min}^n \leq y \leq y_{\max}^n\}.
$$

Assume that the current ROI can be moved by δ in the x- and y- directions. Therefore, the ROI in the following iteration, i.e., Ω_{n+1} is defined by:

$$
\Omega_{n+1} \triangleq \begin{cases} (x, y)| \max(x_{\min}^n - \delta, 1) \leq x \leq \min(x_{\max}^n + \delta, \mathrm{W}), \\ \max(y_{\min}^n - \delta, 1) \leq y \leq \min(y_{\max}^n + \delta, \mathrm{H}) \end{cases}
\tag{14}
$$

5 Analysis of Results and Comparisons

The algorithm was implemented using the Microsoft Visual Studio development platform with an Open CV (Computer Vision) library.

5.1 Comparison with Existing Methods

We use the exact subset of a runway as the initial curve (see Fig. 3(b)), the results by our method and Li's are shown in Fig. 3. Figure 3(d) illustrates the curve has a bigger size than the true runway after 200 iterations. At the same time, it is worth pointing out that our method can automatically provide an initial contour leading to the accurate runway, which has practical significance in batch processing.

It is obvious that the difference of gray values between runways and touch zones (see Fig. 1) is subtle. Chan's model [3,4] detects the runway without image gradient information. Thus, the final result based on Chan's method is likely to include parts of the touch zone by mistake, as shown in Fig. 4(d). In this case, our method prevails in accuracy due to the edge indicator, like Fig. 4(b), which can help differentiate between the runway and the touch zone. The final result of our method is shown in Fig. 4(c).

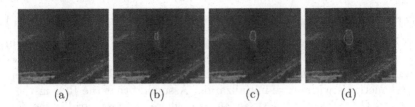

Fig. 3. Comparison with Li's method: (a) original image; (b) initial contour (c) final result based on our method; (d) contour based on Li's method.

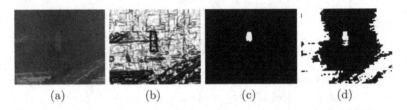

Fig. 4. Comparison with Chan's method: (a) original image; (b) edge indicator image; (c) runway region based on our method; (d) runway region based on Chan's method.

5.2   Time Performance

Compared to other existing methods, our proposed method has significantly better time performance. The average execution time of Li's method and ours using the same computer configuration (CPU: Intel(R) Core(TM) i7-4790 (3.60 GHZ), RAM: 16 GB and OS: Windows 10 (64 bit)) is listed in Table 1. Our processing speed is 28f/s, which meets the demand for real time processing. It was reported that Balla-Arabe's method [2] reaches 0.7 s per frame for 481×321 plane images (CPU: AMD Athlon(TM) 5200 2.3 GHZ, RAM: 2 GB, Matlab 2010b). Shi [10] proposed a real time algorithm to segment the plane image in 0.0249 s (CPU: Intel 1.6 GHZ). Nevertheless, a circle outside the plane should be plotted manually as an initial curve beforehand, which is not realistic in batch processing.

Table 1. Algorithm execution time (s/f).

Processing time	Min	Max	Average
Li's method [7]	0.172	1.844	0.821
Proposed method	0.015	0.063	0.035

6   Conclusion

Although synthetic vision can generate virtual runways in real time, if there are errors in either the navigation data or in the 3D scene database, it is impossible for pilots to verify whether this information is correct or not. Hence, structures such as the runway, river, freeway, overpass and other landmarks detected in real time provide pilots with reliable visual cues. We design a framework for runway detection based on synthetic vision and an ROI level set method. This strategy is applicable for real time processing without any manual intervention. In future work, we will focus on generating more reliable synthetic vision input.

Acknowledgment. The work was supported in part by the Open Project of the Key Lab of Enterprise Informationization and Internet of Things of Sichuan Province under Grant No. 2017WZY01, Natural Science Foundation of Sichuan University of Science and Engineering (SUSE) under Grant Nos. 2015RC08, 2017RCL54 and JG-1707. The authors would like to thank National Natural Science Foundation of China under Grant No. 11705122, NSERC, Canada, for their financial support of this research.

References

1. Arnold, V.I.: Geometrical Methods in the Theory of Ordinary Differential Equations. Springer, New York (1983)
2. Balla-Arabe, S., Gao, X., Wang, B.: A fast and robust level set method for image segmentation using fuzzy clustering and lattice Boltzmann method. IEEE Trans. Cybern. **43**(3), 910–920 (2013)
3. Chan, T.F., Sandberg, B.Y., Vese, L.A.: Active contours without edges for vector-valued images. J. Vis. Commun. Image Represent. **11**(2), 130–141 (2000)
4. Chan, T.F., Vese, L.A.: Active contours without edges. IEEE Trans. Image Process. **10**(2), 266–277 (2001)
5. Farrell, J.: Integrated Aircraft Navigation. Elsevier, Amsterdam (2012)
6. Korn, G.A., Korn, T.M.: Mathematical Handbook for Scientists and Engineers: Definitions, Theorems, and Formulas for Reference and Review. Courier Corporation, Chelmsford (2000)
7. Li, C., Xu, C., Gui, C., Fox, M.D.: Level set evolution without re-initialization: a new variational formulation. In: IEEE Computer Society Conference on Computer Vision and Pattern Recognition (CVPR), vol. 1, pp. 430–436. IEEE (2005)
8. Osher, S., Sethian, J.A.: Fronts propagating with curvature-dependent speed: algorithms based on Hamilton-Jacobi formulations. J. Comput. Phys. **79**(1), 12–49 (1988)
9. Otsu, N.: A threshold selection method from gray-level histograms. Automatica **11**(285–296), 23–27 (1975)
10. Shi, Y., Karl, W.C.: A real-time algorithm for the approximation of level-set-based curve evolution. IEEE Trans. Image Process. **17**(5), 645–656 (2008)
11. Shi, Y., Karl, W.C.: A fast level set method without solving PDEs. In: The 30th International Conference on Acoustics, Speech, and Signal Processing (ICASSP), pp. 97–100. IEEE (2005)
12. Yu, H., Zhang, X., Wang, S., Hou, B.: Context-based hierarchical unequal merging for SAR image segmentation. IEEE Trans. Geosci. Remote Sens. **51**(2), 995–1009 (2013)

Learning

Detection-Based Online Multi-target Tracking via Adaptive Subspace Learning

Jyoti Nigam[✉], Krishan Sharma, and Renu M. Rameshan

Indian Institute of Technology, Mandi, H.P., India
jyoti_nigam@students.iitmandi.ac.in

Abstract. Multi-target tracking is a challenging task and becomes more so when both camera and targets are in motion and the targets have similar appearances with frequent occlusions. To maintain a proper track in such scenarios, individual target representation and accurate data association methods are prime requirements for a robust multi-target tracker. We observe that a target can be modeled as a subspace by using its feature vectors over several consecutive frames. We propose an adaptive subspace model to handle the large range of target variations throughout the track. We also develop a novel two-step parallel scheme for data association which exploits scale and location information along with appearance information to distinguish the targets. The track results for challenging videos (containing occlusions and variations in pose and illumination) indicate that the proposed method achieves better/comparable tracking accuracy in comparison to several recent trackers.

1 Introduction

Multi-target tracking (MTT) can be seen as a mid-level task in computer vision which plays an important role for high-level applications such as visual surveillance, human computer interaction and virtual reality. The key steps in a multi-target tracking system are (i) locating multiple targets, (ii) sustaining their identities (*ids*) and (iii) predicting their individual trajectories in successive frames of a video. In addition to the usual challenges which occur in single target tracking (SST) such as target scale change, out-of-plane rotations and illumination variations, MTT has to handle additional problems which include determining the number of objects which varies with time, maintaining the identities of targets, frequent merge and split, initialization and termination of trajectories, appearance similarity, and interactions among targets. Based on how the targets are initialized MTT algorithms can be categorized into two groups: Detection-Based Tracking (DBT) and Detection-Free Tracking (DFT) [9]. DFT requires manual initialization of a fixed number of targets in the first frame, whereas in DBT new objects are discovered and disappearing targets are terminated automatically. In DBT, the targets are first detected and then mapped to the trajectories. There are two broad categories of tracking-by-detection methods - online and offline tracking methods. In offline tracking methods, the detections from both past and

© Springer Nature Switzerland AG 2018
A. Basu and S. Berretti (Eds.): ICSM 2018, LNCS 11010, pp. 285–295, 2018.
https://doi.org/10.1007/978-3-030-04375-9_24

future frames are used whereas online tracking methods employ detections only from the current and past frames. The performance of DBT is limited to the performance of the object detector used; any advancement in object detection field can be directly adopted to tracking techniques. Recently, a family of advanced object detectors [11] have been made available which enhance the performance of MTT directly. To make the prediction more accurate, target representation is usually learned to describe the appearance of the target. The target appearance models for MTT can be based on region color histogram, kernel density, GMMs [19], conditional random fields or learned subspaces [13]. Among these appearance models, subspace based models attract much attention due to their robustness [18]. For generating appearance models [14] for different targets we construct subspaces for each tracked target.

Contributions of this work are as follows: (1) We propose an adaptive subspace learning method for MTT, in which selected new observations are incorporated into the learned subspace. This approach prevents the unbounded growth of subspace which makes our tracker computationally amenable as opposed to [18]. (2) A novel two-step parallel framework for data association is proposed. (3) We address the problems of merge and split and occlusion by using reconstruction errors and by not updating the subspace corresponding to the occluded person, respectively. We present the results of the proposed method for online MTT on a large number of challenging datasets. The datasets used are from *MOTChallenge* benchmark, which were released as 2D *MOT15*, *MOT16* and *MOT17*. Since subspace based methods for tracking [13] have high computational complexity, we utilize a parallel computation. The paper is organized as follows: in next section, the related tracking methods are reviewed. The proposed method for data association and adaptive learning of subspaces is presented in Sect. 3. In Sect. 2 tracking framework is explained. Section 4 gives experimental results followed by conclusions in Sect. 5.

2   Related Work

In this section, we review related MOT algorithms and works related to subspace based appearance modeling. Among the detection free tracking (DFT) algorithms, [18] propose Riemannian subspace learning algorithm in which, under the log-Euclidean Riemannian metric, image feature covariance matrices which describe spatial relations among pixel values are mapped to a vector space. Furthermore, a log-Euclidean block-division appearance model is constructed which finds the global and local spatial information about object appearance. While tracking, to represent the object they choose to pick recent fifty observations. However, in our algorithm instead of employing recent observations alone, we retain related features to represent changes in the object. In [17], Yoon *et al.* propose an online tracking method which exploits structural constraints with frame by frame data association that assigns objects to correct detection. Unlike the aforementioned methods, our method exploits location and size information along with appearance information and adaptively update all subspaces. In [7], a joint graphical model is proposed for point trajectories and object detections where motion segmentation and multi-target tracking are solved by multi-cuts. The work in [6] incorporates several detectors into a tracking system and cast the tracking problem as a weighted graph labeling problem, resulting in a binary quadratic program. The tracker can take information from many frames and different detectors holistically into account.

In [4], an online multi-target tracker is proposed which uses features from multiple layers of CNN whereas our algorithm works on subspace based representation and gives better results. The work in [3] deals with data association ambiguities, especially in crowded scenarios by performing detection scene analysis and detection-detection analysis. In [2], the authors cope up with high frame rate videos with the help of potential use of a wide range of object detectors along with interaction over union information (IOU). In our proposed method we use detections from a single detector and form subspaces corresponding to each target. In the next section, we explain the proposed method which addresses multi-target tracking using subspace representation.

3   Proposed Method

The proposed MTT algorithm can be split into three parts. The algorithm begins with the formation of initial subspaces followed by data association *i.e.* matching detections with existing trajectories. The third part is the adaptive subspace learning which helps the algorithm in keeping track of changes in target appearance which may occur throughout the length of the video. The main assumption is that a moving target forms a low dimensional subspace in some feature space [15]. The following subsections describe the three parts in detail.

3.1   Formation of Initial Subspaces

In this section, our objective is to model a target using the detection responses from the initial few frames. To model a target we form a subspace corresponding to each target, for which the first step is clustering of data. Since for clustering, a single frame is not sufficient, we consider the detection responses from initial ten frames. It may be noted that this leads to a reduction in performance. The following challenges arise during the clustering process. (1) A detector may predict multiple detections per frame for a single pedestrian or may generate false positives. (2) The exact number of targets to be tracked (number of subspaces) is not known a priori.

To handle the first problem we estimate intersection over union (IOU) values among all detection responses from the previous frame. We keep the detection response of current frame if it obtains the maximum overlap with any detection response of the previous frame with the condition $IOU > threshold$. The chosen threshold is dependent on fps and the value is empirically fixed at 0.5 for fps in the range 15–30 fps. This process is repeated for each pair of frames

---

Algorithm 1. Feasible set

Require:

  Given set of detections for initial ten frames $\mathcal{D}_t = \{d_t^1, \cdots, d_t^{M_t}\}$, where d_t^j is the jth detection in the tth frame and M_t is the number of targets in t^{th} frame.

Ensure:

  Feasible set: Subset of all detections

1: **for** $t = 2$ to 10 **do**
2:    IOU among detections d_{t-1}^m and d_t^n, is calculated for $1 \leq m \leq M_{t-1}$, $1 \leq n \leq M_t$;
3:    **for** $m = 1$ to M_{t-1} **do**
4:      $\hat{n} = \max_n IOU(d_{t-1}^m, d_t^n)$
5:      **if** $(IOU > 0.5)$ **then**
6:        $P_m = \{d_t^m, d_{t-1}^{\hat{n}}\}$, $im = im \bigcup\{m\}$, where im is the set of indices of detections which have $IOU > 0.5$ and it is initialized as empty set.
7:      **end if**
8:      $F_t = \bigcup_{i \in im} P_i$,
9:    **end for**
10:   $F_d = \bigcup_{2 \leq t \leq 10} F_t$.
11: **end for**

---

and we obtain a subset of detections which is named as **feasible set**. Feasible set (F_d) is a set which contains the series of detections assigned with a tentative identity which may lead to some trajectories. The generation of this feasible set is discussed in Algorithm 1. To deal with the second problem we consider those targets (i) which have at least eight consecutive entries in F_d, *i.e.* $d_t^i, d_{t+1}^i, \cdots, d_{t+8}^i$. All detections corresponding to such targets are placed in a set F_d' ($F_d' \subset F_d$). The number of distinct trajectories in F_d' is the number of subspaces. In order to form subspaces, the appearance information also needs to be incorporated for handling cases where the trajectories intersect. To represent the targets based on their appearance we do clustering using HOG features, and the features are extracted from the detections in the feasible set. The detections in F_d' have varying bounding box sizes. All the patches are resized to a fixed size which is chosen as the average of the largest and smallest bounding boxes containing pedestrians. This information is available in the dataset. Each bounding box in F_d' is described using a vector of d dimensional HOG feature thus $\mathcal{R}^d$ becomes the feature space. The subspaces are obtained by collecting these feature vectors and clustering using Local Subspace Analysis (LSA) [16]. The number of subspaces is N and these subspaces may or may not have the same dimension. The LSA algorithm has two main advantages while used for subspace clustering. First, outliers are likely to be not accepted as they are far from all the points and not used as neighboring points of the inliers. Second, LSA requires very less number of data points when compared to other clustering algorithms such as GPCA [15] and SSC [5] and SSC.

3.2   Data Association

In this section, we discuss how the proposed data association process couples subspace representation for appearance modeling and IOU information for location and size information of a target. Given a set of trajectories maintained till $(t-1)^{th}$ frame and a set of detections at t^{th} frame, we extend the trajectories by associating the available detections to these existing subspaces. The tracking process can be seen as finding a mapping between the existing set of trajectories and current set of detections. As discussed above, it can be observed that due to the limited performance of a detector, some of the detection responses may not have an associated trajectory and similarly few trajectories may not have a corresponding detection response.

To deal with this problem we use the observation that a target moves in the proximity of its previous location in the successive frames. With this observation we create two groups of detection responses, the first group is named $\mathcal{D}_{accept}$ and contains the detections which have associated targets and rest of the detections are grouped as $\mathcal{D}_{extra}$. $\mathcal{D}_{extra}$ keeps the track of entries of new targets. The presence of a target corresponding to a detection is estimated utilizing intersection over union (IOU) values calculated over the detections and previous bounding boxes of all trajectories.

Similarly, we create two sets of trajectories named as $\mathcal{T}_{accept}$ and $\mathcal{T}_{extra}$ where $\mathcal{T}_{accept}$ contains the trajectories having an associated detection. The entries in $\mathcal{T}_{extra}$ do not have an associated detection leads to lose of track when the target is actually present. The creation of all the four sets is discussed in Algorithm 2.

(a) **Appearance Information:** Firstly, we formulate the mapping procedure as finding the subspace with minimum reconstruction error corresponding to a detection. In particular, our formulation ensures that a detection gets mapped to a subspace which has the closest appearance model to that detection. We assume that a detection can only belong to one trajectory, which is achieved by considering the minimum reconstruction error constraint.

$$e_n = \|f_i - U_n U_n^T f_i\|_2, \tag{1}$$

where e_n is the distance of f_i from S_n; f_i is the feature vector extracted from i^{th} detection and $n \in \{1, \cdots, N\}$ indexes the subspaces, S_n. U_n is the basis of a subspace. Note that all the computations are done in a parallel environment. Since the first step of association is only dependent on appearance model, it does not resolve the ambiguity of appearance conflict. Appearance conflict occurs when there are two far apart targets having a similar appearance and they try to get mapped to same subspace. The reconstruction error for two different detections comes significantly low for a single subspace which may result in the erroneous association. To overcome this conflict we incorporate the location and size information in the second step by computing the IOU with current detection and previous locations of targets.

(b) **Combining Location and Size Information:** It is observed that the detection which comes in the proximity of a target gives high IOU value in

---

Algorithm 2. Feasible sets

Require:

Given $\mathcal{D}_t$ be the set of current detections in frame f_t and $\mathcal{T}_t$ be the set of existing N trajectories corresponding to N subspaces, $\mathcal{D}_t = \{d_t^1, \cdots, d_t^{M_t}\}$, $\mathcal{T}_t = \{T_1, T_2, \ldots, T_N\}$, where trajectory of jth target (T_j) defined as $T_j = \{(b_1^j, id), \cdots, (b_{t-1}^j, id)\}$, where b_t^j is bounding box $(x, y, width, height)$ of jth target in t^{th} frame.

Ensure:

Feasible sets: $\mathcal{D}_{accept}, \mathcal{T}_{accept}, \mathcal{D}_{extra}, \mathcal{T}_{extra}$.

1: **for** $m = 1$ to M_t **do**
2:     **for** $n = 1$ to N **do**
3:         $\hat{n} = \max_n IOU(d_t^m, b_{t-1}^n)$
4:     **end for**
5:     **if** $IOU(d_t^m, b_{t-1}^{\hat{n}}) > 0.5$, **then**
6:         $t_m = \{(m, \hat{n})\}$, $im = im \bigcup \{m\}$, Note that all detections having $IOU > 0.5$, has an entry in I_n, where
7:         $I_n = \bigcup_{m \in im} t_m$
8:     **end if**
9:     $F_t = \bigcup_{i \in im} P_i$,
10: **end for**
11: Let $r_n = \{m_1, m_2, \cdots, m_l\}$ be the detections which have maximum IOU with trajectory n, $\hat{m} = \max_{m \in r_n} IOU(d_t^m, b_{t-1}^{\hat{n}})$
12: A new set I_n' is obtained from I_n by discarding all pairs $(m, n), m_i \in r_n, m_i \neq \hat{m}$. Any ties are resolved using a coin toss.
13: $I_n' = \{(m_1, n_1), (m_2, n_2), \cdots, (m_k, n_k)\}$, where $|I_n'| = k$ and $k \leq N$.
14: $\mathcal{D}_{accept} = \{d_t^m | (m, *) \in I_n'\}$, $\mathcal{T}_{accept} = \{b_t^n | (*, n) \in I_n'\}$.
15: $\mathcal{D}_{extra} = \mathcal{D}_t \setminus \mathcal{D}_{accept}$, $\mathcal{T}_{extra} = \mathcal{T}_t \setminus \mathcal{T}_{accept}$, where $\setminus$ is a set difference.

---

comparison to other far apart targets. A desirable property of the combining of IOU value with appearance information is to map the detection to an appropriate subspace. $\mathcal{E}_n = e_n.w_n$, where $w_n = (1 - IOU(d_t^i, b_{t-1}^n))$ is the weight factor arising from location and size information. For computing $\mathcal{E}_n$, we are using the information from appearance model as well as location and size of bounding boxes to estimate the nearness of a target to a trajectory. The effect of combining the two can be analyzed for four cases which are as follows: (1) $d_t^i \in S_n$, $(i, n) \in I_n'$; e_n and w_n both are small, (2) $d_t^i \in S_n$, $(i, n) \notin I_n'$; e_n is small, w_n is high, (3) $d_t^i \notin S_n$, $(i, n) \in I_n'$; e_n is high, w_n is small, (4) $d_t^i \notin S_n$, $(i, n) \notin I_n'$; e_n and w_n both are high.

Cases 1 and 4 are favorable since the product brings the value of $\mathcal{E}_n$ very low or very high making the data association process discriminative. Cases 2 and 3 could lead to errors in data association process when w_n/e_n is small enough to make $\mathcal{E}_n$ the lowest. In case 2, the current detection is not close to a particular trajectory (low IOU) but its features are related (low error) to the target belonging to the trajectory. This case may occur when the target moves by a large value in the consecutive frame and IOU value falls below a threshold. Case 3 arises when two targets appear very close say at frame f_{t-1} with their detections still mapping to their respective subspaces and in the next frame f_t, they switch their locations and their detections give high IOU values with respect to different trajectories. Both the cases are very unlikely to occur because in our experiments we use videos with 15–30 fps and at this high fps such a fast movement in targets can be captured easily. The mapping of identities is done as discussed below, for the computed error $\mathcal{E}_n$, $1 \leq n \leq N$,

$$\mathcal{E}_{m_1} = \min_n \mathcal{E}_n, \quad i_{m_1} = \arg\min_n \mathcal{E}_n, \quad \mathcal{E}_{m_2} = \min_{n, n \neq i_{m_1}} \mathcal{E}_n, \qquad (2)$$

$\mathcal{E}_{m_1}$ and $\mathcal{E}_{m_2}$ are first and second minimas and an identity is assigned to a detection if $\mathcal{E}_{m_1} - \mathcal{E}_{m_2} > 0.5$. This threshold of 0.5 is fixed empirically. The identity under this condition is

$$id = i_{m_1}, \quad T_{id}(t) = (d_t^i, id). \qquad (3)$$

After modifying the trajectory we modify the subspace to take care of possible deformations as described in Sect. 3.3. This process is repeated for all $d_t^i \in \mathcal{D}_{accept}$. Mis-detections and occlusion are handled as below.

Fig. 1. (a) Merging of targets, (b) example of false negative and false positive

(c) Merge and Split: The presence of occlusion *i.e.* merging of targets is captured by computing IOU among detections present in D_{accept}. If two detections overlap by a significant amount, it shows that there is an occlusion between these two targets as shown in Fig. 1(a). The detection of occluded target contains features from both targets *i.e.* occluded and occluding. This combination of features gives a similar reconstruction error for all subspaces. Although we can find the smallest error value, it will not be significantly smaller than other error values. In such cases, our data association method does not map the detection to any of the subspaces, and these detections are not used to adapt the subspaces.

(d) False Negatives: The bounding boxes in $\mathcal{T}_{extra} = \{b_{t-1}^{n_1}, \cdots b_{t-1}^{n_{N-k}}\}$ are those which do not have an assigned detection. This can occur either due to target moving out, or due to mis-detection in which case a false negative occurs as shown by Fig. 1(b). The recovery of a missed target is done by searching for the target in a polar region (in f_t), around the previous location of the target and this process is done for each bounding box in $\mathcal{T}_{extra}$, $\mathcal{C}_{n_i} = \{x + \Delta x, y + \Delta y | \Delta x^2 + \Delta y^2 \leq r^2\}$, where (x, y) is location in previous frame and n_i is the index of a bounding box, $n_i \in \{n_1, n_2, \cdots, n_{N-k}\}$. All the candidates in $\mathcal{C}_{n_i}$ are resized to the fixed size and HOG feature vectors $f_{c_{n_i}}$ are extracted for computing the reconstruction error for all subspaces, here c is the index of locations in $\mathcal{C}_{n_i}$.

$$\hat{c}_{n_i}, \hat{n} = \arg\min_{c_{n_i}, n} \|(f_{c_{n_i}} - U_n U_n^T f_{c_{n_i}}))\|_2. \tag{4}$$

The presence of the target is inferred by dissimilar reconstruction error values corresponding to different subspaces. If the feature vector lies in one of the existing subspaces it gives significantly low reconstruction error for that subspace. The bounding box for this target of f_t is obtained as the bounding box at $\hat{c}_{n_i}$ with width and height same as that in the previous frame.

Table 1. Comparison to the online MOT trackers on the *MOTChallenge15* dataset (pedestrian sequences). For FP, FN, IDsw and FG metrics * shows that our experiments are done on entire training sequences and only on one testing sequence.

Method	MOTA	IDF1	MT	ML	FP	FN	IDsw	FG	Hz
Proposed	**42**	**50**	**28.5%**	38%	2,679*	14,450*	259*	587*	0.5
APRCNN_Pub	38.5	47.1	8.7%	**37.4%**	4,005	33,203	586	1,263	6.7
JointMC	35.6	45.1	23.2%	39.3%	10,580	28,508	457	969	0.6
SCEA	29.1	37.2	8.9%	47.3%	6,060	36,912	604	1,182	**6.8**

Table 2. Comparison to the online MOT trackers on the *MOTChallenge17* dataset (pedestrian sequences). For FP, FN, IDsw and FG metrics * shows that our experiments are done on entire training sequences and only on one testing sequence.

Method	MOTA	IDF1	MT	ML	FP	FN	IDsw	FG	Hz
Proposed	51.0	**51.5**	**22.6%**	37.2%	11,406*	124,321*	2,126*	2,327*	0.5
FWT	**51.3**	47.6	21.4%	**35.2%**	24,101	247,921	2,648	4,279	0.2
EDMT17	50.0	51.3	21.6%	36.3%	32,279	247,297	2,264	3,260	0.6
IOU17	45.5	39.4	15.7%	40.5%	19,993	281,643	5,988	7,404	**1.9**

3.3 Adaptive Subspace Learning

The dimension of subspaces is varied adaptively by keeping track of largest and smallest eigenvalues of a matrix (B_n) which contains feature vectors. B_n initially contains the ten feature vectors of nth target. Only those additional feature vectors which changes the eigenvalues considerably are added to B_n. From the experimental results it is observed that the dimension remains fixed and changes only by one when there is a large change in appearance.

4   Experiments and Results

In this section, we have investigated the experimental evaluation of our proposed detection using online multi-target tracking method and presented the comparison against the state-of-the-art methods. Our tracker has been implemented on a machine with 8 GB RAM and 1080 GTX NVIDIA GPU where GPU has been used for parallel array operations. Although we compare our proposed method with state-of-the-art algorithms, it may be noted that none of them have utilized the subspace learning method. We have discussed some subspace based tracking methods in Sect. 2, where Zang *et al.* in [18] have proposed a method for a single as well as multi-target tracking but it is a detection free tracking methods. Due to the detection free tracking method, it tracks only a fixed number of targets that are manually initialized. Whereas our proposed method comes under detection based tracking, that obtains a varying number of targets as the time progresses and tracks them. In addition to this, the tracking method in [18] does not provide its evaluation in terms of the parameters provided by *MOTChallenge* benchmark, so we have not compare our results with [18]. Fig. 2 shows the tracking result of our proposed method for three different targets, in thirty consecutive frames.

Fig. 2. Prediction of three different trajectories in thirty frames.

Benchmark Dataset: In this work, we use video sequences available on *MOTChallenge* benchmark which provides a large set of annotated testing video sequences, unified detection hypotheses, standard evaluation tools, *etc.* Detections for all the sequences are available for this large collection of datasets. In *MOT17* release, all sequences have been used with a new and more accurate ground truth. Note that the data contains the same set of fourteen sequences as *MOT16* but the length of sequences is three times. This dataset specifically focuses on a centralized evaluation of multiple object tracking. In addition to this, the dataset provides several challenging subsets of data for specific tasks such as 2D and 3D tracking, sports analysis and surveillance.

Evaluation Metrics: The multi-target tracking performance measurement can be grouped into two categories. First, tracking accuracy which shows the count of mistakes by the tracker in the form of misses, false positives, mismatches, failure in recovery of tracks *etc.* In the next category, tracking precision shows how well exact positions of targets are predicted. In this work the performance metrics proposed in [1] are used namely, multi-object tracking accuracy ($MOTA$), $IDF1$, mostly tracked MT, mostly lost ML, fragment FG False positives FP, false negatives FN, identity switches ($IDsw$), fragment FG and time in Hz. $MOTA$ [10] is a measure which combines three error sources: false positives (FP), missed targets and identity switches (FN and $IDsw$). Measures like MT, ML and FG [12] indicate how properly the tracking of real trajectories have been done. FG is the count of the interruptions in a ground truth trajectory while tracking and Hz represents time complexity.

Evaluation on 2D $MOT15$ and $MOT17$: We evaluate the proposed algorithm over eleven training sequences and one testing sequence of 2D $MOT15$ [8] as well as of $MOT17$. For the dataset 2D $MOT15$ we compare our result with the state-of-the-art MOT methods including SCEA [17], APRCNN_Pub [4], and JointMC [7] and in particular the values for $MOTA$, $IDF1$ and MT for the proposed algorithm are better than other methods. For the dataset $MOT17$ the proposed algorithm gives results comparable to that of the state-of-the-art MOT methods including FWT [6], EDMT17 [3], and IOU17 [2]. In Tables 1 and 2, we provide the results for $MOT15$ and $MOT17$, respectively. In $MOT15$ dataset since the videos are not very complex the proposed algorithm outperforms other algorithms by a large margin in terms of $MOTA$. Whereas over $MOT17$ dataset the improvement is marginal since the videos are more complex.

As we have discussed above, that $MOTA$ combines three error sources: false positives, missed targets and identity switches. In order to take care of false positives, we have pruned extra detections at two different stages, for missed targets we keep check for the presence of target whenever a target does not find a corresponding detection. The combination of IOU information with subspace representation makes the data association more robust thus reducing the mismatches. Altogether, these steps increase the $MOTA$ and $IDF1$ values. In order to achieve a higher MT value, we keep accumulating the extra detections to form new additional subspaces which take care the entrance of new targets and start tracking them on time. In the case of ML, we could not achieve the best performance because some subspaces cannot be initialized against the targets as soon as they enter in the frame due to inconsistent detection responses.

5 Conclusion

In this work, we address the problem of multi-target tracking subject to varying number of targets, change in appearance due to motion in camera as well targets along with pose and illumination variation. We propose a method to assign target identities and locations where each target is modeled as an adaptive subspace constructed from its appearance over several consecutive frames. We explore the useful information provided by singular values of constructed subspaces at the time of expansion of these subspaces. Performance metrics show that the proposed tracker performs better than some of the existing trackers and exhibits a comparable performance with others.

References

1. Bernardin, K., Stiefelhagen, R.: Evaluating multiple object tracking performance: the clear mot metrics. J. Image Video Process. (2008)
2. Bochinski, E., Eiselein, V., Sikora, T.: High-speed tracking-by-detection without using image information. In: 2017 14th IEEE International Conference on Advanced Video and Signal Based Surveillance (AVSS) (2017)
3. Chen, J., Sheng, H., Zhang, Y., Xiong, Z.: Enhancing detection model for multiple hypothesis tracking. In: 2017 IEEE Conference on Computer Vision and Pattern Recognition Workshops (CVPRW) (2017)
4. Chen, L., Ai, H., Shang, C., Zhuang, Z., Bai, B.: Online multi-object tracking with convolutional neural networks. In: 2017 IEEE International Conference on Image Processing (ICIP) (2017) (2017)
5. Elhamifar, E., Vidal, R.: Sparse subspace clustering. In: IEEE Conference on Computer Vision and Pattern Recognition 2009. CVPR 2009. IEEE (2009)
6. Henschel, R., Leal-Taixé, L., Cremers, D., Rosenhahn, B.: Improvements to Frank-Wolfe optimization for multi-detector multi-object tracking. CoRR (2017)
7. Keuper, M., Tang, S., Yu, Z., Andres, B., Brox, T., Schiele, B.: A multi-cut formulation for joint segmentation and tracking of multiple objects. CoRR
8. Leal-Taixé, L., Milan, A., Reid, I.D., Roth, S., Schindler, K.: Motchallenge 2015: Towards a benchmark for multi-target tracking. CoRR (2015)
9. Luo, W., Zhao, X., Kim, T.: Multiple object tracking: a review. CoRR
10. Milan, A., Leal-Taixé, L., Reid, I.D., Roth, S., Schindler, K.: MOT16: a benchmark for multi-object tracking. CoRR (2016)
11. Ren, S., He, K., Girshick, R.B., Sun, J.: Faster R-CNN: towards real-time object detection with region proposal networks. CoRR (2015)
12. Ristani, E., Solera, F., Zou, R.S., Cucchiara, R., Tomasi, C.: Performance measures and a data set for multi-target, multi-camera tracking. CoRR (2016)
13. Ross, D.A., Lim, J., Lin, R.S., Yang, M.H.: Incremental learning for robust visual tracking (2008)
14. Shirazi, S.A., Sanderson, C., McCool, C., Harandi, M.T.: Improved object tracking via bags of affine subspaces. CoRR (2014)
15. Vidal, R., Ma, Y., Sastry, S.: Generalized principal component analysis (GPCA). IEEE Trans. Pattern Anal. Mach. Intell
16. Yan, J., Pollefeys, M.: A general framework for motion segmentation: independent, articulated, rigid, non-rigid, degenerate and non-degenerate. In: Leonardis, A., Bischof, H., Pinz, A. (eds.) ECCV 2006. LNCS, vol. 3954, pp. 94–106. Springer, Heidelberg (2006). https://doi.org/10.1007/11744085_8
17. Yoon, J.H., Lee, C.R., Yang, M.H., Yoon, K.J.: Online multi-object tracking via structural constraint event aggregation. In: 2016 IEEE Conference on Computer Vision and Pattern Recognition (CVPR) (2016)
18. Zhang, X., Luo, W., Li, X., Hu, W., Maybank, S., Zhang, Z.: Single and multiple object tracking using log-Euclidean Riemannian subspace and block-division appearance model. IEEE Trans. Pattern Anal. Mach. Intell
19. Zhou, S.K., Chellappa, R., Moghaddam, B.: Visual tracking and recognition using appearance-adaptive models in particle filters (2004)

A Deep Learning Approach to Predict Crowd Behavior Based on Emotion

Elizabeth B. Varghese[1,2] and Sabu M. Thampi[1(✉)]

[1] Indian Institute of Information Technology and Management-Kerala (IIITM-K),
Thiruvananthapuram, Kerala, India
{elizabeth.varghese,sabu.thampi}@iiitmk.ac.in
[2] Cochin University of Science and Technology, Kochi, Kerala, India

Abstract. In a visual surveillance system, predicting crowd behavior has recently emerged as a crucial problem for crowd management and monitoring. Specifically, potential dangers and disasters can be avoided by correctly detecting crowd behavior. In this paper, we propose an approach to forecast crowd behavior using a deep learning framework and multiclass Support Vector Machine (SVM). We extract spatio-temporal descriptors using 3D Convolutional Neural Network (3DCNN) based on crowd emotions. In particular, the learned emotion based descriptors help to build the semantic ambiguity in classifying crowd behavior. The effectiveness of our approach is validated with 3 benchmark datasets: Motion Emotion Dataset (MED), ViolentFlows and UMN. The obtained results prove that our approach is successful in predicting crowd behavior in challenging situations. Our system also outperforms existing methods that use local feature descriptors, which reveals that emotions from spatio-temporal features are beneficial for the correct anticipation of crowd behavior.

Keywords: Crowd emotion · Crowd behavior
Spatio-temporal features
3D Convolutional Neural Network (3DCNN)
Multiclass Support Vector Machine (SVM)

1 Introduction

A crowd is a group of people assembles in a place at a specific instance for a particular purpose [22]. Whether crowds gather to protest or for entertaining; chances are there for fatalities and anomalous incidents. Therefore, intelligent crowd behavior analysis techniques are essential for observing and tracking emergency situations occurring in crowded scenes, including busy roadways, sports stadiums, open-air concerts and pilgrimages. Large numbers of cameras are deployed in urban areas and public gathering spots for this purpose and they provide an enormous amount of video. The main challenges in analyzing the crowded scenes from the video data are occlusion among the crowd subjects, uncertainties in crowd density, ambiguities in the description and perception of

© Springer Nature Switzerland AG 2018
A. Basu and S. Berretti (Eds.): ICSM 2018, LNCS 11010, pp. 296–307, 2018.
https://doi.org/10.1007/978-3-030-04375-9_25

the meaning and natures of crowd anomalies. For handling those problems, modeling of all (or most of) the crowd behaviors by analyzing their basic rudimentary aspects is unavoidable [20].

Over the past years, many works were published on analyzing crowded scene by exploiting mainly the motion pattern of the crowd. These works were focused only on partial modeling of crowd behavior such as panic escape, wrong way movement and so on. Moreover, almost all of them use low-level visual features for further analysis [4]. Since crowd behaviors depend mainly on contexts and highly ambiguous in the semantic level, low-level features are not sufficient to define all the high-level diverse behaviors. Therefore, in addition to visual clues, identifying personality traits are also very helpful in detecting crowd behavior which can bridge the linguistic gap between high-level crowd behaviors and low-level features [10]. So, in our work, we are bridging this gap by classifying crowd behavior based on personality trait such as emotions namely *angry, sad, scared, happy* and so on. The process of emotion is a concept centered on individuals, which can be directed to specific events by the estimation of inherent features and have a strong impact on body and behavior [18]. According to the Convergence Theory of collective behavior of crowd [17], crowd behavior is influenced by individual behaviors and hence crowd emotions can be identified in the same way as individual emotions. That is, similar appraisal events may cause similar emotion in both individuals and in a crowd.

In this work, we propose a deep representation framework for crowd behavior classification based on crowd emotions. In variation with the previous emotion-based approaches [5, 10, 13, 21], instead of using appearance or motion features or other low level features to model the crowd behavior patterns, we are proposing deep spatio-temporal features learning to discriminate crowd emotions using a 3D Convolutional Neural Network (3DCNN) [16]. Finally, we introduce a multiclass Support Vector Machine (SVM) to predict multiple heterogeneous crowd behaviors as SVMs are considered to be one of the most popular selective classification algorithms [3]. The features from the 3DCNN encapsulate information from video frames related to different emotions such as *angry, happy, excited, scared, sad* and *neutral.* The emotions are mapped to their corresponding crowd behaviors using SVM and our method is able to predict six different behavioral classes such as *fight, normal, abnormal object, panic, cheerful* and *congested* which is more than most of the state of the art methods and is explained in Sect. 4. We use the Motion Emotion Dataset (MED) proposed in [11] to extract the emotion features as the dataset have video frames annotated with emotions which are very useful in extracting features using 3DCNN.

To summarize, our contributions are listed below

- We propose a 3D Convolutional deep learning framework to learn spatio-temporal features that can segregate crowd emotions from a video.
- We introduce a multiclass SVM to map the emotion features to 6 different crowd behaviors.

- The proposed deep framework with the multiclass model outperforms the methods that use low-level features to classify crowd behavior and abnormal activity classification.

The rest of the paper is structured as follows. Section 2 gives a review of the related works. The technical details of our 3DCNN framework and emotion estimation are introduced in Sect. 3. An outlook of our multiclass SVM model is presented in Sect. 4. Section 5 discusses the experiments and results obtained that evaluates our framework and model. Finally, we conclude the paper with some future perspectives in Sect. 6.

2 Related Works

Effective crowd management in a public surveillance system demands precise recognition and prediction of crowd behavior to detect abnormal activities. Crowd behavior analysis has been tried in the early research of computer vision particularly in simulation and graphics field [15]. Recent approaches to crowd behavior analysis are mainly based on the motion patterns of individuals. These approaches extract the low-level motion/appearance features such as Motion Boundary Histogram (MBH), Histogram of Gradients (HOG), Histogram of Oriented Tracklets (HOT), Histogram of Optical Flow (HOF) etc. [7,9,19] from video data that can be directly mapped to behavior by machine learning algorithms. Moreover, Social Force Models and Fluid Dynamics are also explored in analyzing crowd behavior [8,24]. Most of the methods in literature rely mainly on low level features to extract high level crowd behavior which may lead to an ambiguous categorization of behaviors. For example, individuals who hug each other might be considered as fighting, whereas they are emotionally happy and behaving normally. Thus, we are trying to link this linguistic chasm between the high level and low level features by interpreting the underlying emotions of crowd before classifying behavior.

Emotions are explored in crowd simulation models [2,13,21] which lack the real time parameters of crowd behavior. Moreover, these methods cannot handle the uncertainty of human behavior under unusual situations. Therefore, for effective analysis of crowd behavior, experiments on video data are essential. Rabiee et al. [10] proposed an attribute based approach and developed a new dataset to analyze crowd behavior from videos, where the attribute is the crowd emotion. But this method also relies on low level features to classify emotion(s).

Unlike existing works that depend on low-level features and appearance information between consecutive frames in the video, more advanced methods using deep learning are available for extracting spatio-temporal features [14,23]. Spatio-temporal computational methods are widely used when data are collected across time as well as space and has spatial and temporal properties. Since video data is rich in both spatial and temporal phenomena that exist at a certain time t and location x, we can exploit such properties for feature extraction. Spatio-temporal feature extraction is utilized in the deep fully convolutional neural network (FCNN) proposed by Sabokrou et al. [12] to classify the crowd behavior as normal or suspicious or abnormal. The suspicious behavior is further processed to classify again as either normal or abnormal. Tran et al. [16] learn spatio-temporal features using a 3DCNN which acts as a good feature descriptor, which consists of information related to objects, scenes, and actions in a video. Thus, 3DCNN is also pertinent in behavior analysis as it is generic, compact and efficient [16].

While the main choice of crowd behavior analysis is to predict and classify crowd behaviors, one universal shortcoming in the existing works is to categorize the behaviors which are mostly ambiguous on the semantic level. Therefore we provide a robust and adaptable framework using 3DCNN to segregate crowd behaviors based on human psychological factors such as emotions. These emotions are then mapped to normal and abnormal activities related to crowd behavior, which would help the authorities to take proactive decisions before the occurrence of any catastrophe.

3 Emotion Identification from Spatio Temporal Features

This section deals with the main contributions of our work, particularly emotion estimation from crowd videos using spatio temporal features. Our aim is to capture temporal patterns of emotion that occur at different spatial resolution by leveraging the visual patterns from different convolutional levels. We employ a 3D convolutional neural network (3DCNN) to learn spatio-temporal crowd features and utilize them to discriminate emotions. 3DCNN consists of 3D convolution and 3D pooling operations for the preservation of 3D temporal information of the input signals [16]. Also, a third dimension in the 3D kernels helps to capture useful motion information that is essential for crowd emotion classification. The coming subsections explain our 3DCNN network configuration and also illustrates how the network is used for emotion identification.

3.1 Configuration of 3DCNN Framework

Our 3DCNN framework takes video clips as inputs and allocates emotions which belong to 7 different classes based on MED ground truth data [11]. The network configuration of our deep model is diagrammatically shown in Fig. 1. Each input video is split into non overlapped p-frame clips resulting in the input dimension of $c \times Row \times Col \times p$, where c is the number of channels and $Row \times Col$ denotes the size of the video frame. The value for c is 3 as the input videos have Red, Green and Blue channels. The network consists of 3 convolution layers, 3 pooling layers, one fully connected layer and a soft max loss layer to classify emotions. For the first convolution layer, we employ a filter size of 16 and for the consecutive layers, filter size is 32. Size of the convolution kernel is $convw \times convh \times convd$, where $convw, convh$ and $convd$ are the width, height, and depth of the kernel respectively with stride S. Max Pooling layers also apply a kernel size $poolw \times poolh \times poold$ with stride S. In our work, value for S is taken as 1 as this helps to encode more temporal information from the video. The loss function for each attribute is cross entropy for multitask learning and the activation function for all the layers is Rectified Linear Unit (ReLU) given by Eq. 1.

$$f(x) = max(0, x) \tag{1}$$

The output from the fully connected layer is given to the soft max layer for the emotion classification which is explained in Sect. 3.2.

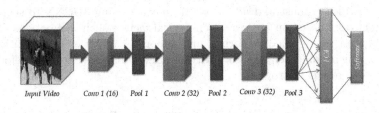

Input Video   Conv 1 (16)   Pool 1   Conv 2 (32)   Pool 2   Conv 3 (32)   Pool 3

Fig. 1. 3DCNN network. The network has 5 layers (3 convolutions, 1 fully connected and 1 soft max). Each convolution layer is followed with max pool layers. The number of filters in each convolution layer is shown in brackets. (Color figure online)

3.2 Emotion Estimation

Estimation of emotions are based on the annotation given in the Motion Emotion Data set (MED) [11]. The available ground truth emotions are *Angry, Happy, Excited, Scared, Sad* and *Neutral*. Also for each video, there are fragments with abnormal object or no crowd which is annotated as *Nothing*.

We represent each input video as $V = (f_i)_{i=1}^n$ where f_i is the i_{th} frame of the video and n is the total number of frames. The video, V is split into non overlapped clips of p frames. All the extracted frames are vectorized and concatenated to get the final representation of the video V as $T \in \mathbb{R}^{c \times Row \times Col \times p}$. Similar methods are applied for all the K input videos to obtain $X_T = (T_i)_{i=1}^K$, which is fed into the convolution network. Emotion labels em_i are also appended to X_T based on the annotation from the data set. Feature maps are generated from the network by applying the convolution kernel of $convw \times convh \times convd$ to the convolution layers. The detailed explanation of our convolution framework is explained in Sect. 3.1. Emotion probabilities associated with each input video is extracted as the output of the soft max layer using Eq. 2.

$$E(em)_j = \frac{e^{em_j}}{\sum_{k=1}^{fc_n} e^{em_k}} \tag{2}$$

where j is 1, 2, 3...em emotion labels and fc_n is the number of outputs in the fully connected layer, which is 256 in our case. The probabilities of each emotion are then used to a train a multi-class SVM for the correct prediction of crowd behavior b_i of an unseen test video clip and are explained in Sect. 4.

4   Crowd Behavior Classification

An intelligent visual surveillance system should recognize the types of crowd behavior to ensure the safety of the public. In order to build such a system, we are trying to analyze behavior based on emotions using 3DCNN framework discussed in the previous section. The emotions estimated using our framework is beneficial to classify behavior, as they are the driving factors for understanding distinct behaviors of a crowd. The soft max layer of our deep framework gives the probability of occurrence of emotions in each input video. We utilize these probabilities to train a multiclass Support Vector Machine (SVM) using crowd behavior labels to classify and predict behavior. Instead of classifying behavior as normal or abnormal, we are aiming to categorize the type of crowd behavior based on emotions. According to the Motion Emotion Dataset (MED) [11], we have estimated 6 different emotions such as Angry, Happy, Excited, Scared, Sad and Neutral. Also if there is no crowd, or if there are only objects in the scene, it is given as the label "Nothing". The emotion to behavior label mapping is done according to [10] and is illustrated in Table 1. We have also devised one additional behavior label "Cheerful" to map the Happy and Excited emotion labels as guided by [17]. Thus, our SVM could predict 6 different crowd behaviors from input videos. The following subsection gives an outlook of our SVM classifier to predict crowd behaviors.

Table 1. Emotion to behavior mapping.

Emotions	Behaviors
Angry	Fight
Happy	Cheerful
Excited	Cheerful
Scared	Panic
Sad	Congestion
Neutral	Normal
Nothing	Abnormal object

4.1   Multiclass SVM for Behavior Classification

Support Vector Machines (SVMs) are discriminative classifiers and considered to be one of the most popularly used classification algorithms [3]. They were initially designed for twofold classification in the form of a hyper plane, but later, many approaches have been proposed for multiclass classification due to their efficient performance in dealing with multiple classes that consist of multi-dimensional data with real numbers. Therefore, in our approach, we adopt a multi-class SVM with dual decomposition for optimization as proposed in [3]. The multi-class

SVM in our work classifies an input array of emotion probabilities $E \in \mathbb{R}^{K \times em}$ into one of the b classes using the rule in Eq. 3 [3]:

$$\hat{b} = \underset{m \in [b]}{\mathrm{argmax}} \, w_m^T E \tag{3}$$

where w_m is the prototype representing m_{th} class and $w_m^T E$ is the inner product that serves as the score of class m with respect to emotions E. The behavior class with the highest score is chosen using Eq. 3. Emotion probabilities E_i associated with each class and their corresponding behavior labels b_i are trained according to Algorithm 1.

Algorithm 1. Multiclass SVM Training

1: **Require:** $(E_1, b_1), \ldots\ldots(E_N, b_M)$
2: **procedure** TRAINSVM($E, b, niter, nsamples$)
3:     Initialize primal and dual coefficients
4:     Initialize $n \leftarrow \sqrt{\sum(E^2)}$ // Normalize Emotion Values
5:     t $\leftarrow 0.01$ // Initialize tolerance parameter
6:   **for** each i in $niter$ **do**
7:       $criteria \leftarrow 0$
8:       **for** each k in $nsamples$ **do**
9:           $i \leftarrow ind[k]$
10:          $g \leftarrow$ gradient (E, b, i)
11:          $criteria \leftarrow$ calccriteria (g, b, i)
12:          criteriatot$\leftarrow$criteriatot $+$ criteria
13:          **if** $(criteria < 1e - 12)$ **then**
14:              $\delta \leftarrow$ projecttosimplex(g, b, n, i)
15:          **end if**
16:          Update primal and dual coefficients using δ
17:      **end for**
18:      **if** $(i == 0)$ **then**
19:          initcriteria $\leftarrow$ criteriatot
20:      **end if**
21:      endcriteria $\leftarrow$ criteriatot / initcriter
22:      **if** $(endcriteria < t))$ **then**
23:          Stop Training : Convergence Attained
24:      **end if**
25:   **end for**
26: **end procedure**

The algorithm takes emotion probabilities E as training samples and original crowd behavior labels b as target values. The algorithm also initializes primal and dual coefficients as SVM utilizes the primal-dual relationship to find optimal solution. SVM is a classifier which can solve the quadratic optimization problem of primal w over dual α and is given in Eq. 4. Initially, the primal and dual coefficients are set to zero and later updated during each iteration using the value of delta calculated from Euclidean projection to simplex as given in [3] to avoid the restricted optimization problem in SVM.

$$w_m(\alpha) = \sum_{i=1}^{N} \alpha_i^m E_i \ \forall m \in b \quad (4)$$

For each iteration, a partial derivative g is calculated with respect to α and this is used to update *criteria* to find optimal solution. The procedure, *calccriteria* in the algorithm modifies the value of *criteria* using the equation given in 5

$$criteria_i = \max_{m \in [b]} g_i^m - \min_{m \in [b]: \alpha_i^m < C_i^m} g_i^m \quad (5)$$

The algorithm can be stopped if the value of criteria is less than a given tolerance parameter, t, $\forall i \in [N]$, where N is the total number of training samples. The tolerance parameter in our experiment is set to 0.01 as we get good convergence using this value. With our SVM model, we successfully mapped emotion probabilities to 6 behavior classes with an average accuracy of around 90%. The details of the implementation and the results are presented in the next section.

5   Experimental Results and Discussions

We evaluate our framework and model with Motion Emotion Dataset (MED) proposed in [11] which have videos with emotion annotation. The dataset comprises 31 videos with 44,000 normal and abnormal clips which are recorded in 30 frames per second with a resolution of 554×235. We perform data augmentation by splitting the video based on ground truth data which results in 106 videos. The size of the video frames are fixed to 200×200. Thus, the dimension of each input video to the 3DCNN framework is $3 \times 200 \times 200 \times 15$ as each video is split into non overlapped 15-frame clips. All the convolution layers in our network use a kernel of size $3 \times 3 \times 3$ whereas kernel of max pooling layer is $2 \times 2 \times 2$. The stride factor of both convolution and the max-pooling layer is 1. The last layer of 3DCNN is a softmax layer which takes 256 inputs from the fully connected layer and gives emotion probabilities of each video as output.

The resultant emotions from each video are given as input to a multiclass SVM for behavior classification. Section 4 presents the details of SVM training and classification. We randomly split the emotion probabilities from 106 videos into training and test sets with a ratio of 6:4. The results of experiments performed on the MED data set are disclosed in the form of a confusion matrix (Fig. 2(a)). It is clear from the matrix that by extracting spatio-temporal features using 3DCNN based on emotion and classifying behavior using SVM is very efficient in detecting crowds in cases such as *Cheerful, Panic, Congestion* and *Normal*. Although we don't get 100% for *Abnormal Object* and *Fight*, it is understandable from the matrix that 80% and 75% respectively of them are correctly classified.

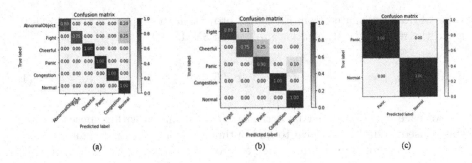

Fig. 2. Confusion matrix of (a) Motion emotion dataset (b) Violent flows dataset (c) UMN dataset

We also compared our method with the crowd behavior classification approach proposed by authors in [10] and the accuracy in percentage for each behavior class is shown in Table 2. They used emotion as an attribute for representing the crowd behavior. It is very evident from the table that our method is very good in classifying behavior compared to [10]. In their method, all the classes have less than 50% accuracy except for the *Panic* behavior, which we got 100% accuracy. Furthermore, we have one more additional behavior class to detect *Cheerful* crowd, which is normally spectators and audience in concerts or stadiums.

Table 2. Comparison with emotion attribute approach [10]

Behavior classes	Our method	Emotion attribute
Abnormal object	80	33.2
Fight	75	34.4
Cheerful	100	Class not present
Panic	100	71.9
Congestion	100	30.7
Normal	100	48.1

We validate our approach with two benchmark datasets: Violent Flows [6] and UMN [1]. Violent Flows consists of 246 real world videos with violence and non-violence annotation whereas UMN composed of 11 clips of normal and panic crowd behavior. We extract spatio-temporal features from the videos using our 3DCNN framework and emotion probabilities are calculated. They are given to SVM for behavior prediction. The outcome of the classifier is presented as confusion matrices and is shown in Fig. 2(b) and (c) for Violent Flows and UMN respectively. We assure that 'violence' videos in Violent Flows are predicted as either *Panic, Congestion* or *Fight* with 90,100 and 89% prediction accuracy respectively whereas 'non-violence' videos as *Cheerful* or *Normal* which have 100 and 75% respectively. Similarly, in the case of UMN, videos with 'Abnormal' annotation are successfully predicted as the crowd with *Panic* behavior. Since the emotion probability of *Nothing* label is 0 in Violent Flows, we skip the *Abnormal Object* class for behavior prediction. Similarly for UMN also, only two classes are needed for prediction. It is clear from the matrices that almost all videos in both datasets are successfully predicted. The results reveal that our 3DCNN framework is efficient enough to extract spatio-temporal features for identifying emotions in a crowded scenario and our SVM model is very effective in predicting crowd behavior in diverse environments.

Table 3. Average accuracy and precision of our approach in different datasets

Datasets	Accuracy	Precision
MED	90.9	97
ViolentFlows	90.6	91
UMN	100	100

Table 4. Performance of our approach compared with low level features in MED

Methods	Accuracy
HOG [7]	38.80
HOF [7]	37.69
MBH [19]	38.53
Dense trajectory [19]	38.71
Emotion attribute [10]	43.6
Our approach	**90.9**

In all the experiments, we employ average accuracy and precision as evaluation criteria. The average precision and accuracy percentages in Table 3 disclose that our framework is successful in predicting crowd behavior in varying situations. It is also noticeable from the table that we have got very high precision which reveals that the false positive rate of our approach is very low which is very substantial in real environments.

Our approach is also compared with state of the art methods that extract low-level features such as HOG [7], HOF [7], MBH [19], Dense Trajectory [19], HOT [9], Optical Flow [8] and SFM [8]. According to the results demonstrated in Tables 4 and 5, it is very evident that our method outperforms all other methods in all 3 data sets. All the above methods extract low-level motion features for behavior classification whereas our method uses deep spatio-temporal features based on emotion. It is very apparent that our method can assimilate more linguistic information which is very helpful in correctly predicting crowd behavior in confronting situations than any of the state of the art low-level feature extraction methods.

Table 5. Performance in terms of accuracy of our approach compared with methods use low level features in violent flows and UMN dataset

Methods	ViolentFlow	Methods	UMN
HOG [7]	59.82	HOG [7]	97.02
HOF [7]	56.68	Optical flow [8]	78
HOT [9]	81.30	SFM [8]	90
Our approach	**90.6**	Our approach	**100**

6   Conclusions

In this paper, we proposed a persuasive approach to detect and predict crowd behaviors from spatio-temporal features based on emotion. These features have the advantage of considering individual interactions to find the type of emotions in a crowded scene which can encode the semantic information of crowd behavior. The effectiveness of the extracted crowd behaviors is validated with three datasets and found that our method is relevant for real-time crowd behavior prediction. We also obtained promising results by comparing with state of the art local feature descriptors, which showed that emotions extracted from spatio-temporal features are outstanding in bridging the linguistic gap between low-level descriptors and high-level discrete crowd behaviors. In future, we are planning to predict crowd behavior class without training and with automatic mapping of emotion to behavior. We are also aiming to incorporate multimodal data to further improve the performance of crowd behavior analysis and also for finding suspicious activities in smart surveillance environment.

References

1. Detection of Unusual Crowd Activity. http://mha.cs.umn.edu/proj_events.shtml/crowd. Accessed 7 Apr 2018
2. Baig, M.W., Barakova, E.I., Marcenaro, L., Rauterberg, M., Regazzoni, C.S.: Crowd emotion detection using dynamic probabilistic models. In: del Pobil, A.P., Chinellato, E., Martinez-Martin, E., Hallam, J., Cervera, E., Morales, A. (eds.) SAB 2014. LNCS, vol. 8575, pp. 328–337. Springer, Cham (2014). https://doi.org/10.1007/978-3-319-08864-8_32
3. Blondel, M., Fujino, A., Ueda, N.: Large-scale multiclass support vector machine training via euclidean projection onto the simplex. In: 2014 22nd International Conference on Pattern Recognition, ICPR, pp. 1289–1294. IEEE (2014)
4. Dupont, C., Tobías, L., Luvison, B.: Crowd-11: a dataset for fine grained crowd behaviour analysis. In: Proceedings of the IEEE Conference on Computer Vision and Pattern Recognition Workshops, pp. 9–16 (2017)
5. Guy, S.J., Kim, S., Lin, M.C., Manocha, D.: Simulating heterogeneous crowd behaviors using personality trait theory. In: Proceedings of the 2011 ACM SIGGRAPH/Eurographics Symposium on Computer Animation, pp. 43–52. ACM (2011)

6. Hassner, T., Itcher, Y., Kliper-Gross, O.: Violent flows: real-time detection of violent crowd behavior. In: 2012 IEEE Computer Society Conference on Computer Vision and Pattern Recognition Workshops, CVPRW, pp. 1–6. IEEE (2012)
7. Laptev, I., Marszalek, M., Schmid, C., Rozenfeld, B.: Learning realistic human actions from movies. In: IEEE Conference on Computer Vision and Pattern Recognition, CVPR 2008, pp. 1–8. IEEE (2008)
8. Mehran, R., Oyama, A., Shah, M.: Abnormal crowd behavior detection using social force model. In: IEEE Conference on Computer Vision and Pattern Recognition, CVPR 2009, pp. 935–942. IEEE (2009)
9. Mousavi, H., Mohammadi, S., Perina, A., Chellali, R., Murino, V.: Analyzing tracklets for the detection of abnormal crowd behavior. In: 2015 IEEE Winter Conference on Applications of Computer Vision, WACV, pp. 148–155. IEEE (2015)
10. Rabiee, H., Haddadnia, J., Mousavi, H.: Crowd behavior representation: an attribute-based approach. SpringerPlus 5(1), 1179 (2016)
11. Rabiee, H., Haddadnia, J., Mousavi, H., Kalantarzadeh, M., Nabi, M., Murino, V.: Novel dataset for fine-grained abnormal behavior understanding in crowd. In: 2016 13th IEEE International Conference on Advanced Video and Signal Based Surveillance, AVSS, pp. 95–101. IEEE (2016)
12. Sabokrou, M., Fayyaz, M., Fathy, M., et al.: Fully convolutional neural network for fast anomaly detection in crowded scenes. arXiv preprint arXiv:1609.00866 (2016)
13. Saifi, L., Boubetra, A., Nouioua, F.: An approach for emotions and behavior modeling in a crowd in the presence of rare events. Adapt. Behav. 24(6), 428–445 (2016)
14. Shao, J., Kang, K., Change Loy, C., Wang, X.: Deeply learned attributes for crowded scene understanding. In: Proceedings of the IEEE Conference on Computer Vision and Pattern Recognition, pp. 4657–4666 (2015)
15. Amir Sjarif, N.N., Shamsuddin, S.M., Mohd Hashim, S.Z., Yuhaniz, S.S.: Crowd analysis and its applications. In: Mohamad Zain, J., Wan Mohd, W.M., El-Qawasmeh, E. (eds.) ICSECS 2011. CCIS, vol. 179, pp. 687–697. Springer, Heidelberg (2011). https://doi.org/10.1007/978-3-642-22170-5_59
16. Tran, D., Bourdev, L., Fergus, R., Torresani, L., Paluri, M.: Learning spatiotemporal features with 3D convolutional networks. In: 2015 IEEE International Conference on Computer Vision, ICCV, pp. 4489–4497. IEEE (2015)
17. Turner, R.H., Killian, L.M., et al.: Collective Behavior. Prentice-Hall, Englewood Cliffs (1957)
18. Urizar, O.J., Barakova, E.I., Marcenaro, L., Regazzoni, C.S., Rauterberg, M.: Emotion estimation in crowds: a survey (2017)
19. Wang, H., Kläser, A., Schmid, C., Liu, C.L.: Dense trajectories and motion boundary descriptors for action recognition. Int. J. Comput. Vis. 103(1), 60–79 (2013)
20. Wang, J., Xu, Z.: Spatio-temporal texture modelling for real-time crowd anomaly detection. Comput. Vis. Image Underst. 144, 177–187 (2016)
21. Xu, M., et al.: Crowd behavior simulation with emotional contagion in unexpected multi-hazard situations. arXiv preprint arXiv:1801.10000 (2018)
22. Yogameena, B., Nagananthini, C.: Computer vision based crowd disaster avoidance system: a survey. Int. J. Disaster Risk Reduct. 22, 95–129 (2017)
23. Zhang, L., Feng, Y., Han, J., Zhen, X.: Realistic human action recognition: when deep learning meets VLAD. In: 2016 IEEE International Conference on Acoustics, Speech and Signal Processing, ICASSP, pp. 1352–1356. IEEE (2016)
24. Zitouni, M.S., Bhaskar, H., Dias, J., Al-Mualla, M.E.: Advances and trends in visual crowd analysis: a systematic survey and evaluation of crowd modelling techniques. Neurocomputing 186, 139–159 (2016)

Object Tracking in Hyperspectral Videos with Convolutional Features and Kernelized Correlation Filter

Kun Qian[1]($\boxtimes$), Jun Zhou[2], Fengchao Xiong[3], Huixin Zhou[1], and Juan Du[1]

[1] Lab of Optoelectronic Imaging and Image Processing, Xidian University,
Xi'an, People's Republic of China
kunqianmhy@gmail.com
[2] School of Information and Communication Technology, Griffith University,
Brisbane, Australia
[3] College of Computer Science, Zhejiang University,
Hangzhou, People's Republic of China

Abstract. Target tracking in hyperspectral videos is a new research topic. In this paper, a novel method based on convolutional network and Kernelized Correlation Filter (KCF) framework is presented for tracking objects of interest in hyperspectral videos. We extract a set of normalized three-dimensional cubes from the target region as fixed convolution filters which contain spectral information surrounding a target. The feature maps generated by convolutional operations are combined to form a three-dimensional representation of an object, thereby providing effective encoding of local spectral-spatial information. We show that a simple two-layer convolutional networks is sufficient to learn robust representations without the need of offline training with a large dataset. In the tracking step, KCF is adopted to distinguish targets from neighboring environment. Experimental results demonstrate that the proposed method performs well on sample hyperspectral videos, and outperforms several state-of-the-art methods tested on grayscale and color videos in the same scene.

Keywords: Target tracking · Hyperspectral video · Correlation filter Convolutional networks

1 Introduction

Hyperspectral imaging plays an important role in remote sensing as it provides hundreds of contiguous, narrow spectral bands [1]. With the advantage of rich spectral information, hyperspectral images (HSIs) have been widely used in many applications involving image classification [2] and segmentation [3], such as land cover detection and mining. However, to the best of our knowledge, there is very little work focusing on hyperspectral video processing. The main reason is that it is difficult to capture hyperspectral videos with low speed imaging devices. It

© Springer Nature Switzerland AG 2018
A. Basu and S. Berretti (Eds.): ICSM 2018, LNCS 11010, pp. 308–319, 2018.
https://doi.org/10.1007/978-3-030-04375-9_26

is not until the last a couple of years that low cost hyperspectral video cameras become available, making it possible to collect hyperspectral videos at a high frame rate.

In this paper, we introduce one of the very first work on object tracking in hyperspectral videos. Object tracking is an important research topic in computer vision and multimedia. Most tracking methods [4–8] were developed on grayscale or RGB videos. Discriminative correlation filter (DCF) [4–6,9] based framework explores supervised visual object tracking. The DCF trains the filters very efficiently in the frequency domain via fast Discrete Fourier transform (DFT). It learns a correlation filter to localize the object in consecutive frames. The learned filter is applied to estimate the target location by calculating the maximum response. Bolme et al. introduced the minimum output sum of squared error filter (MOSSE) tracker [9] which utilizes grayscale features and achieves an impressive speed in tracking application. Other features used for tracking include the incorporation of kernels and histogram of gradient (HOG) features [6], the addition of color name features [4], adaptive scale [10], and the integration of deep learning features [11]. The kernelized correlation filter (KCF) method [6] circularly shifts the training samples and exploits the advantage of multichannel HOG features with the kernel trick. Zhang et al. proposed the Spatio-Temporal Context (STC) [7] tracker, which explores the correlation filter in terms of the probability theory, and utilized the dense sampling to track the object of interest.

In recent years, deep learning methods have shown success in object tracking [11–13]. Several works [14,15] have combined deep learning with the correlation filter based framework. Instead of using hand-crafted features such as HOG, the DCF trackers use features automatically learnt by convolutional neural network (CNN). This significantly improves the robustness of the tracking. Zhang et al. proposed the lightweight convolutional network based tracker (CNT) [16] which has a simple architecture and yet effectively constructs a robust representation. This tracker demonstrates that a two-layer CNN without pooling and training process can obtain competitive results on a benchmark dataset with 50 challenging videos, and outperforms the first deep learning based tracker (DLT) [8] by a large margin.

In this paper, we propose a novel convolutional feature based tracker for hyperspectral video processing. The videos were captured by a hyperspectral camera of 14 bands in the range of 470–620 nm. We first defined convolution filters from a set of normalized three-dimensional cubes surrounding a target. The convolutional operations generate a set of feature maps that are combined to form a three-dimensional representation of an object, which is used in the tracking process. In the tracking step, KCF is adopted to distinguish targets from neighboring environment. We extend the KCF method so it can cope with hyperspectral data.

The remainder of this paper is organized as follows. In Sect. 2, we first present the convolutional feature for hyperspectral images. Then, we briefly describe the KCF tracker, and how it can be extended for multichannel convolutional features for hyperspectral tracking. In Sect. 3, experimental results are presented to verify the performance of the proposed method on hyperspectral video sequences. Our method is also compared with the state-of-art methods on grayscale and RGB videos of the same scene. Finally, conclusions are drawn in Sect. 4.

2   The Proposed Tracking Algorithm

In this section, we describe the details of the proposed method. We first introduce convolutional features in the 3D spectral-spatial domain. Then we describe the KCF method and its extension to hyperspectral data.

2.1   Convolutional Features for Hyperspectral Target

Motivated by the success of convolution network on visual tracking [16], we utilize this method to extract the local hyperspectral information. Given a target template, the proposed hierarchical representation architecture contains two steps. First, local features which contain spectral information are extracted from a bank of three-dimensional filters convolving with the input image at each position. Then, these features are stacked together to form a three-dimensional representation. This feature extraction process is shown in Figs. 1 and 2.

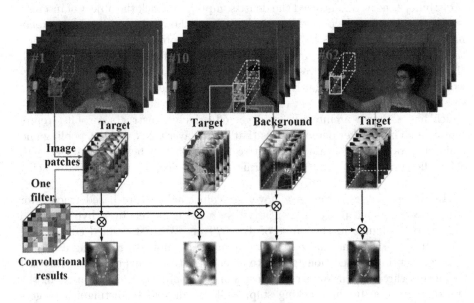

Fig. 1. 3D convolution process.

The image patches in Fig. 1 are generated from local hyperspectral image cube $I \in R^{n \times n \times d}$, where n and d denote patch size and the number of spectral bands, respectively. A set of overlapping local image patchs $Y_i (i = 1, 2, \ldots, l) \in R^{w \times w \times d}$ centered at each pixel position is densely sampled inside the image patch I through a sliding window of size $w \times w$, where $l = n \times n$. In the first frame of the video, several filters $f_j (j = 1, 2, \ldots, d)(d < l)$ are selected randomly from $Y_i(i = 1, 2, \ldots, l)$, the responses on the image patch I are denoted with feature maps $S_j \in R^{n \times n}$, which can be expressed as

$$S_j = I \bigotimes f_j \qquad (1)$$

where $\bigotimes$ is the convolution operator.

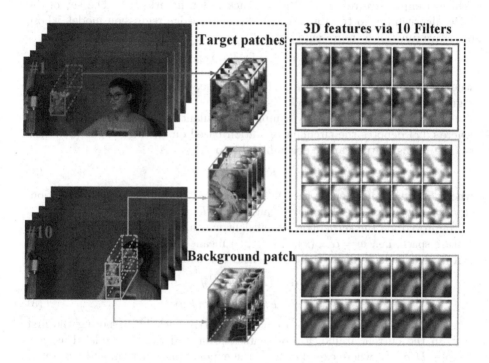

Fig. 2. Stacked features.

Figure 1 shows that the 3D filter, which is localized, can extract local structural features for the hyperspectral cubes. Furthermore, convolutional results of three target templates (at the bottom of Fig. 1) are similar in geometric layout, which demonstrates that the local filter f_j is effective in extracting the target features despite their appearance variation. For negative templates (see the third image patch in the bottom row of Fig. 1), its convolutional result are very different from the target templates. As shown in Fig. 2, 3D features generated by 10 filters have similar properties. Therefore, the convolution results and the generated features represent the inner structure of the tracking target.

2.2   Tracking Framework

The output of the filtering operation are stacked to form a three-dimensional representation. This can be considered as the multichannel feature which is required as the input to the kernelized correlation filter (KCF) tracker. In this section, we firstly briefly describe the KCF tracker [6], and then extend it to use the effective features introduced in the above section.

The KCF Tracker. Our approach is built on the KCF tracker which has achieved impressive results on Visual Tracker Benchmarks [17]. The key of the KCF algorithm is to train a classifier through a ridge regression model, whose objective function is represented as

$$\min_{w}((w^T x - y)^2 + \lambda \|w\|^2) \tag{2}$$

where y, λ and w represent the regression value, regularization parameter and regression coefficient, respectively.

The KCF approach densely samples a circulant sample matrix $X = C(x)$, where $C(x)$ denotes the circulant operation based on the first row x (i.e., base sample). This matrix can be decomposed into

$$C(x) = F \cdot diag(Fx) \cdot F^H \tag{3}$$

where F and $diag(\cdot)$ denote the DFT matrix and the diagonalization function, respectively. F^H is the Hermitian transpose of F, which is a constant.

Improved via the kernel trick, coefficient w is mapped to a high-dimensional feature space, i.e., $w = \alpha^T \varphi(x)$, where $\varphi(\cdot)$ means the mapping function and α is a new coefficient. Then, the coefficient α can be formulated as

$$\alpha = (K + \lambda I)^{-1} y \tag{4}$$

$$F\alpha = ((Fk^{xx}) + \lambda)^{-1}(Fy) \tag{5}$$

where kernel matrix K is also a circulant matrix with k^{xx} denoting the first row. In the current frame, y represents a prior and can be modeled as $y = b\exp(-|D/\sigma_1|^\beta)$, where $\exp(\cdot)$ denotes the exponential function, and b is a normalization constant. D denotes the Euclidean distance between the target and a pixel in the neighborhood. σ_1 and β represent a scale parameter and a shape parameter, respectively.

In Eq. (5), k can be computed based on the Gaussian function, i.e.,

$$k^{xz} = \exp(-\frac{1}{\sigma^2}(\|x\|^2 + \|z\|^2) - 2F^{-1}((Fx) \otimes (Fz))). \tag{6}$$

Subsequently, the object tracking task is transformed to a detection problem. The image patch z of the current frame at the same target location is treated as the testing base sample, therefore, the response map is expressed as:

$$f(z) = F^{-1}((Fk^{xz}) \otimes (F\alpha)) \tag{7}$$

where x and α are learnt before the current frame. An intuitive description is that the response $f(z)$ is a linear combination of the neighboring kernel value k^{xz} with the weighted coefficient α.

Multichannel Convolutional Features of HSI. Suppose the multichannel representation x (which has been reshaped to one row matrix, i.e., vector) in the current frame is composed of $x = [x_1, x_2, \ldots, x_d]$, where x_d denotes the d-th target representation. Since the kernels are based on the dot-product, which can be computed by summing the individual dot-products for each channel, Eq. (6) can be rewritten with the multichannel representation z in the next frame as

$$k^{xz} = \exp(-\frac{1}{\sigma^2}(\|x\|^2 + \|z\|^2) - 2F^{-1}(\sum_d (Fx_d) \otimes (Fz_d))) \qquad (8)$$

Therefore, the 3D stacked convolutional features can be seen as multichannel features referring to a pixel of the target object in KCF.

3 Experimental Results and Analysis

In this section, we introduce the dataset used for the experiments, and provide details on the experimental setting, results, and comparison with alternatives.

3.1 Experimental Dataset

We performed experiments on nine image sequences. They are named as $apple - Gray$, $apple - RGB$, $apple - HSI$, $deer - Gray$, $deer - RGB$, $deer - HSI$, $people - Gray$, $People - RGB$, $People - HSI$, respectively. The sequences contain three scenes and each scene has three videos corresponding to grayscale, color, and hyperspectral format, respectively. The color scene and hyperspectral scene are the same, which were captured using a Nikon D600 camera and a Photonfocus or an Ximea hyperspectral camera. These two types of cameras were put side by side when capturing the videos. The hyperspectral cameras captured frames of 16 bands with active range of 460–630 nm at 30 frames per second. After spectral calibration, the HSI is transformed into a three-dimensional data cube with 14 channels for the Photofocus camera or 11 channels for the Ximea camera. The grayscale video is formed by band image at 490 nm of the HSI sequences. Therefore, the grayscale sequences are the same as the HSI sequences in the size and number of the frames, the video content, and the target location.

3.2 Experimental Setup

To better analyze the strength and weakness of the tracking algorithm, we considered 6 attributes [17] based on different challenging factors including background clutters (BC), out of view (OV), in-plane rotation (IPR), fast motion (FM), Deformation (DEF), and Occlusion (OCC), which are summarized in Table 1.

The proposed convolutional network based hyperspectral tracking (CNHT) method was implemented in MATLAB and ran at 1 frame per second on a PC with Intel i7-7700HQ (2.8 GHz) and 32 GB RAM. To validate the performance

Table 1. Summary of video sequences.

Sequence	No. of frames	Image size	Target size	No. of bands	Description
apple − Gray	182	512 × 272	32 × 30	1	OCC, FM and BC
apple − RGB	422	1980 × 1080	133 × 123	3	OCC and BC
apple − HSI	182	512 × 272	32 × 30	14	OCC, FM and BC
deer − Gray	114	512 × 272	50 × 65	1	OCC, OV and FM
deer − RGB	230	1980 × 1080	170 × 240	3	OCC and OV
deer − HSI	114	512 × 272	50 × 65	14	OCC, OV and FM
people − Gray	641	512 × 272	45 × 70	1	OCC, BC, IPR and DEF
people − RGB	676	1980 × 1080	180 × 280	3	OCC, BC, IPR and DEF
people − HSI	641	512 × 272	45 × 70	14	OCC, BC, IPR and DEF

of the CNHT approach, we compared it with some state-of-the-art algorithms, including deep network based trackers DLT [8] and CNT [16], and correlation filter based trackers STC [7] and KCF [6]. The experimental results of the comparison are shown in Figs. 3, 4 and 5. For convenience, we display the results on grayscale and hyperspectral sequences in the same images as their scene are identical.

For four comparative methods, we only changed the parameter on the search scope (e.g., in STC, the search scope is fixed at 6 times of the target size), in order to adapt to fast motion of the object. In our tracker, the state of the target (i.e., size and location) in the first frame was given by the ground truth, which is carefully manually labelled. The size of the filter was set to $6 \times 6 \times 14$ ($w = 6$, $d = 14$), the number of filters was set to a small number of 10 for high speed tracking. The size of the base sample was set as 0.2–3 times of the initial target size, in order to handle fast motion. The other parameters with respect to the KCF method remain unchanged as in the original paper.

3.3   Qualitative Comparison

Background Clutters. Figures 3 and 5 show some screenshots of the tracking results in sequences where the background and the target have similar color in the RGB images. In the *apple − RGB* sequence, the color of the apple and its neighbourhood are red. The CNT method undergoes large drift in the entire sequence. The DLT, STC and KCF track the target well at the beginning of the sequence (e.g. #18), but lose the target at the final stage (e.g. #372). The tracking result of the KCF method on the grayscale video is more accurate, which is shown in Fig. 3(b). Utilizing the spectral information, our tracker is the only one that performs well on the entire sequence. The target people in the *people − RGB* sequence is wearing a green jumper which is similar to the color of the plants. The CNT tracks the object stably, even in the *people − Gray* sequence. The DLT tracker drifts away from the target from the beginning to the end. The STC and KCF approaches lock on parts of background when the people walks in front of the tree (e.g. #176). Furthermore, the KCF faces the

(a) Sampled tracking results on RGB sequence.

(b) Sampled tracking results on grayscale and HSI sequences.

━━ DLT ━━ STC ━━ CNT ━━ KCF ━━ ours

Fig. 3. Qualitative results on the apple sequence. (Color figure online)

(a) Sampled tracking results on RGB sequence.

(b) Sampled tracking results on grayscale and HSI sequences.

━━ DLT ━━ STC ━━ CNT ━━ KCF ━━ ours

Fig. 4. Qualitative results of the deer sequence. (Color figure online)

same problem as in the grayscale image. However, the convolutional network based KCF approach handles color similarity well thanks to the fact that it exploits the characteristic of hyperspectral features.

Partial Occlusion. The targets in all sequences contain partial occlusion. In Fig. 3, the apple is frequently occluded by the fingers. In the gray sequences, the KCF and CNT methods are able to re-detect the object when the target reappears in the screen (e.g., #125). In Fig. 4, the deer is partial occluded by the camera (e.g., #62 of the grayscale sequence and #148 of the RGB sequence). All trackers achieve favorable results because targets of interest are large compared

(a) Sampled tracking results on RGB sequence.

(b) Sampled tracking results on grayscale and HSI sequences.

━ DLT ━ STC ━ CNT ━ KCF ━ ours

Fig. 5. Qualitative results of the people sequence. (Color figure online)

with the size of frames and have different appearance from the background. However, the target moves out of the screen at #72 of the RGB sequence or #30 of the grayscale sequence, in which frame the DLT method drifts to the background. In Fig. 5, the location estimation of the people is possibly disturbed by the thick bush (e.g., #176 of either grayscale or RGB video). The KCF method does not performs well (e.g., #483 of either grayscale or #498 of RGB video). Nevertheless, the proposed method obtains a stable tracking target on the hyperspectral video with much better accuracy than the alternatives on the grayscale video and the RGB video.

3.4   Quantitative Comparison

Figure 6 shows the performance of all tracking algorithms in terms of precision which is defined as the ratio of successful frames whose tracking output is within the given threshold (in pixels) from the ground-truth, measured by the center distance between bounding boxes. The precision of the proposed algorithm on the HSI sequence ranks the highest (0.982), which is followed by the CNT (0.927) on grayscale sequences. The CNHT method takes advantages of the KCF method, hyperspectral information, and convolution method. Thus, it outperforms the KCF method, which uses only one band of the hyperspectral video, by 83%. The precision of STC and CNT on apple sequences are much lower than those over the deer and people sequences. This is because the apple is small and moves fast. More importantly, it has similar color as the background. As shown in Table 2, the proposed CNHT method runs at 1 frame per second, which is acceptable in consideration of the multiple bands in hyperspectral videos. The algorithm efficiency can be improved in the future via running on GPUs which increase the speed of DLT method by at least 16 times.

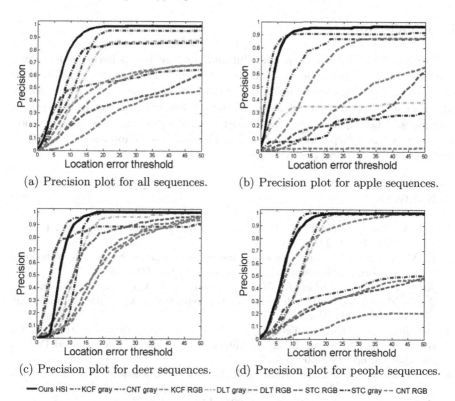

(a) Precision plot for all sequences. (b) Precision plot for apple sequences.

(c) Precision plot for deer sequences. (d) Precision plot for people sequences.

— Ours HSI --- KCF gray --- CNT gray -- KCF RGB --- DLT gray -- DLT RGB — STC RGB --- STC gray -- CNT RGB

Fig. 6. Precision plot.

Table 2. Precision and FPS

Algorithm	Video type	Mean precision (20 px)	Mean FPS
DLT	Gray	80.4%	0.8/20 (CPU/GPU)
STC	Gray	82.8%	365
CNT	Gray	92.7%	0.5
KCF	Gray	53.6%	278
DLT	RGB	21.5%	0.6/10 (CPU/GPU)
STC	RGB	34.6%	13
CNT	RGB	53.1%	0.5
KCF	RGB	45.8%	65
CNHT	HSI	98.2%	1

4 Conclusions

In this paper, we introduce a convolutional feature based kernelized correlation filter approach for hyperspectral video tracking. The hyperspectral features are extracted via two-layer convolutional network. They provide discriminative information and can be used as multichannel features for the KCF tracking framework. The experimental results demonstrate that the presented method performs well in a hyperspectral dataset. This lays the foundation for developing future hyperspectral tracking methods.

References

1. Bai, X., Zhou, J., Kelly, A.: Pattern recognition for high performance. Pattern Recogn. **82**, 38–39 (2018)
2. Li, Y., Xie, W., Li, H.: Hyperspectral image reconstruction by deep convolutional neural network for classification. Pattern Recogn. **63**, 371–383 (2017)
3. Alam, F., Zhou, J., Alan, A., Jia, X., Chanussot, J., Gao, Y.: Conditional random field and deep feature learning for hyperspectral image segmentation. arXiv preprint arXiv:1711.04483 (2017)
4. Danelljan, M., Khan, F., Felsberg, M., Weijer, J.: Adaptive color attributes for real-time visual tracking. In: IEEE Conference on Computer Vision and Pattern Recognition, pp. 1090–1097 (2014)
5. Henriques, J.F., Caseiro, R., Martins, P., Batista, J.: Exploiting the circulant structure of tracking-by-detection with kernels. In: Fitzgibbon, A., Lazebnik, S., Perona, P., Sato, Y., Schmid, C. (eds.) ECCV 2012. LNCS, vol. 7575, pp. 702–715. Springer, Heidelberg (2012). https://doi.org/10.1007/978-3-642-33765-9_50
6. Henriques, J., Caseiro, R., Martins, P., Batista, J.: High-speed tracking with kernelized correlation filters. IEEE Trans. Pattern Anal. Mach. Intell. **37**(3), 583–596 (2015)
7. Zhang, K., Liu, Q., Wu, Y., Yang, M.: Robust visual tracking via convolutional networks without training. IEEE Trans. Image Process. **25**(4), 1779–1792 (2016)
8. Zhang, K., Zhang, L., Liu, Q., Zhang, D., Yang, M.-H.: Fast visual tracking via dense spatio-temporal context learning. In: Fleet, D., Pajdla, T., Schiele, B., Tuytelaars, T. (eds.) ECCV 2014. LNCS, vol. 8693, pp. 127–141. Springer, Cham (2014). https://doi.org/10.1007/978-3-319-10602-1_9
9. Bolme, D., Beveridge, J., Draper, B., Lui, Y.: Visual object tracking using adaptive correlation filters. In: IEEE Conference on Computer Vision and Pattern Recognition, pp. 2544–2550 (2010)
10. Li, Y., Zhu, J.: A scale adaptive kernel correlation filter tracker with feature integration. In: Agapito, L., Bronstein, M.M., Rother, C. (eds.) ECCV 2014. LNCS, vol. 8926, pp. 254–265. Springer, Cham (2015). https://doi.org/10.1007/978-3-319-16181-5_18
11. Nam, H., Han, B.: Learning multi-domain convolutional neural networks for visual tracking. In: IEEE Conference on Computer Vision and Pattern Recognition, pp. 4293–4302 (2016)
12. Choi, J.W., et al.: Context-aware deep feature compression for high-speed visual tracking. In: IEEE Conference on Computer Vision and Pattern Recognition (2018)

13. Wang, L., Ouyang, W., Wang, X., Lu, H.: Visual tracking with fully convolutional networks. In: IEEE International Conference on Computer Vision, pp. 3119–3127 (2015)
14. Ma, C., Huang, J., Yang, X., Yang, M.: Hierarchical convolutional features for visual tracking. In: IEEE International Conference on Computer Vision, pp. 3074–3082 (2015)
15. Danelljan, M., Hager, G., Khan, F., Felsberg, M.: Convolutional features for correlation filter based visual tracking. In: IEEE International Conference on Computer Vision Workshops, pp. 58–66 (2015)
16. Wang, N., Yeung, D.: Learning a deep compact image representation for visual tracking. In: Advances in Neural Information Processing Systems, pp. 809–817 (2013)
17. Wu, Y., Lim, J., Yang, M.: Online object tracking: a benchmark. In: IEEE Conference on Computer Vision and Pattern Recognition, pp. 2411–2418 (2013)

Learning 3DMM Deformation Coefficients for Rendering Realistic Expression Images

Claudio Ferrari$^{(\boxtimes)}$, Stefano Berretti, Pietro Pala, and Alberto Del Bimbo

Media Integration and Communication Center (MICC), University of Florence,
50134 Florence, Italy
{claudio.ferrari,stefano.berretti,pietro.pala,alberto.delbimbo}@unifi.it

Abstract. Analysis of facial expressions is a task of increasing interest in Computer Vision, with many potential applications. However, collecting images with labeled expression for many subjects is a quite complicated operation. In this paper, we propose a solution that use a particular 3D morphable model (3DMM) that, starting from a neutral image of a target subject, is capable of producing a realistic expressive face image of the same subject. This is possible thanks to the fact the used 3DMM can effectively and efficiently fit to 2D images, and then deform itself under the action of deformation parameters that are learned expression-by-expression in a subject-independent manner. Ultimately, the application of such deformation parameters to the neutral model of a subject allows the rendering of realistic expressive images of the subject. In the experiments, we demonstrate that such deformation parameters can be learned even from a small set of training data using simple statistical tools; despite this simplicity, we show that very realistic subject-dependent expression renderings can be obtained with our method. Furthermore, robustness to cross dataset tests is also evidenced.

Keywords: 3D morphable model · Deformation components learning
Facial expression synthesis

1 Introduction

Facial expressions are one of the most important way of person-to-person non-verbal communication, by which humans convey, either deliberately or in an unconscious way, their emotional state. The way humans perform and perceive expressions has been studied for long time, with the seminal works by Ekman et al. [10] showing that human facial expressions can be categorized into six *prototypical* classes, namely, *angry, disgust. fear, happy, sad,* and *surprise* that are invariant across different cultures and ethnic groups. Later studies have also shown that it is possible to think of expressions as the facial deformations induced by the movement of one or more muscles; such atomic deformations have been classified according to a Facial Action Coding System (FACS) [11], where a code is used to identify an Action Unit (AU) corresponding to the effect of individual or groups of muscles.

© Springer Nature Switzerland AG 2018
A. Basu and S. Berretti (Eds.): ICSM 2018, LNCS 11010, pp. 320–333, 2018.
https://doi.org/10.1007/978-3-030-04375-9_27

In Computer Vision and Multimedia applications there is an increasing interest in developing methods for either *recognizing* or *synthesizing* expressions in an automatic way. In fact, this has both theoretical interest in disciplines as different as Cognitive Sciences, Medicine or Psychology, as well as in practical applications, like surveillance by analysis of human emotional state, monitoring for fatigue detection, gaming or Human Computer Interaction, to cite a few. While for long time automatic analysis of facial expressions from images and videos has been based on the careful design of hand-crafted features, now the success of neural networks, and deep learning solutions in particular, has drastically changed the scenario: the idea is to let the network learn the low- and intermediate-level features that are best suited to describe the training data, and then use them in any classification or recognition task. This moves most of the criticisms to the networks design and the collection of the data used for their training. In doing so, the amount of the data and their variability play a fundamental role in learning significant representations. In the case of facial expressions, this has some additional difficulties since obtaining large quantities of ground truth data with accurate expression labels is a complicated and time consuming task if executed by human annotators. Thus, an idea that is making its way is to synthetically generate such training data. To this end, solutions based on parametric models, like the 3D Morphable Model (3DMM), as originally proposed in [2], and its variants are among the most promising. The idea here is to fit such models to 2D target images so as to reconstruct a coarse 3D shape of the face. Then, this 3D face model can be deformed to exhibit a target expression and render a corresponding image. Of course, this process requires the deformation components that change the neutral model to an expressive one are known for each expression. This, by itself, is not an easy task since most of the 3DMMs have been trained without using any expressive scan [4]. Some recent works also applied Generative Adversarial Networks (GANs) for the task of generating expressive face images from neutral ones [15,23]. Usually this is done using 2D images as training, while 3DMM is capable of generating new expression directly in 3D. However, also for GANs, 3DMMs can play a role in generating the images used for training.

Motivated by the above considerations, in this paper, we develop on the idea of generating visual data of human behavior with specific interest for facial expressions. To this end, we start with a particular variant of the 3DMM, which is characterized by its capability of reproducing facial expressions starting from the average model. This is possible thanks to two specific aspects of this 3DMM (called Dictionary Learning, DL-3DMM [12]): *(i)* differing from most existing 3DMMs it is trained also with 3D expressive facial scans; *(ii)* its deformation components are learned as a dictionary of atoms using a *dictionary learning* approach; differently from the standard approach that learns deformation components by Principal Component Analysis (PCA) so that each component acts globally on the model, the atoms identified by the dictionary learning solution capture quite well local deformations of the face. This 3DMM can be efficiently fit to a target 2D face image using a closed form solution generating a coarse

3D model of the target subject. Our goal here is to deform such 3D neutral model so as to realize a given expression of the subject ultimately rendering a 2D expressive image. To this end, we design a learning procedure that identifies the weights of the atoms corresponding to each prototypical expression. The procedure is composed of two main steps: first, the 3DMM is fit to a face image in neutral expression, producing a person-specific 3D reconstruction; then, this reconstruction is used to fit an expressive face image of the same subject and the deformation parameters are collected. This allows us to separate between the deformations modeling identity traits and the ones modeling expressions. Once all these parameters are collected, we look for recurrent patterns in the parameters that identify prototypical expressions and use such parameters to control the 3DMM deformation and generate expressive models. Such parameters are expression-specific, but can also be mixed together so as to generate more complex expressions. Experiments show that this strategy permits us to recover such parameters pretty easily, and that we can effectively generate expressive and realistic models also in a cross-dataset fashion. In particular, the main contributions of this work are as follows: *(i)* we propose a simple yet effective framework that enables the extrapolation of 3DMM parameters that control expression-specific deformations, and successfully apply them to generate expressive renderings starting from face images in neutral expression; *(ii)* we showcase the potential and versatility of the DL-3DMM in handling and generating expressions; *(iii)* we demonstrate the generalization capability of our solution by showing that more complex expressions can be generated by combining different prototypical expression parameters.

The rest of the paper is organized as follows: In Sect. 2, the works in the literature that are most closely related to our proposed solution are discussed; In Sect. 3, we summarize the 3DMM used in this work and the characteristics that make it effective in modeling facial expressions; In Sect. 4, we present the methods used to learn the deformation coefficients related to each expression; These coefficients are then used to generate expressions starting from the neutral 3DMM for new identities; a qualitative evaluation is reported in Sect. 5; Finally, discussion and conclusions are drawn in Sect. 6.

2   Related Work

In the following, first, we report on solutions that define and use a 3DMM to derive the 3D face model of a target subject starting from his/her 2D neutral image; then, we summarize some methods that learn modes of deformations to transform a neutral 3D model to an expressive one.

Blanz and Vetter [2] first presented a complete solution to derive a 3DMM by transforming the shape and texture from a training set of 3D face scans into a vector space representation based on PCA. However, the training dataset had limited face variability (200 neutral scans of young Caucasians), thus reducing the capability of the model to generalize to different ethnicity and non-neutral expressions. Despite these limitations, the 3DMM has proved its effectiveness in image face analysis, inspiring most of the subsequent work. The 3DMM was further refined into the Basel Face Model by Paysan et al. [22]. This offered higher shape and texture accuracy thanks to a better scanning device, and a lower number of correspondence artifacts using an improved registration algorithm based on the non-rigid Iterative Closest Point (ICP) [1]. However, since non-rigid ICP cannot handle large missing regions and topological variations, expressions were not accounted for in the training data also in this case. In addition, both the optical flow used in [2] and the non-rigid ICP method used in [22] were applied by transferring the vertex index from a reference model to all the scans, so that the choice of the reference face can affect the quality of the detected correspondences, and the resulting 3DMM. The work by Booth et al. [5] introduced a pipeline for 3DMM construction. Initially, dense correspondence was estimated applying the non-rigid ICP to a template model. Then, the so called LSFM-3DMM was constructed using PCA to derive the deformation basis on a dataset of 9,663 scans with a wide variety of age, gender, and ethnicity. However, the face shapes were still in neutral expression. Following a different approach, Patel and Smith [21] showed that Thin-Plate Splines (TPS) and Procrustes analysis can be used to construct a 3DMM. In [7], Cosker et al. described a framework for building a dynamic 3DMM, which extended static 3DMM construction by incorporating dynamic data. This was obtained by proposing an approach based on Active Appearance Model and TPS for non-rigid 3D mesh registration and correspondence. Results showed this method overcomes optical flow based solutions that are prone to temporal drift.

3DMM has been used at coarse level for face recognition and synthesis. In one of the first examples, Blanz and Vetter [3] used their 3DMM to simulate the process of image formation in 3D space, and estimated 3D shape and texture of faces from single images for face recognition. Later, Romdhani and Vetter [25] used the 3DMM for face recognition by enhancing the deformation algorithm with the inclusion of various image features. In [29], Yi et al. used the 3DMM to estimate the pose of a face image with a fast fitting algorithm. This idea was extended further by Zhu et al. [31], who proposed fitting a dense 3DMM to an image via Convolutional Neural Network. Hu et al. [13] proposed a Unified-3DMM that captures intra personal variations due to illumination and occlusions, and showed its performance in 3D-assisted 2D face recognition for scenarios where the input image is subjected to degradations or exhibits intra-personal variations. Recent solutions also used deep neural networks to learn complex non-linear regressor functions mapping a 2D facial image to the optimal 3DMM parameters [9,27].

In all these cases, the 3DMM was used mainly to compensate for the pose of the face, with some examples that performed also illumination normalization. Expressions were typically not considered. Indeed, the difficulty in making 3DMM work properly in fine face analysis applications is confirmed by the almost complete absence of methods that use 3DMM for expression recognition. Among the few examples, Ramanathan et al. [24] constructed a 3D Morphable Expression Model incorporating emotion-dependent face variations in terms of morphing parameters that were used for recognizing four emotions. Ujir and

Spann [28] combined the 3DMM with Modular PCA and Facial Animation Parameters (FAP) for facial expression recognition, but the model deformation was due more to the action of FAP than to the learned components. In [8], Cosker et al. used a dynamic 3DMM [6] to explore the effect of linear and non-linear facial movement on expression recognition through a test where users evaluated animated frames. Huber et al. [16] proposed a cascaded-regressor based face tracking and a 3DMM shape fitting for fully automatic real-time semi dense 3D face reconstruction from monocular in-the-wild videos.

3   3D Morphable Model

From the discussion of existing solutions for generating a 3DMM, it is quite evident the existence of some aspects that play a major relevance in characterizing the different solutions: *(1)* the human face variability captured by the model, which directly depends on the number and heterogeneity of training examples; *(2)* the capability of the model to account for facial expressions; also this feature of the model directly derives from the presence of expressive scans in the training. One of the few 3DMM existing in the literature that exposes both these features is the Dictionary Learning based 3DMM (DL-3DMM) proposed by Ferrari et al. [12]. Since our contribution mainly develops on this model, to make the paper as self-contained as possible, below we describe the peculiar features that make this particular 3DMM formulation suitable for our purposes.

3.1   DL-3DMM Construction

The first problem to be solved in the construction of a 3DMM is the selection of an appropriate set of training data. This should include sufficient variability in terms of ethnicity, gender, age, so as to enable the model to include a large variance in the data. Apart for this, the most difficult aspect in preparing the training data is the need to provide dense, *i.e.*, vertex-by-vertex, alignment between the 3D scans. In the original work of Blanz and Vetter [2] this was solved with the optical-flow method that provided reasonable results just in the case of neutral scans of the face. Several subsequent works used non-rigid variants of the Iterative Closest Point (ICP) algorithm, thus solving some problem related to the optical-flow, but without the explicit capability of addressing large facial expressions in the training data. The dense alignment of the training data for the DL-3DMM was obtained with a different solution based on the detection of landmarks of the face, and their use for partitioning the face into a set of non-overlapping regions, each one identifying the same part of the face across all the scans. Re-sampling the internal of the region based on its contour, a dense correspondence is derived region-by-region and so for all the face. Such method showed to be robust also to large expression variations as those occurring in the Binghamton University 3D facial Expression (BU-3DFE) database [30]. This latter dataset was used in the construction of the DL-3DMM.

Once a dense correspondence is established across the training data, these are used to estimate a set of deformation components that will be used to generate novel shapes. In the classic 3DMM framework [2], new 3D shapes $\mathbf{S}$ are generated by deforming an average model $\mathbf{m}$ with a linear combination of a set of M principal components $\mathbf{C}$, usually derived by PCA as follows;

$$\mathbf{S} = \mathbf{m} + \sum_{i=1}^{|M|} \mathbf{C}_i \alpha_i. \tag{1}$$

The DL-3DMM is instead constructed by learning a dictionary of deformation components exploiting the *Online Dictionary Learning for Sparse Coding* technique [19]. Learning is performed in an unsupervised way, without exploiting any knowledge about the data (*e.g.*, identity or expression labels). Then, the average model is deformed using the dictionary atoms $\mathbf{D}_i$ in place of $\mathbf{C}_i$ in Eq. (1).

Dictionary learning is usually cast as an ℓ_1-regularized least squares problem [19]; however, the sparsity induced by the ℓ_1 penalty to the dictionary atoms, can lead to discontinuous components and ultimately in a noisy or punctured 3D shape. To address this issue, the dictionary learning is formulated as an *Elastic-Net* regression, mitigating the sparsity effect of the ℓ_1 penalty with an ℓ_2 regularization that forces smoothness. By defining $\ell_{1,2}(\mathbf{w}_i) = \lambda_1 \|\mathbf{w}_i\|_1 + \lambda_2 \|\mathbf{w}_i\|_2$, where λ_1 and λ_2 are, respectively, the sparsity and regularization parameters, the problem can be formulated as (using N training scans):

$$\min_{\mathbf{w}_i, \mathbf{D}} \frac{1}{N} \sum_{i=1}^{N} \left(\|\mathbf{v}_i - \mathbf{D}\mathbf{w}_i\|_2^2 + \ell_{1,2}(\mathbf{w}_i) \right), \tag{2}$$

where $\mathbf{v}_i \in \mathbb{R}^{3m}$ is the vector of deviations between scan i and the average model (being m the number of points in the scans), the columns of the dictionary $\mathbf{D} \in \mathbb{R}^{3m \times k}$ are the basis components, $\mathbf{w}_i \in \mathbb{R}^k$ are the coefficients of the dictionary learning, and k is the number of basis components of the dictionary. Note that the number of components (dictionary atoms) is fixed and pre-determined. The coefficients vector $\mathbf{w} \in \mathbb{R}^k$ provides an estimate of the degree of importance that each atom had in reconstructing the training set; in comparison with the classic framework based on PCA, these can be interpreted similarly to the eigenvalues. A favorable characteristic of the DL-3DMM is that, oppositely to PCA, larger dictionaries lead to more accurate reconstructions and are likely to include sparser and complementary atoms; this facilitates the identification of the atoms that involve particular face areas. More details on the dictionary learning procedure can be found in [12].

The average model $\mathbf{m}$, the dictionary $\mathbf{D}$ and $\mathbf{w}$, constitute the DL-3DMM.

3.2   DL-3DMM Fitting

Fitting a 3DMM to a 2D face image allows a coarse 3D reconstruction of the face. To this end, estimating the 3D pose of the face, and the correspondence between 3D and 2D landmarks are prerequisites. In order to estimate the pose, a set of 49 facial landmarks $\mathbf{l} \in \mathbb{R}^{2 \times 49}$ is detected on the 2D face image using the technique proposed in [17], while an equivalent set of vertices $\mathbf{L} \in \mathbb{R}^{3 \times 49}$ is manually annotated on the average 3D model. Under an affine camera model [20], the relation between $\mathbf{L}$ and $\mathbf{l}$ is:

$$\mathbf{l} = \mathbf{A} \cdot \mathbf{L} + \mathbf{T}. \tag{3}$$

The affine matrix is directly estimated with a closed-form least squares solution since, by construction, facial landmark detectors do not permit outliers or unreasonable arrangement of the landmarks. The 2D translation is instead recovered as $\mathbf{T} = \mathbf{l} - \mathbf{A} \cdot \mathbf{L}$. The estimated pose $\mathbf{P}$ is represented as $[\mathbf{A}, \mathbf{T}]$ and used to map each vertex of the 3DMM onto the image.

Using the learned dictionary $\mathbf{D} = [\mathbf{d}_1, \ldots, \mathbf{d}_k]$, the average model is non-rigidly transformed such that the projection minimizes the error in correspondence to the landmarks. The coding is formulated as the solution of a regularized *Ridge-Regression* problem:

$$\arg\min_{\alpha} \left\| \mathbf{l} - \mathbf{PL} - \sum_{i=1}^{k} \mathbf{Pd}_i(\mathbf{I}_v)\alpha_i \right\|_2^2 + \lambda \left\| \alpha \circ \mathbf{w}^{-1} \right\|_2, \tag{4}$$

where $\circ$ is the Hadamard product and $\mathbf{I}_v$ are the indices that correspond to the vertices of the landmarks in the 3D model. By defining $\mathbf{X} = \mathbf{l} - \mathbf{L}$ and $\mathbf{Y} = \mathbf{PD}(\mathbf{I}_v)$, the solution can be found in closed form as follows:

$$\alpha = \left(\mathbf{Y}^T \mathbf{Y} + \lambda \cdot \operatorname{diag}(\mathbf{w}^{-1}) \right)^{-1} \mathbf{Y}^T \mathbf{X}. \tag{5}$$

Again, for a detailed description of the procedure the reader can refer to [12]. A fitting example obtained using this solution is shown in Fig. 1; the 3D model is deformed according to the target face image, the vertices of the model can be projected onto the face image exploiting the estimated pose so that we can sample its texture.

Fig. 1. Examples of DL-3DMM fitting on expressive face images from the Cohn-Kanade (CK+) dataset [18]

4   Learning Expression Coefficients

Given the DL-3DMM as described above, the result of the fitting procedure is a set of coefficients α that are used to deform the average model using Eq. (1).

Considering a generic face image, the latter coefficients codify the global shape deformation (*i.e.*, the identity) along with other deformations (*i.e.*, expressions). Our main goal is to derive the set of coefficients that reproduce expressions; in order to do so, we first need to isolate the identity component from the deformation. To this aim, we first fit the DL-3DMM to a face image in neutral expression to account for the identity and obtain the coefficients α_{id}; subsequently, the fitted model is used in place of the average model to fit an expressive face image of the same subject. In this way, we obtain a set of coefficients α_{expr} that codify the expression. The procedure is depicted in Fig. 2. The final and crucial step is to find a recurrent pattern in the α_{expr} coefficients, separately for each expression. To this end, we propose to investigate and compare the appropriateness of different methods using: *(i)* statistical indicators; *(ii)* regressors.

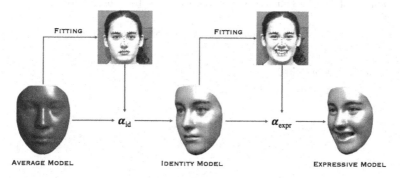

Fig. 2. Workflow of the proposed procedure to extract the expression-specific deformation coefficients from the DL-3DMM fitting

Statistical Indicators – First, we have investigated some basic statistical indicators, namely *mean, median* and *mode*. Best results have been obtained with the latter, which we estimated using the *mean-shift* algorithm. Using a Gaussian kernel

$$K(x_i - x) = e^{-c||x_i - x||^2},$$

a centroid x_i at iteration t is updated with $x_i^{t+1} = x_i^t + m(x)$, at iteration $t+1$, with

$$m(x_i) = \frac{\sum_{x_j \in N(x_i)} K(x_j - x_i)x_j}{\sum_{x_j \in N(x_i)} K(x_j - x_i)}.$$

In this latter equation, $N(x_i)$ is a neighborhood of x_i, that is the set of points such that $K(x_i) \neq 0$, and $m(x)$ is the *mean shift vector*. The centroid updating is repeated till the convergence of $m(x)$. The only parameter used in this algorithm is the *bandwidth*, *i.e*, the radius of the gaussian region. In our case, we search for the centroid best representing the data distribution. To this end, we started with a fixed *bandwidth* and repeated the mean shift iteration by increasing the radius;

the procedure terminates when an individual point is returned; this centroid is assumed as the vector representing the data distribution of a given expression.

At this stage, we also used the mean-shift algorithm to investigate the data distribution. To this end, first, we fixed the *bandwidth*, applied the algorithm, took the resulting number of centroids and counted how many samples fall in the region of influence of the centroids. Table 1 reports the results for each expression. It can be observed as the first centroid, located at the maximum peak of the data distribution, is the most representative of the samples: arguably, this is due to the fact the other maxima capture possible outliers or errors included in the dataset.

Table 1. For each expression, the number of centroids found by fixing the *bandwidth*, and the percentage of vectors that fall in the region of the first centroid are reported. Expressions in the Cohn-Kanade (CK+) dataset have been used here

Expression	#Centroids	% vectors first centroid
Angry	4	93%
Contempt	5	73%
Disgust	2	98%
Fear	2	96%
Happy	5	92%
Sadness	3	93%
Surprise	2	95%

As a further analysis, we iterated the algorithm by augmenting the *bandwidth* so as to find two centroids. Then, we have compared the faces obtained by applying both the weight vectors corresponding to the two maxima for each expression. Results indicated that the deformed faces obtained from the weight vector of the first maximum are the same as those obtained using a single maximum; applying the weight vector corresponding to the second maximum, instead, resulted in non-realistic faces.

Regressors – In the following, we model the problem of estimating the deformation coefficients of the 3DMM as a regression one, using the Support Vector Regression (SVR) technique. A cross validation process has been used to determine the train/test splits. The coefficients vectors have been used as "multi-labels" that are predicted using a *multi-output* regressor, which repeats the estimate for each component of the array. The regressor is controlled by parameters that do not depend on the dimensionality of the feature space. In our case, a 4-fold cross validation has been performed to determine the best kernel and the values of the parameters C and ϵ of the regressor.

As a result, for both the methods, we obtained for each expression a set of coefficients α_{est} that allow the application of an expression to a subject-specific model in neutral expression.

Fig. 3. Qualitative examples of synthetically generated expressive renderings of two subjects from the CK+ dataset. The leftmost column reports the 3DMM fitting to the neutral face images of the two subjects, while the other columns report the models derived from the neutral ones by applying the deformation coefficients corresponding to each expression, from *disgust* to *happy*, left-to-right

5   Experimental Results

Experiments have been performed on the Extended Cohn-Kanade (CK+) dataset [18], which includes about 600 sequences of 123 subjects showing 7 different expressions, namely *Disgust, Surprise, Angry, Sadness, Fear, Contempt, Happy*; for each sequence the neutral (first) and expressive (last) frames have been used. The DL-3DMM has been deformed to each of these frames using the fitting procedure illustrated in Sect. 3.2; we used a dictionary of 300 atoms. A subset of the 123 individuals has been used to learn the parameters so as to test on different identities. For neutral frames, these coefficients capture the shape information of the individual; for expressive scans, we first deformed the 3DMM on the neutral frame of the same subject, then from this to the expressive frame, following the procedure of Fig. 2. In this way, the coefficients capture the shape deformation to pass from a neutral to an expressive scan for a specific identity.

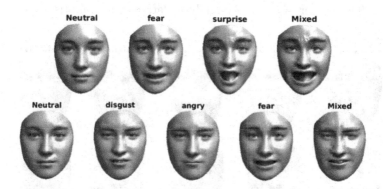

Fig. 4. Qualitative examples of mixed deformations on one subject of the CK+ dataset; two (top row) or three (bottom row) prototypical expressions have been used

In order to derive qualitative results, we fitted the DL-3DMM to some neutral faces of the dataset and applied the estimated deformation coefficients α_{est} so as to generate expressive scans for each expression. Figure 3 shows some examples of generated expressive renderings starting from the neutral one and applying the deformation. The magnitude of the deformations can be controlled with a parameter λ, useful to emphasize subtle expressions that do not sufficiently change the neutral face (*e.g.*, contempt). The expressive models generated from the neutral 3DMM according to the learned deformation vectors are rendered for qualitative evaluation. Some examples can be appreciated in Fig. 3; starting from the neutral expression, we can effectively generate expressive renderings applying the expression-specific parameters separately.

Figure 4 shows another interesting application of our method, that is the generation of complex expressions by combining the parameters of the single prototypical expressions. This feature allows us to mix an arbitrary number of expressions and further demonstrates the meaningfulness of the estimated parameters. The examples in Fig. 4 are generated using a combination of 2 (top row) or 3 (bottom row) basic expressions. A drawback of this application is that if the weights of the single expressions are not balanced, the final model can result noisy or excessively deformed.

In Fig. 5, we show a comparison between the different techniques used to estimate the α_{est} coefficients; the generated images are rather similar to each other, even using basic statistical indicators as the mean. This suggests us that the elements of the dictionary are effective in separating the identity and expression components and that our methodology allows us to easily extrapolate expression-specific patterns within the deformation coefficients.

Finally, Fig. 6 shows the application of our expression transfer method to face images coming from different datasets, demonstrating the generalization capability of our approach in a cross-dataset scenario. Specifically, Fig. 6 (top row) shows a face image from the Bosphorus dataset [26], while in Fig. 6 (bottom row) a face image coming from the Labeled Faces in The Wild dataset (LFW) [14] is shown. The former is a 3D face analysis dataset and comprises face images

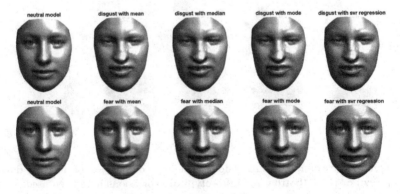

Fig. 5. Qualitative comparison of the different parameters estimation methods

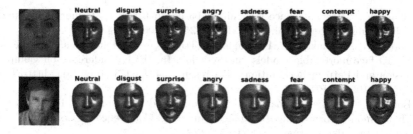

Fig. 6. Cross-dataset evaluation of the proposed method on sample images from the Bosphorus (top row) and LFW (bottom row)

along with their 3D models captured in controlled conditions; the LFW, instead, is composed of "in the wild" face images and is used to address the face verification problem. For both the examples, we are able to transfer the expression of the subject from neutral to any of the learned expressions; this because the 3DMM is independent from the dataset which is applied to.

6 Conclusions

In this paper, we have proposed a method to isolate the expression-specific deformation parameters of a 3DMM and applied them to synthetically generate expressive renderings of subjects in neutral expression. We exploited a peculiar 3DMM implementation based on a dictionary learning technique, able to reproduce expressions thanks to the inclusion of expressive scans in the training set. We showed that our two-step 3DMM fitting methodology is effective in removing the identity component from the 3DMM fitting, and that expression-specific recurrent patterns can be easily found within the parameters used to fit the subject-specific model to its own expressive image. Moreover, the recovered parameters can be effectively mixed so as to generate more complex expressions. However, our solution is not exempt from limitations: first, expressions might be more or less subtle; this means that they must be weighted accordingly in order not to produce exaggerated or imperceptible deformations. Another issue arose is that the textured renderings might result somewhat unnatural at times when trying to generate expressions that are very diverse from the neutral one. Indeed, we can assume that even a very slight expressiveness might be present in "neutral" frames. As a future work, we are considering an extension of the technique to the texture component of the images.

References

1. Amberg, B., Romdhani, S., Vetter, T.: Optimal step nonrigid ICP algorithms for surface registration. In: IEEE International Conference on Computer Vision and Pattern Recognition, Minneapolis, MN, pp. 1–8, June 2007
2. Blanz, V., Vetter, T.: A morphable model for the synthesis of 3D faces. In: ACM Conference on Computer Graphics and Interactive Techniques (1999)

3. Blanz, V., Vetter, T.: Face recognition based on fitting a 3D morphable model. IEEE Trans. Pattern Anal. Mach. Intell. **25**(9), 1063–1074 (2003)
4. Booth, J., Antonakos, E., Ploumpis, S., Trigeorgis, G., Panagakis, Y., Zafeiriou, S.: 3D face morphable models "in-the-wild". In: IEEE Conference on Computer Vision and Pattern Recognition (CVPR), pp. 5464–5473, July 2017. https://doi.org/10.1109/CVPR.2017.580
5. Booth, J., Roussos, A., Zafeiriou, S., Ponniahand, A., Dunaway, D.: A 3D morphable model learnt from 10,000 faces. In: IEEE Conference on Computer Vision and Pattern Recognition, pp. 5543–5552 (2016)
6. Cosker, D., Krumhuber, E., Hilton, A.: Perception of linear and nonlinear motion properties using a FACS validated 3D facial model. In: ACM Applied Perception in Graphics and Vision (2010)
7. Cosker, D., Krumhuber, E., Hilton, A.: A FACS valid 3D dynamic action unit database with applications to 3D dynamic morphable facial modeling. In: International Conference on Computer Vision (2011)
8. Cosker, D., Krumhuber, E., Hilton, A.: Perceived emotionality of linear and nonlinear AUs synthesised using a 3D dynamic morphable facial model. In: Proceedings of the Facial Analysis and Animation, FAA 2015, p. 7:1. ACM (2015)
9. Dou, P., Shah, S.K., Kakadiaris, I.A.: End-to-end 3D face reconstruction with deep neural networks. In: IEEE Conference on Computer Vision and Pattern Recognition (CVPR), pp. 1503–1512, July 2017. https://doi.org/10.1109/CVPR.2017.164
10. Ekman, P.: Facial expression and emotion. Am. Anthropol. **48**(4), 384–392 (1992)
11. Ekman, P., Friesen, W.: Facial Action Coding System: A Technique for the Measurement of Facial Movement. Consulting Psychologists Press, Palo Alto, CA (1978)
12. Ferrari, C., Lisanti, G., Berretti, S., Del Bimbo, A.: A dictionary learning-based 3D morphable shape model. IEEE Trans. Multimedia **19**(12), 2666–2679 (2017). https://doi.org/10.1109/TMM.2017.2707341
13. Hu, G., et al.: Face recognition using a unified 3D morphable model. In: Leibe, B., Matas, J., Sebe, N., Welling, M. (eds.) ECCV 2016. LNCS, vol. 9912, pp. 73–89. Springer, Cham (2016). https://doi.org/10.1007/978-3-319-46484-8_5
14. Huang, G.B., Ramesh, M., Berg, T., Learned-Miller, E.: Labeled faces in the wild: a database for studying face recognition in unconstrained environments. Technical report 07-49, University of Massachusetts, Amherst, October 2007
15. Huang, Y., Khan, S.M.: DyadGAN: generating facial expressions in dyadic interactions. In: IEEE Conference on Computer Vision and Pattern Recognition Workshops (CVPRW), pp. 2259–2266, July 2017. https://doi.org/10.1109/CVPRW.2017.280
16. Huber, P., Kopp, P., Rätsch, M., Christmas, W.J., Kittler, J.: 3D face tracking and texture fusion in the wild. CoRR abs/1605.06764 (2016). http://arxiv.org/abs/1605.06764
17. Kazemi, V., Sullivan, J.: One millisecond face alignment with an ensemble of regression trees. In: IEEE Conference on Computer Vision and Pattern Recognition (2014)
18. Lucey, P., Cohn, J.F., Kanade, T., Saragih, J., Ambadar, Z., Matthews, I.: The extended Cohn-Kanade dataset (CK+): a complete dataset for action unit and emotion-specified expression. In: IEEE Conference on Computer Vision and Pattern Recognition-Workshops (2010)
19. Mairal, J., Bach, F., Ponce, J., Sapiro, G.: Online dictionary learning for sparse coding. In: International Conference on Machine Learning (2009)

20. Masi, I., Ferrari, C., Del Bimbo, A., Medioni, G.: Pose independent face recognition by localizing local binary patterns via deformation components. In: International Conference on Pattern Recognition (2014)
21. Patel, A., Smith, W.A.P.: 3D morphable face models revisited. In: IEEE Conference on Computer Vision and Pattern Recognition (2009)
22. Paysan, P., Knothe, R., Amberg, B., Romdhani, S., Vetter, T.: A 3D face model for pose and illumination invariant face recognition. In: IEEE International Conference on Advanced Video and Signal Based Surveillance (AVSS), pp. 296–301 (2009)
23. Qiao, F., Yao, N., Jiao, Z., Li, Z., Chen, H., Wang, H.: Geometry-contrastive generative adversarial network for facial expression synthesis. CoRR abs/1802.01822 (2018). http://arxiv.org/abs/1802.01822
24. Ramanathan, S., Kassim, A., Venkatesh, Y.V., Wah, W.S.: Human facial expression recognition using a 3D morphable model. In: International Conference on Image Processing (2006)
25. Romdhani, S., Vetter, T.: Estimating 3D shape and texture using pixel intensity, edges, specular highlights, texture constraints and a prior. In: IEEE Conference on Computer Vision and Pattern Recognition (2005)
26. Savran, A., et al.: Bosphorus database for 3D face analysis. In: Schouten, B., Juul, N.C., Drygajlo, A., Tistarelli, M. (eds.) BioID 2008. LNCS, vol. 5372, pp. 47–56. Springer, Heidelberg (2008). https://doi.org/10.1007/978-3-540-89991-4_6
27. Tran, A.T., Hassner, T., Masi, I., Medioni, G.: Regressing robust and discriminative 3D morphable models with a very deep neural network. In: IEEE Conference on Computer Vision and Pattern Recognition (CVPR), pp. 5163–5172, July 2017
28. Ujir, H., Spann, M.: Facial expression recognition using FAPs-based 3DMMM. In: Tavares, J., Natal Jorge, R. (eds.) Topics in Medical Image Processing and Computational Vision. LNCVB, vol. 8, pp. 33–47. Springer, Dordrecht (2013). https://doi.org/10.1007/978-94-007-0726-9_2
29. Yi, D., Lei, Z., Li, S.Z.: Towards pose robust face recognition. In: IEEE Conference on Computer Vision and Pattern Recognition (2013)
30. Yin, L., Wei, X., Sun, Y., Wang, J., Rosato, M.: A 3D facial expression database for facial behavior research. In: IEEE International Conference on Automatic Face and Gesture Recognition (2006)
31. Zhu, X., Lei, Z., Liu, X., Shi, H., Li, S.Z.: Face alignment across large poses: a 3D solution. In: IEEE Conference on Computer Vision and Pattern Recognition (2016)

Semi-supervised Adversarial Image-to-Image Translation

Jose Eusebio, Hemanth Venkateswara$^{(\boxtimes)}$, and Sethuraman Panchanathan

Center for Cognitive Ubiquitous Computing (CUbiC), Arizona State University,
Tempe, AZ, USA
{jeusebio,hemanthv,panch}@asu.edu

Abstract. Image-to-image translation involves translating images in one domain into images in another domain, while keeping some aspects of the image consistent across the domains. Image translation models that keep the category of the image consistent can be useful for applications like domain adaptation. Generative models like variational autoencoders have the ability to extract latent factors of generation from an image. Based on generative models like variational autoencoders and generative adversarial networks, we develop a semi-supervised image-to-image translation procedure. We apply this procedure to perform image translation and domain adaptation for complex digit datasets.

Keywords: Image-to-image translation · Domain adaptation
Generative adversarial networks · Variational autoencoders

1 Introduction

Image-to-image translation attempts to extract the meaning or content of an image and express it in a new domain. Some examples of images from two domains are; the image of a city skyline during the day versus during the night, or a photograph of a person versus a pencil-sketch of the same person. In the above examples, the content or meaning of the image is the same, whereas its representation changes. Image-to-image translation requires two components; content-consistency and domain-consistency. The new image must retain the same content as the original, but look similar to other images in the domain it is translated to. Image-to-Image translation differs from other style transfer methods like [4] and [14], in its focus on understanding ideas portrayed in the original image and explicitly making sure that the content is the same throughout translation. The definition of 'content' is determined by the context for the translation and in our work, content is represented by the image category. In this work we develop models to translate between domains while keeping the category of the image constant. For example, a webcam image of a bus is translated into the clipart domain resulting in a clipart image of the bus.

One of the applications of such image-translation is domain adaptation [3,10]. In unsupervised domain adaptation, we have a source domain of labeled images

A. Basu and S. Berretti (Eds.): ICSM 2018, LNCS 11010, pp. 334–344, 2018.
https://doi.org/10.1007/978-3-030-04375-9_28

and a target domain of unlabeled images, belonging to the same set of categories. The goal is to determine the labels of the target images using the labeled source data. Image-translation procedures translate target images into source images and a source classifier is then trained to classify the translated target images [2,9]. In this work we present a robust image-translation procedure that can be used for domain adaptation.

We develop the Semi-supervised Adversarial Translation (SAT) model based on Variational Autoencoders (VAE) [6] and Generative Adversarial Networks (GAN) [5]. VAEs help to extract latent generative factors [1], of an image, which can be useful for image translation. Images are projected to a latent space where the 'content' of the image can be extracted and combined with the domain information, to generate a translated image. GANs are used to maintain category consistency and domain consistency using adversarial losses. In this work, we present the SAT model using a coupled system of VAEs and GANs for the source and target domains. In the following sections, we describe the SAT model and conduct experiments with challenging digit datasets from multiple domains.

2 Unsupervised Image-to-Image Translation

In unsupervised image translation we have two domains, a labeled source domain X_S, and an unlabeled target domain X_T, with $x_S \sim X_S$ and $x_T \sim X_T$ representing images from these domains. Each source image has an associated one-hot label vector y_S belonging to label space Y_S with K categories, where $y_S \in \{0,1\}^K$. The target images also belong to the same set of K categories. The goal is to translate images from the source domain into the target domain and vice-versa, with the constraint that the image category does not change during translation. For example, if the two domains were clip-art images and webcam images, then the image of a pen in clipart translates to the image of a pen in webcam and vice-versa. We achieve this by training a network consisting of two coupled VAE-GANs [7], with each VAE-GAN handling the interpretation and synthesis of images from either the source or target domains. The source VAE-GAN consists of an encoder E_S, a decoder G_S, a domain discriminator $D_{S,D}$ and a category discriminator $D_{S,C}$. Similarly, the target VAE-GAN consists of E_T, G_T, $D_{T,D}$, and $D_{T,C}$. Figure 1 depicts the different components of the network.

The encoders E_S and E_T map the source and target images x_S and x_T to z_S and z_T respectively, where z_S and z_T belong to the latent space Z. The source decoder G_S converts the latent vectors z_S and z_T to source images $G_S(z_S) = \tilde{x}_S^{S \to S}$ and $G_S(z_T) = \tilde{x}_T^{T \to S}$ respectively. Likewise, the target decoder G_T converts the latent vectors z_S and z_T to target images $G_T(z_S) = \tilde{x}_S^{S \to T}$ and $G_T(z_T) = \tilde{x}_T^{T \to T}$ respectively. The domain discriminators $D_{S,D}$ and $D_{T,D}$ are binary classifiers designed to distinguish between real and generated images. The category discriminators $D_{S,C}$ and $D_{T,C}$ are designed to classify the source and target images into K-categories. In the following sub-sections, we outline the objective functions for each of the network modules.

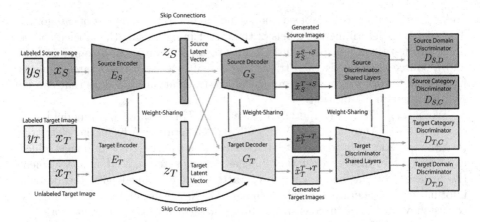

Fig. 1. The proposed semi-supervised adversarial translator framework. Input images x_S and x_T are encoded into latent vectors z_S and z_T using encoders E_S and E_T, respectively. The latent vectors z_S and z_T can be decoded by either decoder G_S into a source image or by decoder G_T into a target image. Cross-domain image-to-image translation occurs when these latent vectors are decoded into the other domain. Each domain has a multi-purpose discriminator that branches into a category discriminator ($D_{S,C}$ and $D_{T,C}$) and a domain discriminator ($D_{S,D}$ and $D_{T,D}$) that ensure that the model is able to synthesize images that conserve the original contents while being stylistically similar to the new domain.

Variational Autoencoders: In each domain, the paired encoder and decoder can be viewed as a VAE. For the source domain, E_S and G_S together form VAE_S. The encoder E_S acts as a variational inference network, mapping input x_S to latent code z_S in the latent space Z, which is assumed to be conditionally independent and have a normal distribution. Given input x_S, the encoder E_S outputs a mean vector $E_{S,\mu}(x_S)$ and variance vector $E_{S,\sigma^2}(x_S)$, which are representative of the image's latent code. These outputs are then used as the parameters of distribution $q_S(z_S|x_S)$, which is sampled from in order to obtain $z_S \sim q_S(z_S|x_S)$. The decoder G_S is a deep neural network that takes latent codes z_S and z_T to generate $\tilde{x}_S^{S\rightarrow S} = G_S(z_S)$ and $\tilde{x}_T^{T\rightarrow S} = G_S(z_T)$, respectively. VAE_S is trained by minimizing the variational upper bound of the objective function given by:

$$L_{\text{VAE}_S} = \gamma_1 \mathbb{E}_{\substack{z_S \sim q_S(z_S|x_S); \\ x_S \sim X_S}} [-\log p_{G_S}(x_S|z_S)] + \gamma_2 \text{KL}(q_S(z_S|x_S)||p(Z)). \quad (1)$$

In the objective function, $p(Z)$ is the prior distribution of Z which is $\mathcal{N}(0, I)$. The first term ensures that the reconstructed image $G_S(z_S)$, is similar to the original input x_S. The KL stands for Kullback-Leibler divergence, which is a measure of disparity between the prior probability distribution of $p(Z)$ and the encoder's distribution of $q_S(z_S|x_S)$. The hyper-parameters, γ, control relative importance of the reconstruction and divergence. The VAE for the target domain VAE_T is governed by a similar objective function given by:

$$L_{\text{VAE}_T} = \gamma_1 \mathbb{E}_{\substack{z_T \sim q_T(z_T|x_T); \\ x_T \sim X_T}} [-\log p_{G_T}(x_T|z_T)] + \gamma_2 \text{KL}(q_T(z_T|x_T)||p(Z)). \quad (2)$$

Generative Adversarial Networks: Attached to each VAE is a discriminator that provides feedback to the generator concerning both the content and realism of the generated image. The discriminator is a deep convolutional network that branches out into two subnetworks, a domain discriminator and a categorical discriminator. Each branch shares the weights of their early layers but also utilize unique layers used to perform their specific function.

Domain Discriminator: In the source domain, the network learns to discriminate between real images x_S and generated images, $\tilde{x}_S^{S \rightarrow S}$ and $\tilde{x}_T^{T \rightarrow S}$. Each domain discriminator forces its associated decoder to generate domain-like images using latent vectors from either domain. The source domain discriminator accomplishes this using the objective function,

$$\begin{aligned} L_{GAN_{S,D}} = \ & \gamma_3 \mathbb{E}_{x_S \sim X_S} [\log D_{S,D}(x_S)] \\ & + \gamma_4 \mathbb{E}_{z_S \sim q_S(z_S|x_S)} [\log(1 - D_{S,D}(G_S(z_S)))] \\ & + \gamma_4 \mathbb{E}_{z_T \sim q_T(z_T|x_T)} [\log(1 - D_{S,D}(G_S(z_T)))]. \end{aligned} \quad (3)$$

This objective function is maximized w.r.t $D_{S,D}$. The first term ensures that inputs from the original source domain are categorized as real images. The second and third term attempt to classify the generated images as unreal images. The adversarial role of the discriminator trains the generator $G_S(.)$ to generate source like images. Similarly, the target domain discriminator is trained with an objective function given by,

$$\begin{aligned} L_{GAN_{T,D}} = \ & \gamma_3 \mathbb{E}_{x_T \sim X_T} [\log D_{T,D}(x_T)] \\ & + \gamma_4 \mathbb{E}_{z_T \sim q_T(z_T|x_T)} [\log(1 - D_{T,D}(G_T(z_T)))] \\ & + \gamma_4 \mathbb{E}_{z_S \sim q_S(z_S|x_S)} [\log(1 - D_{T,D}(G_T(z_S)))]. \end{aligned} \quad (4)$$

Category Discriminator: The category discriminators classify the category of the input image. The category discriminators are necessary to maintain the original input image category through reconstruction or translation. In the source domain, the category discriminator $D_{S,C}$ is trained to correctly classify original source images through minimizing the cross-entropy (CE) between the predicted conditional distribution $\mathbf{p}(y_S|x_S, D_{S,C})$ and the true label y_S given by,

$$\text{CE}[y_S, \mathbf{p}(y_S|x_S, D_{S,C})] = -\sum_{i=1}^{K} y_{S,i} \log p(y_{S,i}|x_S, D_{S,C}), \quad (5)$$

where $\mathbf{p}(y_S|x_S, D_{S,C}) = [p(y_{S,1}|x_S, D_{S,C}), p(y_{S,2}|x_S, D_{S,C}), \ldots, p(y_{S,K}|x_S, D_{S,C})]^T$ and $y_{S,i} = 1$ if the label of x_S is i otherwise, $y_{S,i} = 0$. The following objective is minimized to ensure the real and generated images of the source domain are correctly classified,

$$L_{GAN_{S,C}} = \gamma_5 \mathbb{E}_{x_S \sim X_S, y_S \sim Y_S} \Big[\mathrm{CE}[y_S, \mathbf{p}(y_S | x_S, D_{S,C})] \Big]. \tag{6}$$

3   Semi-supervised Image-to-Image Translation

Semi-Supervision: The Semi-Supervised Adversarial Translation model (SAT) is inspired by the UNIT [9], and utilizes a few labels in the target domain for more robust performance when the domains are very different and challenging. This change to the model requires the addition of classification losses in the category discriminators related to these new labels for the target domain. We introduce the classification loss for the labeled target images and the translated source images. The objective function is given by,

$$L_{GAN_{T,C}} = \gamma_5 \mathbb{E}_{\substack{x_T \sim X_T; \\ y_T \sim Y_T}} \Big[\mathrm{CE}[y_T, \mathbf{p}(y_T | x_T, D_{T,C})] \Big]$$
$$+ \gamma_6 \mathbb{E}_{\substack{z_S \sim q_T(z_S | x_S); \\ x_S \sim X_S; \\ y_S \sim Y_S}} \Big[\mathrm{CE}[y_S, \mathbf{p}(y_S | G_T(z_S), D_{T,C})] \Big]. \tag{7}$$

Similarly, for the source domain, we add a classification loss based on the translated versions of the labeled target images as well as a classification loss based on $\tilde{y}_T$, which are target images with pseudo-labels [12]. These pseudo labels are obtained using the category classifier $D_{T,C}$. Since these pseudo labels are not guaranteed to be correct, the weighting in the objective function is set to be substantially lower than other factors. The modified objective function of $D_{S,C}$ is given by,

$$L_{GAN_{S,C}} = \gamma_5 \mathbb{E}_{\substack{x_S \sim X_S; \\ y_S \sim Y_S}} \Big[\mathrm{CE}[y_S, \mathbf{p}(y_S | x_S, D_{S,C})] \Big]$$
$$+ \gamma_6 \mathbb{E}_{\substack{z_T \sim q_T(z_T | x_T); \\ x_T \sim X_T; \\ y_T \sim Y_T}} \Big[\mathrm{CE}[y_T, \mathbf{p}(y_T | G_S(z_T), D_{S,C})] \Big] \tag{8}$$
$$+ \gamma_7 \mathbb{E}_{\substack{z_T \sim q_T(z_T | x_T); \\ x_T \sim X_T, \tilde{y}_T}} \Big[\mathrm{CE}[\tilde{y}_T, \mathbf{p}(\tilde{y}_T | G_S(z_T), D_{S,C})] \Big].$$

Image-to-Image Translation and Domain Adaptation: The SAT model is able to translate images between the source and target domains by using the encoder of the original domain and the decoder of the opposite domain. In general, successful image-to-image translation has two requirements. The first is to maintain category consistency between the original input and the generated image. The second requirement is to create an image that could have originated from the target domain. The objective functions of the SAT work together to optimize both of these requirements. A trained SAT can also be used to perform domain adaptation by translating images from the target domain into the source and then labeling the translated target image using the source category discriminator.

Domain Coupling and Skip Connections: Figure 1 depicts shared layers (coupling) between the subnetworks of each domain. Images from either domain are assumed to share certain characteristics. It follows that they share certain lower level features common to all natural images and certain higher level features corresponding to the category. This is implemented by having the subnetworks share layers across domains in the encoders, decoders and discriminators. This weight sharing enforces the features that are evaluated to be similar in each domain. Each VAE also makes use of skip connections between some of the shared layers of the encoder and decoder in order to transfer certain feature components that may be lost when encoding to a latent space.

Training: The SAT network is trained using the objective functions discussed above. The model is trained similarly to the original GAN in an iterative two-step procedure [5]. In the first step, the parameters of the discriminators are adjusted to optimize their part of the objective function. In the next step, the parameters of the encoders and decoders are trained. Training occurs by having the discriminator and generator play a two-player minimax game with the following objective function,

$$\min_{\substack{E_S,E_T,G_S,G_T; \\ D_{S,C},D_{T,C}}} \max_{D_{S,D},D_{T,D}} = L_{\text{VAE}_S} + L_{\text{VAE}_T} + L_{GAN_{S,D}} + L_{GAN_{T,D}}$$

$$+ L_{GAN_{S,C}} + L_{GAN_{T,C}}. \tag{9}$$

4 Experiments

Datasets: We conduct experiments with challenging image translation tasks consisting of digit images from 0–9. The datasets used are SVHN [11], MNIST [8], and MNIST-V, a modified version of MNIST. Digit datasets are used because they contain relatively simple images (although translation is hard) and have a consistent amount of categories and the datasets are large. SVHN, or the Street View House Numbers Dataset, contains real-world images of house numbers taken from Google Street View with many degrees of variation. MNIST contains normalized and fixed-size handwritten digits. This normalization causes there to be much less variation in the domain. MNIST-V contains MNIST images with random scale shifts and random pixel value multipliers.

Semi-Supervised Translation: A SAT network is trained to translate combinations of MNIST, MNIST-V, and SVHN datasets. In these results, images from the source domain are translated into a target domain that had 100 labels, or 10 labels for each category. Each combination of the three datasets provides some meaningful insights into the way the model performs as the choice of source and target domains dramatically affects translation performance.

The first set of results found in Fig. 2 are the translations from source MNIST images into the MNIST-V and SVHN domains. Translating from MNIST into

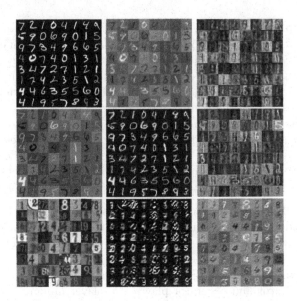

Fig. 2. Original and translated versions of images obtained using the SAT. Top row: MNIST (left) translated into MNIST-V (middle) and SVHN (right). Middle row: MNIST-V (left) translated into MNIST (middle) and SVHN (right). Bottom row: SVHN (left) translated into MNIST (middle) and MNIST-V (right).

MNIST-V yields images that demonstrate content consistency and domain consistency. Translating MNIST into SVHN achieves relatively good content consistency, but translated images do not necessarily look like images from the SVHN domain. The colors of the translated images are consistent with other images of the domain, but the style of the numbers are still similar to MNIST images. Throughout experimentation, content consistency is given priority when setting the parameters and the result is a visible trade-off with the domain consistency or image fidelity. Typically, GANs can produce higher quality images, but with the severe trade-off of not correctly translating the original image. The translation of MNIST images into SVHN images is the most difficult of these sets of translations because of the steep domain shift between the simple source domain and complex target domain. Similar unsupervised solutions, like the UNIT [9] model, will generate very realistic images, but with incorrect digits. An example of this content inconsistency during translation is shown in Fig. 3.

The next set of results are the translations from MNIST-V into MNIST and SVHN. The digits in the generated images look similar to the digits of the original image except with a black background and white digit. These results are the best example of translation because the source domain is more complex than the target domain and the domain shift between MNIST-V and MNIST is relatively small. Translating images from MNIST-V into SVHN yields higher quality images than the translation of MNIST into SVHN because of the added complexity in MNIST-V. The variety in MNIST-V that is introduced when adding

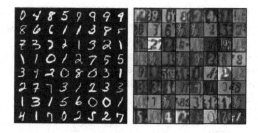

Fig. 3. Translation of MNIST data (left) into SVHN domain (right) using a UNIT [9] network.

noise to the original MNIST dataset forces the SAT to learn a better representation of MNIST-V, which in turn makes the data representation more robust and well-suited to understand the target SVHN dataset.

The last set of translation results are the translations from SVHN into MNIST and MNIST-V. Translating from SVHN into MNIST yields images that preserve the original content, but a subset of these translations contain large amounts of artifacts. In this case, the target decoder is not able to handle the large number of variations of the SVHN dataset's background and foreground color. Since the MNIST dataset only contains images with a black background and a white digit, the associated decoder learns to best handle images with little variation. Translating from SVHN into MNIST-V yields images that preserve the original digit and contain fewer artifacts than the translations into MNIST, because the variation found in the MNIST-V dataset is able to better express the variations found in the SVHN dataset.

Semi-supervised Domain Adaptation: To evaluate the domain adaptation capabilities of the SAT model, a SAT network was trained to translate between pairs of datasets MNIST, MNIST-V, and SVHN, where one dataset is considered as source domain and the other dataset is the target domain. In these results, images from a sparsely labeled target domain are translated into the labeled source domain. The goal is to estimate the labels of the unlabeled target domain images using only labeled source images and a few labeled target images. The classification results of the SAT on translated target data is compared to a classifier based on a convolutional neural network trained with the same numbers of labels as well as a classifier that utilizes deep features obtained from a pre-trained imagenet network [13], using the same number of labels. Results from the SAT consistently outperform these two methods as depicted in Table 1.

Further, domain adaptation comparisons were made with the unsupervised UNIT [9], model to analyze the effects of the addition of target labels with results reported in Table 2. When the target domain is more complex than the source, like MNIST (source) → SVHN (target) or MNIST-V (source) → SVHN (target), there are very clear improvements in performance. However, in other situations, the semi-supervised domain adaptation of the SAT is worse than

Table 1. Recognition accuracies (%) on the MNIST, MNIST-V, and SVHN datasets across multiple semi-supervised algorithms with varying amounts of labeled target data. CNN is a Convolutional Neural Network with an architecture similar to LeNet. Deep features trains a CNN using deep features of the input obtained from VGG-16 trained on imagenet. SAT is the proposed semi-supervised adversarial translator utilizing various source domains. SAT(MNIST) implies MNIST is the source domain. The best results are in bold.

Target domain	Target labels	CNN	Deep features	SAT (MNIST)	SAT (MNIST-V)	SAT (SVHN)
MNIST	50	60.34	61.45	-	**92.40**	67.14
MNIST	100	73.29	68.23	-	**92.66**	76.27
MNIST	200	78.73	79.40	-	**93.15**	82.59
MNIST	1000	88.65	90.42	-	**94.29**	90.67
MNIST-V	50	25.90	51.03	50.79	-	**57.84**
MNIST-V	100	31.63	58.35	55.23	-	**64.28**
MNIST-V	200	41.10	67.85	59.16	-	**71.04**
MNIST-V	1000	77.70	85.30	**85.62**	-	80.47
SVHN	50	16.51	19.05	23.8	**48.33**	-
SVHN	100	20.28	28.03	27.2	**52.55**	-
SVHN	200	33.08	30.66	37.0	**54.97**	-
SVHN	1000	57.72	44.12	62.6	**69.31**	-

the unsupervised domain adaptation of the UNIT network. This decrease in performance can be attributed to the additional complexity introduced by the target labels. Adding more objective terms to an already complex model gives more sub-tasks to each component of the network. In some cases, this helps the network to model more complex domain shifts, but in others cases, this pulls the parameters of the networks in different directions away from the optimal solution.

Table 2. Recognition accuracies (%) of the UNIT and SAT models on images from the target domain while utilizing knowledge and labels from the source domain. The numbers appended to SAT is the total number of labels used during training.

Source domain	Target domain	UNIT	SAT-50	SAT-200
MNIST	MNIST-V	98.07	50.79	59.16
MNIST	SVHN	23.46	23.82	37.20
MNIST-V	MNIST	99.01	92.40	93.15
MNIST-V	SVHN	29.00	48.33	52.55
SVHN	MNIST	83.52	51.03	82.59
SVHN	MNIST-V	85.23	57.84	71.04

5   Conclusions

Because of inherent differences in domains, attempting to fully represent the different generative factors of multiple domains in a compressed latent space can be a challenging task. As seen in the evaluation on semi-supervised translation, despite the use of labels in the target domain, perfect domain consistency and label consistency was not attained. This indicates that there is some conflict between these two objectives stemming from how they are represented in the latent space. Fully containing the information necessary to recreate two drastically different domains in a single shared latent space can be challenging. For better performance, fine-tuning the different hyper-parameters for each specific problem context may lead to a better balance of the various learning factors of the model and better performance.

Domain adaptation and transfer learning capabilities will always be important to the advancement of machine learning and artificial intelligence. Semi-supervision, if available, will always be an option to increase performance compared to the unsupervised counterparts. The problem of the SAT is that the model is set up so that the objectives of content-consistency and domain-consistency are in conflict. Further work on the model should include adjustments to the way that data is represented in the latent space that will either better balance the two objectives and allow both to accomplish their objectives well.

Acknowledgements. The authors thank Arizona State University and National Science Foundation for their funding support. This material is partially based upon work supported by the National Science Foundation under Grant No. 1116360.

References

1. Bengio, Y.: Deep learning of representations for unsupervised and transfer learning. In: Proceedings of ICML Workshop on Unsupervised and Transfer Learning, pp. 17–36 (2012)
2. Bousmalis, K., Silberman, N., Dohan, D., Erhan, D., Krishnan, D.: Unsupervised pixel-level domain adaptation with generative adversarial networks. In: CVPR (2017)
3. Ganin, Y., Lempitsky, V.: Unsupervised domain adaptation by backpropagation. In: ICML (2015)
4. Gatys, L.A., Ecker, A.S., Bethge, M.: Image style transfer using convolutional neural networks. In: CVPR, pp. 2414–2423. IEEE (2016)
5. Goodfellow, I., et al.: Generative adversarial nets. In: NIPS (2014)
6. Kingma, D.P., Welling, M.: Auto-encoding variational Bayes. In: ICLR (2014)
7. Larsen, A.B.L., Sønderby, S.K., Larochelle, H., Winther, O.: Autoencoding beyond pixels using a learned similarity metric. In: ICML (2016)
8. LeCun, Y., Cortes, C., Burges, C.J.: The MNIST database of handwritten digits (1998)
9. Liu, M.Y., Breuel, T., Kautz, J.: Unsupervised image-to-image translation networks. In: NIPS (2017)

10. Long, M., Cao, Y., Wang, J., Jordan, M.I.: Learning transferable features with deep adaptation networks. In: ICML (2015)
11. Netzer, Y., Wang, T., Coates, A., Bissacco, A., Wu, B., Ng, A.Y.: Reading digits in natural images with unsupervised feature learning. In: NIPS Workshop on Deep Learning and Unsupervised Feature Learning (2011)
12. Russo, P., Carlucci, F.M., Tommasi, T., Caputo, B.: From source to target and back: Symmetric bi-directional adaptive GAN. In: CVPR (2018)
13. Simonyan, K., Zisserman, A.: Very deep convolutional networks for large-scale image recognition. CoRR abs/1409.1556 (2014)
14. Zhu, J.Y., Park, T., Isola, P., Efros, A.A.: Unpaired image-to-image translation using cycle-consistent adversarial networks. In: ICCV (2017)

A Step Beyond Generative Multi-adversarial Networks

Aman Singh[✉]

Department of Computing Science, University of Alberta,
Edmonton, AB T6G 2E8, Canada
amansing@ualberta.ca

Abstract. In this paper we modify the structure and introduce new formulation to improve the performance of the Generative adversarial networks (GANs). We achieve this based on the discriminating capability of the Generative Multi-Adversarial Network (GMAN), which is a variation of GANs. GANs in general has the advantage of accelerating training at the initial phase using the minimax objectives. On the other hand, GMAN can produce reliable training using the original dataset. We explored a number of improvement possibilities, including automatic regulations, boosting using Adaboost and a new Generative Adversarial Metric (GAM). In our design, the images generated from noisy samples are reused by the generator instead of adding new samples. Experimental results show that our image generation strategy produces better resolution and higher quality samples as compared to the standard GANs. Furthermore, the number of iterations and the required time for quantitative evaluation is greatly reduced using our method.

Keywords: Multi-discriminators · Generators · Adversarial
Minimax · GAN · GMAN · GAM

1 Introduction

Generative adversarial networks (GANs) is a powerful subclass of generative modeling. It had received a tremendous amount of success when applied to image generation, editing, domain adaptation and semi-supervised learning [1]. GANs [2] provides a structure for the implementation of a generative model based on the concept of a two-player minimax game. There is player one (the generator), who tries to generate realistic images from the noisy samples. The model tries to learn a deterministic transformation G from a simple distribution p_z, with only one objective to match the data distribution p_d. A feedback is provided by the discriminator to the generator showing how realistic the produced samples are in comparison to another player. The discriminator has to determine whether the samples are produced by the generator, or drawn from the actual dataset.

In this study, our implementation is based on the Deep Convolutional GANs (DCGAN), which is a variation of the state-of-art GANs structure. We incorporated a new and improved formulation of Generative multiple-Adversarial Metric

© Springer Nature Switzerland AG 2018
A. Basu and S. Berretti (Eds.): ICSM 2018, LNCS 11010, pp. 345–356, 2018.
https://doi.org/10.1007/978-3-030-04375-9_29

(GMAN) [3]. GMAN uses multiple discriminators and is also a variation of GAN. We modified the structure of GMAN and used a pre-trained GMAN to get better image resolution and quality. Experiments were conducted using the CIFAR-10 dataset [4].

In the remaining paper, Sect. 2 reviews related work. In Sect. 3, we describe the structure of GANs. Section 4 presents our proposed structure and the new formulation. Sections 5 and 6 shows the experimental setup and results respectively. Finally, we conclude the paper in Sect. 7. Future work is given in Sect. 8.

Our main contribution in the research of GANs are: (a) the images generated from noise are used again by the generator instead of taking new samples; (b) A new methodology for GMAN, a multi-discriminator GAN framework with the reuse of images generated from generator; (c) A new a generative multi-adversarial metric (GMAM) formulation for separately trained frameworks to perform pairwise evaluation on them;

2   Related Work

There are ongoing challenges in the study of GANs, which include convergence properties [5] and stability in terms of optimization [6], but researchers believe that the most critical and difficult challenge is the quantitative evaluation of GANs. The most classical approach towards evaluating generative models is based on the likelihood of the models which in most cases is intractable. Additionally, the log-likelihood can be approximated for distributions on low-dimensional vectors but when it comes to the context of complex high-dimensional dataset the task becomes extremely overwhelming and challenging [7]. In [8] a sampling algorithm to estimate the hold-out log-likelihood was proposed, which had many drawbacks. The key drawback was the assumption of the Gaussian observation model which carried over all issues of kernel density estimation in high-dimensional spaces. A partial solution to this was provided by Theis et al. [9], in which the likelihood was higher but visual quality and latency was low. Furthermore, it was argued that using Parzen window density estimates as the likelihood estimation provides incorrect results, and thus ranking the models based on this estimation was highly discouraged.

In recent developed GAN frameworks, the algorithms between learners are carefully formulated so that Nash equilibrium should harmonize with appropriate set of criteria. Nash equilibrium is a system involving two participants interacting with each other and these participants cannot gain over the other by changing the strategies if the strategies of the other participant remain the same. Initially the main idea behind the development of GANs was on generating images (e.g., MNIST [10]) and CIFAR [11]. However, it has been proven that GANs can be applied on a variety of application domains, which include transferring of domain knowledge [12], imitation of the expert policies [13] for better understanding the system, censored representation learning system [14], learning of features [15] to evaluate models in a better manner, extending the work of GANs to semi-supervised learning [16] and improving the image generation [17] process and methodology. All these fields of study have presented a lot of potential and successful results. Considering all these successes, GANs are still very tedious, critical and difficult to train, and thus have room to improve. So far research to improve the training techniques focuses on understanding and generalizing GANs with the aim of providing better results in terms of quality of generation instead of generation running time.

3   Overview of GAN

The logic behind GANs is a minimax game between the generator and the discriminator. In this minimax game, the following function is expected to be optimized:

$$\min_G \max_D V(D,G) = E_{x \sim P_d(x)}[\log(D(x))] + E_{z \sim P_z(z)}[\log(1 - D(G(z)))] \quad (1)$$

where the true (correct) data distribution is assumed to be $p_d(x)$ and simple distribution can be assumed to be $p_z(z)$, which can generally be fixed and is easy to draw samples [2,3]. The differentiation of the functional space of discriminator, D and the elements of the functional space is performed by using various differential methods. At the same time, it is assumed that for generator the distribution induced is $p_{G(x)}$ for the functional space $G_\theta(z)$ and lastly, D and G are the deep neural network which is usually the case in generative adversarial models.

In the introductory and initial work on GANs [2], it was anticipated that with the optimal discriminator $D^* = arg \max_D V(D,G)$ from oracle, with sufficient network capacities and capabilities, the minimization function (stochastic gradient descent) on $p_G(x)$ will provide the required solution, $p_G(x)$ equal to $p_d(x)$, which can be applied to match the generator distribution exactly with data distribution to produce the high quality results for the enhancement of the gradient signals and better approximation. In practice, it was found that it required to replace the second term of the equation, $\log(1 - D(G(z)))$ with $-\log(D(G(z)))$ at the very beginning of the game so that the game will no longer be considered as a zero-sum game. In the convergence and optimality proof using oracle, the provided $D*$, can give a minimization only over G:

$$\min_G V(D^*,G) = \min_G C(G) = -\log(4) + 2JSD(p_{data}||p_G) \quad (2)$$

where JSD stands for Jensen-Shannon divergence, C(G) is the function which is necessary to minimizes JSD. However, very little is known about D* when the minimization of $V(D,G)$ is attempted [2]. This insight leads to the development of a model that tries to minimize maximum mean discrepancy (MMD) for all of the moments of $p_G(x)$ with $p_d(x)$ [18]. In one of the other approaches known as EBGAN [19], the objective of the generator and discriminator is to take real-valued "energies" as the input to the functions instead of using the probabilities. Different perspectives of JSD have been extended for GANs to achieve more general divergences [20,21].

In a recent paper [22] on the training dynamics of generative adversarial networks, the authors described the problems and possible solutions in training GAN. In the training process of GAN, people have found that as the discriminator gets better, the updates to the generator get consistently worse; if we just train D until convergence, its error will go to zero. The authors argue that this is because of the discontinuous distributions and distribution supports lie on low dimensional manifolds. In the case of GANs, the distribution of current sample x is defined via sampling from a simple prior $z \sim p(z)$. If the dimensionality of z is less than the dimension of x (as is the typical case in GAN), then it is impossible for the distribution to be continuous. It is also proved that if the two distributions we care about have supports that are disjoint or lie on low dimensional manifolds, the optimal discriminator will be perfect and its gradient will be zero almost everywhere.

4   Backpropagation in Generative Adversarial Networks (GANs)

In order to address some of the deficiencies in GANS and inspire further improvements, we implemented a framework of backpropagation for the generated images based on two main variants of the GANs: (a) Deep Convolutional Generative Adversarial Network (DCGAN) [1]; (b) Generative Multi-Adversarial Network (GMAN) [3].

4.1   Deep Convolutional Generative Adversarial Network

We consider using Deep Convolutional Generative Adversarial Nets (DCGAN), a topologically constrained variant of conditional GAN, as our basic GAN structure and baseline. DCGAN is by far the most cited basic GAN structure and remains as a base line or reference architecture for other models. It has outstanding performance in dealing with image processing tasks. In our study, we trained the model on the CIFAR-10 dataset [4]. We used the backpropagation of generated image methodology to improve the results of current methods by changing the parameters and structure of the system. DCGAN pairs learnt a hierarchy of representations from object parts level to scene level in both the generator and discriminator [1]. We find that comparing to other models, DCGAN is stable to train and is useful to learn unsupervised image representations.

- Structure of DCGAN
  In the DCGAN model, we introduced the following changes to the CNN architecture [1].
    - Replace pooling layers with strided convolutions (discriminator) and fractional-strided convolutions (generator), which allows the network to learn its own spatial down-sampling.
    - Eliminate fully connected layers on top of convolutional features.

- Use batch normalization in both generator (all layers except output layer) and discriminator (all layers except input layer). This helps to resolve training problems that arise due to poor initialization and helps the gradient flow in deeper models.
- Use ReLU activation in generator for all layers except the output, which uses Tanh to break the linearity and keep the values between 1 and -1, Use LeakyReLU activation in the discriminator for all layers.

Here are some of the parameters that are used for DCGAN in our research:
- Minibatch with minibatch size of 64.
- Generated image with imageSize of 64.
- Slope of leak = 0.1 for LeakyReLU.
- Learning rate = 0.0001, $\beta 1 = 0.3$
- Weights initialized with 0 centered normal distribution with standard deviation = 0.01

4.2 Generative Multi-adversarial Networks

We propose an improvement to Generative Multi-Adversarial Networks (GMANs) [3] by providing a modified formulation. GMANs differ from the traditional GANs in that multiple Discriminators are used with the Generator to improve the output of the system [3]. In GMANs there are four important components: (1) Maximizing $V(D,G)$, where D and G are the discriminator and Generator respectively, (2) Boosting, (3) Soft-Discriminator and (4) Automating Regulation. This architecture improves the output of the system and reduces the turnaround time and throughput of the system. In GMANs, Boosting of N weak discriminators is done to enhance the output of the system. The Soft-Discriminators provide realistic samples so that the generator receives a positive feedback from the discriminator [3]. The Use of Automating Regulation allows the generator to reduce the performance of the discriminator when necessary and also encourages the generator to challenge itself to be more efficient towards more accurate adversaries. Comparing to other models, GMANs are able to generate better quality images and it can be trained on a wide variety of datasets when using restricted domains of images. But the proposed methodology [3] has some problems - the booster does not generate comparative results and Generative Adversarial Metric (GAM) type of evaluation does not consider the performance of intermediate discriminators.

To address the above issue, we consider two approaches for training of discriminator in GMAN as suggested in [3] and made improvement to the original model structure: (a) a larger discriminating D using AdaBoost (for the better approximation of $\max_D V(D,G)$ (b) a better formulation of GAM type metric.

We studied a multiple-discriminators variant [3], which attempts to do a better approximation on $\max_D V(D,G)$ by providing a tough and strong critic to the generator, so that the generator has an opportunity to do a better evaluations on the reused images.

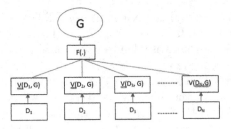

Fig. 1. (GMAN) The generator is trained using feedback from multiple discriminators and the image is being reused by the generator.

Figure 1 shows the basic system structure of GMAN. As we mentioned before, we use DCGAN as our basic GAN structure. Thus, deep convolution networks for Discriminators and Generator are used instead of the normal neural networks. Initially, from the noise signal a random image is generated which is given to the discriminators along with the images from the dataset for evaluation. The discriminators provide feedback to the generator to improve results. In the second cycle, instead of generating a new set of noisy images, the generator uses the image created in the initial step and tries to improve the created images which are then provided again to the discriminators.

Boosting Using AdaBoost. The boosted discriminator takes the maximum value from the N discriminators. In this process the discriminator is given a sample to predict whether the sample comes from the generator or the dataset [3]. The booster takes the reference of N weaker discriminator predictions and then makes a prediction of its own to evaluate the dataset. In our experiment we trained the weak discriminators using boosting and then for optimality we used *AdaBoost.OL* [23]. To get the comparative images for the boosted discriminators, the generator needs to have a mechanism to automatically decrease the performance of the discriminator whenever necessary. This is because there can be problems keeping both the discriminator and generator in the balance, e.g., unstable dynamics, oscillatory behavior and generator collapse [3]. Although the generator dampens the discriminator's performance, the dampening is restricted so that the generator still drives itself towards more accurate adversaries [3]. As described in [3], we use the following equation:

$$\min_{G, \lambda > 0} F_G(V_i) - l(\lambda) \tag{3}$$

Here $l(\lambda)$ is monotonically increasing in λ. In our experiments, $l(\lambda) = k\lambda$ where k is a constant which in our case is initially set to 0.005. In order to compete against the best available adversary produced by the boosted algorithm and increase λ at the same time, the generator is given a relaxation to reduce its objectives [3]. In our work, the boosting produced quite impressive results on the image generation tasks.

GMAM Metric. The authors in [3,17] introduced the Generative Adversarial Metric (GAM) for the comparison of independently trained GAN models by allowing a pairwise comparison between them. They believed that the generator and discriminator pairs (G_1, D_1) and (G_2, D_2) system should be capable to understand and learn the relative performance by evaluating the generator under the reference of the opponent's discriminator. However, there are two issues: (a) No evaluation of intermediate results derived from the GMAM metric. (b) $V \leq 0$ does not always hold for all evaluations. We suggest to modify the formulation of the Generative Multi-Adversarial Metric (GMAM). Our modified metric is adaptable for multiple discriminator training and can overcome some existing shortcomings.

$$GMAM = \log(\frac{F_{G_a}^b(V_i^b)}{F_{G_b}^a(V_i^b)} / \frac{F_{G_b}^b(V_i^a)}{F_{G_a}^a(V_i^b)}) \tag{4}$$

where a and b represent the two different variants of GMAN. The idea behind this method is that if generator 1 performs better than generator 2 with respect to both discriminator 1 and 2, then GMAM ≥ 0.5 and ≤ 1. If generator 1 performs better in both cases, then GMAN ≥ 0 and ≤ 0.5. This way, intermediate cases are taken into consideration.

5   Experimental Setup

The experiments for GMAN are performed under similar architecture as DCGAN [1]. For G a convolutional transpose layer and for D strided convolutions are being used with the exception for the input of G and the final layer of D. In this experimentation single step gradient method [20] is being used and for each of the generated layers we used the batch normalization. The training on various discriminators were performed with different dropout rates ranging between [0.2, 0.8]. We used two different ways to effect variations in the discriminators. First, the architecture was changed by changing the number of filters in the discriminator layers which was reduced by the factors of 2, 4 and so on, and at the same time changing the dropout rates. Second, the training samples of the discriminator were decorrelated by splitting the minibatch across the discriminators. The code has been written in Pytorch and run on Nvidia GTX 1060 GPUs. The details about MNIST architecture and training process are as follows:

- The architecture of Generator transpose layers: $(4, 4, 128), (8, 8, 64)$, $(16, 16, 32), (32, 32, 1)$.
- The architecture of Discriminator: $(32, 32, 1), (16, 16, 32), (8, 8, 64)$, $(4, 4, 128)$..
- Slope of leak = 0.1 for LeakyReLU.
- Learning rate = 0.0001, $\beta 1 = 0.3$
- Weights initialized with 0 centered normal distribution with standard deviation = 0.01

- In the variants tests are performed by removing either convolution 3 $(4, 4, 128)$ or by dividing all the filter sizes by 2 or 4 that is $(32, 32, 1)$, $(16, 16, 16), (8, 8, 32), (4, 4, 64)$ or $(32, 32, 1), (16, 16, 8), (8, 8, 16), (4, 4, 32)$.
- ReLu activation, Tanh activation and Sigmoid activation is taken respectively for all the hidden units, output units of the generator and output of the discriminator.
- The training of MNIST was performed for 25 epochs with a minibatch of size 64.
- CIFAR dataset was trained over 25000 iteration with a minibatch of size 64.

6   Results

Note that in the original work [2], the authors reported that log likelihood estimates from Gaussian Parzen windows does not perform properly in high dimensions and has high variance. To evaluate the performance of our new GMAN structure in addressing this issue, we conducted two experiments on the MNIST [10] and CIFAR-10 [11] datasets. Tables 1 and 2 compare the performance of our approach with the standard GMAN (Figs. 2, 3, 4, 5 and 6).

Table 1. The selection of the models on MNIST with standard deviation for pairwise GMAM. The positive values for GMAN for each column represent the better performance, similarly the degraded performance is represented by negative values. These scores are obtained by doing the summation of each variant's column.

Score [3]	Score (ours)	Variant	GMAN*	GMAN-0	GMAN-max	Mod-GAN
0.127	**0.124**	GMAN*	-	-0.019 ± 0.008	−0.027 ± 0.018	−0.078 ± 0.035
0.007	**0.006**	GMAN-0	0.019 ± 0.008	-	−0.01 ± 0.014	−0.015 ± 0.026
−0.03	**−0.027**	GMAN-max	0.027 ± 0.018	0.01 ± 0.014	-	−0.01 ± 0.023
−0.122	**−0.13**	Mod-GAN	0.078 ± 0.035	0.015 ± 0.026	0.01 ± 0.023	-

Table 2. Results for 5 iterations on MNIST for the pairwise evaluation of GMAN/stddev (GMAN) considered for GMAN -λ and GMAN* (λ*)

Score [3]	Score (ours)	λ	$\lambda*$	$\lambda = 1$	$\lambda = 0$
0.028	**0.024**	$\lambda*$	-	−0.007/±0.008	−0.018/±0.009
0.001	**0.0005**	$\lambda = 1$	0.007/± 0.008	-	−0.007/±0.009
−0.025	**−0.020**	$\lambda = 0$	0.018/±0.009	0.007/±0.009	-

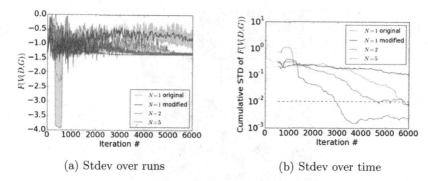

(a) Stdev over runs   (b) Stdev over time

Fig. 2. Plot (a) shows the plot for *stdev* over runs. It shows $V(D, G)$ average for iterations on MNIST. It can be seen with the increase in number of discriminators the acceleration of $V(D, G)$ converges to a steady state (solid line) and the variance is reduced to σ^2 (filled shadow $\pm\sigma$). Part (b) of the figure provides an alternative proof of $GMAN^*$'s accelerated convergence. Plot (b) shows the plot for *stdev* over time. In this plot *stdev*, σ, of the generator objective over a sliding window of 500 iterations is taken. It can be seen that lower values shows a more steady-state. $GMAN^*$ achieves a steady-state with $N = 5$ at a speed equivalent of 2.2x in comparison to the speed of GAN for $(N = 1)$.

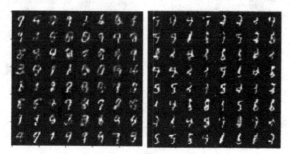

Fig. 3. Training result on MNIST dataset

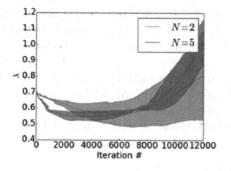

Fig. 4. The difficulty of the game is regulated by the adjustment of λ for $GMAN^*$. At first, G tends to reduce the value of λ to ease out the learning process and then continuously increases the value of λ to make the environment more challenging for the learning process.

Fig. 5. Training result on CIFAR-10 dataset on DCGAN.

(a) Cifar-10 on GMAN   (b) Real data sample

Fig. 6. Generated images trained on Cifar-10 dataset for GMAN-variant

7   Conclusion

In this paper we propose to use a new formulation of GAM type metric for Generative Multi-Adversarial Network and further explored many roles and methods for the implementation of discriminators to find the optimal results. The implementation of boosting with automatic tunning of the generator for the generation of images totally outperformed the GANs with only one discriminator on MNIST, faster convergence was achieved without any milkiness or blurriness at a stable state on various processes with respect to the measurement performed by a GAM-type metric (GMAM) at variation of GMAN.

8   Future Work

The experiment results shown in this paper demonstrate the potential of GMAN method. In future work, considering the difficulty in training generator against discriminator, it is natural to choose multiple generator as new working direction.

Moreover, we will look into more sophisticated models like conditional GANs and GANs using different loss evaluation functions; we will also test our method on other dataset and provide detailed analysis of the performance of this method.

References

1. Radford, A., Metz, L., Chintala, S.: Unsupervised representation learning with deep convolutional generative adversarial networks. arXiv preprint arXiv:1511.06434 (2015)
2. Goodfellow, I., et al.: Generative adversarial nets. In: Advances in Neural Information Processing Systems, pp. 2672–2680 (2014)
3. Durugkar, I., Gemp, I., Mahadevan, S.: Generative multi-adversarial networks. arXiv preprint arXiv:1611.01673 (2016)
4. Krizhevsky, A., Nair, V., Hinton, G.: The CIFAR-10 dataset (2014). http://www.cs.toronto.edu/kriz/cifar.html
5. Arora, S., Ge, R., Liang, Y., Ma, T., Zhang, Y.: Generalization and equilibrium in generative adversarial nets (GANs). arXiv preprint arXiv:1703.00573 (2017)
6. Salimans, T., Goodfellow, I., Zaremba, W., Cheung, V., Radford, A., Chen, X.: Improved techniques for training GANs. In: Advances in Neural Information Processing Systems, pp. 2234–2242 (2016)
7. Lucic, M., Kurach, K., Michalski, M., Gelly, S., Bousquet, O.: Are GANs created equal. A Large-Scale Study. ArXiv e-prints (2017)
8. Wu, Y., Burda, Y., Salakhutdinov, R., Grosse, R.: On the quantitative analysis of decoder-based generative models. arXiv preprint arXiv:1611.04273 (2016)
9. Theis, L., Oord, A., Bethge, M.: A note on the evaluation of generative models. arXiv preprint arXiv:1511.01844 (2015)
10. LeCun, Y.: The MNIST database of handwritten digits (1998). http://yann.lecun.com/exdb/mnist/
11. Krizhevsky, A., Hinton, G.: Learning multiple layers of features from tiny images (2009)
12. Yoo, D., Kim, N., Park, S., Paek, A.S., Kweon, I.S.: Pixel-level domain transfer. In: Leibe, B., Matas, J., Sebe, N., Welling, M. (eds.) ECCV 2016. LNCS, vol. 9912, pp. 517–532. Springer, Cham (2016). https://doi.org/10.1007/978-3-319-46484-8_31
13. Ho, J., Ermon, S.: Generative adversarial imitation learning. In: Advances in Neural Information Processing Systems, pp. 4565–4573 (2016)
14. Edwards, H., Storkey, A.: Censoring representations with an adversary. arXiv preprint arXiv:1511.05897 (2015)
15. Donahue, J., Krähenbühl, P., Darrell, T.: Adversarial feature learning. arXiv preprint arXiv:1605.09782 (2016)
16. Chen, X., Duan, Y., Houthooft, R., Schulman, J., Sutskever, I., Abbeel, P.: InfoGAN: interpretable representation learning by information maximizing generative adversarial nets. In: Advances in Neural Information Processing Systems, pp. 2172–2180 (2016)
17. Im, D.J., Kim, C.D., Jiang, H., Memisevic, R.: Generating images with recurrent adversarial networks. arXiv preprint arXiv:1602.05110 (2016)
18. Li, Y., Swersky, K., Zemel, R.: Generative moment matching networks. In: International Conference on Machine Learning, pp. 1718–1727 (2015)
19. Zhao, J., Mathieu, M., LeCun, Y.: Energy-based generative adversarial network. arXiv preprint arXiv:1609.03126 (2016)

20. Nowozin, S., Cseke, B., Tomioka, R.: f-GAN: training generative neural samplers using variational divergence minimization. In: Advances in Neural Information Processing Systems, pp. 271–279 (2016)

21. Uehara, M., Sato, I., Suzuki, M., Nakayama, K., Matsuo, Y.: Generative adversarial nets from a density ratio estimation perspective. arXiv preprint arXiv:1610.02920 (2016)

22. Arjovsky, M., Chintala, S., Bottou, L.: Wasserstein GAN. arXiv preprint arXiv:1701.07875 (2007)

23. Beygelzimer, A., Kale, S., Luo, H.: Optimal and adaptive algorithms for online boosting. In: International Conference on Machine Learning, pp. 2323–2331 (2015)

Adversarial Training for Dual-Stage Image Denoising Enhanced with Feature Matching

Xinyao Sun, Navaneeth Kamballur Kottayil, Subhayan Mukherjee, and Irene Cheng[✉]

Multimedia Research Center, University of Alberta, Edmonton, Canada
locheng@ualberta.ca

Abstract. We propose a dual-stage convolutional neural network, augmented with adversarial training, to address the shortcoming of current convolutional neural networks in image denoising. Our dual-stage approach, coupled with feature matching, is especially effective in recovering fine detail under high noise level. First, we use residual learning denoising to output a preliminary denoised reference image. Then, an image reconstruction denoiser uses a multi-scale feature selection layer, which deploys skip-connections and ResNet blocks to recover the image detail based on the noisy image and the reference image. This dual-stage denoising is augmented with the feedback from a discriminator, which forms an adversarial training framework and guides the denoising towards a clean image construction. The feature matching process embedded in the discriminator ensures that the framework can be generalized to a diverse collection of image content. Experimental results show better denoising performance in public benchmark datasets compared with the state-of-the-art approaches.

Keywords: Image denoising · Adversarial training · Generative Residual learning · Feature matching

Images and videos can be contaminated with noises at various stages along the processing pipeline, e.g., acquisition, compression and transmission. Noise can affect the quality of subsequent processing and user visualization. Thus, image denoising [19] is a necessary step for many applications. Although noise patterns vary, an additive white Gaussian noise (AWGN) is commonly discussed in the literature, and related de-nosing approaches have been exploited extensively by modelling image priors and solving optimization problems, e.g., nonlocal self-similarity (NSS) models [3,7], sparse representations models [9,18] and gradient-based models [20,23]. These conventional methods target mainly low to medium noise levels, involve time-consuming optimization processes, and require hand-crafted image priors, which in general is insufficient for denoising complex and diverse scene content with fine detail. Recently, deep neural networks (DNNs), especially deep convolutional neural networks (CNNs), have shown promising

© Springer Nature Switzerland AG 2018
A. Basu and S. Berretti (Eds.): ICSM 2018, LNCS 11010, pp. 357–366, 2018.
https://doi.org/10.1007/978-3-030-04375-9_30

performance in image denoising. These deep CNNs use a discriminative denoising model, e.g., MLP [4], RED-Net [19] and DnCNN [25]. Their success is mainly attributed to CNNs' modeling capability and the deep network training. These deep-learning based discriminative methods show better performance than conventional model-based methods. However, when an image is distorted with high noise, these discriminative learning approaches are insufficient.

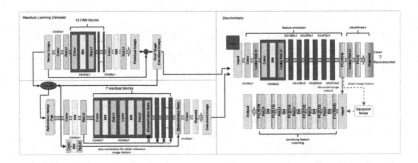

Fig. 1. Architecture of proposed AADNet with corresponding kernerl size (k), number of feautre maps (n) and stride (s) indicated for each convolutional layer.

We propose an Adversarial Augmented Dual-stage neural Network (AAD-Net) for image denosing, which includes two stages of discriminative denoising process: (1) a residual learning denoiser is used to generate a residual image from a noisy input image and construct a reference image, and (2) a full CNN model is designed to output the final denoised image by using the preliminary reference and noisy image pair. To improve the dual-stage denoising, we introduce an adversarial training framework. Adversarial training is first described in Generative Adversarial Nets (GANs) [11]. Different from current GANs, which aim to achieve generative tasks, our adversarial training is augmented with feature matching [22] and classification capability for image denoising, which enables our adversarial training to cover a diverse collection of image content. Our goal is to recover the latent clean image from its corrupted observation. The dual-stage denoising process uses trained data from the discriminator, while the discriminator receives input from the dual-stage denoisers for training and generates feedback. Our contribution lies in:

- Introducing a dual-stage net for image denoising, to address the shortcoming of single denoiser design deployed by existing CNN-based networks.
- Proposing adversarial training to provide feedback for the dual-stage image denoising. While current nets are trained for specific objects, our adversarial training framework can achieve better results with its feature matching and classification capability to cover a diverse collection of complex content with fine detail.

The rest of this paper is organized as follows: Related work is given in Sect. 1. We present our proposed AADnet in Sect. 2. Experimental results and analysis are in Sect. 3. In Sect. 4, we give the conclusion and future work.

1 Related Work

Image denoising is a popular research topic in the literature [5,7,9,20]. In general, these techniques follow image prior modeling to solve optimization problems. They remove noises but also tend to over-filter the content, especially fine detail. As deep learning methodology emerges, neural network based discriminative denoising methods show better performance than conventional model-based techniques in many applications. An advantage of using neural networks, in particular CNN based models, is that the network parameters for image denoising can be learned from the training data, based on pairs of clean and corrupted images rather than pre-defined hand-crafted image priors. This powerful learning capability makes deep neural network attractive. To take full advantage of deep learning, and avoid the computational cost of training too deep, a symmetrically encoder-decoder skip-layer connection was introduced [19], which shows faster training and better denoising performance. Residual network (ResNet) [14] is designed for a similar purpose but to train an extremely deep CNN. As an alternative, DnCNN [25] adopts the residual learning formulation. It deploys identity shortcuts and a single residual unit to generate a residual image instead of outputting the latent clean image directly. In a classical CNN architecture, a fixed size kernel is used at each layer, which means that all necessary features characterized by different kernel sizes can only be extracted by exploring multiple layers. In order to extract multi-scale features at the same layer, GoogLeNet [21] applies multiple sets of convolutional filters on the image. The resulting activations are then stacked together and passed to subsequent layers.

As technology evolves, Generative Adversarial Nets (GANs) have become a popular approach. GANs are based on a two-player min-max game between two models. They aim to generate realistic synthetic images. Ideally, network discriminator is expected to learn distinct features from real data, which the generator can imitate. To achieve this, an optimal point should be reached when real data and synthesized data are indistinguishable. However, in practice, it is hard to train GANs as desired; it is challenging to balance the relative capacities of the two models in an adversarial network. This is due to the lack of an unambiguous and computable convergence criterion. A solution is to add an augmented training process to GANs by directing the generator network towards a probable configuration of abstract discriminative features [22]. In our work, we propose an image denoising framework AADNet, which not only has the merits of existing methods, but also introduces a new dual-stage denoising net, augmented by adversarial training with embedded feature matching and classification.

2   Proposed AADNet Framework

There are three major components in our AADNet: (1) A residual learning based denoiser (Fig. 1 Top-left), (2) a full image reconstruction denoiser with skip-connections and ResNet blocks (Fig. 1 Bottom-left), and (3) a discriminator for distinguishing denoised images from clean images (Fig. 1 Right). All three components interact in an adversarial training environment. In a classical image degradation model $\mathbf{y} = \mathbf{x} + \mathbf{v}$ [25], the denoiser is trained to estimate the difference between the input noisy image $\mathbf{y}$ and a clean image $\mathbf{x}$. At our first stage, a residual image $\hat{v}$ is obtained from a noisy input image $\hat{y}$. The preliminary output (reference) is denoted by $\hat{x}_{s1} = \hat{y} - \hat{v}$. At the second stage, a full CNN model obtains a denoised image by inputting the reference & noisy image pair tensor (concatenating $\hat{y}$ and $\hat{x}_{s1}$ along the last dimension). The final denoised output is denoted by $\hat{x}_{s2}$.

2.1 1st Stage: Residual Learning Denoiser $\mathbf{D_{s1}}$

$\mathbf{D_{s1}}$ is trained to learn the mapping function $\mathbf{D_{s1}(y)} = \mathbf{v}$. The clean image can be predicted as $\mathbf{D_{s1}}$'s output $\hat{x}_{s1} = \mathbf{y} - \mathbf{D_{s1}(y)}$. The parameter in $\mathbf{D_{s1}}$ is trained by computing the mean square error (MSE) or L2 loss (Eq. 1), between the residual and the model predication.

$$\mathcal{L}_{\mathbf{L2}}^{\mathbf{D_{s1}}}(\mathbf{x}, \mathbf{y}, \mathbf{D_{s1}}) = ||\mathbf{D_{s1}(y)} - (\mathbf{y} - \mathbf{x})||_2 \tag{1}$$

$\mathbf{D_{s1}}$ is used for estimating the noise rather than reconstructing the de-noised image. Residual learning can be used for image denoising, but it usually over-filters and is not effective in recovering complex structure [25]. To resolve this issue, we introduce dual-stage denoising.

2.2 2nd Stage: Full Image Reconstruction Denoiser $\mathbf{D_{s2}}$

Existing end-to-end CNN based denoising methods use a noisy and clean image pair to train the model for full image reconstruction. In our AADNet, we have an output of $\mathbf{D_{s1}}$ from the first stage as a preliminary denoised reference, which already has the Gaussian Noises partly or mostly removed. We concatenate the original noisy image and $\hat{x}_{s1}$ to form a reference-noisy pair tensor as input to the (second stage) full image reconstruction denoiser $\mathbf{D_{s2}}$. The output is the final denoised image $\hat{x}_{s2}$. Batch-normalization [15] and Res-Net [14] blocks, as well as Skip-connections [19], are used for improving training efficiency and stability. More detail about these techniques can be found in [14]. Note that, for an image denoising task, we want to avoid noisy information affecting subsequent layers during training. Therefore, different from other methods, which pass feature maps generated from the entire input, we select feature maps generated from the preliminary denoised reference image only. These feature maps are passed to the end layer via skip-connection as illustrated in Fig. 1 (bottom-left). The parameter in $\mathbf{D_{s2}}$ is trained by minimizing the L2 loss (Eq. 2) between the desired clean image and the model's reconstruction.

$$\mathcal{L}_{L2}^{\mathbf{D_{s2}}}(\hat{\mathbf{x}}_{s1}, \mathbf{y}, \mathbf{D_{s2}}) = ||\mathbf{D_{s2}}(\hat{\mathbf{x}}_{s1}) - \mathbf{x}||_2 \tag{2}$$

2.3 Adversarial Training with Feature Matching

AADnet is trained to recover the fine detail visually masked under noise degradation. We apply adversarial training using a discriminator $\mathbf{D}$ to learn whether the input image is a clean image or an image reconstructed after denoising. We split $\mathbf{D}$ into two components based on the denoising feature matching technique [22]. $\mathbf{D}$ takes $\mathbf{x}$, $\hat{\mathbf{x}}_{s1}$ and $\hat{\mathbf{x}}_{s2}$ as input. A feature extractor then extracts a feature vector of length 1024 and then pass it to a classifier generating a logits for classification. The loss function for $\mathbf{D}$ is given in Eq. 3:

$$\mathcal{L}_{\mathbf{D}}(\hat{\mathbf{x}}_{s1}, \hat{\mathbf{x}}_{s2}, \mathbf{x}, \mathbf{D}) = -\mathbb{E}\left[log\mathbf{D}(\mathbf{x})\right]-$$
$$\frac{1}{2}(\mathbb{E}\left[log(1 - \mathbf{D}(\hat{\mathbf{x}}_{s1}))\right] + \mathbb{E}\left[log(1 - \mathbf{D}(\hat{\mathbf{x}}_{s2}))\right]) \tag{3}$$

In order to maximize clean image content, we impose optimization adv loss $\mathcal{L}_{adv}^{\mathbf{D_{s1}}}$ and $\mathcal{L}_{adv}^{\mathbf{D_{s2}}}$ on each denoiser as shown in Eq. 4 & 5

$$\mathcal{L}_{adv}^{\mathbf{D_{s1}}}(\hat{x}_{s1}, \mathbf{D}) = \mathbb{E}\left[log(1 - \mathbf{D}(\hat{\mathbf{x}}_{s1}))\right] \tag{4}$$
$$\mathcal{L}_{adv}^{\mathbf{D_{s2}}}(\hat{x}_{s2}, \mathbf{D}) = \mathbb{E}\left[log(1 - \mathbf{D}(\hat{\mathbf{x}}_{s2}))\right] \tag{5}$$

As mentioned before, feature matching is necessary because current GANs are content or object specific [22], which is ineffective for real-world content covering a diverse collection of objects. A robust denoising net should target not only a narrow class of content, but also a wide collection of complex scenes. To address this issue, we embed a feature denoiser trained using extracted features from a feature extractor. Let F_{clean} denote a clean image feature vector. Feature matching denoiser $\mathbf{FD}$ is trained to reconstruct the clean image feature vector from its corrupted version F_{clean}^C by minimizing the MSE loss function (Eq. 6), where F_{clean}^C is generated by adding Gaussian noise to F_{clean}.

$$\mathcal{L}_{\mathbf{FD}}(F_{clean}, F_{clean}^C, \mathbf{FD}) = ||F_{clean} - \mathbf{FD}(F_{clean}^C)||_2 \tag{6}$$

$F_{\mathbf{D_{s1}}}$ and $F_{\mathbf{D_{s2}}}$ denote feature vectors extracted from the dual-stage denoised output. When $\mathbf{FD}$ performs the inference process directly on $F_{\mathbf{D_{s1}}}$ and $F_{\mathbf{D_{s2}}}$, the difference between $\mathbf{FD}$'s input feature vector and its output reconstructed feature vector is an additional cost to the two denoisers. Once $\mathbf{FD}$ is well trained with clean image features, minimizing the difference between denoised image features and its $\mathbf{FD}$ output will push the denoised image towards higher probability configuration following the clean data distribution in the feature space [22]. The two denoisers' feature matching loss functions are defined by Eqs. 7 and 8 respectively.

$$\mathcal{L}_{\mathbf{FD}}^{\mathbf{D_{s1}}}(F_{\mathbf{D_{s1}}}, \mathbf{FD}) = ||F_{\mathbf{D_{s1}}} - \mathbf{FD}(F_{\mathbf{D_{s1}}})||_2 \tag{7}$$
$$\mathcal{L}_{\mathbf{FD}}^{\mathbf{D_{s2}}}(F_{\mathbf{D_{s2}}}, \mathbf{FD}) = ||F_{\mathbf{D_{s2}}} - \mathbf{FD}(F_{\mathbf{D_{s2}}})||_2 \tag{8}$$

Now the final loss functions $\mathcal{L}^{\mathbf{D_{s1}}}$ and $\mathcal{L}^{\mathbf{D_{s1}}}$ for the two denoisers have all the components as shown in Eqs. 7 and 10. α, β and γ are heyperparameters. In the current implementation, we set them as 1, 10^{-3} and 10^{-3} respectively. All components described above can be trained in synchronization to form an end-to-end framework.

$$\mathcal{L}^{\mathbf{D_{s1}}} = \alpha\mathcal{L}^{\mathbf{D_{s1}}}_{\mathbf{L2}} + \beta\mathcal{L}^{\mathbf{D_{s1}}}_{adv} + \gamma\mathcal{L}^{\mathbf{D_{s1}}}_{\mathbf{FD}} \tag{9}$$

$$\mathcal{L}^{\mathbf{D_{s2}}} = \alpha\mathcal{L}^{\mathbf{D_{s2}}}_{\mathbf{L2}} + \beta\mathcal{L}^{\mathbf{D_{s2}}}_{adv} + \gamma\mathcal{L}^{\mathbf{D_{s2}}}_{\mathbf{FD}} \tag{10}$$

2.4   Learning Configuration

The parameters of all convoluntional layers and fully connected layers are initialized using Xavier method [10]. Residual learning denoiser and Full image reconstruction denoiser are trained using Adam optimizer [16] with $\beta_1 = 0.9$, $\beta_2 = 0.999$, $\epsilon = 10^{-8}$. Learning rate was set from 10^{-2} to 10^{-4}. The feature matching denoiser was also trained by Adam optimizer with the same configuration but learning rate was set from 10^{-5} to 10^{-6}. The discriminator was trained using stochastic gradient descent (SGD) with momentum 0.9. The reason why not use Adam optimizer for training discriminator is for improving the stability of the adversarial training. This is suggested by recent empirically studies related to GAN [13][2]. The learning rate was set from 10^{-1} to 10^{-4}. The network was trained using 40 epochs with min-batch size of 64.

3   Experimental Results

We evaluate our AADNet using two well-known public benchmark datasets: 14 widely used images (Fig. 2) and the BSD200 dataset [19]. The network was implemented using TensorFlow-1.4 [1] GPU version. All experiments were run on Compute Canada Cedar GPU instance with NVIDIA P100 Pascal graphic processor and Intel Xeon E5-2650 v4 CPU. The network took about two days for training 40 epochs.

Fig. 2. The 14 widely used test images

Table 1. Average PSNR and SSIM results of σ 30, 50, 70 for 14 widely used images.

σ	BM3D	EPLL	NCSR	PCLR	PGPD	WNNM	RED30	DnCNN-S	AADNet
PSNR									
30	28.49	28.35	28.44	28.68	28.55	28.74	29.17	29.20	**29.30**
50	26.08	25.97	25.93	26.29	26.19	26.32	26.81	26.81	**27.11**
70	24.65	24.47	24.36	24.79	24.71	24.80	25.31	25.32	**25.58**
SSIM									
30	0.8204	0.8200	0.8203	0.8263	0.8199	0.8273	0.8423	0.8377	**0.8420**
50	0.7427	0.7534	0.7415	0.7538	0.7442	0.7517	0.7733	0.7669	**0.7830**
70	0.6882	0.6717	0.6871	0.6997	0.6913	0.6975	0.7206	0.7206	**0.7318**

3.1 Training and Testing

Similar to related work in the literature, we used gray-scale images. We applied three noise levels, i.e., $\sigma = 30$, 50 and 70, to train AADNet with additive white Gaussian noises (AWGN). 300 images from the Berkeley Segmentation Dataset were used. Preprocessing was done by cropping each image to 40×40 patches with stride of 10. The output was then randomly scaled, flipped and rotated to produce a larger training set (about 0.45M). For each noise level, we used extracted patches as ground truth and added AWGN to get noisy samples for training. All the patches were scaled to [0,1]. The reason to choose AWGN is because (1) there is no specific prior information on noise score, and (2) real-world noise can easily be approximated locally as AWGN [19]. During testing, there is no need to perform the feed-forward computation on our discriminator. The final denoised output is obtained by running inference on the dual-stage denoisers. Although the model is trained on local patches, there is no fully connected layer in our denoiser net. Note that AADNet can perform denoising on arbitrary image size.

Table 2. Average PSNR and SSIM results of σ 30, 50, 70 for BSD200 images.

σ	BM3D	EPLL	NCSR	PCLR	PGPD	WNNM	RED30	DnCNN-S	AADNet
PSNR									
30	27.31	27.38	27.23	27.54	27.33	27.48	27.95	28.55	**28.61**
50	25.06	25.17	24.95	25.30	25.18	25.26	25.75	26.30	**26.43**
70	23.82	23.81	23.58	23.94	23.89	23.95	24.37	24.94	**25.08**
SSIM									
30	0.7755	0.7825	0.7738	0.7827	0.7717	0.7807	0.7993	0.8152	**0.8195**
50	0.6831	0.6870	0.6777	0.6947	0.6841	0.6928	0.7167	0.7323	**0.7451**
70	0.6240	0.6168	0.6166	0.6336	0.6245	0.6346	0.6551	0.6785	**0.6913**

3.2 Evaluation

To objectively assess the performance of AADNet, we use Peak Signal-to-Noise Ratio (PSNR) and Structural SIMilarity (SSIM) to measure dissimilarity between the original noise-free and denoised images. BM3D [7], EPLL [26], NCSR [8], PCLR [6], PGPD [24], WMMN [12], RED30 [19], and DnCNN-S [25] are compared with our AADNet. We used the publicly available source code of DnCNN-S to generate its scores. Scores of other methods are taken from [19]. Table 1 & 2 reports the PSNR and SSIM results of $\sigma = 30, 50$, and 70 on the 14 commonly tested images and BSD200 images. Some visual examples are shown in Fig. 3. The zoom-in view at the bottom right of each image demonstrates that AADNet preserves fine detail better.

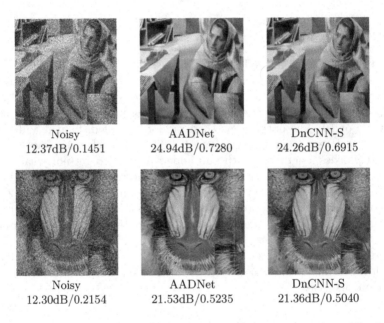

Noisy	AADNet	DnCNN-S
12.37dB/0.1451	24.94dB/0.7280	24.26dB/0.6915

Noisy	AADNet	DnCNN-S
12.30dB/0.2154	21.53dB/0.5235	21.36dB/0.5040

Fig. 3. Visual comparison examples - (Left to right): noisy image ($\sigma = 70$), denoised by AADNet and denoised by DnCNN-S. The zoom-in view shown at the bottom right of each image demonstrates that AADNet preserves fine detail better.

4 Discussion and Conclusion

Quantitative (PSNR, SSIM) and qualitative (visual) comparisons show that our AADNet achieves better results at all test noise levels in the BSD200 dataset and the 14 images widely used in the literature. There are only a few methods outperforming BM3D by more than 0.3dB [17], but AADNet has a higher PSNR (almost 1.0dB) compared with BM3D. When comparing to a pure residual learning network DnCNN-S, AADNet also outperforms at all noise levels.

SSIM results indicate that AADNet surpasses other methods by a large margin, especially under high level noise conditions. Visual comparisons in Fig. 3 show that AADNet can preserve sharp edges and fine structural details better than the original DnCNN-S on high noise level ($\sigma = 70$). Therefore, we conclude that AADNet is more robust than other methods in recovering image detail. AADNet's better performance is attributed to our dual-stage denoising and adversarial training strategy.

In this paper, we propose a novel adversarial augmented dual-stage denoising network, which outperforms existing state-of-the-art conventional and learning based approaches. The dual-stage is composed of residual learning for preliminary noise removal, and full image reconstruction for recovering fine detail. Dual-stage denoising is complemented by adversarial training, with embedded feature matching and classification to augment learning. Experimental results confirm that our method gives better results at all test noise levels. AADNet is expected to perform well on image restoration tasks in general. In future work, we will test our denoising approach in other real-world scenarios.

References

1. Abadi, M., et al.: TensorFlow: a system for large-scale machine learning. OSDI **16**, 265–283 (2016)
2. Arjovsky, M., Chintala, S., Bottou, L.: Wasserstein generative adversarial networks. In: International Conference on Machine Learning, pp. 214–223 (2017)
3. Buades, A., Coll, B., Morel, J.M.: A non-local algorithm for image denoising. In: IEEE Computer Society Conference on Computer Vision and Pattern Recognition, CVPR 2005, vol. 2, pp. 60–65. IEEE (2005)
4. Burger, H.C., Schuler, C.J., Harmeling, S.: Image denoising: can plain neural networks compete with BM3D? In: 2012 IEEE Conference on Computer Vision and Pattern Recognition (CVPR), pp. 2392–2399. IEEE (2012)
5. Chatterjee, P., Milanfar, P.: Clustering-based denoising with locally learned dictionaries. IEEE Trans. Image Process. **18**(7), 1438–1451 (2009)
6. Chen, F., Zhang, L., Yu, H.: External patch prior guided internal clustering for image denoising. In: Proceedings of the IEEE International Conference on Computer Vision, pp. 603–611 (2015)
7. Dabov, K., Foi, A., Katkovnik, V., Egiazarian, K.: Image denoising by sparse 3-D transform-domain collaborative filtering. IEEE Trans. Image Process. **16**(8), 2080–2095 (2007)
8. Dong, W., Zhang, L., Shi, G., Li, X.: Nonlocally centralized sparse representation for image restoration. IEEE Trans. Image Process. **22**(4), 1620–1630 (2013)
9. Elad, M., Aharon, M.: Image denoising via sparse and redundant representations over learned dictionaries. IEEE Trans. Image Process. **15**(12), 3736–3745 (2006)
10. Glorot, X., Bengio, Y.: Understanding the difficulty of training deep feedforward neural networks. In: Proceedings of the Thirteenth International Conference on Artificial Intelligence and Statistics, pp. 249–256 (2010)
11. Goodfellow, I., et al.: Generative adversarial nets. In: Advances in Neural Information Processing Systems, pp. 2672–2680 (2014)
12. Gu, S., Zhang, L., Zuo, W., Feng, X.: Weighted nuclear norm minimization with application to image denoising. In: Proceedings of the IEEE Conference on Computer Vision and Pattern Recognition, pp. 2862–2869 (2014)

13. Gulrajani, I., Ahmed, F., Arjovsky, M., Dumoulin, V., Courville, A.C.: Improved training of Wasserstein GANs. In: Advances in Neural Information Processing Systems, pp. 5769–5779 (2017)

14. He, K., Zhang, X., Ren, S., Sun, J.: Deep residual learning for image recognition. In: Proceedings of the IEEE Conference on Computer Vision and Pattern Recognition, pp. 770–778 (2016)

15. Ioffe, S., Szegedy, C.: Batch normalization: accelerating deep network training by reducing internal covariate shift. In: International Conference on Machine Learning, pp. 448–456 (2015)

16. Kingma, D.P., Ba, J.: Adam: a method for stochastic optimization. arXiv preprint arXiv:1412.6980 (2014)

17. Levin, A., Nadler, B.: Natural image denoising: optimality and inherent bounds. In: 2011 IEEE Conference on Computer Vision and Pattern Recognition (CVPR), pp. 2833–2840. IEEE (2011)

18. Mairal, J., Bach, F., Ponce, J., Sapiro, G.: Online dictionary learning for sparse coding. In: Proceedings of the 26th Annual International Conference on Machine Learning, pp. 689–696. ACM (2009)

19. Mao, X., Shen, C., Yang, Y.B.: Image restoration using very deep convolutional encoder-decoder networks with symmetric skip connections. In: Advances in Neural Information Processing Systems, pp. 2802–2810 (2016)

20. Rudin, L.I., Osher, S., Fatemi, E.: Nonlinear total variation based noise removal algorithms. Physica D: Nonlinear Phenomena 60(1–4), 259–268 (1992)

21. Szegedy, C., et al.: Going deeper with convolutions. In: CVPR (2015)

22. Warde-Farley, D., Bengio, Y.: Improving generative adversarial networks with denoising feature matching (2016)

23. Weiss, Y., Freeman, W.T.: What makes a good model of natural images? In: IEEE Conference on Computer Vision and Pattern Recognition, CVPR 2007, pp. 1–8. IEEE (2007)

24. Xu, J., Zhang, L., Zuo, W., Zhang, D., Feng, X.: Patch group based nonlocal self-similarity prior learning for image denoising. In: Proceedings of the IEEE International Conference on Computer Vision, pp. 244–252 (2015)

25. Zhang, K., Zuo, W., Chen, Y., Meng, D., Zhang, L.: Beyond a Gaussian denoiser: residual learning of deep cnn for image denoising. IEEE Trans. Image Process. 26(7), 3142–3155 (2017)

26. Zoran, D., Weiss, Y.: From learning models of natural image patches to whole image restoration. In: 2011 IEEE International Conference on Computer Vision (ICCV), pp. 479–486. IEEE (2011)

IVUS-Net: An Intravascular Ultrasound Segmentation Network

Ji Yang, Lin Tong, Mehdi Faraji$^{(\boxtimes)}$, and Anup Basu

Department of Computing Science, University of Alberta,
Edmonton, AB T6G 2E8, Canada
{jyang7,ltong2,faraji,basu}@ualberta.ca

Abstract. IntraVascular UltraSound (IVUS) is one of the most effective imaging modalities that provides assistance to experts in order to diagnose and treat cardiovascular diseases. We address a central problem in IVUS image analysis with Fully Convolutional Network (FCN): automatically delineate the lumen and media-adventitia borders in IVUS images, which is crucial to shorten the diagnosis process or benefits a faster and more accurate 3D reconstruction of the artery. Particularly, we propose an FCN architecture, called IVUS-Net, followed by a post-processing contour extraction step, in order to automatically segments the interior (lumen) and exterior (media-adventitia) regions of the human arteries. We evaluated our IVUS-Net on the test set of a standard publicly available dataset containing 326 IVUS B-mode images with two measurements, namely Jaccard Measure (JM) and Hausdorff Distances (HD). The evaluation result shows that IVUS-Net outperforms the state-of-the-art lumen and media segmentation methods by 4% to 20% in terms of HD distance. IVUS-Net performs well on images in the test set that contain a significant amount of major artifacts such as bifurcations, shadows, and side branches that are not common in the training set. Furthermore, using a modern GPU, IVUS-Net segments each IVUS frame only in 0.15 s. The proposed work, to the best of our knowledge, is the first deep learning based method for segmentation of both the lumen and the media vessel walls in 20 MHz IVUS B-mode images that achieves the best results without any manual intervention. Code is available at https://github.com/Kulbear/ivus-segmentation-icsm2018.

Keywords: Intravascular · Segmentation · Ultrasound · IVUS
Deep learning

1 Introduction

Convolutional Neural Networks (CNNs) play an important role in visual image recognition. In the past few years, CNNs have achieved promising results in image classification [12,13,15,22,23] and semantic segmentation [4,5,16,19,20]. Fully Convolutional Networks (FCNs) [16] have become popular and used to solve the problem of making dense predictions at a pixel level. There are two major

© Springer Nature Switzerland AG 2018
A. Basu and S. Berretti (Eds.): ICSM 2018, LNCS 11010, pp. 367–377, 2018.
https://doi.org/10.1007/978-3-030-04375-9_31

differences between FCN and the type of CNNs which are primarily designed for classification [15,22,24]. First, FCN does not have fully-connected layers therefore can accept any arbitrary size of inputs. Secondly, FCN consists of an encoder network that produces embedded feature maps that are followed by a decoder network to expand and refine the feature maps outputted by the encoder. Skip connections are also common in the architecture to connect corresponding blocks in the encoder and decoder [2,4,7].

Segmentation of the acquired IVUS images is a challenging task since IVUS images usually comes with artifacts. Particularly, a successful separation of the interior (lumen) and exterior (media) vessel walls in IVUS images plays a critical role to diagnose cardiovascular diseases. It also helps building the 3D reconstruction of the artery where the information of the catheter movements has been provided using another imaging modality such as X-Ray. The segmentation of IVUS images has been a well-investigated problem from a conventional perspective where numerous ideas and approaches of computer vision and image processing such as in [17,18,25,26,30] have been employed. One of the best segmentation results have been achieved in a very recent work [8] where authors proposed a two-fold IVUS segmentation pipeline based on traditional computer vision methods [9,10]. Although no learning method was used, it outperforms existing methods from both the accuracy and efficiency perspective. Although the reported performance of [8] is very close to the ground truth label (0.30 mm error of the segmented lumen and 0.22 mm error of the segmented media from the gold standard), we believe that the deep learning technique has the potential to perform better.

In this paper, we propose an FCN-based pipeline that automatically delineates the boundary of the lumen and the media vessel walls. The pipeline contains two major components: a carefully designed FCN for predicting a pixel-wise mask which is called IVUS-Net, followed by a contour extraction post-processing step. In addition, the FCN is trained from scratch without relying on any pretrained weights. We evaluated the proposed IVUS-Net on the test set of a publicly available IVUS B-mode benchmark dataset [3] which contains 326 20MHz IVUS images consist of various artifacts such as motion of the catheter after a heart contraction, guide wire effects, bifurcation and side-branches. Two standard metrics, namely, Jaccard Measure (JM), alternatively called Intersection over Union (IoU), and Hausdorff Distance (HD) were used for evaluation.

The contributions of the proposed work can be summarized as follows:

- We propose a pipeline based on a FCN followed by a post-processing contour extraction to automatically delineate the lumen and media vessel walls.
- We show that the proposed work outperforms the current state-of-the-art studies over a publicly available IVUS benchmark dataset [3] which contains IVUS images with a significant amount of artifacts. This shows that the proposed work has the potential to be generalized to other IVUS benchmarks as well.

- To the best of our knowledge, there is no previous work based on deep architecture that can produce segmentation for both the lumen and media vessel walls in B-mode IVUS images.

The rest of the paper is organized as the follows: Sect. 2 contains a detailed description of our proposed work. In Sect. 3, we demonstrate multiple experiments that reinforce our contribution. Finally, we conclude the work briefly in Sect. 4.

2   Proposed Method

In this section, we first introduce the dataset we used to train the deep model. Then, we present the architecture, IVUS-Net, that produces binary prediction mask for either the lumen or media area, followed by a contour extraction step to delineate the vessel wall.

2.1   Dataset

We used a publicly available IVUS dataset [3] that contains two sets (train and test) of IVUS gated frames using a full pullback at the end-diastolic cardiac phase from 10 patients. Each frame has been manually annotated by four clinical experts. The train and test sets consist of 109 and 326 IVUS frames, respectively. Also, test set contains a large number of IVUS artifacts including bifurcation (44 frames), side vessel (93 frames), and shadow (96 frame) artifacts. The remaining 143 frames do not contain any artifacts except for plaque.

2.2   IVUS-Net

IVUS-Net is designed based on fully convolutional network (FCN) [16], with inspirations from aggregated, multi-branch architectures such as ResNeXT [27] and the Inception model [24]. Both SegNet [2] and U-Net [21] can be considered as a base version of our proposed work according to the network architecture design. It has two major components:

1. An encoder network that can downsample and process the input to produce a low-resolution deep feature map.
2. A decoder network that can restore the resolution of the deep feature map outputted by the encoder network towards original size.

The output feature map is sent to one more convolutional layer followed by a sigmoid activation to produce the final result.

The encoder network contains 4 encoding blocks where the decoder network contains 3 decoding blocks. Each decoding block receives feature map from its previous block and extra information from the encoder network by skip-connections. The entire architecture is therefore symmetric as shown in Fig. 1.

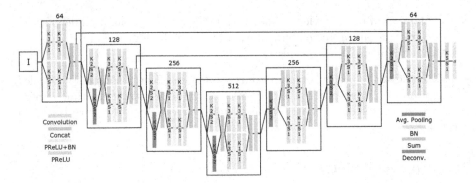

Fig. 1. The IVUS-Net architecture. Every convolutional layer in the same block has the same output depth as labeled on the top of the block. The figure should be read from left to right as we omitted arrow heads to save the space.

There are minor differences among the blocks in the architecture. We give a brief illustration for the design and also show the intuitions behind.

Except for the first encoding block, each encoding block contains a downsampling branch that downsamples the input feature map, then followed by a two-branch convolution path, as shown in Fig. 2(a). We build and expand downsampling branches in order to avoid losing information due to using the pooling. In fact, the downsampling branch facilitates reducing the spatial resolution of the input. It employs a 2-by-2 average pooling layer and a 2-by-2 convolutional layer with a stride of 2 at the same time, and finally concatenate the two outputs together, this aggregation idea is similar to [24,27].

After the downsampled, aggregated feature map outputs by the downsampling branch is passed to two subsequent branches, namely the refining branch and the main branch. First, we follow the design in [2,21] to include a branch with consecutive convolutional layers followed by activation and batch normalization, here we call it "main branch". A recent trend is to use small kernel size for the feature map refinement [4,19]. So we intentionally design a "refining branch" that has one convolutional layer with a 3-by-3 kernel size followed by a convolutional layer with a 1-by-1 kernel size produces similar but refined feature map. The outputs from the main branch and refining will be summed up and pass to the next block and its corresponding decoding block.

Decoding blocks need a slightly different configuration, as shown in Fig. 2(b). Every decoding block receives the feature map from both its previous block and its corresponding encoding block. Only the feature map received from the previous block is upsampled by a 2-by-2 deconvolution and then concatenated with the feature map from its corresponding encoding block. Note that this concatenated feature map will only be passed to the main branch, where the refining branch handles the upsampled feature map only.

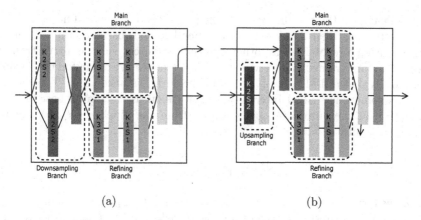

(a)   (b)

Fig. 2. A detailed illustration of the encoding block and the decoding block. Note the first encoding block does not have the downsampling branch, therefore the main branch and refining branch will directly accept the raw image as the input. (a) An encoding block with downsampling branch, followed by the main branch and the refining branch. (b) A typical decoding block that accept feature map from both the previous block and the skip-connection.

The activation used in the IVUS-Net is the **P**arametric **R**ectified **L**inear **U**nit (PReLU) [11].

$$\text{PReLU}(x) = \max(0, x) - \alpha \max(0, -x) \tag{1}$$

Compared with the ordinary ReLU activation, PReLU allows a part of the gradients flow through when the neuron is not activated, where ReLU only passes gradients when the neuron is active. As suggested in [11,28], PReLU outperforms ReLU in many benchmarks and also has a more stable performance.

Finally, the output feature map from the last decoding block is refined by a 5-by-5 convolutional layer, which is experimentally proved to be helpful on improving performance. As we want IVUS-Net to produce binary masks, the last activation is a sigmoid function.

2.3 Post-processing

Generally, as it has been proposed in [8], since the shape of the lumen and media regions of the vessel are very similar to conic sections, representing the predicted masks by fitting an ellipse on the masks can increase the accuracy of the segmentations. Therefore, we follow the same process explained in [8] to post-process the predicted masks in order to extract the final contours.

3 Experiments

The evaluation is based on a publicly available IVUS B-mode dataset [3], which has been widely used in the IVUS segmentation literature [6,8,17,26,30]. There are 109 images in the training set, 326 images in the test set and no official validation set is provided. Models are trained end-to-end, based on only the given dataset without involving any other external resources such as extra training images and pre-trained model weights. Two metrics are used for the evaluation, namely Jaccard Measure (JM) and Hausdorff Distance (HD). The Jaccard Measure, sometimes called Intersection over Union, is calculated based on the comparison of the automatic segmentation from the pipeline (R_{pred}) and the manual segmentation delineated by experts (R_{true}).

$$JM = \frac{R_{pred} \cap R_{true}}{R_{pred} \cup R_{true}} \tag{2}$$

The Hausdorff Distance between the automatic (C_{pred}) and manual (C_{true}) curves is the "greatest distance of all points belonging to C_{pred} to the closest point" [8] in C_{true} and is defined as follows:

$$HD = \max\{d(C_{pred}, C_{true}), d(C_{true}, C_{pred})\} \tag{3}$$

3.1   Data Augmentation

The training set contains only 109 images, which is considered as a relatively small training set for training a deep model from scratch. We then employ data augmentation on all the available training images. The augmentation is twofold. First, every original IVUS image and its corresponding ground truth masks are flipped (1) left to right, (2) up to down, and (3) left to right then up to down, to generate three new image-mask pairs. Secondly, we add heavy noises to input images. The methods we use to add noises to the input image include giving additive Gaussian noise, as suggested by [29], or converting the input image to entirely black. No modification is done on the ground truth masks. The effectiveness of data augmentation is discussed in Sect. 3.3.

3.2   Training the Model

All the models are trained and evaluated on a computer with a Core i7-8700K processor, 16 GB of RAM, and a GTX 1080 8 GB graphics card. Training a model from scratch generally takes less than 2 h to complete. To make the training faster and use a relatively large batch size, we downsized every frame of the dataset by a factor of 0.5.

We implement IVUS-Net with TensorFlow [1]. The weights in the model are all initialized randomly. Then we train the model with Adam optimizer [14]. The learning rate is set to be 0.0001 with no decay scheme. The augmented training set is used to train each model for 96 epochs, with a batch size of 6 and 144 iterations in total for each epoch. Note that we need two groups of models to predict the lumen area and the media area since the output activation is a sigmoid function:

$$\sigma(x) = \frac{1}{1 + e^{-x}} \tag{4}$$

For training each model, we randomly select 10 original IVUS images as the validation set to monitor the average Jaccard Measure without extracting contours. The given prediction by a single model is a probability map that has equal dimensions to the input image size. We follow the ensemble practice in [5] to produce the final result.

3.3   The Effectiveness of Data Augmentation

We validate the effectiveness of data augmentation with a small experiment. In each case, 5 models with identical configurations are trained and we use the ensemble strategy illustrated in [5] to produce the final prediction. The result is shown in Table 1a. Note that this result is based on the predictions produced directly by the ensembling without contour extraction. No matter which type of vessel segmentation the model predicts, we can safely conclude that the augmentation helps to improve the segmentation performance.

Table 1. Data Augmentation and Refining Branch Validation.

(a) Data augmentation evaluation result					(b) Refining branch evaluation result				
	Lumen		Media			Lumen		Media	
	Jacc.	Acc.	Jacc.	Acc.		Jacc.	Acc.	Jacc.	Acc.
Aug. data	0.86	98.6	0.84	96.8	W/ ref path	0.86	98.6	0.84	96.8
Orig. data	0.83	97.6	0.79	96.1	W/O ref path	0.84	97.9	0.80	96.0

3.4   On Evaluating the Refining Branch

Does refining branch really help? We use the exact same configuration to train two groups of 5 models. One group includes the proposed model, another group is the proposed model without the refining branch. The evaluation procedures and metrics are as same as we did for the data augmentation evaluation, the result is shown in Table 1b. There are, indeed, improvements made by the refining branch.

3.5   Segmentation Results

In this section, we present and discuss experimental results on the IVUS dataset [3]. We train 10 models with the configuration mentioned in Sect. 3.2 and ensemble the predictions followed by contour extraction to produce the final prediction mask.

The quantitative result is shown in Table 2. As we can see, IVUS-Net outperforms existing methods by a significant margin. According to the Jaccard Measure, we achieve 4% and 8% improvement for the lumen and the media, respectively. If we look at the Hausdorff distance, IVUS-Net obtains 8% and 20% improvement for the lumen and the media, respectively.

Table 2. Performance of the proposed IVUS-Net with contour extraction. Measures represent the mean and standard deviation evaluated on 326 frames of the dataset [3] and categorized based on the presence of a specific artifact in each frame. The evaluation measures are Jaccard Measure (JM) and Hausdorff Distance (HD).

		Lumen		Media	
		JM	HD	JM	HD
All	Proposed	**0.90 (0.06)**	**0.26 (0.25)**	**0.86 (0.11)**	**0.48 (0.44)**
	Faraji et al. [8]	0.87 (0.06)	0.30 (0.20)	0.77 (0.17)	0.67 (0.54)
	Downe et al. [6]	0.77 (0.09)	0.47 (0.22)	0.74 (0.17)	0.76 (0.48)
	Exarchos et al. [3]	0.81 (0.09)	0.42 (0.22)	0.79 (0.11)	0.60 (0.28)
No artifact	Proposed	**0.91 (0.03)**	**0.21 (0.09)**	**0.92 (0.05)**	**0.27 (0.23)**
	Faraji et al. [8]	0.88 (0.05)	0.29 (0.17)	0.89 (0.07)	0.31 (0.23)
Bifurcation	Proposed	**0.82 (0.11)**	0.50 (0.58)	**0.78 (0.11)**	0.82 (0.60)
	Faraji et al. [8]	0.79 (0.10)	0.53 (0.34)	0.57 (0.13)	1.22 (0.45)
	Downe et al. [6]	0.70 (0.11)	0.64 (0.27)	0.71 (0.19)	0.79 (0.53)
	Exarchos et al. [3]	0.80 (0.09)	**0.47 (0.23)**	0.78 (0.11)	**0.63 (0.25)**
Side vessels	Proposed	**0.90 (0.04)**	**0.23 (0.12)**	**0.83 (0.14)**	**0.59 (0.49)**
	Faraji et al. [8]	0.87 (0.05)	0.24 (0.11)	0.73 (0.60)	0.74 (0.18)
	Downe et al. [6]	0.77 (0.08)	0.46 (0.19)	0.74 (0.16)	0.76 (0.47)
	Exarchos et al. [3]	0.77(0.09)	0.53 (0.24)	0.78 (0.12)	0.63 (0.31)
Shadow	Proposed	**0.87(0.06)**	**0.27 (0.25)**	0.76 (0.12)	0.80 (0.45)
	Faraji et al. [8]	0.86 (0.07)	0.29 (0.20)	0.58 (0.13)	1.24 (0.39)
	Downe et al. [6]	0.76 (0.11)	0.55 (0.26)	0.74 (0.16)	0.77 (0.48)
	Exarchos et al. [3]	0.80 (0.10)	0.46 (0.19)	**0.82 (0.11)**	**0.57 (0.28)**

IVUS-Net performs particularly well on images with no artifact. Furthermore, it improves the performance by a large margin for segmenting both the lumen and the media according to the Hausdorff distance. The reason why IVUS-Net does not exceed all the methods in every single categories of [3] can be addressed from two perspectives. First, the training set is too small to capture all the common artifacts in the real world and even the test set. But the architecture is still considerably effective as the training set contains only 1 image with side vessels artifact while the test set contains 93 frames with side vessel artifacts. Secondly, the shadow artifacts are generally overlapped with parts of the media area that makes the segmentation becomes much more challenging since the media regions leak to the background. Some predictions are illustrated in Fig. 3.

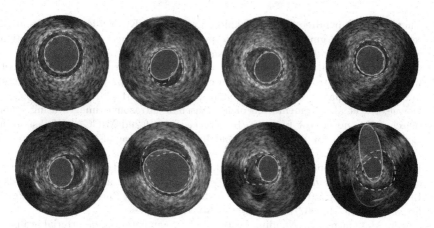

Fig. 3. Lumen and media segmentation results. Segmented lumen and media have been highlighted by cyan and red colors, respectively. The yellow dashed lines illustrate the gold standard that have been delineated by four clinical experts [3]. (Color figure online)

4   Conclusion

In this paper, we proposed IVUS-Net for the segmentation of arterial walls in IVUS images as well as a contour extraction post-processing step that specifically fits for the IVUS segmentation task. We showed that IVUS-Net can outperform the existing conventional methods on delineating the lumen and media vessel walls. This is also the first deep architecture-based work that achieves segmentation results that are very close to the gold standard. We evaluated IVUS-Net on a publicly available dataset containing 326 IVUS frames. The results of our evaluation showed the superiority of IVUS-Net output segmentations over the current state-of-the-arts. Also, IVUS-Net can be employed in real-world applications since it only needs 0.15 s to segment any IVUS frame.

Acknowledgment. The authors would like to thank the PhD students in the Multimedia Research Centre at University of Alberta. Special thanks to Xinyao Sun for the discussions on the related work and the network architecture figure design.

References

1. Abadi, M., et al.: TensorFlow: large-scale machine learning on heterogeneous systems (2015). Software: https://www.tensorflow.org/
2. Badrinarayanan, V., Kendall, A., Cipolla, R.: SegNet: a deep convolutional encoder-decoder architecture for image segmentation. IEEE Trans. Pattern Anal. Mach. Intell. **39**(12), 2481–2495 (2017)
3. Balocco, S., et al.: Standardized evaluation methodology and reference database for evaluating ivus image segmentation. Comput. Med. Imaging Graph. **38**(2), 70–90 (2014)

4. Chen, L.C., Papandreou, G., Kokkinos, I., Murphy, K., Yuille, A.L.: DeepLab: semantic image segmentation with deep convolutional nets, atrous convolution, and fully connected CRFs. arXiv preprint arXiv:1606.00915 (2016)
5. Ciresan, D., Giusti, A., Gambardella, L.M., Schmidhuber, J.: Deep neural networks segment neuronal membranes in electron microscopy images. In: Advances in Neural Information Processing Systems, pp. 2843–2851 (2012)
6. Downe, R., et al.: Segmentation of intravascular ultrasound images using graph search and a novel cost function. In: Proceedings of 2nd MICCAI Workshop on Computer Vision for Intravascular and Intracardiac Imaging, pp. 71–9. Citeseer (2008)
7. Drozdzal, M., Vorontsov, E., Chartrand, G., Kadoury, S., Pal, C.: The importance of skip connections in biomedical image segmentation. In: Carneiro, G., et al. (eds.) LABELS/DLMIA -2016. LNCS, vol. 10008, pp. 179–187. Springer, Cham (2016). https://doi.org/10.1007/978-3-319-46976-8_19
8. Faraji, M., Cheng, I., Naudin, I., Basu, A.: Segmentation of arterial walls in intravascular ultrasound cross-sectional images using extremal region selection. Ultrasonics 84, 356–365 (2018)
9. Faraji, M., Shanbehzadeh, J., Nasrollahi, K., Moeslund, T.B.: EREL: extremal regions of extremum levels. In: 2015 IEEE International Conference on Image Processing (ICIP), pp. 681–685. IEEE (2015)
10. Faraji, M., Shanbehzadeh, J., Nasrollahi, K., Moeslund, T.B.: Extremal regions detection guided by maxima of gradient magnitude. IEEE Trans. Image Process. 24(12), 5401–5415 (2015)
11. He, K., Zhang, X., Ren, S., Sun, J.: Delving deep into rectifiers: surpassing human-level performance on ImageNet classification. In: Proceedings of the IEEE International Conference on Computer Vision, pp. 1026–1034 (2015)
12. He, K., Zhang, X., Ren, S., Sun, J.: Deep residual learning for image recognition. In: Proceedings of the IEEE Conference on Computer Vision and Pattern Recognition, pp. 770–778. IEEE Computer Society (2016)
13. Huang, G., Liu, Z., van der Maaten, L., Weinberger, K.Q.: Densely connected convolutional networks. In: Proceedings of the IEEE Conference on Computer Vision and Pattern Recognition (2017)
14. Kingma, D.P., Ba, J.: Adam: a method for stochastic optimization. arXiv preprint arXiv:1412.6980 (2014)
15. Krizhevsky, A., Sutskever, I., Hinton, G.E.: ImageNet classification with deep convolutional neural networks. In: Advances in Neural Information Processing Systems, pp. 1097–1105 (2012)
16. Long, J., Shelhamer, E., Darrell, T.: Fully convolutional networks for semantic segmentation. In: Proceedings of the IEEE Conference on Computer Vision and Pattern Recognition, pp. 3431–3440 (2015)
17. Mendizabal-Ruiz, E.G., Rivera, M., Kakadiaris, I.A.: Segmentation of the luminal border in intravascular ultrasound b-mode images using a probabilistic approach. Med. Image Anal. 17(6), 649–670 (2013)
18. Mendizabal-Ruiz, G., Kakadiaris, I.A.: A physics-based intravascular ultrasound image reconstruction method for lumen segmentation. Comput. Biol. Med. 75, 19–29 (2016)
19. Peng, C., Zhang, X., Yu, G., Luo, G., Sun, J.: Large kernel matters-improve semantic segmentation by global convolutional network. arXiv preprint arXiv:1703.02719 (2017)
20. Rajpurkar, P., et al.: ChexNet: radiologist-level pneumonia detection on chest x-rays with deep learning. arXiv preprint arXiv:1711.05225 (2017)

21. Ronneberger, O., Fischer, P., Brox, T.: U-Net: convolutional networks for biomedical image segmentation. In: Navab, N., Hornegger, J., Wells, W.M., Frangi, A.F. (eds.) MICCAI 2015. LNCS, vol. 9351, pp. 234–241. Springer, Cham (2015). https://doi.org/10.1007/978-3-319-24574-4_28

22. Simonyan, K., Zisserman, A.: Very deep convolutional networks for large-scale image recognition. In: International Conference on Learning Representations (ICRL), pp. 1–14 (2015)

23. Srivastava, R.K., Greff, K., Schmidhuber, J.: Highway networks. arXiv preprint arXiv:1505.00387 (2015)

24. Szegedy, C., et al.: Going deeper with convolutions. In: Computer Vision and Pattern Recognition (CVPR) (2015)

25. Taki, A., et al.: Automatic segmentation of calcified plaques and vessel borders in IVUS images. Int. J. Comput. Assist. Radiol. Surg. 3(3–4), 347–354 (2008)

26. Unal, G., Bucher, S., Carlier, S., Slabaugh, G., Fang, T., Tanaka, K.: Shape-driven segmentation of the arterial wall in intravascular ultrasound images. IEEE Trans. Inf. Technol. Biomed. 12(3), 335–347 (2008)

27. Xie, S., Girshick, R., Dollár, P., Tu, Z., He, K.: Aggregated residual transformations for deep neural networks. In: 2017 IEEE Conference on Computer Vision and Pattern Recognition (CVPR), pp. 5987–5995. IEEE (2017)

28. Xu, B., Wang, N., Chen, T., Li, M.: Empirical evaluation of rectified activations in convolutional network. arXiv preprint arXiv:1505.00853 (2015)

29. Zhang, C., Bengio, S., Hardt, M., Recht, B., Vinyals, O.: Understanding deep learning requires rethinking generalization. In: International Conference on Learning Representations (ICLR) (2017)

30. Zhu, X., Zhang, P., Shao, J., Cheng, Y., Zhang, Y., Bai, J.: A snake-based method for segmentation of intravascular ultrasound images and its in vivo validation. Ultrasonics 51(2), 181–189 (2011)

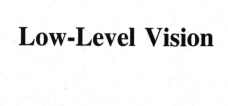

Low-Level Vision

A Simplified Active Calibration Algorithm for Focal Length Estimation

Mehdi Faraji$^{(\boxtimes)}$ and Anup Basu

Department of Computing Science, University of Alberta, Edmonton, Canada
{faraji,basu}@ualberta.ca

Abstract. We introduce new linear mathematical formulations to calculate the focal length of a camera in an active platform. Through mathematical derivations, we show that the focal lengths in each direction can be estimated using only one point correspondence that relates images taken before and after a degenerate rotation of the camera. The new formulations will be beneficial in robotic and dynamic surveillance environments when the camera needs to be calibrated while it freely moves and zooms. By establishing a correspondence between only two images taken after slightly panning and tilting the camera and a reference image, our proposed Simplified Calibration Method is able to calculate the focal length of the camera. We extensively evaluate the derived formulations on a simulated camera, 3D scenes and real-world images. Our error analysis over simulated and real images indicates that the proposed Simplified Active Calibration formulation estimates the parameters of a camera with low error rates.

Keywords: Active Calibration · Self calibration
Simplified Active Calibration · SAC · Pan tilt zoom camera · PTZ

1 Introduction

Many 3D computer vision applications require knowledge of the camera parameters to relate the 3D world to the acquired 2D image(s). The process of estimating the camera parameters is called *camera calibration* in which two groups of parameters (intrinsic and extrinsic) are estimated.

In order to calibrate a camera, conventional calibration methods need to acquire some information from the real 3D world using calibration objects such as grids, wands, or LEDs. This imposes a major limitation on the calibration task since the camera can be calibrated only in off-line and controlled environments. To address this issue, Maybank and Faugeras [1,2] proposed the so-called *self-calibration* approach in which they used the information of matched points in several images taken by the same camera from different views instead of using known 3D points (calibration objects). In their two-step method, they first estimated the epipolar transformation from three pairs of views, and then linked it to the image of an absolute conic using the Kruppa equations [1]. Not long after

© Springer Nature Switzerland AG 2018
A. Basu and S. Berretti (Eds.): ICSM 2018, LNCS 11010, pp. 381–390, 2018.
https://doi.org/10.1007/978-3-030-04375-9_32

the seminal work of Maybank and Faugeras, Basu proposed the idea of Active Calibration [3,4] in which he included the concept of active camera motions and eliminated point-to-point correspondences.

The main downside of the Active Calibration strategies (A and B) in [3–5] is that it calculates the camera intrinsics using a component of the projection equation in which a constraint is imposed by the degenerate rotations. For example, after panning the camera, the equation derived from vertical variations observed in the new image plane is unstable. Furthermore, the small angle approximation using $\sin(\theta) = \theta$ and $\cos(\theta) = 1$ decreases the accuracy of strategies when the angle of rotation is not very small. Also, rolling the camera [6] is impractical (without having a precise mechanical device) because it creates translational offsets in the camera center. In this paper, we propose a Simplified Active Calibration (SAC) formulation in which the equations are closed-form and linear. To overcome the instability caused by using degenerate rotations in Active Calibration, we calculate focal length in each direction separately. In addition, we do not use small angle approximation by replacing $\sin(\theta) = \theta$ and $\cos(\theta) = 1$. Hence, in our formulation we only refer to the elements of the rotation matrix. Moreover, the proposed method is more practical because it does not require a roll rotation of the camera; only pan and tilt rotations, which can be easily acquired using PTZ cameras, are sufficient.

The rest of the paper is organized as follows. In Sect. 2 we present our proposed Simplified Active Calibration formulation. Section 3 reports and analyzes the results of the proposed method on simulated and real scenes. Finally, conclusions are drawn in Sect. 4.

2   Simplified Active Calibration

Simplified Active Calibration (SAC) has been inspired by the novel idea of approximating the camera intrinsics using small angle rotations of the camera which was initially proposed in [3,4] and extended in [5,6]. Imposing three constraints on the translation of the camera generates a pure rotation motion. In addition, using small angle rotations allows us to ignore some non-linear terms in order to estimate the remaining linear parameters. The estimated intrinsics can then be used as an initial guess in the non-linear refinement processes.

In general, SAC can be used in any platform in which information about the camera motion is provided by the hardware, such as in robotic applications where the rotation of the camera can be extracted from the inertial sensors or in the surveillance control softwares that are able to rotate the PTZ cameras by specific angles. Having access to the rotation of the camera, we propose a 2-step process to estimate the focal length of the camera. In the first step, we present a closed-form solution to calculate an approximation of the focal length in the v direction (f_v) using an image taken after a pan rotation of the camera, assuming that v and u represent the two major axes of the image plane. In the second step, we estimate the focal length of the camera in the u direction (f_u) using an image taken after tilt rotation of the camera. Therefore, to estimate the two main components (focal length) of the intrinsic matrix, namely f_v, f_u, two pairs of images are required, one taken before and after a small pan rotation, and another taken before and after a small tilt rotation.

2.1 Focal Length in the V Direction

We assume that the camera is located at the origin of the Cartesian coordinate system and is looking at distance $z = f$ where the principal point is specified. Every 3D point $\mathbf{X} = [X \ Y \ Z]^T$ in the world that is visible to the camera can be projected onto a specific point $\mathbf{u} = [v \ u \ 1]^T$ of the image plane where the coordinates of the principal points are denoted by $[v_0 \ u_0]^T$. With modern cameras it is reasonable to assume that image pixels are square so that the value of the camera skew is zero.

Every point $\mathbf{u} = [v \ u]^T$ in an image seen by a stationary camera (that freely rotates but stays in a fixed location) is transformed to a point $\mathbf{u}' = [v' \ u']^T$ in another image taken after camera rotation. The mathematical relationship between $\mathbf{u}$ and $\mathbf{u}'$ when the camera is panned is denoted by $w\mathbf{u}' = \mathbf{K}\mathbf{R}_y^T\mathbf{K}^{-1}\mathbf{u}$ and after expanding the equation, the relationship is thus represented by:

$$v' = \frac{r_{11}(v - v_0) + r_{31}f_v}{r_{13}\dfrac{v - v_0}{f_v} + r_{33}} + v_0 \tag{1}$$

$$u' = u_0 - \frac{u_0 - u}{r_{13}\dfrac{v - v_0}{f_v} + r_{33}} \tag{2}$$

where r_{ij} is an element of the rotation matrix around Y-axis at row i and column j. After simplification of Eq. 2:

$$\frac{v - v_0}{f_v} = \frac{\dfrac{u_0 - u}{u_0 - u'} - r_{33}}{r_{13}} \tag{3}$$

Note that after a pure pan rotation, the u coordinates of the new image will not be affected by the transformation. (The reader is referred to [7] for a detailed explanation and analysis about this fact.) In other words, image pixels only move horizontally. Thus, the rate of change in the u direction before and after the pan rotation is close to one, viz:

$$\frac{u_0 - u}{u_0 - u'} \approx 1 \tag{4}$$

Substituting Eq. 4 into Eq. 3 and then replacing the equation obtained for the term $\dfrac{v - v_0}{f_v}$ in the Eq. 1, we have:

$$v' \approx \frac{r_{11}(v - v_0) + r_{31}f_v}{r_{13}\dfrac{1 - r_{33}}{r_{13}} + r_{33}} + v_0 \tag{5}$$

The above substitution changes the value of the denominator to 1 and hence simplifies the whole projection equation.

$$v' - r_{11}v \approx r_{31}f_v + (1 - r_{11})v_0 \tag{6}$$

Knowing that the principal point is close to the center of the image ($c_u = h/2, c_v = w/2$), where h and w represent the image height and width respectively, we replace v_0 with c_v in Eq. 6. Thus, we can derive a suitable linear equation to estimate the focal length in the x direction from an image taken after a pan rotation.

$$f_v \approx \frac{v' - r_{11}v - (1 - r_{11})c_v}{r_{31}} \tag{7}$$

Equation 7 needs only one point v in the reference image that corresponds to v' in the transformed image. If there are more point correspondences, we can easily use the average of these points to obtain more robust results.

2.2 Focal Length in the U Direction

So far, we could estimate f_v by the information provided from an image taken after a pan rotation. We repeat the same procedure to approximate f_u. This time, we need an image taken after a pure tilt rotation of the camera. Thus, the projection equation is characterized by replacing $\mathbf{R}$ with the proper rotation matrix that describes rotation of the camera around X-axis. Following the same reasoning as in Sect. 2.1, a closed-form solution to estimate the focal length of the camera in the u direction is obtained by:

$$f_u \approx \frac{r_{22}u - u' + (1 - r_{22})c_u}{r_{32}} \tag{8}$$

3 Results and Analysis

Based on our proposed method, focal length in the v and u directions can be estimated using Eqs. 7 and 8, respectively. Only one point correspondence is required to calculate the focal length. Figure 1 shows the estimated focal lengths using various pan and tilt angles on a 3D synthetic scene of a teapot taken by a simulated camera. It can be seen that when the pan and tilt angles are small, the estimated focal lengths are very close to the ground truth.

In another experiment, we calculate the proposed simplified active calibration formulation on 1000 different runs of 500 randomly generated 3D points for small pan and tilt angles. The mean and standard deviation of the results obtained are shown in Table 1. As we can see, our proposed active calibration formulation attains results very close to the ground truth. Specifically, the error in focal length estimates is less than 1 pixels.

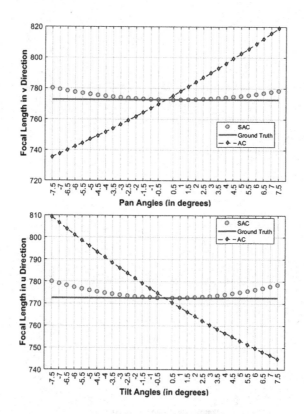

Fig. 1. Focal lengths calculated in the v and u directions using Active Calibration Strategy B (AC)[6] versus SAC for various angles of rotations. In SAC we only use one point correspondence.

Table 1. Results of the proposed simplified active calibration on 1000 separate 3D random points for various small pan and tilt angles. In the table, GT denotes the Ground Truth, SD represents the Standard Deviation. The error values are in pixels.

Pan	Tilt		f_v	f_u
		GT	772.55	772.55
1°	−1°	Mean	772.61	772.76
		SD	0.02	0.09
		Error	0.06	0.21
−1.5°	1.5°	Mean	773.02	772.73
		SD	0.13	0.07
		Error	0.47	0.19

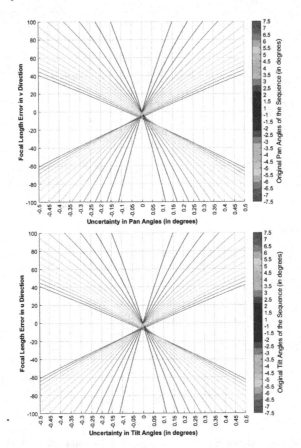

Fig. 2. The error caused by uncertainty in determining the angle of the camera. Top: The effects of the uncertainty of the camera pan rotation on calculating the focal length in the v direction by SAC. Bottom: The effects of the uncertainty of the camera tilt rotation on calculating the focal length in the u direction by SAC.

3.1   Angular Uncertainty

Acquiring the rotation angles requires either specific devices such as gyroscopes or a specially designed camera called a PTZ camera. Even using these devices does not guarantee that the extracted rotation angles are noise-free. To simulate the noisy conditions of a real-world application, we contaminated the angles of the above-mentioned teapot sequences with increasing angular errors.

While the point correspondences are kept fixed for all of the pan and tilt rotations, we calculate the focal length (Eqs. 7 and 8) using contaminated pan and tilt angles. The results are shown in Fig. 2. Specifically, Fig. 2(a) and (b) show the error of our proposed formula for estimating the focal length when the pan and tilt angles are not accurate. Every sequence has been colored based on its rotation angle, ranging from blue indicating smaller angles to red for larger angles. For focal length estimation, Fig. 2(a) and (b) illustrate that the sequences taken with smaller angles have steeper slopes than the sequences acquired with larger rotation angles. This shows that focal lengths are more sensitive to angular noise when the camera is rotated by smaller angles rather than larger angles.

Overall, when the camera is rotated by small angles, the influence of the angular noise on SAC equations is higher. On the other hand, SAC tends to use the benefit of rotating the camera by small angles. Therefore, to avoid magnifying the effect of noise it is important not to rotate the camera by very small angles.

3.2 Point Correspondence Noise

Another type of noise that affects the SAC equations is the noise in the location of features used for matching. To simulate such conditions, we assume that the location of every teapot point is disturbed by a Gaussian noise with zero mean and variance σ_{pixel}. Then, we calibrate the camera using SAC for all σ_{pixel} in the range of 0 to 3. The intrinsic parameters obtained are illustrated in Fig. 3.

Figure 3(a) and (b) illustrate the influence of pixel noise on the estimation of focal length (Eqs. 7 and 8). Colors are distributed based on the rotation angles of the camera and, hence, the distribution of the colors reveals how noise affects the SAC equations. In fact, the high concentration of red, yellow, and orange points around the zero error line in Fig. 3(a) to (b) reveals that when the angle of the camera rotation is not very small, SAC achieves low-error estimates for focal lengths. This corroborates the claim that very small camera rotations can cause results from the SAC formulations to have high error.

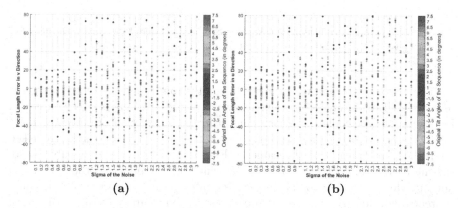

(a)   (b)

Fig. 3. The error caused by uncertainty in location of points. **(a)** Error of the estimated focal length in the v direction using SAC when the location of the teapot points are disturbed by different values of σ_{pixel}. **(b)** Error of the estimated focal length in the u direction using SAC under the same conditions as in (a).

3.3 Real Images

We studied the proposed SAC formulations on real images as well. We used the Canon VC-C50i PTZ camera that is able to freely rotate around Y-axis (pan) and X-axis (tilt). The camera can be controlled by a host computer using a standard RS-232 serial communication. Therefore, the required pan and tilt rotation angles can be set in a specific packet and then be written into the camera serial buffer to rotate the camera based on the assigned rotation angles.

Using the above-mentioned procedure, we captured four sequences of images for evaluating the proposed SAC formulations. Figure 4 shows a sequence of our bookshelf scene. All sequences were taken using a fixed zoom. While keeping the zoom of the camera unchanged, another 30 images were acquired from various viewpoints of a checkerboard pattern. The ground truth of intrinsic parameters were found by applying the method of Zhang [8] on the checkerboard images.

(a)   (b)

Fig. 4. A sequence of real images taken for SAC. **(a)** Image taken after panning the camera by $0.5625°$. **(b)** Image taken after tilting the camera by $-0.675°$.

The performance of SAC formulations on the four sequences of real images is reported in Table 2. For every sequence, we only used the images in the sequence. For example, to calculate the focal length in the v direction of Sequence 1, we found the point correspondence between a reference image and the image taken after the pan rotation of the camera (Fig. 4(a)). Then, we used only one of the matched points that is closer to the center of the image. Although we did not include the lens distortion parameter into the SAC formulation (because it creates non-linear equations), we decrease the inaccuracy of the focal length estimates by using a matched point that is closer to the center of the image and, thus, is less affected by the lens distortion. A similar procedure was adopted with the image taken after a tilt rotation of the camera (Fig. 4(b)) for calculating the focal length in the u direction of Sequence 1.

Table 2. Results of the proposed simplified active calibration on four sequences of real images. All angles are in degrees. $\delta_{f_v}, \delta_{f_u}$ are the percentage errors from the corresponding ground truth acquired by the method of Zhang [8].

#	Pan	Tilt	f_v	f_u	δ_{f_v}	δ_{f_u}
1	0.5625°	−0.675°	880.42	−999.07	15.3	5.33
2	−1.8°	2.025°	1052.1	−966.35	1.18	1.88
3	−4.6125°	−4.1625°	1067.9	−970	2.70	2.26
4	−7.9875°	−7.425°	1069.6	−986.58	2.87	4.01

The errors reported by applying SAC on four different sequences of real images in Table 2 show that despite the presence of various types of noise, such as angular uncertainties, point correspondence noise and lens distortion, focal lengths estimated by SAC are close to the results of the method of Zhang [8], except when the angles of rotations are very small ($< 1°$).

4   Conclusion

Inspired by the idea of calibrating a camera through active movements of the camera, in this paper we presented a Simplified Active Calibration formulation. Our study provides closed-form and linear equations to estimate the parameters of the camera using two image pairs taken before and after panning and tilting the camera.

A basic assumption about the rotation of a fixed camera was made; i.e., to solve the proposed equations, knowing the rotation angles of the camera is necessary. The proposed formulation can be used in practical applications such as surveillance, because in PTZ and mobile phone cameras accessing the camera motion information is straightforward.

The proposed closed-form formulations for estimating the focal lengths can be solved with only one point correspondence. Finding the correspondence point is straightforward. Due to the recent developments in feature extractors, one may use [9,10] to extract repeatable regions from a pair of images. This is especially useful for applications that prefer no point correspondences; where instead of the reference and transfered points in Eqs. 8 and 7, the average of the edge points or the centroid of the regions can be used.

The results of solving our proposed formulations on randomly simulated 3D scenes indicated a very low error rate in estimating the focal lengths. We evaluated our proposed SAC formulation for two different noise conditions, namely angular and pixel noise. The simulated results showed that if the angle of rotation is not very small, the SAC formulation can robustly estimate the focal lengths. This conclusion was later verified in our experiment with real images. Our future work will focus on deriving linear equations for calculating the location of the principal point and also including lens distortion parameters into the Simplified Active Calibration equations.

References

1. Maybank, S.J., Faugeras, O.D.: A theory of self-calibration of a moving camera. Int. J. Comput. Vis. **8**(2), 123–151 (1992)
2. Faugeras, O.D., Luong, Q.-T., Maybank, S.J.: Camera self-calibration: theory and experiments. In: Sandini, G. (ed.) ECCV 1992. LNCS, vol. 588, pp. 321–334. Springer, Heidelberg (1992). https://doi.org/10.1007/3-540-55426-2_37
3. Basu, A.: Active calibration. In: Proceedings of 1993 IEEE International Conference on Robotics and Automation, pp. 764–769. IEEE (1993)
4. Basu, A.: Active calibration: alternative strategy and analysis. In: Proceedings of 1993 IEEE Computer Society Conference on Computer Vision and Pattern Recognition, CVPR 1993, pp. 495–500. IEEE (1993)
5. Basu, A.: Active calibration of cameras: theory and implementation. IEEE Trans. Syst. Man Cybern. **25**(2), 256–265 (1995)
6. Basu, A., Ravi, K.: Active camera calibration using pan, tilt and roll. IEEE Trans. Syst. Man Cybern. Part B (Cybern.) **27**(3), 559–566 (1997)
7. Junejo, I.N., Foroosh, H.: Optimizing PTZ camera calibration from two images. Mach. Vis. Appl. **23**(2), 375–389 (2012)
8. Zhang, Z.: Flexible camera calibration by viewing a plane from unknown orientations. In: The Proceedings of the Seventh IEEE International Conference on Computer Vision, vol. 1, pp. 666–673. IEEE (1999)
9. Faraji, M., Shanbehzadeh, J., Nasrollahi, K., Moeslund, T.B.: Erel: extremal regions of extremum levels. In: 2015 IEEE International Conference on Image Processing (ICIP), pp. 681–685. IEEE (2015)
10. Faraji, M., Shanbehzadeh, J., Nasrollahi, K., Moeslund, T.: Extremal regions detection guided by maxima of gradient magnitude. IEEE Trans. Image Process. **24**, 5401–5415 (2015)

Automatic Computation of Fundamental Matrix Based on Voting

XinSheng Li[1,2] and Xuedong Yuan[1,2(✉)]

[1] College of Computer Science, Sichuan University, ChengDu, China
lixinsheng@scu.edu.cn,yxdongdong@163.com
[2] Key Laboratory of Fundamental Synthetic Vision Graphics and Image
for National Defense, Sichuan University, ChengDu, China

Abstract. To reconstruct point geometry from multiple images, a new method to compute the fundamental matrix is proposed in this paper. This method uses a new selection method for fundamental matrix under the RANSAC (Random Sample And Consensus) framework. It makes good use of some low quality fundamental matrices to fuse a better quality fundamental matrix. At first, some fundamental matrices are computed as candidates in a few iterations. Then some of the best candidates are chosen based on voting the epipoles of their fundamental matrices to fuse a better fundamental matrix. The fusion can be simple mean or weighted summation of fundamental matrices from the first step. This selection method leads to better result such as more inliers or less projective errors. Our experiments prove and validate this new method of composed fundamental matrix computation.

Keywords: Fundamental matrix · Vote · Fusion · RANSAC

1 Introduction

Now there is more and more demand for 3D models in computer graphics, virtual reality and communication. Much progress of multi-view stereo (MVS) algorithms with a surge of interest has been made in recent years, both in terms of precision and in terms of performance. Fundamental matrix F computation is a basic problem in multi-view geometry to reconstruct the 3D scenario.

Usually eight-point method (8-point), seven-point method (7-point), five-point method (5-point) and golden distance method [2] are all based on the RANSAC (RANdom Sample And Consensus) framework. All of them can have very accurate result if the picture quality and feature matching are good enough. The Sampling method is based on the distance from feature points to the epipolar lines. All the epipolar lines cross the same one point, epipole. This is the epipolar theory.

The RANSAC framework is also used to compute fundamental matrix F like most of the other ordinary algorithms. New computation method for F is proposed, which votes and fuses of multiple reasonable F rather than only

© Springer Nature Switzerland AG 2018
A. Basu and S. Berretti (Eds.): ICSM 2018, LNCS 11010, pp. 391–396, 2018.
https://doi.org/10.1007/978-3-030-04375-9_33

depending on projective distance from pixel to its epipolar line in projective space. This modification improves the quality of F which most of time has more inliers or less average distance to epipolar lines.

2   Previous Research

Lots of works have been done on fundamental matrix computation in the past 30 years, like 8-point method, 7-point method, 5-point method and golden distance method. This is a well developed area in computer vision. Some traditional methods have very good result which means very low projective errors to the epipolar lines. But there still are some papers published every year on computing fundamental matrix in computer vision.

The 5-point method finds the possible solutions for relative camera pose between two calibrated views if five corresponding points are given. The algorithm consists of computing the coefficients of a tenth degree polynomial in closed form and subsequently finding its roots. Kukelova et al. [3] proposed polynomial eigenvalue solutions to the 5-point and 6-point relative pose problems, which can be solved using standard efficient numerical algorithms. It is somewhat more stable than solutions by Nister [5,6] and Stewenius [7].

Even two-point fundamental matrix method [1] was proposed. It makes use of the epipolar theory to estimate the fundamental matrix based on three corresponding epipolar lines instead of seven or eight corresponding points.

3   Algorithm Overview

The input data of our algorithm is two photographs of a scene to be reconstructed, which are taken with a hand-held camera having fixed focal length.

3.1 F Computation in Multi-view Geometry

The most basic F computation is based on the linear equations

$$Af = 0 \tag{1}$$

where

$$f = \begin{bmatrix} F_{11} & F_{12} & F_{13} & F_{21} & F_{22} & F_{23} & F_{31} & F_{32} & F_{33} \end{bmatrix}^T \tag{2}$$

$$A = \begin{bmatrix} x'_1 x_1 & x'_1 y_1 & x'_1 & y'_1 x_1 & y'_1 y_1 & y'_1 & x_1 & y_1 & 1 \\ x'_2 x_2 & x'_2 y_2 & x'_2 & y'_2 x_2 & y'_2 y_2 & y'_2 & x_2 & y_2 & 1 \\ \vdots & \vdots & \vdots & \vdots & \vdots & \vdots & \vdots & \vdots & \vdots \\ x'_n x_n & x'_n y_n & x'_n & y'_n x_n & y'_n y_n & y'_n & x_n & y_n & 1 \end{bmatrix} \tag{3}$$

Here $u = [x \ y \ 1]^T$ and $u' = [x' \ y' \ 1]^T$ are the coordinates of the matching features on 2-view images. It is usually called 8-point method because at least 8 matching point pairs are needed to determine this equation.

If constraint $\det(F) = 0$ is added to Eq. 1, only 7 matching pairs are necessary to solve the equation. So this is usually called 7-point method [2]. With more constraints being added in Eq. 1, less matching pairs are indispensable. In the extreme occasion as mentioned in Sect. 2, only two matching pairs are needed [1].

Most of the time RANSAC robust estimation is widely used because error on matching pixels coordinates of real image exists and RANSAC can remove or reduce the error on matching. For example, automatic feature matching methods such as SIFT, SURF etc. always has some wrong matchings. Otherwise, the precision of features coordinates sometimes is not high enough because camera distortion or objects occlusion on image. The steps of the RANSAC framework are as follows.

1. Normalize the matching point coordinates by Ref. [2].
2. Repeat for N samples:
   (a) Select a random sample of 8 correspondences and compute the fundamental matrix F as Eq. 1.
   (b) Calculate the distance d from feature pixel to epipolar line for each putative correspondence.
   (c) Compute the number of inliers consistent with F by the number of correspondences for which $d < T$ pixels. T is the threshold which is a constant.
3. Finally, choose the F with the largest number of inliers.

3.2 F by Voting

A voting method to calculate the fundamental matrix F is proposed. Its steps are as follows:

1. Calculate F_i by traditional 8-point method in RANSAC framework in ith iteration and record it in the memory.
2. Adjust F_i to satisfy $\det(F_i) = 0$. Usually, the result of 8-point method is $\det(F_i) \neq 0$. let $F_i = UDV^T$ be the SVD of F_i, where D is a diagonal matrix. After replace the least eigen value of F_i in D with 0, which means $F_i = U diag(r, s, 0) V^T$. r, s is the other two bigger eigen values. Now F_i is $\det(F_i) = 0$ after adjustment.
3. Compute corresponding epipole of F_i. It is the null space of F_i which is denoted as $Null(F_i)$.
4. Iterate the up three steps 1) to 3) n_I times. Then we have n_I F_i matrices.
5. Choose the best n_F $Null(F_i)$s or top 25% of $Null(F_i)$ based on projective distance to epipolar line. Here best $Null(F_i)$ is determined by the least average distance to the epipolar lines.
6. Average these n_F amount of F_i as the final F. Or summarize n_F F_i by designed weights as the final F.

The Step 2 can be omitted if we adjust the final F to $det(F) = 0$ after the last step. Even if we do not adjust the final F, reasonable results can still be achieved sometimes. This result always has less inliers or bigger average distance error to epipolar lines because constraint $det(F) = 0$ limits the solution space of F.

In addition to the above, weighted summarization is applied to this our method as a further fusion based enhancement. The weight of F_i depends on the distance from epipole to the mass center of all epipoles of n_F F_i candidates. Smaller distance has bigger weight for fusion.

4   Experiment

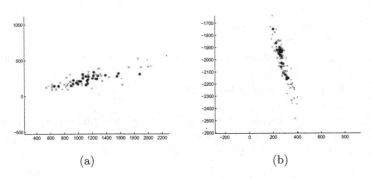

(a)   (b)

Fig. 1. The epipoles of three different scenarios from voting method. (a) Kitchen (b) Lion. The symbols represent that black asterisk ranking top 25%, red x ranking best 25%~50%, blue dot ranking best 50%~75%, green cross ranking last 75%~100%. Most of the best 25% epipoles (black asterisk) locate nearer to center of mass center of all epipoles than the rest worse 75% epipoles. (Color online figure)

Figure 1 shows three typical results for algorithm in Sect. 3.2 for images from datasets Kitchen and Lion. The best 25% epipoles (black asterisk) locate nearer to center of mass center of all epipoles than the rest worse 75% epipoles. This phenomenon proves epipoles can be used to judge the quality of F. Of course $det(F) = 0$ is enforced for our voting method here.

Figure 2 is part of the typical feature pixels and their corresponding epipolar lines. The features denoted as green cross are produced by SIFT [4]. As we can see, the pixels are close enough to the epipolar lines. It validates this voting method.

Table 1 compares performances of different methods 8-point [2], 7-point [2], 5-point [3] and our voting method (VM). Two rows represent three scenarios Kitchen and Lion scenario. The numbers in the brackets are the inlier numbers for each method. 5-point method is based on the 3D metric distance which is re-projection errors projecting X to $[u, u']$ rather than the distance to epipolar line because it recovers the 3D metric scene of X.

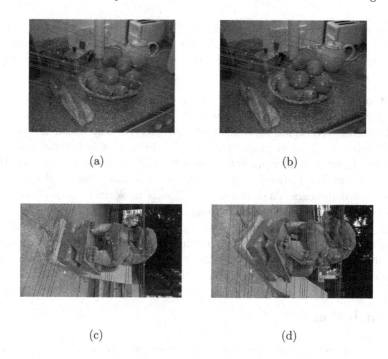

Fig. 2. The epipolar lines and their feature pixels.

Table 1. Method performance compare for three scenario

Scenario	Feature number	8-point	7-point	5-point	VM
Kitchen	716	0.22 (682)	1.16 (194)	2.05(201)	0.49(715)
Lion	445	0.01 (395)	0.45 (203)	2.12(371)	0.5(382)

As we can see in Table 1, different methods have different performance. 8-point method has very small epipolar distance which seems 8-point is the best method. But 8-point does not satisfy $\det(F) = 0$. This is not a good property. 7-point method results in longer epipolar distance for Kitchen and smaller number of inliers especially for Kitchen and Lion. 5-point has very large re-projection distance from X to $[u, u']$ and the inliers are less than the 8-point and VM methods. It does not mean this method is bad because it recovers the essential matrix $E = K'^T F K$ where K is the intrinsic matrix of camera. E reconstructs the 3D metric space of X. For our voting method (VM), it almost has comparatively more inliers and short average distance to epipolar line. That is the advantage of our voting scheme under RANSAC.

About $\det(\mathbf{F}) = \mathbf{0}$. In our experiment, this is a useful and necessary but a weak constraint. It is useful because it adds one equation to reduce one point pair input. It is useful because epipole has to be within this constraint. It is weak because it affects the result very much. Most of time without this constraint, the better projective error or average epipolar lines distance are achieved although this does not mean it will result in better 3D construction result. When this constraint is applied to the algorithm, an advantage is to compute the epipoles on corresponding images.

Weight of F_i. When iterations are run n_I times, n_I fundamental matrices F_i are worked out. To make good use of them we need to set appropriate weights for different F_i. Averaging F_i is a simple and effective way which uses every F_i evenly. Giving F_i of lower projective error higher weight is another reasonable way. When F_i with smaller projective error is weighted more, the final synthetic F will have smaller projective error too, but less inliers are included in the final correct matchings. And vice versa. This is reasonable because the small projective error weeds out the matchings with big error. Or weighing F_i by the distance from epipole to the mass center of all epipoles of n_F F_i candidates is reasonable too. F_i with smaller distance has bigger weight. In our experiment, these three ways of weighting have similar or slightly different performance. So average of all candidates F_i is applied in this paper.

5   Conclusion

We have proposed a novel framework for the fundamental matrix computation problem. Experimental results show that our voting scheme has good result for different data compared with other methods such as 8-point, 7-point and 5-point method. In future work, we would like to explore theoretical proof to provide stronger evidence to support our voting framework.

References

1. Ben-Artzi, G., Halperin, T., Werman, M., Peleg, S.: Two points fundamental matrix. arXiv preprint arXiv:1604.04848, April 2016
2. Hartley, R., Zisserman, A.: Multiple View Geometry in Computer Vision. Cambridge University Press, Cambridge (2003)
3. Kukelova, Z., Bujnak, M., Pajdla, T.: Polynomial eigenvalue solutions to the 5-pt and 6-pt relative pose problems, pp. 1–10 (2008)
4. Lowe, D.G.: Distinctive image features from scale-invariant keypoints. Int. J. Comput. Vis. 60(2), 91–110 (2004)
5. Nister, D.: An efficient solution to the five-point relative pose problem. IEEE Trans. Pattern Anal. Mach. Intell. 26(6), 756–777 (2004)
6. Nister, D., Hartley, R.I., Henrik, S.: Using Galois theory to prove structure from motion algorithms are optimal. In: 2013 IEEE Conference on Computer Vision and Pattern Recognition (CVPR), pp. 1–8. IEEE (2007)
7. Stewenius, H., Engels, C., Nistèr, D.: Recent developments on direct relative orientation. ISPRS J. Photogramm. Remote Sens. 60(4), 284–294 (2006)

Adapting Texture Compression to Perceptual Quality Metric for Textured 3D Models

Navaneeth Kamballur Kottayil[1](✉), Irene Cheng[1](✉),
Kumaradevan Punithakumar[2](✉), and Anup Basu[1](✉)

[1] Multimedia Research Center, University of Alberta, Edmonton, AB, Canada
{kamballu,locheng,basu}@ualberta.ca
[2] Department of Radiology and Diagnostic Imaging, University of Alberta,
Edmonton, AB, Canada
punithak@ualberta.ca
http://crome.cs.ualberta.ca/mrc/
https://sites.ualberta.ca/punithak/

Abstract. 3D textured models are an integral part of modern computer graphics. The geometry of these models is represented by a 3D polygonal mesh and the textures by 2D images. 3D textured models occupy more storage space than conventional images, since we need to store both the mesh and the texture. Thus, they can be expensive to store and transmit. One way to reduce these costs is to compress the mesh and texture in 3D models. Compression invariably leads to the loss of visual quality. Therefore, a method for objectively measuring the perceived loss in visual quality is important. There are studies that can mathematically model the perceptual impact of 3D mesh compression. However, there are only a few studies on the perceptual impact of texture compression. In this paper, we perform a subjective experiment to measure the perceived loss of quality of a 3D model caused by JPEG compression of the model's texture. We propose a simple modeling function that can determine the perceived quality of a 3D model with JPEG compressed texture.

1 Introduction

3D graphics is an integral part of modern multimedia with applications in various areas, including video games, medical data transmission, and virtual reality. 3D models are a fundamental part of 3D computer graphics. The most common method to represent the 3D model is by using a triangular mesh to describe the 3D geometry and one or more 2D images to represent the texture. We will be referring to 3D models used in graphics represented this way as *tex-mesh* in this paper.

With the recent push towards cloud storage and interactive 3D graphics, a significant part of the information exchange is happening over the Internet. The information in 3D graphics consists mainly of tex-meshes. Given the limited

© Springer Nature Switzerland AG 2018
A. Basu and S. Berretti (Eds.): ICSM 2018, LNCS 11010, pp. 397–405, 2018.
https://doi.org/10.1007/978-3-030-04375-9_34

bandwidth and a high amount of tex-mesh data to be transmitted, there is a significant drop in transfer speed, and hence, the quality of user interaction with a graphics application can become unacceptably slow. One way to increase the speed is to compress the data, which leads to loss in perceived quality. This in turn leads to a bad quality of experience for the user. Thus, it is extremely important to find a tradeoff between compression and perceived quality. Such a trade-off requires a model that can predict the perceived quality of a tex-mesh at a given compression level.

A popular method for increasing the efficiency in the representation of multimedia data, that is meant to be perceived by the human visual system (HVS), is to remove perceptually irrelevant information. Identification of perceptually irrelevant information requires subjective studies, where user opinion about quality is collected. Since this is not feasible in every situation, a perceptual quality model can be used to mimic the HVS. Perceptual quality models analyze a given tex-mesh and give a score or rating to the quality of the tex-mesh that would be similar to what a human would score or rate. The literature is rich with studies that model the perceptual quality of 3D meshes (without texture). However, the texture is an important part of the tex-mesh representation, as it contributes to the visual appeal of a model as well as act as a mask to hide some geometric imperfections in the mesh. Despite its importance, there is insufficient amount of research that deals with perceptual effects of texture on tex-mesh. [5] is one of the only study that, took both texture and geometry into account while estimating the quality. The method attempts to fit a curve that satisfies the observed quality levels under different texture and mesh resolutions. The model was a global approach and is very fast as it does not require complex calculations. This approach is useful in controlling the perceptual quality during transmission given limited bandwidth. This model is however restricted to the effect of texture resolutions. The effect of compression is an area where more research needs to be done. Our goal is to understand and model the perceptual quality resulting from texture compression. In principle, there is a possibility that this can make the tex-mesh storage and transmission pipeline more efficient.

In this paper we study the effects of JPEG compression of the texture on the perceived quality of a tex-mesh. We do this by a subjective experiment. After collecting observations based on ratings, we model these observations using parametric mathematical functions.

2   Motivation

Most tex-mesh representations make use of uncompressed texture formats for the sake of preserving quality. Hence, most applications have large texture sizes consuming requiring large file size and bandwidth during transmission. A good analysis of what texture resolution to use vs. quality of the mesh given a limited bandwidth is given in [5]. The study, however, did not look into the impact of texture compression.

JPEG is one of the most popular image compression methods to date and is widely used. Most applications involving subjective judgments on quality use a fixed compression ratio that is heuristically decided. For JPEG, the compression ratio is decided by the Q factor used for compression of the images. There are however no guidelines on how to select this Q factor. Determining the ideal compression could be greatly beneficial towards transmission and optimization of 3D models.

One could argue for the use of 2D image metrics for evaluation like the [7], [3] or [4] to assess the quality of texture in tex-mesh. This question was investigated by [6]. The authors conducted perceptual experiments with an animated 3D mesh and a still picture of a 3D mesh without any interaction. The users were asked to give quality scores based on the degree of simplification and considering different lighting conditions. Based on the fact that there was no conclusive relationship between the scores for still images and animated meshes, the paper concludes that 3D geometry quality cannot be assessed by image quality assessment methods.

We found no other studies exploring the effect of texture compression on 3D meshes though there are many unsolved research problems in this area.

3   Experimental Setup

Perceptual experiments were conducted with a rating based subjective experiments on a custom interface. The design and details of the experiments are described in this section.

3.1   Design Considerations

Number of references: Providing a reference to subjects while taking opinion scores allows precise control of the variable we want to study (in this case texture compression). Additionally, in studies like ours, self-consistency of results between the subjects are extremely important. The importance and positive results of these factors are shown in [5] and analysis can be found in [1]. Providing a reference allows the subjects to set an internal scale for the range of distortions. This helps them to assess the range of distortions in the experiments and hence helps in improving self-consistency.

3.2   Interface

The interface developed for the study shows the users three different models. The leftmost model is the model with the maximum amount of texture compression (Q factor 1), the rightmost is the best texture quality possible (Q factor 100) and the middle is a model with variable texture quality. The user can interact with the model by using the mouse. The interactions allowed are rotation and scaling of the models. These interactions are synchronized for all of the three models displayed. The ratings on the interface allows recording the user opinions. The ratings are labeled with adjectives: "Bad", "Poor", "Fair", "Good", and "Excellent". This translates to a rating score in the range [0,5]. The interface

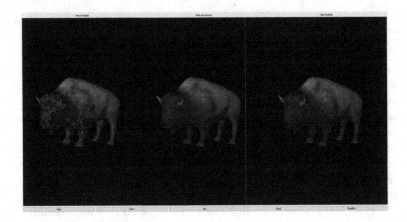

Fig. 1. Screen shot of the interface used for rating based experiment.

is blanked after a time limit of 30 s. The user can rate during this period, but cannot see the model (Fig. 1).

Selection of the Next Model. Upon selection of a rating, the interface selects the next model pseudo-randomly. This goes against the conventional practice of a purely random selection. However, we found that a random selection gives highly skewed results with few models having very few user responses. To ensure that we have a uniform number of user responses for each quality we follow an alternate procedure. Until we obtain a minimum number of user response per model, we maintain a pool of models that do not have enough user responses. We then randomly select from the models in the pool and display it for a subjective rating. Once a model has enough number of responses, the model is removed from the pool. Once we ensure that all the models have a minimum number of responses, we select models whose response have larger variance by using the same model pool based method above. This ensures that the models where there is a large variance in user score are examined by a greater number of users; hence reducing the error.

3.3   Experimental Conditions

The subjective experiments were performed with the interface displayed on an AOC 27 inch screen with factory color calibration. The subjects viewed the screen at a distance of approximately 70 cm. The subjects had 30 s to make a decision. The computer used to perform the experiments had an i7 processor with 16 GB RAM and Nvidia GTX660 GPU.

3.4   Stimuli Generation

We select from a total of 6 models. The visualization of the models are shown in Fig. 2. The details of models used are provided in Table 1. We limit the resolution of the model to a width of 480 pixels.

Table 1. Details of 3D models used for psychovisual experiment.

Model	#Vertex	#Texture shape	File size	
			Mesh	Texture
Apple	6738	480 × 480	1.04 MB	184 KB
Bison	3821	480 × 480	883 KB	188 KB
Dwarf	6167	480 × 480	1.12 MB	188 KB
House plant	6608	480 × 480	58 KB	61 KB
Treasure chest	6792	960 × 480	43 KB	294 KB
Barrell	42284	480 × 480	7.03 MB	100 KB

3.5 Experiments

Each subject was initially briefed about the purpose of the study and informed about the reference models, time limits and mode of interaction in a short demonstration session. The subjects were then asked to rate the center model on the scale of the interface. Each user is asked to rate 30 times.

We chose from a set of 6 different models with 6 levels of texture compression (Q factors 1, 20, 40, 60, 80, 100) giving us 36 textured models to assess subjectively.

Fig. 2. Visualization of models used in experiment.

4 Mathematical Modeling

An initial assessment of the data was done by analyzing the average user rating for each Q factor. The plots of the average user rating collected from 9 subjects are shown in Fig. 3. From the figure, we obtain an average score that is monotonically increasing with the Q factor; consistent with the general intuitions on the effect of compressed texture on quality.

To model our results mathematically, we started with the results by [5]. We refer to this as a *generic tex-mesh model* from now on. The generic tex-mesh model can be summarized by Eq. 2. The model describes the perceived quality of a tex-mesh with normalized variables for texture and geometry level. Since our texture resolution and the range of quality levels are normalized in a fixed range, we can model the overall effect of texture compression by modulating the texture variable t in the generic tex-mesh model.

Outlier Detection. Detection and removal of outliers was performed by using the modified z score method proposed in [2] because of its robustness. We follow the recommendations of the paper and remove the points above $M_i > 3.5$.

$$M_i = 0.6745\frac{x_i - \tilde{x}}{MAD} \tag{1}$$

where x_i represents the ith user score for a particular Q factor, $\tilde{x}$ represents the median of the user scores and MAD represents the median absolute deviation. This is repeated for every Q factor.

4.1   Analysis

After outlier removal, we can see the effect of compression on quality by looking at the average quality score for each compression level. On this data, we can fit a generic log function of the form $y = a * log(b + cx)$ where x is the Q factor and a, b, c are the parameters of the fitting. The motivation for this stems from the fact that generally the quality drops observed in 2D image compression follow this trend. The results are shown in Fig. 3. Similar to observations of texture resolution in previous studies, here also we find that till a certain compression level, we have an extremely small drop in quality. Hence we verify that, the transmission of data with high Q factor leads to wasteful utilization of the bandwidth.

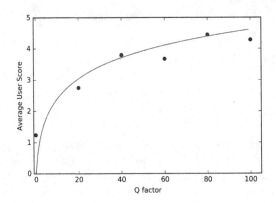

Fig. 3. Change in perceived quality for each Q factor.

From the generic tex-mesh model we have the perceived quality Q for a model with geometry level g and texture resolution t as:

$$Q(g,t) = \frac{1}{\frac{1}{m+(M-m)t} + (\frac{1}{m} - \frac{1}{m+(M-m)t})(1-g)^c)} \tag{2}$$

where m and M are the minimum and maximum bounds of quality, g and t are graphical and texture components scaled into a [0,1] interval, and c is a constant.

Our observations of texture compression can be integrated into generic tex-mesh model by substituting t with $\tilde{t}$ described by Eq. 3.

$$\tilde{t} = t * (a'log(cx + b))$$

$$a' = \frac{a}{5} \tag{3}$$

We can determine a, b, c from the data we have from our experiment. From our results, we found the values of a, b, c is 1.02, 1.13 and 1.08 respectively. We multiply a by $\frac{1}{5}$ to scale the data in the same range of original experiment.

Information about the file size of the texture also provides the same information as above, albeit in a different form.

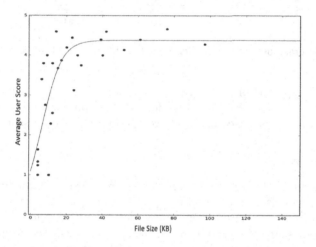

Fig. 4. Change in perceived quality for different texture file sizes.

As stated earlier, in our experiment we standardize the texture dimensions for controlling the number of unknown variables in the experiment. Hence, we find that the overall texture sizes are generally similar (refer to Table 1). The scatter plot of the image file sizes (which is actually impacting the bandwidth usage) against subjective rating is shown in Fig. 4. These observations are similar to the observations on mesh resolution in the generic tex-mesh model, i.e., we see a saturation of perceived quality after a certain file size. Similar to the mesh quality in [5], we can fit a curve of the form $y = \frac{a}{b - exp(cx)}$ with parameters a, b, c. The upper limit would be M as described in the original paper. From our results, we found the values of a, b, c is 1.08, 0.24 and 0.19 respectively.

The result can be integrated into generic tex-mesh model by substituting t with $\tilde{t}$ described by Eq. 4.

$$\tilde{t} = t * \frac{a'}{b - exp(cx)}$$

$$a' = \frac{a}{5}$$

(4)

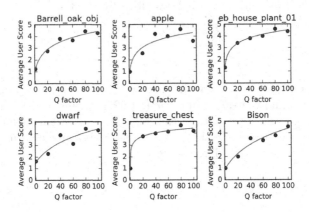

Fig. 5. Average user score for each model at different levels of compression.

We can use spearmann rank order correlation (SRCC) to compare the performance of our system. A larger value for SRCC implies a better performance. When using the values based on Eq. 3, we obtain a correlation score of 0.849.

4.2 Future Work

Further insights can be obtained when curves are fitted individually on ratings of each of the models with different compression factors. The results of this step are shown in Fig. 5. An interesting observation here is that for certain models where the models are animate (alive), we find that the decrease in quality is more linear. This opens up the possibility of the model content influencing the rate at which the global texture quality deteriorates. This, however, is beyond the scope of this paper and will be pursued in future work. In addition, we will extend our current quality metric by incorporating mesh compression and simplification.

5   Conclusion

In this paper, we study the effects of JPEG texture compression on the perceived quality of a textured 3D model. We performed a rating based subjective experiment to measure human responses to degradation in texture caused by JPEG compression. We found that the user responses can be related to the Q factor and texture file sizes by Eqs. 3 and 4. We then integrated our results into an existing model by [5].

References

1. Guilford, J.P.: Psychometric methods (1954)
2. Iglewicz, B., Hoaglin, D.C.: How to Detect and Handle Outliers, ASQC Basic References in Quality Control. American Society for Quality Control, Milwaukee (1993)
3. Larson, E.C., Chandler, D.M.: Most apparent distortion: a dual strategy for full-reference image quality assessment. In: Proceedings of SPIE, vol. 7242, pp. 72,420S–72,420S–17 (2009)
4. Mittal, A., Soundararajan, R., Bovik, A.C.: Making a "completely blind" image quality analyzer. Sig. Process. Lett. IEEE **20**(3), 209–212 (2013)
5. Pan, Y., Cheng, I., Basu, A.: Quality metric for approximating subjective evaluation of 3-D objects. Trans. Multimedia **7**(2), 269–279 (2005). https://doi.org/10.1109/TMM.2005.843364
6. Rogowitz, B.E., Rushmeier, H.E.: Are image quality metrics adequate to evaluate the quality of geometric objects? vol. 4299, pp. 340–348 (2001). https://doi.org/10.1117/12.429504
7. Zhang, L., Zhang, D., Mou, X., Zhang, D.: FSIM: a feature similarity index for image quality assessment. IEEE Trans. Image Process. **20**(8), 2378–2386 (2011). https://doi.org/10.1109/TIP.2011.2109730

A Novel Data Clustering Method Based on Smooth Non-negative Matrix Factorization

Chengcai Leng[1,2,3(✉)], Hai Zhang[1,4], and Guorong Cai[5]

[1] School of Mathematics, Northwest University, Xi'an 710127, China
zhanghai@nwu.edu.cn
[2] Department of Computing Science, University of Alberta, Edmonton,
AB T6G 2E8, Canada
chengcai@ualberta.ca
[3] School of Mathematics and Information Sciences,
Nanchang Hangkong University, Nanchang 330063, China
[4] Faculty of Information Technology, State Key Laboratory of Quality Research
in Chinese Medicines, Macau University of Science and Technology, Macau,
People's Republic of China
[5] College of Computer Engineering, Jimei University, Xiamen 361021, China

Abstract. Non-negative matrix factorization (NMF) is a very popular dimensionality reduction method that has been widely used in computer vision and data clustering. However, NMF does not consider the intrinsic geometric information of a data set and also does not produce smooth and stable solutions. To resolve these problems, we propose a Graph regularized Lp Smooth Non-negative Matrix Factorization (GSNMF) method by incorporating graph regularization with Lp smooth constraint. The graph regularization can discover the hidden semantics and simultaneously respect the intrinsic geometric structure information of a data set. The Lp smooth constraint can combine the merits of isotropic (L_2-norm) and anisotropic (L_1-norm) diffusion smoothing, and produce a smooth and more accurate solution to the optimization problem. Experimental results on some data sets demonstrate that the proposed method outperforms related state-of-the-art NMF methods.

Keywords: Graph regularization
Smooth Non-negative Matrix Factorization (SNMF) · Data clustering

1 Introduction

Low-rank matrix factorization has become an increasingly popular data analysis method in computer vision [1], data clustering [2, 3], hyperspectral unmixing (HU) [4, 5] and high-dimensional data analysis [6]. Most of the dimensionality reduction methods such as Principal Component Analysis (PCA), ISOMAP [7], Locally Linear Embedding (LLE) [8], Laplacian Eigenmap [9], Isometric Projection [10] and Path-Based Isometric Mapping [11], usually allow both the basis vector and reconstruction coefficients to contain negative values [3]. In practical applications, some types of real-world data such as images and audios are usually non-negative. Therefore, there is a new paradigm of factorization, i.e., Non-negative Matrix Factorization (NMF) that

© Springer Nature Switzerland AG 2018
A. Basu and S. Berretti (Eds.): ICSM 2018, LNCS 11010, pp. 406–414, 2018.
https://doi.org/10.1007/978-3-030-04375-9_35

differs completely from the above dimensionality reduction methods, which incorporates the non-negativity constraint and thus obtains the parts-based representation by only allowing additive, and not subtractive combinations; as well as enhancing the interpretability [12].

NMF is a parts-based representation method proposed by Lee and Seung [13] by exploiting the non-negativity property. NMF has been successfully used in many fields such as data clustering [2, 14] and image or data analysis [15, 16]. Recently, many researchers have proposed different forms of NMF models by incorporating additional constraints into the original NMF. In order to exploit the manifold property, Cai et al. [17] proposed a graph regularized NMF (GNMF) method which can discover the intrinsic geometric structure information of the scatter of data points. Liu et al. [18] used the label information as an additional hard constraint and proposed a constrained NMF method; the central idea of this method is that the data points from the same class should be merged together in the new representation space.

In order to produce a smooth and more accurate solution, and discover the intrinsic geometric structure information of a data set, we propose the Graph regularized Lp Smooth Non-negative Matrix Factorization (GSNMF) method by incorporating graph regularization and an Lp smooth constraint. The proposed method not only discovers the hidden semantics and simultaneously respects the intrinsic geometric structure information of a data set, but it can also fully retain a smooth and more accurate solution of the optimization problem. We provide the corresponding update rules. Experimental results on data sets demonstrate that the proposed method outperforms related state-of-the-art NMF methods.

The rest of this paper is organized as follows. Section 2 introduces some related work. We propose the GSNMF method including multiplicative updating rules in Sect. 3. Section 4 reports experiment results, before we draw the conclusions in Sect. 5.

2   Related Work

NMF is a powerful and special parts-based method for low-dimensional data representation. NMF aims to find two non-negative matrices $W \in R^{m \times r}$ and $H \in R^{r \times n}$ that provide a good approximation to the original data matrix V, i.e., $V \in R^{m \times n}$, where each column of V is an m-dimensional data point, and the objective function is given as follows:

$$O_{NMF} = \|V - WH\|_F^2 \text{ s.t.} W \geq 0, H \geq 0 \tag{1}$$

where $\| \cdot \|_F$ denotes the Frobenius norm.

The objective function in Eq. (1) is convex in W only or H only, but it is not convex in both variables W and H. The objective function in Eq. (1) can be optimized by the multiplicative update rules as follows [19]:

$$W_{ik} \leftarrow W_{ik} \frac{(VH^T)_{ik}}{(WHH^T)_{ik}} \tag{2}$$

$$H_{kj} \leftarrow H_{kj} \frac{(W^T V)_{kj}}{(W^T WH)_{kj}} \tag{3}$$

The objective function in Eq. (1) is non-increasing, as proved by Lee and Seung [19] under the above multiplicative update rules proposed in Eqs. (2) and (3).

3 Graph Regularized *Lp* Smooth Non-negative Matrix Factorization

3.1 The Objective Function

Based on graph regularization and the *Lp* smooth constraint, the proposed GSNMF model is given as follows:

$$O_{GSNMF} = \|V - WH\|_F^2 + \lambda \mathrm{Tr}(HLH^T) + 2\mu\|W\|^p \quad s.t. W \geq 0, H \geq 0 \tag{4}$$

where $1 < p < 2$, λ and μ are the positive regularization parameters balancing the reconstruction error in Eq. (4) in the first term. With graph regularization being represented in the second term and smooth regularization represented in the third term. The term $Tr(\cdot)$ denotes the trace of a matrix and $L = D - S$ is a Laplacian matrix characterizing the data manifold, S is a weight matrix that measures the similarities among data samples [1] and D is a diagonal matrix with column sums of S as its diagonal entries, i.e., $D_{ii} = \sum_{j=1}^{n} S_{ij}$ [20].

3.2 Multiplicative Update Rules

The objective function in Eq. (4) is minimized with respect to W and H, and we can find an iterative update algorithm to obtain a locally optimal solution, which can be rewritten as:

$$\begin{aligned} O_{GSNMF} &= \mathrm{Tr}\big((V - WH)(V - WH)^T\big) + \lambda \mathrm{Tr}(HLH^T) + 2\mu\|W\|^p \\ &= \mathrm{Tr}(VV^T) - 2\mathrm{Tr}(VH^T W^T) + \mathrm{Tr}(WHH^T W^T) \\ &\quad + \lambda \mathrm{Tr}(HLH^T) + 2\mu\|W\|^p \end{aligned} \tag{5}$$

We use the Lagrange multiplier φ_{ik} and ϕ_{kj} for constraint $w_{ik} \geq 0$ and $h_{kj} \geq 0$ respectively, with $\Psi = [\varphi_{ik}]$ and $\Phi = [\phi_{kj}]$. The Lagrange function L can be rewritten as:

$$\begin{aligned} L &= \mathrm{Tr}(VV^T) - 2\mathrm{Tr}(VH^T W^T) + \mathrm{Tr}(WHH^T W^T) + \lambda \mathrm{Tr}(HLH^T) \\ &\quad + 2\mu\|W\|^p + \mathrm{Tr}(\Psi W^T) + \mathrm{Tr}(\Phi H) \end{aligned} \tag{6}$$

The partial derivatives of L with respect to W and H are given by:

$$\frac{\partial L}{\partial W} = -2VH^T + 2WHH^T + 2\mu p W^{p-1} + \Psi \tag{7}$$

$$\frac{\partial L}{\partial H} = -2W^T V + 2W^T WH + 2\lambda HL + \Phi^T \tag{8}$$

Using the Karush-Kuhn-Tucker (KKT) condition $\varphi_{ik} w_{ik} = 0$ and $\phi_{kj} h_{kj} = 0$, we get the following equations for w_{ik} and h_{kj}:

$$-(VH^T)_{ik} w_{ik} + (WHH^T)_{ik} w_{ik} + \mu p (W^{p-1})_{ik} w_{ik} = 0 \tag{9}$$

$$-(W^T V)_{kj} h_{kj} + (W^T WH)_{kj} h_{kj} + \lambda (HL)_{kj} h_{kj} = 0 \tag{10}$$

From Eqs. (9) and (10), the following multiplicative update rules are obtained:

$$w_{ik} \leftarrow w_{ik} \frac{(VH^T)_{ik}}{(WHH^T + \mu p W^{p-1})_{ik}} \tag{11}$$

$$h_{kj} \leftarrow h_{kj} \frac{(W^T V + \lambda HS)_{kj}}{(W^T WH + \lambda HD)_{kj}} \tag{12}$$

Theorem 1. The objective function O_{GSNMF} in Eq. (4) is non-increasing under the update rules in Eqs. (11) and (12). Theorem 1 guarantees that the objective function O_{GSNMF} converges to a local optimum under the update rules in Eqs. (11) and (12). In addition, the related theory and proof can also be found in [16, 17, 19].

4   Experimental Results

In order to evaluate the performance of the proposed GSNMF method, we compare results for data clustering with several related state-of-the-art methods, e.g., NMF [13], graph regularized NMF (GNMF) [17], and graph dual regularization NMF (DNMF) [2]. We use two popular data sets. The experimental conditions are similar to those in [17] as much as possible.

4.1   Data Sets

The clustering performance is evaluated on two widely used data sets, including COIL20 and ORL. The important statistical information of the two data sets is summarized in Table 1 with more details given in [18].

Table 1. Statistics information of the two data sets.

Data sets	Size	Dimensionality	# of classes
COIL20	1440	1024	20
ORL	400	1024	40

4.2   Evaluation Metrics

In order to evaluate the clustering performance, the accuracy (AC) and the normalized mutual information (NMI) are used to evaluate the clustering performance by comparing the cluster label of each sample with the label provided by the data set. Please see [21, 22] for the detailed definitions of these two metrics.

4.3   Performance Evaluations and Comparisons

In order to demonstrate the clustering performance, we compare our method with NMF, GNMF and DNMF methods under the same conditions, same parameters and the same iteration times on two well-known data sets. In all the experiments we use the F-norm formulation as the objective function and use the 0–1 weighting scheme for constructing the k-nearest neighbor graph with $k = 5$. In addition, the parameters λ and μ are the same and set to 100, as recommended in [2, 17]. Tables 2 and 3 give the clustering results based on the proposed method with $p = 1.7$ compared to the other three methods on the COIL20 and ORL data sets respectively which have been normalized and measured by the AC and NMI algorithms. We can make some interesting observations from these experiments from Tables 2 and 3. The NMF method is the worst of the four clustering methods on the COIL20 and ORL data sets tested for the different cluster numbers for 100 iterations, without adding any regularization or extra information. The GSNMF method is better than GNMF and DNMF methods. This is

Table 2. Clustering results comparisons on the COIL20.

k	Accuracy (%)				Normalized mutual information (%)			
	NMF	GNMF	DNMF	GSNMF	NMF	GNMF	DNMF	GSNMF
5	66.181	70.486	70.764	**78.125**	76.187	84.343	86.828	**87.175**
10	60.347	70.556	77.014	**80.625**	71.952	84.860	87.220	**88.242**
15	61.875	75.556	75.972	**82.153**	72.809	89.131	86.320	**90.430**
16	60.347	74.653	74.653	**75.417**	73.295	85.897	86.075	**87.912**
17	67.708	76.458	77.014	**77.167**	77.615	86.749	87.545	**87.782**
18	65.764	79.722	77.569	**81.181**	74.246	87.209	87.766	**89.419**
19	67.639	73.333	75.972	**77.569**	75.632	85.749	87.420	**88.673**
20	67.569	76.319	80.486	**84.653**	75.907	88.313	88.511	**90.128**
Avg.	64.679	74.635	76.181	**79.611**	74.705	86.531	87.210	**88.720**

because the graph regularization can discover the hidden semantics and simultaneously respect the intrinsic geometric structure information in the data set. At the same time, the Lp smooth constraint can combine the merits of the isotropic and anisotropic diffusion smoothing, and produce smooth and more accurate solution. In addition, the DNMF method simultaneously considers the geometric structures of both the data manifold and the feature manifold, which has better performance than GNMF.

Table 3. Clustering results comparisons on the ORL dataset.

k	Accuracy (%)				Normalized mutual information (%)			
	NMF	GNMF	DNMF	GSNMF	NMF	GNMF	DNMF	GSNMF
5	51.750	52.750	53.500	**58.000**	72.035	72.918	73.922	**75.946**
10	51.000	54.500	55.000	**56.750**	70.994	73.791	74.643	**75.979**
15	50.000	53.500	57.000	**58.500**	69.682	74.328	75.099	**76.198**
20	50.250	55.000	56.500	**57.750**	70.643	74.227	74.494	**75.062**
25	50.000	51.250	53.750	**55.250**	71.783	73.028	74.418	**75.105**
30	51.250	55.250	56.000	**56.500**	70.708	75.086	74.723	**75.301**
35	51.500	54.250	56.750	**57.000**	69.673	73.101	74.892	**75.663**
40	51.000	53.000	55.750	**56.500**	70.545	73.526	73.571	**74.754**
Avg.	50.844	53.688	55.531	**57.031**	70.758	73.751	74.470	**75.501**

4.4 Parameter Selection

In order to test the stability of the proposed GSNMF method for various parameter settings there is a variable parameter $1 < p < 2$ which can control the diffusion speed, and combine the merits of the isotropic and anisotropic diffusion smoothing. The other parameters λ and μ are the same and set to 100 as recommended in [2, 17], with the iterations set to 50. Therefore, we only adjust the variable parameter p to test stability. Figure 1 (a) and (b) show the performance comparisons including the criterion to measure accuracy and normalized mutual information with the parameter p varying from 1.1 to 1.9, considering different number of classes such as 10 and 20 on the COIL20 data set.

As we can see, the performance of GSNMF is very good for different values of parameter p and it also has higher accuracy than all others in most cases. From the experimental results, the parameter p can control the clustering performance, but the clustering performance is relatively low under some clusters such as the $k = 10$ with $p = 1.3$ and $p = 1.6$, and $k = 20$ with $p = 1.3$ and $p = 1.8$.

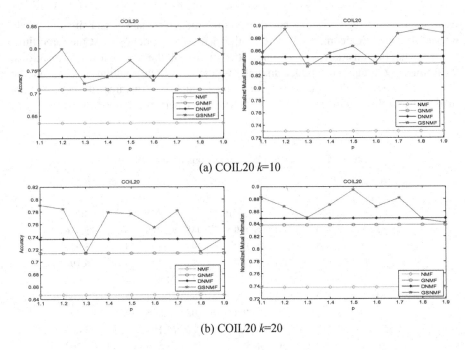

(a) COIL20 k=10

(b) COIL20 k=20

Fig. 1. Performance comparisons for varying parameter p on the COIL20 data set.

5 Conclusions

We proposed the Graph regularized Lp Smooth Non-negative Matrix Factorization (GSNMF) method by incorporating graph regularization and Lp smooth constraint. The purpose was to discover the intrinsic geometric information of a data set and produce smooth and stable solutions during the process of data representation. Furthermore, multiplicative update rules were provided to solve the optimization problems. Experimental results on two data sets demonstrated that the proposed method outperforms related state-of-the-art methods for clustering.

Acknowledgments. This work is supported by the National Natural Science Foundation of China under Grant Nos. 61702251, 61363049, 11571011, 61501286, the State Scholarship Fund of China Scholarship Council (CSC) under Grant No. 201708360040, the Natural Science Foundation of Jiangxi Province under Grant No. 20161BAB212033, the Natural Science Basic Research Plan in Shaanxi Province of China under Program No. 2018JM6030, the Key Research and Development Program in Shaanxi Province of China under Grant No. 2018GY-008, the Doctor Scientific Research Starting Foundation of Northwest University under Grant No. 338050050 and Youth Academic Talent Support Program of Northwest University.

References

1. Lu, G.F., Wang, Y., Zou, J.: Low-rank matrix factorization with adaptive graph regularizer. IEEE Trans. Image Process. **25**(5), 2196–2205 (2016)
2. Shang, F.H., Jiao, L.C., Wang, F.: Graph dual regularization non-negative matrix factorization for co-clustering. Pattern Recognit. **45**(6), 2237–2250 (2012)
3. Wang, D., Gao, X.B., Wang, X.M.: Semi-supervised nonnegative matrix factorization via constraint propagation. IEEE Trans. Cybern. **46**(1), 233–244 (2016)
4. He, W., Zhang, H.Y., Zhang, L.P.: Sparsity-regularized robust non-negative matrix factorization for hyperspectral unmixing. IEEE J. Sel. Top. Appl. Earth Obs. Remote Sens. **9**(9), 4267–4279 (2016)
5. Fan, F., Ma, Y., Li, C., Mei, X.G., Huang, J., Ma, J.Y.: Hyperspectral image denoising with superpixel segmentation and low-rank representation. Inf. Sci. **397**, 48–68 (2017)
6. Li, Z.C., Liu, J., Lu, H.Q.: Structure preserving non-negative matrix factorization for dimensionality reduction. Comput. Vis. Image Underst. **117**(9), 1175–1189 (2013)
7. Tenenbaum, J.B., Silva, V.D., Langford, J.C.: A global geometric framework for nonlinear dimensionality reduction. Science **290**(5500), 2319–2323 (2000)
8. Roweis, S., Saul, L.: Nonlinear dimensionality reduction by locally linear embedding. Science **290**(5500), 2323–2326 (2000)
9. Belkin, M., Niyogi, P.: Laplacian eigenmaps and spectral techniques for embedding and clustering. In: Advances in Neural Information Processing Systems, Vancouver, BC, Canada, vol. 14, pp. 585–591 (2001)
10. Cai, D., He, X. F., Han, J. W.: Isometric projection. In: Proceeding of the National Conference on Artificial Intelligence, Vancouver, BC, Canada, vol. 1, pp. 528–533 (2007)
11. Najafi, A., Joudaki, A., Fatemizadeh, E.: Nonlinear dimensionality reduction via path-based isometric mapping. IEEE Trans. Pattern Anal. Mach. Intell. **38**(7), 1452–1464 (2016)
12. Wang, Y.X., Zhang, Y.J.: Nonnegative matrix factorization: a comprehensive review. IEEE Trans. Knowl. Data Eng. **25**(6), 1336–1353 (2013)
13. Lee, D.D., Seung, H.S.: Learning the parts of objects by non-negative matrix factorization. Nature **401**(6755), 788–791 (1999)
14. Zeng, K., Yu, J., Li, C.H., You, J., Jin, T.S.: Image clustering by hyper-graph regularized non-negative matrix factorization. Neurocomputing **138**, 209–217 (2014)
15. Li, G.P., Zhang, X.Y., Zheng, S.Y., Li, D.Y.: Semi-supervised convex nonnegative matrix factorizations with graph regularized for image representation. Neurocomputing **237**, 1–11 (2017)
16. Leng, C.C., Cai, G.R., Yu, D.D., Wang, Z.Y.: Adaptive total-variation for non-negative matrix factorization on manifold. Pattern Recognit. Lett. **98**, 68–74 (2017)
17. Cai, D., He, X.F., Han, J.W., Huang, T.S.: Graph regularized nonnegative matrix factorization for data representation. IEEE Trans. Pattern Anal. Mach. Intell. **33**(8), 1548–1560 (2011)
18. Liu, H.F., Wu, Z.H., Li, X.L., Cai, D., Huang, T.S.: Constrained nonnegative matrix factorization for image representation. IEEE Trans. Pattern Anal. Mach. Intell. **34**(7), 1299–1311 (2012)
19. Lee, D.D., Seung, H.S.: Algorithms for non-negative matrix factorization. Adv. Neural. Inf. Process. Syst. **13**, 556–562 (2000)
20. Chung, F.R.K.: Spectral Graph Theory. American Mathematical Society, Providence (1997)

21. Xu, W., Liu, X., Gong, Y.H.: Document clustering based on non-negative matrix factorization. In: Proceedings of the Annual International ACM SIGIR Conference on Research and Development in Information Retrieval (SIGIR 2003), Toronto, Canada, pp. 267–273 (2003)
22. Cai, D., He, X.F., Han, J.W.: Document clustering using locality preserving indexing. IEEE Trans. Knowl. Data Eng. 17(12), 1624–1637 (2005)

Miscellaneous

Subjective Quality of Spatially Asymmetric Omnidirectional Stereoscopic Video for Streaming Adaptation

Igor D. D. Curcio[1($\boxtimes$)] [iD], Deepa Naik[2], Henri Toukomaa[1], and Alireza Zare[1]

[1] Media Technology Research, Nokia Technologies, Tampere, Finland
{igor.curcio, henri.toukomaa, alireza.zare}@nokia.com
[2] Department of Signal Processing, Tampere University of Technology, Tampere, Finland
deepa.naik@tut.fi

Abstract. Asymmetric video coding is a well-studied area for bit rate reduction in stereoscopic video coding. Such video coding technique is possible because of the binocular fusion theory which states that the Human Visual System (HVS) is capable of fusing views from both the eyes. As a result, past literature has shown that the final perceived quality of different left and right quality images is closer the highest quality of the two views. In this paper, we investigate spatially asymmetric omnidirectional video in subjective experiments using a Head Mounted Display (HMD). We want to subjectively verify to what extent the binocular fusion theory applies in immersive media environments, and also assess to what degree reducing the omnidirectional video streaming bandwidth is feasible. We prove that (1) the HVS is capable of partial suppression of the low-quality view up to a certain resolution; (2) there is a bandwidth saving of 25% when 75% of the spatial resolution is used for one of the views, while ensuring a subjective visual quality with a DMOS of 4.7 points; (3) in case of bandwidth adaptation using asymmetric video, bit rate savings are in the range 25–50%.

Keywords: Omnidirectional video · Virtual reality streaming
Subjective quality evaluation · Asymmetric video · Streaming adaptation

1 Introduction

Streaming omnidirectional video over a network is very bandwidth demanding, due to the huge bit rate requirement of 360-degree video at 4 K or higher resolutions. The research community is focusing its efforts towards searching for means to reduce the streaming bit rates as much as possible, while at the same time ensuring a high subjective video quality. These means include optimization techniques in video coding, transport or content creation.

At any point of time, out of the whole transmitted 360-degree video, only a limited field of view of the stream is viewed by the user. Therefore, streaming the whole 360-degree video at high quality is not efficient in terms of bandwidth and decoding

© Springer Nature Switzerland AG 2018
A. Basu and S. Berretti (Eds.): ICSM 2018, LNCS 11010, pp. 417–428, 2018.
https://doi.org/10.1007/978-3-030-04375-9_36

complexity. Viewport Dependent Streaming (VDS) is one of the techniques that has been proposed in the literature, with the purpose of reducing the streaming bandwidth. With this scheme, only the current user viewport is streamed at high quality, and the remainder of the video is streamed at lower quality. This technology saves streaming bandwidth considerably. However, there is still scope for further reducing the network bandwidth requirements for streaming omnidirectional video.

In general, a 3D scene can be represented by using a single view plus depth or by two stereo channels where two images which are captured by slightly different viewpoints are presented to the left and right eyes. The brain combines these images to give the perception of depth. So, stereoscopic video requires two times more data than monoscopic video. Efficient video compression or transport is of great importance here, especially when the streaming bandwidth is limited.

In order to efficiently reduce the bandwidth required for stereoscopic video, one of the technologies that can be applied for video streaming is asymmetric video transmission. With such scheme, one of the views is transmitted with lower quality video either in terms of SNR quality or spatial quality, compared to the other view. The major processing of the raw information perceived through the eyes takes place in the brain. However, the brain does not process all the information supplied to it. If two images given to the brain are of two different qualities, the brain partially suppresses the image with lower quality, and the final fused perceived quality is closer the image with higher quality [1].

In this paper we mainly focus on running subjective video quality assessments that reconfirm this theory for immersive omnidirectional video when users make use of Head Mounted Displays. We also show that there is a significant bandwidth saving of 25% when 75% of the spatial resolution is used for one of the views, while at the same time ensuring a subjective quality level of DMOS = 4.7.

The paper is structured as follows: Sect. 2 introduces the related work in the area. Section 3 presents the test setup of our subjective quality assessment experiment. Section 4 presents the results, while Sect. 5 concludes the paper.

2   Related Work

Some of the relevant literature in the field mainly deals with reduction of stereoscopic video streaming bandwidth and increasing compression efficiency. When a stereo pair is used, various asymmetric techniques between two views can be used to achieve a better compression efficiency. Some of the most common are: asymmetrical SNR quality between left and right views, asymmetrical resolution, asymmetrical frame rates, etc.

In [2], asymmetric quality between two views is used for bandwidth reduction. One of the views is low pass filtered, whereas the other view is kept at high quality. Subjective results of this study show that the use of low pass filter efficiently reduces the bandwidth requirements, while subjective quality remains close to the original video, following the suppression theory of a binocular system [1]. In [3], subjective and objective evaluations of full and mixed resolution stereo coding are reported. Subjective results show that mixed resolution is preferred when a sequence is encoded especially at lower bit rate, and full resolution is preferred otherwise (not encoded).

In [4], rather than applying the asymmetrical criteria to one of the views, the authors divide the video frames into slices. Low-pass filtering is applied to the odd slices of one of the views and even slices of the other view. Subjective results of the experiments show that the perceived depth, sharpness and quality of the stereoscopic view is close to the original view, despite there is a degradation in quality of both the views. In [5] a different filtering method for up-sampling the down-sampled frames at the decoder is proposed. In [6], asymmetric resolution is applied by down-sampling the color channel. Subjective results show that the depth perception remains the same with down-sampling. However, in order to keep the perceived image quality close to the original, the chroma channel was filtered.

In [7], uneven quantization is applied to luma samples for different views along with down-sampling. The proposed method is subjectively comparable with full resolution symmetric stereoscopic video coding and mixed resolution stereoscopic video coding. Results show that the HVS is capable of fusing views with different types of quality degradation. In [8], mixed resolution of stereo images is explored to check the perception of image quality subjectively. Here the left view is provided with full resolution, and the right view provided with different resolution levels (1/4, 1/2, Full). Images meant for left and right were shown by opening and closing the shutter glasses synchronously. Subjective results showed that this asymmetric technique can effectively be used to reduce the transmission bandwidth, while retaining the depth, sharpness and quality as close as possible to the original image.

The work in [9] answers the question about to what extent the binocular fusion theory can mask the low quality and a subject can perceive the high visual quality when the asymmetric resolution is used. In other words, what is the threshold for which the mixed resolution is viewed close to the full resolution symmetric view. Here, the test sequences were displayed on a Hyundai P240W 24″ polarizing stereoscopic screen. Subjective results of their study showed that full resolution is preferred over the mixed resolution. In case of mixed resolution, down-sampling by a factor of half horizontally and vertically is acceptable. If the downsampling was beyond a certain ratio, the test subjects rated the quality poorly.

Finally, recent developments of omnidirectional video streaming have led towards the development of Viewport Dependent Streaming (VDS) as method to reduce the streaming bandwidth. Subjective evaluation of VDS against Viewport Independent Streaming (VIS) (i.e., full sphere constant quality omnidirectional video streaming) has been analyzed by the authors in [10]. Results have shown that VDS can bring a considerable bandwidth reduction of over 40%. The authors have also introduced a methodology for subjective quality assessment of omnidirectional video as well as the Similarity Ring Metric (SRM) for assessing the degree of watching pattern similarity within-subject or between-subjects [11]. In [12], the authors propose a machine learning mechanism to predict the viewer motion and also the accuracy. Based on this data they propose a transmission scheme that reduces the transmission bandwidth by 45%. The paper [13] proposes an adaptive VR video streaming strategy to save up to 72% bandwidth. However, this is not formally validated via subjective results. In [14] the authors explain the problem of finding the optimum random access point that helps to reduce the transmitted bit rate, while ensuring that the user watches most of the time high resolution content.

3 Experimental Setup

3.1 Test Environment and Procedure

The implemented setup in this experiment consists of an omnidirectional video streaming server which was MPEG DASH compliant with the needed extensions, a streaming client run on a Samsung Galaxy S8 phone, and a number of subjects that watched the clips using the Gear VR 2016 HMD. Such setup requires a test subject to wear the HMD for the duration of the test session and assume a convenient sitting position on a rotating chair or a standing position for free movement. This allows the test subjects to freely look around the whole omnidirectional space.

The average age of the subjects was between 20 and 40 years and there were 27 people participating to our experiment. Subjects were informed about the possible side effects of the tests. Any subject with health conditions such as epilepsy, pregnancy, strong nausea or hangover, etc. were excluded from the test. Once the preliminary screening was performed, the recruited subjects were screened for their vision [15]. The vision and color tests performed were similar to another earlier experiment we reported in [11].

For the evaluation of the video, some perceptual quality metrics for stereoscopic video have been studied in literature. See for example [16]. However, to comply as much as possible with standards-based assessment methods, we selected the single-stimulus Absolute Category Rating with Hidden Reference (ACR-HR) based on DMOS [15, 17, 18]. With this method, the stimuli are displayed to the subject in random order.

The participants were requested to score the videos on a category scale. A 5-grade fractional scale (with adjective category judgment) was used [19] to rate visual quality as follows: 1-Bad, 2-Poor, 3-Fair, 4-Good, 5-Excellent. A hidden reference was presented to the subjects like any other stimuli, and the participants were unaware of the reference. Subjects were expected to score the reference as either Good or Excellent.

It is advised that the entire test session not be longer than an hour. Out of this time, in our experiment, the recommended session wearing the HMD was 25–35 min long, which included breaks of 2 to 5 min. The HMD could be removed during the break session in order to relax. One-hour session was divided into several sub-sessions which included instructions, pre-test visual fatigue questionnaires, training session, break, actual test session, breaks in between required to continue the next session, and post-test visual fatigue questionnaires.

In the instruction part, the goal of the test and the assessment methodology were explained to the participants. People were also informed about the possible side effects that might occur after the test. A training session was also utilized for the purpose of assisting and familiarizing the participants to the watching environment of the omni-directional video, and also to the voting procedure. Clips in the training session were selected in such a way that they possibly included the whole quality ranges of the clips that the subjects watched in the actual sessions, including the reference.

In the beginning of the actual test session, the subjects were presented with stabilizing sequences for the purpose of statistically stabilizing the rankings [17]. These clips were selected randomly from the actual test clips. In order to improve the statistical results, it is recommended to use a number of repetitions of the sequences [17]. The same test clips were presented in pseudo-random order to the different participants. Also, the repetition of the clips follows a pseudo random order [15, 18]. Before beginning the test session, participants were requested to calibrate the Inter-Pupillary Distance (IPD) nob of the HMD by focusing on a still picture, in order to match their actual IPD.

3.2   Test Stimuli

The video sequences were selected to cater different genres from sports ("Pole Vault") to military ("JET") and adventure ("Bear Attack"). Equirectangular panorama video with 4 K resolution (3840 × 1920 pixels) was selected and encoded with HEVC at 30 frames per second.

The horizontal Field of View (FoV), the vertical FoV and the down-sampling ratios were chosen in such a way that, after down-sampling, in the horizontal and vertical directions, the resolution was divisible by 64 in order to match the coding block unit. So, the selected horizontal FoV was 192 degrees (the remaining FoV was displayed black; see Fig. 2); the vertical FoV was 96 degrees (the top and bottom areas were 42 degrees and were displayed black, see Fig. 2). The horizontal and vertical spatial resolutions after down-sampling of 1/4, 1/2 and 3/4, in addition to Full, are shown in Table 1. In all the cases, the aspect ratio of 2:1 was maintained after down-sampling. The selected Quantization Parameters (QPs) were 22, 24 and 26 which were producing bit rates that were comfortably streamed by the client over a private high-bandwidth WLAN 802.11ac tri-band access point.

Table 1. Spatial resolutions of the videos used in the experiment

Initial resolution (pixels)	1/4 down-sampling (pixels)	1/2 down-sampling (pixels)	3/4 down-sampling (pixels)	Full (pixels)
3840 × 1920	512 × 256	1024 × 512	1536 × 768	2048 × 1024

For all the sequences, the left view was assigned full resolution, and for the right view was assigned one of the four rightmost resolutions mentioned in Table 1. Since eye dominance is invariant, this choice was well justified.

4 Experimental Results

When the subjects collectively rank the video sequences, the Mean Opinion Score (MOS) can be used for data analysis. However, in our methodology, two stimuli are used: a hidden reference and the test stimulus. Due to this, the vote measures can change between the two versions of the stimuli. Therefore, the Differential Mean Opinion Score (DMOS) is computed between the test stimulus and its corresponding reference [20].

The primary goal in our experiment was

1) to reconfirm the binocular suppression and fusion theories in immersive environment when the content is displayed over a HMD;
2) find the optimal asymmetric resolution combination between two views that can be used, such that the perceived quality is the highest possible, and the required bandwidth is the lowest, and deal with the best bandwidth adaptation strategy.

Figure 1 shows the subjective DMOS values for different video sequences. Here the bars on the X axis are ordered by increasing QP values, and then by increasing spatial resolution. The Y axis shows the DMOS values.

The results show invariance against content genre for the sequences we considered. For each of the 12 test cases, we calculated the *Maximum DMOS Difference (MDD)* between the sequence which resulted in the highest DMOS and the one that resulted in the lowest DMOS. The average MDD across all 12 cases was 0.5 (with a standard deviation of 0.3). A second result showed that the MDD calculated only by similar resolutions, produced lower MDD values as soon as resolutions tended towards the full resolution (average MDD = 0.3). These set of results show that the findings of our experiment could be generalized.

Since our main goal was that of reducing the streaming bit rate as much as possible, the results in Table 2 have been sorted according to the last column, i.e., the total average bit rate saving percentage for all 12 test cases across the three sequences using different QP values. The second last column of the table shows the total average DMOS across all three video sequences.

From the last two columns of this table, it is possible to draw the following conclusions about asymmetric omnidirectional video transmission:

a) A spatial resolution scale of 1/4 in one of the stereo views can yield bit rate savings up to 76%, compared to full resolution at high quality (QP = 22) delivered to both views. However, the subjective quality is pretty poor (DMOS = 1.9–2.5). This suggests that it is not convenient to use such a strong down-sampled spatial resolution for omnidirectional stereoscopic asymmetric video streaming;
b) A spatial resolution scale of 1/2 in one of the stereo views can yield bit rate savings in the range 41–73%, compared to full resolution at high quality (QP = 22) delivered to both views. In this case, the subjective quality is in the range of almost Fair to almost Good. This level of asymmetric stereoscopic video delivery may be acceptable for some applications;
c) A spatial resolution scale of 3/4 in one of the stereo views can yield bit rate savings in the range 25–66%, compared to full resolution at high quality (QP = 22)

delivered to both views. In this case the subjective quality is in the range of more than Fair up to almost Excellent. In particular, the best subjective quality is achieved for QP = 22, which offers just a 0.3 DMOS subjective video quality degradation, and a streaming bit rate saving of 25%.

It is also possible to conclude that stereoscopic omnidirectional video delivery can take advantage of asymmetric delivery for bandwidth adaptation purposes also in immersive environment. For example, it would be perfectly feasible to deliver asymmetric stereoscopic video during the low bandwidth periods, in order to adapt to the network conditions, and deliver symmetric stereoscopic video during the periods of good network conditions.

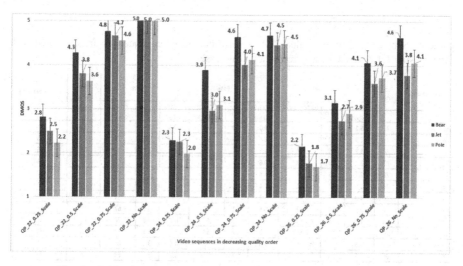

Fig. 1. Subjective quality results (DMOS) for different video sequences.

With the goal of using asymmetric stereoscopic video delivery for performing bandwidth adaptation, we could make the hypothesis of fixing two operational points:

A. A good level adaptation mechanism with a guaranteed subjective DMOS in the range of 4.0–4.5 during the adaptation periods.
B. An optimal level adaptation mechanism with a guaranteed subjective DMOS in the range 4.5–5.0 during the adaptation periods.

With reference to Table 2, case A results are highlighted in yellow color. For such a case, the average bit rate saving using asymmetric stereoscopic video is 51%. Case B results are highlighted in green color. For such a case, the average bit rate saving using asymmetric stereoscopic video is 25% (with a maximum of 60% on the Bear Attack sequence).

The results so far considered are quite good if considered in isolation. However, given our experiment was designed to include several QP levels by means of which the

SNR quality can vary, a deeper analysis of Table 2 results for the same A and B cases leads to the following additional conclusions:

- For the case A, full resolution (i.e., symmetric omnidirectional video delivery) with a higher QP level (i.e., lower SNR quality) yields an average bit rate saving of 56%, which is 5% additional bit rate reduction compared to asymmetric video delivery;
- For the case B, full resolution (i.e., symmetric omnidirectional video delivery) with a higher QP level (i.e., lower SNR quality) yields an average bit rate saving of 35%, which is 10% additional bit rate reduction compared to asymmetric video delivery. When looking at the individual sequences results, it can be seen that the bit rate savings of this configuration may reach up to 69% (for the Bear Attack sequence), which is 44% additional bit rate reduction compared to asymmetric video delivery;

Table 2. Subjective quality results (DMOS) of different video sequences are compared with bitrate saving for different spatial resolution scale cases

Spatial Resolution Scale	QP	Jet			Pole			Bear			Total Average DMOS	Total Average Bit rate saving %
		Bit rate (Mbps)	DMOS	Bit rate saving %	Bit rate (Mbps)	DMOS	Bit rate saving %	Bit rate (Mbps)	DMOS	Bit rate saving %		
Full Scale	22	5.1	5.0	0	9.0	5.0	0	22.6	5.0	0	5.0	0
3/4	22	3.9	4.7	24	6.8	4.6	24	16.2	4.8	28	4.7	25
Full Scale	24	3.9	4.5	24	5.6	4.5	38	12.6	4.7	44	4.6	35
1/2	22	3.2	3.8	37	5.6	3.6	38	12.1	4.3	47	3.9	41
1/4	22	2.7	2.5	47	4.8	2.2	47	11.9	2.8	47	2.5	47
3/4	24	3.0	4.0	41	4.4	4.1	51	9.1	4.6	60	4.2	51
Full Scale	26	3.0	3.8	41	3.8	4.0	58	7.0	4.6	69	4.1	56
1/2	24	2.5	3.0	51	3.6	3.1	60	7.5	3.9	67	3.3	59
1/4	24	2.1	2.3	59	3.0	2.0	67	6.7	2.3	70	2.2	66
3/4	26	2.3	3.6	55	3.0	3.7	67	5.3	3.1	77	3.5	66
1/2	26	1.8	2.7	65	2.5	2.9	72	4.4	3.1	81	2.8	73
1/4	26	1.6	1.8	69	2.1	1.7	77	3.8	2.2	83	1.9	76

- All highlighted test case results for the operational points A and B, confirm that adaptation using full resolution symmetric stereoscopic video with different SNR quality levels yields more streaming bit rate reduction compared to an adaptation scheme based on asymmetric stereoscopic video delivery. This is a side effect result out of our experiment, but very important when searching for a global strategy for optimizing the streaming bandwidth on omnidirectional video streaming. These results completely confirm the early findings of the authors in relation to using lower resolution in background (non-visible tiles) during omnidirectional tiled video streaming [10].

With this analysis, we gave an answer to the second of our primary questions. We will deal now with the first question, i.e., reconfirm the binocular suppression and fusion theories in immersive environment when the content is displayed over a HMD.

The first thing we performed was an objective video quality evaluation. We adopted the omnidirectional video quality assessment framework developed in [21] to objectively evaluate QoE. According to this framework, a rectilinear view with 90 × 90-degree FoV (e.g., cubemap) can sufficiently estimates the viewing environment in different HMDs available in the market.

In Fig. 2, the outer rectangle shows the original omnidirectional content, and the central white rectangle shows part of the content presented to the viewers, which covers an area of 192 × 96 degrees. In the grey area there was no content; hence the viewers were asked to watch along the equator over the central rectangle. In order to measure the QoE, 7 pre-defined orientations called Quality Assessment Views (QAVs) were selected, each 15 degrees apart. The choice of 15 degrees interval was made to have a reasonably fine evaluation of all possible viewing orientations. The blue dots in Fig. 2 show the centers of the QAVs. In this work, it is assumed that the viewers looked at different orientations with the same probability. Hence, the quality is reported as an average PSNR over the 7 QAVs.

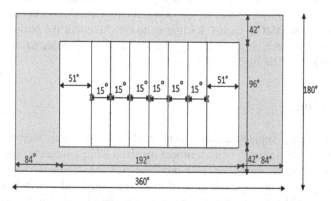

Fig. 2. Quality Assessment View for objective video quality evaluation. (Color figure online)

Table 3. Objective quality results (Y channel PSNR) of different video sequences and their corresponding bit rates for different spatial resolution scale cases

QP	Full Scale		3/4 Resolution			1/2 Resolution			1/4 Resolution		
	Bit rate (Mbps)	Y-PSNR (dB)	Bit rate (Mbps)	Y-PSNR (dB)	PSNR loss (dB)	Bit rate (Mbps)	Y-PSNR (dB)	PSNR loss (dB)	Bit rate (Mbps)	Y-PSNR (dB)	PSNR loss (dB)
Jet											
22	5.1	44.5	3.9	40.1	-4.4	3.2	39.3	-5.2	2.7	38.3	-6.2
24	3.9	43.6	3.0	39.5	-4.1	2.5	38.7	-4.9	2.1	37.8	-5.8
26	3.0	42.6	2.3	38.8	-3.8	1.8	38.1	-4.5	1.6	37.2	-5.4
Pole											
	Bit rate (Mbps)	Y-PSNR (dB)	Bit rate (Mbps)	Y-PSNR (dB)	PSNR loss (dB)	Bit rate (Mbps)	Y-PSNR (dB)	PSNR loss (dB)	Bit rate (Mbps)	Y-PSNR (dB)	PSNR loss (dB)
22	9.0	43.4	6.8	39.5	-4.0	5.6	38.1	-5.3	4.8	36.3	-7.1
24	5.6	42.5	4.4	38.9	-3.6	3.6	37.6	-4.9	3.1	35.8	-6.6
26	3.8	41.6	3.0	38.3	-3.4	2.5	37.0	-4.6	2.1	35.3	-6.3
Bear Attack											
	Bit rate (Mbps)	Y-PSNR (dB)	Bit rate (Mbps)	Y-PSNR (dB)	PSNR loss (dB)	Bit rate (Mbps)	Y-PSNR (dB)	PSNR loss (dB)	Bit rate (Mbps)	Y-PSNR (dB)	PSNR loss (dB)
22	22.6	41.7	16.2	37.8	-3.9	12.1	36.5	-5.2	11.9	34.9	-6.8
24	12.6	40.6	9.1	37.0	-3.5	7.5	35.8	-4.7	6.7	34.3	-6.3
26	7.0	39.5	5.3	36.3	-3.2	4.4	35.2	-4.3	3.8	33.7	-5.8

The Table 3 shows the PSNR values for the three different content genres. It also shows the PSNR loss against the full scale. For the full scale, at different QP levels, the PSNR is calculated as average of the 7 pre-defined orientations for each view. The PSNR values obtained for the left and right views are then averaged. For all other reduced resolution cases, the left view PSNR remains the same, while the right view PSNR is the average of 7 orientations at reduced resolution. The left and right PSNRs are then averaged. By comparison with Table 2 results, two exemplary test cases from Table 2 have been highlighted in blue color in Table 3. The first is a case for the Jet sequence with subjective DMOS = 4.7 and DMOS loss = −0.3 (see Table 2) and PSNR loss = −4.43 dB (see Table 3). The second case is for the Bear Attack sequence that shows a subjective DMOS = 4.8 and DMOS loss = −0.2 (see Table 2) and PSNR loss = −3.92 dB (see Table 3). According to [22], each 0.1 MOS points in the MOS = [4..5] range, maps approximately to 1.2 dB PSNR points. The results above show that the calculated PSNR loss is proportionally much more than the DMOS loss. This lead us to conclude that the binocular suppression and fusion theories hold also in the immersive environment case of video watched over HMDs. In fact, subjective results show higher DMOS values, leading us to conclude that the brain fuses the left and right views in such a way that the resulting quality is closer to that of the full resolution view, i.e., the higher quality one.

5   Conclusions

This paper presented subjective assessment results of asymmetric stereoscopic omni-directional video streaming. The experiment involved 27 test subjects. The aim was to verify the assumptions based on past literature that the binocular suppression and fusion theories apply also for the case of omnidirectional video watched on a head mounted display. The assumption has been verified by means of additional objective results. A second aim of the paper was to find optimal configuration settings for reducing the bandwidth during an adaptive streaming session. Results show that with 75% of spatial resolution scale, it is possible to achieve an average bandwidth reduction of 25% by ensuring a subjective quality with a DMOS of 4.7, making asymmetric stereoscopic video transmission an effective method for optimizing bandwidth in streaming sessions in either a static or an adaptive scenario, where bit rate savings are in the range 25–50%. Additional results confirmed early results that adaptation by using SNR quality can yield more streaming bit rate savings compared to asymmetric stereoscopic video delivery.

References

1. Blake, R.: Threshold conditions for binocular rivalry. J. Exp. Psychol. Hum. Percept. Perform. 3(2), 251–257 (1977)
2. Valizadeh, S., Azimi, M., Nasiopoulos, P.: Bitrate reduction in asymmetric stereoscopic video with low-pass filtered slices. In: IEEE International Conference on Consumer Electronics (ICCE), Las Vegas, NV, USA, 13–16 January 2012

3. Brust, H., Smolic, A., Mueller, K., Tech, G., Wiegand, T.: Mixed resolution coding of stereoscopic video for Mobile devices. In: IEEE 3DTV Conference, Potsdam, Germany, 4–6 May 2009

4. Azimi, M., Valizadeh, S., Li, X., Coria, L.E., Nasiopoulos, P.: Subjective study on asymmetric stereoscopic video with low-pass filtered slices. In: IEEE International Conference on Computing, Networking and Communications (ICNC), Maui, HI, USA, 30 January–2 February 2012

5. Chung, K.-L., Huang, Y.-H., Liu, W.-C.: Quality-efficient upsampling method for asymmetric resolution stereoscopic video coding with interview motion compensation and error compensation. IEEE Trans. Circuits Syst. Video Technol. 24(3), 430–442 (2014)

6. Aksay, A., Bilen, C., Akar, G.B.: Subjective evaluation of effects of spectral and spatial redundancy reduction on stereo images. In: IEEE 13th European Signal Processing Conference, Antalya, Turkey, 4–8 September 2005

7. Aflaki, P., Hannuksela, M.M., Hakala, J., Häkkinen, J., Gabbouj, M.: Joint adaptation of spatial resolution and sample value quantization for asymmetric stereoscopic video compression: a subjective study. In: IEEE 7th International Symposium on Image and Signal Processing and Analysis (ISPA), Dubrovnik, Croatia, 4–6 September 2011

8. Stelmach, L., Tam, W.J., Meegan, D., Vincent, A.: Stereo image quality: effects of mixed spatio-temporal resolution. IEEE Trans. Circuits Syst. Video Technol. 10(2), 188–193 (2000)

9. Aflaki, P., Hannuksela, M.M., Gabbouj, M.: Subjective quality assessment of asymmetric stereoscopic 3D video. SIViP 9(2), 331–345 (2015)

10. Curcio, I.D.D., Toukomaa, H., Naik, D.: Bandwidth reduction of omnidirectional viewport-dependent video streaming via subjective quality assessment. In: ACM International Workshop on Multimedia Alternate Realities at ACM Multimedia Conference, Mountain View, CA, USA, 27 October 2017

11. Curcio, I.D.D., Toukomaa, H., Naik, D.: 360-degree video streaming and its subjective quality. In: SMPTE Annual Technical Conference and Exhibition, Hollywood, CA, USA, 23–26 October 2017

12. Bao, Y., Wu, H., Zhang, T., Ramli, A.A., Liu, X.: Shooting a moving target: motion-prediction-based transmission for 360-degree videos. In: IEEE International Conference on Big Data, Washington, DC, USA, 5–6 December 2016

13. Hosseini, M., Swaminathan, V.: Adaptive 360 VR video streaming: divide and conquer! In: IEEE International Symposium on Multimedia, San Jose, CA, USA, 11–13 December 2016

14. Sanchez, Y., Skupin, R., Hellge, C., Schierl, T.: Random access point period optimization for viewport adaptive tile based streaming of 360° video. In: IEEE International Conference on Image Processing (ICIP 2017), Beijing, China, 17–20 September 2017

15. ITU – Radiocommunication (ITU-R), Recommendation BT.2021-1: Subjective methods for the assessment of stereoscopic 3DTV systems, February 2015

16. Battisti, F., Carli, M., Stramacci, A., Boev, A., Gotchev, A.: A perceptual quality metric for high-definition stereoscopic 3D video. In: Image Processing: Algorithms and Systems XIII [939916], SPIE Conference Proceedings, vol. 9399

17. ITU – Radiocommunication (ITU-R), Recommendation BT.500-13: Methodology for the subjective assessment of the quality of television pictures, January 2012

18. ITU – Standardization (ITU-T), Recommendation P.910: Subjective video quality assessment methods for multimedia applications, April 2008

19. ITU – Radiocommunication (ITU-R), Recommendation BT.2021-1: Subjective methods for the assessment of stereoscopic 3DTV systems, February 2015

20. ITU – Standardization (ITU-T), Recommendation P.915: Subjective assessment methods for 3D video, March 2016

21. Zare, A., Aminlou, A., Hannuksela, M.M.: Virtual reality content streaming: viewport-dependent projection and tile-based techniques. In: IEEE International Conference on Image Processing (ICIP), Beijing, China

22. Zinner, T., Abboud, O., Hohlfeld, O., Hossfeld, T., Tran-Gia, P.: Towards QoE management for scalable video streaming. In: 21th ITC Specialist Seminar on Multimedia Applications - Traffic, Performance and QoE, Miyazaki, Japan

A Model-Based Approach for Arrhythmia Detection and Classification

Hongzu Li and Pierre Boulanger[⊠]

University of Alberta, Edmonton, AB, Canada
{hongzu,pierreb}@ualberta.ca

Abstract. Automatic real-time ECG patterns detection and classification has great importance in early diagnosis and treatment of life-threatening cardiac arrhythmia [7]. In this paper, we developed an algorithm which could classify abnormal heartbeat at more than 85% accuracy. The ECG data of this research are provided by MIT-BIH Arrhythmia Database from Physionet. We extracted seven features from each ECG record to represent the ECG signal. Furthermore, Support Vector Machine and Multi-Layer Perceptron Neural Network are used for classification. We were able to achieve over 85% accuracy and with only 10% difference between sensitivity and specificity.

Keywords: ECG · Machine learning · Pattern recognition
Support vector machine · Neural network

1 Introduction

An arrhythmia is an abnormal heart rhythm. It often occurs when the electrical signals to the heart that coordinate heartbeats are not working properly. For instance, some people experience irregular heartbeats, which may feel like a racing heart or fluttering [4]. However, during a long ECG record, it is time-consuming and difficult for doctors to find irregular heartbeats since most of the heartbeats are normal heartbeats. Automatic arrhythmia detectors can have high impact on the quality of life preventing the risk of stroke or sudden cardiac death in high-risk cardiac patients. Hence, there is a need for quick and early detection of various cardiac arrhythmia conditions [7] in continuous cardiac sensing.

Health condition of heart is generally reflected in shapes of the ECG waveform and the rate at which it beats. Most of the important information in the ECG signal is concentrated in the P wave, QRS complex and T wave. Position as well as magnitude of these waves along with time intervals such as PR interval, QRS width, QT interval and ST segment also play an important roles in arrhythmia detection [7].

© Springer Nature Switzerland AG 2018
A. Basu and S. Berretti (Eds.): ICSM 2018, LNCS 11010, pp. 429–436, 2018.
https://doi.org/10.1007/978-3-030-04375-9_37

2   Data Description

2.1   Data Source

MIT-BIH Arrhythmia Database from Physionet provides a huge amount of ECG recording that contain various type of heartbeats. The database has 48 fully annotated half-hour two-lead ECGs obtained from 47 subjects studied by the BIH Arrhythmia Laboratory between 1975 and 1979. The records were digitized at 360 samples per second per channel with 11-bit resolution over a 10 mV range. Two or more cardiologists independently annotated each record. The ECG records are two lead ECGs. In most records, the upper signal is a modifies limb lead II, obtained by placing the electrodes on the chest. The lower signal is usually a modified lead V1 (occasionally V2, V4 or V5), as for the upper signal, the electrodes are also placed on the chest. Since normal QRS complexes are usually prominent in the upper signal, we only used these ECG signals.

2.2   Beats Description

There are several types of heartbeats. The types are normal beats(N), left bundle branch block beat(L), right bundle branch block beat(R), Atrial premature beat(A), Aberrated atrial premature beat(a), Nodal(junctional) premature beat(J), Supraventricular premature or ectopic beat(S), Premature ventricular contraction(V), Fusion of ventricular and normal beat(F), Atrial escape beat(e), Atrial escape beat(e) and Atrial escape beat(E). Although there are 12 different heartbeat types, but many of those heartbeats occur very rarely in the entire ECG database. For example, there are only 2 supraventricular premature or ectopic beats and 16 atrial escape beats events in the entire database. Comparing to the number of normal beats, they are significantly small since there are about 2000 normal heartbeats in one ECG record. Therefore, all heart could fall into 2 classes: normal heartbeat and abnormal heartbeat.

3   Feature Extraction

3.1   Data Prepossessing

In most of the real-world ECG data acquisition system, the recording are contaminated with several types of artifacts/noise such as base-line wanderings, muscle noise, etc. To eliminate some of those artifacts a Butterworth band-pass filter was used to reduce such noises. The frequency band of the filter is 0.5–100 Hz.

3.2   Beat Extraction

In this research, cardiologist's annotations of R-peaks were used for selecting individual beats from the ECG records. With the position of R-peaks, it is easy to acquire the RR intervals in the ECG records. The RR interval is shown in Fig. 1. Then, by subtracting half of the former and later RR intervals, the starting

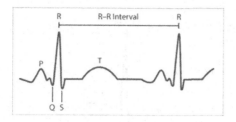

Fig. 1. Two consecutive heartbeats

point and the ending point of a heartbeat can be calculated. Therefore, all the heartbeats can be extracted using the starting and ending points.

In heartbeats classification, not all the heartbeats are used for the training and testing. The first and the last heartbeats are discarded since they only have one related RR interval. In addition, since the heart rate can only exist between 30 and 220 BPM, it makes sense to threshold the RR intervals that would not follow this heart rate range [6]. So, if the RR intervals is not in the range of 30 to 220 BPM, the corresponding heartbeats are being discarded too.

For each heartbeat, 7 features are extracted to represent the heartbeat. The first feature is the duration of the heartbeat. As stated above, the duration of the heartbeat is extracted using RR-interval. Therefore, the heartbeat duration contains the information from RR-interval which indicates the heart rate.

3.3   Skewness and Kurtosis

The second and the third features are statics features, which are skewness and kurtosis. These two features represent the shape of the heartbeat signal.

The skewness is a measure of symmetry, or more precisely, the lack of symmetry. A distribution, or data, set, is symmetric if it looks the same to the left and right of the center point [3]. The skewness of a distribution is defined as:

$$s = \frac{E(x - \mu)^3}{\sigma^3} \tag{1}$$

where μ is the mean of x, σ is the standard deviation of x, and E(t) represents the expected value of t. The kurtosis is a measure of whether the data are heavy-tailed or light-tailed relative to a normal distribution. Data sets with high kurtosis tend to have heavy tails or outliers. Data sets with low kurtosis tend to have light tails or lower amount of outliers [3]. The kurtosis of a distribution is defined as:

$$k = \frac{E(x - \mu)^4}{\sigma^4} \tag{2}$$

Where μ is the mean of x, σ is the standard deviation of x, and E(t) represents the expected value of quantity t.

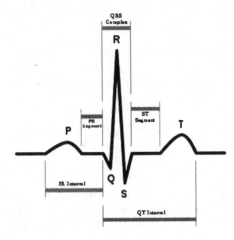

Fig. 2. Normal ECG

3.4   QRS Complex Features

The next four features are related to the QRS complex region in the heartbeat signal. The QRS complex is a name for the combination of three of the graphical deflections seen on a typical electrocardiogram (EKG or ECG). It corresponds to the depolarization of the right and left ventricles of the human heart. It normally lasts 0.06 to 0.1 s in adults. The QRS complex contains three waves: Q wave is any downward deflection after P wave; R wave follows an upward deflection; S wave is any downward deflection after the R wave [2] (see Fig. 2). As stated above, the annotation provides the position for each heartbeat. Therefore, one can used the position as a start point to seek the highest value in the ECG, and the highest the value is the R peak of the QRS complex as shown in Fig. 2. Then the R peak value is recorded as one feature of the ECG records. In addition, the position of R peak is recorded to acquire other features. The position of the R peak can be used as a start position to seek the minimum of the Q wave and the minimum of the S wave. Also, the duration of the QRS complex is the last feature for the ECG.

To sum up, the features used for training the models are the duration of the heartbeat; skewness of the heartbeat; kurtosis of the heartbeat; R peak of the QRS complex; Q value of the QRS complex; S value of the QRS complex; duration of the QRS complex.

4   Machine Learning Algorithm

One needs balanced data sets for training and testing, the training and testing was hand-picked, so that the normal heartbeats and abnormal heartbeats were of similar size. The 12 ECG recording were picked as the training data, and 4 ECG recording were picked as the testing data. In the training data set, there are 29842 heartbeats signals in total. Among all training heartbeats, there are 14653 normal heartbeats and 15189 abnormal heartbeats. As for the testing data set, there are 6003 heartbeats in total. Among all testing heartbeats, 3516 heartbeats are normal heartbeats and 2487 heartbeats are abnormal heartbeats. In both data sets, the amount of normal heartbeats is similar to the number of abnormal heartbeats. Therefore, the trained model will not overfit to one label. The training and testing data set are performed using a Support Vector Machine algorithm and Multi-layer perceptron neural network.

4.1   Support Vector Machine (SVM)

Support vector machine is a supervised learning algorithm that analyze data used for classification and regression analysis. Given a set of training data, the model categorizes the data into two classes [1].

The kernel function of our support vector machine algorithm use a radial basis function (RBF). The slack variables' trade-off parameter C as is optimized by grid search within the range of 1 to 103 and the scale of the RBF kernel is optimized by grid search within the range of 0.1 to 8 [5].

4.2   Multilayer Perceptron Neural Network (MLP)

Multilayer perceptron is a class of feed-forward artificial neural network. An MLP consists of at least three layers nodes. Except for the input nodes, each node is a neuron that uses a nonlinear activation function [5]. The multilayer perceptron neural network was trained using a scaled conjugate gradient algorithm while varying the number of nodes (N_{ij}) in the hidden layer from 50 to 100 and choosing the topology that gave the highest accuracy on a validation set. The Fig. 3 shows the neural network structure with 150 hidden layers. For this purpose, the training set was divided into 70% training, 15% validation and 15% testing [1].

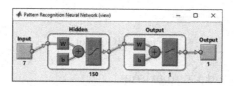

Fig. 3. Multilayer perceptron neural network structure

The confusion matrix shown in Fig. 4 sum-up the training result of the multilayer perceptron neural network. The accuracy of the training set is 97%, and the accuracy for detecting both classes are very similar. So, the network should not have over-fitted the problem. In addition, by looking at ROC plot in Fig. 5, one can see that the model should perform well in both classes.

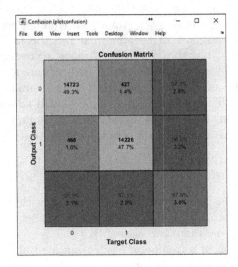

Fig. 4. Confusion matrix

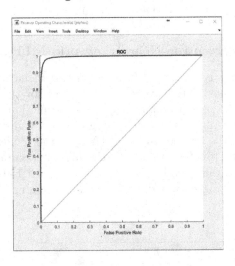

Fig. 5. ROC plot

4.3   Test Result and Comparison

The training time for SVM and MLP neural network are very similar. Both algorithms take around 15 min of for training.

Table 1. Test result of SVM and MLP

Model	ACC	F1-score	SEN	SPC
SVM	86.39%	0.88	90.88%	80.90%
MLP	88.22%	0.9	92.22%	83.26%

As shown in Table 1 above, SVM and MLP neural network produced a similar result and they both performed well. The SVM had 86.39% accuracy and MLP had 88.22% accuracy. For sensitivity, SVM had 90.88% and MLP had 92.22%. On the other hand, both algorithms had lower specificity, where SVM had 80.90% and MLP had 83.26%. However, the difference between sensitivity and specificity is not very high. It is only around 10% difference. The reason for that might be that there were much more abnormal heartbeat classes than normal heartbeat classes. As stated in Sect. 2, we have 11 abnormal heartbeat classes, and only 1 normal heartbeats class. The difference between all the abnormal heartbeats might be even larger than the difference between abnormal heartbeat and normal heartbeat. Therefore, the classification of abnormal heartbeats could be much harder than the classification for normal heartbeats.

5 Conclusion

In this paper, we introduced an algorithm to classify the heartbeats from single lead ECG signal. In our experiment, we have processed ECG records from MIT-BIH Arrhythmia Database from Physionet to extract all the heartbeats. There are 12 different types of heartbeat contained in this database. Due to the lack of certain types of heartbeats, the heartbeats were categorized into two classes which are the normal heartbeat and abnormal heartbeat. For each heartbeat, we have extracted seven features to represent signal which are heartbeat duration, the skewness of the heartbeat, the kurtosis of the heartbeat, QRS complex duration, Q wave valley value, R wave peak value, and S wave valley value. Then we have used Support Vector Machine and Multi-level perceptron Neural Network to training the data.

For training and testing, 12 ECG records were picked to be the training data set, and 4 ECG records were pick to be the testing data set. To get balanced data sets, the ECG records were hand-picked. There are 14653 normal heartbeats and 15189 abnormal heartbeats in the training data set. In the testing data set, 3515 heartbeats are normal, and 2487 heartbeats are abnormal. Since the data sets are manually balanced, the trained models will not over-fit to one label. Furthermore, two machine learning algorithms were trained on the data sets for training and testing, which are SVM and MLP neural network. The results for SVM and MLP neural network are very similar and excellent. They both have over 85% accuracy, and there is only 10% difference between sensitivity and specificity. So, we know that the models did not over fit to one label. Our next step is to use a automated QRS complex detection algorithm to replace the annotation, then we could test the algorithm on the ECG signal without annotation. In addition, we also plan the add more classes to the heart beat types, doing so the algorithm could report the actual heart beat type.

References

1. Clifford, G., Lopez, D., Li, Q., Rezek, I.: Signal quality indices and data fusion for determining acceptability of electrocardiograms collected in noisy ambulatory environments. In: Computing in Cardiology, pp. 285–288. IEEE (2011)
2. Cortes, C., Vapnik, V.: Support-vector networks. Mach. Learn. **20**(3), 273–297 (1995)
3. Natrella, M.: NIST/SEMATECH e-Handbook of Statistical Methods (2010)
4. Nordqvist, C.: Arrhythmia: causes, symptoms, types, and treatment (2017). https://www.medicalnewstoday.com/articles/8887.php
5. Sathyanarayana, S.: A gentle introduction to backpropagation (2014)
6. Tat, T.H.C., Xiang, C., Thiam, L.E.: Physionet challenge 2011: improving the quality of electrocardiography data collected using real time QRS-complex and t-wave detection. In: Computing in Cardiology, pp. 441–444. IEEE (2011)
7. Tuzcu, V., Nas, S.: Dynamic time warping as a novel tool in pattern recognition of ECG changes in heart rhythm disturbances. In: 2005 IEEE International Conference on Systems, Man and Cybernetics, vol. 1, pp. 182–186. IEEE (2005)

EREL Selection Using Morphological Relation

Yuying Li and Mehdi Faraji[✉]

Department of Computing Science, University of Alberta, Edmonton, Canada
{yuying5,faraji}@ualberta.ca

Abstract. This work concentrates on Extremal Regions of Extremum Level (EREL) selection. EREL is a recently proposed feature detector aiming at detecting regions from a set of extremal regions. This is a branching problem derived from segmentation of arterial wall boundaries from Intravascular Ultrasound (IVUS) images. For each IVUS frame, a set of EREL regions is generated to describe the luminal area of human coronary. Each EREL is then fitted by an ellipse to represent the luminal border. The goal is to assign the most appropriate EREL as the lumen. In this work, EREL selection carries out in two rounds. In the first round, the pattern in a set of EREL regions is analyzed and used to generate an approximate luminal region. Then, the two-dimensional (2D) correlation coefficients are computed between this approximate region and each EREL to keep the ones with tightest relevance. In the second round, a compactness measure is calculated for each EREL and its fitted ellipse to guarantee that the resulting EREL has not affected by the common artifacts such as bifurcations, shadows, and side branches. We evaluated the selected ERELs in terms of Hausdorff Distance (HD) and Jaccard Measure (JM) on the train and test set of a publicly available dataset. The results show that our selection strategy outperforms the current state-of-the-art.

Keywords: Extremal regions · Extremum level · EREL
Morphological relation · Correlation coefficient · Compactness measure

1 Introduction

This work focuses on segmentation of arterial wall boundaries from Intravascular Ultrasound (IVUS) images. Our goal is to develop an automatic way to extract the luminal border of an IVUS image. Various approaches have studied this topic such as artificial neural network [1], computational methods that tried to minimize probabilistic cost functions [2], and fast-marching and region growing methods [3–5]. Another state-of-the-art method is known as Extremal Regions of Extremum Level (EREL) [6,7], a region detector that is capable of extracting repeatable regions from an image. This work is a derivation of [8] in the context of Intravascular Ultrasound (IVUS) image segmentation in which the EREL detector is applied to each IVUS frame and extracts several regions. Each EREL

© Springer Nature Switzerland AG 2018
A. Basu and S. Berretti (Eds.): ICSM 2018, LNCS 11010, pp. 437–447, 2018.
https://doi.org/10.1007/978-3-030-04375-9_38

is fitted by a closest ellipsoid since the intrinsic shape of coronary artery is similar to a conic section [8]. Among these fitted ellipsoids, we expect one of them to have the smallest Hausdorff Distance (HD) [9] to the ground truth luminal border labeled by clinical experts and the goal is to find and represent this ellipse as a segmentation of the luminal region. In order to select the best EREL, every extracted regions in each IVUS sample is analyzed and the two-dimensional (2D) correlation coefficients between the current region and each of the other ERELs are computed. The morphological relationship between each EREL region and its fitted ellipse is studied and used as a compactness measure. These two metrics are combined as a selection strategy to find the EREL with the best performance.

In comparison to other data analysis tasks; out of 435 20 Mhz IVUS frames of this dataset, the training set takes only 25.65% of the total data. Also, the training and testing dataset have a large variation in terms of the number of ERELs and the distribution of ground truth in each sample. In training data, an IVUS frame has an average of 30 ERELs; whereas in testing set, an IVUS frame has an average of 7 ERELs. This shows that the test set contains a significantly higher number of artifacts. Table 1 reports a comparison between both datasets. Also, distributions of ground truth in both datasets are presented in Fig. 1. As a consequence, most feature learning methods such as convolutional neural networks that are highly dependent on the quantity and quality of datasets, may fail in extracting the relationship between ERELs and will eventually lead to overfit on the training data.

Table 1. Comparison between training dataset and testing dataset [9].

	Training set	Testing set	Overall
Number of IVUS frames	109	326	435
Percentage in total dataset	25.65%	76.71%	100%
Best matching HD (lumen)	0.19701	0.22872	0.2260
Total number of ERELS	3207	2206	5413
Average number of ERELs	29.61	6.77	12.7871
Maximum number of ERELs	43	7	43
Minimum number of ERELs	6	3	3

In order to deal with this issue, each EREL is treated as an independent entity in the proposed method. The key relationships between ERELs are extracted and the performance of each EREL is evaluated and compared to the others. Based on the variation of the number of ERELs in each sample, we assume that there is one and only one EREL that possesses the best matching qualifications regardless of the number of competitors. These qualifications are evaluated by computing two morphological metrics for each EREL: the correlation coefficient

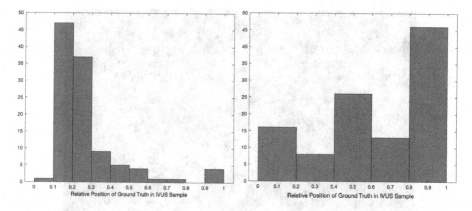

Fig. 1. Distribution of the relative position of ground truth in training and testing set calculated by the index of ground truth divided by the total number of ERELs. The ground truth ERELs are found by comparing the Hd distance of each EREL with the gold standard and choosing the EREL with the lowest Hd distance.

and the compactness measure. The details are given in the next section. Several advantages of the proposed method include:

- This method operates immediately on ERELs by extracting them from the original IVUS frames as binary or grayscale regions such that the result is not influenced by other factors where the characteristics of these ERELs can be closely analyzed.
- This method treats each EREL as an independent entity. Therefore, it works regardless of the number of ERELs in each sample.
- This method uses two passes where the first pass takes the ERELs with high correlation coefficients and the second pass takes the ERELs with high compactness measures. As a result, accuracy is guaranteed in two folds.

Fig. 2. Images from left to right represent: the original IVUS frame, the IVUS frame with the highlighted EREL region, the EREL region extracted in binary format, the EREL region extracted in grayscale format, respectively.

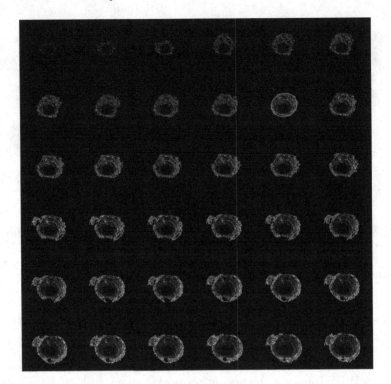

Fig. 3. Visualization of EREL regions generated from a sample IVUS frame in dataset. ERELs are visualized in grayscale format, the ground truth EREL is circled in green. (Color figure online)

2   Method

The proposed method works based on the pattern observed from EREL regions in each IVUS sample. Some major patterns can be summarized as follows:

1. EREL regions in each sample are ordered in an increasing fashion in terms of the size of detected features. Therefore, features in current EREL are also preserved in the following ones.
2. An EREL feature detector may be influenced by noises such as shadow and bifurcation that lead to irregular shapes of the resulting EREL regions.
3. The ground truth lumen region is relatively stable in terms of the growing trend and also tighter elliptical shapes compared to the others.

The procedure in selecting EREL includes several steps. First, EREL regions are preprocessed into binary and grayscale regions respectively (note that in this paper, we refer to $EREL^+$ that are filtered based on their distance to the center as $EREL^1$). Next, the relationships among ERELs are studied that we process

---

[1] The process of EREL filtering has been explained in [8].

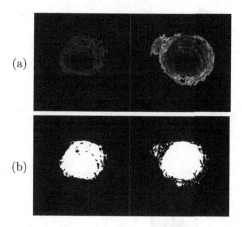

Fig. 4. (a) Comparison between the ground truth (left) and the last EREL (right). (b) Comparison between the ground truth (left) and the approximate lumen region (right) in binary format.

on the last EREL of each sample to extract the possible lumen region. After that, a 2D correlation coefficient is computed between this extracted region and each EREL to only keep the ERELs with high correlations. Then, we further process on these EREL regions with their fitted ellipse to find the EREL with the highest compactness measure to the selected EREL. The details about each step are given as follows.

2.1 Preprocessing

In the dataset, each EREL is represented by a set of pixel coordinates. In order to analyze their characteristics and relationships, these ERELs are extracted in binary form and grayscale form respectively, shown in Fig. 2.

2.2 Correlation Evaluation

Figure 3 visualizes EREL regions for an IVUS sample in grayscale form, where the ground truth EREL is circled. As we investigate these ERELs, we can see that the intensity and general shape of the ground truth EREL is preserved in all the subsequent ERELs. A direct comparison between the ground truth EREL and the last EREL in this sample is shown in Fig. 4(a). In the last EREL, the low intensity region in the middle tends to be the lumen region and the idea is to process on this frame to keep the possible lumen region. Then a 2D correlation coefficient r is computed for each EREL (denoted by A) and the approximate lumen region (denoted by B):

$$r = \frac{\sum_m \sum_n (A_{mn} - \bar{A})(B_{mn} - \bar{B})}{\sqrt{(\sum_m \sum_n (A_{mn} - \bar{A})^2)(\sum_m \sum_n (B_{mn} - \bar{B})^2)}} \tag{1}$$

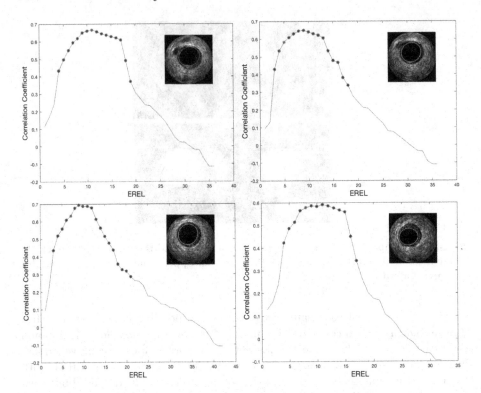

Fig. 5. Correlation plots of sample IVUS frames where the correlation coefficients are computed using Eq. 1. IVUS frames are presented in top-right corner of each plot with ground truth contour highlighted in green. Blue markers on each plot represent those selected ERELs with correlation coefficients higher than the threshold. The red marker on each plot represents the ground truth EREL. (Color figure online)

where $\bar{A}$ is the average intensity of A, $\bar{B}$ is the average intensity of B and m, n represent columns and rows of A, B respectively. Presumably, the ground truth should have a high correlation with this region.

Therefore, the average intensity of the last EREL is calculated as a threshold. We process the last EREL to keep only the low intensity pixels. The result is shown in Fig. 4(b). The region on the left is the ground truth region in a binary form and the region on the right is the extracted region. As we can see these two regions are close and they should have a high correlation.

Some sample plots for correlation are shown in Fig. 5. It can be observed that these plots tend to be right-skewed and the ground truth ERELs (marked in red) are located around the peak of each plot. Without missing any ERELs, we are setting the average of these correlations as a threshold, and output all the ERELs with correlations higher than this threshold. Hence, the resulting list of ERELs is guaranteed to contain the ground truth EREL.

Fig. 6. EREL region before (left) and after (right) dilation using disk-shaped structuring element of radius = 6.

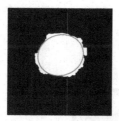

Fig. 7. Illustration of masking an EREL region. Images from left to right represent: the EREL region after dilation, the EREL region and its fitted ellipse in green, intersected area of EREL and its fitted ellipse, respectively. (Color figure online)

2.3 Compactness Evaluation

An EREL region is eventually defined by its contour; however, they may subject to internal cracks since ERELs in their nature are regions selected from a set of extremal points [6,7]. Therefore, a morphological dilate operation is performed on each EREL. This dilation ensures that some insignificant cracks are filled to some extent, and gaps between ERELs caused by bifurcations can be narrowed where the general shape of an EREL is still preserved (shown in Fig. 6).

Due to the intrinsic shape of a luminal border, each EREL region is described by an elliptical contour [8]. The intuitive idea behind this step is that among all the EREL regions, the best matching EREL should have the tightest relationship with the fitted ellipse. Therefore, the ellipse is used as a boolean mask and the intersection between the EREL region and the ellipse is extracted (shown in Fig. 7).

For each EREL region, two measurements will be calculated:

1. The intersection between EREL and its fitted ellipse over the fitted ellipse:

$$M_1 = \frac{Area_{ellipse} \cap Area_{EREL}}{Area_{ellipse}} \tag{2}$$

This measurement guarantees a minimal amount of missing pixels within the fitted elliptical region after the dilation operation. Especially, it can effectively screen out those ERELs with shadow and bifurcation inaccurately included within the detected area.

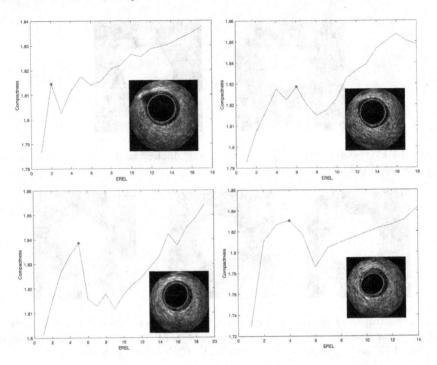

Fig. 8. Compactness plots of sample IVUS frames where the compactness values are computed as $M1 + M2$ where $M1, M2$ are calculated from Eqs. 2 and 3. IVUS frames are presented in bottom-right corner of each plot with ground truth contour highlight in green. The red marker on each plot represents the ground truth EREL in the corresponding IVUS sample. (Color figure online)

2. And the intersection between EREL and its fitted ellipse over the whole EREL region:

$$M_2 = \frac{Area_{ellipse} \cap Area_{EREL}}{Area_{EREL}} \tag{3}$$

This measurement guarantees that most of the detected pixels are fitted into the ellipse. It can also effectively exclude those EREL regions with bifurcation and shadow outside of the fitted ellipse that cause irregular boundary of the EREL.

Then these two measurements, M_1 and M_2, are summed and used together as a compactness standard to define the suitability of an EREL region. A qualified EREL region is expected to have a higher value in this metric than the others in the same IVUS frame sample. Later, these measurements are arranged with the same ordering as the ERELs and the next subsection will describe how the best matching EREL is extracted.

2.4   EREL Selection

Figure 8 visualizes the compactness plots for some sample frames, where the ground truth ERELs are marked in red. We can conclude that these plots obey a similar growing trend and the best matching EREL locates at one of the local maxima of each plot. It is also worth noting that other local maxima may correspond to the shadowed area within the lumen, the media border, and also some intermediate regions with conformance to elliptical shape.

Without loss of generality, for IVUS frames where several local maxima exist, the best matching EREL is selected from the first few local maxima where they have a high possibility to represent lumen. For samples with small number of ERELs where the compactness measure continuously grow and local maximum does not exist, the global maximal EREL is chosen. The result of this method is presented and analyzed in the next section.

3   Experimental Results

The performance of this method is summarized in Table 2. Also a comparison between the proposed method and the result in original work [8] is shown in Table 3. Among all the EREL regions, the one with the shortest Hausdorff Distance (HD) to the hand-annotated ground truth is taken as the golden standard. These numbers represent the best result that an algorithm can achieve in this EREL selection task. The performance of the proposed strategy is evaluated under five categories: the general performance, performance of the proposed method on frames with no artifacts, with bifurcation, with side vessels and with shadow.

Table 2. Performance of the proposed method in lumen detection. The metrics being used are Hausdorff Distance (HD) and Jaccard Measure (JM) evaluated in average and standard deviation. Performance is evaluated under five dataset categories: the general performance, frames with no artifacts, frames with bifurcation, frames with side vessels and frame with shadow. GT denotes the reported Ground Truth.

	Dataset	HD (GT)	HD (Proposed)	JM (GT)	JM (Proposed)
General	Training	0.1970 (0.09)	0.3159 (0.17)	0.9123 (0.03)	0.8761 (0.07)
	Testing	0.2287 (0.14)	0.2952 (0.24)	0.8906 (0.06)	0.8747 (0.07)
No artifact	Training	0.1861 (0.06)	0.3080 (0.16)	0.9138 (0.03)	0.8755 (0.07)
	Testing	0.2076 (0.16)	0.2771 (0.25)	0.8978 (0.06)	0.8864 (0.06)
Bifurcation	Training	0.2490 (0.19)	0.3805 (0.22)	0.9021 (0.05)	0.8706 (0.06)
	Testing	0.4230 (0.10)	0.5544 (0.19)	0.8854 (0.04)	0.7791 (0.11)
Side vessels	Training	0.2426 (0.00)	0.2426 (0.00)	0.9269 (0.00)	0.9269 (0.00)
	Testing	0.1914 (0.15)	0.2406 (0.24)	0.8809 (0.06)	0.8872 (0.06)
Shadow	Training	0.1987 (0.07)	0.2848 (0.13)	0.9153 (0.02)	0.8851 (0.05)
	Testing	0.2333 (0.12)	0.2906 (0.22)	0.8835 (0.04)	0.8591 (0.08)

Table 3. Comparison between the state-of-the-art [8] and the proposed method in lumen detection. The metrics being used are Hausdorff Distance (HD) and Jaccard Measure (JM), performance is evaluated in average and standard derivation.

	HD [8]	HD (Proposed)	JM [8]	JM (Proposed)
General	0.30 (0.20)	0.2952 (0.24)	0.87 (0.06)	0.8747 (0.07)
No artifact	0.29 (0.17)	0.2771 (0.25)	0.88 (0.05)	0.8864 (0.06)
Bifurcation	0.53 (0.34)	0.5544 (0.19)	0.79 (0.12)	0.7791 (0.11)
Side vessels	0.24 (0.11)	0.2406 (0.24)	0.87 (0.05)	0.8872 (0.06)
Shadow	0.29 (0.20)	0.2906 (0.22)	0.86 (0.07)	0.8591 (0.08)

4   Discussion and Conclusion

The proposed method in this paper uses the morphological characteristics of EREL regions as metrics to evaluate these ERELs. Other feature learning methods may require pixel-to-pixel comparison between every two EREL regions and would result in high computational consumption; where this proposed method operates on independent ERELs which makes it fast and straightforward.

Nevertheless, there are still some improvements needed for this method. In the first pass, this method extracts a possible lumen region from the last EREL in each series and computes the correlation coefficient between each EREL and this extracted region. For a small IVUS sample where the last EREL is similar to all the other ones, this method fails to extract a possible lumen region which may lead to negative correlation in all comparisons. The second pass works on the basis of the compactness of an EREL region and its fitted ellipse. A major issue comes from this method is that any EREL conformed to elliptical shape may be wrongly chosen as a suitable representation. Therefore, incorporating the characteristics of lumen into this method is necessary and beneficial to eliminate these interferences.

Furthermore, considering the simplicity and power of this combined correlation and compactness evaluations, it is also likely to produce a better result if the these metrics can be used as supplementary tools in other EREL selection algorithms to screen out the inappropriate ERELs.

The original study also involves assigning an EREL as media region of human coronary where in this work we focus on lumen only. EREL selection as media adopts a similar idea with some variations due to the particular characteristics of media, this task will be assigned as the future work of this study.

References

1. Su, S., Hu, Z., Lin, Q., Hau, W.K., Gao, Z., Zhang, H.: An artificial neural network method for lumen and media-adventitia border detection in IVUS. Comput. Med. Imaging Graph. **57**, 29–39 (2017)
2. Head, J.D., Zerner, M.C.: A Broyden—Fletcher—Goldfarb—Shanno optimization procedure for molecular geometries. Chem. Phys. Lett. **122**(3), 264–270 (1985)
3. Destrempes, F., Cardinal, M.H.R., Allard, L., Tardif, J.C., Cloutier, G.: Segmentation method of intravascular ultrasound images of human coronary arteries. Comput. Med. Imaging Graph. **38**(2), 91–103 (2014)
4. Hamdi, M.A., Ettabaa, K.S., Harabi, M.L.: Real time IVUS segmentation and plaque characterization by combining morphological snakes and contourlet transform. Int. J. Imaging Robot.™ **11**(3), 57–67 (2013)
5. Chen, F., Ma, R., Liu, J., Zhu, M., Liao, H.: Lumen and media-adventitia border detection in IVUS images using texture enhanced deformable model. Comput. Med. Imaging Graph. **66**, 1–13 (2018)
6. Faraji, M., Shanbehzadeh, J., Nasrollahi, K., Moeslund, T.B.: Extremal regions detection guided by maxima of gradient magnitude. IEEE Trans. Image Process. **24**(12), 5401–5415 (2015)
7. Faraji, M., Shanbehzadeh, J., Nasrollahi, K., Moeslund, T.B.: EREL: extremal regions of extremum levels. In: 2015 IEEE International Conference on Image Processing (ICIP), pp. 681–685. IEEE (2015)
8. Faraji, M., Cheng, I., Naudin, I., Basu, A.: Segmentation of arterial walls in intravascular ultrasound cross-sectional images using extremal region selection. Ultrasonics **84**, 356–365 (2018)
9. Balocco, S., et al.: Standardized evaluation methodology and reference database for evaluating IVUS image segmentation. Comput. Med. Imaging Graph. **38**(2), 70–90 (2014)

EREL-Net: A Remedy for Industrial Bottle Defect Detection

Nikunjkumar Patel[1]([⊠]), Subhayan Mukherjee[1], and Lihang Ying[2]

[1] University of Alberta, Edmonton, AB T6G 2R3, Canada
{nikunjku,mukherje}@ualberta.ca
[2] Together Solution Inc., Edmonton, Canada
lihang.ying@togethersolution.com

Abstract. Product defect detection is an integral part of quality control process in any manufacturing industry. In many cases, this problem is solved by a specific designed system for each type of product, which often requires parameter tuning for each product model. In this paper, we propose a generic method for defect detection that can be deployed for various kinds of products and models. We detect defects on bottle surface and classify bottles accordingly. Bottle defect detection is a challenging task due to several factors like no sufficient training data, reflective (metallic) bottle surface, and visually similar defects with design patterns on bottles. To overcome these challenges, we first use a computer vision-based region detection technique called EREL to extract multiple regions of interest from training images and thus increase the volume of training data. The extracted regions are manually labelled as defective/non-defective. Then, we train our proposed CNN classifier to discriminate between defective and non-defective regions, based on the extracted regions and labels. Experimental results demonstrate superior performance on non-reflective bottles and acceptable performance of the proposed method with 77% accuracy on overall unseen test images, considering various kinds of bottles and challenging reflective metallic bottles. With a current modest personal computer, our method takes around 2.4 s to process an input image to generate final image with bounding boxes localizing the defects (if any).

Keywords: Defects detection · Quality control · EREL
Region extraction

1 Introduction

Challenge of defect detection on bottle surface involves identification of minor dents, scratches or any other imperfections. It requires significant amount of efforts to manually inspect. Also, it is difficult for human to perform inspection consistently due to tiredness, mood and other factors. Therefore, it is necessary to automate this process of detecting defects in order to reduce the repetitive labour and more importantly consistent production standards.

© Springer Nature Switzerland AG 2018
A. Basu and S. Berretti (Eds.): ICSM 2018, LNCS 11010, pp. 448–456, 2018.
https://doi.org/10.1007/978-3-030-04375-9_39

Defect detection can be achieved by various computer vision techniques ranging from conventional algorithms to modern generalized learning using deep neural networks. Conventional algorithms such as Speeded Up Robust Features (SURF) [1], scale invariant feature transform (SIFT) [9], etc. are widely used for keypoint detection and description. Extremal Regions of Extremum Levels (EREL) [3,4] is a recently proposed region detector technique that can extract nested regions from an image with high repeatability. Extracting EREL is of most interest since the method is flexible and based on several input arguments that user has the opportunity to tune for various industrial applications. For instance, one can extract regions between desired minimum and maximum areas. Also the smoothness ability of the method can be set by changing the parameter $alpha$ that is useful when the images are contaminated by noise. This recent detector has been employed even in other types of applications such as face recognition [8] or medical image segmentation [2].

Due to the high repeatability and flexibility of EREL to detect the important regions from the image, it is likely that our region of interest (i.e. defect in this case) is detected by EREL. However, detected keypoints may also contain other features such as edges, corner, etc. which are not defects, and thus, need to be filtered out from our set of true defects.

On the other hand, there has been paradigm shift in the field of computer vision after deep convolutional neural network (CNN) based classifier model won the ILSVRC competition in 2015 [7]. Since then, different architectures such as GoogleNet [13], ResNet [5], Faster-RCNN [11], etc. have been proposed, which greatly advanced the field of deep learning. Deep learning techniques have been proven to be robust and accurate in many tasks such as image classification, object detection, etc. However, it has its own shortcomings and is not scalable to domains for which model is not trained. Additionally, it requires significant amounts of training data.

1.1 Our Contribution

To identify the tiny dents, scratches, etc. on the surface of bottles, we proposed a method called EREL-Net which is a combination of the newly proposed EREL region detection technique followed by convolutional neural network (CNN) classifier trained over very sparse dataset of bottles. To the best of our knowledge, we are the first to propose combination of these techniques to address defect detection. In addition, despite other techniques that extract ERELs from an image, we propose to extract EREL from an Edge Amplified (EA) image in which the presence of the defect is strengthened. EREL-Net can be trained by a small number of images and yet generates correct classification results.

The rest of this paper is organized as follows: Sect. 2 presents detailed description of the proposed method. Section 3 reports the results and finally we conclude the paper and describe future works in Sect. 4.

2   EREL-Net

EREL-Net is designed for defect detection process. It is broadly divided into two major steps: (1) Region detection and (2) Region Classification. Figure 1 shows all the steps involved in the entire EREL-Net pipeline. The region detection step extracts all regions which fall within threshold values of EREL parameters. Region classification step uses convolutional neural network to discriminate regions with defects from regions without defects. Finally, defects are visualized in the last step.

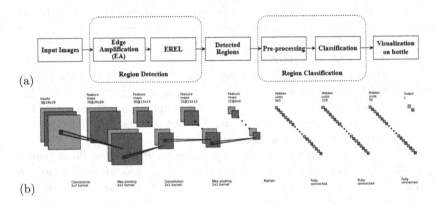

Fig. 1. EREL-Net: (a) Pipeline of proposed EREL-Net. (b) CNN architecture of EREL-Net

2.1   Region Detection

The region detection task is implemented in two steps. Before passing the input image to EREL region detector, an Edge Amplification (EA) process is done that helps amplifying parts of the image which are defected. EA is described as follows.

Edge Amplification (EA). We perform this task by first calculating the gradient of each color component (3 channels) of the input image individually. Then, we select only the maximum value out of the gradient of three channels. It can be represented using Eq. 1 as,

$$EA = Max[GMag^R, GMag^G, GMag^B] \qquad (1)$$

Here, $GMag$ represents the gradient magnitude for the respective channel. Figure 3 shows the edge amplified output images for some input images shown in Fig. 2. These edge-amplified images are now fed to the EREL region detector.

Fig. 2. Sample input images consisting bottles of different sizes, shapes, colors and build material with different type of defects on the surface.

Fig. 3. Edge amplified output

Extremal Regions of Extremum Level (EREL). EREL is a recently proposed region detector that extracts nested regions in the image using the union-find structure [3,4]. The time complexity of EREL is almost linear [4] which is very suitable for industrial applications that need the system that perform in real time in the production line. The output results of EREL on an EA image will be several regions of interest that are accurately localized as it is shown in Fig. 4. We assume that if there is a defect in the image, it should be among these detected ERELs.

2.2 Region Classification

Not all the regions extracted by EREL are defects. Therefore, in this step, we need a classifier that can tell us whether a region is a defection or not. For this specific task we use a convolutional neural network (CNN).

Pre-processing. EREL region detector outputs the coordinates (x, y) of all pixels inside a region that might differ in size for various regions, but CNN requires a fixed rectangular or square image with pixel values as input. Therefore, we extracted total 784 pixels (28 pixels height, 28 pixels width) around the centroids (x_c, y_c) of all the regions detected by EREL. Figure 5 shows the extracted regions by EREL technique for sample images given in Fig. 4. Additionally, we ignored all the regions located near the boundary of an image to reduce the unnecessary computation time. The rationale behind this is that there is no bottle there, hence no defects.

Fig. 4. Detected regions from 4 bottles (shown by yellow ellipses) consisting of true defects as well as other regions (Color figure online)

Next, we manually label all the detected regions with '1' if it is defected and '0' if it is not. We then flattened the image into (1,784) vector to feed it as input for our classifier.

Classification. Our CNN model is binary classifier which has 2 convolutional layers with kernel size of (3,3) and (2,2), each followed by a max-pooling layer of size (2,2). Following these, there are three dense layers with progressively decreasing size with each layer. Dropout [12] of 0.25 is added after the second max-pooling layer as a regularizer to prevent overfitting. Rectified Linear Unit (ReLU) [10] is used as activation function except last layer which is activated by

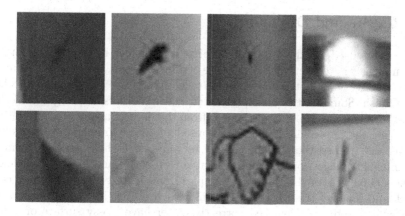

Fig. 5. Several extracted blocks for classifications around EREL regions

softmax. Loss function was categorical cross-entropy and Adam [6] is selected as optimizer with the default parameter values used in the original paper i.e. learning rate of 0.01, beta1 and beta2 values of 0.9 and 0.999 respectively and no decay. Input to the classifier is (1,784) sized vector (flattened 28 × 28 image) with its corresponding label '1' (defective) or '0' (non-defective). Output of the CNN is binary, resulting '1' if detected region has defect else '0'. We trained our model with total 1772 labeled images extracted from 44 images of defected and perfect bottles combined in a batch of 32 images. This simple classifier model is able to classify the regions with over 94% accuracy.

2.3 Evaluation and Visualization

To evaluate our method, we passed the bottle images through the same steps as shown in Fig. 1 (except training our classifier). We used our trained classifier model to classify the regions. The output of the classifier is label '1' or '0' describing presence or absence of defect respectively. For all the detected regions that are classified as defects, bounding boxes of size (28,28) are drawn around the (x_c, y_c) coordinates provided by EREL region detector for the corresponding regions. Figure 6 shows the final output highlighting the defects by square bounding boxes around them.

Fig. 6. Final output. Defects on the bottles are highlighted by bounding boxes

3   Results and Discussion

The dataset used for this project comprised 55 images in training set and 13 unseen images in test set. The bottles are of different sizes, shapes, colors, surface materials, etc. Some bottles have glossy/reflective surface and some bottles have matte finish. Some bottles have plain surface while others have logos or designs printed on their surface. Sample images from the dataset are shown in the Fig. 1.

During the implementation, we only used 44 out of 55 images to extract the regions and trained the classifier model by only using those regions. From the remaining 11 images, our method was able to identify and localize the defects on the 10 images. For the 13 unseen samples from the test set, our method could detect and localize true defects in 10 images resulting in 77% accuracy. The bottles that were not identified correctly either have glossy surface or defects overlap with the bottle logo or the design printed on the bottle.

To further evaluate our method, we created confusion matrix for total 11 images of test set by calculating number of True Positives (TP), False Positives (FP), True Negatives (TN) and False Negatives (FN). To calculate the number of TPs and FPs, we take the coordinates of blocks that are classified as '1' and check the summation of pixel values of (28,28) block in the ground truth image. If summation is non-zero then we consider it as TP else FP. In case of TNs and FNs, we take the coordinates of blocks that are classified as '0' and do the same. If sum value is zero then it's TN otherwise FN. From the confusion matrix we calculate various other terms for each bottle image as shown in Table 1.

Number of False Negatives for each test image are close to zero. This increased performance of our method can be attributed to EREL algorithm's tendency of rejecting False Negatives and selecting regions of interests. Our first step of region detection reduces the stress on CNN classifier. In other words, region detector technique and CNN classifier complements each other. And this can be visible by the last two columns of the Table 1. Average accuracy of proposed method for 11 images in test set is 98.93% and precision is 78%. The reason behind such value of precision is that the system is unable to find any defect in two images which are glossy and has design overlaps with defect. Which leads to 0 precision value for those two images.

The bottles in the dataset were captured in different environmental conditions where position of bottle, camera angle, camera exposure and lighting conditions varied. In a real-world scenario, the results can be further improved by controlling the aforementioned factors as well as larger data set to train the classifier.

Our method takes around 2.4 s to process an input image to generate final image with bounding boxes when executed on MATLAB 2018 with 4 working cores on the system having Intel i7-7700HQ processor and Nvidia GTX 1060 video card.

Table 1. System evaluation parameters

Image No.	Misc. Classification Rate	True Positive Rate	False Positive Rate	Specificity	Prevalence	Positive Predict Value	Negative Predict Value	False Discovery Rate	False Omission Rate	Precision	Overall Accuracy
1	0	100	0	0	100	100	0	0	0	100	100
2	0	100	0	100	33.33	100	100	0	0	100	100
3	11.11	100	14.28	85.71	22.22	66.67	100	33.33	0	66.67	88.89
4	0	100	0	100	50	100	100	0	0	100	100
5	0	100	0	100	50	100	100	0	0	100	100
6	0	100	0	100	24.14	100	100	0	0	100	100
7	0	0	0	100	0	0	100	0	0	0	100
8	0	100	0	100	25	100	100	0	0	100	100
9	0	0	0	100	0	0	100	0	0	0	100
10	0.62	100	0.68	99.33	8.07	92.86	100	7.14	0	92.86	99.39
11	0	100	0	100	75	100	100	0	0	100	100

4   Conclusion and Future Work

We propose a novel bottle defect detection approach called EREL-Net which uses the state-of-the-art region detector EREL to detect candidate regions of interest (ROI). These ROIs are subsequently classified as either 'good' or 'defective' by our trained CNN model. Our method is robust enough to detect defects in presence of specular reflections and similarity of defects with design prints on bottle surface, with very few missed detections. With a current modest personal computer, the current method runs in 2.4 s, which we want to improve in our future work by speeding up EREL.

This paper only reports the preliminary work of generic defect detection for diverse products and models. Future work include:

1. Deploying and evaluating the system in the real product assembly line, capturing significant more defective bottle images and updating the trained model in real time.
2. Extending the experiments to more product types and evaluating whether the system can adapt effectively.

References

1. Bay, H., Ess, A., Tuytelaars, T., Van Gool, L.: Speeded-up robust features (SURF). Comput. Vis. Image Underst. **110**(3), 346–359 (2008)
2. Faraji, M., Cheng, I., Naudin, I., Basu, A.: Segmentation of arterial walls in intravascular ultrasound cross-sectional images using extremal region selection. Ultrasonics **84**, 356–365 (2018)
3. Faraji, M., Shanbehzadeh, J., Nasrollahi, K., Moeslund, T.B.: EREL: extremal regions of extremum levels. In: 2015 IEEE International Conference on Image Processing (ICIP), pp. 681–685. IEEE (2015)
4. Faraji, M., Shanbehzadeh, J., Nasrollahi, K., Moeslund, T.B.: Extremal regions detection guided by maxima of gradient magnitude. IEEE Trans. Image Process. **24**(12), 5401–5415 (2015)
5. He, K., Zhang, X., Ren, S., Sun, J.: Deep residual learning for image recognition. In: Proceedings of the IEEE Conference on Computer Vision and Pattern Recognition, pp. 770–778 (2016)
6. Kingma, D.P., Ba, J.: Adam: a method for stochastic optimization. arXiv preprint arXiv:1412.6980 (2014)
7. Krizhevsky, A., Sutskever, I., Hinton, G.E.: Imagenet classification with deep convolutional neural networks. In: Advances in Neural Information Processing Systems, pp. 1097–1105 (2012)
8. Lin, J., Chiu, C.T.: LBP edge-mapped descriptor using MGM interest points for face recognition. In: 2017 IEEE International Conference on Acoustics, Speech and Signal Processing (ICASSP), pp. 1183–1187. IEEE (2017)
9. Lowe, D.G.: Distinctive image features from scale-invariant keypoints. Int. J. Comput. Vis. **60**(2), 91–110 (2004)
10. Nair, V., Hinton, G.E.: Rectified linear units improve restricted Boltzmann machines. In: Proceedings of the 27th International Conference on Machine Learning (ICML 2010), pp. 807–814 (2010)
11. Ren, S., He, K., Girshick, R., Sun, J.: Faster R-CNN: towards real-time object detection with region proposal networks. IEEE Trans. Pattern Anal. Mach. Intell. **39**(6), 1137–1149 (2017)
12. Srivastava, N., Hinton, G., Krizhevsky, A., Sutskever, I., Salakhutdinov, R.: Dropout: a simple way to prevent neural networks from overfitting. J. Mach. Learn. Res. **15**(1), 1929–1958 (2014)
13. Szegedy, C., et al.: Going deeper with convolutions. In: CVPR (2015)

Author Index

Printed in the United States
By Bookmasters